Afghan Village Voices

Afghan Village Voices

Stories from a Tribal Community

Compiled and Edited by Richard Tapper

with Nancy Lindisfarne-Tapper

I.B.TAURIS

LONDON · NEW YORK · OXFORD · NEW DELHI · SYDNEY

I.B. TAURIS
Bloomsbury Publishing Plc
50 Bedford Square, London, WC1B 3DP, UK
1385 Broadway, New York, NY 10018, USA
29 Earlsfort Terrace, Dublin 2, Ireland

BLOOMSBURY, I.B. TAURIS and the Diana logo are trademarks
of Bloomsbury Publishing Plc

First published in Great Britain 2020
Reprinted 2020, 2022

Cover design: Catherine Wood
Cover image © Nancy Lindisfarne-Tapper

A catalogue record for this book is available from the British Library.

A catalog record for this book is available from the Library of Congress.

ISBN: HB: 978-0-7556-0085-4
       PB: 978-0-7556-0086-1
       ePub: 978-0-7556-0088-5
       ePDF: 978-0-7556-0087-8

Typeset by RefineCatch Limited, Bungay, Suffolk
Printed and bound in Great Britain

To find out more about our authors and books visit www.bloomsbury.com
and sign up for our newsletters.

For the Piruzai people of Konjek and Khârkash

Contents

List of Maps, Tables and Figures

Maps

Tables

Figures

List of Illustrations

Credits: Nancy Lindisfarne-Tapper, except Richard Tapper 1, 2, 11, 17;
Margaret Ruschill 21.

Preface

Afghan Village Voices is a book of stories told by a people whose voices have rarely been heard: semi-nomads and farmers from rural Afghanistan. They were recorded in the early 1970s, just before that unfortunate country was swept up by the cycle of disasters that have continued well into the twenty-first century.

The book begins with a Prologue that provides an introduction to the Piruzai, a community of some 200 families of Durrani Pashtuns who winter and farm in the Sar-e-pol region of northern Afghanistan, and who take their flocks to summer pastures high in the Hazârajât mountains in the centre of the country. The book consists of thirteen Chapters and an Epilogue, containing a variety of stories introduced with brief notes to set the scene and introduce the narrators and the protagonists. The stories range widely: some are memories of the Piruzai migration a half-century earlier, from Nawzâd and Musâ-qala in Helmand to Sar-e-pol in the north. Some are accounts of the doings of powerful khans, and feuds and ethnic strife. Others are about falling in love, elopements and marriages, childbirth and the world of spirits. Still others are of the economy, and the skills and skulduggery people need to survive. They are interspersed with folk tales that echo many of the themes in the stories.

Afghan Village Voices is not about current events, but about the lives of rural Afghans many of whose children and grandchildren have been major actors in those events.

Since the US response to the Al-Qaeda attacks of 11 September 2001, the international media have daily featured news stories of the Taliban and the American war. Yet for much of the twentieth century the country was virtually unknown in Europe and America except as a remote, exotic land, a destination for adventurous tourists, or a stop on the 'hippy trail' to India and Nepal.

Despite its remoteness Afghanistan has long been a cross-roads or bridge between the Middle East, Central Asia and India, and therefore has of course been a focus of foreign interest for millennia. In the nineteenth century the Russian empire spread east to the northern borders of Afghanistan; to counter the Russian threat the British in India fought no less than three Afghan wars before the country became independent in 1919.

In the ensuing decades Afghanistan did not apparently have the natural resources that brought wealth to some neighbours. Things changed after the Second World War. During the Cold War, the USSR and the USA competed to develop basic infrastructure and services in the country, yet it remained among the world's least developed. The small urban elite had little interest or influence in rural affairs. But until the 1970s, Afghanistan was at peace and welcomed foreign visitors and researchers, including anthropologists.

The stories in *Afghan Village Voices* were recorded by Nancy Tapper (now Lindisfarne) and myself when we lived with the Piruzai during ethnographic fieldwork in 1971–72.

We first visited Afghanistan in summer 1968, hoping to find nomadic groups we could compare with the Shahsevan, Turkic-speaking nomads of north-western Iran, with whom we had lived between 1963 and 1966. We found that Turkic nomads existed, but only in the remote north-east, inaccessible to us. However, during a month touring the north-central provinces of Jawzjân and Fâryâb, we encountered many Pashtun nomads, who had arrived from southern Afghanistan around half a century earlier. We learned of hostilities between these Pashtun newcomers, especially the khans of the large Es'hâqzai tribe, and the indigenous Uzbek Turks and others. We decided to attempt a study of Pashtun nomads and their relations with other groups in the region. (See Map A.)

We returned to Afghanistan in late 1970. After some weeks negotiating permits in Kabul we spent another month touring Pashtun camps and villages in Jawzjân and Fâryâb, looking for a suitable community that would agree to host us. The most feasible plan was to study one of the many Es'hâqzai groups based in Sar-e-pol, then a sub-province of Jawzjân.

After a further visit to Kabul to extend our permits, in late winter 1971 we joined the Piruzai, an Es'hâqzai sub-tribe, semi-nomadic pastoralists (*mâldâr*) but also (unlike the Shahsevan in Iran) much involved in village-based farming. After two months in their spring camps, we trekked with them to the central mountains, then in late summer back to their villages and farmlands, where we had to leave them before the autumn set in. Next summer (1972), we spent another two months in the villages.

Our hope for our fieldwork was that we could accurately describe the world of the Piruzai and capture something of the depth and colour of their lives. I spent most of my time with the men, and paid particular attention to tribal organization, regional ethnic relations, livestock raising and agriculture. Nancy stayed mostly with the Piruzai women and learned of their lives through their domestic work, their marriages and their hopes and fears for their families and friends. This division of labour suited us and, more importantly, was acceptable to our hosts and fitted their sensibilities.

Our fieldwork was intensive. Our Piruzai hosts were pleased that we hoped to write a book about their lives, and were unfailingly helpful and welcoming. We had close relationships with numerous individuals. Among the materials we collected were the stories in this book. We tape-recorded interviews and conversations as a way of focusing our and our narrators' attention on particular topics, and as a supplement to our normal note-taking.

In the first days of our stay, we heard vivid stories of recent events – scandals, violence, intrigue – involving our hosts and their neighbours and enemies. At first, we could not believe them: they must be pulling our legs. Only later did we learn that those events had happened, and that our hosts were not merely sharing public knowledge with us but also attempting to establish their versions, their interpretations, to pre-empt any other versions we might be told.

Early on we had a stroke of luck. Nancy refused to play back to our host Haji Tumân a recording she had just made of a spirited argument among women at a wedding. Haji's angry reaction seemed likely to jeopardize our stay with his family. But after a few days, a shooting occurred in pastures some distance away from the camp; as headman, Haji commandeered me and our Land Rover to take him to help sort things out. When we returned, Haji let the matter of the recording drop.

This saga established that we were making tapes for ourselves, which we would not play back locally without the permission of those whose voices were recorded. However useful and interesting it might have been for us to record listeners' reactions, it was more important to maintain the confidentiality we had fortuitously guaranteed early on.

Other incidents, involving either their rivals or government agents, convinced our hosts that we would not betray their trust, particularly that we would not pass on any confidences that they shared with us. At the same time, we made sure to collect alternative versions where possible, so that, for example, the narratives of the 'runaways' (Chapter 3) and of the 'feud' (Chapter 4) differ in detail from Nancy's composite accounts and analyses in her book *Bartered Brides*, where she also draws on information recorded only in our note-books.[1]

We left Afghanistan expecting to return for further fieldwork, but this was not to be. In 1973, after a forty-year reign of peaceful stagnation, the Afghan King Zâher was deposed by his cousin Sardâr Dâ'ud, bringing the 226-year-old monarchy to an end. Since then, the Afghan people have hardly known a year of peace and security, but have undergone rebellion, revolution, invasion, occupation, civil war, drought, famine and other catastrophes.

The Prologue provides background to the Piruzai arrival in Sar-e-pol and their position in the local economy in 1970–72. A short Epilogue summarizes what little we know or can guess of the fate of the Piruzai in the years since we left. Briefly, in the mid-1980s, during the Soviet occupation, they had to abandon their homes and lands in the north. They moved south, first to refugee camps in Pakistan, then back to Helmand province, where they have ancestral homes in Nawzâd and Musâ-qala. These districts, and indeed the Es'hâqzai tribe, have figured prominently in the international press since 2001 as the main centres of both opium production and Taliban resistance to government and international forces. Appendix 2 gives more detail on the history of Sar-e-pol and Afghanistan since 1972.

So these stories are the only account, in Afghan voices, of rural life before Dâ'ud's 1973 coup. They tell of times long past, and the lives of a people whose relatives and descendants have been major actors in recent events in Afghanistan. And this book offers a unique testimony to people we cared for deeply, and whose humanity and humour shine out in the stories.

---

[1] N. Tapper (1991). She has written at length on the circumstances of our fieldwork (1991: 3–13). See also Tapper and Tapper (1989). In Appendix 3, I describe how the tapes were translated, selected and edited.

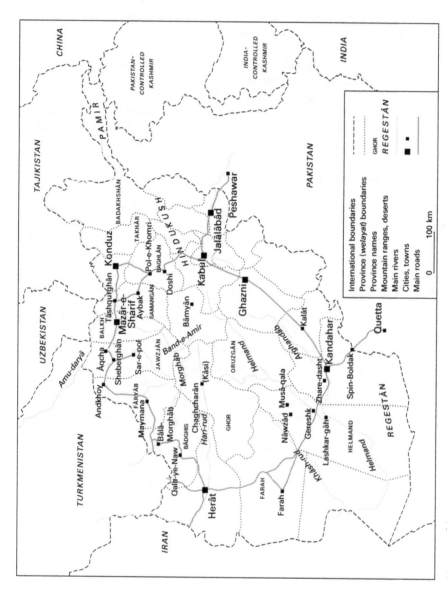

Map A Afghanistan (in 1970).

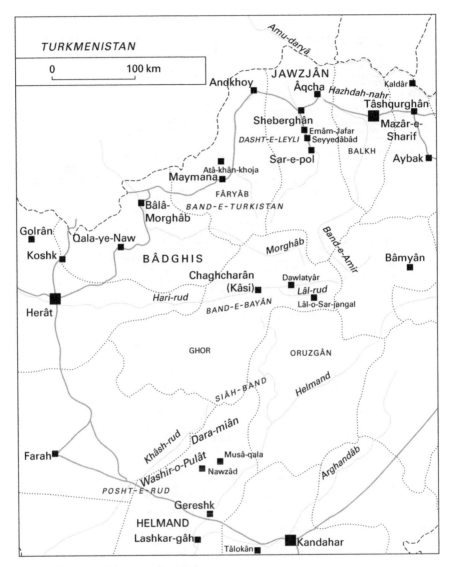

Map B Western Afghanistan (in 1970).

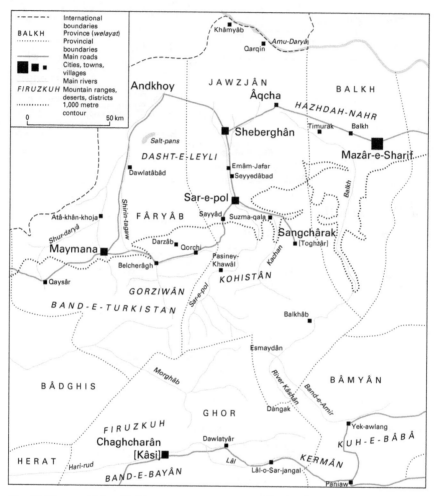

Map C Western Afghan Turkistan.

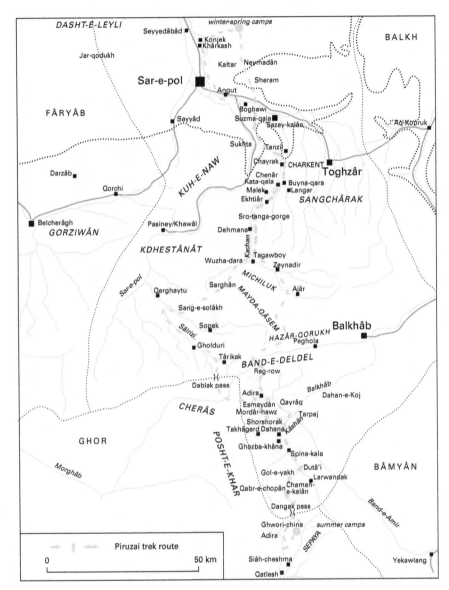

DASHT-É-LEYLI
winter-spring camps
BALKH
Seyyedâbâd
Konjek
Khârkash
Jar-qodukh
Kaltar Neymadân
Sheram
Sar-e-pol
Angut
FÂRYÂB
Boghawi
Sayyâd
Suzma-qala
Âq-Kûpruk
Sazay-kalân
Sukhta
Tanzi
Darzâb
Chayrak
CHARKENT
Toghzâr
Chenâr
Qorchi
Kata-qala
Buyna-qara
Malek
Langar
Ekhtiâr
SANGCHÂRAK
Belcherâgh
Sro-tanga-gorge
GORZIWÂN
Pasiney/Khawâl
Dehmana
KDHESTÂNÂT
Tagawboy
Wuzha-dara
Zeynadir
MICHILUK
Qerghaytu
Sarghân
Ajâr
Sang-e-solâkh
Sopak
HAZÂR-QORUKH
Balkhâb
Gholduri
Peghola
Târikak
BAND-E-DELDEL
Reg-row
Dablak pass
Balkhâb
Adira
Dahan-e-Koj
CHERÂS
Esmaydân
Qayrâq
Mordâr-hawz
Tarpaj
Shorshorak
Takhâgerd Dahana
GHOR
Ghozba-khâna
Spina-kala
Dutâ'i
Gol-e-yakh
Larwandak
BÂMYÂN
Morghâb
Qabr-e-chopân
Chaman-e-kalân
Dangak pass
Ghwori-china
summer camps
Adira
Siâh-cheshma
SEPAYA
Yekawlang
Qatlesh

Piruzai trek route
0   50 km

Map D From the steppe to the mountains.

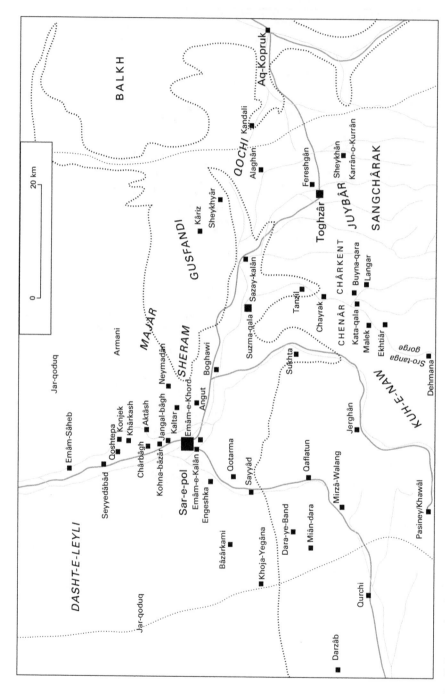

Map E Sar-e-pol and Sangchârak.

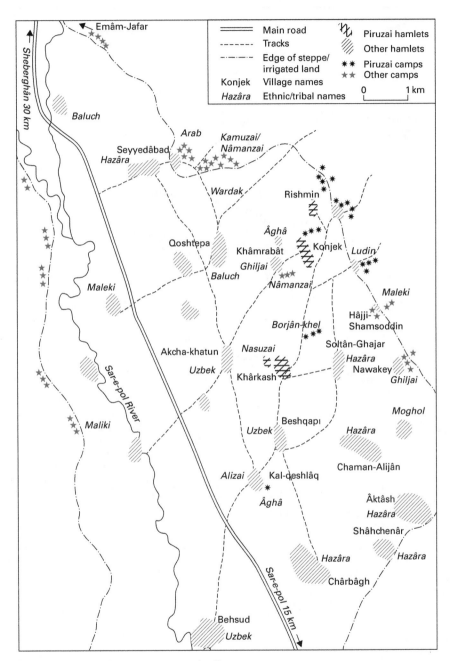

Map F Piruzai settlements in Sar-e-pol valley.

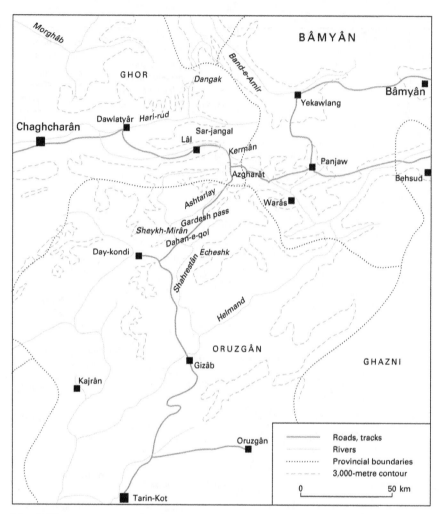

Map G The runaways, Day-kondi.

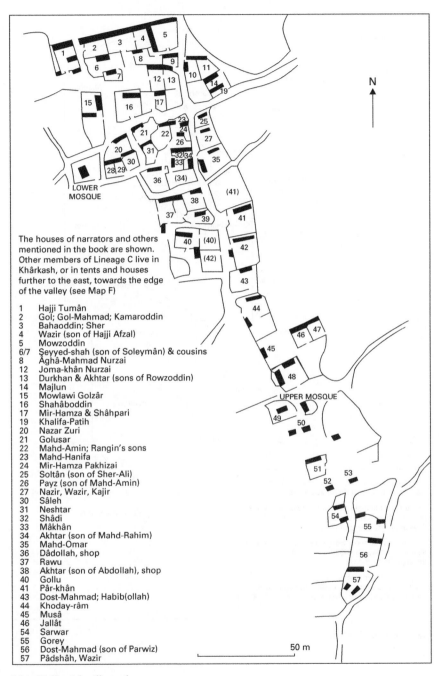

The houses of narrators and others
mentioned in the book are shown.
Other members of Lineage C live in
Khârkash, or in tents and houses
further to the east, towards the edge
of the valley (see Map F)

1	Hajji Tumân
2	Gol; Gol-Mahmad; Kamaroddin
3	Bahaoddin; Sher
4	Wazir (son of Hajji Afzal)
5	Mowzoddin
6/7	Şeyyed-shah (son of Soleymân) & cousins
8	Âghâ-Mahmad Nurzai
12	Joma-khân Nurzai
13	Durkhan & Akhtar (sons of Rowzoddin)
14	Majlun
15	Mowlawi Golzâr
16	Shahâboddin
17	Mir-Hamza & Shâhpari
19	Khalifa-Patih
20	Nazar Zuri
21	Golusar
22	Mahd-Amin; Rangin's sons
23	Mahd-Hanifa
24	Mir-Hamza Pakhizai
25	Soltân (son of Sher-Ali)
26	Payz (son of Mahd-Amin)
27	Nazir, Wazir, Kajir
30	Sâleh
31	Neshtar
32	Shâdi
33	Mâkhân
34	Akhtar (son of Mahd-Rahim)
35	Mahd-Omar
36	Dâdollah, shop
37	Rawu
38	Akhtar (son of Abdollah), shop
40	Gollu
41	Pâr-khân
43	Dost-Mahmad; Habib(ollah)
44	Khoday-râm
45	Musâ
46	Jallât
54	Sarwar
55	Gorey
56	Dost-Mahmad (son of Parwiz)
57	Pâdshâh, Wazir

50 m

Map H Konjek village plan.

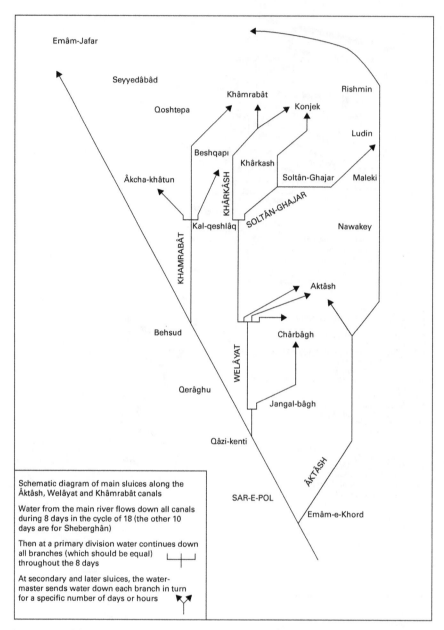

Emâm-Jafar

Seyyedâbâd

Rishmin

Khâmrabât

Qoshtepa

Konjek

Ludin

Beshqapı

Khârkash

Âkcha-khâtun

KHÂRKÂSH

Soltân-Ghajar

Maleki

KHAMRABÂT

Kal-qeshlâq

SOLTÂN-GHAJAR

Nawakey

Aktâsh

Behsud

Chârbâgh

WELÂYAT

Qerâghu

Jangal-bâgh

Qâzi-kenti

Schematic diagram of main sluices along the
Âktâsh, Welâyat and Khâmrabât canals

Water from the main river flows down all canals
during 8 days in the cycle of 18 (the other 10
days are for Sheberghân)

ÂKTÂSH

Then at a primary division water continues down
all branches (which should be equal)
throughout the 8 days

SAR-E-POL

Emâm-e-Khord

At secondary and later sluices, the water-
master sends water down each branch in turn
for a specific number of days or hours

Map I Canal diagram.

Prologue: Introducing the Piruzai

Great Games in Afghanistan

Afghanistan has had a rich and eventful history, and at times very much preoccupied European governments, particularly during the nineteenth-century 'Great Game' between the British and Russian empires, which treated the country as a 'buffer state' between them. In the north, as the Russians absorbed the khanates of central Asia (later to crystallize into the states of Turkmenistan, Uzbekistan and Tâjikistan), the present frontier was established on the Oxus river (Amu-daryâ). In the 1880s an Anglo-Russian Boundary Commission marked out the north-western land frontier. In the south and east, following the first two Afghan wars (1839–42 and 1878–80), the British drew the Durand Line (1893) to separate Afghanistan from India (eventually Pakistan). Britain continued to control Afghan foreign relations until the third Afghan war (1919). (See Map A.)

Afghanistan's most marked geographical feature is the Hindu-Kush mountain massif and its extensions, the western end of the Himalayas. In the nineteenth century the central mountains were inhabited by Persian-speaking Tâjiks, Aymâqs and Hazâras. In the north, Tâjiks and Turkic-speaking Uzbeks and Turkmens occupied the foothills and plains of Afghan Turkistan. Pashtu-speakers predominated in the south, east and west.

None of these political, geographic or ethno-linguistic boundaries were impermeable. Pashtun-dominated Afghan governments never accepted the Durand Line, which bisects Pashtun lands, though it divides only a few tribes. The northern frontier similarly was and is a political not an ethnic reality – Turkmens, Uzbeks, Tâjiks and others live on both sides. Mountain peoples, notably Hazâras, have long migrated to Iran, India, Pakistan and elsewhere for trade and work, while Pashtun and other nomads of the plains traditionally trekked seasonally into the mountains or across the Durand Line.

After the Second World War, a new 'Great Game' began, this time as a peaceful competition between the USA and the USSR to provide aid and infrastructure to neutral Afghanistan. 'Development' – the spread of education, industrialization and other manifestations of modernity – proceeded slowly; too slowly for many in the urban educated classes. A series of events began in the 1960s that were to restore the country to the centre of world attention in ensuing decades. Though a new constitution and a reformed parliament with democratic elections were instituted in 1964, the

Kabul government was weak and ineffective, particularly in dealing with the severe drought of 1970–71, the subsequent harsh winter, and the spring 1972 famine that killed many thousands in the west and north-west. This failure was a major factor leading to Dâ'ud's coup in July 1973.[1]

Afghan Turkistan: the setting

North-central Afghanistan – the western part of Afghan Turkistan, between Mazâr-e-Sharif and Maymana – is both fertile and ethnically diverse. From the steppes and sandy deserts of low elevation near the northern frontier, the land rises in rolling loess hills southward towards the Band-e-Turkistan mountains, the north-western spur of the Hindu-Kush, with peaks up to 3,500 metres. Higher mountain chains lie further south in Ghor and Bâmyân provinces. Springs and snow runoff from these ranges feed streams and rivers flowing north, cutting deep, spectacular canyons across the mountains before being consumed by irrigation. Summers and winters in Turkistan are extreme. In the mountains, summers are pleasant but short, winter snow often lying in the valleys for over six months of the year. (See Map B.)

During the nineteenth century this region experienced decades of internecine warfare and raiding, cholera epidemics and famine, and by the 1880s it was under-populated. The steppes and foothills, traditionally the lands of the Uzbeks, provided fine winter and spring grazing, used by Arab and Turkmen nomads, while Uzbek and Tâjik farmers struggled to maintain the irrigation systems in the Sar-e-pol, Shur-daryâ and Shirin-tagaw river valleys. The main towns (Maymana, Andkhoy, Âqcha, Sheberghân, Sar-e-pol) were seats of small Uzbek khanates.[2]

Uzbeks were tribally organized, and once included semi-nomadic pastoralists. By the 1960s, however, all Uzbeks in this region were settled, though many, particularly the better-off, continued to spend summer months in felt-covered mobile huts set up in orchards near their houses. Most craftsmen and tradesmen in the towns are Uzbek.[3] Uzbek farmers tend fruit orchards and vineyards in the valleys near the market centres of Sar-e-pol, Sangchârak/Toghzâr, Gorziwân, Belcherâgh and Maymana; they also grow rainfed wheat on the hillsides up to 2,000 metres.

Turkmens are few in Sar-e-pol but numerous in the northern districts of Sheberghân and Andkhoy. Linguistically and culturally related to the Uzbeks, but distinct and seen as such by all, the Turkmens are still tribally organized and largely pastoralists, though they do not normally practise long-range migrations. A dominant feature of Turkmen economic organization is livestock corporations, headed by chiefs and producing karakul lambskins for the world market. They are also prominent in the carpet-weaving industry, for which western Turkistan is noted.

Numerous communities of Arabs live in the Sar-e-pol and Suzma-qala districts. They too are mainly pastoralists, specializing in the *Arabi* breed of sheep, producing lambs and yearlings for local and national meat-markets. They claim descent from

---

[1] See Barry (2002: 216–17), Parenti (2011: 100–2).
[2] See Lee (1996).
[3] From here on, I use the 'ethnographic present' for the situation in 1971–72.

Arab tribes of the original Muslim conquests, but they are Persian-speaking and have adopted both Uzbek and Turkmen cultural features.

The Sar-e-pol river rises in the highlands of Sar-e-pol and Sangchârak sub-provinces, running north through Sar-e-pol town to Sheberghân, centre of Jawzjân province. To the south, Hazâras, Tâjiks and Aymâqs inhabit the mountain valleys at 1,500 to 3,000 metres, where fast-flowing streams irrigate a limited amount of wheat and barley. On the slopes above, they grow precarious crops of rainfed wheat. After the snows melt, there is good if rocky pasturage over 3,000 metres, and flocks of hardy mountain sheep can be raised locally if enough fodder is grown in the valleys for use in the long winters. In the scattered settlements, houses are closely packed for protection against extreme cold.

The Hazâras[4] are mainly Shi'a Muslims, whereas the large majority of the population of Afghanistan are Sunni. Their mountain homeland, the Hazârajât, covers Bâmyân, Oruzgân, eastern Ghor, southern Jawzjân and parts of several other provinces. Here they long defended their independence as a nation of about a million people, until they were overcome and integrated into the state in 1893 by Amir Abdor-Rahmân (1880–1901). Many Hazâras are settled in the lowlands, for example in several large villages near Sar-e-pol town, where they are known as industrious farmers and have an influential chief. In close economic and social contact with people of other ethnic groups, they retain their distinctive identity and maintain ties with relatives in the mountains, who practise mixed farming of wheat and barley, together with *Hazâragi* sheep – which have a high milk yield and contribute much of the ghee that all groups in the region value. In the Hazârajât, society is still dominated by powerful local Mirs.

Tâjiks in Sar-e-pol are Persian-speaking Sunnis. They are often confused – and confuse themselves – with Aymâqs. In Sar-e-pol there are outposts of Firuzkuhi and Taymani, two of the main Chahâr-Aymâq ('Four-Tribes') of western Afghanistan, but most of them have forgotten their original identity and lost contact with their fellow-tribesmen; they often call themselves Tâjik. Some who called themselves 'Aymâq' – especially in the Kachan valley and in Sangchârak – are plausibly thought to have been Hazâras recently converted to Sunni Islam; Kachani 'Aymâqs' have marriage links in the Hazârajât. Tâjiks, Aymâqs and Kachanis are mixed farmers, cultivating grain, fodder and fruit; they also raise sheep and cattle, and many have summer camps on the slopes above their villages.

These mountain-dwellers are territorially quite well defined and often isolated – two to three days' journey even in good weather from the nearest market or administrative centre. They rarely leave their valleys, let alone the region. For knowledge of the outside world they rely on military conscripts, the few locals who travel to market, and the nomads who pass through their lands in spring and late summer.

Pashtuns come to Sar-e-pol

In the 1880s, as Turkistan came under the control of Kabul, Amir Abdor-Rahmân, keen to have his northern domains repopulated and his frontiers defended, promoted a

---

[4] Mousavi (1998), Ibrahimi (2017), Monsutti (2005, 2018).

major immigration of his fellow-Pashtun tribespeople, especially from the two rival confederations, the Durrani and the Ghiljai. The colonization came from two directions. First, he sent large numbers of Ghiljai and other tribes from south-eastern Afghanistan – often his political opponents – to settle and farm in the north-east. Some of these immigrants moved west to Sheberghân and Maymana. Then (see Chapter 2) in 1886 he ordered Tâju Khân Khânikheyl of the Es'hâqzai tribe to take several thousand families of *mâldâr* – nomadic or semi-nomadic pastoralists – from the south-west to guard Bâdghis and the north-western frontier. These were Durrani, like the amir and all but one of Afghanistan's rulers between 1747 and 1978. Abdor-Rahmân trusted his fellow-tribesmen's loyalty. Spurred on by drought conditions in their homeland, the migrants were granted land rights in favoured spots and advances to help them settle and cultivate, though few of them did so then.[5] Many of the *mâldâr* later moved eastward to Maymana and Turkistan.

At first only small groups of Pashtuns arrived in Sar-e-pol, where they occupied vacant lands with little local opposition. Then, from 1900, more Durrani arrived from the west and south-west, mainly Es'hâqzai from Nawzâd and other parts of Posht-e-Rud – districts of Kandahar, but today's Helmand province – where severe droughts drove some farmers off the land and some *mâldâr* to seek new pastures. In their summer quarters (the Band-e-Bayân mountains in Ghor) they had met *mâldâr* from Turkistan, who told them that conditions there were much better than in Helmand.

In the early 1900s the *mâldâr* newcomers in Sar-e-pol thrived in the lush conditions, having ousted local Arab and Turkmen pastoralists. In summer they trekked south to their traditional pastures in Ghor; there they sold surplus livestock to Pashtun nomad traders from the east, who set up large tented bazaars, selling cloth, guns and other wares brought from India and Pakistan, to the locals and to pastoral nomads from south, west and north. When the bazaars closed in late summer, some traders moved north to continue trading in the Sar-e-pol region, returning eastwards in autumn.

In the 1920s and 1930s, many Pashtun *mâldâr* learned the value of karakul sheep from the Turkmens. Having formerly marketed livestock on the hoof in the central mountains, now they sold lambskins to dealers in the north who took them to Kabul by road, so they had less reason to trek to the mountains. Some Pashtun immigrants acquired farmlands, but at first they barely cultivated them – the extensive irrigation networks in the Sar-e-pol valley remained unusable. However, as the northern population grew, the pastures filled up, and by the 1950s the canals were restored and all the irrigable land was back under cultivation. Landowning *mâldâr* found their investment bringing greater and more reliable returns than their flocks, and with less hardship. Wherever possible they built houses and adopted a fully mixed economy. In 1971, many who have not acquired farmland are experimenting – not always successfully – with rainfed crops in the steppe pastures. Another trend is for wealthy settled *mâldâr* to send their flocks to seasonal pastures accompanied only by hired shepherds.

---

[5] See N. Tapper (1983), Kakar (1979), Lee (1996).

The population of Sar-e-pol sub-province in 1971 is around 150,000 (25,000 households). Uzbeks are the largest ethnic group, totalling (together with the small numbers of Turkmens) about 60,000 (10,000 households). Persian-speakers (Seyyeds, Arabs, Aymâqs, Tâjiks and Hazâras) number nearly the same. The remaining 30,000 to 40,000 (6,000 households) are Pashtuns, including about 15,000 Durrani (2,500 households). Persian is the lingua franca of northern Afghanistan, used by most Pashtu- and Turkic-speakers in daily interaction with friends, neighbours, customers, clients and traders from other ethno-linguistic groups, as well as the local authorities. Table 1 gives estimates for ethnic group membership in Sar-e-pol sub-province as a whole.

In 1971, fourteen Es'hâqzai sub-tribes, averaging 150 to 200 households, have villages and winter quarters in Jawzjân, mostly near Sar-e-pol town. The sub-tribes vary in situation and character. Seven (the Akhtarkheyl, Amânkheyl, Sufikheyl, Akbarkheyl sections of the Kamuzai, and sections of the Omarzai, Dawlatzai and Torkheyl), numbering up to 1,000 households, are pastoralists with winter tent-villages west of the Sar-e-pol river valley, in the dry hill-steppes of the Dasht-e-Leyli, where they are relatively isolated from administrative control and from Uzbek villagers. During their trek to the mountains (Chaghcharân and Upper Morghâb) they conduct trade and other economic exchange with Aymâqs and Tâjiks.

A few hundred households of tent-dwelling pastoralists from four sub-tribes (another Kamuzai section, two sections of Nâmanzai, and a small section of Omarzai) camp most of the year beside the Sar-e-pol valley, some miles north of the town. They have greater contact with local Uzbek, Hazâra, Arab and Aymâq villagers, both in the Valley and during their trek to the mountains (Esmeydân and Lâl-o-Sar-jangal). Few of them own valley farmlands, though they often dry-farm nearby steppe pastures.

About 1,000 households from five sub-tribes (Nazarzai, Pakhizai, Piruzai, Sheykhânzai and Torkheyl) are semi-settled, having villages in or beside the Valley, where most of them own lands and have houses. All are in regular contact with members of several other ethnic groups, though fewer than half the families trek to the mountains (Kohistân, Lâl-o-Sar-jangal).

Two of this last group of sub-tribes are of particular interest to us. The Nazarzai include the khans who dominated the region from their arrival until the 1970s; we shall hear more about them. The Piruzai are the main subjects of this book.

Table 1 Ethnic groups in Sar-e-pol sub-province, 1971.

Ethnic Group	Language	Sect	No. of households	Percentage
Uzbek and Turkmen	Turkic	Sunni	10,000	40
Aymâq, Tâjik, Kachani	Persian	Sunni	5,000	20
Hazâra	Persian	Shi'ite	2,500–3,000	10
Arab and Seyyed	Persian	Sunni	1,000–1,500	5
Durrani Pashtuns	Western Pashtu	Sunni	2,500	10
Other South-western Pashtuns	Western Pashtu	Sunni	2,500	10
Ghiljai and eastern Pashtuns	Eastern Pashtu	Sunni	1,000	4
Total			about 25,000	100

The Piruzai

In 1971, the Piruzai sub-tribe in Sar-e-pol number about 1,900 people, in 272 households. They have two villages and various smaller hamlets and camps some fifteen kilometres north of Sar-e-pol town, to the east of the main (unpaved) road to Sheberghân. These settlements are officially named Upper, Middle and Lower Khârkash; locally, only the first is known as Khârkash (headman Nâder-shâh); the second is called Konjek (headman Haji Tumân), and the group of hamlets constituting Lower Khârkash is known after a leading man, Rishmin.[6]

The sub-tribe is of mixed composition. Four core Piruzai lineages number 177 household heads: A, *awlâd* (descendants) of Khoday-dâd, 77 households; B, Nasuzai, 15 households; C, *awlâd* of Ezzat, 70 households; D, *awlâd* of Mir-Âzâr, 15 households. Lineages A and B are recognized as *awlâd* of Piru. Lineages C and D claim equal rights with them but are suspected of other origins. The remaining 95 households are more or less transient clients (*hamsaya*, 'neighbours') from other tribal and ethnic groups.

In the nineteenth century, Piruzai were based in Dara-miân, a valley north-west of Nawzâd. Some had farmland there, dependent on irrigation from *kâriz*, underground water-channels, but all were tent-dwelling *mâldâr* and trekked north to Ghor in spring. Close neighbours included Khânikheyl, the Es'hâqzai chiefs.[7] In mid-century, the *kâriz* failed in a severe drought, disrupting both farming and pastoralism. Then, people tell us, the Piruzai became scattered. The ancestors of today's Lineage C (see below) moved to Washir-o-Pulât, then to Tâlokân, between Gereshk and Kandahar, to join the Piruzai leader Malek-Mahmad. This history, and the fact that they had no land, later threw doubt on Lineage C's claims to Piruzai ancestry: as former dependants of Khânikheyl they are suspected of Fârsibân (non-Durrani) origins; and Es'hâqzai in the north say that unless you owned land in Dara-miân, you are not Es'hâqzai.[8] A century later, Lineage C are still – behind their backs – called 'Pulâdi', doubtless because they came from Pulât district, but the name resembles those of many Fârsibân groups. Lineage C members too privately refer to themselves as Pulâdi.

The Piruzai heard about Sar-e-pol through connections such as Seyf Âkhondzâda Nazarzai, who, before he went north with Tâju Khân, was Malek-Mahmad Piruzai's mullah. In the early twentieth century, when another drought struck their homeland and famine conditions prevailed, some Piruzai were persuaded to try their luck in the north. Joma-khân, grandson of Lineage A ancestor Khoday-dâd, went to visit Sar-e-pol; he came home enthusiastic about conditions there and intent on leading a Piruzai

---

[6]   See Map F. Google Maps labels Konjek 'Abrishamin'; the other villages are not named. Some earlier maps name Khârkash correctly, but label Konjek 'Khâm-rabât Haji Shamsoddin' which is actually the name of a settlement nearby to the east.

[7]   A 'Pirozay' settlement is marked on Google Maps, alongside 'Idizay' and 'Khani kheyl', in a valley some 10 km north-west of Nawzâd centre. The Idizai are closely related to the Piruzai, and both were probably clients of Tâju Khân Khânikheyl. Also marked is Kârez-i Dara-ye Miân, about one kilometre up the valley from 'Khani kheyl'.

In the *Hilmand Province District Atlas* (OCHA 2014), p. 12, the three villages are 'Edo zai', 'Ferozi' and 'Khani Khail'. 'Washer' is a nearby district and district centre; 'Folad (= Pulât)' is very close to the centre.

[8]   See N. Tapper (1979: 180, n. 11).

migration north. To gain further followers for his expedition, he fetched the Pulâdi back, arranging two pairs of exchange marriages with them. As Durrani girls may not marry non-Durrani, these marriages recognized the Pulâdi as Durrani, and Joma-khân further dispelled suspicions of their Fârsibân origins by persuading Tâju Khân's son Jamâl Khân to 'make them Durrani' by exempting them from a tax he was levying on all non-Durrani in Kandahar. Thereafter the Pulâdi have insisted on their Piruzai identity. (See Fig. 1.)

Joma-khân's expedition came north around 1920. A bare majority were Piruzai. Lineage A, led by ancestor Khoday-dâd's son Arz-begi and his sons Joma-khân and Karim-dâd (father of Khârkash village headman Nâder-shâh), were 24 households. Lineage C (Pulâdi), led by ancestor Ezzat's grandson Afzal, were twelve households; being landless, they had done long-distance trading to supplement their pastoral income; Joma-khân's invitation offered them an opportunity to revive their pastoral economy, and it seems they all agreed to follow him. Associated with the Pulâdi were

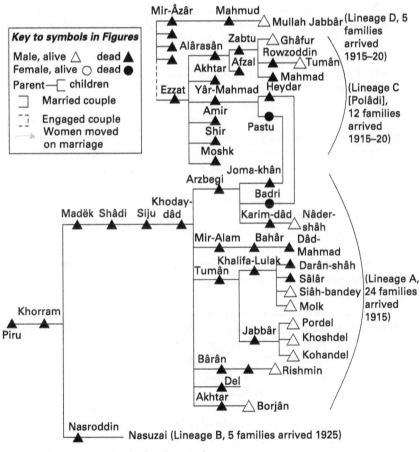

Figure 1 Piruzai ancestors and early arrivals.

five other households of uncertain origins, the *awlâd* of Mir-Âzâr. Ezzat's father, people said, had found the infant Mir-Âzâr 'in a mosque' and his wife nursed him. Mir-Âzâr's mother was supposedly an Alizai Durrani; his father was probably Alizai too, but Mir-Âzâr 'became Durrani through the milk' and his *awlâd* came north as Lineage D, led by Mullah Jabbâr. There were no marriages between them and Lineage A, though both had intermarried with a group of Alekozai Durrani.

Joma-khân's party was completed by twenty-five households from other Es'hâqzai and Durrani tribal groups and at least two different Fârsibân tribes, all of whom had marriage links with the Piruzai. In 1971, some of their descendants continue to live near the Piruzai, others have gone on to Balkh but still intermarried with the Piruzai, while yet others have recently left the Piruzai to take up farming in Konduz. In all, around 70 households followed Joma-khân to Sar-e-pol, where the Piruzai formed a single settlement of 55–60 households. All the migrants came north as *mâldâr*. None were wealthy, and no leader had much authority over any but his immediate relatives. The lineages were intermarried; but tension between Lineages A and C later exploded in feud, as we shall hear later.

The Piruzai migrants spent their first winter near Emâm-Ja'far, the home of Gholâm-Rasul Khân Nazarzai, official chief of the northern Durranis. Next year they moved about 20 km south and camped in the Valley in what was then an uncultivated, thorn-ridden wilderness (*jangal*). Arab nomads who had occupied this land fled into the nearby steppe. The Piruzai found that land, water and food were plentiful, and they began to prosper.

The two decades after their arrival were relatively uneventful – apart from a brief interethnic war in 1929, at the time of the Saqawi revolt (see below). The Piruzai learned karakul sheep husbandry and their pastoral enterprises thrived in the abundant grazing. For many years they continued to trek to their former summer quarters in the Band-e-Bayân mountains near Chaghcharân (Kâsi), which they knew as Siâh-band; then they shifted to more accessible grazing lands in eastern Ghor, first in Kermân then in Lâl-o-Sar-jangal. In the mountains they sold their surplus stock, traded and returned north with goods such as cloth.

Soon after they had established a pastoral base, Joma-khân died and was succeeded as head of Lineage A and the Piruzai by his half-brother, Karim-dâd. Karim-dâd recruited two further important groups of migrants, following Joma-khân's precedent of using exchange marriages to reunite distant kinsmen – a useful and quick means for a leader to gain followers.

Around 1925, five households arrived to form Lineage B; they were Nasuzai, an established Piruzai branch, most members of which stayed in Kandahar. However, they had come north earlier and lived for some years with Baluch nomads in the steppe west of the Sar-e-pol valley. Karim-dâd sought out these distant kin and persuaded them to join him in Khârkash. To cement the alliance he arranged a pair of exchange marriages between them and his own closest agnates in Lineage A.

Then around 1930 other migrants arrived from the south: four households of descendants of Lineage A ancestor Khoday-dâd, but by a different wife from Arz-begi's mother. This group is now known as Borjân-kheyl after their leading man. Again Karim-dâd arranged exchange marriages with his own family, but the exchanges were never completed. For many years the two groups quarrelled and several times Borjân-kheyl left Sar-e-pol.[9]

Not long after the Piruzai started camping in the Valley, the owner of the surrounding lands, Abdol-Kâder Alizai (remembered as Tahsildâr, the tax collector), offered to sell them to the Piruzai, as he wanted to move east. There was little interest in the offer; after the disasters in the south, the leaders were disillusioned with farming and were content with the easy life pastoralism offered in the north. But Karim-dâd of Lineage A and Afzal of Lineage C – realizing that 'land is a golden tent-peg' (*zamin mikh-e-zarin*) – bought the lands, with associated water rights, for 4,000 rupees (afghanis), which was very cheap. The total area of land sold was 3,000 *jeribs* (600 hectares); 150 *jeribs* went to local Uzbek villagers, the remaining 2,850 were registered to the Piruzai leaders in the initial deeds. I was unable to discover how accurate these figures were.

Karim-dâd and Afzal divided the lands into five equal shares and distributed them among five leading men of Lineages A and C. Each share was further subdivided, and eventually parcels were distributed to all forty-one households of the two lineages. Lineage D too received a quarter portion of one of the Lineage C shares; but no non-Piruzai households received land. Nasuzai and Borjân-kheyl had not arrived in time for the distribution. Later, several Piruzai acquired large parcels of land elsewhere.

At a pace that matched the population increase in the region, the Piruzai began to hire local villagers to restore the canals and cultivate their rich valley lands, and learned the techniques of intensive irrigated agriculture. In the early 1930s the leaders built the first fixed dwellings in their farmlands.

Despite the initial lack of interest, in due course the distribution of farmland became a major factor defining relations among the Piruzai. A division emerged between landowners and the rest, who became their clients. Disputes over land sharpened social cleavages within and between Lineages A and C, which now occupied distinct settlements – Khârkash and Konjek – and they rarely trekked together to the mountains. The first major conflict was the outbreak, in 1936–37, of a feud between the two main lineages, with men killed and wounded on both sides (see Chapter 4). The Es'hâqzai chief made peace with difficulty, arranging the customary marriages between the sides, but the hostility between them lingered. Lineages A and C are linked by a series of marriages, some dating from before the feud, some contracted at its end, others since, usually between relatives by existing marriages. The villages have different mosques and graveyards, and celebrate the Ids separately, both the Greater Id of Sacrifice and the Lesser Id after Ramazan.

By 1971, the four core lineages number 177 households (Table 2). The heads of the 162 households of Lineages A, C and D descend from the migrants who received land in the original distribution. Lineage B has lands elsewhere. Many households have already lost their land, bought or seized by more powerful relatives, but about half of all Piruzai households own and benefit directly from shares in irrigated lands, totalling

---

[9] Nancy examines the complicated story of the political consequences of these exchange marriages in detail (N. Tapper 1979: 348ff.). Lineage A consider the intransigent attitude of Borjân-kheyl during this quarrel to be a legacy of their Hazâra ancestress, Khoday-dâd's second wife.

over 5,000 *jerib*s (1,000 hectares). Others also farm dry-lands nearby. Nâder-shâh, headman of Khârkash village and wealthiest man in the sub-tribe, is reckoned a 'khan'; his main rival is Tumân, headman of Konjek village. Both men inherited substantial shares of land and bought additional large holdings elsewhere.[10]

Table 2 Composition of Piruzai sub-tribe, 1920 and 1971.

		c. 1920	1971
Core Lineages			
Lineage A	*awlâd* of Khoday-dâd	24	77
Lineage B	(5 households joined *c.* 1925), Nasuzai		15
Lineage C	*awlâd* of Ezzat, Pulâdi	12	70
Lineage D	*awlâd* of Mir-Âzâr	5	15
Clients (*hamsaya*)			
	Piruzai relatives	14	24
	Other Es'hâqzai and Durrani	*c.* 5	56
	non-Durrani	*c.* 10	15
Totals		70	272

The Piruzai economy

The Piruzai usually operate a surplus economy, that is, the crops grown on irrigated valley lands owned by members of the sub-tribe, and the wool and meat produced by their flocks, are adequate for the needs of all. Deficits in grain and milk products are more than made up by proceeds from the sale of lambskins and cash crops such as cotton.

A 'typical' pastoral household of three adults and four children, owning no land, can live off a flock of 60 ewes. The flock will produce enough milk and meat for their annual consumption. A cash income of 10,000 rupees (£50 at that time) from skins and 1,000 rupees from fleeces will allow a minimum of bought goods: flour, rice, fat and incidental items. A household without flocks needs 10 *jerib*s (2 hectares) of good irrigated land to allow similar consumption.

A day-labourer can earn 50 rupees a day or up to 800 rupees a month, but employment is very seasonal. A domestic servant or a herding assistant receives food and clothing for himself and a cash wage of 200–500 rupees a month. Even the maximum annual wage of 6,000 rupees (£30) is insufficient for a small family of two adults and two children, particularly in years of high grain prices like 1970–71. Such jobs are usually taken by young men without dependents, who can save most of the cash wage towards the cost of a future marriage. Most servants and labourers with dependents survive only on charity. A chief shepherd receives food and clothing and 10 per cent of his charges' produce, including lambs and skins: his average income is worth about 10,000 rupees, though it can range from nothing to more than 20,000

[10] For more on Piruzai land tenure, see N. Tapper (1991).

rupees in a good year. A farmhand who contracts his labour for a year may earn produce worth over 10,000 rupees, but even if the crop fails completely he is guaranteed around half a ton of wheat, on which a family of four can just live for a year.

Although they had known extreme differences of wealth in the south-west, the Piruzai who came north – at least the core lineages – had been relatively homogeneous in this respect. After their purchase and eventual cultivation of irrigated valley lands, and most recently with the rise in land values, wealth differences have once more widened, ranging between those who own several hundred animals and a hundred or more *jeribs* of land, to those who have no such capital at all and depend on selling their labour.

Table 3 shows the distribution of wealth in the 67 households of Lineage C in 1971. This lineage is the major, and more permanent, part of the population of Konjek village. The 'sample' is skewed in favour of the better-off members of the community, in that it does not include the dozen or so transient 'client' households living in the same village and camps. Khârkash village is substantially wealthier, so the sample plausibly represents the middle range of people; and it certainly depicts a population in the process of settlement.

I have grouped the households into four quartiles, using wealth units of 1,000 rupees, equivalent to 1 ewe or 0.1 *jerib*.

The wealthiest quartile own 65 per cent of all productive assets (60 per cent of the irrigated farmland and 76 per cent of the flocks); all have sheep and go to spring pastures, and their tents and flocks constitute the majority of those going to the mountains.

In the two middle quartiles, 23 out of 34 households have sheep and 22 go to spring pastures, while 11 of 17 in the poorest quartile go to spring pastures even though only three of them have sheep.

Table 3 Household wealth and size.

Wealth quartiles	I	II	III	IV	Totals
Number of households	16	17	17	17	67
Total no. of people	217	130	109	84	540
Persons per household	13.6	7.7	6.4	4.9	8.1
No. of households owning land	16	17	14	0	47
Total units (0.1 *jerib*) of land owned	5895	3180	745	0	9820
Land units per person	27	24	7	0	18
No. of household owning ewes	16	13	10	3	42
Total number of ewes owned	3560	635	414	54	4663
Ewes per person	16	5	4	1	9
No. of households owning land or ewes	16	17	17	3	53
Total units of land and ewes	9455	3815	1159	54	14483
Mean household wealth in units	591	224	68	3	216
Percentage of total wealth	65	26	8	0	99
1971 households (all or part) in					
spring pastures	16	12	10	11	49
summer pastures	11	4	1	0	16
Households with members employed outside	4	6	15	16	42

All households in quartiles I and II, and most in III (14 of 17), have land, though none of IV do. Altogether 47 of the 67 households have land; holdings average over 20 *jeribs* (4 hectares).

Forty-two households have sheep, with a mean of 111 ewes each.

Fourteen households have no assets at all, but some expect to inherit land in due course.

There is a clear correlation of household wealth and size: the wealthiest households have a mean size of nearly 14 persons, while the poorest average five. The overall mean household size is eight. But it is striking that the top two quartiles have similar holdings of irrigated land per person, while the top quartile has much larger average flocks. In flock sizes, on the other hand, the second quartile differs little from the third, which has a much lower average land holding.

In other words, large-scale pastoralism has become an enterprise for wealthy households with more male members than are needed for farming. Very few households depend exclusively, or even predominantly, on pastoralism. Half of all households can expect enough income from their capital holdings to be fundamentally self-sufficient. Such households with property and wealth are said to be 'full' (*sir, mor*), well off and secure (*tayyâr*), while this is certainly not the case for many in the third quartile and all of the fourth, who are known as 'hungry' (*wëzhey, gushna*). Households with little or no capital are 'poor' (*khwâr, gharib*) and 'light-weight' (*spëk*). In fact only 25 households depend entirely on production from their own land and/or flocks, so that 42 gain some or all of their income from outside employment or by engaging in trade.

The Piruzai still speak of themselves as *mâldâr,* and many are still much involved with livestock. They own over 10,000 breeding ewes; half the households have flocks of twenty to several hundred head, and most flock-owners make the annual trek to mountain pastures. But population pressure and the volatility of national and world markets in karakul skins, their main pastoral product, has long encouraged them to look elsewhere for economic security. More than three-quarters have mud-brick dwellings (with flat, timber-beamed roofs) – though this in itself is no index of settlement. The rest still live in tents only. But most people spend most of the year in the villages. Village communities and camps form a single arena, and political and economic decisions made in the villages, for example over agricultural concerns, are likely to have a direct effect on pastoral activities, and vice versa. At the same time, the Piruzai economy affords them a wider range of solutions to political and economic problems than those available to other local groups that are more exclusively either pastoralists or farmers. The Piruzai are well aware of this advantage and seem likely to continue their dual economy for the foreseeable future.

Population growth and change

Settlement in villages of itself brings little cultural and social change for the Pashtuns. Real change follows only from population pressure on resources and consequent increasing inequalities of wealth and power. A generation or two earlier, when the region was under-populated, government writ did not extend far outside the administrative centres, being concerned mainly with the collection of taxes and military recruits. Most farming was confined to the irrigated river valleys, much of which was uncultivated 'jungle'. As government control and public security improved and taxation lightened, population increased, and a land rush followed.

Now the wide river valleys near Sar-e-pol are cultivated to the full; moreover, the pastureland in the surrounding steppes and mountain slopes has begun to disappear beneath rapidly expanding rainfed cultivation, although this is often a risky enterprise. Like Afghanistan as a whole, the region depends for survival on a successful rainfed wheat crop. In a good year Sar-e-pol can export a surplus, but after years like 1970 and 1971 famine threatens as wheat prices are grossly inflated, not only because of bad local harvests, but also as a result of speculation and the immigration of destitute peoples from even less fortunate areas to the west.

By 1971 it seems that the region has as much population as it can support with given resources and technologies. Both crafts and trades have expanded, as has employment in government service. The Tefahosât oil and gas extraction company, based in Mazâr-e-Sharif and Sheberghân, is active at Jarqoduq and Angut, not far from Sar-e-pol. Run by Soviet and Kabuli engineers, it offers about the only industrial jobs available to locals. There is continual emigration to less crowded and developing provinces in the north-east.

Population pressure near Sar-e-pol is reflected in the ethnically complex settlement pattern. Travellers on the road to Sheberghân pass in quick succession villages of the following ethnic groups: Uzbek, Durrani, Maleki, Durrani, Uzbek, Hazâra, Durrani, Baluch, Arab, Seyyed, Durrani, Ghiljai, Durrani. With acute pressure on resources, and the dominant position of the Pashtun khans, competition and hostility tend to focus in common opposition to Pashtuns by the rest. Few Pashtuns live in the mountains south of Sar-e-pol, however, where the population remains relatively homogeneous, Uzbek, Aymâq and Hazâra territories being still distinct.

A further reflection of population growth is the emergence of a fourfold class structure: a traditional power-elite of landowners, khans, wealthy merchants and others; a 'bourgeoisie' of independent propertied tribesmen and peasants and established traders and artisans; a property-less and dependent rural and urban 'proletariat'; and a new 'intelligentsia' of young, educated townspeople, especially teachers and senior officials, including some educated and even employed in Kabul. There are also officials and traders from outside the region, often from ethnic groups not otherwise represented locally. This class structure does not coincide with ethnic divisions, nor do occupational categories – e.g. *mâldâr* (pastoralist), *molkdâr* (landowner), *gharibkâr* (labourer, usually casual), *dokândâr* (shopkeeper), *dehqân* (farm-worker) – have ethnic implications. Although most pastoralists are Pashtun and most townspeople and educated youth are Uzbek, both Pashtuns and Uzbeks and most others contribute significant numbers to each of the four emergent classes.[11]

In 1971, however, like much of rural Afghanistan, Sar-e-pol is still a 'feudal' society. Despite the presence of government organs, in most contexts power is in the hands of

---

[11] For more on 'class' in Sar-e-pol, see R. Tapper (1984). Jebens (1983) is a thorough geographical study of Sar-e-pol in the 1970s, with a focus on textile production and trade.

the power-elite, dominated by wealthy, landed tribal khans – predecessors of more recent 'warlords'. The khans have large entourages of servants and paid thugs. In ordinary life, villagers and townspeople conduct their economic and social activities without much interference by the khans; but certain extreme actions, like homicide and large-scale theft, usually lead to intervention by both government and khans – which entails ruinous expense for ordinary people, often quite innocent of any offence. In desperate cases a whole community (a village or even groups of villages) can unite to confront and resist oppression – there will be violence, but the resistance can succeed: as the Piruzai say, 'community strength is God's strength'.[12]

In Sar-e-pol, claimants to the status of Durrani Pashtun must trace descent from a recognized ancestor, and ensure that their sisters and daughters marry only Durrani men. For Durrani, differences among them are insignificant compared to their distinction from members of other ethnic groups. All Durrani, as 'cousins', Sunni Muslims and Pashtu-speakers, are ideally equal. In 1971, for many Durrani in Sar-e-pol this ideal diverges dramatically from reality. The growing value of farmland and other sources of wealth, and the expansion of local government bureaucracy, make economic and political inequality a fact of life, both within local communities and between powerful khans and ordinary tribespeople. The egalitarian ethic is transformed into ideals of independence and self-sufficiency, which mean, at the local level, highly competitive economic behaviour: every household for itself.

Tribalism too is being transformed. A generation or two earlier, tribal rules of co-responsibility and blood compensation still operated. Talking of such events, which they do reluctantly, Durrani express both regret and relief that such a succession of killings is now impossible. Violence occurs, but 'there are two things the government will not tolerate now: rustling and murder', and revenge killings are rare in the Sar-e-pol region.

There is still a strong ideal that descendants (through males) of a common ancestor should be both neighbours and politically united, and the strength of this ideal is greater the closer the ancestor; but people continually regret the degeneration of the times, such that nowadays one can no longer rely on one's paternal relatives; brother fights brother, father fights son – all moreover regarded as signs of the impending end of the world.

It is, of course, impossible to be sure that the Sar-e-pol Durranis did not always have this attitude to relatives, but evidence to hand indicates that in practice the strength of kinship is not what it was. There are several reasons for this change. Improved security has lessened the need for trekking nomads to move together in large, lineage-based groups. Increased government intervention has reduced the possibility of interethnic warfare and consequent demands for solidarity at that level. Settlement as close neighbours leads to intensified hostilities between close relatives who, as nomads, can simply avoid each other, while individual ownership of, and now pressure on, agricultural land leads to widening inequalities and ample grounds for dispute. Families are now ruthlessly competitive. The evidence indicates that this was not always so.

---

[12] *dë woles zur dë khoday zur*; strictly speaking, *vis populi vis dei*. See also p. 95.

Durrani see clearly that when land and pasture were abundant, 'everyone had adequate means, people had *qawmi* (tribal solidarity)'. Even more fundamentally, they recognize the major change as arising from the fact of landowning itself. As one man puts it, 'In the old days there were no powerful khans; every headman or white-beard was of some consequence, and independent. They were called *maleks* and were *khân bi-sterkhân*' – khans without tablecloths: that is, unlike khans, hospitality played no part in relations with their followers. 'That was before people had land,' he explains; 'a man's opportunities were the same as his father's. Now land enters the question, and inheritance, power and wealth pass from father to son.'

Village life in 1971

Piruzai lands and villages are in the broadest part of the river valley between the western and eastern steppes, just south of the border between Sar-e-pol and Sheberghân sub-provinces. A track, jeep-able but criss-crossed by irrigation ditches, runs from the main north–south road first to Khârkash and Konjek, then out into the eastern steppe. Neighbouring villages are varied: other Es'hâqzais; Alizai Durranis; Ghiljai, Kâkar, Wârdak and Ludin Pashtuns; Arabs, Uzbeks and several large Hazâra settlements not far away.

Villages are compact, though houses are sometimes strung out in a line. Land for houses (from large compounds to simple houses and one-room huts) is all privately owned and the landless must ask permission to pitch a tent or build a house. For domestic water, houses near a canal-head (such as those of Khârkash) have ponds filled every cycle; in villages further down (such as Konjek), where canal water does not always reach, 30-metre wells provide sweet water.

Wealthier households have high-walled compounds, with gateways and separate guestrooms; inside or adjacent to the compound, there is often a well or a pond, and sometimes a small orchard or garden. Poorer households have separate one- or two-roomed huts, either outside or possibly inside the compound of a wealthier relative or patron. The village alleys run between the high compound walls.

Most villages like Khârkash and Konjek are divided into two 'quarters', typically Upper and Lower, each with its own mosque, built by wealthy men or communally by people of the quarter. Mosques serve as public meeting-places for men, a neutral ground for recreation as well as for airing and resolving disputes. Houses and compounds are private spaces, and where possible no windows look onto the alleys. In practice, apart from the mosques, the whole village or quarter is private space, home territory within which women move around freely – more so than men. Nancy describes and explains in some detail (N. Tapper 1991: 101–11) the lack of gender segregation inside villages and camps. Outside, women's movements are restricted to occasional visits to relatives, and more occasional visits to shrines or even to town for medical reasons.

The narrators

After we left, we worried that enemies of the Piruzai might read our writings on them and use them to harm individuals if we mentioned them by name. So, in Nancy's doctoral thesis (1979) and monograph (1991) and in all our published articles, we have adopted the ethnographic convention of pseudonyms for individuals, their sub-tribe and their villages.

The Piruzai abandoned these villages in the 1980s. If there are survivors, which we dearly hope, it is hard to imagine at the time of writing – nearly half a century later – how they could be harmed by what we publish about them now. Besides, the late Daniel Balland, without consulting us, in an article in *Encyclopedia Iranica* (1998b), 'outed' the sub-tribe we had named Maduzai/Madozai as 'Pirozi'. So, with Nancy's agreement, I have restored the original names, except in the story of 'The pimp'.

A note on names and titles

Many men and women have both a birth name and a common name, and at least one nickname. There are no family names as such; people are known as son or daughter, sometimes as brother or sister, or husband or wife, of so-and-so. Narrators commonly add kinship terms or terms of respect when they mention names, especially of elders, the powerful, or the dead. For younger people or co-evals, diminutives are common; for both men and women, suffixes like -ak/-a, -ey/-gey. I have omitted additions, but I sometimes use a nickname and/or diminutive in the text (and Figures), when the person's 'proper' name was not recorded.

Khan: 'XX Khân' denotes a male member of the Nazarzai khan family; 'khan' is the class and family; '-khân' as suffix (e.g. Baya-khân) is just part of a male name. Another common suffix is '-shâh' (Seyyed-shâh, Nâder-shâh), while Shah after a monarch's name, and other ranks or titles (e.g. Haji, Seyyed, Wazir) before a name, are capitalized. Many male personal names are compounded with prefixes such as Abdol-, Mahmad-. Mohammad is usually shortened, in both speech and writing, to either Mahmad (prefix or suffix) or Mahd- (prefix only). Such compounds are usually further shortened in daily use: e.g. Mahmad-Afzal becomes Afzal, Abdol-Manân becomes Manân; though Abdol-Mahmad becomes Abdol.

Among the narrators there are two Pâdshâhs and two Seyyed-shâhs, distinguished in each case by adding their father's name. Some names can be both male and female, e.g. Tumân, Sarwar, Wazir.

Most narrators are close relatives of our host, Haji Tumân, known as 'Little Haji', and his uncle Haji Ghâfur, known as 'Big-Haji'.

The narrators (in bold) and their relations

The key character in the recent history of Konjek was Haji Afzal, Piruzai leader when they migrated north to Turkestan. He was, by all accounts, both saintly and hospitable. He died in about 1961, leaving numerous descendants.

Haji Ghâfur is one of the few living Piruzai who remember times before they came north. His father Haji Zabtu was Afzal's elder brother. Ghâfur is wealthy and much respected, but is pitied in his old age because, despite having had five wives, two still alive, he has only four living sons, all by his present wife Keshmir, and none thought to be much good. Keshmir herself is regarded as a hard-working and devoted wife and mother, but young people call her 'crazy'. Their large compound is on its own, near the village of Kal-qeshlâq, south of Khârkash but near their main farmland and the main road. They have a large flock of sheep, which Keshmir and some of her sons usually take to the mountains in spring.

Ghâfur's eldest son, **Gol-Ahmad**, is literate, has travelled around the country, and is good company, but is commonly considered rather ineffectual. He is married to his cousin Negâr, Afzal's daughter, but they have only one child, Boghak, a bright girl of about six; one son and two other daughters died in infancy. Most of the work (herding, farming, housework) is done by employees, under the care of second son Joma-khân. Joma is married to Bâbu, who was 'given' to Ghâfur by an admirer, Zarin Tâjik; they have a small son. Ghâfur's other two sons, Ajab-khân and Alef-khân, are teenagers.

Ghâfur has six daughters by three of his wives (including the present two, Keshmir and Bibiwor). All have been strategically married to close and distant cousins. Two are involved in exchanges, Mumin going to Gol-Mahmad, son of Afzal's eldest son Mahd-Karim, in exchange for his sister Khânamir for Alef-khân; and Golak going to Tumân's son Manân in exchange for his sister Khurak (see below) as second wife for Gol-Ahmad.

Headman of Konjek is **Tumân**, late forties, son of Ghâfur's younger brother Rowzoddin. Tumân has three wives. He received the first, **Maryam**, in the 1930s after the feud, as compensation for her brother's killing of his father Rowzoddin. They were both children at the time. Having borne seven sons and three daughters, Maryam is now past childbearing. As a Khârkashi in Konjek, she is defensive of her own family; her brothers do not come to visit her, but she and her children visit them on formal occasions. Maryam speaks reasonable Persian, larded with Pashtu words and phrases, but her narratives are not always easy to follow. Her daughter-in-law **Pâkhâl** frequently corrects or contradicts her on facts and dates.

Maryam's oldest son, Khâni-Âghâ, around thirty, is on military service (1970–72) throughout our stay; he comes home for a few days' leave in spring 1971. In 1964 he married a cousin, Bâdâm, daughter of Haji Wahâb; they have three small children. Bâdâm becomes a close friend to Nancy, but in summer 1971, having remained in the village while we trekked to the mountains, she tragically dies. Maryam and the family take care of her children until Khâni-Âghâ returns in autumn 1972, after we left.

Maryam's second son, **Pâdshâh**, in his late twenties, married Mahd-Amin's daughter **Pâkhâl**, a distant cousin, in a direct exchange involving Maryam's second daughter, Zeytun, and Mahd-Amin's son Payz-Mahmad. The wedding, in 1960 (before Khâni-Âghâ's) was lavish. In summer 1971 Pâdshâh and Pâkhâl stay in the village to look after the farmlands. The following winter they live out in the steppe with the sheep; in Chapter 6, the couple relate how they suffered catastrophic losses from cold and hunger. In Chapter 12, Pâkhâl narrates the birth of her first daughter that winter, to add to her three small sons. In the village, she and her mother-in-law, Maryam, are constant companions. Pâdshâh is an authority on herding, farming and village affairs, and acts as deputy when both his father and his elder brother are absent.

Maryam's third son, **Darwiza**, 25, is an expert shepherd. He stays in the village in summer 1971, starting his military service that autumn. Engaged some years earlier to a second cousin, Haji Afzal's daughter Sawur, they are expected to marry when he returns.

Baya-khân, the fourth son, about 22, accompanies us to the mountains, and records more tapes for us than anyone else. In particular, he tells the best folk tales. He is not yet engaged, but there is an active search for a suitable bride. There is much competition in the neighbourhood to give a daughter to Tumân's son, and thereby acquire powerful local in-laws.

The fifth son, **Kala-khân,** 20, nicknamed 'Sheykh', is a religious student; he knows nothing of farming or herding. Probably he will become the family mullah. The sixth son, Nasib, a teenager, is gaining experience as a shepherd. (Abdul-)**Kayum,** Maryam's youngest son, about twelve, helps with farming and the flocks.

Tumân married his second and favourite wife, Pâkiza, in the late 1950s. She has borne him two surviving sons and three daughters. Her firstborn son, Sadr-e-Azam, died of smallpox at a tender age, but not before he was engaged to a paternal cousin, Haji Ghâfur's daughter Bâbak. Ghâfur should have transferred Bâbak to Pâkiza's second son Manân, but he reneged and gave her to another cousin, Afzal's son Shir.

Pâkiza's eldest surviving son (Abdul-)**Manân,** about twelve, is studying like Kala-khân, and does no work in the fields or with the animals. After the dispute about Bâbak, Ghâfur has agreed to give Tumân another daughter, Golak, for Manân, in exchange for Manân's eldest sister Khurak, aged about nine, as a second wife for Gol-Ahmad; the exchange is sealed in spring 1971, though the weddings will not be held until the girls grow up.

Pâkiza's son, Ridigol, and daughters, Golpeyda and Maygol, are small children.

Tumân's third wife, Sarwar, is an Uzbek widow from Buyna-qara, a village south of Sar-e-pol; she lived with Tumân and his family briefly, but bore no children, and eventually returned to her home village, though he still visits her occasionally. Konjek people remember her fondly and with respect.

Ghâfur has two surviving half-brothers, Jân-Mahmad and **Abdol**(-Mahmad), living in a joint household. Tumân too has two half-brothers, Dur-khân and Akhtar (-Mahmad), also in a joint household. Both joint households are riven by tensions between the brothers' wives; but Tumân manages to keep the whole family united in most situations.

Neshtar, second cousin of Ghâfur, is a widow in her late forties, with three sons, two of them married. Their household is not well off, but Neshtar is the most important woman in Konjek, known, half-jokingly, as the women's 'headman' (*qariyadâr*). As a widow with sons, she can move around independently. She is admired for her ability to organize other women for ceremonies such as wedding parties and for general gatherings. She used to lead the singing at parties, and is known as an entertaining and charismatic conversationalist. Male elders regularly consult her on community issues, not just women's affairs. She also organizes funeral washing for women.

Other narrators

Seyyed-shâh, son of Neshtar's brother Golusar.

Pâdshâh, son of Parwiz, a leading figure of Upper Konjek.

Jamâl-khân, young son of Golgol, son of Haji Wahâb and Ghâfur's sister Saduzi.

Mullah Kadir, son of Mowzoddin, brother of Neshtar and Golusar.

Chârgol, brother of Tumân's second wife Pâkiza, son of Mullah Jabbâr of Khârkash.

Seyyed-shâh, son of Soleymân Kharoti and Ghâfur's sister Belanis.

Karim, hired shepherd, Aymâq from Taghawboy in Kachan valley.

Hâshem, professional cook, from prominent Sar-e-pol Uzbek family.

Gholâm-Rasul Khân, chief of Bâbakzai sub-tribe, important Es'hâqzai leader in Fâryâb province – with whom we begin.

2

The Es'hâqzai Come North

The move north

As we tour the north in January 1971, we pitch our aims in ways that we hope will make sense to potential hosts. An obvious one is an interest in origins and history: although we are quite well-informed on the subject, now we seek local accounts.[1] We meet many local khans, and ask them to talk about tribal history. None is so helpful as the leading Pashtun of Fâryâb province, Gholâm-Rasul Khân of the Bâbakzai Es'hâqzai. We visit Gholâm-Rasul Khân at home in Atâ-khân-khoja village, and would have accepted his offer of further hospitality, if it were not too close to the Soviet frontier for us to obtain government permission to stay there. We record several stories from him, including this narrative of how the Es'hâqzai migrated to Turkistan under Tâju Khân.

Amir Abdor-Rahmân Khân [*reigned 1880–1901*] summoned Tâju Khân Khânikheyl Es'hâqzai: 'There are vast pastures in the borderlands of Morghâb and Bâdghis; you're *mâldâr*, take some of your tribes to live there.' The Amir wrote to the governors of Kandahar, Farah and Herat, saying, 'Cooperate with Tâju Khân, help him and his people move to the borderlands of Bâdghis and Morghâb.'

Tâju Khân called his tribes together and they decided to send off 1,200 families, drawn from every [*Durrani*] tribe: Es'hâqzai, Nurzai, Alizai, Hat-Mâku, Khugyâni. When they got to Chaghcharân, they missed their ancestral homelands, and some of them went back; the others followed. This was a tribal decision, not a government order.

Next year, the lunar year 1304 [*1886–87*], the same order was given, and people from every tribe again left Kandahar: Es'hâqzai, Nurzai, Alizai, Kâkeri; this time they found there was plenty of room for *mâldâri*, and they weren't quite so homesick, so they stayed. But they scattered; from Koshk-e-Golrân, to the borders of Andkhoy, Sheberghân, Sar-e-pol, Mazâr-e-Sharif, on to Qataghan, Aybak, Tashqurghân. The Es'hâqzai mostly stayed in Golrân, Mazâr-e-Sharif, Sar-e-pol.

When they came, Tâju Khân was leader of the Mandinzai Es'hâqzai. After him was Seyf Âkhondzâda, father of Gholâm-Rasul Khân Nazarzai, leader of the Sar-e-pol

---

[1] Nancy had researched British archives relating to the Pashtun move north. While we awaited our research permit in Kabul, Richard scoured the pages of the standard history, Faiz Mohammad's *Serâj al-Tawârikh*, and we submitted an article to the journal of the Afghanistan historical society. It was turned down because it dealt with matters that were still politically sensitive. Nancy later published a revised version (N. Tapper [1973] 1983). See also Kakar (1979: 131–35), Lee (1996).

people, and my grandfather Qâzi Jân-Mahmad Bâbakzai. Seyf Âkhondzâda was just a mullah with a small group of five families, but he was a good, upright man, and he treated different tribes and peoples justly and equally, so he won everybody to his side, and was recognized as leader by all the Es'hâqzai who came to Turkistan: Nazarzai, Chokhâzai, Khânikheyl, Mahmudkheyl, Kamuzai, Sheykhânzai, Bâbakzai, Bârânzai.

Early leaders of the Pashtun mâldâr newcomers to the north-west were Tâju Khân Khânikheyl's sons Kamâl Khân, Jamâl Khân and Âghâ-Mahmad Khân, but in Turkistan they were replaced by Seyf Âkhondzâda. By 1910 Seyf's sons, led by Gholâm-Rasul Khân, had gained control of much of the best and most convenient farmlands: they became khans themselves. Based in Emâm-Ja'far, north of Sar-e-pol, they conducted extensive pastoral activities but quickly settled down to live in comfort on the income from their lands, cultivated by local villagers. They also acquired tax-farming and other lucrative privileges and posts. They oppressed the local Uzbeks, Arabs, Aymâqs and Hazâras, as well as previous Pashtun arrivals, forcing many of them to emigrate from the region.

From Kandahar . . .

One group that came north in about 1920 was the Piruzai – an Es'hâqzai sub-tribe not mentioned by Gholâm-Rasul Khân Bâbakzai.

In late winter 1971 we join the Piruzai in Sar-e-pol, settling with Haji Tumân and his large family in their steppe pastures. Some elderly Piruzai, like Tumân's uncle, the wealthy Haji Ghâfur, recall life before the migration north. One evening we visit Ghâfur's nearby tent; helped and prompted by his eldest son Gol-Ahmad, he tells us more of life in the south.

Note that all our narrators refer to Pashtuns as 'Afghans', as will be explained later.

Tâju Khân gave his daughter to the Amir [*Abdor-Rahmân*]. He took her with a party of elders by camel to the royal palace, where they held the wedding. The Amir had seven wives, I believe. He asked the Qâzi, 'How many wives does the Book allow?' The Qâzi didn't answer. 'No, tell me, how many wives does the Book permit?' He replied, 'Amir-seb, forgive me, four wives are permitted, no more.' So he said, 'okay, if they aren't permitted, let Tâju Khân's daughter and the others go.' He divorced four wives, leaving three.

Tâju Khân was very annoyed. He took his daughter home, and later married her to Darwiza Khân of Maymana; but first he betrothed his sister to the Amir. The Amir agreed to take Tâju Khân's sister. He wanted to please these Afghans who had struggled hard and helped the throne so much at the time of the upheavals. To avoid upsetting them, he agreed to become *khish*, in-laws: *khishi* is something that lasts 100, 1,000 years – and we're people who think in the long term.

Our own ancestor, Ezzat, was a wealthy man. Mullah Jabbâr says that his ancestors were four brothers, while Ezzat was their half-brother, from a different mother. The others would mistreat Ezzat; they'd put a yoke on his back. He was scared of them, being on his own. But he worked hard and finally took three wives and had many sons: Amir, Moshk, Shir, Alârasân, Akhtar-khân, Yâr-Mahmad. His descendants multiplied, but his half-brothers' are still few. They got separated, and became Alizai. Later they came back to join us.

Grandfather Ezzat lived in Srë-kala[2] ['*Red-fort*'], where there were many Atsakzai and Nurzai. It wasn't like Turkistan; one year there was famine, next year something else. We had to leave the fort and flee to Washir-o-Pulât; our ancestor settled there, with Malek-Mahmad Khân's son Rostam Khân. Before Seyf Âkhondzâda left for Turkistan, he was Rostam Khân's mullah, a holy man who made charms and spells. [*See Map B*]

My father Haji Zabtu used to buy and sell guns; he brought silk from Herat. Trade was his business. That year when the sheep died, his brother Afzal went to buy sheep. I said, 'I'm dying of hunger, I can't go'. Afzal wrapped half a seer[3] of corn in a white felt. I went to a place where many people were dying of hunger. I came to a home with a newly married bride. As it was raining, I pleaded with her husband, but he wouldn't let me in. I sat there a while ... then I told his wife, 'Sister, bring a griddle.' She brought it; I threw in some corn and made popcorn. When one flew up, her husband grabbed it and ate it. I roasted a few more, gave them some and ate some myself. His wife said, 'If you'd let him in at once, he'd have given us both some more.' He said, 'I didn't know, did I? The Muslim's a traveller, he passes the night, and doesn't eat your food.'

I went and bought 160 Kandahari ewes and some goats, about 200 animals in all. Then we had lashings of milk. There was somebody with a vineyard, an apricot orchard and so on, I can't recall the name of the place. He was like a khan, and he'd sold so much wheat to the people, but finally he died of hunger himself. His place was abandoned, green with alfalfa; we took the sheep and camels there. That year there was incredible abundance.

Our summer quarters were near Chaghcharân. Nowadays many Kandahar *mâldârs* still come to Chaghcharân. Not long ago I had some business in Dawlatyâr on the Hari-rud, a little above where it joins the Lâl river; I met Haji Shari Nâmanzai, who'd come from Kandahar to his summer quarters at Chaghcharân.

On our way to the mountains, we'd load our camels with wool in gunnysacks, and take them to the shrine – was it the Holy Cloak in Kandahar? No, it was on a hilltop, a good shrine called Paruy Bâbâ, where you could leave your stuff as long as you liked, nobody would steal it. As we went by, we'd leave our wool and pots and everything there; they were quite safe until we collected them again in autumn; though we took the wool to the mountains to sell.

Our trek to the mountains took forty daily stages, both coming and going. It was hard, many gorges and passes, along the Khâsh Rud, across the sand desert of Tayalmân, which would take a mountain man over two days to cross. All the Baluch flocks are there.

Those Baluch speak Baluchi and don't understand Pashtu. For sheep they say *gorek*, for ram *pas*. Bread is *yarak*, water is *dir*. Those of us who were literate talked Persian with them; Persian is sugar after all, everybody knows a little. I was literate, I'd learned our Five Books [*see p. 354*]. I could read and write, but now I can't see properly.

---

[2]   Not the one near Gereshk, but in Nawzâd.
[3]   One seer (*sir*) locally is about seven kilograms; it divides into sixteen *paw* (pounds).

After Seyf Âkhondzâda left Washir-o-Pulât, we went to a place the Baluch call 'desert' [*Registân*], and lived there for some time. The Baluch chief was Mahd-Rasul Khân. He had 700 camels, 500 of them females, which he milked, looking after their calves; he made a milk-churn and gave people buttermilk. There was no tea, nobody'd heard of it. Every evening he had forty guests. Seven maidservants with seven hand-mills would grind flour from evening to morning, making such a noise; then they baked bread from morning to evening. He was a real khan. When he died, all those camels wept, and ran away to India; they scattered, not five were left; and all his wealth disappeared. Animals understand some things.

The Baluch have Marri camels, called *bâdi*, 'like wind'. They go faster than horses; if you let them run, you couldn't catch them in your car. They're the same size as our camels here, but two people can ride one, like a horse. They have two-man saddles, and silvered bridles with reins you use to steer them. They're really lively. People rode these *bâdi* camels to battle. Horses were rare, and these camels were worth 10,000 rupees. They looked just like the camels we have here in Turkistan, but when we came to Turkistan, we found that they couldn't survive here. I brought one; someone said it would be all right, but others said Turkistan is all steep hills with lots of canals and rivers, and those camels can't cope. I exchanged it for a local camel and a gun.

Grazing in Kandahar is sparse but very strong. There's a plant called saxaul, which we Afghans call *ushmargey*; also *katasar*, *zhuzhgey*. The land's all sand desert; we got water from shallow wells, *kâriz* underground canals. In those days I bought wheat for one *tanga* – half a *qerân* – per *nimcha*.[4]

When we married in Kandahar, we didn't give sheep; we gave cash: 500, 2,000, 3,000 rupees. Now wives have become much more expensive.

... to Turkistan

One summer evening in 1972, Gol-Ahmad speaks for his father, describing how the Piruzai got together for the move north, though he himself was born long after their arrival.

Seyf Âkhondzâda came many years before us. He had seven sons; they set off for Turkistan with one black tent. Before them, no Kandahari *mâldârs*, no Hazâras, had come here; it was all Turks, they called it Turkistan. [*See Map C*]

The year we left Kandahar, my father said, flock losses were even worse than this year. We had sixty sheep left, uncle Haji Afzal and us. He said, 'Haji Afzal and I went and bought 1,200 rams at 5 *qerâns* and 600 yearlings at 1 *qerân*.'

Seyf Âkhondzâda wasn't with us. Our ancestors were originally with Rostam Khân, but we came to join the ancestors of these Khârkashis. Some of them, like Haji Dâd-Mahmad, had come a year or two earlier. We didn't know each other before, but now we intermarried and became one *qawm*,[5] and they persuaded us to come with them: 'Turkistan is such a nice country'. [*See Fig. 1*]

---

[4] *Qerân*: an old coin worth half an Afghan rupee; the rupee was later replaced by today's Afghani, colloquially still called the rupee (*rupya*). A *nimcha* is about 10 kilograms.
[5] This is a key term, with meanings ranging from family to tribe to ethnic group, according to context.

We intermarried with them, and they brought us along. We were one camp under Jamâl Khân and Âghâ-Mahmad Khân [*Tâju Khân's sons*] with 300 sheep. There were four or five families of Khârkashis: Joma-khân, Arz-begi and Tumân. We were another four or five families. Then there was Jallât-khân Nâmanzai. Several little groups of families made a total of fifty-one houses. Jamâl Khân was the leader of the whole group, and after him Joma-khân. But Jamâl Khân and Âghâ-Mahmad Khân and many of their people went back to Kandahar.

Also with us was Patih, father of Haji Mahd-Omar Payluch, who now lives in Maymana; they were a few families. In those days people would work for bread. Patih was a young man, who came and asked to be our servant; he asked for two chapattis in the morning with some cheese, two in the evening; that's all. Some time later there was no buttermilk left in our churn-skin. Who's eating it? My father's mother told Afzal's wife, 'Wait until evening, then watch the servant.' She hid in the sleeping-place, and saw the servant at the churn, eating – you've seen how women tie the churn up at night then shake it in the morning. She hit him on the neck; he let go of the churn and ran off, covered in milk. But the dogs – there were fifty tents, remember – thought it was a thief … anyway, they got him, and brought him back.

We came to Sar-e-pol via Bâdghis, Gorziwân, and Sayyâd, travelling as nomads[6] with our families, just like when you and I travelled together last year to Dangak via Kachan and Esmeydân. My father told me the whole story, all the places they stopped at, but I'm afraid I've rather forgotten it!

This land belonged to Turkmens and Arabs; there were many of them – you can still see their campsites. When our people came, they drove the Turkmens out, after a lot of fighting. In the Saqawi war[7] they took many of our animals, and we took many of theirs. They took our donkeys, so we went and beat up their shepherds and brought back sheep.

In Kandahar, my father said, we hadn't heard of melons. In Turkistan, there are melons in Sar-e-pol, Âqcha and Mazâr, but not in mountain areas like Sar-jangal and Kachan – they're also part of Turkistan.[8] We'd been to those mountains and such places, but when we came here, we saw a melon-patch ten times as large as ours today. There was a warden guarding it, he said. Jamâl Khân told us to go and bring some melons, so we took camels and donkeys and started collecting. Then uncle Shir – I was a kid, and he was bigger than me – sat on the pile, claimed it for himself, and wouldn't move. So we went for him, ten or twenty of us, and beat him so badly he couldn't walk. Finally somebody brought him back and Jamâl Khân rebuked him, 'Curse you, Shir, what were you doing, was that your father's melon-patch? You should just have brought back your lot.' Then, father said, the melon-warden's boss wrote to Jamâl Khân, 'Is this how people behave?' He wrote back, 'Forgive us, we're just desert-mountain people, you can spare us a few melons.' So they shut up, and at night we went and loaded up the melons. Shir was ill for a month; every day he went to the mosque, and Jamâl Khân scolded him for what he'd done.

---

[6] He says *kuchi*; narrators use this word of themselves, rather than *mâldâr*, very rarely and only when emphasizing movement and migration. See Tapper (2008).

[7] In 1929, the nine-month reign of Habibollah II, 'Bacha-ye-Saqaw'.

[8] The Piruzai came to Sar-jangal and Dangak only after they had moved north, hence Gol-Ahmad's classification; strictly speaking they are in the Hazârajât.

My father said that after they came to Turkistan, they used to take the spring wool all the way up to Dangak and sell it there, 3 to 4 rupees a seer. That's what life was like. He said, 'You simply have no idea of the troubles we've seen.' When we came here and got some land, things became easier. In Kandahar we never mowed hay for the sheep, and we didn't need fodder. It's only now, he said, that straw's become fashionable.

He said, 'The year we went on Hajj [1958], I thought of going to Kandahar; we've lost touch but they've sent several letters asking us to come back.' Khalifa-Patih and Mowlawi Golzâr [*religious figures living in Konjek*] were there recently, and they visited Rostam Khân, who said, 'I've heard that Seyf's sons have become khans, is that true?' 'Sir, they've become the most powerful khans in Turkistan'. He said, 'Here, Seyf was our mullah; look, this was his cell; how did he become khan? But I'm not surprised that my kinsmen have become their subjects.' He added, 'If you give me some land, I'll come too; if you can't, then come back here, all of you, and I'll give you land here; I feel strongly about my own people.'

Konjek village headman Tumân, known as 'Little Haji' after his pilgrimage in early 1971, is 'Big-Haji' Ghâfur's nephew. Tumân took us to the mountains in 1971. Like his cousin Gol-Ahmad, Tumân was born in Turkistan. One evening in August 1972, sitting in his village yard with Mahd-Amin – his friend, and his second son Pâdshâh's father-in-law – Tumân recalls his youth.

At that time, the people of Hazârajât were very rebellious. At night we'd have to guard the sheep. We couldn't stand it, so we went to summer in Tell-e-khoshk. There we had a Kabuli[9] friend, Ajib-Rishmin; our grandfathers were very friendly with him, we went to his house a lot when I was a boy. He gave me a nice bandolier to put around my neck. I was young – you don't forget these things! Just like us today, talking together – we won't forget this!

One day they heard that the government had dispatched a treasure caravan from Herat: cash, gold, and so on, loaded onto mules, with a *tahsildâr* and an escort of 40 to 50 troops. Government work! In those days aeroplanes hadn't been invented, there weren't even motor vehicles. There was the *dak* postal service, carried on the back. The government had no planes, no artillery; they loaded it all onto mules.

Ajib-Rishmin heard about them, got some of his Kabulis together and went and held up the caravan. They emptied the soldiers' guns and took away whatever they could carry. Nobody asks, even now, what happened to that government property. He was poor, but this new wealth made him a real Big-Man; he acquired livestock, Hazâra land. After he died, his son Nasim got one or two estates in Hazârajât. I don't know whether he's now paying for it or not.

Later we summered at Karaney for a few years, then we moved to Michiluk in Sarghân. We didn't go there last year; you remember where we stopped in that gorge, up from Tagawboy? [*Map D*] Michiluk is a full stage east of that. Twenty years we summered there – only us; the rest of Piruzai went to the mountains. When I grew up,

[9]   Not literally from Kabul, but from one of the eastern Pashtun tribes.

I went to join them, but Haji Ghâfur refused to come to the mountains and went over to Ghawsoddin Khân's at Isâr. After some years he did leave Sar-e-pol with us, but he stayed in Chârkent.[10] When we returned from the mountains we stopped with him for a few days. He stayed on while we came home and mowed the hay. Haji prepared a place in Chârkent, then in November he sent for us: 'Bring the camels!' We'd take some people and the camels, then after one or two days we'd bring him home, with all the barley, wheat and raisins: one day to Chayrak, one at Suzma-qala, the next at Boghawi, another at Kaltar, and then home.

Not long after arriving in Sar-e-pol, Ghâfur and others acquired lands in neighbouring Sangchârak, esp. vineyards in the Chârkent/Chenâr valley, which is four or five stages along the migration route to the Hazârajât. Ghâfur used to spend the summer months there, and many of his relatives, such as Tumân, still spend several weeks there in late summer for the grape harvest.

Resisting the khans

As our narrators have admitted, their new homeland was not empty, and the immigrants were not welcomed by the local inhabitants: Turkmen and Arab semi-nomadic pastoralists, and Uzbek, Aymâq, Hazâra and Tâjik village farmers and townspeople. But, with government support, the Pashtuns acquired much of the pastures and farmland. Their leaders – the Nazarzai family – had already seized the best and most convenient irrigated lands and reduced the resident farmers to serf status. These khans dominated economic and political life in most parts of the north. But there were revolts against this oppression, often harshly put down, but sometimes successful.

In 1929, when a Tâjik known as Bacha-ye-Saqaw reigned briefly in Kabul as Habibollah II, the Uzbeks, Turkmens and Aymâqs of Sar-e-pol rose against the Nazarzai khans, drove them into the mountains, and set up a Saqawi supporter as hâkem *in the town. In Mazâr-e-Sharif, however, Gholâm-Rasul Khân Nazarzai rallied his Es'hâqzai followers and drove the rebels out. Nâder Khân, the last shah's father, terminated the revolt and restored Durrani rule in Kabul. In Sar-e-pol, the Nazarzai khans regained power and commenced reprisals. They recovered their former lands and seized more – even lands belonging to Hazâras and Arabs, the only local groups to have sided with the khans against the Saqawi rebels.*

Gol-Ahmad continues.

When Seyf Âkhondzâda and his sons arrived in Turkistan, they started collecting taxes for the government, 100 or 200 rupees per house. People also paid duty for bringing animals across from Russia. All at once Seyf became wealthy, and attracted followers; they managed to buy some lands, to seize others, and so on. His grandson, Re'is Abdol-Ghâfur Khân, was *hâkem* (sub-province governor) here in Sar-e-pol for

---

[10] A small district in Sangchârak (Maps D, E); not the larger district of the same name in Balkh province.

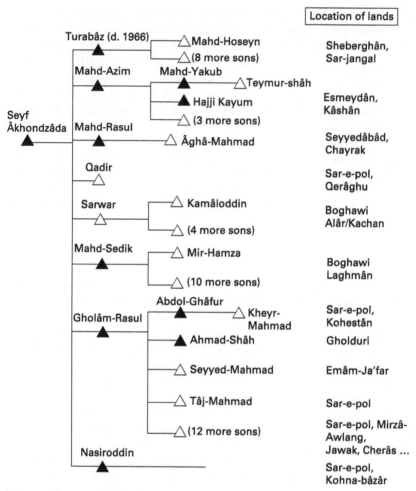

Figure 2 The Nazarzai khans.

some years. As the khans divided their inheritance, they multiplied. When people resisted their land seizures, they found that instead of one khan, there were ten. [*See Fig. 2; Map D*]

Seyf had a place at Dahana, in the Kâshân valley: you remember, there's a castle near the bridge. After he died – I don't know whether in Turkistan or in the south – his son Mahd-Azim Khân, father of Haji Kayum, went to Kâshân and asked the Hazâra people there for land to build a mosque: 'I want to say my prayers, please make it halal for me.' The people were simple, so they sold him some land; at that time it was cheap, 10 to 20 rupees a *jerib* [*0.2 hectare*]. He gave them a document and became their headman; then every year he collected cash, ghee and so on.

None of the locals had ID cards, nobody was literate; they didn't do military service, but served the khan himself. The government had scarcely heard of Kâshân and

Esmeydân and those places, and they put them into Balkhâb district, though afterwards they were transferred to Sar-e-pol.

There were two men called Mahd-Azim: one was this Mahd-Azim Khân, the other was a Hazâra. Each produced a deed stating that the land was Mahd-Azim's. Then fifteen years ago the khans stole some cows and fodder belonging to Haji Mamadi of Esmeydân. The villagers of Ghozba-khâna, Takhâgerd, Tâjik-hâ and Spina-kala united under his leadership, and paid him to fight for them against the khans.

Haji Mamadi took his complaint to Sar-e-pol, Sheberghân, and eventually Kabul. Then all the people abandoned their villages and scattered, to Sangchârak, Sar-e-pol. The khans killed some people, seized their animals. For two years or so the land remained uncultivated. Then the khans said, 'You're our tenants, we're your khans, come back, give us what you gave before, okay?' They gathered them and brought them back. A year passed, then they all girded themselves for battle. They fought, and for some years the khans were quite unable to go there. The villagers returned one by one, saying, 'We'll give neither ghee nor cash; the land is ours. You may have lands in Kandahar, but not here.' The dispute continues. Again the khans killed some of them. They say that the other day Haji Kayum brought an Order that 7,000 *jeribs* should be handed to him, and so on. But I don't believe it. The Hazâra people now have lots of guns and things, and they've sworn never to let the land go, to die defending it.

Ahmad-shâh Khân [*son of Re'is Abdol-Ghâfur*] had a castle among the Aymâqs in Gholduri; you saw it. Then Mirzâ Boy and the others rose up against him, and took their land back.

In the Saqawi years [*1929*], these Fârsibâns stole much of our property. Now the government has become much harsher. At first, we Afghans stole their animals. They didn't know anything about Afghans; they hadn't seen a black tent before – just like when you first came here, you wanted to know, what are the Afghans like, men and women, what do they do, what do they eat?

The khans have no interests now at Tarpaj, Qayrâq, Esmeydân, Nawa-ye-Darâz, Adira; they can't control those people. Only Teymur-shâh Khân [*Haji Kayum's nephew*] has planted himself there; he has his thugs with guns and ammunition, and refuses to give in; he stays there, winter and summer.

Tumân's fourth son Baya-khân, about 22 years old and unmarried, tells me more one morning.

Previously, all the Aymâqs of Cherâs, Gholduri, Sâlrizi and Târikak were subject to Ahmad-shâh Khân. The Aymâqs had to do whatever he said. For many years he was like their padishah. He behaved just like a *hâkem* who now oppresses the people. He built that cliff-top castle above Gholduri – it's ruined now, one side's fallen down. But he exhausted the people; they were very downtrodden, but finally they got fed up and said, 'We'd rather die than put up with this life any longer!' He had a warehouse, and one year they got together and plundered it. He'd put his livestock in there and gone up the mountain behind his castle; they seized his livestock, shot at him, and took back their lands. They said, 'By God, if he comes here again, he'll have to kill us all, or we'll kill him.'

Teymur-shâh Khân in Esmeydân is just as powerful and ruthless now. All the other khans used to come down to Sar-e-pol for the winter; but Teymur-shâh doesn't come down then or any other time, he stays on his land, at a stand-off with the Hazâras. The khans once seized all the Hazâra lands there; but they're now in dispute. It's been going on for years. The Hazâras didn't recognize the government, but they've grown in numbers and strength, and now they can collect money to give the government. The khans used to beat the Hazâras, seize their sheep and cows, their ghee and so on; but now nobody can touch them.

Pashtun mâldâr *like the Piruzai benefited from the dominance of their fellow-tribesmen, the khans; consequently the local Hazâras resented them too.*

But the khans also ill-treated ordinary Pashtuns. Late one night, Baya-khân's mother Maryam tells Nancy of an incident in her childhood when the Piruzai united to defeat Teymur-shâh Khân at Esmeydân. Maryam is from Lineage A, and later married Tumân as part of the settlement of the Lineage A/Lineage C feud. For her, those were the good old days, when she was with her family of birth – but she denies the hostility with her husband's people, and insists that all the Piruzai were united.

We camped at Shorshorak; next we went and pitched camp where the Kâshân river joins the Balkhâb. We turned off the main river and came up to the traders' meadow at Qayrâq and camped there. Next we moved on to Esmeydân. At around midday, all the ewes were asleep near the river: Haji Khalifa-Lulak's flock, Haji Jabbâr's, Haji Karim-dâd's [*Lineage A elders*], all were asleep in one hollow, where there were lots of stones and wormseed, as well as some wood for fuel.

All at once, a large herd of mares came by, driven by Mahd-Azim Khân's son [*Teymur-shâh Khân*] and Sarwar Khân's son [*Kamâloddin Khân*]. He drove the mares among our ewes and scattered them. Uncle Haji Khalifa-Lulak was a powerful man; nobody could knock him down. He and his son Sâlâr took clubs and beat Mahd-Azim Khân's son about the head and knocked him off his horse. He fell down unconscious, his clothes covered in blood. He took pity on him and had him brought back to his tent, cleaned his wounds and washed his clothes. As the boy lay there, Haji Khalifa put his hand on his head to calm him, saying, 'I didn't recognize you when I hit you like that, I thought you were a Hazâra or an Uzbek; I wouldn't have beaten you, you're Nazarzai, you're one of us.' But he was one of the khans, and as he got back on his horse, he said, 'You'll never come this way again, you'll never pass our castle; we'll kill you.'

That afternoon, as the men were saying their prayers, the mullahs in front, the rest in rows behind, somebody looked round the corner towards the Esmeydân gorge and saw a great army of the khans' people approaching, carrying guns and clubs. There were three or four parties of Kabulis: Bakhtyâri, Khalili, Breti, Moghol, all the khans' dependents, and Nâmanzai and Torkheyl too. They were all camped near the khans' place there at Esmeydân. They started hitting our men, who didn't respond with clubs or guns, but threw stones at them; we were all gathered there, the women too – I was a young girl at the time, I used to watch the lambs. Many people cried, others were laughing at the battle – the local Hazâras were happy that we Afghans were fighting each other!

Well, they tried to round up all our men: Khalifa's sons Sâlâr, Darân-shâh, Siâh-bandey, Molk, and [*my brothers*] Pordel, Kohandel, Khoshdel. Haji [*Tumân*]'s father Rowzoddin was there too, and Haji Ghâfur, Haji Mahmad, Haji Afzal, and Mullah Jabbâr's family too - all were there, we were one *qawm*, we all moved and camped together. Then some others arrived and managed to rescue our men. But the khans said, 'You'll never pass this way again, we'll kill you all in that gorge.'

Next day, we struck camp around dawn, loaded the camels and the whole community [*woles*] set off together. Everyone gathered near the khans' castle at Esmeydân - you've seen it - and we went right past. No one came out. We led the camels right through the middle of their camp, and went on through the gorge, then up the long climb of Reg-row, and camped on the ridge at the top. We kept looking back, but nobody came. They'd gone into hiding. They never said, 'Why did you beat up my son, break his head and his arm?'

So the battle finished, and those years passed.

Wazir Mahmad-gol Mohmand

In the early 1930s, following the Saqawi revolt, Interior Minister Mahmad-gol Mohmand restored Kabul's control of Turkistan. Despite fiercely pro-Pashtun sentiments, he refused to allow the oppression perpetrated by the Nazarzai khans, and he appears to have dealt fairly with petitions brought against them by Uzbeks and Aymâqs from throughout Sar-e-pol and its hinterland. Gholâm-Rasul Khân was put under house arrest in Kabul, where he later died. Other khans were arrested and placed in temporary custody. Mahmad-gol also balanced the Durranis from Kandahar by introducing more eastern Pashtuns, especially as landowners between Âqcha and Balkh.[11]

On one of our last evenings, Tumân talks of Mahmad-gol's tour of Turkistan - he was a child at the time.

In those days [*1930s*] the government wasn't so strong. Our khans here did very well; they grabbed the best lands of the people of Kohestân and elsewhere, and settled in all the best places. They seized people's best mares, and slaughtered their lambs. Everywhere the khans did what they wanted; in Qazzâq village, Qayum Khân would tie up the Uzbeks all day, beat them, fine them, imprison them, take their money, register their lands in his own name. It was like that everywhere; there were khans in Maymana, Kandahar, Herat. Oppressed and distressed, people got really angry.

The king told Wazir Mahmad-gol to go round Afghanistan: 'You have complete authority, don't let anyone oppose you; if somebody disobeys your orders, use the troops, or telegraph Kabul so that we can send whatever you need.' The wazir went to Ghazni, Kalat, Kandahar, Gereshk, Farah, Herat, Qala-e-Naw, Maymana, dealing with the khans. He arrested them and sent them to Kabul. Some he killed, others surrendered: 'Whatever you do, you're the boss, we accept your authority.'

---

[11] See Ghobar (2001: 56–58), McChesney (2002: 85–87), Nasar (2005).

In Kandahar, the Alizai khans rebelled against the livestock tax, one *tanga* [*half a rupee*] per sheep. 'We can't pay this *tanga*, it'll ruin our people.' He said, 'If people refuse to pay, what should the King do? How will he pay for the army, ministers, governors, judges, all these things? Tax revenues are too small. If you don't pay now, tomorrow others will refuse. So I have to collect it.' They repeated, 'We're not paying.' So he summoned the troops, attacked the khans, killed many of their men, and finally captured the khans alive. Even then they wouldn't submit, so he shot some from the cannon's mouth. All the people of Afghanistan cried, 'See what Mahmad-gol's done!'

He went to Herat to collect the livestock tax, and the people paid. Then he came to Maymana. Stopping only one day in Sheberghân – just a district centre then – he arrived in Mazâr, our provincial government centre. There he stayed; he built a mosque, brought his family, built his own house; people visited all day long.

In those days, the lands of Hazhdah-nahr[12] were unoccupied; there were few people around. So he summoned Afghans from everywhere, from east, south, all directions, and gave them land there. If they said, 'We're ten families,' for example, he gave them enough land for ten families. He gave land to any Afghan who applied for it, but not to others. He gave a lot to Kabulis, especially Shinwâris and above all his own tribe, Mohmand, in places like Timurak. Most of the people of Hazhdah-nahr today are Ghiljai and Kabuli Afghans. The Mohmands have the best lands. He gave better land to Kabulis than to Kandahari Afghans.[13]

The wazir spent several years there. Some people made petitions, saying, 'So-and-so is oppressing me.' He'd investigate, summon the village, and ask who was in the right. If five elders said this side was right, not that one, he'd beat the latter, put them in prison, get whatever they'd taken from the former and return it to them. The Aymâqs from Supak, led by Ruzi-Diwâna, collected 6 seers [*42 kg*] of petitions against Ahmad-shâh Khân and took them to Mazâr. The wazir arrested several of the [*Nazarzai*] khans: Re'is Abdol-Ghâfur Khân, Ahmad-shâh Khân, Sarwar Khân, Haji Kayum, Âghâ-Mahmad Khân – but not Turabâz Khân or Mir-Hamza Khân – and told them, 'You stay here in Mazâr, as long as I'm here.' As it happened, Ahmad-shâh Khân fell ill there, and was sent to Kabul, where he died. Finally, the khans too managed to get petitions together, and after they'd promised not to do such things again he freed them and sent them back home.

In Sheberghân he spent little time on investigations, probably only a day or two. The only khan there was Turabâz Khân, and he didn't have much influence; he had some 23 *paykâl* [*1,800 hectares*] of land, several flocks of sheep, and no interest in extorting people's money – he had plenty of his own. He had four wives, but no sons.

The wazir once came to Sar-e-pol, for three days – after the Supak Aymâqs had submitted their petitions. He asked people, 'How are your khans?' The Afghans said they were good, but the Uzbeks and Fârsibâns all made complaints against the khans. After three days of that, he left, that's all.

---

[12] '18-canals', the land between Mazâr-e-Sharif and Âqcha, irrigated by the Balkhâb/Band-e-Amir river.

[13] Northern Pashtuns – and others – call Durrani and associated southern tribes 'Kandahari', while Shinwâri, Mohmand, Wardak and other eastern tribes are 'Kabuli'.

He gave very good justice, and took not a penny in bribes. They raised his salary for his piety; he had land in Aybak [*Samangân province*], and income from it. Finally he said he was too old and sent in his resignation. Several times the Prime Minister turned it down, but he insisted that he couldn't work any more, so they released him, and he retired to Aybak, where he settled and quickly built a mosque and said his five daily prayers, praying to God to forgive his sins. He died a few years ago [*1964*]; he had a son or two, but they're not up to much.

He was a brave and strict man, astute and just; he knew people so well, Richard, that, if two men came before him, he could tell at once who was innocent, who was guilty. He'd tell the latter, 'Off you go and if you come again with a complaint against this man I'll skin you alive.' People were terrified and trembled before him. After he killed those khans in Kandahar, he got a reputation, and people didn't dare approach him. He made these parts, Turkistan, really safe and secure. If this progress had continued, Turkistan would have become a paradise; khans and beys and thieves would have disappeared. He hated thieves; he didn't rest until they were caught. He'd kill them, skin them alive. But after he retired, the khans rose again, and behaved like khans and beys once more.

The wazir told his tribesmen, 'Go to the Pamirs, get some of those nice two-humped Bactrian camels, the females, and you can sell them for ten to twenty thousand rupees.' People like the Shinwâris and the Ahmadzai Ghiljais followed his advice, fetched some of those Bactrians, and sold them for up to 30,000 rupees. They mated the male Bactrians to dromedary females, which then bore the lovely hybrids – Yes, we saw some today! That's how the Shinwâris and Ahmadzais became wealthy.[14]

The khans in 1970

The khans continued to dominate economic and political life in Sar-e-pol and neighbouring districts until the 1970s. Gholâm-Rasul's son Abdol-Ghâfur was for many years hâkem *in Sar-e-pol; until his death in 1969 he was director (re'is) of the Mazâr Company, exporting locally produced skins and dried fruit from Mazâr-e-Sharif. In the 1960s and 1970s the khan family controlled regional affairs informally through governors appointed from Kabul. In 1970 the head of the family, Abdol-Ghâfur's son Haji Kheyr-Mahmad, recognized as khan by all Jawzjân Es'hâqzai, lived in Sar-e-pol town. Other family members lived on and supervised their estates, scattered throughout Jawzjân, mainly in Sar-e-pol districts but including one each in Sheberghân, Sangchârak and Esmeydân in the mountains. The khans continued to be vigorously opposed by both fellow-Pashtuns and others.*

Tumân himself, though, had a special relationship with Turabâz, the only Nazarzai khan to live in Sheberghân district, who also controlled and extracted rents for the Hazârajât lands where the Piruzai summered.

Baya-khân tells how Tumân tricked Turabâz Khân out of some of these lands, putting his rival Nâder-shâh of Khârkash in his debt.

---

[14] On camel hybrids, see Tapper (2013).

Many years ago Haji, my father, went around with Mahd-Hoseyn Khân's father, Turabâz Khân. The khan was very fond of him, and took him wherever he went; he wouldn't go if Haji didn't want to go. Haji was his secretary; he read his letters for him, slept in his guest tent and didn't come home for days. In the mountains, while the khan sat in his tent, Haji organized his men and got the work done; for example, he'd send men to collect pasture dues.

Most of the Dangak mountain land – pastures, farmland and the rest – belonged to Turabâz Khân. Nâder-shâh had some land there too, not much: a campsite and a little alfalfa meadow at the confluence – where he pitched his guest tent last summer, you remember. He'd tried to get deeds for it, but failed. About ten years ago, he pleaded with Haji to get the deeds from Turabâz Khân. The khan was old and blind. Haji – let's be honest – stole the deeds and gave them to Nâder-shâh, who couldn't have got them otherwise. After that, Haji didn't go back.

Turabâz Khân found out what he'd done and was furious, but Haji had a large community behind him. The khan took him to court in Kabul, but in the end he lost the lands. Then he died. When Nâder-shâh got the deeds, they were for all the Dangak land. He spent a lot of money, and the community contributed. After Turabâz Khân died, the local MP (*wakil*) [*his cousin Kamâloddin Khân*] told Mahd-Hoseyn Khân, 'This is a whole community, they won't give in. If you try to bully them it won't work. They're 300 or 400 families, and we're no more than 100. And if it's a question of money, we can't beat them. So you'd better forget about those lands; you already have plenty.' And Re'is Abdol-Ghâfur Khân also told him to forget about it, so Mahd-Hoseyn Khân had to let it go.

The place where we camped last summer, the east side of Sepaya, the watershed between Gol-e-yakh and Sarcheshma, belongs to Nâder-shâh. The other side – including the place where Gol-Ahmad and Abdol camped – belongs to Mahd-Hoseyn Khân. We still went there for two more years, and Mahd-Hoseyn Khân couldn't complain. He collected the pasture dues, and we paid like everyone else. Haji didn't go; Pâdshâh and I went and handed it over. After two years Nâder-shâh told Haji, 'You got those lands for me, now take whatever place you want for your summer quarters; I won't take any rent.' The following year Haji didn't go to the mountains, but he told us where to go. One year we were with Mastuk, at Kala-khân and Shahâboddin's campsite. The next year we moved to our present site; we felt good there; water's plentiful, and there's a meadow for the sheep. If we'd gone this year, we'd have camped there again.

3

Ethnic Politics in Sar-e-pol

Elections

Afghanistan has had parliaments since the early twentieth century, with local representatives chosen by local elders. Then the 1964 Constitution and subsequent electoral law provided for two chambers, elected by universal male and female suffrage: a People's Assembly (wolesi jerga), *with representatives* (wakil) *from each sub-province* (woleswâli), *and a Senate or Assembly of Elders* (mëshërâno jerga), *with one senator from each province* (welayat).

The first two such elections were held in 1965 and 1969 (for the 12th and 13th parliaments); the third is due in 1973.[1] Each sub-province constituency has a number of polling stations. For Sar-e-pol sub-province there are polling stations in (a) Sar-e-pol town; (b) Khoja-Yegana in the western steppe, which includes some Uzbek villages, but is the winter quarters of Pashtun nomads, mostly Es'hâqzai, i.e. subjects of the Es'hâqzai khans; and (c) Khawâl-Pasiney, the centre of Kohestânât alâqadâri *(district). For Sangchârak sub-province, there were polling stations in (a) Toghzâr town; (b) the eastern steppe; (c) Balkhâb district centre. (See Map E)*

The narrator is Hâshem, a professional cook in his late forties from a prominent Uzbek family in Sar-e-pol town. His father, Khalifa Ebrâhim, is a respected pir *(spiritual guide) of many local people, including Pashtuns. One uncle is Qâri Azim, a distinguished scholar, who has served as both local Member of Parliament and* hâkem *elsewhere; another uncle, Mirzâ Mahmad-Qâsem, has been local MP. His first cousin (father's sister's son), Seyyed-Hakim 'Shari', is a Soviet-educated political activist who stood unsuccessfully for parliament in both elections. (In 1978–79, Shari was Minister of Justice in the Communist government before the Soviet invasion.)*

Hâshem, like most local Uzbeks, speaks fluent Persian, but he also speaks Pashtu, and has a wide circle of contacts in the region. He has worked for oil exploration groups (including Soviet engineers), and is often employed by government officials for occasions like electoral campaigns. He justifies our hiring him as servant and cook by the local information and insights he can supply; his father has land in a nearby village; but he has a big mouth, and many of our Pashtun hosts resent his presence for just this reason, though they appreciate his cooking, and sometimes his stories.

---

[1] Dupree (1980: 587f., 651f.).

Hâshem was involved in both the 1965 and 1969 electoral campaigns in Sar-e-pol sub-province, working for his cousin Shari, the popular candidate, who on both occasions was widely believed to have been victim of government-approved vote-rigging in favour of Kamâloddin Khân, 'Re'is' Abdol-Ghâfur Khân's nephew and cousin of the current Es'hâqzai chief Haji Kheyr-Mahmad Khân.

In August 1972, Hâshem describes the campaigning and polling procedures, then narrates events in which he was personally involved. The dominant politics are both ethnic (Pashtun versus Uzbek) and class (khans versus the rest). Evidently, many ordinary Pashtuns are already inclined to join the Uzbeks in supporting the popular, anti-khan candidate, Shari.

Previous elections were done differently, by acclamation; they went to all the villages, Afghan, Uzbek, Hazâra, and asked, 'Who do you want as *wakil*?' People took sides, and whichever side was larger won the election. For example, 100 families would come and say, 'We want Seyyed-shâh.' Then I might come, and if 150 people liked me, I'd win. Then they'd pray, collect money for the *wakil*, and off he went to parliament. The first *wakil* was my uncle Qâri Azim, for many years; later he was *woleswâl* of Sorkh-o-Pârsâ sub-province [*Parwân province*] for three years; then he resigned. Other *wakils* included my kinsman Abdor-Rahmân; Abdol-Jabbâr Khân, son of Gholâm-Rasul Khân; my uncle Mirzâ Mahmad-Qâsem; Mirzâ Mahmud, who died – he was Uzbek too. Then we had Kamâloddin Khân, who's now been *wakil* for four terms.

The new system has operated for two terms; next year [*1973*] will be the third. Elections start in late August; people register as candidates two months earlier. Anyone can apply to register. Each candidate must have agents that people know. Anyone with an ID card has the right to vote. Campaigning starts on 25 August, once Jashn[2] is over. For every electoral district, five full days. In Sar-e-pol that means three places: the first five days in Sar-e-pol town, then out in Khoja-Yegana; then up in Kohestân. It'll be the same next year.

Each candidate has his own ballot box with his photograph on one side and his symbol on the other – they choose a symbol such as a sheep, or wheat. Hazâras usually like a kilim (*gelim*), because they're kilim-weavers. Afghans choose a sheep; Kamâloddin Khân chose a karakul pelt. Shari always has the wheat-ear. People hold up placards with these symbols, like the wheat-ear.

Elections for People's Assembly 1965

In the first elections, I was in charge of expenses. The candidates were Haji Amân Hazâra, Yusuf Boy's son, Shari and Kamâloddin Khân. Yusuf Boy's son withdrew on the third day; then Shari should have had a majority of 1,200 votes. What did they do? They bought the votes. In just one night Shari's majority disappeared. Three sacks of IDs got 'lost'; they couldn't vote. When Shari realized this, he went to Kabul. He'd brought several tape recorders, cameras and stuff, so that when the judge and the *hâkem* let the Afghans in and not the Uzbeks, he taped and snapped it all, and took it off to Kabul.

---

[2] Independence Day, 19 August.

Shari had to go up to Kohestân campaigning himself. He'd sent an agent called Haji Sattâr, but Kamâloddin gave him 20,000 rupees cash and promised him another 20,000 – which in fact he never paid. They also tricked the judge, promising him a car and 50,000 rupees; and they gave the school principal 10,000. After the fight they bribed [*local police commandant*] Mahmad-Ali Khân. I was there, in a dark corner behind a wall, my turban wrapped round my face, trying to pretend I was an Afghan. Nobody knew me; when they asked me in Pashtu, 'Where are you from?' I said, 'Kâriz.' Mahmad-Ali kept refusing what they offered, but finally he accepted 20,000 cash and a nice *chapân* cloak. When I got back, Shari asked me what had happened; I said, 'Tell the goldsmith, no one else will understand!' He sighed and said, 'The elections are decided by a rainbow-coloured cloak!' The same night I asked the commandant, 'Was it all in thousand-rupee notes?' He just laughed. The same commandant as now.

Elections for Senate 1969

In the elections for the Senate, there were four candidates in Jawzjân: Sharif-jân, an Afghan from Sheberghân; Seyyed-Pâdshâh from Âqcha, I don't know him; Majid, originally from Istâlef; and my kinsman Dâmollah, an Uzbek from Sar-e-pol.

We began in Sar-e-pol. Dâmollah had a team of four, and he sent them round the districts. Here in Sar-e-pol there was his brother, Sattâr-jân; Dâmollah himself went to Sangchârak; Qâri Es'hâq represented him in Qârqin and Khâmyâb; somebody else in Sheberghân.

When they counted the votes here, Dâmollah had a majority of 250. The next morning we left town to campaign in Khoja-Yegana. The khans supported Seyyed-Pâdshâh, ordinary people supported Dâmollah. When we arrived, there was a fight with the khans' men. The khans gave the local headman 10,000 rupees; he picked a fight with Sharmiqu, a respected local notable, so people there didn't vote. The local villages split into two factions. One of our people went out onto the street and knifed one of the khan's supporters. He paid the judge and the commandant 5,000 rupees; they let him go, and instead arrested a mullah – a very good man, one of our supporters – and sent him to Sheberghân. But the local people were angry and didn't vote for us. There in Khoja-Yegana, Seyyed-Pâdshâh polled 150 more votes than Dâmollah.

After five days there, we came back to Sar-e-pol. The next morning we left to campaign in Pasiney-Khâwâl, the Kohestân centre. There Dâmollah won, with 650 votes. Seyyed-Pâdshâh got 160, and 60 went to Sharif-jân. When the polling was over we returned to Sar-e-pol at night.

In Sangchârak, Sharif-jân won by buying votes at 250 rupees; overall he spent 1,800,000 rupees. Dâmollah spent only 200,000; he wasn't wealthy but his relatives and the people of Sar-e-pol helped, collecting 100,000 rupees for him. In the end he trounced the khans.

Elections for People's Assembly 1969

Kamâloddin Khân and Mr Shari were the two candidates. Many people in Sar-e-pol, both Afghan and Uzbek, supported Shari. When Kamâloddin Khân's team saw that he was lagging behind, they sent someone to Kabul; he brought back a letter from the Chief Justice to the judge and the *wâli* (provincial governor) of Jawzjân, who ordered the Sar-e-pol judge, 'Do whatever's needed to make sure Kamâloddin Khân, not Shari, becomes *wakil* – or we'll get you dismissed.'

They counted the votes for Sar-e-pol district in the Bâlâ-Hesâr [*municipal offices*]. That evening crowds gathered, the khans' people and ours, there wasn't an inch to spare. Every ten steps there was an armed soldier, they wouldn't let anyone near. The provincial police commandant, the Sar-e-pol *hâkem*, the judge and others did the counting. Kamâloddin Khân was there, but the commandant put Shari in his car and drove him off, until the people – the Uzbeks in front – stopped the cars and asked, 'How did the votes go? Where's Shari? Has he won?' They said, 'He's here, with the commandant.' Shari rose to speak, but they told him to sit down and keep quiet; he asked the people to stay calm.

The commandant took Shari home. Everybody came to his house carrying lamps. There was no room inside, people flowed out into the street. Shari got onto the roof and started talking, to calm them and prevent violence. 'I swear I've won by a big majority,' he said. 'Go home, don't worry.'

As the crowd dispersed, he turned and told me to follow him inside. 'I won both these elections,' he said, 'but as you know, the government doesn't like me, they won't let me be elected. Will you come with me to Khoja-Yegana?' I said, 'Yes, even to the grave.'

So next morning we went to Khoja-Yegana. Polling for that district was previously held in Kolaboy, but this time Haji Kheyr-Mahmad Khân had arranged things in his uncle Haji Qâsem's place in Kâriz: black tents, canvas tents, traders' stalls, a large yard, cooking-pots, and so on. As we arrived in Kâriz, Shari asked, 'Is it here?' I said, 'No, the polling station's some distance further on;' but he wanted to stop there. Up came Din-Mahmad Qariyadâr [*government liaison officer for nomads*] and Kheyr-Mahmad Khân, who said, 'Mr Shari, it's nice here, why go to that nasty place?' He answered, 'I've nothing to say to you, let me go and talk to the judge.' He went and asked the judge where the polling was held before; he said, 'In Kolaboy, but the road there's very bad, your car will break down.' Shari said, 'I don't accept that; will you come with me? If not, I'll go by myself. We'll wait, and if you haven't come after an hour, we'll record that polling in Khoja-Yegana has been completed.'

Off we went, and the judge was forced to follow us. Before he arrived we'd already had something to eat. They set up a tent and some kilims near the village melon-fields, and slaughtered some sheep, so we started cooking. After they'd sat down and eaten too, polling began. It was late before anybody came; none of our people knew it was happening, but that afternoon 250 Afghans voted. The next morning 100 of the khans' supporters voted; then our people began to arrive in large numbers; they even came out from Sayyâd and Qaflatun, although those places are close to Sar-e-pol town and the khans had wanted them to vote there.

When the khans saw that Shari was being so firm and resolute, they tried some tricks. They brought along a photographer; they'd get a fellow to vote using his own ID, then they'd shave off his beard, take his photo and issue him a temporary ID with this photo, saying, 'He's a nomad, he doesn't have a proper ID,' so he'd go and vote again.

That morning Haji Qâsem's son Rangin came to our tent, along with Din-Mahmad. We served them tea, then Mahmad-qul Khân, leader of the Sayyâd Uzbeks, who was sitting there too, introduced Rangin to Shari: 'This is the son of Haji Qâsem, Haji Kheyr-Mahmad Khân's maternal uncle; he's a great *châpandâz*,[3] and my good friend.' Rangin first went and voted that morning with his ID, then around mid-afternoon he voted with another ID, where he had a beard down to here. Shari said to him, 'I know you, you're Haji Qâsem's son Rangin; this isn't your ID; did you have a beard?' 'No, I've never had a beard.' 'Well, this ID has a picture of a bearded man!' So Shari put the ID in his pocket and told the judge to arrest him. They handcuffed him and sent word to town.

Haji Kheyr-Mahmad was very annoyed that Shari had his cousin arrested. He was worried how the Afghans would react, so he told two of his retainers to go and beat up the commandant. I had two pots on the fire and was busy with one of them, when all of a sudden, Richard, stones started flying in from the khans' place; it was raining sticks and stones! The commandant ordered his men to hit back, but when he approached we could see he was covered in blood from head-wounds. The police and the gendarmes got hold of the sticks, and they began beating and arresting the Afghans. Two of our people were outside, busy slaughtering goats and sheep, and a stone struck one of them; otherwise, there was no one but me. Haji Kheyr-Mahmad came by and sent his uncle Turabâz to make sure that no one hit the cook. Tâj-Mahmad Khân was standing on top of the mosque throwing stones at my pot; thank God it didn't break, but another person, Abdollah-jân, brother of Abdor-Rahmân Wakil, came and kicked the pot over, and half the meat fell out. I said, 'Bravo, what a hero! You'd better not come to Sar-e-pol.' Then I saw them trying to upend the tent. There was only Senator Dâmollah inside. I thought things were getting dangerous; there was a pistol inside the tent, so I went in to get it. Dâmollah asked, 'What are you doing?' 'I need the pistol that Shari brought.' 'Have many died?' 'Only a few!' I told him. Dâmollah wouldn't let me go, he was afraid I'd make things worse; but he started swearing at the Afghans, 'What the hell are they up to, behaving like this at the polling station, in front of the mosque?'

Then up came the judge, followed by Shari: 'What's up?' 'Come and see!' They saw that the tent and pots had been upset. Shari laughed and got onto a 200-litre drum. The soldiers brought the Afghans, took their photos, and peace and order were restored. The commandant said, 'Mr Shari, this is your doing!' Shari replied, 'You're right, my men were fighting. I have five men; three of them have gone hunting, leaving these two: one cook, one uncle!'

That night our people didn't come, so they set guards to prevent the Afghans attacking us and stealing things. Next morning news of the affair reached Sar-e-pol, and two truckloads of Uzbeks came out, armed with pistols and clubs. The commandant and the *hâkem* saw that things might turn violent, so they asked Shari to deal with them. He said he'd send them home. They came and ate, then Shari said, 'Go home, we'll follow when the votes have been counted.' The two truckloads of men left, but they stopped and blocked the road at Sardawa, opposite Sayyâd.

---

[3]   In buzkashi, the Afghan 'national' sport: mounted *châpandâz* compete to carry off a headless calf. See Azoy (2012).

When they counted the votes, Kamâloddin Khân had 300 more than Mr Shari, who had 764 – they'd boasted that he wouldn't get one. We set off back to town, our car in front, then Haji Kheyr-Mahmad and the judge. When we got to the roadblock, Shari asked 'What's all this?' They said, 'We've been waiting for you; we won't let the khans past.' He said he'd won the election, and we all got back in the cars. Shari told the others, 'You go first, I'm coming.' When we arrived near the shrine [*Emâm-e-Kalân, just outside Sar-e-pol town*], there were about fifty people waiting with lamps; others lined the road to Shari's house.

We went home and slept. In the morning they went up to Kohestân district centre at Khawâl for the polling. The provincial commandant, the Sar-e-pol *hâkem*, Haji Seddiq, the late Abdollah Khân, all went in the same car. The government wouldn't let any of us go, but one of our people from Jerghân was an official there, and he and a mullah called Haji Rasul later told us what happened. People gathered at the mosque waiting for the car and for polling to begin. When the *hâkem* arrived, he kicked an important village headman called Sohrâp, who shouted to the commandant, 'Why d'you let him kick me?' The commandant answered, 'Your candidate [*Shari*] is an atheist and a communist!' At that, he jumped on the commandant, cursing him. The commandant drew his pistol and threatened him. Sohrâp challenged, 'Shoot me then!' The commandant couldn't shoot, but dragged him to the car, where he calmly proceeded to sit in the commandant's seat! When Abdollah Khân said, 'That's the commandant's seat,' he turned round and punched him. The commandant said, 'Why don't you sit over there?' He said, 'I'm sitting right here.' When the car started, a hundred men with clubs blocked the road, asking 'Where are you taking him? You'll have to kill fifty of us before you take him anywhere!' The commandant was scared and let him go.

Later, they sent up a Special Commandant from Sar-e-pol with four officers and about twenty gendarmes. They handcuffed Sohrâp the headman and three others, brought them back, and for half an hour that day they interrogated them. Then a truckload of people from Jerghân arrived in the centre of town. They cut staves from the willows outside the government offices. When the commandant saw the situation, he told Shari, 'Do something about it! Unless I release your people, we'll get ourselves killed.' So he released the prisoners, and the people dispersed.

As for the nomads, Kamâloddin went long ago and said, 'We have all these people, *kuchis*, who have no land, no home, no ID,' and he got an official voucher for 1,700 votes. Seven hundred of these 1,700 people actually voted. He lied: there aren't so many nomads without ID. He brought along some boys, saying they were nomads without ID; in fact, they were all from wealthy landed families.

When the polling was concluded, Kamâloddin won, not by popular vote, but by government decision. They say Shari actually got 10,000 votes, while Kamâloddin Khân got only 1,000. That's how government works!

If the government hadn't interfered in those two elections, Shari would've won. Shari himself didn't spend one penny on the election. The people collected 200,000 rupees, of which he spent 150,000 and then personally divided the remaining 50,000 among the poor. He didn't take a penny for himself, saying he didn't need it.

In Kohestân, Kamâloddin Khân has 120 employees – farmhands, sharecroppers and so on. Twenty would have voted for him, a hundred for Shari. But he didn't let them vote; an officer and fifteen men went round the villages and stopped them coming. Shari was up in Kohestân a month earlier, before Jashn, when the *mâldârs* were coming down from the mountains. Everywhere he went, he talked to the people. If you go around Kohestân, Shari's picture is up in every guesthouse and mosque. A friend printed out 3,000 copies for him. And his picture is up in mosques and shops all over Sar-e-pol town. His proper name is Seyyed-Hakim; Shari is his pen-name (*takhalos*) – he's a poet too. In Uzbeki he's Yildirim, and in Pashtu something else. He knows twenty-four languages. He was offered a judgeship, but he turned it down, saying he's still a child – he's 30 this year.

Many Afghans from the villages didn't want to vote for Kamâloddin Khân, as he knew very well. The Seyyedâbâd Hazâras supported him, but there aren't many of them. All the other Hazâra villages – Chârbâgh, Chabuk, Boghawi, up to Mirzâ-wâlang over there, Miân-dara – all these were on Shari's side. Hazâras collected 50,000 rupees for him.

The Arabs, in the daylight, seemed for Kamâloddin Khân – they were under some pressure! But they voted for Shari. There are thousands of them out there in the eastern steppe, as I learned during the elections – I couldn't make out where so many Arabs had come from! I was on guard there during the polling. One Arab told me he'd lost a shoe; I teased him, 'Ask Kamâloddin Khân, he has a whole truckload of shoes, and another of boots, which he'll give to anybody who's lost one.' He went over to Kamâloddin and said, 'My dear Mr Wakil, I've lost my shoe, what shall I do?' The judge looked at him then turned to Kamâloddin Khân, 'Go on, Mr Wakil, give him a shoe.' So he forked out a hundred rupees! The *wakil* upbraided me, the judge laughed, and the Arab thanked me and kissed my beard!

For Shari's sake, some pickpockets stole a lot of Afghan ID cards and would have burned them, but Shari stopped them. They'd come and eat with us in the evening and report, 'Today we got fifty IDs; one of us got ten, one five.' They wouldn't take money for them, that's not why they did it. Some of them came with us for the polling. Once the judge asked one of them, 'Show me your ID.' He had a hundred of them somewhere, but he said 'I haven't got one,' so the judge told him to get lost.

There was much unrest during the elections. The Uzbeks and the Afghans fell out, the Hazâras . . . If, God forbid, violence should break out, it would be really bad. I know that many Afghans here, people like Nâder-shâh, dislike Kamâloddin and the khans; they're unhappy with their fellow-tribesmen. Even so, when the elections come, the khans know lots of tricks. Nâder-shâh called us to his place and swore to vote for Shari, but Shari said, 'I'm not asking you to vote for me. Kamâloddin Khân is one of your people. Vote for whoever will bring you what you want; when you enter the polling booth it's entirely up to you whether you put your ballot in my box or another one, or tear it up. Everyone is their own *wakil*, makes their own choice; and when they leave, only they know what they've done.'

Some of the khans' men came to fetch Nâder-shâh, but he wouldn't go. Then one evening Abdor-ra'uf Khân, Seyyed-Mahmad Khân, Kheyr-Mahmad Khân, Tâj-Mahmad Khân all appeared at Nâder-shâh's gate, with Korans hanging from their necks and their turbans tied like this – you see, I know all about it! – to persuade him to break his oath. They took some people off to the polls, though not many of them voted. We were there, Shari and I and many others, when Nâder-shâh came. When he saw Shari, he hid his head in shame; he wasn't able to look him in the face.

Kheyr-Mahmad Khân was responsible for all the trouble. Otherwise, Kamâloddin Khân would have conceded on the second day. It was a bad business. On polling day, there was a fight in the town centre, by the Bâlâ-Hesâr. Two Uzbek lads were knifed, one of them in the stomach, but thank God it was just a flesh wound. The other was knifed just here. Shari took pictures of the wounds but he wouldn't allow either of them to lodge a complaint. He immediately sent for a doctor, who stitched them up, and they went straight off and voted. One is son of the barber below the café.

Another day Tâj-Mahmad Khân drew his gun on Ja'far Khân Hazâra of Chârbâgh. The khans' people were smart enough to hide Tâj-Mahmad Khân in the cinema; otherwise the Uzbeks and Hazâras would have killed him. We had a man in the khans' place, and he reported to us every evening.

Once I was in Darzâb when a truckload of men came. I was behind the wall. Kheyr-Mahmad Khân asked in Pashtu, 'Do you have IDs?' 'Yes we do, Khân-seb!' So he told them to come and vote. They said, 'But we already voted at Jar-qoduq before coming here.' He said, 'It doesn't matter, come and vote here too.' Then he saw me and said, 'O son of the Pir, where did you spring from?' I said, 'I've got your tail, I'll follow you wherever you go!' He laughed, but he took them off; he hid their IDs, then gave them fake IDs and let them through. Now I calmly tell these stories of an evening, and he has to laugh.

In Sangchârak there are few Afghans, and no Es'hâqzai. Seyyed Es'hâq Hazâra won the election. The Aymâq khans quarrelled among themselves, because during the Senate elections Sharif-jân the Afghan had given Ghawsoddin Khân Aymâq 20,000 rupees, and he didn't share the money. Ghawsoddin Khân's cousin would have been *wakil*; Mirzâ Azizollah at first supported him, but he turned against him after Ghawsoddin and the others didn't vote for Dâmollah as senator. He said, 'You sold your own people out for 20,000 rupees and voted for Sharif-jân as Senator; I won't vote for your *wakil*, I'll vote for the Hazâra.' Ghawsoddin Khân's sons beat Mirzâ Azizollah badly and dishonoured him. Mirzâ Azizollah made a complaint; there was a major row, but he wasn't powerful enough, and they were rich, so they bribed the *wâli* and others, that's all. But the people went in Seyyed Es'hâq's trucks and voted for him.

Seyyed Es'hâq lives among the Gusfandis near Karrân-o-Kurrân, beyond Sheykhân, I've seen it. He's very wealthy, Richard, and he's well respected among his people, the Hazâra Seyyeds; he's their spiritual leader, and he's a good speaker. He's done many good things for the people of Sangchârak, who're very happy with him.

Sharif-jân is senator of the whole province; *wakil* of Sheberghân is Khalifa-seb Turkmen's son from Qezel-ayâq. The Andkhoy *wakil* was a powerful man, a Turkmen, and the government killed him. They say the Afghans could do nothing against him; he turfed out the gendarmes and set up twenty to thirty armed men of his own, and anybody he didn't like, he wouldn't let them vote. That's how he won the election.

We'll see what happens in the elections next year. Shari won't stand. Only two people want to stand, Haji Amân and possibly my uncle, Mirzâ Mahmad-Qâsem, who lives in Kabul; he's been *wakil* before, and people pressed him to stand again.

Ethnic Categories

Each ethnic group has a different view of its own and others' cultural attributes, and of the political and moral hierarchies among them. Here, Tumân's sons explain how 'Afghans' (Durrani Pashtuns) are different and superior to 'Fârsibâns/Pârsiwâns' ('Persian-speakers'), a category that, for them, includes several groups of Pashtu-speakers, as well as Turki-speaking Uzbeks.

'Afghan' and 'Fârsibân'

Pâdshâh, Tumân's second son, in his late twenties, articulates the standard 'Afghan' perspective.

In Afghanistan there are all kinds of peoples. Some Afghans, if they're Mahmadzai, Saduzai, Es'hâqzai, Nurzai, Alizai and a few others, consider themselves superior, noble. They reckon Maleki, Khalili, Kharjuli, Breti and Baluch among the Fârsibân.

We Afghans call all Fârsibâns *khâm-kala*, 'raw-minded', whereas all the Afghans of Afghanistan have 'cooked' minds. Fârsibâns are rather simple-minded; Afghans easily fool them. Some things please them, some fool them. Our king is Afghan, so is our prime minister. Why aren't they Fârsibân: Hazâra, Uzbek? All the great people in Kabul are Afghans. The king won't make anyone else ambassadors, ministers, *wakils*. The reason is that if a Fârsibân were king or minister or whatever, he'd immediately come down on the Afghans if he could; he wouldn't deal justly with us. So Fârsibâns are never allowed to be high-ranking officials; lower ranks yes, but not higher ones.

If we marry a woman from another *qawm* – Uzbek or Aymâq, say – they have different customs, so there are difficulties. With Uzbeks, on the whole, we neither take nor give women. If an Afghan does take an Uzbek wife, it's difficult for him. He won't understand Uzbeki, but they'll both understand Persian and they'll get along. Some Uzbeks learn Pashtu, which is easy; others don't – like you, they understand some but can't speak it properly. But that's okay, they learn gradually. But some of our women don't know Persian, and they'll make fun of her. He won't learn her language, only her little children learn it. Uzbeki is really difficult. Adults can't learn it; perhaps we'll understand a little, like you, but we can't speak it.

An Uzbek wife and mother is hard-working, she's very good with guests, serving them tea and food; but she'll complain to her husband, 'Why haven't you brought me something from the bazaar?' You have to bring her clothes, or something for her stomach; because she's an Uzbek, you'll always be squabbling with her. That's why Afghans don't like Fârsibân women.

An Afghan woman from a good family gets on well with her husband. Even if she has only rags to wear, she'll care for her husband's comfort and wellbeing. If her husband is wealthy, then she'll ask for things; but if he's eating barley bread, she'll never demand wheat bread, rice, meat, nice clothes; 'My husband's so thin and naked, how can I ask him to bring me anything?' An Afghan wife acts according to her husband's wishes. She won't demand that he go out to work as a servant or a herdsman, to earn money to buy things for her. No, that's not good behaviour for an Afghan; it looks bad, all Afghans would laugh at her: 'Look, her poor husband can't find even barley bread, yet she tells him to buy her fine clothes!'

If you take a Fârsibân wife, her children are like other children with the same father. A few turn out well, but when they grow up they'll stay rather immature; they don't come out as good as Afghans and they'll fight with everybody; they'll be incapable of getting on with Afghans. Some children take after their father, others after their mother; the 'strain' (*rag*) goes to one side rather than the other. What do we mean by 'strain'? If the father's strong, he draws the children his way; if he's weaker than his wife, they'll tend to her direction. You'll see it when they grow up and start talking; when they're sitting in company and they get up, you'll see how mature or immature they are, whether they're smart or dumb.

If you marry a Baluch wife, it's not such a problem. But some Afghans say, 'A Baluch woman is Fârsibân, we won't marry her.' Otherwise, Baluch understand our language, though we don't understand theirs. If a child's mother's Baluch and his first language is Baluchi, not Pashtu, that doesn't matter. A small child learns the language spoken by those who bring him up, whether it's Baluchi, Uzbeki or Persian – but he'll soon learn Pashtu.

Kabulis like the Shinwâri speak a rather different Pashtu; we understand it all, but we don't like it. In Afghanistan, the first language is Persian; second is Pashtu; third is Turkmeni. We like Uzbeki and Persian, but not Turkmeni, which is very peculiar.

Darwiza, Tumân's third son, aged 25, is even more explicit about the difference between Afghans and Fârsibâns, beginning with the ban on allowing Afghan women to marry Fârsibân men. He is himself engaged to a cousin; and like Pâdshâh, he is talking in August 1971, in the immediate aftermath of the scandalous elopement of a Piruzai girl with a Hazâra boy, which we shall hear about later.

The way you tell a Fârsibân from an Afghan is this: even if he's dying of hunger, even if he has nothing and you give him a room full of loot, an Afghan won't give his daughter or his sister to a Fârsibân: Hazâra, Uzbek, Taymani, Aymâq, Arab, Turkmen. But an Afghan can take a Fârsibân wife. That's how you tell Afghan from Fârsibân.

The Maleki call themselves Afghan, so do the Baluch, but they aren't, they're Fârsibân. The same with Khalili, Breti, Moghol: they call themselves Afghan; if they see an Afghan, they speak Pashtu, but if they're at home, with no Afghans present, they all speak Persian; they're Fârsibân. They give women to Fârsibâns. And Baluch exchange women with Maleki, and give and take them for brideprice too, so they're not Afghan. If they didn't give women to Maleki, they'd be proper Afghans.

Mind you, these aren't real Baluch; they're Jeghjegh. The real Baluch live near Herat – or is it Kandahar? – and have their own language. They're very tall, like Richard, but pitch black all over, with yellow eyes. Those real Baluch are good people; they count as Afghans. But the Baluch here are Fârsibân.[4]

---

[4] There are many Baluch in northern Afghanistan; they speak Pashtu, use Durrani-style tents, and follow Durrani customs, but they don't trace descent to Durrani ancestors. They are related to, but long separated from, the Baluchi-speakers of south-western Afghanistan, western Pakistan and south-eastern Iran. Darwiza's rather strange view is widely shared, but almost certainly far from reality.

The Bakhtyâri too aren't real Durrani Afghans; but they aren't exactly Fârsibân. All groups with *zai* in their name, like Nurzai, Atsakzai, Saduzai, Mamadzai, Jamâlzai, Bâdenzai, Pakhizai, Nazarzai, they're real Afghans. Bakhtyâri have no *zai*, so they aren't. Others without a *zai*, like the Tâjiks, are in-between. The ancestor of the Torkheyl was Tor, hence their name, but their real *-zai* is Bâdenzai. A real Afghan is someone whose name has *-zai* in it.

Ghiljai, such as Shamsoddin-kheyl – Nancy, you went there with Neshtar – are neither Afghan nor Fârsibân, something in-between. Teymur [*distant cousin*] gave his daughter to Shamsoddin, when he was desperate from hunger. He did it secretly. Once the mullah's prayed over her, with five elders to witness that 'we've given so-and-so's daughter to so-and-so's son', once that's done, there's no way to reverse it. Teymur came and apologized to my father and Nâder-shâh, who'd never have allowed it if they'd known. When people heard about it, they were very reproachful. Teymur couldn't do it openly; they were starving, it was like this year, they had nothing and were heavily in debt to the Ghiljais: that's why he gave her. Anyone who has money won't even take a Fârsibân woman; he'll say, 'She'll ruin my lineage, my offspring will go bad, they'll be mongrels.'

As for Durrani, we are *dur-andish*, which means 'far-looking'.[5] The difference between Afghan and Fârsibân is this: suppose I have a quarrel with a Hazâra, whose father was a good friend of ours; if he attacks me, with words or even blows, I won't retaliate; I'll realize that one day his parents may complain, 'Why did you hit us? We were good friends.' If he can, an Afghan looks ahead like that, thinking what his wife, his father or mother might say, and whatever he hears he stays calm. But however close our friendship, if we fight, that Hazâra won't have the same thought – that one day my parents may blame him. After all, he's a Hazâra, he's impatient, he looks at his feet, saying, 'Today I'm stronger than him, I'll beat him or kill him.' That's how you tell an Afghan from a Fârsibân. A Hazâra, a Fârsibân, is *kutâ-fekr*, 'short-thought'; when he's stronger than you, he won't hesitate to kill you. If two Hazâras fight, they'll go to court and demand compensation for a single drop of blood. We Afghans laugh at that, it's not our custom.

If an Afghan with a *-zai* takes a Hazâra wife, it doesn't really matter. We take after our fathers, not our mothers. A man from generations of Afghans is wise, has patience, looks far ahead, doesn't talk loosely to anyone. If my mother were pure Hazâra, I'd still be Afghan, but I'd have a wrong 'strain' [*rag*], and one day I might do something short-sighted, like attack my own father or a neighbour, or fight with my brother; and everyone would laugh and say, 'After all, he was "wrong-mother", *mâdar-khatâ*, he had a Hazâra strain.'

My father has another wife in Buyna-qara – you know about her? – Sarwar, an Uzbek widow. She spent one or two years here. Like you when you first came, she didn't understand our language and we didn't understand hers. She had a young son, but she didn't bear any children here, and she went back; she lives there now, and we pay her expenses. Her son – what's his name? Rawuk – has finished his military service; she found him a wife, and he has a child.

---

[5] This 'folk-etymology' is popular with the Piruzai. The usual etymology relates that the first ruler of Afghanistan, Ahmad Shah, adopted the title Dorr-e-Dorrân (Pearl of Pearls) and changed his tribal name from Abdâli to Durrani (Dorrâni).

Now an Afghan, no matter how destitute, will never give his daughter to a Fârsibân, even if offered five lacs of rupees, even ten lacs.[6] An Afghan won't marry a Fârsibân woman unless he's poor, or the woman comes freely by calling out 'This is my husband!' or because she attracted him by a magic charm; then it won't matter to him. A well-to-do Afghan will marry an Afghan woman; he won't take a Fârsibân even if she's offered free.

The Piruzai have a fund of jokes and stereotypes about other Es'hâqzai sub-tribes and other Durrani tribes. Baya-khân tells one joke to an appreciative audience.

An Atsakzai, who's never heard Persian or seen a Fârsibân, goes to town. He asks a shopkeeper, 'What is this Fârsi?' The shopkeeper, realizing he's a dumb, ignorant hick, tells him to go and come back next market-day, when he'll give him a nice Fârsi. Off he goes. The shopkeeper fetches a jar of grape-syrup; he puts some in a red hornet's mouth, and when the other hornets come and get stuck in the jar, he puts the lid back on. The next market-day the Afghan hick returns, delighted to be coming to fetch his Fârsi. The shopkeeper tells him to finish his business around the bazaar and come back in the afternoon, while he completes his work. He comes back and asks for his Fârsi. He pays 4,000 rupees, and the shopkeeper hands over the jar, telling him, 'Take it home, put it in a room, make sure there are no holes in the walls, then all of you, young and old, go in, shut the door, take off all your clothes, then open the jar.' [*Audience convulsed by laughter*]. So that's what they all do; they gather inside, lock the door, all so happy that they're going to learn Fârsi; they take their clothes off and open the jar. Out come the hornets. [*Laughter takes over*]. They have a white-haired old woman in there with them, called Anna; she too wants to learn Fârsi. She manages to get out, with twenty hornets attached to her bum, and disappears. Somebody says, 'I saw a red Fârsibân stuck to Anna's bum; she's gone, over there!'

Pâdshâh tells another Atsakzai joke, not quite so well as his younger brother.

Another story about an Atsakzai. In the mosque, mullah and *mowlawi* announce, 'Ramadan arrives this morning.' An Atsakzai says, 'Ah Mullah-seb, which direction is this Ramadan coming from?' Mullah answers, 'From Mecca'. 'What's it like, this Ramadan that's coming?' Mullah realizes he's a simpleton, and answers, 'It's a white thing, and it's nearly here.' The Atsakzai starts to think, goes home, gathers his community and tells them, 'We mustn't let this Ramadan come! Let's stop it!' He gathers an armed posse of ten people and they set off in the direction of Mecca. He sees a white camel – like our foal, except it's female – and thinks, 'This must be Ramadan!' So he calls out to his grandfather, 'Over here! It's the thing that mullah and *mowlawi* said was coming.' They all shoot at the camel until it's holed like a sieve. Atsakzai are simple-minded people . . . or they were of old; not so much now.

There are few Atsakzai in the north; but there are many Nurzai, a Durrani tribe closely related to the Es'hâqzai – who have a poor opinion of them, as Baya-khân tells.

---

[6]   Lac or lakh = 100,000. In 1970, £1 = 200 Afghan rupees; $1 = 70 Afghan rupees.

We call the Nurzai 'Donkey-eaters', because in earlier times they were great thieves. They'd case a village, looking for a place where a camel was tethered, planning to steal it at night. One day some Nurzai passed a house, and the man there had a ram with a huge fat tail; so they planned to come and steal it that night. The householder realized what they were planning: 'They've seen my ram; they'll come and steal it.' Now he had a donkey that had just given birth, so that evening he tied up the foal in place of the ram. He said, 'Don't move, these thieves are coming tonight.' In the dark of night the thieves came and quickly hoisted the foal onto their backs, thinking it was the ram, took it home, killed it and skinned it the same night, putting its head aside. In the morning they gathered to eat the meat, and one of them said, 'Bring the ram's head.' They were surprised to see it was a donkey foal's head; and since then they've been known as 'Donkey-eaters'!

Early in our stay, we spend an evening with Haji Ghâfur's family. I ask Gol-Ahmad about their hired shepherds: his answers are not very serious.

Our best shepherd was Lâljân Baluch; nobody was better than him. After him, the best was Aydak the Arab, very loyal. My father got Aydak betrothed to a girl, Mir-Âzâr's daughter. Somebody asked him, 'Ghâfur Bey, where are you off to?' He said, 'I'm off to get my shepherd married.' He said, 'Ghâfur Bey, you can't do that, that sort of thing isn't done; Mir-Âzâr won't give her to you.' My father replied, 'God knows; we'll see, maybe he will.' He got her for 30,000 rupees, this wife for Aydak, who was a very loyal man.

And he got Lâljân Baluch a wife for 30,000 rupees; he still owes 19,000. He's a Fârsibân. A Fârsibân is short-sighted, he looks at his feet; a Durrani Afghan thinks ahead, looks at distant places, not at his feet.

Our present shepherd, Abdollah-jân here, is from Boghawi. We think he's a Breti; he says, 'No, my father is Alekozai; we happen to be among the Breti, so people call us Breti; what can we do? we can't fight them!' He may look like an Alekozai, but if you consider his short-sightedness and his lies, then he must be a Breti. I don't know if you've looked at him, Richard; can you tell which he is? We can't!

Someone said to a Breti, 'Do you prefer sheep or God?' He answered, 'How can I decide between two friends?' The worst thing about the Breti is that in the beginning there was just one sheep in all Afghanistan. One person led it with a rope, another drove it from behind, with a dog; they took it night-grazing. 'For God's sake, how can you take just one sheep night-grazing?' Ever since then, everybody does night-grazing; if the Breti hadn't done it, we'd never have had such a headache! That's the one bad thing about the Bretis.

If I talk any more rubbish, Abdollah-jân will get angry!

There are several Breti groups in Sar-e-pol; Baya-khân explains.

For us, the Baluch, Breti and Maleki are all the same, they're Fârsibân; but actually they're distinct. The Breti have their own tribal sections, such as Bârakzai, Achakzai and so on; just like the rest of us and like the Hazâras.[7]

---

[7] On Breti/Barec see Balland (1988a).

Pâdshâh/Parwiz, a cousin we got to know well in 1972, adds a few details.

The Ludins aren't Fârsibâns, they're . . . what are they? They're Durranis. Hazrat Seb, our pir, was a Ludin.[8] My wife Golak's a Kabuli, from Mesrikheyl. When a woman comes from a different people, with different customs, it's easy for them to change. They change into our style of clothes, just as Nancy did. Kabulis do have a funny way of talking Pashtu; but they change this too.

Mahmad-Joma's son Mahmad-yâr is poor; he has nothing, he works as a watchman, or a gleaner. His wife Seyyedak comes from the Tâheri, who have land in Sangchârak, and also in Qataghan. They lived among us; and Mullah Jabbâr's aunt was married there. The Tâheris are Afghans, even though they have no -zai; they're not to be confused with the Turis, who are Fârsibâns, a kind of gypsies who have their own language. The Turis hunt foxes with their *tazi* [*Afghan hounds*].

One of the families that joined the Piruzai early on, and became attached to Ghâfur and Tumân's family through intermarriage, is that of Seyyed-shâh son of Soleymân, and his cousin Jamâloddin. They claimed to be seyyeds, descendants of the Prophet; among seyyeds, first sons carry the title. However, 'Seyyed-shâh' is a common name, borne by men who are neither seyyeds nor shahs.

Pâdshâh/Tumân tells how they learned who Seyyed-shâh and Jamâloddin really were.

They aren't really seyyeds, they're Kharoti from Wardak. A few days ago – it was the night that Baya-khân was telling stories – someone came here from Hazhdah-nahr, selling melons; he called out to me, 'Brother, there are two families of Kharoti here, my relatives, where are they?' I asked, 'Who are they?' He said, 'One is Seyyed-shâh, the other Jamâloddin.' Seyyed-shâh looked crushed, he was so ashamed. I brought them together and they greeted each other and Seyyed-shâh took him off to his house. [*See Fig. 3*]

We already knew they were Kharoti, but since it was a shameful matter we didn't mention it; if we had, Seyyed-shâh would have attacked us or been really mad at us. It's bad for an Afghan to be exposed as a fake, as a Hazâra or an Uzbek. It's like guns, a Saduzi is genuine, a Zafir is fake.

When Seyyed-shâh's father Soleymân first came, and we gave them women like Bibikuh, we knew he was a Kharot from Wardak, that kind of seyyed, but they were a large household from a good family, with lots of land. In those days people were simple-minded, not cunning and calculating as they are now. Grandfather Haji Zabtu gave them two daughters; Bibikuh to Seyyed-shâh's brother Dâ'ud-shâh for brideprice, and Belanis to his uncle Zolâboddin in exchange for Bibiwor, Haji Ghâfur's wife.[9] He also got Seyyed-shâh's sister Eyjab for Abdol-Mahmad. Seyyed-shâh's sister Negâr went to Shir for 30,000 rupees brideprice, but she died, leaving one son, Omar.

People talked, a lot; but we knew who they were, and once we've become in-laws [*khishân*], the tie can't be broken, even if they'd been Hazâras. However hard you tried

---

[8] There is a Ludin settlement close to Konjek. On the Hazrat of Shur-Bâzâr, see p. 431.
[9] Padshâh gets the arrangements wrong: Belanis married Seyyed-Soleymân, while Bibikuh went first to his brother Zolâboddin, then when he died, to Dâ'ud-shâh; see Fig. 3.

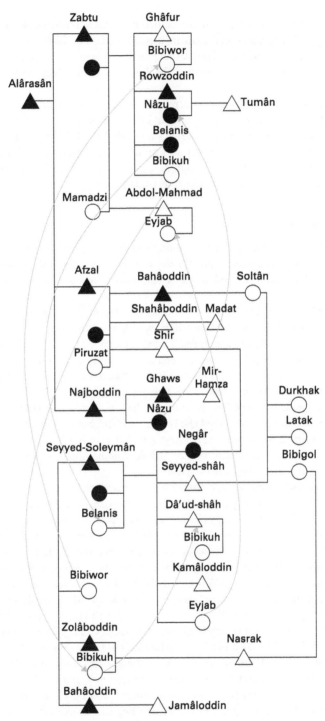

Figure 3 Lineage C and the Kharoti Seyyeds.

to cut it, the women would still visit each other; it's women's business. No doubt it's the same with you; if you marry an American, then no matter how bad your relations with America, you still visit with her family. That's the way it is with us. If you take a Baluch wife, even if you quarrel with the rest of the Baluch, you must keep up relations with her family.

Sometimes people in the village quarrel with Seyyed-shâh, and he threatens to go to Hazhdah-nahr or Chenâr, where he has land. Then someone persuades him to stay. After all, he can't go to Chenâr, one family among all those Uzbeks; and he can't go to Hazhdah-nahr because he doesn't get on with his people there, so he's forced to stay here. If the community drove him out, he'd join the Baluch of Qoshtepa and find himself a place there. He won't go back to Hazhdah-nahr.

Uzbeks and others

As outlined earlier, Uzbeks are the most numerous ethnic group in the plains and foothills of Turkistan. Piruzai, however, especially the women, often refer to all non-Pashtuns as 'Uzbeks', which Hâshem, our cook, a 'real' Uzbek, resents. He sets the record straight.

There are lots of Uzbeks in Sar-e-pol, from many different clans. My people are called Qâzikheyl, descendants of Mir-Rowzadâr; we're Seyyeds, we have family in Balkh. Originally, Balkh and Bokhara were one. Our street is called Qâzi Street, because we've been Qâzis [*judges*] for at least seven generations, up to my father, who was Qâzi in the year of Saqaw [*1929*]. Six months later when Haji Kheyr-Mahmad Khân's father, Re'is Abdol-Ghâfur Khân, became *hâkem*, my father resigned saying, 'Now the oppression starts.' They appointed Saluk, an old man, and he was useless. My father got a letter from Kabul, 'You've been appointed Qâzi of Sheberghân'; but he refused.

We're known in Sar-e-pol as Qâzikheyl. Another clan is Ulqâni, they're Fârsibân ['*Persian-speakers*']; then Awchi, they're Uzbek. Another one's named Baluch, but they're Uzbek too. Then there are the Tigan.

Yusuf Boy and Yaqub Boy [*prominent local Uzbeks*] are Ulqâni. They're known as Fârsibân because I think they came originally from Ulqân, towards Bokhara. My uncle Qâri Azim says that in the history books they're known as Il-khân.

Hâtam Beg and his associates were real Uzbeks, from Kâriz in Sangchârak. He was a rebel. The year before last, someone from Kâriz became my father's disciple; he told me, 'Hâtam Beg, Ebrâhim Beg, Khâldâr Beg and many others of our people came here from the USSR; Khalta-ye-Turkmen in Sheberghân – his son's there now – came to Hâtam Beg and asked for help: "We'll make you king."' Many soldiers came from Kabul, and they fought all over the place: here, in Mazâr, and towards Badakhshân. This was after the Saqawi war; I remember some of it. Such battles, Richard! There are still some of his followers in Sar-e-pol. They tell how he'd sit in the square and as soon as he saw a soldier he'd send four armed horsemen straight off – they rode like this, head under the horse's belly and one foot tied to the stirrup – and they'd swoop on the soldier, seize him and slice his head off. His four men managed to put a whole regiment to flight. That's how he fought, they say: Hâtam Beg was an extraordinary man. [*See Map E*]

After the fighting, Ebrâhim Beg returned to Bokhara, but Hâtam Beg stayed here. He often went into Kâriz, where he broke into people's houses to steal their goods.

Finally Wazir Mahmad-gol Khân told the local *hâkem*, 'Catch him or we'll kill you.' So the government put an end to him. One evening people were sitting in his tent listening to a *bakhshi* singing Gorogli,[10] which was a favourite of Hâtam Beg's. The *bakhshi* sang on and on and Hâtam Beg fell asleep. 'We tricked him,' they said. 'We tethered his horse in a shed with its legs hobbled, locked the door, then we all gathered, twenty armed men. When the guard was asleep, we entered the tent; six people jumped on him, two men shut his mouth; he threw them off, but we were too many and tied him up. He said, "Don't take me like this, cut my head off!" He had huge moustaches.' They cut off his head, put it in a sack and took it to Wazir Mahmad-gol Khân in Mazâr. When he saw it, he cried, 'What a head!'

So they killed Hâtam Beg and took his horse; but they didn't understand what it ate. It wouldn't eat hay, only sheep's tail and sheep-droppings. 'We offered it straw but it refused, it wasn't used to it.' Finally, they say, it was taken to Kabul and died of hunger.

Khâldâr Beg now has a shop and some land in Mazâr, and he has workers there. He's a very rich man. Hâtam Beg's followers were outlaws; many were fugitives in Kandahar, they didn't come this way. They were eighteen years under sentence of death. I heard the story from one of his followers in Sar-e-pol, an old man called Bubarinjugar. If you look at his feet, Richard, they're riddled with bullet wounds. He was released about ten years ago.

Even now the people of Kâriz are of Hâtam Beg's clan. They're called Qochi ['*Ram-people*']. You know Sazay-kalân, on the road to Toghzâr? Turn off east by the spring there, on the track towards Mazâr; it goes via Kâriz. After Alaghân village, there's Sheykhyâr, Kandali, Kâriz and so on – the Qochi. They all had *kâriz* canals, but they're now ruined and they use wells.

When you've passed Fereshgân and Toghzâr, there's a village called Sheykhân; beyond that the people are Karrân-Kurrân, in Juybâr ['*Riverine*'] district, the Seven-Valleys of Sangchârak; and then Gusfandi ['*Ewe-people*'] ...

Every village belongs to one clan. Each has a name: Sheykhyâr, Kandali, Bura-qezel, Kâriz, Kolamâ'i, Ulkâr, Chârshanger, Qezel-kent – what names the Uzbeks have given their villages! I've been to them all with my father; they're all his murids.

In the Sar-e-pol *woleswâli* there are 12,000 Uzbeks with ID cards, 5,000 Afghans, 3,000 Hazâras. I don't know how many Arabs, but they're numerous, especially in the steppe and various places around Sar-e-pol town. All the Arabs in Engeshka, on the outskirts of town, have land, houses, orchards. The Uzbeks have some melon crops there, on Arab land. Beyond is Qotarma; the people are Arabs, and own their land. Then beyond Qotarma is Bâzârkami; they too are Arabs. There are Arabs scattered everywhere. Most Sar-e-pol townspeople are Uzbeks. There aren't so many Hazâras in Sar-e-pol town; there's no special Hazâra quarter, and they don't own land there, rather they rent. Only Ebrâhim-jân the treasurer owns some land, on the way to Âsiâbâd; he lives near Emâm-e-Khord.

---

[10] See Javadi (2009), Youssefzadeh (2009).

Seyyed-shâh/Soleymân – the outsider who married into the Piruzai, but was 'outed' as a non-Durrani – has land in Chârkent, an Uzbek district of Sangchârak sub-province, which lies on the Piruzai migration route. Like many Pashtun landowners, he has recently found local Uzbeks refusing him his share of the crop. In August 1971, camped in Chârkent with his in-laws Tumân and Gol-Ahmad, without whose patronage he could not hope to keep his land, Seyyed-shâh voices his resentment.

All Sangchârak belonged to the Uzbeks; the Sar-e-pol lands were all Arab. When the Afghans arrived in numbers, under Gholâm-Rasul Khân Nazarzai, the Arabs made themselves scarce. Most Sar-e-pol land now belongs to Afghans, because Re'is Abdol-Ghâfur Khân was *hâkem* of Sar-e-pol, and Turabâz Khân was tax collector in Sheberghân, so they controlled government and got all the land registered in their names. Now nobody has as much land as the khans; but the Uzbeks kept Sangchârak. There were no Hazâras around here then.

The best vine-growers in Sangchârak are the people of Khojagi-o-Tadil valley. The other Uzbeks of Juybâr and Chârkent are good too. Not the Afghans. Here the people are Juybâri; they have plenty of water. With flowing rivers, vines, water-mills, Juybâr people are much better off than the Gusfandi, over in the other valleys and the steppe, who are short of sweet water and have few vineyards; their living conditions are tough – they're mostly stockmen, but some do rainfed farming.

At buzkashi time, Gusfandi and Juybâri people compete with each other. There's no other team in Sangchârak. Of course, if only Juybâri turn up, then the different valleys form teams. There are many Hazâras here in Juybâr; if only Hazâras come, then they put the Juybâr Hazâras on one side, and the Gusfandis on the other. There are also Afghan and Hazâra Gusfandi. Juybâri are better at buzkashi than Gusfandi; and they have better relations with government.

I've been to many places, to the south, to Maymana, Hazhdah-nahr, met many people, Turkmens, Afghans, Hazâras; but I've never known such untrustworthy people as these Uzbeks. One year we cultivated flax on our land by the spring. The crop came to about 100 Kabul seer. Then one night the farmhand, Mullah Jura, brought three camels and grabbed the lot. We came in the morning and said, 'Let's divide the crop in two.' We didn't know he'd already taken it all. He was a 70-year-old Haji! I heard the other day that he'd died; shameless in this world and the next!

It's not the proper way to do things. The people of Afghanistan, Turkistan, Sangchârak are all good and trustworthy, but not these people of Chârkent, especially Kata-qala and Buyna-qara villages, including their Hajis. They don't understand right and wrong. They agree to sharecrop our land for half the crop; they farm it, then take the harvest and don't even give us one-tenth. They offer silly excuses, but they're quite unreliable. However hard you try being friendly with them, it means nothing. Nobody can understand either their friendship or their hostility.

Ten years ago, when their elders were alive, they were very good people, very straight, kept their word, behaved like friends and brothers. We had good relations with them. We used to camp right here; the grapes were ours, the hay was ours, the firewood was ours. Now, the very day we arrive, we have no control over our own vineyards.

Times have changed, things get worse every day. Our Afghanistan is corrupt. The moment you touch something, someone gets up and complains. We don't understand these times. Now, if a man's house falls down, his brother's happy. One man has pilaw to eat, and won't help his poor and debt-ridden brother.

When we arrived from Kandahar forty years ago, they begged us to buy their land. We were stockmen, *mâldâr*, we didn't want farmland. But they persisted, 'Come, buy our land; it's a good thing.' So we bought it. Now they say, 'We were too young,' or 'It was my brother who sold it.' Another says, 'My daughter claims a share.' So it's all turned to shit.

They have no rights. But they don't fear God. We go to the government, and what do they do? Judge Morât knows very well that we've been farming the land for years, that the land's ours; but bribes are what counts. He takes money from here, from there, and in the end, having filled his pockets, he says, 'Go and sort it out yourselves.' What sort of justice is that? Ask five people, 'Did we take this land by force or by consent?' They sold it to us freely, took our money, and one man spent it on a Hajj, another on a wedding for his son, or for his father. Now they've started a huge dispute with us. Where's the justice in our Afghanistan?

Âktâsh and Chârbâgh are the two largest Hazâra villages near Sar-e-pol. The Piruzai have contacts there, as they do among the Hazâras near their summer pastures in Lâl-o-Sar-jangal. Baya-khân and Pâdshâh tell something of what they know of Hazâras.

The mountain Hazâras, like those of Âktâsh and Chârbâgh, have different tribes, like Gheyratzai, Meraka, Jamâli, Jaghori, Pacha-palang, Qezelbâsh. The Qezelbâsh – they're in Chârbâgh – say they're the purest. The Jaghori are strong, loud, lively, enthusiastic people; not like other Hazâras.

Some call themselves seyyeds; they say, 'We're descendants of the Prophet.' They wear black or green turbans, and they're called *âghâ*. If a black-turban comes to a village, other Hazâras will kiss his hands, saying, '*âghâ's* come!' One year, on our way down from the mountains, our brother Khâni-âghâ went to find some wheat. With him was Seyyed Amir, from Khâdem's place. Khâni-âghâ's turban was black too. They went to a place called Diwâlak, far away from the wheat, and entered a hut. Their houses are dark, even at midday, as you saw. Several other Hazâras came in and kissed Seyyed Amir's hand, but they also kissed Khâni-âghâ's. When they found out, they attacked him: 'This Seyyed Amir is a descendant of the Prophet, but you're no *âghâ*, you're an Afghan. Why didn't you tell us, why'd you let us kiss your hand?' Several of them grabbed his shirt and roughed him up, until Seyyed Amir cried, 'He's my friend, let him go.' They're very simple people!

Soltân's mother Yeli was quite a woman. She used to collect weeds; one day she went to visit the Hazâras. In the month of Moharram, the Hazâras hold sacrificial feasts every day, then at night they pray in the mosque, and while the mullah recites they beat themselves here on the chest with their fists, very hard, and chant 'Hasan, Hoseyn!' They also flog themselves with chains. During this month, when they hold these feasts, laughter's forbidden. They sit quietly; they can talk, but not laugh. Anyway, Yeli and Sâf-khân, Shâhpari's brother, decided to go to one of these Hazâra feasts. They ate the food, then came outside; but when the Hazâras were busy beating themselves, Yeli couldn't stop herself bursting into laughter. The Hazâras were infuriated and leapt after her. She ran like hell, and they chased her back as far as the edge of our village – they were going to beat her like a donkey! When she got back she was exhausted and had a high fever for several days.

Kala-khân, Tumân's fifth son, aged 20, a religious student, mutters:

Our Prophets were Fârsibâns, from the beginning . . .

Baya-khân tells of two other important groups, the Arabs and the Turkmens.

Before the Afghans arrived, all *mâldârs* here were Arabs, who had lots of sheep. They occupied the whole Sar-e-pol valley, and they took their vast flocks of sheep up to Sar-jangal, as we do today. Hazâra elders and seyyeds there say that nobody'd heard of Afghans, all the *mâldârs* in Sar-jangal were Arabs, who'd come and visit them. All the Hazâra valleys there were forested. Then they founded villages, cut down the trees for their houses and for winter fuel, and the forest disappeared.

When the Afghans came from Kandahar and seized the Sar-e-pol valley, the Arabs moved to the steppe, places like Sheram, Neymadân, Jar-qoduq, Dara-ye-band, Majar and Armani, where they camped on the hilltops. In the old days, in a good year with rain and *barakat*, rainfed crops did very well in the steppe, but the Arabs prefer their sheep and the steppe, where there's plenty of grass. They didn't like irrigated land; they'd say, 'Our feet and our sheep get stuck in the mud in winter; the steppe's better.'

Arabs marry among themselves. We don't give them women, but some Afghans, like Teymur-shâh Nâmanzai, marry Arab wives. There are no Arab women in our village. Âghâ-Mahmad Khân's brother Seyyed-Mahmad Khân had an Arab wife; he died, and his nephew Shâh-Mahmad Khân took her. People say uncle Shahâboddin's mother was half-Arab; but it was his mother's mother, not his mother.

The Arabs in Holy Mecca are noble, good people. These Arabs aren't the same, but they're all right; we're the same religion, not like the Hazâras. The Arabs have many different tribes, like our Es'hâqzai, Nâmanzai, Piruzai: the ones I've heard of are Hazhdah-Diwâna ['*Eighteen-Crazies*'], Chelkappa – they really do have a tribe called Hazhdah-Diwâna, I'm not joking, ask Hâshem. I don't think they speak Arabic now; as far as I know, they all speak Persian.

Turkmens don't give women to anyone; we don't give them women, or take from them. Nobody can understand their language. Turkmens claim to be pure-bred, but they're not, only Afghans are.

During the Saqawi revolt [*1929*], Turkmens attacked the Pakhizai [*an Es'hâqzai sub-tribe*] and abducted many women. The Pakhizai fled to our villages and told our grandfathers, 'The Turkmens came, stole our women and plundered us!' They raped three Afghan women for several nights and when they gave birth, their children were like Turkmens. Some of the Pakhizai today are very well built; people say they're the result of that Turkmen attack. Examples are Sâleh's wife Badri and her twin brother

Lâlu, who has a big head like a Turkmen. Several Pakhizai women completely disappeared. It was a long time ago.

Marrying strangers: Rangin and Golshâh Taymani

Piruzai much prefer to marry other 'Afghans', people they know and have other ties with. But many Piruzai men have married 'Fârsibân' women, not always with happy results. Konjek village headwoman Neshtar tells what happens when Afghan men marry strangers.

It's better to marry among ourselves, people from the same ancestor. Marrying a stranger brings problems. I mean, you have to provide more wedding goods than usual, it's a matter of honour and rivalry. If the partners are close, nobody fusses about the goods; whatever they bring, it's fine. When someone marries an Uzbek or an Aymâq wife, we do Afghan-style ceremonies. We give lots of goods, as you saw last year; whereas the Aymâqs give only a couple of blankets, a pair of pillows, two mattresses, a small felt, one storage bag; they just don't provide goods on the same scale as us. We'll make up what's missing – nice pillows, felts, rugs and so on. If she's smart and hard-working, she'll soon find what she needs.

As soon as we've married such a woman, we make her wear nice Afghan clothes and throw away her Aymâqi things. She'll never wear them again. If you take a Fârsibân wife, she soon learns Pashtu. My brother-in-law Shâdi took an Aymâq wife, and so did his uncle Khalifa-Patih. They learned perfect Pashtu within one year. Every Fârsibân woman who's brought here learns Pashtu, and her children of course won't speak Persian; they take after their father, not their mother.

One extreme case is that of Neshtar's half-brother Rangin, who grew up in Ghor among his mother Kheyru's people, Taymani Aymâqs. He was raised as a Taymani, married a Taymani, Golshâh, and failed to acknowledge his 'Pashtun' identity – though he had property and relatives among the Piruzai. (See Fig. 4; Map C)
Neshtar tells the story.

My father Golnur married Kheyru, a Taymani from Ghor. Soon after they married, she got pregnant with Rangin, who was born nine months later. Golnur and his family were in Kandahar at the time. When Rangin was ten months old, Kheyru gave birth to another child, but both she and the baby died, leaving Rangin motherless. His Taymani aunt and granny came and said, 'For God's sake, give us the infant, we'll look after him and suckle him.' My mother Mabu, who'd just had her own baby, said, 'No, I'll look after them both,' but the aunt insisted, 'He's my nephew, let me look after him.'

So they gave Rangin to his maternal relatives to raise. When he was seven years old, my father went to Ghor on horseback – there weren't any motors then – and said, 'I've come to fetch my son.' His aunt and gran refused to let him go but Golnur put him on the horse. The boy was suddenly seized with a coughing fit and fainted. His granny and aunty repeated their plea to keep the boy, who was clearly unwell; so my father left him and came back.

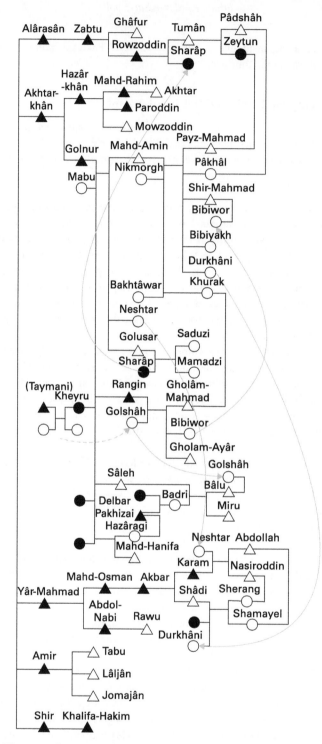

Figure 4 The story of Rangin and Golshâh.

Rangin became a teenager. Once again Golnur went to fetch him. The boy didn't recognize his father; he was scared and ran away: 'An Afghan wants to carry me off, I won't go with him!' – of course, he was a Persian-speaker. So once more his father left him.

He grew up in Ghor, and got engaged to Golshâh; then he headed north with two companions. The word went round, 'Golnur's son's coming!' Golnur himself wasn't around when his brothers Mahd-Amin and Paroddin heard the news, so they rode off into the steppe, taking an extra horse. Three days later they brought Rangin home, with his companions. He said, 'I'm engaged to marry Golshâh, but I can't afford the wedding.' My father gave him 30,000 rupees – a lot of money then – to spend on clothes for his wife. He also gave him clothes for himself.

Rangin spent several months here, then went back and spent a few more years there; then he returned. My father Golnur asked him, 'Have you held the wedding?' 'Yes, I have, and I have a son, but now I have to do my military service.' So my father gave him another 30,000 for his expenses. Two more years passed, then Mahd-Amin and Khalifa-Hakim – my father's cousin – rode off to fetch them home. They went to the mountains of Ghor, where the Taymanis live. When they found Rangin, they said, 'You're our brother, now you're coming home with us.' He replied, 'No, I'm not going anywhere; my heart is here; when my heart wants go north, I'll come, but not now.' Mahd-Amin got angry and said, 'Aren't you my brother?' Khalifa also spoke: 'We've come all the way from Turkistan, you must come with us.' But he stayed.

A few years later we were in the mountains, in Michiluk. Rangin had gone to Cherâs, and left his wife there with Khalifa. We migrated to Târikak, and one afternoon Rangin arrived. Everyone was so happy that he'd come. He said, 'My wife's here, with my daughter Bibiwor at her breast. I've left them both at Khalifa's house in Cherâs.' He stayed with us, while two boys took several donkeys and fetched his wife and household.

After a few years Rangin said, 'Give me my share of the family property.' They gave him a camel, twenty sheep, some land, a tent, and some household things: they made him a home. He spent about six years here; then, about eight years ago, he died. That was his story.

Rangin's Pashtu was laughable. He understood it, but he wouldn't speak – people would laugh. When we spoke Pashtu to him he'd laugh himself. He'd say, '*Balé, balé* (yes, yes),' but he wouldn't speak Pashtu. They said, 'Speak Pashtu, you're Golnur's son, you're shaming us.' However hard we tried, he laughed and refused to speak. Then he died . . . When he came here, he adopted our clothes, our customs. His wife Golshâh too, when she came, didn't understand Pashtu; she spoke Persian. But she adopted our way of life: clothes, chador, all our customs.

Neshtar continues Golshâh's story in a later chapter.

The Runaways

Our narrators have made it clear that 'Afghans' never allow their daughters to marry non-Afghans. Exceptions to this rule are rare. But although Piruzai have many Hazâra contacts, even friends, in both Sar-e-pol and the mountains, their Shi'a religious identity

*is one among many differences between them that makes intermarriage inconceivable.
The worst possible breach of the rule would be an Afghan girl eloping with a Hazâra; yet
this is just what happens in summer 1971.*

We are with the mâldâr *in summer quarters in Lâl-o-Sar-jangal district, Ghor
province, in the western Hazârajât. Askar, from Chârbâgh, a large Hazâra village near*

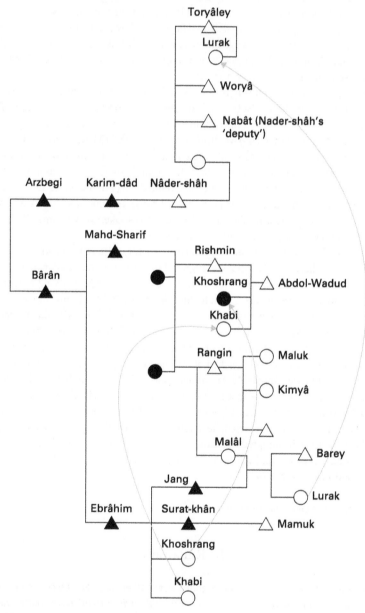

Figure 5 Chasing the runaways.

the Piruzai settlements in Sar-e-pol, rides up to the mountains, ostensibly to visit some relatives. He stops for a few nights with his former Piruzai employer, a different Rangin (Lineage A), then leaves. That evening Rangin's daughter Kimyâ follows him, dressed in Hazâra clothing he has left for her, taking a large amount of her father's cash. Discovering her absence, Rangin in shame spends two days looking for the runaways alone, before informing Nâder-shâh and asking for help.

The story is mainly about relations between Pashtuns and Hazâras; but we learn that there is a considerable back-story about relations between Rangin and his half-brother Rishmin, who have had a complex and sometimes violent quarrel. Tumân has spent much of the spring trying to reconcile them – Rishmin is one of his closest friends. A year before, Rishmin's son got another of Rangin's daughters pregnant; the affair was hushed up. In the spring, a valuable gun of Rangin's went missing; he put the blame on Rishmin, who was forced by a jirga to pay compensation; but it seems Kimyâ gave it to Rishmin's son, who passed it to Askar to sell – thus facilitating the elopement.

Tumân takes a leading role in the search for the runaways. In August 1972, having, as will become clear, spent much of the intervening year in a fruitless chase, he tells us the story. The Piruzai have been deeply dishonoured. The Hazâras, clearly counting this as a coup in their long-standing hostilities with the Pashtuns, are uncooperative at best. As with his even more laconic account of his Hajj pilgrimage earlier in 1971 (see pp. 354–55), Tumân focuses on details of time and place; apart from the odd expression of exasperation and weariness, his feelings must be inferred from the narrative.[11]

Let me tell the story of Rangin's daughter. Last year on 15 Saratan [6 *July*] Rangin's daughter eloped at midnight with a Hazâra. We heard about it three days later. Fifteen of us assembled with our guns, and we all went to inform the Lâl *woleswâli* office. They said, 'We've noted it, now we'll telephone around; you go and see what you can find, and we'll keep in touch.' [*See Fig. 5; Map G*]

Five of us set off south-east towards Day-kondi; five others went north-east to Yekawlang, and five more westwards into Ghor. We went by truck and came via Kermân to Azgharât, where we got off, as the truck was going east to Kabul via Panjaw, while our way went south. It was evening before another truck came from Kabul, heading our way.

The quest in Day-kondi

We were: myself, Mâmuk, Rishmin, Worya and Toryâley. In the morning we went all the way down the Ashtarley gorge, as far as the Gardesh pass. Just before the climb up the pass there were four or five shops; we got out, and the truck went on. We asked all around the place, but no one would tell us anything. There was a khan there, Anwar Khân, and we went to see him. One of his farmhands told us, 'Three days ago, I was in such-and-such a valley, repairing the pond that we fill for watering the wheat we have there. As I was doing this I saw a man coming along on foot with a woman on horseback behind

[11] See N. Tapper (1991: 61–62, 90–91, 226–27).

him. The woman asked him in Pashtu, "Why's he doing this?" and he replied in Pashtu, "He's fixing the pond so he can fill it with water and irrigate the wheat; if he lets the water out when there isn't much in it, it won't go very far." The woman was an Afghan, but I think the man was a Hazâra,' the fellow told us. We asked him which direction they were heading, and he said, towards Khoshak, a place the other side of Day-kondi.

We stayed there that night and all the following day. In the evening I said to Worya, 'Come on, let's take our handguns and go on towards Khoshak, since the trail leads that way; the others needn't come, we can catch them by ourselves.' We'd brought a Hazâra with us from Lâl. The khan advised us to take someone else as well, but we couldn't do that.

After dusk prayers we set off up the Gardesh pass, *hala-hala-hala*. At midnight we reached the top. On we went, and by morning we were down the other side. As we came down we met an old man coming up, with a basket of apricots on his back. We asked where he was coming from, and he said, 'From Chârbâgh, at Dahan-e-qol, where there are apricots. I spent the night there and in the morning I bought two seers of apricots; I'm taking them back for my kids.' We asked him to sell us a few pounds, but he said, 'No, I've taken so much trouble bringing them all this way on my back, I can't give you any. You'll be there yourselves in a couple of hours.'

So we said, 'Okay, too bad, but can we ask you some questions?' 'What?' We said, 'We have land and farm-workers in Lâl; one of our men – registered on our land – went off on military service, but he deserted and came home. At first he said an officer had given him a month's leave, and he'd be going back. But after two or three days he ran off, taking his wife and all their clothes and belongings. He got away early. The military police came after him to Lâl; then the day before yesterday they took us in and ordered us to go find him. So we've come after him.' We described them for him. 'We're not after the woman, only the man.'

The old man answered, 'These days if you ask somebody, "Can you see that camel?" he'll be sure to say no, for fear that, if he says yes, he'll end up with a chain round his neck.'

We said, 'No, brother, we're not like that; we swear by God and the Koran, we'll never mention your name to anyone as having told us anything, and we'll give you some sweets.'

He had a Koran with him. He took it out and said, 'Will you swear by this if I tell you?' and we said, 'We swear by this that we won't tell anyone what you tell us.'

So he said, 'Two days ago, this woman ... wasn't she tall?' We said yes. 'Well, I was carrying apricots, when I met a man and a woman coming from the other direction. I saw that the woman wore a chador on her head, and she'd put a cloth over it. She was an Afghan, but the man was Hazâra. I saw them right here. I know this woman was in hiding round here until yesterday.'

We said, 'Fine, if she's in hiding, please go and find out where, which village, and what the situation is, who's hiding her; then we'll give you anything you want.'

He said, 'If that's the case, first let me take my apricots home, over there, then I'll come back, and if you give me 100 rupees I'll bring you news of the woman.'

We agreed, gave him 100 rupees and sent him off. He went home, unloaded the apricots and returned, saying, 'Let your Hazâra man come with me; you two go down into the village and sit there; as soon as I've found some information I'll tell him and he'll bring it to you.'

We entered the village. We were hungry and thirsty, but they wouldn't give us anything. We paid 20 rupees for two pounds of wheat and wondered what to do with it; we took it to a place where they hand-ground it for 6 rupees, and then had the flour made into dough in another place; they put some cumin with it, and we also bought some ghee for 12 rupees. We cooked the bread, but we couldn't eat it dry, so we bought some buttermilk for 5 rupees and ate the bread with that.

It was hot, and we were very tired; we asked if someone could lend us a felt so that we could sleep under a tree. A man brought us a felt and we lay down and had a nap. Then we got up and said our midday prayers; we were strolling around in the trees, when our man appeared. He said, 'This very morning she's been taken to Echeshk; the fellow with her, Askar, has a sister who's married to someone there; anyway, that's where she is, he's taken her to his sister's house in Echeshk.'

We realized that we'd never be able to bring her back if we went to Echeshk; we were only two people and the Hazâras were powerful. So we told our companion, 'Brother, now the matter's clear.' 'Don't worry,' he said, 'they're in Echeshk. She's settled there and they won't go anywhere else.'

So we left that evening, walked all night, and at prayer-time we reached the bottom of the Gardesh pass. There we met Nâder-shâh coming towards us in a truck. We all stopped and Nâder-shâh got out and asked, 'What's the news?' 'We've tracked her down, but if we go there now we'll never be able to get her. Let's go to the government office and see if they'll do something for us.'

We stayed there the rest of that day, waiting for another truck. The next morning one finally came, so we set off, *hala-hala-hala*, and at two o'clock we arrived at Day-kondi district government centre. We left the truck, hungry and thirsty. The first thing we did was to have some food and tea.

Nâder-shâh said, 'Let's find somebody to act as intermediary.' I said, 'Why bother looking for an intermediary? Why don't we two go together to the *hâkem*; we can talk to him ourselves.' So we went to the *hâkem* and greeted him. He asked us where we were from, and we said, from Lâl.

'Where are you going?' 'We've just arrived; one of our women has eloped with a Hazâra and it seems she came here.'

He said, 'Two days ago I received information that a fellow called Askar brought a woman and they're at Khoshak. A village headman called Akram Khân said he'd go after them, but the commandant said, "No, the fellow will just say, 'This is my wife and I brought her from such-and-such a place.' There's no point going after them until they've been tracked down." Well, now you've tracked them down!'

He quickly put together a commission: the commandant, Akram Khân, and three or four soldiers. We hired a jeep for 1,000 rupees and set off at noon. By evening we reached Shakhnaw, which is as far as the jeep could go. We went to the local *wakil*'s house and spent the evening there, then at midnight we left – we also had with us Anwar Khân from Ashtarley, whose farmhand had told me that the woman came that way. We went on foot, *hala-hala-hala*; and in the morning we arrived at Juy-sorkh, Anwar Khân's place – he had one house there, and another at Ashtarley.

Tumân does not state it, but we can assume that the hâkem *and the commission members, i.e. government agents, were Pashtuns, except Akram khan and Anwar khan: that they are Hazâras can be inferred from the rest of the account.*

The khan called out, and his men brought food and tea and hot milk. After we'd eaten and drunk, he told Barey and me, 'You set off down that valley, we'll follow you.' We took two of the soldiers; we'd sent the others to find horses, but they hadn't yet come back. *Hala-hala-hala*, we went a long way down that river valley. It was a godforsaken place; the track was very hard going, the river way down below us. Down we went, *hala-hala-hala*, nearly overcome by fatigue, until about midday.

Meanwhile the others, the khan and the commissioners, had passed us on horseback. Finally, along came the soldiers with two horses for Barey and me. We mounted them, and left the soldiers behind on foot. *Hala-hala-hala*, until we came to Dahan-e-Echeshk. There we asked a local Hazâra, who pointed up the mountain track opposite and said that Akram Khân, Anwar Khân and the commandant had gone that way. So we set off after them, *hala-hala-hala*.

You can't imagine how high that bloody mountain was. The track was unbelievably steep; there's a village right at the very top above Echeshk. We found the commissioners there; they'd collected the villagers. They gave us some tea, and when we'd drunk it, the commandant told me, 'You and your companion go outside, we have to talk with the Hazâras.' So we went and washed and said our prayers, then we returned.

The commandant told me, 'We've found the woman; they brought her here, but two days ago they took her to another village. She's now secured. Take your companion and these soldiers, off you go, and I'll bring the woman, along with the other commissioners Akram Khân and Anwar Khân.'

I said, 'Brother, why did you bring us here? Don't send us away now! We'll go with you, or follow you.'

But he said, 'We brought you with us in case your story was a hoax; now it's proved true, and they've assured us that the woman's in that village and that they'll hand her over to me, but not those Afghans; "If those Afghans are there," they said, "there'll be a massacre; they're honour-bound to shoot either the woman or the man or both."'

I said, 'Brother, take my knife and our guns, we won't do anything; send us ahead of you or behind you. If there's a stone in front of us, remove it. I mean: we're going with you.'

The commandant said, 'That's quite impossible. If you're going to take this woman from anyone, it'll be from me; we're the commission, and you'll get the woman from me in the district centre.'

I said, 'For God's sake, don't do that! Take our guns and ammunition; what else can we kill them with? Why have we come? We're with you; why are you making it difficult?'

But he wouldn't change his mind. So they forced us two to leave, with two of the soldiers. He told us to return to Anwar Khân's place, and they'd eventually bring the woman there. So we mounted our horses and set off, *hala-hala-hala*. After a night on the road we came to the khan's place. We spent the day there, but there was no sign of the commission, the commandant or the woman.

Anwar Khân arrived the following afternoon, with the commission secretary. He greeted us and said, 'The woman's gone.' 'What! Where?' 'She's gone to another district; we've lost her.'

'What do you mean by telling us such dreadful news?'

'I swear, she's gone.'

I said, 'Okay, if she's gone, she's gone.'

So there we sat until nightfall. They brought water and we washed our hands, and food came, but when they put it before me I said, 'By God, I won't eat this food.'

The khan asked why. I said, 'You've acted like our enemy; they've paid you one or two lacs of rupees to leave the woman there; I'm not going to eat your food.'

He tried to make me eat, but I was damned if I would. Then he swore, 'I'll give you the woman, but only on condition that you give me lots of money and leave the man to me. I'm not giving you the man.' I said, 'Okay, keep the man but give us the woman; she's ours; but I'm not paying any money.'

He wouldn't accept that. In the end he said, 'Eat your food and we'll reach an agreement.' He brought the Koran and we both swore, and I ate the food.

Then he said, 'I've found the woman, she's in such-and-such a place, but if you don't give me one lac of rupees I shan't hand her over.'

I said, 'We'll give you a lac if you also give us the man.' But he said, 'No, we'll give you the woman but not the man.'

So we argued. We were five strangers in Day-kondi, in the Hazârajât, what could we do against 92,000 people? We were forced to agree with the khan and the secretary that they'd deliver the woman to us for 50,000 rupees, and we all swore not to make the affair official. Then in the morning the khan gave us a letter for the commandant: 'I've arranged the matter we talked about, so send the woman; we'll meet the day after tomorrow in Day-kondi town.'

In the middle of the night we set off on foot, *hala-hala-hala*. We couldn't find either a jeep or a horse. We couldn't find a thing, by God. The Hazâras knew what was going on; they're such well-informed people. When they saw us, they wouldn't give us any food however much we asked; when we offered 100 rupees to hire a 50-rupee horse, they refused. After two days on the road we arrived at Day-kondi. We found Nâder-shâh and asked if they'd brought the woman. He said, 'No, the commandant isn't back yet.' I said, 'But he was on horseback and we were on foot, he should have got here first.' We'd arrived at noon, and by nightfall there was still no sign of him. Early next morning I went to the mosque to say my prayers, and as I came back I passed some Gardezi shopkeepers who said, 'The commandant came back at midnight, without the woman; he was exhausted.'

I went straight to Nâder-shâh and told him the news. He got up, and we both went to the commandant's house. He was lying in bed, groaning, 'I'm dead, God help me!'

We asked, 'What happened, Commandant-seb?' 'The Hazâras beat me up; Arbâb Akbar's son and Durjân and his nephew Karbalâ'i Abbâs; these three people collected 500 men and cut us off; they shot at us; we fired back, but without effect, and when our ammunition ran out they attacked, separated me from the soldiers, beat me up, stole my pistol, my watch and 3,000 rupees, took the woman back by force, and got away with her.'

We went to the *hâkem*; he said he'd already been to see the commandant, who'd told him the story of how they'd taken the woman back. 'What can I do?' he asked, 'They took the woman by force; we're not strong enough to do anything about it. Let me call the *wâli*.'

So in the morning he called the Oruzgân provincial centre Tarin-Kot. The *wâli* said, 'Please put the receiver down while I call Kabul to ask for guidance.' He called the Interior Ministry, and they said, 'Please wait for a couple of weeks, right now the government is in confusion and there's nobody in office; the Prime Minister's forming a new cabinet.[12] When they've sorted themselves out, then we'll give you instructions.'

The *hâkem* told us what the *wâli* said. We answered, 'How can we sit here for two weeks until you get some directive? We should go right now and deal with those people.'

But the *hâkem* said, 'Ah brother, the commandant was my sword and my right hand; now they've beaten him up and broken two of his ribs. If he were all right we might have done something, but now I can do nothing. Take my advice, go to Kabul. Nothing can be done from here. You can't get the woman back from here. That's the truth of it.'

We spent several days trying to change his mind, saying, 'You're the government here, you're sitting in the government office. Those people who sent the commandant packing, they're subjects, they can't do such strong-arm stuff on you. Go along yourself and bring them in.'

He replied, 'I swear, I can't do anything now. If you do as I suggest and go to Kabul, with any luck they'll send me a commission or a company of troops, and then I'll be able to do something. But now, I'm not close enough to Kabul to telephone there myself and be heard. I can do nothing.'

We failed to change his mind. So we went and hired a truck from the Prospecting Company for 1,000 rupees to take us as far as Sheykh-Mirân, halfway back to Azgharât. The company was surveying the mountains in search of minerals, and the driver told us, 'Don't worry, for 5,000 rupees I'll get you to Azgharât, one way or another!' All fifteen of us came, and we all got onto the truck.

He dropped us at Sheykh-Mirân, where he went to see his boss, a Hazâra chief, who told him, 'You're crazy, I won't let you take them any further, even for 20,000 rupees; get back to work.' So he abandoned us. Late in the evening, around this time, we got back on the road, and walked on until dawn.

By morning we reached a valley, I forget the name, where there was a teahouse. Exhausted from walking all night, we sat there and had tea and killed two or three chickens to eat. Then, thank God, two Prospecting Company jeeps came by, with some foreigners riding inside. We asked the drivers to take us to Azgharât for 6,000 rupees. They said, 'Wait here, we'll take the foreigners to where they're working, then we'll tell them some story and come back and take you where you want to go. Don't worry, we'll be back.' So the two jeeps went off and delivered the foreigners; an hour later they returned and in we got; *hala-hala-hala*, finally we arrived at Azgharât in the late afternoon. They set us down and we gave them 6,000 rupees.

---

[12] A new prime minister, Dr Abdol Zâher, was appointed after the fall of Nur Etemadi's government in May. See Dupree (1980: 663–64).

At Azgharât there are shops and a road junction; the road to the left goes to Lâl, the other one to Kabul. There was no truck from Lâl for Kabul, but one came from Kabul heading for Lâl, so we put everyone in that except Nâder-shâh, Rishmin and me. We stayed the night, then around one o'clock in the morning a jeep came and we got the driver to take us to Kabul for 200 rupees each. That day we got as far as Behsud, spent the night there, and at about two the following day we reached Kabul.

Petitioning the government in Kabul

We had a meal before going to find our *wakil*, Kamâloddin Khân. As we didn't know the way to his place, we got a guide and hired a car. When we arrived we exchanged greetings; eventually he asked, 'What's up? What brings you here at this time?' So we told him the whole story, from beginning to end. 'We don't know what to do; we went to Day-kondi but we couldn't do anything there, so now we've come to ask you for help.'

He told us to go and prepare some petitions, one to the King himself, one to the Prime Minister, and one to the Interior Minister. 'At one o'clock I'll go to the Interior Ministry; prepare a petition in the following fashion, and I'll present it. I'll do all the talking and I'll collect the directive and instructions. It's an easy business, it'll be sorted out, I'll see it through, and in two or three weeks, God willing, I'll be able to send you home.'

He showed us where to find a good scribe; we got the petitions written as he told us. We went back to the Ministry and waited for him. At one o'clock he came, took the petitions from us and presented one to the Minister; the others he delivered himself, to the Prime Minister and the King's office. He told us, 'Come back the day after tomorrow; I'll find out how the petitions are going.'

For two days we wandered about, then we returned to the Ministry. Kamâloddin brought back our petition, and we saw that there was a directive to the *wâli*. We told him, 'This won't work unless the Ministry sends a commission. The *wâli* can do nothing on his own.'

He said, 'No, it's not like that. If we get a directive to the *wâli*, then he's obliged to produce both the woman and the man.'

We said, 'But the *wâli*'s no good, he can't do anything, the Hazâras are stronger than him. This is a waste of time and effort!'

'No,' he said, 'You go and rest for a week, I'll make that *wâli* produce the woman.'

A week passed, then another and then another. We kept asking what he'd done. 'I've called the *wâli*, and he's forced people; they'll bring her today, tomorrow,' and so on. But nothing happened.

Then it was Jashn holiday [*19 August*]. Kamâloddin said, 'Go home to your families for the four days of Jashn, then come back.' We had to agree, so we set off on the first day of Jashn and arrived home in the evening. We stayed for a week, and then the rumour spread that they'd brought the woman to Kabul. Who said so? Everyone said that someone else had said it; you couldn't find a single reliable person in the whole place: everyone said they heard it from somebody else!

So Nâder-shâh and I were forced to go back to Kabul. 'Oh, if only the woman's there!' When we arrived we found no woman, nothing. All that had happened was that a commission had gone from the provincial government, and they were doing this and that. So we stayed another month; but whatever we did, nobody came, no man, no woman. In the end Nâder-shâh and I got fed up and came home.

God knows what happened. We paid out 53,000 rupees, 30,000 to the Ministry of the Interior, and 23,000 rupees to the *wâli*. I came home and spent a few days here. My family was in Chenâr, so I went to spend Ramadan [*21 Oct–19 Nov 1971*] there. After the fast I came back here.

In December Nâder-shâh and I went back to Kabul, because it was said that all the Hazâra people had come. When we got there we found that they'd brought several of their khans, nothing else. We asked these khans what they'd done with the woman, and they said, 'She's gone, she's crossed into Iran.' 'How did this happen?' 'We don't know.'

We argued with them endlessly, and we went to the Interior Ministry every day for a month. We said, 'Give us the woman'; they said she was gone. *Hala-hala-hala*, finally we got the upper hand, and the government got a letter from nine Hazâras promising, 'We'll produce the woman in Kabul shortly.' But they didn't actually fix the period: one month, twenty days; they just put, 'shortly'.

So again we petitioned the Interior Minister: 'What do you mean by "shortly"? One day, ten days, a hundred days?' The Ministry wrote back, 'We can't set a deadline; if they fail to meet it, government loses face. You must accept "shortly" as right for both you and us. Don't worry, you'll get the woman from us. Winter's come, go home for a couple of months. When the roads are clear, come back; we'll produce the woman and the man by April, God willing.' The Commandant-General and the Interior Minister told us, 'Off you go, wait out January and February, then at the end of March come back and you'll get the woman from us.'

The very day we left Kabul, the rain started. It was raining in Kabul itself, there was snow at the Kheyr-khâna pass, rain at Chârikâr, and at Jebel-Sarâj the road had disappeared under the snow. At Sâlang the snow was really deep. We got over to Doshi, and there was snow as far as Doshâkh. That evening we arrived at Mazâr. During the night it snowed hard there; in the morning we left for Sheberghân, and there was snow all the way home.

Then it was snow, snow, snow. Our fodder ran out. Every day we went out to look for fodder, enough to get through the night. This went on until the end of March. Nothing was left, the hay didn't last, the money ran out, and our sheep died of hunger.[13]

And we still haven't got our hands on that woman. We're exhausted!

The fallout

A month after the elopement, Darwiza articulates sentiments and ideals that were constantly on people's lips in the following months.

If an Afghan had abducted Rangin's daughter, it wouldn't be so shameful for us, and people wouldn't make such a fuss. Rangin would have the right to two girls, even three,

---

[13] For Baya-khân's and other accounts of this dreadful winter, see Chapter 6.

as compensation: one to replace his daughter; another for his reputation, which he lost when someone took his daughter; and the elders might award him a third, as a fine. Rangin would say, 'I'll let you off one girl, just give me the two,' but he'd have the right to all three. As soon as she disappeared, he'd defend himself through a mediator, such as his father or his brother, or some other relative.

For seven generations, our elders say, none of our women had run away; perhaps you didn't know. Now, after seven generations with no runaways, she's gone – and with a Hazâra! Not only has she gone, but several lacs of rupees have been spent trying to get her back. When they do get her, they'll kill her. If they don't, they say, one day another woman will do the same.

A year later, Baya-khân reflects on the consequences for the protagonists.

You saw how that whore Kimyâ ran away with a Shi'a. We call the Hazâras Shi'a; they're a different sect, they have a different Book. If she'd gone with a Sunni, such as an Uzbek or an Arab, it wouldn't have been so bad; we have the same religion, and we would've made peace and accepted compensation. If the Arabs had taken her, we would've taken a girl, or money. But she went with a Hazâra, who took her to a province where all the people are Hazâra. It was far away, and the Hazâras closed ranks. It was impossible for anyone to fight them there.

Nâder-shâh and my father spent a lot of time in Kabul last year. The bastards there have taken all their petitions and their money, but the case seems to have gone to sleep. There used to be rumours, but they've dried up. Sometimes it was said that they're bringing the girl. Now they say the Hazâra's in prison. If they do get her back, they'll kill her for sure. It would've been better if she'd just disappeared without anyone knowing who'd taken her. But everybody knew it was that Hazâra bastard, and that he came all the way from Sar-e-pol to fetch her; they'd planned it all in advance.

Rangin's back in Kabul. He says he won't come home until they give him back his daughter. But he'll have to come home. He's deeply ashamed; he can't even look a small boy in the eye. For example, this little rascal, my nephew Tâjak, called out to Rangin when he passed by, 'Hey, Uncle Rangin, what have you done with Kimyâ?' and laughed at him. What an insult! His father Pâdshâh hit him hard: 'How dare you say that to a grown man?' Now if the women in their tent see someone passing, but a long way off, they'll put the tent-flaps down out of shame. People laugh at them, 'Look, Rangin's daughter ran off with a Hazâra! Why didn't she take an Afghan husband? Don't Afghan men have the right stuff? Aren't there enough of them?'

Kimyâ was rather plain, dark-skinned, with grey eyes – did you see her? Rangin told his nephew to marry her, but he refused and asked for Rangin's other daughter, Maluk; but he wouldn't give her. Then Kimyâ ran away. Now nobody'll take Maluk; she's already grown up. Perhaps some destitute fellow will marry her, nobody else will. People would taunt him, 'Your sister-in-law ran off with another man, how do you know your wife won't do the same tomorrow?' As for Rangin's son, he'll find a wife. Relatives, the Es'hâqzai, won't give him one, but an Alizai, some poor man, or one of the many refugees who come here, will give him a wife, saying, 'After all, Rangin's a man of property.'

Baya-khân and Chârgol, his step-mother Pâkiza's brother, discuss the latest rumours.

(*Baya-khân*) – Kuk [*Lineage A, son of Tumân's aunt Bakhtâwar; close companion of Khârkash headman Nâder-shâh*] said that Rangin's gone by plane to Oruzgân and Day-kondi; Wakil Kamâloddin put him on the plane, promising to pay whatever he needed. He was alone. Nobody else will help him now. The *wakil* didn't go, he just gave him a letter.

(*Chârgol*) – None of his relatives will give him money now. Three times now, everyone, including the poor and the weak, has dipped into their pockets for him. Why should they do it again?

(*Baya-khân*) – People will contribute to a fund once or twice, but no more.

(*Chârgol*) – Everyone knows that if they give Rangin money, well, his daughter went one way and now his money's gone the other. His credit's now zero.

(*Baya-khân*) – He's gone through two brideprices' worth of money; some 2 lacs.

(*Chârgol*) – Kamâloddin was up against twelve Hazâra *wakils* in Parliament. What can one *wakil*, Kamâloddin, do against twelve who're united, with their own people behind them? You've seen those mountains, and the Hazâras. I can tell you, he'll never achieve anything. Will the monarchy ruin itself over one woman? She wasn't taken by force, or by guns or cannon. That boy won her heart by some charm or talisman – or perhaps telepathy! However he did it, he got her.

(*Baya-khân*) – It's a free country. Rangin has pawned some land, 20 to 25 *jerib*s. He was going to pawn it to a Chârbâgh Hazâra, but people prevented him and took it back from them, and Alâoddin and Qâsem took it instead.

(*Chârgol*) – He's borrowed money on interest, the idiot.

(*Baya-khân*) – He took a 50,000-rupee loan from Haji Yusuf [*Hazâra*] of Chârbâgh. Last year he sold some sheep, thirty or forty of them. And he sold lots of wheat too.

(*Chârgol*) – This year those Chârbâgh people really went over the top. Straw was more expensive than gold, and if you went to Chârbâgh to buy some, I'm told they'd say, 'Here come our in-laws!' They got quite light-headed, each of them would give a basket or two of straw, saying, 'He's our in-law!' They were taunting us about Rangin: 'He's lost his sheep, his wealth has run out, and he's lost his daughter. The big camel's taken a fall!'

(*Baya-khân*) – Nobody will give him any more money; they've none left to give. Nobody will take his daughters now. Rangin's women are very bad. They're delighted when Hazâras and other strangers come to their house; they really like the Hazâras! Last year he hired a Hazâra farmhand; people told him not to, but he did it again, and now his brother Rishmin too has a Hazâra farmhand.

A Moral Tale of Abduction and Revenge

Shortly after narrating the search for Kimyâ, Tumân told the following tale.[14]

---

[14] Tumân rarely if ever gives his characters names, unlike Baya-khân in his tales. I failed to ask why.

Once in Mazâr-e-Sharif there was a wealthy Afghan *mâldâr* with lots of sheep: a real *Boy*.[15] He had a son, who was a womanizer and a pederast (*bacha-bâz*). His father wanted him to settle down and help look after their property. 'Your uncle has several daughters, choose one; or any woman in Mazâr, or more than one; but stop your debauchery.'

His son paid no attention. Finally the *Boy* decided to invite all his son's friends to a party. He asked them, 'Be my guests, bring my son with you, and help me persuade him to change his way of life, to settle down and work in the family business. Let him choose a wife – or two or more, he's allowed up to four. I'll pay for them all.'

The friends promised to come on the day fixed for the party. So he went and bought supplies, meat and rice and stuff; he was rich, he could afford anything. Twenty of so of his son's friends came, and the *Boy* entertained them all for three days and nights. They urged his son to choose one of his cousins to marry, but he refused. In the end, however, the combined pressure of his friends, his father and his uncle was too much for him, and he had to accept one of the girls. That very night, as they insisted, the contract was signed, and they were married.

The next morning he let his friends go, and stayed at home. A few days later, as it was early spring, people moved out to the spring pastures. They loaded the tents, household goods and supplies and went and pitched camp alongside their flocks of ewes, which were in the middle of lambing. Everybody was busy, but the boy said, 'I'm going away for a few days; I've got business in Tâshqurghân, a debt to collect.'

Now it so happened that he and his new wife had fallen in love; she'd become very dear to him, and he didn't really want to be away from her. Even so, he set off for Tâshqurghân, leaving his wife behind. A few days later they realized they were short of water. In the afternoon, the mother-in-law said, 'Come, dear daughter, let's go for water.' She agreed, and off they went. The spring was about as far as Shamsoddin's village from here. They were sitting there, filling their water-skins, when a man rode up on a fine glossy horse. He asked the two women, 'Give me some water.' The mother-in-law offered him a bowl of water, but he said, 'I won't take it from you, let the girl give it to me.' They were frightened, but they were too far from the village to cry for help, so she told the girl in Pashtu, 'You give it to him, what's the difference?' The girl filled the bowl from her water-skin and handed it to him, but as she did so he grabbed her by the wrist, swung her up behind him on his horse, and rode off with her.

The woman ran after them, but they were soon gone. She came back to the spring, collected the skins, went home and told her husband what had happened. That evening a search party went out with lamps and torches, but it was sandy and any tracks had disappeared. In the morning they searched once more, without success.

They wondered what to tell the boy. Two days later he came home. Now one tent in the camp was his, and another, some way off, belonged to his uncle. The boy asked his mother, 'Where's my wife?' 'In her father's house.' 'What's she doing over there? Call her back!' 'She'll be back in the morning.' 'No, I want her back now!'

Several times she tried to divert him, but he wouldn't let go, so eventually she said, 'My son, your wife has gone. I went with her to fetch water, and a fellow came and

---

[15] *Boy, Bey,* or *Bay*: title for a rich man, widely used in Turkistan, by and of Pashtuns as well as others.

carried her off. We searched everywhere, but they left no tracks. What could we do? She's gone; forget her and marry another of your cousins.'

He said, 'Never! Now you've cuckolded me, you expect me to forget her and take another wife? I won't! By God, if I don't find my wife ...'

His father and his uncle too tried to persuade him that there was no point looking for his wife. 'God knows who it was that took her; perhaps it was a jinn or a fairy. He was mounted on such a fine great horse, who knows who he is, or where he's taken her; there's no point in going after them.'

'No,' he said, 'By God, I'm not going to let it go.' He rejected his father's and uncle's words, saying, 'You can't stop me; I didn't want the girl in the first place; now I've finished with her, but my only concern is that you've cuckolded me.'

The following morning, he packed a saddlebag with gold, a fine gun, cartridges, and fine clothes, and mounted his horse. He set off northwards. He was riding along, occupied with his thoughts, when he came upon a wandering dervish, who called out, 'Friend, where are you going? You'll never find the thief dressed like that!' He dismounted at once and threw himself at the dervish's feet, amazed: 'You obviously know that someone's stolen my wife!' The dervish said, 'I didn't know, I guessed; but as I said, you'll never find her or get her back dressed like that. Take my clothes and go around like a dervish.' He agreed, and having kept some money in his pocket he gave the dervish everything else, his clothes, his horse, his gun and so on. Having become a dervish himself, he went on, down to the banks of the Amu-daryâ [*Oxus*].[*See Map B*]

For six months, he wandered through all the lands and villages, house by house, chanting like a dervish: *hu-ya-hu, hu-man-hu*, and looking for his wife; but he found no trace of her. He couldn't face going home, so he decided to cross the river to the other side, where nobody knew him; better to disappear.

He inflated a skin to make a raft and threw it into the great river; climbing onto it, he paddled across to the other side. On he went for a year or more, looking everywhere, until eventually he came to a place with six of those fine Turkmen tents, you've seen them. There was also a guest tent, so he went in and sat down.

It was midday. There were no men or boys around, but an old woman came and brought him food. She asked, 'Young lad, where are you from?' 'I'm from such-and-such a place, but I can't go home, I'd like to find some work here.' But she said, 'You don't need to work; I have six sons and six tents. You can stay here in the guest tent. Put on these clothes, and you can be another son to me.' He agreed.

After some time, it was the Feast of Sacrifice, when people go visiting, and he got homesick and started crying. His new mother said, 'What's the matter?' 'You've never asked me anything about myself.' 'I didn't want to offend you; now tell me about yourself.'

He told her about losing his wife. She asked what the woman was like, and he described her as an Afghan woman, and so on. She said, 'Well, one of my sons-in-law brought back an Afghan woman. He's a very rich man; he has two superb horses, finer than the Russian ones. Tomorrow, go and have a look and see if she's your wife or not.'

So he went off to her son-in-law's camp, and saw that it was indeed his wife. But she told him, 'If you say anything, I'll have you killed; go back where you came from.'

He came and asked his new mother to help him with a horse and a gun. It was spring, but the son-in-law and his Afghan woman were staying in their winter camp, having sent his other wife – the old woman's daughter – off with the flocks. She called her sons together and said, 'Go and get that Afghan woman as a wife for this boy I've adopted as my son.' They said, 'But your son-in-law is rich and well-armed, what can we do?' She said, 'I have a plan. In two days, you go off and rebuke him for sleeping with his Afghan wife while thieves have come and raided the sheep and beaten up your sister. If he gets up, this'll give the boy a chance to catch the girl and ride away with her.'

Two of them went and tried this, but the man didn't want to move. Then all six sons and the mother went together to upbraid him, and he got angry and went off, armed, on horseback. The young man seized the girl and tied her on the back of his horse. But she'd brought a feather pillow, and as they galloped away she left a trail of feathers. The Turkmen, who'd found nothing amiss with his flocks, set off after them.

They rode for six days, and then the boy had to rest. As he was sitting there, the Turkmen came up and they started shooting at each other. When they ran out of ammunition, they wrestled fiercely, until the girl tripped the boy up. The Turkmen told her in Turki to kill him, but she said, 'Not until I've made love to you with him watching; I swore this when he seized me.'

They tied the boy up, and made love, then they fell asleep. The boy managed to free himself, vowing to Ali Lion-of-God[16] to sacrifice 100 of his father's sheep at Ali's shrine in Mazâr. He wondered what to do with the couple, because if he killed them there nobody at home would believe he had; and if he cut off their heads the heads would go bad before he got them home. But he did cut off the Turkmen's head.

He set off home with his wife, who now regretted what she'd done; *hala-hala-hala*, they passed a town where they bought some supplies. On they went *hala-hala-hala* until they came to the Amu-daryâ. He put all their things on one horse, stripping the other bare and tying himself and the woman tight onto its back; then he whipped both horses on, and they plunged into the river. You probably haven't seen it, but horses swim very well, using their front legs. Anyway, they came out the other side just fine, but completely soaked, their clothes and everything.

They found themselves on a plain; they soon came to an old domed hut. They collected some fuel, made a fire and got themselves nice and dry. Then they slept for a while, and spent a night or two, as they had plenty of supplies. Then they set off again and came to Kaldâr, where they had a meal before going on to Tâshqurghân, where he'd originally been to collect a debt. They came to the same man's house; he welcomed them in, treated them well, killed a lamb for dinner and sent a man on horseback to buy cakes from the bazaar.

After the first night, their host pressed them to stay, but our boy said, 'No, now the news has reached home, I must go.' So they mounted their horses again, and set off, accompanied by several people including their host, who said, 'Why don't you tell us the story, how did you find her?' 'I'll tell you the story when we get there, I can't do it now.'

---

[16] Shir-e-Khodâ: common title for the Prophet's son-in-law Ali, also known as Sakhi; reputedly buried in the shrine at Mazâr-e-Sharif, known as Sakhi-Bâbâ.

As he got closer to home, his father, his uncle and all their relatives, a crowd of 100 people, with guns and drums, came out to greet them, like a wedding. Once they were home, people gathered round and said, 'Tell us, how did you find her!' He said, 'No, I'm tired, let me rest for three days.' He sent the girl to her father's house, he didn't want her staying near him.

When three days had passed, he said, 'Go and fetch that girl.' They brought her, and he told the story from beginning to end: how he met the dervish, exchanged clothes with him, went and searched without success, then crossed the river, wandered some years over there, was adopted by a woman, and finally found his wife and went to her.

'Don't you remember,' he said to her, 'how I asked you, "cousin, how are you?" And you said, "My God, why didn't you come earlier?" I swear that's true,' he said. She said, 'Ha.' So he told them the whole story, all of it, right up to where they were now.

His father, mother, brother, uncle, all took the woman out and made her a target and shot 1,000 bullets at her, until she was like a sieve, *tika-tika*. His father said, 'Marry another of your cousins.' He replied, 'I've had enough of wives; I don't need one!'

They stayed in their house, and I came here. Good night!

Baya-khân adds the obvious moral.

If we'd found Kimyâ, we'd have done the same to her.

4

Tribal Politics

Murder and Revenge

Pashtuns have strict traditional rules about what happens when someone is killed. Ideally, the victim's close male relatives receive women/girls in compensation, a Pashtun custom now reported and condemned in western media as baad/bad.[1] *For Piruzai* badi *means feud or vendetta, but we did not hear the term used for compensation marriages.*

Baya-khân outlines the ideal.

Suppose two men have a fight, and one is killed. The family won't be satisfied until they're given a girl, or two girls, and some money in compensation. If a girl is given, they'll make peace, but if not, there'll probably be another fight. For one man killed, our people give two girls. Some give one girl plus some wealth: money, land. If someone kills a woman, it's the same; he must give a daughter or sister of his own, or a lot of money. Whatever it takes to placate the victim's father. The actual compensation is negotiated, and people gather to decide it; if they take the matter to the government, the killer will be sentenced to several years in prison.

If the killer's known but escapes, they'll take a relative such as a cousin hostage, and force him to give the girls. When girls are given, they don't bring a trousseau – perhaps one or two things. There's no wedding party; after all, they've lost a man and they're in mourning; they just bring her. When people – the elders or the government – have gathered and made peace, they go to the killer's house and bring his daughter to the victim's house, for his brother or another close relative. Sometimes they'll beat that poor woman hard, saying, 'Why did you kill my brother?' But people differ; sometimes the husband comes to love his wife. It's a very difficult matter.

Baya-khân expresses some sympathy for the fate of a girl so given; his mother Maryam was one. His older brother Darwiza gives a more nuanced version.

Suppose I fight someone, and – God forbid – kill him, then our custom is this. We get five elders, such as a mullah, a holy man, a religious leader, and take them to that man's father, or his brother or his mother, to persuade them to forgive and not demand

---

[1] See Anwari et al. (2004); press references and NGO reports since then are too numerous to list here.

restitution. It's the Afghan custom to forgive that very day; if you've killed a man, or shot and wounded him, whether he died or recovered, if you go straight to his house, they'll forgive you. That's the custom in all four corners of Afghanistan, from the ancestors of all Afghans: Kamuzais, Alizais, all the tribes. But not the Fârsibâns. If they were Uzbeks or Arabs or Hazâras, even if you went a hundred times they wouldn't forgive you until either you paid them something or they killed you.

Or we do it this way: one of their elders says, 'We forgive it, we don't want anything.' Our elders will say, 'No, one of your people has been killed, you shouldn't forgive it like this.' They'll say, 'As far as we're concerned, we've forgiven you; whether you give us something or not, we still forgive you, we shan't go after you.' Our people insist, 'Don't forgive like this; even if you do, we'll give you one woman.' Then we promise them two or three women; or it might be land, or cash. They'll accept this, and they'll swear an oath together, saying, 'We'll never go after you, we won't make any demands or try to kill one of your men,' and so on. Then the mullahs and the elders recite the *do'â-o-takbir* prayers – elders like my father, or Haji Ghâfur, Haji Jallât, Haji Wahâb, Rawu, Mahd-Amin, Khalifa-Patih, Rishmin, Nâder-shâh, Mowlawi, Mayoddin-jân Âghâ, men like that who went as mediators. Then the matter's finished, once the women are given. The victim's people are satisfied, they let the offenders go: 'There's nothing more between us, we owe each other nothing.'

The elders say, 'If the dead boy's father or brother still tries to catch these people and beat or kill them, then may his house be ruined.' If, in spite of declaring his forgiveness, he later changes his mind and says, 'I shan't let Richard go, he's killed my brother Darwiza,' then, after the prayer those mullahs and elders recited, his house would be ruined: either he'd die himself, or all his possessions would disappear; his camel would die, or his sheep, his horse, his donkey, his cow, so that he couldn't even make a living by begging; he'd be destitute, ruined, just as the elders said.

We asked for examples. Darwiza first refers to events in spring 1971, in which I participated, following the shooting of a young Kamuzai by some Piruzai in a dispute over a debt. Then he mentions a more recent case of physical violence. The main concern today is clearly to avoid government intervention, which can lead to the ruin of anyone involved – and many not.

It's happened to many people. When Nayib was shot by Mâmuk and the others, despite being urged to send a delegation to Nayib's father to ask for reconciliation, the offenders hadn't the courage to go. If they'd gone, he'd immediately have responded, 'Even if my son dies, we forgive you.' But they didn't go. We tried repeatedly to bring them together to talk about it. Then, the very day the Afghans got back from the mountains, Nayib's father went to Mâmuk and said, 'We overlook that matter; it's up to you and the government.' The government is now so oppressive, they won't let it rest until they've had your hat and put you in prison. You must go to the *hâkem* and confirm: 'We've no quarrel with this person, it's finished.' But the government decides for itself; even if Nayib asks for them to be freed, they take their money and put them in prison.

As for the man who beat up Haji's shepherd, his cousin came here just today. The shepherd, a Breti, was my father's follower and gave him the authority: 'Haji, you're the elder of our whole community; whatever you say, people will accept it; that'll be the end of it.' The cousin came to our house and sat down. Haji forgave him on behalf of the Breti; he recited a prayer over him and told him, 'Go; it's forgiven.' If they'd complained to the government, it would have cost both sides money. It's our Afghan custom that if one man hits another, breaks his arm, cracks his skull, then people will laugh if this person demands compensation: 'Is he so hungry? Curses on his father! He'd have done better to hit him back!' It's not Afghan custom to demand compensation.

On another occasion, Baya-khân sketches public knowledge of two recent local cases. First, a case that involved the khans, and reached national level.

Abdol-Hakim Baluch, his son and a servant were murdered. People say that Seyyed-Mahmad Khân's men killed them because a Maleki killed his son the previous year in Sheberghân. This meant a feud between the khans and the Malekis, and Baluches were killed because they supported the Malekis. The Malekis are related to the Baluches of Qoshtepa; they exchange women.

The Maleki who killed the khan's boy was Abdor-Rauf's son. I think Abdor-Rauf was married to Abdol-Hakim's sister, so his son was the latter's nephew; at any rate, they were some kind of close relatives. The Baluches didn't support the Malekis openly, they were scared of the khans; but they contributed money privately. Here, money's everything; the government favours whoever gives them most money.

This is what I heard: late one evening the khan's thugs went to Abdol-Hakim's home. He'd undressed and gone to sleep in his own room, which was by the gateway to his compound. Inside the house his servant and his son were still up. All at once the dogs started barking outside the gate. The servant came and opened the gate to find several men with torches in their hands; how could he know they were intruders? They shot him. The dogs were still barking, so Abdol-Hakim came out of his room to see what all the noise was. When he saw the men with torches, he tried to escape, but one of them shot him down at the door of his room, and he died right there.

After killing these two men, the intruders were leaving through the gateway, when Abdol-Hakim's son came up behind them, took hold of one and pulled him back inside – but he was unarmed. As they struggled, the thug called out to his companions, 'You bastards, where are you going? I've been caught.' They turned back. They couldn't get a clear shot, but one of them grabbed the boy by the foot and dragged him from his antagonist, then they shot and killed him too. Then they left. Their tracks led into the steppe past the Wardak compound[2] and on to Seyyed-Mahmad Khân, who paid them well. The government took the khans' side.

You remember how last year, when we were in the mountains, the radio reported that a Baluch *wakil* from Kandahar asked about this affair in parliament: why was there no enquiry about the Baluch killings? 'These days one can't kill three chickens, but here are three Baluches, my kinsmen, who've have been unjustly killed, and the government's done nothing. What's going on? Why doesn't the king ask how and why they were killed so openly?' and so on.

---

[2] A Wardak family bought land and built a substantial compound not far from Kunjek a few years before. The Wardaks are a prominent tribe from the province of the same name, near Kabul.

Now there have been several commissions of enquiry. The Baluches and the khans are daggers drawn; but the khans are very rich, each one readily contributes a lac – they'll never run out of money. In one day they can collect ten or twenty thousand. When they need more, they just go around, collecting a few thousand at a time, from the Uzbeks. For several years Tâj-Mahmad Khân was headman over 800 to 900 houses of Uzbeks, over towards Sayyâd. All day long, dozens of people would bring him their problems – land disputes, sheep theft, assault. He took four to five thousand rupees from each party and made peace between them. In those years he completely plundered those people, so how could his money run out? Some people lodged complaints about him, and he was dismissed, but he continues to settle many of their affairs.

The Sâtu case, which occurred in early 1971 just before we arrived, impoverished several Piruzai who weren't actually involved. Sâtu's killers included the sons of Delbar Pakhizai and Hazâragi, half-sister of headwoman Neshtar: they live in Konjek. Baya-khân goes on to outline the case.

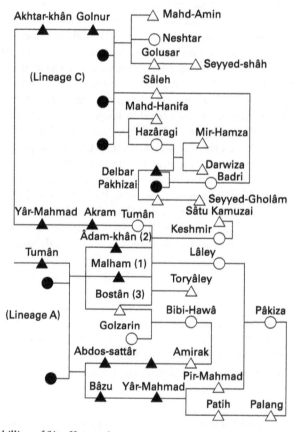

Figure 6 The killing of Sâtu Kamuzai.

People are very unhappy with aunt Hazâragi, because her sons Mir-Hamza and Darwiza[3] are thieves. My father can't tell them to leave; whatever he says, they'll answer, 'It's none of your business; it's not your land, where we're living.' They're thieves, with terrible reputations. Any robbery, they immediately get the blame. I've never known them do any real work. They go off thieving in places like Hazhdah-nahr and Maymana. During the day they scout around; when they see animals, they watch to see if they're guarded; or they look at the dogs and reckon whether the house is empty. Then at night they come and steal the animals. Hazâragi says nothing; she's quite happy with what they do. If they steal a sheep and kill it for her, she'll eat the meat. [*See Fig. 6*]

They were involved in murdering Sâtu Kamuzai. Sâtu was a rich man, with 300 sheep and lots of money, but few relatives. His wife Keshmir, daughter of Âdam-khân Piruzai, didn't much like him. She invited her maternal half-brother Toryaley and his friends to come and steal the sheep and money. They were a party of ten; Palang, Amirak, Toryaley from Piruzai; Mir-Hamza and Darwiza, sons of Delbar Pakhizai [*and Hazâragi*]; and others, from Torkheyl. Sâtu was killed. All were caught and are now in jail, except Mir-Hamza, who's disappeared. Toryaley was the worst and got 18 years; he confessed, incriminating Delbar's sons, who tried to kill him in revenge. He also implicated their uncles Mahd-Amin, Golusar, Sâleh and Mahd-Hanifa, who had to sell or pawn most of their land to pay to clear themselves. Sâleh's married to Delbar's daughter Badri, who's as bad as her brothers.

Seyyed-shâh, Golusar's son – not to be confused with his namesake Seyyed-shâh/ Soleymân – tells how the Sâtu case affected his family.

Sâtu was murdered the year before you came. Government officials first took money from Sâleh, then they came to Mahd-Amin and my father [*Golusar*] and explained what they wanted; but they arrested two of Mahd-Amin's sons, and me, and Sâleh and his son.

They took 60,000 to 65,000 rupees from Mahd-Amin and us. We had sixty sheep, and Mahd-Amin had forty or fifty. We took them to town to sell, but nobody would pay more than 500 rupees for them; they knew we'd been arrested and thought, 'They're stuck; let's do nothing; if the government presses them, they'll sell for 400.' We sold the sheep in the second-hand bazaar! We had three *jeribs* of the land where Borjân's now built a house; we had to sell that to Haji Wahâb, for just 12,000. We're still dealing with that business today.

Toryaley, Delbar's nephew Seyyed-Gholâm, Palang and Amirak did the killing; they were all sentenced to 18 years. They claimed that we'd instigated it. Haji Tumân was away in Tehran when this happened; Nâder-shâh dealt with the khans for us. Darwiza got his sentence shortened; now he has two years left. But we've suffered great losses, both money and reputation.

Seyyed-shâh and Baya-khân talk of some other recent local murders.

---

[3] Ghaws and Shâhpari had two sons of the same names, see pp. 337–39.

(Seyyed-shâh) – Black-Abdollah, who's with [*yet another*] Rangin, gave his daughter Hawa to Rangin's nephew. She bore a son, then said, 'I'm not having him as a husband!' and called out for another boy: 'I'll marry him!' Everybody was talking about it. One evening Abdollah called her into the house and put a rope round her neck; he took one end, Haji Golân took the other and they strangled her. In the morning they buried her, saying, 'Last night she got diphtheria (*khorzak*) and died;' they sacrificed a kid over her mouth—

(Baya-khân) – So people would think she just died.

(Seyyed-shâh) – —and told the government they'd buried her. Then some officials came and took Haji Golân and Black-Abdollah off to town. This was about seven years ago. Abdollah had sixty sheep; now he's lost the sheep and his daughter, and he's just a shepherd himself.

(Baya-khân) – Haji Golân lost money too. If you ask me, she was a good woman, but her husband was useless. She didn't like him; he was a silly, stupid fellow, he wandered around without thinking of his wife. His name is Zhermâr, he's with Kamâl; he has long moustaches, they called him Whiskers Zhermâr; now he's called Whiskers Wimp. He's a Nurzai, like Black-Abdollah. His face is black.

Haji Golân also murdered his own son, people say, on the trek. That idiot has a terrible temper; if he's got something in his hand, he'll hit you.

(R) – Which of his sons?

(Seyyed-shâh) – Gogey, a fine young man, older than Baya-khân. Haji Golân got him engaged that year. When they went to the mountains, the boy had several rings made for his fiancée. Haji Golân's wife told him, 'Gogey's had some rings made.' So he asked, 'Is this true? Where'd you get the money?' Gogey admitted what he'd done. Haji Golân picked up a boot and hit him on the ear, and he fell down dead. People die quickly if you hit them on the ears. It was in Sar-jangal, and they buried him there. His wife, an Omarzai, went to his brother Kayem.

(Baya-khân) – Also, two years ago Rangin's daughters [*including the runaway Kimyâ*] murdered their cousin Shefik's mother Zhwar; they said that an evil spirit came into their tent and struck her, but in fact they killed her.

(R) – Why?

(Baya-khân) – She was bad. One night they seized her, put a rope around her neck and strangled her. They buried her in grandfather Mullah Shir's graveyard. Rangin had gone to Lâl or somewhere, but I think he was probably happy about it.

God prevent such a thing happening, but that same year a Kachani called Khâlyâr, a very bad man, was hit on the ear with a single stone the size of a camel turd, and died on the spot.

(Seyyed-shâh) – He was murdered by another Kachani, Qadir Boy's son, Mumin; after the killing, he made himself into a khan in Kachan. Khâlyâr was his uncle, and headman. He came round collecting contributions; he said to Mumin, 'You owe me this much.' They started shouting at each other, then Mumin hit Khâlyâr on the ear with a stone, and he died. His men went straight to the district office at Khawâl, which isn't far away, and the governor and police all came. Mumin Khân's mother said, 'My son has killed my brother; how can we resolve this problem?' They said, 'What do you suggest?' She said, 'I'll give my daughter to his nephew.' They said, 'That won't work.' So she said, 'I'll

weigh my son and give you three times his weight in silver coins, but please let him go.' They said, 'We won't let him go.' So they brought Mumin Khân down to Sar-e-pol and put him in prison. He had another uncle, Rowzoddin, who said, 'You killed my brother; I'm going to kill you!' But Mumin Khân, without going home, managed to kill him, by poison or something in the city. Then he bought his freedom – he had plenty of money – and went to join the Oil Exploration Company; he became an expert driver, and that's how he spent his sentence. That family's wealthy; they probably have at least 20 lacs in old silver coins. Now he's become such a big khan and headman in Kachan. [*See Map E*]

There've been many such affairs. Up there, they say, it was very hard this year. One fellow came all the way from Cherâs, with a cow and a donkey, to find grain. He loaded the donkey with barley and the cow with wheat. On his way home, he spent the night with a friend in Lower Dehmana. His friend said, 'Stay here several nights, you're tired, we'll find you a travelling companion.' He said, 'No, why should anyone hurt me?' As he was passing a hut by that graveyard, he unloaded his donkey, went and found some alfalfa and put it down for the animal. A man came up and said, 'Come with me.' He answered, 'When it's finished eating, I'll set off after you.' He crossed the water, and at once some men seized him, killed him, and threw him into the river. His body stayed afloat, so they loaded stones on top of it, which kept it under for a few days.

I think he'd arranged with his son, 'If I don't return by such a time, come after me.' The son waited. 'My father hasn't come, what's happened?' He came over and went to their friend's house; 'Did my father come here?' 'Yes, he did; he loaded a cow with wheat and a donkey with barley and set off home'. 'How long ago?' 'Several days. Let's go!'

That same night, I think, the water rose and the stones fell off the body, which floated down until it came to the bridge, where its clothes snagged on the struts. It was very swollen, which happens after being in water so long. Haji Sarwar of Dehmana saw it, 'It's a body!' and got some men to take it out. As they did so, along came the son; 'That's my father! It's his clothes!' The bastards who killed him had cut off his nose and stolen his goods.

The young man explained how his father left home, loaded his donkey and cow, stayed the night with a friend and so on. Then his kinsmen came, Taymani people from Cherâs, Qerghaytu and Târikak and took him to the *alâqadâr* (district governor), and they summoned all the men of Dehmana so that only the women were left. Eventually they found the thieves, a band of three, and handed them to the *alâqadâri*. They were taken to Sar-e-pol, then Sheberghân. People say that two of them got twenty years in Deh-Mazang prison in Kabul.

It was a very bad year; many people were murdered . . .

(*Baya-khân*) – This year too, a Cherâsi was murdered in the same place, Dehmana. He was bringing down eighty sheep, together with some companions. Thieves came and cut open some of the sheep's stomachs. They shot at his companions, but missed, and they managed to escape; but he bravely chased the thieves, who shot the poor guy dead. People say they were Seyyed-Mahmad Khân's thugs; but in the morning a commission followed the thieves' trail to the Arabs. They arrested about twenty Arabs, took a lot of their money and jailed them for some days; eventually they all bought their release, except four who're still in prison. Then Mirzâ Khân came from Târikak and accused Seyyed-Mahmad Khân. The case continues.

The murdered man's relatives were Aymâqs from Cherâs. His father was dead, but he had a mother and a small brother in Târikak. The commission brought his body here to Mowlawi Golzâr's house, and left it overnight in our mosque. Everyone here was worried they'd get implicated in the death; we couldn't be sure the commission wouldn't arrest us and cause major trouble. However, next morning they washed the body and buried it – that grave with the big horns planted on it. He was a martyr, blameless, murdered for his property.

The whole village helped to bury him, though most were in the steppe at that time. A while later, the relatives brought rice and a sheep and asked Mowlawi to hold the funeral feast; 'Do a distribution for us, we're very busy and can't do it ourselves.' Mowlawi didn't do a proper distribution; his family ate the food themselves. I admire Mowlawi-seb, but he's not such a good man!

Finally, Baya-khân and Chârgol together tell what happened to Pâr-khân – another case of a Pashtun who bought land from Uzbeks, but now finds he's lost it, and in fact lost everything.

Pâr-khân bought a vineyard from some Uzbeks in Chenâr. There's much hunger there after several bad years. Last year [*1971*], his Uzbek sharecroppers wouldn't give him his share of the raisins, some 20 large seers [*about a ton*]. The vineyard's previous owner died, and one of his relatives – a brother or a cousin – declared, 'This vineyard's mine; he may have sold it, but it's my inheritance.' So they kept all the raisins.

Pâr-khân went to Sheberghân several times to complain. Both sides spent money, but nothing happened. Then Haji Tumân and Seyyed-shâh[/*Soleymân*] took it to court in Kabul on Pâr-khân's behalf. In spring they did this repeatedly; but the court sat on the case, and nothing happened.

Some Wardaks murdered an Uzbek boy – a close relative of Pâr-khân's vineyard-man. The boy had become familiar with Lalabey Wardak's women; Lalabey's son Jahângir told his uncle Shir-Mahmad, 'He's been seen in our house several times; we can't have this; what shall we do? Next time he comes I'll let you know.' Shir-Mahmad said, 'If we get him, we'll have to kill him.'

So one night they took the Uzbek boy off, saying, 'We're taking you to a meal.' He was a smart, able lad, but also a good-for-nothing thief; he stayed in town and rarely went home; and he wore a pistol round his neck all year round. But he was alone, and there were several of them. He fired a couple of shots; one hit Jahângir, the other wounded Shir-Mahmad's son Nawâb; but they killed him. They put his body in the old mosque you may have noticed near Lalabey's house; people don't use it for prayers any more, there's a new mosque. Meanwhile Shir-Mahmad took his son and nephew by car to a doctor in Mazâr, who treated their wounds. The boy's body lay for two nights in the mosque, then, worried that someone would find it, they put it in a sack, took it to the river and hid it under some rocks. There it stayed for several days until they could endure it no more, so at night they took him up onto the Tâwa – you know, on this side of the Valley – and buried him there.

Some bloke informed the government, and investigations began. They beat Jahângir and Nawâb until they confessed. The Uzbeks took advantage of all this to ensnare Pâr-khân. The vineyard-man said, 'Let's get Pâr-khân involved in this affair, then perhaps he'll let the vineyard go and stop bothering us.' The Uzbeks are now lying to the government: that Pâr-khân had arranged to give the Wardaks 50–100,000 rupees for killing that lad.

That's why so many summonses come for Pâr-khân. At first he paid the soldiers 500 or 1,000 rupees to go away; but they came three times a day – the government won't give up. He tried to hide, but he realized that he might as well give himself up. Today, when you were there, he came to get a prayer from the *âghâ*, and then he went with the soldiers. There was nobody with him, he was very worried. He didn't do what the Uzbeks say he did; he knew nothing about it, he was here at the time.

The Piruzai Feud

More serious and complex was the feud between the two main Piruzai lineages, Lineage A (based in Khârkash village) and Lineage C (Konjek). The two lineages came together in the south-west and intermarried before migrating to Turkistan, but from the beginning there was hostility between them: in particular, Lineage A questioned Lineage C's claims to Durrani identity, though usually behind their backs (see Chapter 1).

I: In the mountains

The hostility first turns violent in spring 1936 (or 1937), as the Piruzai caravans trek towards their mountain summer pastures. In a narrow river gorge two flocks get mixed up. The shepherds start fighting. Pordel and his younger brother Khoshdel of Lineage A beat up young Kamaroddin of Lineage C, who is injured and badly shaken. Calming down, the brothers put Kamaroddin on a household camel and take him to Cherâs, the next camping ground.

Three senior Piruzai men – Kamaroddin's uncle Zabtu, Pordel's father Jabbâr, and Karim-dâd, the acknowledged Piruzai leader – are away on pilgrimage to Mecca. The other main leader, Kamaroddin's father Haji Afzal, has stayed in Sar-e-pol. Those present want the whole matter settled peacefully, but Kamaroddin's mother Tumân, a 'short-sighted woman of Fârsibân descent', calls to Zabtu's son Rowzoddin: 'They've injured my son; only a woman wouldn't retaliate.' Shamed by her cry, the hot-tempered Rowzoddin takes his father's horse and gun, rides straight to where the brothers are setting up camp, and shoots Khoshdel, wounding him. The brothers soon recover from the shock and wrest Rowzoddin's gun from him; they club him down, and as he falls Pordel shoots him dead.

Ghâfur, Rowzoddin's elder brother, buries him, while Lineage A move their tents into a side-valley some way from those of Lineage C. Ghâfur sends news to the rest of Lineage C, who are some stages away, but they are most reluctant to come. By the time they arrive, Turabâz Khân, one of the Es'hâqzai khans, is already there.

Turabâz Khân arranges for Pordel's sister Maryam to be given to Rowzoddin's eldest son Tumân, and Ghâfur's eldest daughter Karâr to go to Khoshdel's brother Kohandel. Maryam is married that same night. Her brother takes her, with a few pieces of bedding, to Ghâfur's tent and the nikah marriage ceremony is performed for both girls, though Karâr is still a child and continues to live in her father's house.

While the Piruzai are in the mountains, the pilgrims return from Mecca, and are grief-stricken at the news. When Afzal hears, he is angry that only one woman was given in

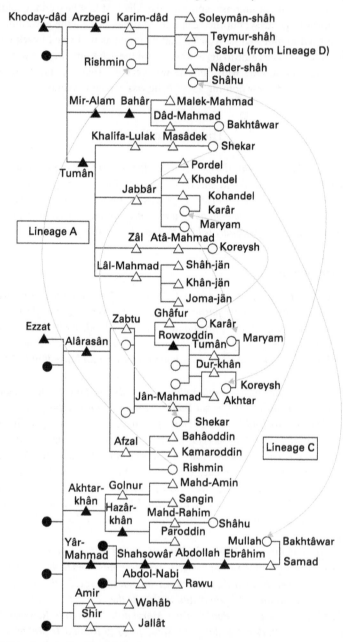

Figure 7 Principals in the Piruzai feud.

compensation for Rowzoddin's death, and insists that his family be given a second woman. Haji Karim-dâd promises two further women, to be given when the nomads return to the Sar-e-pol valley.[4]

Maryam tells Nancy what happened. She witnessed some of the events, and was the first to be given in the peacemaking. A young girl at the time, her memory is sometimes obviously faulty, leading to correction by her daughter-in-law Pâkhâl, who was not born but has heard the story many times from close relatives who were there. (See Fig. 7; Map D)

When Rowzoddin was killed, we were all in the mountains at Cherâs. My father was on pilgrimage to Mecca, with Zabtu and Karim-dâd.

We pitched camp at Târikak, then early next morning we started off up Dablak pass – you've seen it? In the gorge on the other side there's a fast-flowing river, twisting and turning. Our caravan filed along the narrow track on one bank. The sheep had been up on the herding trail along the mountain ridges; now they made their way along the other bank, in a long line, like a rope. There were three flocks, Haji Zabtu's, Haji Afzal's and my father's.

The shepherds got into a fight. My father's shepherd Kamaroddin had his arm broken; he fell down, crying, 'They've beaten me, I'm dying!' But everything was fine, nobody said anything. The sheep went on ahead. They lifted the shepherd up onto a camel, and went out onto the broad Cherâs plateau.

We camped just at the start of that track leading up the ridge beyond. When we arrived, Ghâfur and his people had already pitched their tents, just above us; we could see them. A large crowd had gathered, the families of Jabbâr, Khalifa-Lulak, Dâd-Mahmad, Karim-dâd, Golnur, Jallât, Abdol-Nabi, Amir, Del. We all camped together, and everybody else had pitched their tents. Some of the sheep had arrived, some hadn't. Everything was fine, there was no fighting or quarrelling. The sheep came, and they put the injured shepherd down. It was a flesh wound; nobody paid much heed. Someone said, 'Take him to Ghâfur's and Afzal's place, and send another shepherd with the sheep.'

But at Ghâfur's a woman cried out, 'Hey, Ghâfur, they've brought back the shepherd, they've slaughtered your sheep!' Everything would've been fine, but this woman stirred things up.

(*Pâkhâl*) – But uncle Haji Ghâfur wasn't there, he'd gone hunting.

(*Maryam*) – How do you know? Why are you lying?

(*Pâkhâl*) – Now I'm going to tell the story. My grandmother says they'd stopped and hadn't put up their tents, when Kamaroddin's mother came and called to Rowzoddin, 'Didn't you know, Jabbâr's shepherds have beaten my son.' He grabbed his gun from his wife and got on his horse ...

(*Maryam*) – We hadn't yet unloaded the camels, when suddenly someone cried that a huge mob was approaching, all carrying guns. They looked like they wanted to shoot us, but we hadn't a single gun with us. Right there, Rowzoddin shot someone.

(*Pâkhâl*) – We say Rowzoddin took his father's gun and shot Maryam's brother Khoshdel.

---

[4] See N. Tapper (1991: 74–79).

(Maryam) – We had only five men: my brothers and my cousins Shâh-jân, Khân-jân, Joma-jân. But the others were a whole army, [*Kamaroddin's brothers*] Bahâoddin, Nur-Mahmad, Mahd-Karim. People started spoiling for a fight. As soon as he arrived, my father-in-law Rowzoddin shot my brother Khoshdel; he hit him twice in the thigh, one bullet came out here, and one there. Rowzoddin was killed – they put him on one side, and on the other they put my brother, who was still alive. Why did they have to start fighting? We spent the night there; and they buried the dead man.

In the morning, people wanted us to keep apart. It wasn't a good idea for us all to be in the same place. We moved off in one direction, towards the Posht-e-khar range, and they went in the other, down towards Esmeydân. That night we camped separately, but not far apart. We kept hidden, over a little hill, as far away from them as Khârkash is from here. Before, we'd camped in one place, together with uncles Afzal and Zabtu – after all, we're one people, one clan.

In the morning everyone from Afzal's camp came, with uncle Del and Mullah Ebrâhim. They looked at my brother and took him to task, saying: 'What on earth got into you? Why did this fight start?' He said, 'I didn't start it, he did. We'd just stopped and hadn't even pitched our tents when he came up. I had nobody, my father had gone and my brother wasn't there; I was with the women.'

It was the mother of Shahâboddin, Kamaroddin and Mahd-Karim who started it. She was a strange woman; her son had been beaten, she just lost her temper.

Next morning we broke camp again. They went ahead and we came behind. Some time after we got to the mountain pastures, people said 'Haji Zabtu and Haji Karim-dâd are back from Mecca.' My father Jabbâr had gone too, but he died there. They came straight up to the mountains. In those days there were no cars and buses; it took a whole year to go to Mecca.

Haji Zabtu wept when he heard that his son was dead; so did we, because my father had died. Haji Karim-dâd came and wept with us; they were our people. Then Zabtu's family came to us and said, 'Why did you do this? He was a good man.' They were very upset and reproachful.

While we were in the mountains Haji Karim-dâd and Haji Zabtu arranged the exchange of women. Turabâz Khân was there too; his eyes were fine then, he used to go to the mountains; he aged and went blind later. They gave me [*to Rowzoddin*] in direct exchange with Ghâfur's daughter Karâr [*married to Khoshdel's brother Kohandel*].

Seyyed-shâh/Golusar gives further details. Like his paternal cousin Pâkhâl, he heard the story from close relatives: his mother Sharâp was Rowzoddin's daughter.

Haji Afzal had stayed here in the Valley, but his sons [*Kamaroddin et al.*] and their mother were on the trek. After Kamaroddin was beaten, his mother shouted to Rowzoddin, 'Hey, Rowz! They've beaten my son, he's bleeding; the sheep have scattered,' and so on – as women will. They'd just pitched the tents. My mother told me about it. She said, 'I was small, but I remember it. My father shouldered his gun, put on his cartridge belt, and mounted his mare.' As soon as he got there, he shot Khoshdel in the buttocks. They tried to take his gun from him, but they couldn't, he was very strong.

They clubbed him on the head and cut it open. He collapsed on top of his gun, and they still couldn't get it from him. But they managed to wrest Haji Afzal's son Bahâoddin's gun from him, and they shot Rowzoddin with that. In those days, the latest fashion was the *paj*-style turban; when they shot him, his turban flew into the air and came down like a crow.

My grandfather Golnur and his nephew Paroddin were several stages behind, at Michiluk above the Kachan valley. Ghâfur sent a hired hand, Sâf-khân Alizai from Kaltar, to tell Golnur about the killing, asking him to come. Golnur was busy shearing; he said, 'It's none of my business. If you're doing a sacrificial feast, I'll come; if it's anything else, I won't.' Sâf-khân said, 'We've done a sacrifice, so come.' Without telling the women what had happened, they instructed the servants to break camp, load the camels, trek to Târikak and straight on to Cherâs; then they took their guns and went on ahead.

Meanwhile the elders gathered; but they couldn't make peace – *rowgha*, as we say – until Turabâz Khân came. When my grandfather Golnur arrived, Turabâz Khân was saying, 'You must make peace together.' Golnur got angry and said, 'They've killed Ghâfur's brother; what's that to do with me? It's not my son, my brother, my cousin who's been killed.' They said, 'No, you're a very excitable chap, you could cause a lot of trouble if you don't join in.' He repeated: 'What's it to me?' So they left him alone.

II: At the wedding

When the mâldâr *arrive back in the north in late summer, Lineage C are incensed to hear Lineage A boasting that they have killed a 'Pulâdi' and paid only one woman in compensation.*

Ghâfur speaks to some relatives. He promises one of his own sisters in marriage to Paroddin, a strong and determined young man, if he will kill Rowzoddin's murderer. Paroddin agrees, and also swears to kill Haji Karim-dâd's sons, who are among those boasting most loudly.

Shortly after, there is a wedding party in Seyyedâbâd for Pordel, whose bride is from the Nazarzai khans who live there. Paroddin and three cousins, Bahâoddin, Jallât and Rawu, set off at night and join the party, disguised as women. They slip out and untie the guests' horses; the ensuing disturbance draws the male guests out of the reception tent. Paroddin shoots at the first man to emerge. His single shot hits two sons of Haji Karim-dâd, killing Soleymân-shâh outright and wounding Teymur-shâh. This action effectively unites Lineage A behind Karim-dâd, and they prepare for a major battle with the more numerous Lineage C.

Early the following morning, two men of Lineage C, Mullah Ebrâhim and his kinsman Sangin, set out from Konjek for Sar-e-pol, unaware of what has happened. Before they get far from home they meet a Lineage B man, who tells them about the killing. They disregard his warning, saying it's none of their business, as their close kin are not involved. As they ride past the graveyard halfway to Khârkash, they are ambushed by Malek-Mahmad of Lineage A, who fires on them. Sangin manages to ride to safety, but Mullah Ebrâhim's horse stumbles and he falls. He has been hit twice, but not badly wounded; he pleads for his life, but Malek-Mahmad tells him to say his prayers and, when he has finished, shoots him dead in cold blood.

Seyyed-shâh continues.

After they got back here, these Khârkashis were boasting, 'Look what we've done, we've killed your man, what have you done about it?' As winter approached there was a wedding party. So four men, Haji Afzal's son Bahâoddin, Paroddin – he was a very powerful man – Rawu and Jallât, set off for the party that night, with guns on their shoulders and bandoliers round their necks.

Paroddin said, 'Haji Karim-dâd's son's been boasting; where is he? Wait till I get him, I'll kill him.' He put on a chador and went among the women, looking around until he found Soleymân-shâh. 'If I open fire in here,' he thought, 'innocent people will get hurt, and that's not honourable; I'll let the horses loose.'

So Paroddin came out and untied the horses. The cry went up, 'The horses are loose!' As people came out, he shot down Soleymân-shâh, who died right there; Teymur-shâh was hit in the mouth – you know Haji Teymur-shâh, with the crooked mouth? – and he too fell and lay still. Their honour was gone; and the women started mourning the dead man.

After the killing, Jallât fled in fear of his life; he jumped into the river at Pashm-shuy, and came out again at Salmâzân. Paroddin said, 'Let's go, but where's Jallât?' They waited, but he didn't come, so they went home in the dark, not knowing what had happened to him. They'd shot two people, one dead, the other alive but unconscious. 'It would be good if he died too', Paroddin said. When they got home, though, he was full of remorse: 'Oh God, what have I done? I've killed a man, and now one of us is lost; if they catch him, they'll kill him for sure!'

The next morning, Haji Abdollah's son Mullah Ebrâhim set off for town with my uncle Sangin. They knew nothing about what had happened the previous night. We told them, 'Don't go – we've killed Haji Karim-dâd's son!' But they mounted their horses and went off down the track towards Khârkash. They met Amroddin, Manakey's elder brother, who told them: 'You'd better turn back, or they'll kill you.' Thinking he was just boasting, they rode on. They saw men with guns, but they didn't turn back. As they passed Mullah Jabbâr's place, Ebrâhim's mare stumbled and he fell; the horses went on, leaving him lying there. God decided his time had come. Two bullets hit him. He said to Malek-Mahmad, 'Don't kill me, I'm all right.' Malek-Mahmad took pity on him: 'What's the point of killing him?' But someone else said, 'For God's sake kill him – they killed our man.' Malek-Mahmad turned once more and was about to finish him off, but Mullah Ebrâhim said, 'Don't kill me until I've said my prayers; when I've finished, then you may kill me, my time has come.' So he did his prayers, then took his turban and covered his face, and they shot him and he died there.

When they brought Mullah Ebrâhim's body home there was a great uproar . . .

Pâkhâl takes over.

It was like this. One evening there was a wedding at Seyyedâbâd for Maryam's brother Pordel. Some of our men got together: Ghâfur, Jallât, my uncle Paroddin, and Rawu. Ghâfur told Paroddin, 'Go tonight and kill Pordel, my brother's killer, and I'll give you my sister Bakhtâwar.'

So these three men, Paroddin, Jallât and Rawu, set off for the wedding party; they put black chadors over their heads. There were great crowds of men and women gathered. Among the guests were two of Nâder-shâh's brothers, Soleymân-shâh and Teymur-shâh, as well as Maryam's brother Pordel. They'd just arrived and tied up their horses and were giving them some barley. Jallât, Rawu and Paroddin aimed their guns at them. One shot hit Soleymân-shâh, a second hit Teymur-shâh in the mouth, but they missed Pordel. Soleymân-shâh died at once. Teymur-shâh's still alive – you went to his son's wedding party the other day.

Our three men escaped in the dark by jumping into the river, and they got back home by water. Paroddin's wife came round and woke my father, Mahd-Amin: 'Get up; they're back from the wedding, it looks like they've spilt blood.' If you kill someone, what happens to you? Your eyes go funny, like this. My father went round to Paroddin and asked him what he'd done. He said, 'I've killed someone, I couldn't see who; we shot two of them, but I don't know if they're dead, because we fled.' My father said, 'Well, now the feud will get worse. Why'd you do it, going off at night like that?' 'Ghâfur told me to, and promised me his sister, Bakhtâwar.'

My father came home and went back to bed. Early next morning my uncle Sangin got up to pray. He and Ebrâhim were going to town. They saddled their horses and set off, unaware of what these guys had done the night before. As they passed the hill by the graveyard, up came Wadud saying, 'Ghâfur sent some men who killed Haji Karim-dâd's son and wounded another; don't go on or they'll kill you.' As they turned back, they saw armed men coming after them. My uncle's horse was lively and he galloped away, but when he looked behind he saw those men firing their guns, *tak-a-tak-a-tak*. Ebrâhim's horse stumbled, and they shot him right there. He cried, 'Stop shooting, I'll recover!' But they kept on shooting, and he died there.

It was Malek-Mahmad who shot him. His cousin Haji Peydâ Nâmanzai had seen them coming and told him, 'They're on their way to town, hurry up and you can kill them!' So he caught Ebrâhim and killed him.

When my uncle got home, it was still early morning. He cried out, 'An army came and they've killed Ebrâhim!' My father, who was older than Sangin, wrung his hands, saying, 'What were you thinking of, idiots, going to town?' Sangin replied, 'How were we to know what happened last night? Nobody told us somebody'd been killed.'

III: Peacemaking, marriages

Lineage C closed ranks; they collected Mullah Ebrâhim's body and posted guards round the tents. Both sides prepared for battle. Abdol-Ghâfur Khân, the Es'hâqzai chief who was then hâkem of Sar-e-pol, swiftly intervened; at Khârkash he arrested men from both sides and held them in prison until he had organized a jirga assembly of leading Pashtuns of the province some months later.

Eight marriages were arranged between the lineages: in theory, one woman for each man wounded and two for each man killed. Our narrators disagreed as to what was arranged; as far as we could establish, the following were actually given:

Lineage A (Soleymân-shâh killed, Teymur-shâh and Khoshdel wounded) received:

1. *Ghâfur's daughter Karâr for Khoshdel's brother Kohandel;*
2. *Afzal's daughter Rishmin for Karim-dâd;*
3. *Paroddin's brother Mahd-Rahim's daughter Shâhu for Nader-shâh;*
4. *Mahmud's daughter Sabru, from Lineage D, for Teymur-shâh.*

Lineage C (Rowzoddin and Mullah Ebrâhim killed) received:

1. *Pordel's sister Maryam for Rowzoddin's eldest son Tumân;*
2. *Pordel's cousin Koreysh for Rowzoddin's second son Dur-khân;*
3. *Pordel's cousin Shekar for Rowzoddin's half-brother Jân-Mahmad;*
4. *Malek-Mahmad's niece Bakhtâwar for Mullah Ebrâhim's young son Samad.*

Pâkhâl continues.

They went out to get Ebrâhim's body. It was all cut up, his clothes were drenched in blood, which flowed like a river, reddening the earth before it disappeared. The poor man was innocent and never knew why he was killed, so they buried him in his clothes, without a shroud. This was all because Ghâfur sent them to kill Maryam's brother, saying, 'He killed my brother; if he dies, I'll be content, my heart will cool.'

After Ebrâhim's death, the feud got worse. Our village set guards at night, so did theirs. Our hearts were black. Then after some days they went to town and the government made peace between them. If women are exchanged, then there'll be peace, *rowgha*. They gave Maryam to Tumân, Koreysh to Dur-khân, Shekar to Jân-Mahmad; then we gave uncle Mahd-Rahim and aunt Tunya's daughter Shâhu to Nâder-shâh, and Haji Afzal's daughter Rishmin to Haji Karim-dâd himself because his son was killed. Dâd-Mahmad's daughter Bakhtâwar was given to Ebrâhim's son Samad.

The government arranged it all. They asked, 'Does Rowzoddin have a son?' Answer, 'Yes, he has two, Tumân and Dur-khân'; so each got a wife. Jân-Mahmad was Rowzoddin's brother.

Maryam says they were all direct exchange marriages, but they weren't. They gave women for everyone who was killed; then they made peace. Nobody was kept in prison. After the peacemaking, Paroddin complained to Ghâfur, 'Why didn't you give me your sister Bakhtâwar, as you promised?' Ghâfur said, 'I will give her, don't worry.' But a year later Paroddin died. He was a good man, very powerful. After he died, Bakhtâwar was given to Molk. She was very attractive when she was young, very light-skinned, very plump. Now she's old, but she's still a fine woman.

Headwoman Neshtar gives further detail on the marriages, emphasizing their importance in reconciling the two sides – and the role of the wealthy Ghâfur.

They gave Koreysh to Dur-khân in the peacemaking. They would have given her free, but Haji Ghâfur was a good man, he treated them like relatives and gave a brideprice (*wëlwar*). He said, 'Let's do the right thing, let's let bygones be bygones and put calm back in our hearts.' Of course, he was wealthy and didn't mind spending money. He told them, 'I'll give whatever you ask.' He gave forty or fifty thousand rupees for her.

Ghâfur's daughter Karâr went to Kohandel and Kohandel's sister Maryam to Ghâfur's nephew Tumân as part of the peacemaking, without brideprice. But it was like a direct exchange between relatives, to bring people's hearts together. First they brought Maryam, when Karâr was still very small. We took Karâr to Kohandel when she grew up – by that time Maryam had children: Khâni-âghâ, Pâdshâh and Mesru.

Shekar went to Jân-Mahmad in the peacemaking. At first there was no brideprice, but later Haji Ghâfur gave some 50,000 rupees for her too, and made her wedding a happy one. He said, 'Instead of fighting, we'll be family; the cost of a brideprice is nothing to me.'

Both Shekar and Koreysh had fine weddings. After a feud you take with one hand and give with the other. Maryam they brought on the first day, when tempers were still red-hot. But the others came with joy, with music and dancing.

My uncle Mahd-Rahim's daughter Shâhu was given to Nâder-shâh in the peacemaking; her brideprice was 3,000. And we gave Rishmin to Haji Karim-dâd free, without brideprice.

After Malek-Mahmad killed Samad's father Ebrâhim, he promised him his niece Bakhtâwar [*not to be confused with Zabtu's daughter*]. Samad and his bride were both small, the age of Seyyed-shâh's young son here. When they grew up, there was a quarrel about it. When Samad's guardian – his distant uncle Haji Abdol-Nabi – asked Malek-Mahmad to deliver his daughter, he demanded a brideprice. We objected, but eventually Abdol-Nabi agreed to give 30,000 rupees.

Long before the feud, Zabtu had promised his daughter Bakhtâwar to Khalifa-Lulak for his son Molk, though he didn't tell anyone else. All her cousins, such as Bahâoddin, wanted her because she was a fine girl. But Zabtu kept his word. As we say, *Âdam mordâr, lawz halâl*, a dirty man's word may be clean. On his deathbed, Haji Zabtu said, 'When this girl was small I promised her to Molk.' There was nothing they could do about it. Bakhtâwar went to Molk for 5,000 rupees. Bakhtâwar and I are the same age. For me, it was 2,500, for her 5,000! So it goes.

One other girl was given after the feud. Mullah Jabbâr's cousin Mahmud's daughter Sabru went to Teymur-shâh, or his son. It happened this way. They were our relatives. We're all from one ancestor, Ezzat, but our lineages are separate: Mullah Jabbâr was from one; Haji Afzal and us, another; Haji Amir and Haji Jallât from a different one. In the feud, Mullah Jabbâr's father Mahmud-khân and his brother Jân-Mahmad, Sabru's grandfather, said that each lineage should stand apart; they weren't involved in the fighting. But the rest, Haji Afzal and others, wouldn't accept this, saying, 'If we're to be relatives, we should all contribute.' In the peacemaking, they persuaded young Mahmud to give his daughter, but Haji Afzal said, 'This poor man has nothing, we have plenty,' and he gave him 3,000 rupees to compensate for the loss of brideprice. This was *qawmi* (tribal solidarity); my uncles Haji Afzal, Haji Abdol-Nabi, Haji Amir and my father Golnur all did this *qawmi*. It was a *takila* collection, as we did the other day for the theft, when they went round and collected 100 or 200 rupees from each house.

So Mullah Jabbâr's lineage [*Lineage D*] stood with us in the peacemaking. They hadn't been involved in the killing, but they mourned with us and did *qawmi*. Nâder-shâh's people in Khârkash gave them no woman in return. Mullah Jabbâr's lineage simply wasn't worried about giving the girl free. They helped make peace because they wanted to; everybody wanted it, from goodwill. In those days, we had *qawmi* and goodwill. Nowadays people are less inclined to such generosity and *qawmi*.

Mullah Jabbâr's land was near Khârkash, but at that time they all camped here with us, in Shâhpari's place, you know it? We had no houses then – we didn't know what they were! We were *mâldâr*, we came and went! When we saw others building houses, we did so too. Then they said, 'If we're going to build houses, we'll put them on our own land,' so they went to Khârkash.

Maryam was the first to be given in the peacemaking, but she denies this and insists that all the marriages were direct exchanges (mëkhi), *and that payments were involved. Like Neshtar, she seeks to emphasize peace and solidarity in the Piruzai.*

Our side didn't give a single girl in compensation: all our women were given in direct exchanges or for brideprice. They did the weddings, with the proper prayers: we took their women and they took me. Haji Zabtu was alive, but the following spring he fell ill. His daughter Bibikuh and I looked after him, so did his wife and everyone, but the poor man died. His sons were heartbroken.

I was exchanged with Karâr, Haji Ghâfur's daughter; she was a good girl, my brother Kohandel's wife. Kohandel came courting; Karâr's mother Moshkendi, my cousin, was alive when they betrothed her, and she and her co-wife Bibiwor looked after Kohandel well when he came round; but Moshkendi died before the wedding.

Karâr had a spring wedding, out in the steppe. There were drums and pipes; we brought lots of sheep, and my mother brought a skin full of ghee; at least a maund.[5] I'll bet no one ever brought so much ghee. They served so much rice that everybody ate like dogs, and yet the cauldrons were still full. So they gave my exchange partner Karâr to my brother Kohandel, and thank God she has three fine sons and two grown daughters.

When Koreysh was given to Dur-khân, Haji Ghâfur gave brideprice for her. Shekar too went for brideprice, her aunt Moshkendi persuaded her brother Masâdek to give Shekar to Jân-Mahmad. This was before the feud. Koreysh and I were given afterwards, at the same time.

Later Ghâfur promised his daughter Morid to Dâd-Mahmad's son Ahmad-shâh, but she died in childhood. That was after the feud; people called it peacemaking. He did it to make people's hearts happy. He thought, 'If I give this girl, our hearts will be happy and we'll be one house, like brothers and fathers.'

Now, if I go and visit that house it's like my father's; they've had Haji Ghâfur's daughter there, so their hearts are good again. They've forgotten the sadness. We became like mother and sister. That's why he gave her. So, thank God, there's been no more fighting, nobody else has been killed, we all came back together; people behaved normally, like now; we all visited each other, my brothers came, nobody worried. We were one united community, one *woles*: Haji Karim-dâd, Dâd-Mahmad, Haji Ghâfur, Hajj Afzal, Haji Zabtu. We're one clan, one family, from one mother and one father, all of us.

---

[5] A local maund, *man,* is 8 seers, 56 kg.

Towards the end of our stay we spend an afternoon in Seyyed-shâh/Golusar's house with him, his cousin and friend Pâdshâh/Parwiz, and his aunt Neshtar; we ask more about how feuds are ended.

(R) – Some weeks ago, you told us that if someone's killed in a feud, they have a right to two women?

(Neshtar) – The dead man's family has the right to seven women, according to the Book.

(R) – But they don't take seven, they take two or three.

(Pâdshâh) – Last year there was a fight between two Pakhizai kinsmen. One was killed. For three months the government pushed people around, and put a dozen men in prison. Then one guy gets up and says, 'I killed him, let the others go.' They release the others and this guy gets eighteen years, but they also gave the dead man's family two girls and 50,000 rupees. They did the right thing, because they were kinsmen.

(R) – What happens if someone kills his paternal cousin? He can't give a girl; she'd belong to both sides.

(Pâdshâh) – He'll give the dead man's family a girl, even if they're paternal cousins.

(R) – But what if he has no sisters to give? The dead man's sister can't be given!

(Pâdshâh) – No, no! If he doesn't have a daughter, he'll do *qawmi*; he'll give two girls from among their relatives, and some wealth.

(Seyyed-shâh) – And he'll take the Holy Koran to ask them to excuse the rest, for the Koran's sake; he'll give two women and also pay any penalty the government demands.

(R) – Is there compensation in feuds between Afghans and Uzbeks or Arabs? If you killed an Arab, or he killed an Afghan, what happens? Girls can't be given.

(Neshtar) – No, you can't give women to Fârsibâns; you give wealth.

(R) – You mean, you give enough for a brideprice?

(Pâdshâh) – Yes; for two or three girls.

(R) – But an Afghan brideprice is expensive, while theirs is less.

(Seyyed-shâh) – You give them the price of one of their girls, not of an Afghan girl.

(R) – What if an Arab kills an Afghan? Do they give a brideprice for an Afghan girl?

(Neshtar) – They give a girl.

(Pâdshâh) – No, first they'll take revenge. Then, when they've made peace, they'll give the brideprice of one or two girls at the going rate for Afghans. They wouldn't give Arab girls.

(Neshtar) – Yes, they would.

[They argue briefly]

(Pâdshâh) – They'll give them if the Afghans will take them. Akbar Khân, who recently killed six Uzbeks and burned their bodies, had to pay wealth and property; he was supposed to give land, but he didn't. He was released after a year and a half in jail. They weren't able to take revenge, to kill him.

(Neshtar) – If they'd been Afghans, with a sense of honour, they'd have done something. But they were Uzbeks; they did nothing. Their people died, and nothing happened. They got neither revenge, nor brideprice, nor property.

(Pâdshâh) – If two Afghans fight, and one person from each village is killed, they'll meet and consult together. They'll each take a daughter from the other, and be reconciled.

(*Seyyed-shâh*) – The point is to remove the bad feeling from their hearts.

(*Neshtar*) – Otherwise, if they aren't satisfied, there may be further killings.

We ask again about the Piruzai feud and its legacy. The main speaker is Pâdshâh/Parwiz, a large and engaging character who dominates small group conversations. Pâdshâh often talks of his famously maverick late father Parwiz, joking about his own escapades as trivial by comparison.

(*Pâdshâh*) – The jirga was in Haji Mahd-Omar Maleki's place, where Kadir-khân lives now. People came from there to our mosque here, then they went to the Khârkash mosque. They made peace; and each side gave two girls to the other side. They brought the Koran between them and reconciled them, to get rid of the enmity.

(*Neshtar*) – People from both sides kissed each other on the face; they prayed together and swore that if their children did the same again, if they killed each other, then God curse them and remove all blessings. They should stay peacefully at home.

(*Pâdshâh*) – Some years ago the feud nearly did start up again. Haji Wahâb had sown some corn over in that stubble-field of Nâder-shâh's. Nâder-shâh's brother Heydar-shâh came here and swore at Haji Wahâb, who instantly gave him a beating. A boy went off and told Nâder-shâh, and his shepherd came and beat Haji Wahâb, injuring him in the head. Then ten or fifteen of them came after us; but ten of us – Haji Wahâb, Lâljân and the rest – went out there and beat them black and blue; they beat Heydar-shâh badly, on the head. Nâder-shâh's shepherd was an Arab from Neymadân; a real club-fighter, nobody could touch him. He fought with uncle Lâljân, who's also handy with a club; he can take on ten or twenty men; once his hand's raised, twenty men can't hit him. They fought for a long time, but finally Lâljân hit the Arab on the head and knocked him out.

At the time, I was ploughing with my farmhand, up there beyond the hill. All I had with me was a little stick, a switch. Suddenly I saw people with guns running past down below. Somebody shouted to me, 'They've killed Nâder-shâh's nephew [*brother*], you'd better go home, but go the other way.' So I left my oxen and fled. I was down below the hill when I saw an army coming after me, all with rifles and pistols, so many that they hid the path. God help me! I thought. Somebody called out, 'Run, you bastard, or we'll kill you!' I said, 'Okay, kill me; if it's my day to die, so be it.' A man never knows when his time's come. Well, they surrounded me and set about me with knives and clubs and guns. I hit back at them, at their arms and legs, as best I could, with stones and my little switch, but they were too many for me. Then Nâder-shâh cried out, 'Don't hit him, you bastards! Why are you hitting Parwiz's son? Let him go!' Mullah Amir, a really tough guy, came among them and pushed their clubs aside, but Kolagey's brother took aim at me and cried, 'Out of my way, let me shoot him!' I threw myself on him saying, 'Think you're going to shoot me? I'll see you in Hell first!' Well, I escaped and made it home, but I was pretty nearly done for.

From our side, anybody who had a gun went out, ready for a fight. But the Ludin people intervened, brought the Koran between us.

(*Seyyed-shâh*) – It was Mahd-Amin Omarzai who brought the Koran. Everybody brought their guns, but the Holy Koran came between them.

(*Pâdshâh*) – Yes of course; Mahd-Amin brought the Koran, and separated the two sides. Two days later, ten or fifteen of them came to our mosque, and ten or fifteen of us went to theirs. First they came to us, afterwards we went there. From their side, Nâder-shâh, Haji Malek-Mahmad, Haji Teymur-shâh, Haji Molk, Borjân and some others, together with the mullahs. From our side there was my father Parwiz, God rest his soul; uncle Mahd-Amin, uncle Shahâboddin, Mowlawi Golzâr; Tumân was also among them, and Haji Ghâfur.

(*Neshtar*) – The elders, the greybeards. So they made peace again. No women were exchanged, or money; it wasn't that kind of feud.

(*Pâdshâh*) – A few heads and limbs were cracked, but nobody was killed. It was a near thing; if shooting had started, there'd have been a major clash, lots of killing. This was five or six years ago.

(*Seyyed-shâh*) – Before you and I went on military service.

(*Pâdshâh*) – You're right! So it must have been eight or nine years.

Village Factions

The two main Piruzai villages, Konjek and Khârkash, are located in lands that their leaders bought in the 1920s (see Chapter 1). Khârkash is inhabited mainly by Lineages A, B and D; most Konjek villagers belong to Lineage C; the brothers Rangin and Rishmin, and others from Lineage A, live in hamlets on the edge of the Piruzai lands, as do some of Lineage B. Konjek and Khârkash also include a variety of non-Piruzai and non-Es'hâqzai households. Haji Ghâfur of Lineage C lives in a large compound near his mill, south of Khârkash and close to the village of Kal-qeshlâq. This was Tumân's home for much of his time as headman; closer to both the main road and the Sar-e-pol river, it is ideal for offering hospitality to visitors to the Piruzai villages – and controlling their access. (See Fig. 8; Maps F and H)

Groups

What is the nature of these different settlements? What unites them as Piruzai, and in what circumstances do they constitute different political groups? Some of the answers emerged in this dialogue with Baya-khân.

(*R*) – What's the difference between *qawm, kheyl, tol, woles*?

(*Baya-khân*) – The village is a *woles*. As for *tol*, that's a gathering of people.

(*R*) – Here in Konjek, most people are from one *qawm*; but some, like Seyyed-shâh[/Soleymân], are from another *qawm*; are they part of your *tol*, or *woles*?

(*Baya-khân*) – If people gather to discuss common affairs, and someone like Seyyed-shâh joins in, then anyone who doesn't like him can say, 'It's none of your business.'

(*R*) – So people like Seyyed-shâh aren't called *qawm*?

(*Baya-khân*) – No. He may be called *qawm*, but not if he gets into a fight with someone.

(*R*) – Is a *woles* bigger than a *këley*?

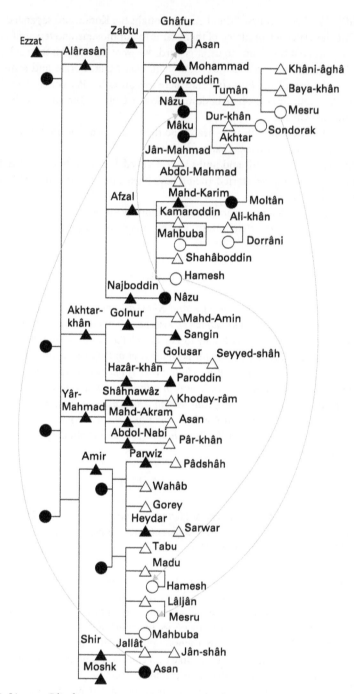

Figure 8 Lineage C leaders.

(Baya-khân) – Yes, a *woles* is a large village. A *këley*'s just a few houses.

(R) – The two villages, Konjek and Khârkash: together, are they a *woles*? The Piruzai *woles*?

(Baya-khân) – For the government, all Piruzai are registered in Khârkash. Among us, this village is known as Konjek; the other one is Khârkash.

(R) – What's the difference between *kheyl* and *këley*?

(Baya-khân) – *Kheyl* and *këley* are the same thing: a few houses in one place. *Woles* is more. When we go to the mountains, twenty or so tents together, it's a *këley*. If there are only two or three, then we refer to them as households: *khâna* or *kur*; otherwise it's a *këley*.

(R) – When a big man has followers from different places, what do you call them?

(Baya-khân) – If he's responsible for four or five *woles* or villages, his followers don't really come together, he solves their disputes individually.

(N) – You often say, if there's a problem, it's good when the *woles* stands together.

(Baya-khân) – One fellow with a sword in his hand, even two people, or ten households, can do nothing on their own against a *woles*. They say, *dë woles zur dë khoday zur*: the *woles*'s strength is God's strength. For example, this year Jallât Khân went to court to grab some of our land. If we hadn't been a *woles*, but only a few households, he'd have succeeded. But the *woles* stood firm, so he achieved nothing. If we collect 10 rupees per household, they'd have to collect 100 per household to match us. When a *woles* of several hundred households stands together, the government can't break them.

(N) – Sometimes people say *haft-posht*, 'seven generations'; what does this mean?

(Baya-khân) – If you're fighting with someone, you may say, 'You won't win, even if you stand there for seven generations.' Also, people [*descended from a common ancestor*] no more than seven generations back are close *qawm*. In this village we're all *qawm*. Beyond that, they're too far to be called *qawm*; in Khârkash, Manakey and his lot [*Lineage B*] belong to our *qawm*, but not the others.

Baya-khân makes two unexpected statements here, first that the Piruzai as a whole are not qawm, *secondly that Lineage B (Nasuzai) are closer genealogically to Lineage C (Pulâdi) than to Lineage A. Unfortunately we failed to follow them up.*

On another occasion we pursued related questions with Baya-khân, Chârgol (who lives in Khârkash) and Seyyed-shâh/Golusar.

(R) – In Khârkash, there are many people from different tribes like Nurzai, Baluch; they're not Nâder-shâh's *qawm*. Is he their leader too? Do they go to him for dealings with the government?

(Baya-khân) – Yes, if the government's after them, they'll go to him, but he'll take money for it.

(Chârgol) – Villagers who've come from another place go to Nâder-shâh when they get into trouble, even if they're not of his *qawm*.

(Baya-khân) – The other day when a soldier came here after the Nâmanzai, Haji collected money from everybody, including the Baluch visitors.

(*Chârgol*) – If they're after a thief, and the trail comes to the village, everyone who's there will contribute; money will be collected from every house: 10 rupees.

(*N*) – When they collected money for Rangin, I heard that they reckoned it by four 'fathers' (*plâr*), or was it five or six? How was this done?

(*Seyyed-shâh*) – Nâder-shâh collected 10,000 rupees from this village, and 10,000 from the other village too, and Rangin contributed 50,000 of his own.

(*N*) – So they collected by village?

(*Baya-khân*) – We [*in Konjek*] did it by 'father'. We and Shir are one father, and our levy would be 5,000, for example, or 2,000, and so on, by fathers. Then Haji Jallât and Haji Wahâb were another father. Rawu and uncle Mahd-Amin were another.

(*N*) – And another from your lot, from Akhtar?

(*Seyyed-shâh*) – Here we were four 'fathers'; to make 10,000 rupees they levied 2,500 from each 'father'. We did it by 'father', whereas in Nâder-shâh's village they did it by household.

(*Chârgol*) – Yes, in Khârkash it was collected house-by-house. In practice, each family's elders paid up; and the *hamsaya*, if there were any. But they don't collect from every house; nobody would ask the poor and destitute, a cowherd or a beggar, only people of substance.

(*R*) – So they took more per house in Khârkash than here?

(*Baya-khân*) – Yes.

(*N*) – How much did they take from your house?

(*Chârgol*) – I've no idea: I was with you in the mountains at the time!

(*Baya-khân*) – The people of Khârkash are closer *qawm* to Rangin than we are; also, they're more numerous. If they're in some kind of trouble, we point this out and say, 'We'll give money once, but no more.'

(*Chârgol*) – We're not fools, we reckon Nâder-shâh spends all the money on himself. We're all his *qawm*, but when he asks for more, we ask him, 'What have you done with it? Have you spent it all on billiards or chess?'

(*R*) – Did they collect from the outsiders in Khârkash?

(*Chârgol*) – He collected from the *qawm*, and if the outsiders also contributed, fine. Once they did collect from every man, they didn't let anybody off.

(*R*) – So they collect by house, so many rupees per house?

(*Chârgol*) – They take a levy, *andâz*, from each householder.

(*Baya-khân*) – For example, 100 rupees per house.

(*Chârgol*) – It's not to do with *qawmi*, it's everybody who happens to live in the village.

(*R*) – So, nobody will say, 'But I'm not your *qawm*'?

(*Baya-khân*) – No: they'd be thrown out!

(*Chârgol*) – If you don't give, they'll say, 'Get out, brother!'

(*R*) – So someone who settles in Nâder-shâh's village must do whatever Nâder-shâh tells him, or he'll be turfed out?

(*Chârgol*) – Yes. But if he's taken my money once and not achieved the purpose – he hasn't brought Rangin's daughter back – then I can refuse to give any more, and he'll have to shut up. He's 'eaten' my money.

(*Baya-khân*) – People will give money once, but not a second time.

Leaders

Khârkash and Konjek each have a government-recognized headman (qariyadâr), a position instituted in about 1934. Headmen conduct relations between their villagers and government agents, notably the police and the military. This involves both negotiation and bribery, regarded as 'dirty work', unsuited to an elder – and in particular to a Haji. They must command respect, but they and their actions may be subject to approval by village elders, the real leaders. A leader, whether of a household, a village, or a wider entity, is often not the eldest of a set of brothers.

Neshtar, 'headwoman' of Konjek, talks of some past leaders.

Haji Abdol-Nabi was a good man. He was good at speaking in public, good with *qawmi* and everything he did. He solved our disputes by *qawmi*, to general satisfaction. He was the tribal elder. He was like Nâder-shâh in the other *qawm*. He sat at the head in any gathering, and whenever he spoke, whatever he said, nobody else would speak; they did what he said.

He died twelve years ago, after Haji Afzal. They were elders at the same time. Nobody else in the community would speak out. Haji Ghâfur never said anything, he didn't care; only those two were involved in every community gathering. Haji Afzal was senior; he was 100 years old – he grew a new set of milk-teeth – but he got senile and didn't understand things, and Haji Abdol-Nabi took over from him. Haji Abdol-Nabi was a peacemaker; he solved all the disputes. The two of them were close cousins, like brothers. The whole community were like brothers then, not all saying different things like now.

It's excellent if there are two elders who get on together. Now Haji Tumân can do nothing; he's on his own. If there were two elders, and they were on good terms, then the whole community would get on. Now, with Haji acting alone, it doesn't work.

First headman of Konjek was Haji Jallât, still alive. Tumân's son Pâdshâh describes him.

Haji Jallât was headman for a time. You've seen him now, he has difficulty breathing; once he was a huge man, a devil; he made everybody in Khârkash and nearby villages suffer. Whenever someone in the community gave trouble, Jallât went straight to the government in Sheberghân and lodged a complaint. The moment the order came back, he arrested that man.

He pleased the khans – Kheyr-Mahmad Khân, Abdol-Wahâb Khân, Tâj-Mahmad Khân, Abdor-Rauf Khân, and they all got on well with him. Whenever there was a problem here, he went to the khans and told them privately, 'There's money in this for you.'

Pâdshâh/Parwiz adds.

When Haji Jallât was still young, he had a dark grey horse, a very proud animal. When he mounted it, it would rear up in the air, and it took five or six people to hold it down with a bridle. Haji Jallât broke the brass stirrups – that's how strong he was. Now he's an old man.

Baya-khân remembers.

Haji Jallât was just like a wolf in this village; everybody was afraid of him. He ate everyone's wealth. If there was business with the government, and Jallât had to spend 1,000 rupees, he'd come and take 5,000 from Haji Ghâfur, who was scared of him – that's why he gave him Dur-khân's daughter Sondorak for his son Jahân-shâh. When Jallât went on the Hajj, Haji Ghâfur paid all his expenses. Haji Ghâfur's a timid man. Ask my brothers. Everybody took advantage of him. Then my father Tumân grew up and became known to the government, and he stood up to everybody. His own father Rowzoddin was a powerful man. People don't listen to Ghâfur now. He can't do anything if my father's here. When Nâder-shâh isn't around, people from both villages don't go to Ghâfur, they come to Tumân.

Seyyed-shâh/Golusar praises his maternal grandfather Rowzoddin, who was killed in the feud, and his son Tumân, but confides that he doesn't think much of Tumân's own sons.

Rowzoddin was a very good man. Tumân's the only son of Nâzu, my grandmother, and she loved him dearly; he was small when his father was shot. Grandmother said that when Tumân's half-brother Dur-khân was born, he was very sick with a urinary infection; he cried all night. Then, she said, he got better the very day that Rowzoddin died. If Rowzoddin had lived, she said, he'd have held a feast for Dur-khân's recovery.

It was Rowzoddin who bought the lands in Sangchârak; now his brother Ghâfur's had deeds drawn up in his own name. Sometimes I say to him, 'Give me my mother's share!' He answers, 'Where's the land you're claiming?' I say, 'You're profiting from it, let me do so too.' I'm joking of course. Now, whatever my mother's brother Tumân does, I can't complain; God has made him so dear to me. I've done all sorts of things to him, but he's never refused me. He's given me money; I let him name the price. Last year, before he went on Hajj, I gave him 3 seers of corn, which an Uzbek had given me. He said he'd owe me the corn, and gave his radio into my care. When he came back, I didn't go to him at first, but later I went to his house and asked for my corn. He said, 'Why didn't you come before, I'd have given it to you at once.' Tumân is the best man in that family; if it weren't for him, neither his sons nor his relatives could get through a night.

The other day, when Haji Tumân wasn't around, Pâr-khân's son beat Kamaroddin's son, Ali-khân the cowherd, with a stick, shouting, 'Why are you charging 10 rupees for cowherding? Back down: we'll do it for five!' Then he hit Ali-khân's wife Dorrâni, and the boy wasn't brave enough to say, 'How dare you hit my wife!' There was nobody around to help him; if Haji'd been there, he'd have knocked their heads together. His sons wouldn't do anything. If the government sends a message, the sons just sit here. If he has to, Haji borrows from you and me, but he settles the affair, and pays back the money. His sons have no experience of the town, of courts.

Tumân made his mark many years before, not least in his relations with Nâder-shâh of Khârkash: in the late 1950s he beat Nâder-shâh in their rivalry for the hand of Pâkiza, by agreeing to pay her father Mullah Jabbâr (of Khârkash and Lineage D) one lac (100,000 rupees), by far the highest brideprice paid in this area at the time. Then he stole Turabâz Khân's deeds to the mountain pastures for Nâder-shâh, putting him in his debt.

In early 1971 (just before we joined his family) Tumân made the pilgrimage to Mecca. On his return, he hoped that his new status as Haji would allow him to retire from headmanship, but there are no obvious successors, and his services are once again in demand, not least in the affairs of Rishmin and Rangin. Moreover, when we arrived, Nâder-shâh refused to allow us to stay with our first host, Haji Molk of Khârkash; hearing this, Tumân readily volunteered to take complete responsibility for us, thus shaming his rival for timidity.

But Pâdshâh/Parwiz finds Tumân timid in his dealings, compared with his own father, Parwiz, famous for defying several of the Nazarzai khans.

My father, God forgive him, won all his battles; nobody could best him. Whenever I fought with one of the family, he'd say nothing to them, but he beat me: 'Why're you fighting?' He paid no attention to what other people said, the government or the khans.

He had quite a life. When he went to the mountains, Dâ'ud-shâh Khân sent people to steal his animals. My father said, 'When I was a lad I tended the ewes. We had several hundred; there was one shepherd, one *mozdur*,[6] and me on a donkey. Five or six of the khan's men came and said, "We're taking your sheep." I said, "You'll have to kill me first."' They started to grab them, but he lifted his club and knocked one of them down. There was a fight but he knocked them all to the ground, telling the shepherd and *mozdur* to drive the sheep on.

Then he saw the khan's army approaching, several hundred armed men. They tried to reach him, firing at him, but he climbed a cliff and hurled rocks down on them. The fight went on until evening; as it got dark he didn't notice that several men had come up behind him. He said, 'As I stuck my neck out, those guys threw stones that hit me on the back, and I fell.' Before he could get up they'd rushed him, and they took him to town. 'They brought me into the square. I sat there in the dark, while several hundred people walked round me with their lamps; "What sort of man is this, who couldn't be caught by armed men?" I had a fancy-coloured waistcoat. The women rushed out saying, "The bloodthirsty (*khun-khur*) Afghan's come!" When they saw me, they exclaimed, "What – this little man?" "Yes," the men said; "The bastard fought so hard, he's really strong."'

They kept him in custody for one day, then his father, Haji Amir, came, along with Gholâm-Rasul Khân. Amir had called him, 'Hey, Gholâm-Rasul, where's my Parwiz?' Gholâm-Rasul Khân said, 'I don't know him, how should I know where he is?' Amir said, 'He's the "Bloodthirsty" one who fought.' Someone told him where Parwiz was; he came and broke the door down, saying, 'Get up; off you go.' My grandfather was a powerful man; he wasn't afraid of Gholâm-Rasul Khân, who said, 'What are you doing? He's killed several men and he'll kill others if you let him out.' Haji Amir said, 'If you want to jail my son, you should inform me so that I can jail him myself. I'm alive, not dead!' Gholâm-Rasul Khân cried, 'Eh, uncle Haji Amir, I'm sorry, I didn't recognize him.' Amir said, 'Why did you jail him, if you didn't recognize him?'

---

[6] A *mozdur/mazdur* is at the bottom of the regular waged worker heap: herding assistant, farming assistant, houseman/domestic servant.

He said, 'Forget it, the matter's over.' So Amir released Parwiz, and he went off back to the sheep.

'Those were the days,' my father said. 'Everyone who saw me cried out, "There's the Bloodthirsty Afghan".' If a woman saw him, she'd take refuge in her house. Those were the days, indeed. Now look at his sons: look at me! I doubt if I could scare a cat! Eh, Richard? In those days, there were such powerful men. Now you can't fight or hit anyone, and if someone annoys you, you can't say anything back for fear of the government. In those days, the government wasn't so harsh.

One year he swore at Kheyr-Mahmad Khân.[7] It was during the Jashn festival. All the guys had gone to the show. Jallât Khân – who has a land dispute with us – together with Hâshem Khân, the Commandant and the rest, took a beardless boy, Sarfrâz, our neighbour Khoshkyâr Nurzai's son, into the back room of a teahouse, where they wanted rape him, to do *bacha-bâzi*.[8] My father was in town, at our friend Haji Ruzi Boy's place. My brother Wazir (I hadn't gone that day) came and said, 'Father, Jallât Khân, the Commandant and the soldiers have seized that boy from us.' He went out into the main square and called out, in his powerful voice, 'Fuck Haji Kheyr-Mahmad's wife!' and suchlike. They shouted, 'Parwiz has come!' Kheyr-Mahmad Khân rushed out of his house, and the Commandant and Jallât Khân heard as he was crossing the bridge the other side of the Bâlâ-Hesâr [*government offices*]. They were afraid there'd be trouble, so they let the boy go. Kheyr-Mahmad Khân came up and asked him, 'Why're you shouting?' He answered, 'By your grandfather Gholâm-Rasul's wife I'll piss on you, you pimp! You dare let them take my neighbour's son? Tomorrow they'll be taking mine. By God, we won't allow such shameless behaviour!' Kheyr-Mahmad said, 'Brother, for God's sake stop talking like that!' My father called the boy over and turned to Jallât Khân, 'Today you took this boy, my neighbour; if I don't take you to court for this, tomorrow you'll take my son and I'll be unable to do anything. By God, I'll tear your teeth out! You dare do this while I'm still alive?'

Abdor-Rahmân *wakil* came and joined Kheyr-Mahmad, so did his brother Abdor-Rauf Khân, and calmed him down. They were 'eating shit' for having allowed such a thing; they swore at the Commandant, and that night they beat the soldiers. I heard about it that night, and the following morning I went to town early. When I arrived, my father called me, 'Come, don't fight, just listen.' Kheyr-Mahmad came and took us to the festival pavilion he'd built, fed us and pleaded with us to drop the matter. That neighbour left us about fifteen years ago for Sheberghân.

Now Haji Tumân goes around collecting money, pleading with people to contribute. My father never pleaded; if anyone refused, he knocked them down and took it by force. The other day Nâder-shâh recalled him, saying that Jallât Khân would never be meddling with us if Parwiz was alive. But now that Parwiz is dead, Nâder-shâh's lacking a lieutenant and our Haji Jallât is old and confused, Jallât Khân sees his opportunity to get hold of that land.

---

[7] Current leading khan, son of Abdol-Ghâfur Khân and grandson of Gholâm-Rasul. Jallât Khân and Abdor-Rauf Khân are his close relatives.

[8] *Bacha-bâzi*, pederasty, has received much notoriety in the international press since the US invasion of 2001. For earlier analyses, see Centlivres (1992), Lindisfarne (1997).

'Upper' vs 'Lower' Konjek

Konjek, like many villages, is split physically, genealogically and politically into two 'quarters'; each now has a separate mosque. Tumân and the descendants of Ezzat's three eldest sons, Alârasân, Akhtar-khân and Yâr-Mahmad, live in the Lower (more downstream) Quarter; their rivals, descended from the three younger sons, Amir, Shir and Moshk, live in the Upper Quarter.

Gol-Ahmad and Neshtar (both from the Lower Quarter) give different accounts of the origins of the split. As so often, a khan (or seyyed or other holy man) was brought in to make peace.

Gol-Ahmad gives his version.

My father Haji Ghâfur was going to marry Shir's daughter Asan, but then he said, 'I won't have her.' It was when Moshk, Haji Amir and Shir forced us to take a woman. If we had a sister or a daughter, they tried to force an exchange on us. They started a dispute that's lasted until today. I'll be damned if I lie to you – they tricked us! Shir told my father: 'I'm your father-in-law. I don't want anything for my daughter, but I'll go to town to buy her some clothes.' He went and bought lots of clothes, then demanded the money for them: 'I got them for your wife!' So we paid him. Then some time later Shir said, 'You gave 7,000 rupees for Khalifa-Lulak's daughter, so give me 7,000 too, otherwise let my daughter go.' Father said, 'How can you ask for 7,000? Women here are 500 to 600; I paid 7,000 for that woman because I felt like it. I don't need your daughter. You can marry her anywhere, but not with a relative.' So they married her to the Nurzais in Maymana.

They hadn't done a formal betrothal ceremony. They'd agreed the exchange informally. That's what Afghans did in those days: we didn't do formal engagements, a man's word was enough. But it's not like that now: Afghanistan is beset with lies and tricks. You two, when you say something, you mean it; it was like that with us Afghans before.

Neshtar gives her version.

In Upper Konjek, Heydar's son Sarwar the water-master is their elder, he deals with their problems and solves their disputes. His paternal uncles are Haji Amir's sons Haji Wahâb, Gorey, Lâljân, Haji Tabu; Parwiz's son Pâdshâh's his first cousin. If there's any kind of problem with government, Sarwar's the one who deals with it. If there's a levy, he collects it.

It's about twenty-five to thirty years since our bad relations with Upper Konjek started. Haji Afzal and Haji Amir were first cousins [*or nephew/uncle*]. It was Afzal who bought all the village land from Tahsildâr, and then did *qawmi*: he was a good man: he gathered everybody and said, 'I've bought this land, let's all have some and settle in the same place.' So he gave land to all the *qawm*. Land was very cheap then: a *jerib* wasn't even 100 rupees. But if Afzal hadn't bought that land, who in the *qawm* would have bought it? He gave it away, including to Amir, saying, 'We're cousins.' Amir wasn't interested at first, he just took a little. But when land became valuable, he accused Afzal,

'It was far too little.' They argued, and Afzal said, 'I won't give you any more now.' Amir was offended, and took his family back to Kandahar.

They spent two years in Kandahar, then returned. When they got back Amir complained, 'Why do you have so much land and I have so little?' He demanded more. Afzal said, 'I bought it, not you, and I gave you enough to live on.' Haji Amir wasn't satisfied and the ill-feeling continued. They went to the mountains, where they had a big assembly with Haji Turabâz Khân. He arranged for Afzal to give his daughter Hamesh to Amir's son Madu, and Amir to give his daughter Mahbuba to Afzal's son Kamaroddin. Afzal also gave Amir a little more land. The matter was closed. Both parties were satisfied and reunited, their quarrel resolved. Later, though, Amir got upset again, went to Qataghan for a year, then returned.

Tumân's daughter Mesru married Amir's son Lâljân, for 30,000 rupees. It was a sordid mess, involving Moltân, Afzal's son Mahd-Karim's daughter. In truth, all that lot, from Khoday-râm's house upwards, are messy. Lâljân said, 'When my wife died, Mahd-Karim promised me his daughter.' Haji Ghâfur said, 'That's fine, you're no stranger, you can have her.' Lâljân seized on these words, and for two years he pressed for her, saying, 'Ghâfur's given me this girl.' But Mahd-Karim said, 'How can Ghâfur give you my daughter? She may be his niece, but what's it got to do with him? I won't give you Moltân.' Instead, he gave her to Tumân's brother Akhtar. At this, Lâljân made a formal complaint. It went on and on. Then Ghâfur – he was a good Haji – said, 'We don't want bad feeling,' and he gave Tumân's daughter Mesru to Lâljân.

Tumân said nothing, but when it came to brideprice, it was up to him; he insisted on 30,000 cash – a lot of money in those days, and he collected the lot, every single rupee. And he was difficult about the wedding, he kept putting it off. He was really angry with Lâljân.

It was the spring trek. Lâljân loaded fuel and rice and moved to Boghawi; Tumân had camped this side of it, you know the place, and Lâljân stopped at the bottom of the pass. He sent to Tumân, 'I've brought rice and fuel, but you're off to the mountains; why won't you let me have the wedding?' Tumân was very angry; he hadn't prepared any of the proper clothes and things; he told his son Khâni-âghâ and the others to do the wedding, and himself went off to town. So his brothers Akhtar and Dur-khân, uncle Jân-Mahmad and Khâni-âghâ gave the wedding party at Boghawi.

Next morning they went their separate ways. When people behave so badly to their own *qawm*, where's the good in any of it? We all see and talk to each other, things aren't that bad, but the ill-feeling remains; inside, in our hearts, we're really upset. Of course, they're happy they got a woman.

Pâdshâh/Tumân observes.

We used to be wealthier than the Upper-Quarter people – Tabu, Jallât and the others. We had ten times as much land and animals. Then each one of them got a yoke of oxen and started to plough our lands as sharecroppers. Now they're better off than us here below.

The fact is, the people who live above Khoday-râm's house aren't good people; they say all sorts of wild things. They're always picking quarrels. There wasn't a particular incident, but we found that, for example, if you agreed 10,000 for a girl from them, they'd be sure to swear on the Koran that it was 20,000. Before, we used to give and receive women, but now it's finished. None of us, as far as Khoday-râm's, give them women any more. Occasionally someone does, but on the whole we don't give or take. They give and take among themselves. We gave Lâljân one of my sisters; don't ask how much we've regretted that. We haven't given them any other woman, nor will we. And we don't take from them either. Nâder-shâh's Khârkash hasn't given them a single woman; nor do they take any woman from them. Khârkash give women to us and take from us, from Shahâboddin's house downwards. Beyond Shahâboddin's house, they neither give nor take women with Khârkash.

5

A Shepherd's Life[1]

In 1970 the Piruzai talk of themselves as mâldâr, *pastoralists, and there is still a strong feeling that the life of a shepherd* (shpun, chopân) *– unlike the stereotypes maintained by farmers and townspeople – is honourable, requiring capacities of responsibility, intelligence and decisiveness.*

This seems to be the chief moral of the following tale: that shepherds are not just the dumb hicks presumed by local townspeople – and by those in the tale.

The Tale of the Shepherd and the Judge

Maryam's fourth son, Baya-khân, is an excellent storyteller and records the most, and the best, folk tales for us. One August evening in 1972, after a hot and tiring day touring the steppe and dealing with visiting government officials, we sit with Baya-khân and a few neighbours, and he tells this tale.

Once upon a time there was a padishah who had a son and a daughter. The prince went out hunting every day. Meanwhile the princess was secretly having an affair with the vizier's son. They had regular assignations, and one day they agreed to run away together a few nights later; they arranged to pack their things, prepare some horses, and elope.

Now there was a shepherd who, three nights in a row, had the same dream; he thought, 'God has given me three pigeons' – for us, pigeons mean women. After the third dream, he abandoned his flock in the middle of the night and set off for the country where the princess was about to elope – and it was the very night this was to happen. Even though he didn't know the way, God led him to the padishah's castle, and there in front of it he saw a sofa and somebody asleep on it.

The princess had told the vizier's son, 'Bring a sofa and go to sleep on it; when I've got the horses, I'll bring all my things and a bag full of gold and silver; once I'm out of the gate, we'll ride off together.' And so, when the shepherd arrived that night, it was the vizier's son that he found asleep on the sofa. Without waking him, he pushed the vizier's son off the sofa, and went to sleep himself.

When the princess arrived with the horses, she shook the shepherd without saying a word, so as not to wake anybody else. He hadn't a clue what was happening but he got

[1] With nods to Rebanks (2015) and Hudson (1910).

up, keeping quiet – realizing it was a woman and that she was capable. She held his horse's reins tightly, telling him to mount. He still said nothing, as they both rode off.

The princess rode ahead; the shepherd was still light-headed with sleep and fell behind. Then, as the sun came up, she spotted his rustic sandals and realized what had happened. 'What a disaster!' she said, 'I thought I was eloping with the vizier's son, and look who God put in his place!' But she told herself, 'Oh well, that's fate!'

She tried to engage him in conversation to find out who he was, whether he was a cowherd, a shepherd, a camel-herder, or what. But he wasn't answering.

Soon they came across a large herd of cattle grazing in a broad meadow; she said, 'How nice it'd be to have a house here, and to drive a herd of contented cattle home from such rich pasture towards evening!' The shepherd said nothing.

A little further on they came to a field thick with thistles, where one could easily get lost; she said, 'What a nice life it'd be to have a herd of camels, and to bring them home of an evening!' He didn't utter a word.

Then they came to a grass-covered steppe, and she said, 'If one were a shepherd grazing sheep in a place like this, how fat they'd be!' He answered, 'By God, you're right, sheep would really get fat here!' So the princess said, 'You're a shepherd, for sure!'

Next they stopped at a spring, where she got the shepherd to wash himself all over with soap and put on the clothes she'd brought – belonging to the vizier's son – until he looked like a proper gentleman. As he was bathing in the pool, his hand fell on a stone, which he picked up. It was a jewel, worth a padishah's ransom.

By afternoon they came to another country. He told the princess, 'I'll go ahead into town and get a room, you wait here; we'll go in together later.' She said, 'We've plenty of money; get us a nice room with carpets and rugs.' The shepherd knew nothing about carpets, and he got a room with sackcloth on the floor. He came back and said, 'I've got us a nice room with carpets spread around, but it was very cheap.' They went to the room, but when the princess saw it, she said, 'You silly shepherd, there are no carpets here, this is sackcloth! Don't you know the difference?' They found another room. The princess was very beautiful, and everyone who saw her fell in love with her.

They spent some time in that country. The padishah took the shepherd on as his servant. Every day he'd go off to work for the padishah, and in the evening he'd come home. After some time he said to his companion, 'Woman, for many nights we've been living in sin; this won't do, let's get married.' She said, 'This evening I'll cook something; you go to the mosque, find someone to marry us, but don't bring anybody with blue eyes or a red beard; anyone else will do.'

That evening, in spite of what his wife had said, he sent a judge with a red beard. The moment the judge saw the woman he was smitten: 'By God, this is an outstanding woman! She's too good for this fellow, he's just a simple man, from nowhere; I must kill him and take her for myself, nobody will say anything.'

After dinner, the judge said, 'This is not a good evening for the marriage; I've been working hard today, I'm very tired.' They said, 'Fine, judge-seb, come back another day.'

The shepherd continued as the padishah's servant. His wife told him, 'Why don't you give the padishah the jewel you found?' So one morning the servant took the jewel to the padishah, who was sitting with the vizier and the judge. He brought it on a tray and placed it before the padishah, saying, 'Please accept this present, Your Majesty.'

The padishah picked it up and was astonished at its brilliance: 'Look at it; it's so bright, we'd never find anything like it in my country; where did it come from?' He was delighted, and that night, when he placed it by his bed, it lit up the whole room like a gas-lamp.

The judge said, 'Your majesty, wouldn't it be nice if you had a pair of these jewels, one for here and one to keep in your bedroom, to light up both places. Why don't you get him to bring another one.' This mischievous judge was hoping that the servant would be killed in the search for another jewel, leaving his wife a widow, so that he could marry her. But he didn't tell the padishah what a nice wife the fellow had.

Anyway, the padishah told his servant, 'Go and find another such jewel; if you have one at home, fine; otherwise find one somewhere else, so that I can have a pair, that'd really be nice.' The servant told him, 'I haven't got another jewel, that was the only one.' The padishah said, 'Too bad, but I must have another one.' 'Your Majesty, give me a few days off, I'll go and see if I can find one somewhere.' So the padishah gave him a week's leave.

He went home, downcast. His wife asked him what was the matter. He told her what the padishah had said: 'He liked the jewel so much that he wants me to find him another one.' She said, 'God will help you find another jewel. But it'll take some time; have you taken a few days off?' He said, 'Yes, I've taken a week off.' His wife said, 'Go to the pool where we swam, climb up to the source of the spring, and beside it you'll see a cave; go inside and you'll meet a *pari* [*fairy*]; there are lots of houses and gardens, and there's a seven-headed *div* [*demon*] who has a room full of jewels; the jewel you found must have come down to the pool from the spring. Anyway, that *div* has a room full of them. With God's help, if you don't get killed, you'll bring another back.'

He made his way back to the spring, found the cave and went in. There he found a country with forests, gardens, houses and everything, all in bright daylight under the sky. There was a *pari* sitting beside a *div*, which was fast asleep. Now *divs* sleep for seven days at a time, and this one had just started; the *pari* had served it several pots of pilaw, it had scoffed the lot and gone to sleep, the first of seven days of sleep.

When the *pari* saw the man, first she laughed then she cried. He asked, 'Why are you laughing and why are you crying?' She answered, 'I've never seen a man before; but I was crying because this *div* will swallow you in one gulp; it has seven heads, you can't escape it!'

He answered, 'Fine, if that's my fate.' He was exhausted from his journey, so the *pari* made him some nice pilaw and filled him up, then slept with him for three nights, and he rested for three days. On the fourth day he said, 'Find me a good sword. If it's my fate, the *div* will kill me; if not, I'll kill it while it's asleep.'

He took the sword she gave him, said *bismillah*! and cut off one of the *div*'s heads. The *div* didn't wake up. *Divs* sleep really deeply; we have this saying, 'So-and-so won't wake up, he sleeps like a *div*.' He cut off four more heads, and only two were left when the *div* awoke. They fought, but the *pari* helped by knocking the *div* off its feet, and together they managed to cut off the two heads.

He realized, 'I've only two more days' leave, I must go.' She said, 'If you're going, I'm coming too; I've nothing to stay for here in this wilderness. Over there's the room full of jewels, go and take as many as you want.' So he filled his bags with jewels, saddled his horse, put the *pari* behind him, and they sped home to the country where his wife was, arriving the following afternoon.

The padishah heard that his servant had returned; 'We'll see whether or not he's brought what I asked him to bring.' When people came to greet him, the *pari* covered her face – she was so beautiful that if she showed herself people would be struck down. They went home and had a meal. At nightfall, he took another jewel, only one, and brought it to the padishah, who was very pleased.

After a few days, his wife and the *pari* both insisted, 'It's not right for us to be living with you without being properly married. Go and get someone to marry us; a proper person, without a red beard, not someone like the judge.' So they put some food on to cook, and he went to the mosque. He looked all round, but he sent back the same judge. His wife said, 'You fool, why did you send this fellow again?'

The judge arrived and was bowled over by the women. He thought, 'He's brought another one, even more beautiful than the first – or is it the other way round? He's not worthy of them. There aren't such women anywhere in our country.' Once again he said, 'It's Wednesday, it's not a good night for the marriage ceremony, let's do it another night.'

In the morning, the judge went to the padishah and said, 'He has an amazing wife, and he's brought home another one, just as beautiful; he has two wives that are too good for him.'

But the *pari* understood, 'This judge is up to something; we must frustrate his plans.' She told her husband, 'Go and collect all the feathers and hair that you can find – chicken, turkey, goose, sheep's wool, goat hair – and bring them here.' Out he went and got every kind of hair and wool and filled a room with the stuff.

Then she told him to dig a pond near the room, large enough to drown a man. When he'd done that, she said, 'Go to town, buy up all the syrup you can find, bring it home and fill the pond with it.' So he bought up all the syrup in town – they had lots of money, so he paid over the market rate. Then they filled the pond with syrup, enough to drown someone who fell in.

When that was done, the women hid him for three days, 'Don't show yourself; if anybody asks, we'll say you've gone to your own country.' On the third day, they sent someone in the afternoon to the judge saying, 'Come, our husband's dead, there's nobody else, we want you, come and we'll get married.'

The judge was thrilled, 'These women like me, they've even proposed to me themselves, they've sent someone to fetch me so we can get married!' He came and ate his dinner; then they did the marriage contract, and he told the women, 'Lay my place, I want to go to bed now.' They said, 'Take off your clothes ready for bed, we won't let anybody else in.' They'd told their husband, 'Stay hidden until the moment he takes his clothes off, then come out directly and grab him by the neck.'

So the moment the judge took off his clothes, the husband leapt out, grabbed him and put a rope around his neck, saying, 'You've had it, I'm going to kill you!' Then he dragged him to the pond full of syrup and threw him in, and he was completely covered in the stuff. Then he pulled the judge out, took him to the room full of feathers and told him to lie down in them. He lay in the feathers, which stuck to his body, covering him so that only his two eyes were showing. Finally, he took a stick, covered in syrup and feathers, and stuck it up the judge's backside. Then he bound the judge tightly in chains, and that very night he telephoned the padishah and said, 'I've captured a *seyyes!*' – a *seyyes* is a kind of monster, covered in all kinds of feathers and hair, from chickens, sheep, donkeys, cows, goats, foxes and wolves; a ghastly sight that terrifies people.

The padishah was pleased with his servant, 'What a great servant he is; we're raising his wages.' Early in the morning, he gathered his courtiers and told them, 'This servant has captured a *seyyes*, let's go and have a look at it. It's several years since anybody captured one; people go hunting them but can't find them; many people have heard of them, but haven't seen one.'

The servant also announced what was going to happen that morning. He put a rope round the judge's neck and dragged him towards the castle, completely covered in hair and feathers, except his eyes. All the courtiers and the people came out to see the captured *seyyes*. The servant pulled him this way and that by the rope round his neck, saying, 'See how nicely my *seyyes* dances!' The people too were shoving the judge about, thoroughly humiliating him.

The judge's wife came too. She'd told people, 'My husband's missing, he hasn't left a trace.' But when she saw the eyes of the *seyyes*, she told herself – not the people – 'It's him!'

In the evening, the padishah's daughter told her father, 'Bring us the *seyyes*, we want to see it too.' The padishah's servants put chains around its neck and brought it into the castle to his daughter. She had many maidservants, all unmarried and high-spirited. After a grand meal they set on the *seyyes*, dragging him around by the neck; some of them jumped on him, some kicked him. He tried to open his mouth, but they knocked him down – and what could he say? He couldn't admit he was the judge. The women played merry hell with him all evening.

The judge's wife said to herself, 'Let me free my husband, then let's get away and go somewhere else. Nobody else recognized him, but he's my husband after all.' In the middle of the night she came and managed somehow to free her husband and get him home. He had a good bath, and put on some clothes, then they escaped and fled to another country.

In the morning the padishah asked his daughter, 'Where's the *seyyes*? Let's have some more fun with it.' They discovered that it was missing. After some enquiries they found that the judge's family had fled too, and people put two and two together. The servant told the whole story, 'My wives got him to come; he'd failed to marry us; they hid me, and we played this trick on him.'

Then the padishah made his servant judge in place of the other one.

And they went that way and I came this way, and brought you the story.

The Flocks

The Piruzai raise two main sheep breeds, both for market sales: Karakuli (called digil*) for their astrakhan skins (they slaughter male lambs soon after birth, sell their skins, and eat the meat); and Arabi for meat (male lambs being sold for slaughter in their first or second year). With both, the breeding ewes are the core of the flock. Other breeds are* *recognized; goats, kept for milk and hair and as flock-leaders, are less than 10 per cent of the flocks.*

Early in our stay, the cousins Gol-Ahmad and Pâdshâh talk about the different breeds.

(*Gol-Ahmad*) – In Kandahar, all our sheep were Kandahari, there wasn't a single Karakuli. When we came here to Turkistan, we brought our Kandaharis, but they soon finished. We let Arabi rams run among them; when you cross an Arabi ram with a Kandahari ewe, you get an Arabi lamb. Then somebody found a Karakuli ram, and all the sheep here turned into them. Lambskins rose in price, people sold them for 200, 300, 400, 500 rupees.

The Kandahari's best for meat. The Hazâragi's meat is good too. Third is the Karakuli, which is best for lambskins. Fourth is the Arabi. Fifth is the Qataghani.

Hazâragi ewes are tops for milk; they lamb twice a year, so they give lots of milk, twelve months of the year, winter and summer. Hazâras milk three times a day: dawn, midday and afternoon. Their pastures are very rich, full of fat. If a Hazâra has 20 ewes, he'll get 10 seer of butter, which he can sell – we buy it from them. But 500 of our ewes won't make 10 seer of butter.

Arabi sheep also give plenty of milk, but the Karakuli is number one in Afghanistan for lambskins worth 500 rupees. The Arabi can't match that, however much effort and expense you put in. If an Arabi lamb dies, the skin fetches 10 or 15 rupees at most. We keep only a few Arabi male lambs, to sell for meat. Some people have several hundred Arabi ewes, and they make both male and female lambs *barapay*, that is, they put them straight out to graze with their mothers. Then in June they sell the males to the dealers for 500 to 700 rupees, and make a pile of cash. But not many do that. Throughout the Piruzai, there isn't one person with a whole flock of Arabi sheep. Kohestâni people do it, like Haji Yaqub, who has four flocks of 700 head each, one of piebald Arabi, one of black Arabi, one of black Karakuli, one of grey Karakuli. Another is Nawâb the Shinwâri, who has 500 head of Arabi. But we Piruzai Afghans in this steppe have very few; some people have 50 or 100 head, but nobody has more than 200 – Haji Tabu has about 200 Arabi, and about 100 Karakuli, that's all.

(*Pâdshâh*) – At first we Afghans didn't understand, we were primitive and simple-minded; our Kandahari sheep were a different breed, and we herded them differently. The Turkmen people had long kept these Karakuli sheep that we now have. When they were on migration, they herded the lambs separately from their mothers. We Afghans learned from them: as my father told you, we all watched what the Turkmens did with their sheep, how they herded the ewes on migration and how they milked them whenever they pitched camp, then churned the milk into butter.

There are differences between Arabi and Karakuli sheep. If there's grass in a hollow or a meadow, the Arabi stay put; they graze and then lie down, like cattle. With Karakuli, if you let them go they keep moving from hollow to hollow, like deer. In winter, if you put fodder out for them, Arabi sheep eat more than Karakuli; they have larger stomachs, they eat like cattle. When you let in the rams, you keep Arabi and Karakuli separate and put the rams with their respective ewes. You separate them for a month or two, then put them together again. Some people separate them for over two months. Otherwise there are no differences between them, when grazing or herding them at night for example.

They also differ, though, in when they mate. In a hard winter, if an Arabi ewe dies, the lambskin won't sell; it'll fetch 20 rupees at most. So you put the Arabi ram in a couple of weeks later than the Karakuli ram, so that when winter comes the foetuses will be small; they won't grow too soon, and the cold won't get into the mothers' bodies. But if a Karakuli ewe dies, a foetus's skin will fetch even more than a live lamb's: several hundred rupees, maybe 1,000.

And after lambing there's another difference. When an Arabi ewe gives birth, you leave the lamb with it, and as the *mozdur* grazes the ewes, it learns to move after its mother and quickly grows up. With the Karakuli, you kill the males, and some people kill the grey ewe-lambs, for the skins. Nobody kills the black ewe-lambs; you keep them in the house for 35 or 40 days, then a small child will take them out to the steppe, to teach them to graze, until spring migration time.

In earlier times, sheep and their skins weren't worth much, and shepherds had little trouble looking after them. There were few thieves, plenty of grass, plenty of *barakat*. A good skin fetched 20 or 30 rupees. The price rose, gradually, to 100, 200. Now skins go for 600, even 1,000 rupees – even poor ones fetch 500. Meanwhile the place has lost its *barakat*, fodder and hay are scarce, and it gets worse every year, not better. Earlier, it was better in every respect.

There used to be more herds than now. My grandfather had two large herds; so did Haji Abdol-Nabi; everybody had many more animals. The herds were the same size as now: 500, 600, 800 head, sometimes 1,000 head if we joined them together. Some people kept separate herds of black and grey sheep, as a matter of prestige. Some had three herds, one with white heads, or some special markings. People would say, 'So-and-so has four herds: one piebald, one grey, one black, one red', and so on. This doesn't happen any more; except for the Shinwâris, over towards Mazâr. Here too, some people have two herds, but they no longer care about separating colours; they mix the grey and the black.

After the terrible 1972 winter, Baya-khân tells more.

Arabi and Karakuli rams differ. Three years ago, when Karakuli lambskins fetched only 100 or 150 rupees, people favoured Arabi sheep, which have huge fat tails and plenty of meat; when they're mature they sell well, better than Karakuli. If you kept the Arabi lambs with their mothers, they drank plenty of milk and got fat, and you could sell them for 200 to 400. But the trouble with Arabi is that if they die in a bad winter, nobody's interested in their skins. They fetch 20 to 30 rupees, while Karakuli skins now sell well, so people prefer Karakuli to Arabi: an unborn Karakuli lambskin can fetch up to 1,000. This winter some people made a lot of money from skins. Haji Wahâb has 400 ewes that survived and lambed; fewer than 100 skins were poor, so he had 300 lambskins to sell, but the prices were so high in London that they fetched on average 1,000 rupees, whether grey or black. So his 300 skins made 3 lacs of rupees. That's what's so good about Karakuli. But if skins get cheap again, the Arabi will return to favour.

If you put a Karakuli ram to an Arabi ewe, the lamb is neither Arabi nor Karakuli, it's a *karghoza*, a hybrid. I'll show you one: it's very fat, with a huge rear end, a very good tail. It's best to keep it for meat; the lambskin isn't worth much, perhaps 200 rupees; it'll never be worth as much as a Karakuli. With some ewes it works well, and you get nice whorls in the fur. If you put an Arabi ram to a Karakuli ewe, it just ruins the skin. Everything depends on the ram.

Another breed is Maymanagi, khaki-coloured, properly called *shotori*, camel-coloured. Once my father brought two rams from Maymana. We let them run with the ewes but for three years this kind of good khaki colour didn't come out. The first year, the lambs were all grey or black or brown. When you let them breed among themselves, the lambs are camel-khaki. Their wool is good, but the best thing is the skins, which are brown with a nice texture; they fetch a good price, more than the Karakuli. They're used for hats.

Another variety is Siâh-sur (dark-brown). In the old days, they say, a rich man had a flock of these. When the lambs were born, the *mozdur* brought them in every night. One day he found a strange lamb, vivid brown. He showed it to his boss, who said, 'We won't kill this one, let it grow up as a ram.' All Maymana camel-khakis descend from that ram.

Some ewes are eight-tooth, most are six-tooth. An eight-tooth ewe is better, they say, because it doesn't age as quickly as a six-tooth; it'll bear lambs for eight years. If someone buys a good eight-tooth sheep, people comment on it. The eight-tooth aren't a separate breed, it comes from the ram; they're found in all breeds. As an eight-tooth lamb grows up it keeps two of its baby teeth while the others come out. You can see the last two baby teeth until it's two years old, then in the third year it'll lose them and get new ones.

Some sheep are *du-shkamba*, with two rumens inside their stomach instead of one. When a ewe gives birth, if the lambskin's particularly light in colour, people say, 'This one's a *du-shkamba*, let's keep it.' Others prefer to kill it. A *du-shkamba* drinks its mother's milk and soon gets very fat, but after you get to the mountains it can't fill both its huge rumens, so it stays hungry. It drinks a lot of water, and every day its rumens get bigger and it gets thinner; no matter how you care for it, feed it barley and stuff, it won't recover; it'll die. Some people say you can tell from the lamb's tongue; if it's black, it's not *du-shkamba*. I think that's a myth: how can you tell what the insides are like? Generally, though, *du-shkamba* are rare among black sheep; they're commoner in grey ones; perhaps four to five ewe-lambs from 100 ewes. It's chance. Some people get many of them, some a few, some none.

After Parwiz's son Pâdshâh lost all his sheep this year, he bought twenty old ewes, for the skins of the foetuses. He put the ram with them, and if he grazes them well they'll get very fat; then in early winter he'll sell the ewes for 1,500 or 2,000 rupees for their meat, but first he'll remove the foetuses from their bellies, to sell for their skins. A foetus-skin, *takir*, isn't fully formed; it's only just started to make lines and whorls. It fetches a lot of money in early winter. You get the ewe pregnant, fatten it, and it's worth up to 2,000 rupees each for both the meat and especially the lambskin.

The government taxes the sheep; once a year, they collect a rupee per head. Soldiers come to the elders, who hand the money over. That's what happened last time. Everybody's sheep are registered in their name. Or rather, all village sheep are registered in the headman, my father's name. This village was registered years ago for (I think)

2,000 rupees, and they collected one for each sheep. But of course many people understated their holdings in the register; for example, if you had 500 sheep, you had 200 or 300 written down. How could the government know? But we haven't paid for two years now. It's up to the *wakils*; they've been meeting in parliament to discuss it. Some *wakils* don't want the responsibility of collecting the tax and passing it on, but our *wakil*, Kamâloddin Khân of Sar-e-pol, is willing to do so. But he says, 'Why should these hard-working, hungry people pay taxes? They've already enough trouble with their sheep.'

The Nomad Trail

In autumn and winter the Piruzai flocks are out in the steppe (chol) with only hired shepherds and perhaps anxious owners for company. Early March until early May is the best season: rain brings up fresh grazing, lambs are born and spring wool is shorn. Three-quarters of the Piruzai join the steppe-camps to provide the labour required and to supervise the collection of lambskins. Even those without sheep go to stay with relatives and enjoy the flowers and the festive spring atmosphere. They hold wedding parties and other ceremonies. As the heat sets in, members of one-third of the households prepare for the trek up (aylâk-bâlâ) to Siâh-band, 'Black-range', the central mountains. Everyone else returns to the villages for the summer's agricultural activities. (See Map D)

The 300-km trek south takes up to a month, the mâldâr moving almost daily until they arrive by early June in the Lâl-o-Sar-jangal district of Ghor province. While there, as the animals fatten on the rich grazing, young men and women are busy with milk and wool processing. In late July they start the return trek north (aylâk-neshib) to the villages, to supervise or participate in a series of harvests. Piruzai much prefer the return trek to the hard spring slog. Often only the family and the camels go home at this time, leaving the shepherds with the flocks in the mountains for another month; there is still grazing there, and then crop-stubble in the valleys on the gradual trek down. In the steppe there is little forage before the autumn rains.

These treks are essentially 'transhumance', like that common in parts of Europe and North America: stock-keepers move their animals to new grazing grounds in a seasonal cycle of changing altitude; the difference here being that in most cases mâldâr families move too, to help with herding but also to process the milk and wool products. In addition, most mâldâr conduct large and small trade along the treks, in both directions, establishing complex relations with village trading partners (âshnay – 'acquaintances') along the route. Other attractions of the trek for the mâldâr include the abundance of fresh water, at least in spring, various edible or medicinal plants, and, on the return trek, a succession of fruit harvests: apricots, grapes, melons. But there are discomforts and dangers, especially in spring: rain, flash-floods, snow and ice on the high passes, narrow cliff paths, bridges over swollen rivers.

Baya-khân accompanies us on the trek to the mountains in spring 1971. One May afternoon, halfway through the trek, he describes the route and events that typically occur. First, he stresses the need to start an important move on the right day.

When the time comes to move out to the spring camp, people who understand the calculations, like my father and Big-Haji, look for a certain star, and every day they discuss where it's rising. If it's right ahead, they say, 'Don't move today, it may hit somebody, or a camel, and they'll die.' Uncle Jân-Mahmad had a white camel with a two-year-old calf. Big-Haji told Jân-Mahmad, 'It's not yet spring; the star's right ahead: you mustn't move today.' Jân-Mahmad said, 'I'll trust to luck, I'm going.' So he set off, and as he was going down the little pass to the main valley the star struck that camel, and down it fell. It was finished; they had to slaughter it. They told people back here, and they had a public distribution of the meat. Big-Haji asked, 'Why didn't you believe me?' Jân-Mahmad was very sorry, but we all said, 'It's just as well the star didn't strike a person; the camel's taken the fall for you!'

Tumân later explains the astrological reckoning involved.

On certain days we don't move, that is, from anywhere we've stayed for more than a few days, from the village to the spring campsite, or from there to the mountains. There's a star with a cycle of ten days. On the first and second day of the new moon, it's in the east; on the third and fourth it's in the south; on the fifth and sixth it's in the west; on the seventh and eighth it's in the north; on the ninth it's on the earth, on the tenth it's in the sky. First, we don't move on the two days when the star's straight ahead, in the direction we're headed. That's very important. The star will certainly harm anybody who moves then – his property, his animals, his family, or himself. Also, we don't move on the ninth or the tenth. On the ninth, it's very hard to get the tent-pegs into the ground; on the tenth the end of the ridge-pole's hard to shift.

On the eleventh the cycle begins again: the star's in the east, and so on, round the cycle until the thirtieth and then again the next month. The cycle repeats without stopping, every night, every season, twelve months of the year. On four days of the cycle, we can't move, on six we can. The star isn't visible; you tell from the calendar, from a book. We don't know where the star is, but we know it's there. It must be in some corner of the world. It's where the sun rises; then over where the earth ends, a corner of the heavens; then over here where the sun sets. The heavens have four corners; it spends time in each corner, then on the ninth day, I imagine, it goes to the earth's navel, the middle; then on the tenth it rises into one of the seven heavens – I don't know which.

That's the only star we reckon by. In the Book, it has a good Arabic name; we call it simply *storey*, the star. But there's another time we don't move: during the month we call Asan-Oseyn, when those Emams were killed: Muharram. In the first ten days of that month we don't move, nor do we wash our hair or put on new clothes, and we never have ceremonies like engagements or weddings. After noon on the tenth, we carry on as normal.

Then again on the first thirteen days of the month of Safar we absolutely never move, wherever the star is. Those days are very dangerous for us. This has been so from the beginning, since Adam.

Otherwise, we're free to make a new move any time.

Baya-khân's narrative continues.

For the spring trek the lambs move and graze together with the ewes. Some people put three men with the herd, or four if it's very large. My father tells how, years ago, before

I was born, they'd herd ewes and lambs separately on the trek. They milked the ewes every day. When they pitched camp, they tied the ewes to the milking-rope and milked them, before letting the lambs join them. Then they separated them again: the mothers went with the barren ewes, and the lambs with the rams. We don't do that any more. Those days were tough. People were rather simple-minded! Now lambs stay with their mothers until they reach the mountains.

Our first move's from the spring pastures to Neymadân. The sheep are very tired from the heat and the trek. At nightfall the women strike the tents and we pack everything, and at dawn we load the camels. Next we move to Boghawi and pitch the tents there; the sheep are still very tired. Some people look to the horses, some to the camels, some visit their village contacts to collect debts. On to Sukhta, where we give the horses fodder, but the sheep are tired again; and to Chayrak, where the camels go up onto the mountains. Some people go to the village to collect debts, others to get fodder. In the afternoon we strike the tents and that night we move on to Chenâr. There, some go for fodder, some go with the sheep, and we strike the tents again in the afternoon. Everybody's very tired. At dawn we load the camels, and on to Ekhtiâr; in the evening we strike the tents and at dawn we load again and move up through Sro-tanga [*Red-gorge*].

Aunt Keshmir [*Haji Ghâfur's wife*] doesn't sleep, she likes to be up first, to be at the head of the whole train. Sometimes she manages to get in front, sometimes we do, or someone else does.

Then we move to Wuzha-dara [*Dry-valley*]. The sheep go up onto the Deldel range, the train heads for Sang-e-solâkh [*Rock-hole*]. We camp at Sarghân, where there's no water, and Ajab [*Keshmir's son*] has a fight with the local Aymâqs. Then we go on down into Sang-e-solâkh, where there's no fodder for the horses; they and the camels go hungry. More fights with the Aymâqs – their youths are very feisty. We move on to Gholduri; some people pitch their tents there, some don't; in the afternoon we strike them, then at dawn we load. Abdol [*Ghâfur's brother*] and Safar [*his son*] are at the head of the train.

We make it up to Târikak, then we come down into the Cherâs plain. The *mozdurs* bring the herds into camp, and collect their food rations. *Mâldâri* is really hard work, it never stops.

From Cherâs we move on to the Esmeydân [*Horse-plain*] meadows where the horses can graze, and where the Kabuli traders will camp later on. We pass by Teymur-shâh Khân's place. There's plenty of water, we fill up; then up the pass and on to Mordâr-hawz [*Foul-mere*], where there's browse for the camels but nothing for the horses. Some pitch their tents, some don't. At dawn we migrate, and come down to Shorshorak [*Little-falls*], on the Kâshân river. There are lots of trees on the riverbanks, and we let the camels loose to browse. Some people go hunting – in Kâshân there are wild sheep, and lots of partridges. We move on to Ghozba-khâna village, where some go and collect flour they're owed. The river's deep, impossible for camels to ford now, so we use the bridge near the village. Then we migrate on to Spina-kala [*White-castle*], Larwandak and Dutâ'i. Some collect asafoetida [*anj*], others cut branches to make into tent-pegs or spits or even tent poles, which might come in useful in Siâh-band.

Then we move up to Gerdi-chaman [*Round-meadow*], where there are lots of onions; some people collect them, others collect branches for tent-pegs. We load the camels – not at night but mid-morning – and start up the Dangak pass, arriving the other side in the afternoon. We don't pitch the tents, but early in the morning we move on down to Ghwori-china [*Oily-spring*]. We stay three days there before finally moving to our summer campsite.

After a month in Siâh-band, we move to another campsite where the men shear the sheep, then the women make felts: *krâst* and *netsey*. They get tired from carding the wool, colouring it and rolling the felt; it's hard work, and their hands get very sore.

Ten days later we move back to the foot of Dangak pass. The horses have been grazing freely for a month or more. Everybody collects the horses, tethers them and gives them fodder; some people beat thorns with sticks to soften them for the horses to eat.

The return trek starts. We move up and over the pass and pitch camp at Qabr-e-chopân [*Shepherd's-grave*]. Grazing's abundant, horses and camels get full, and people are happy, saying 'We're going home!' Coming down is better than going up: the weather's pleasant, there's no rain; every day you get closer to home, it's a happy time.

On to Kâshân, with its woods and plenty of grass. Some people cut tent-pegs or walking-sticks. We go down the river, stopping at Qayrâq for several days. There you find raisins, grapes, walnuts. Qayrâq's a rock, where people sharpen their knives and ploughshares; it's also a shrine. It's on this side of the river. In spring the river's too full and the camels can't get by, so we go over the mountains, but on the way down the river's lower, so the camel-train comes along the river gorge.

From there we pass Esmeydân, stopping by the Kabuli traders' camp. The Kabulis are Tâghâr, Sak, Niâzi; they put their tents up there, and people call it Bazaar-jay [*Market-place*]. There's a huge meadow where horses can graze their fill. If you have skins and things to sell, you take them to the Kabulis, who'll pay with cloth or cash. People buy all kinds of cloth from them: *jin, gol-e-bahâr, chit, san, tafta*.

Moving on, we camp at the bottom of Reg-row [*Scree-slope*]. That night, Keshmir gets up very early, she can't sleep, she's thinking of coming home to her husband. In the middle of the night we start the long climb up Reg-row. When we reach the top, the Deldel range, it's very cold. We pitch camp in that little gully, but we don't put up the tents. We turn the camels onto the plentiful thorns there. But we tether the horses to eat the fodder we've brought up from Esmeydân.

Next move is all the way to Hazâr-qoruq [*Thousand-meadows*], where again we let the camels go, while we give the horses what's left of the fodder. From there some people go straight down into the Alâr valley, others carry on via Mayda-Qâsem and stop there. These are the most difficult stages on the return trek, on Deldel, between Esmeydân and Kachan. It's bitterly cold up there, with icy winds.

Down in Alâr we find some stubble for the horses; in the evening we bring them straw. As for the camels, we let them roam the hillsides; they soon fill themselves. Next stop is at Zeynadir, where apricots are abundant; the Aymâq people bring them and we give wool in exchange, two-, three- or four-for-one by weight. If you're giving salt, it goes two-for-one; perhaps one-for-one.

Then we arrive in Kachan, where we spend several days. There are masses of apricots. We tether the horses in camp and give them hay, but we send the camels up to roam free on the mountains; every other day we check on them. Everyone has Kachani friends, and gets hay from their yards; your friend gives it free, because he owes you money. Straw and hay are plentiful on the return trek.

Down in Kachan the air's warmer, there's plenty of grass, people are happy; it's like our own home territory. Every day we get further down and it's more enjoyable.

From Kachan we move to Ekhtiâr, then Chenâr, which is nicer. We get grapes from our vineyards there, and fetch lucerne for the horses. Next stop is Chayrak, where we don't stay long, perhaps a day or two; everyone gets hay from his friend's house, and we let out the camels. Then on to Sukhta; there the camels get full, there's straw for the horses. Next stop is Boghawi, where we stay a couple of days, letting the camels out on the hilltops. We ask about the irrigation schedule: if it's Sar-e-pol's turn, we go on, if not, we stay at Boghawi until the Sar-e-pol turn comes. The final stop is by Jangal-bâgh; the next day we arrive home in Khârkash, and everyone goes to his own place.

All the people in Siâh-band are Hazâra. Mountain people have a harder life than we do. Their winters last for six or seven months; they stay inside their houses, where they work, they cook their food, and they sleep with their animals, which live inside all day long. The winters are really cold, and sometimes the snow destroys their crops. Their soil's very stony. They grow grain both up on the plateau and down in the valleys. They harvest the crops and bring them down in sacks, then thresh in front of their houses; it's a lot of trouble. They also bring mountain grasses and thresh them, and fill the houses and store rooms with hay.

The people of Kâshân and Esmeydân are Hazâra too, but their winters are kinder, and the land is good and warm. People can't go up on Deldel in winter, it's too cold; a horse would get lost in the snow. Down in Kachan, the people are Aymâq, as far as Dehmana. The Kachanis grow all their grain up on the plateau; they harvest it then bring it down for threshing – it's hard work. After Dehmana, the people are Uzbek, Breti, Afghan, all kinds.

Maryam didn't come with us in 1971, but she has vivid (if confused) memories of the days when she did go on the trek.

We'd all go to Siâh-band together; we all camped in one place and it was like a wedding. We'd break camp and pitch camp together. As dawn broke, you'd see all the caravans passing, the camels linked together, their loads covered in fine cloths and trappings; the men rode horses, some of them donkeys. That's the way we went, as a clan. We carried a standard, *sar-neyza* – a turban tied to a rifle-barrel. People would come out to watch us go by, all the way to the mountains. When we stopped, the men would do target-practice – as you've seen – setting up stones and shooting at them, *tak-a-tak-a-tak*. In Chenâr, every evening the women sang songs; what fun, what times we had!

The ewes lambed, we killed many for the skins; there was plenty of meat and cheese. The camels too had given birth. They sheared the sheep, we collected the wool, made ropes, halters for the camels. It was time for the spring trek. I struck the tent, and removed several strips to make the tent smaller. My sons Pâdshâh, Baya-khân and Nasib took the sheep to Siâh-band. Pâdshâh's wife Pâkhâl and I usually went together; we churned butter, we carded the wool and made felts, we made ghee and *krut*, dried whey, we did everything, and then we trekked home. Then one year we sent Pâkhâl alone, while my co-wife Pâkiza and I stayed behind. That was the only year Pâkhâl went alone, and I haven't been since. Pâkiza hasn't been often; once or twice she went with my daughter Zeytun. Two or three years Pâkiza and I went together, and we made felts and milked the sheep and made *krut* together. Her sons were small and so were mine. We rode on the camels and made a real show with the load-covers. We made nice halters for the camels, with bells that jingled as we went along. We moved at night and often fell asleep.

One year I went to Siâh-band alone. Pâkiza stayed behind with Tumân. Tumân sent my sons Khâni-âghâ, Pâdshâh, Darwiza and my daughters Zeytun and Mesru with me, and my son Kayum was newly born. In Siâh-band I pegged down two milking-ropes; I milked the ewes at one end and Khâni-âghâ the other. I churned and churned the milk, I made 15 or 20 maunds of ghee, and so much *krut* that it covered the top of the tent; I did this all by myself.

I'd just boiled up the whey for *krut*, when Pâkhâl's brother Payz came. I cut up some meat and put it on to cook, then I went back to rolling whey-balls. There was such a wind! Siâh-band is always windy – those days we camped up on top of the range, along with Dur-khân, Jân-Mahmad and Haji Ghâfur. It's only two years since we came down to the Valley bottom where we camp now.

I was rolling whey-balls for *krut* when my infant son Kayum got burned. I'd just left the *krut* to go fix the trivet in the hearth, when he came up and the cooking-pot overturned and burned his foot. The poor boy howled in pain. I couldn't do anything but bind up his foot and sit with him.

We Afghan women endured many hardships in those times. There was a lot this year too. We struck and pitched camp in the dark. Kayum called out, 'For God's sake let's not go to Siâh-band!'

I saw many such things when I was alone in Siâh-band. My work never stopped. Those years are gone; what do women do now? Nothing!

Once on the way down my son fell into a ditch. We had a wonderful camel, as clever as a human – the red camel we gave to Châri; it's dead now. When we left Spina-kala in Kâshân, he was riding that camel. We set off in the dark, and it was still pitch black when we reached an enormous ditch above a spring. You couldn't see your hand in front of you. The boy fell into the ditch, under the camel's feet, but the camel lifted its feet carefully and avoided stepping on him. Talâk [*Tumân's sister*] cried out, 'A boy's fallen into the ditch!' – and we got him out.

The same morning there were many partridges about. The men galloped after them as fast as they could. The children were laughing, men and women yelling; it was a real party, we had a good time. The camel bells were jingling; Mamazi and Saduzi, twin daughters of Golusar and my sister-in-law Sharâp, rode side-by-side, singing and laughing. People were laughing so much, it was like a wedding party. Everybody looked at the women as they rode by: 'Who are those girls riding on the camels, singing?' 'They're Golusar's daughters.' He was so fond of them.

Wherever we stopped people gathered. The men hunted partridge, antelope and mountain sheep. The women sang as we made felts and baked bread. We bought apricots and mulberries, and we handed them round over the felt. The women went to fetch water; we went down to the river and bathed, the girls first, then the men. The whole day the men were stripped to their pants.

We stopped near the bridge – did you see it? One of Haji's friends arrived with some baskets of apricots. These Hazâras were our friends; they came to our tent and sat down; the women brought things they'd cooked for us, fatty bread, eggs, butter, mushrooms, pot-herbs, cumin and onions, and in return we gave them salt, rice, cloth and *krut*.

We also collected loads of wheat, and took them across the bridge the next day, to Ghozba-khâna and Shorshorak. There were so many camel-trains then, Bakhtyâri, Nâmanzai, Pakhizai; wherever we stopped, many people came together; it was such fun.

At the bridge we saw a rabbit, and the children cried out, 'Look at its ears!' The men on horseback, Baya-khân, Pâdshâh and the others, chased it round; the kids were shouting and the dogs barking, but it got away – it went into the water and disappeared.

Haji Molk had a nice big camel with a beautiful rug spread over the storage bags, which were full of [*Tumân's aunt*] Bakhtâwar's things, her clothes, money and so on. As the camel approached the bridge, the men pulled it forward, but it leaped straight into the river, just like that. It was carried away, and everything, the rug, the bags full of fine clothes, money, cartridges, all were lost. People gathered round, they brought expert swimmers – local Hazâra mountain-men – who jumped into the water. They were good swimmers, but the river was too strong and they couldn't find any sign of the camel or its load. It was swept all the way down to Balkhâb, where it was found later, dead.

Haji Molk's camel was lost. The very next day we were all going along together in procession, together with Haji Abdol-Nabi's son Gollu. At Yekpaya, where the shrine is, the riverbank's very narrow. Gollu's train came along, with his camels strung together two-by-two, and as they passed the shrine, one of a pair fell into the river. Everybody rushed to help; they pulled one camel out and tried to slaughter it properly right there, but it was already dead so they threw away the carcass. They rescued Gollu's stuff, but the water carried off the other camel and it died too.

We climbed Reg-row and camped at the top. Next day we went on to Hazâr-qoruq; then we camped at Mayda-Qâsem, and the next day we went down into Kachan valley and camped at Tagawboy; the local women brought us apricots, grapes and mulberries, and dishes of *âsh* [*noodle broth*]. We were astonished how many women came. We spent three days there, then moved on to Dehmana; the women there too brought us grapes and all kinds of fruit. We gave them wool and salt in exchange.

Then we went on to Ekhtiâr and camped there. Again, crowds of visitors brought melons, watermelons; it was unbearably hot, so I made a little shelter, and the lambs slept on one side, people on the other. We spent a day there, then struck camp and moved on to Malek. Again people came with mulberries and apricots, apples and grapes. Everybody bought some. We spent the night there, and then went on to Chenâr, at the Ishân dervish-house. Once more the women gathered. We went to wash clothes in the river, and we traded our wool for grapes, grape-syrup, whatever we could find. The women went from village to village, buying chickens.

Karim, from Tagawboy in Kachan, is Ghâfur's shepherd. With some exaggeration, half-joking, he reveals something of Kachanis' views of the nomads who pass through their valley twice a year.

When the Afghan *mâldârs* arrive in our Kachan valley, all our camels are up in the mountains. They demand, 'Give us fodder, give us straw, give us wheat, give us money, give us grain.' We collect anything there is to eat in Kachan and take it to them, because we're in debt to them. Here we sell wheat for 30 or 40 rupees a seer, they buy it from us and then go and sell it down in Sar-e-pol for over 1,000. What can we do? We've no alternative; we have to make a living. Some of us go and work as servants or *mozdurs* for six months at 300 rupees. Some years you may earn 2,000 rupees, even 4,000 a year tending the camels. Some people don't need a worker and won't take one. You're helpless then; you have to carry wheat and fodder yourself. It's exhausting!

These Afghans go to the mountains and spend forty days there; then they come down to the Kâshân river, the Shorshorak waterfall, the Esmeydân meadow, the Dahan-e-Koj confluence, and they eat everything they find. When they get to Kachan valley, they eat all the apricots; there are none left. After they've finished the apricots here they go down to Dehmana, and finish them off there, then they go to Chenâr and finish them there. My boss spends a fortnight in Chenâr, then he moves down to camp at Chayrak, then Sukhta, then Boghawi, then to Jangal-bâgh in Sar-e-pol, then finally to his own place in Konjek. Then some of his people go out to the steppe, to guard the new grazing in the campsite until the snow comes.

Baya-khân enthuses over the wild onions and mushrooms that can be found in the mountains.

There are two kinds of wild onion, one with a big bulb, the other without. In the mountains, once you've passed Esmeydân, you can find the larger one, *kuhi-piâz*. Shepherds, camel-herds and others collect them in Kâshân. It has a large bulb like an ordinary onion; you just put them in a sack, then dry the leaves. This onion's very strong: it's very good for someone who's overheated; if he eats some, he'll soon cool down.

The smaller ones, *uraki*, are abundant in the irrigated meadows east of Cherâs; I've been on horseback several times to gather them. They have a root, but very small; they stand up like lucerne, and you cut them down with a sickle. You remove any grass, chop up the onions and dry them in the sun; they too are for the pot. We don't sell these pot-herbs, we use them ourselves – though when the women bring them home, their friends and relatives who didn't go to the mountains come and ask if they've brought any, so you give them a little.

Once, on the trek up, we pitched camp in Kâshân beside Shorshorak, and let the camels loose in the woods. Usually in spring nobody takes the camels across the river, afraid that they'll fall in and drown. But some years there's less snow and the river's less full. Gol had a *maya* hybrid camel. If the hybrid's a real bastard, whenever it sees green grass it'll head straight for it. This camel was browsing in the woods, when suddenly we saw that it had crossed the river to the other side, where there was plenty of grass. Nothing would cross, no Afghans, but the camel did.

But we saw that the water was low, so we took the other camels over. I was on horseback and brought up the rear, in case a calf was knocked over. We got the camels over, and on the other side, opposite where we camped together – the white clay you saw – there's a track that the *mâldârs* from Hazhdah-nahr use on their way to the top of the range they call Miâna-band. We went up that track and found loads of onions; each of us picked a skirt-full and brought them home.

There are onions in Kâshân up to Qabr-e-chopân; beyond that, there are mushrooms instead. The Kâshânis collect them, and Afghans go and buy them for up to 15 rupees a pound, depending on the year. In a rainy year, with thunderstorms in the mountains, masses of mushrooms come up. Shepherds, and people who know where they appear every year, go and fill their skirt or cloak or shawl and bring them back. You chop them small and dry them in the sun for a few days; then you store them in a container for winter. They're very warm, and good for the cold; cook them in ghee and they taste delicious – have you ever had them?

Chârgol's first trip

In late May 1971, Tumân's brother-in-law Chârgol rode up from Khârkash (with Nâder-shâh and others) to join the mâldâr in Siâh-band. It was Chârgol's first time in the mountains. One evening towards the end of the return trek, Chârgol tells us and some of his nephews and in-laws his impressions; Seyyed-shâh/Golusar prompts.

(*Chârgol*) – Before we left home, everybody said what beautiful flowers and grasses there are in Dangak, how the cool water sends you crazy. We started off—

(*Seyyed-shâh*) – Tell us where you stopped, day by day.

(*Chârgol*) – We came to what's-it-called, Behmana [*shrieks of laughter*], no, Dehmana.

(*Seyyed-shâh*) – After leaving home, where did you spend the first night?

(*Chârgol*) [*after much prompting*] – At Shana [*more laughter, corrections*]; at Tanzil.

(*Seyyed-shâh*) – Whose place?

(*Chârgol*) – I can't remember the name . . . forget it!

(*R*) – Who was with you?

(*Chârgol*) – Nâder-shâh; Kandahârey; Kuk; Nur; Wâli-Mahmad; Kalsum; and me.

(*R*) – All on horseback?

(*Chârgol*) – All on horseback. We went on to Dehmana. The gorge left me open-mouthed. What a sight! But my thighs were in agony. The others rode ahead; my horse, Long-legs, was a bone-shaker [*laughter*]. We got a drink of buttermilk. Then we spent the night, where was it? Larwandak?

(*R*) – Tagawboy?

(*Chârgol*) – No, after that; Alâr. We looked into Akhtar Khân's dispute, about sheep; we solved it and took 10,000 rupees from him. In the morning we went over to Reg-row.

(*R*) – Did you go by Band-e-Deldel?

(*Chârgol*) – Yes, we did.

(*R*) – Was it hot there?

(*Chârgol*) – It was so cold, my lips were chapped! We were aghast, we wished we'd never come!

(*R*) – Was it night or daytime?

(*Chârgol*) – Day. As we went down Reg-row that afternoon, we were very hungry and thirsty. We found a flock of Arabi sheep. We 'liberated' a fat ewe, killed it, ate it, and around four we set off again. The khan's men were on the road.

(R) – Teymur-shâh Khân's men?

(Chârgol) – Yes. They invited us in, and we spent the night there. He fed and entertained us very well, respectfully. Next day we went on to Spina-kala, where we found Rishmin's camp. They called us in, but there was no straw or barley to be found, so we went on to Dutâ'i, where we spent the night. We met a couple of Hazâri [*laughter*], I mean Hazâra shepherds. We gave one of them a rupee and sent him to fetch a teakettle and some bread. The other we sent to get a lamb from his large flock. It was night before the man brought us tea and bread. They were very good folk. While we ate and drank, we gave the horses some barley: they ate some 10 seers of barley. At ten o'clock we were settling to sleep, when the Hazâra shepherd arrived with a lamb. So we got up, killed the lamb, and cooked and ate some meat, but we gave half of it back to the Hazâra. Early next morning, after prayers, I mounted Long-legs, and we set off again. We made it over the Dangak pass to Du-bandi. I was so sorry I'd come. It's a terrible place; forget it. That's it, turn the recorder off!

The flash-flood and the dervish

Flash-floods are a major threat on the trek. Haji Tumân recalls a special occasion.

One year I set off on migration, just my family, though we had a *hamsaya*, a permanent guest, with us: Allah-dâd, a Baluch, a greybeard but newly married; a good, honest man, who'd been our *hamsaya* since my grandfather's time. He died here and was buried with our people; his bones are with ours, in the same graveyard.

That year there was foot-and-mouth (*dabbâgh*), and many sheep were lame; the grazing was rather poor too, so I started on the trek before the others. We made our way steadily up, via Chayrak and Chenâr, to Dehmana and Tagawboy; up the slopes of Sarghân, then down into Gholduri; on to Sâlrizi, then up to Târikak and over into Cherâs and Esmeydân, *hala-hala-hala*.

From Esmeydân it rained heavily every day, and it was hard work getting down into the Kâshân valley. The river was very high, so we took the camels over the little bridge at Ghozba-khâna; they went on up the eastern bank, but I came back to Ghozba-khâna because we'd run out of flour. In the village I bought a couple of donkey-loads of flour and hired a Hazâra to bring it, and I went on ahead.

After I got back over the river, down came a flash-flood. This fellow had driven the donkeys into the river to get across, but the floodwater swept one donkey's load off. He called me and I rushed back to join him at the river; with a couple of horses we managed to get the donkeys out, and transferred the remaining load onto the horses. We were soaked. When I got into camp it was still pouring, and I was really exhausted.

The next morning we moved on and pitched camp at Dutâ'i, the junction of the Larwandak and Dangak valleys. That day too it rained. We spent the night there, and in the morning it was still raining. Despite the rain and the foot-and-mouth, the sheep had gone on ahead. Around midday the weather was better, so we set off up the Dangak valley.

A little way along there's a meadow. When we got there, it started raining again, so we pitched camp. As the camels were hungry and the trees weren't yet leafy enough for them to browse, I sent the boys on horseback to Gol-e-yakh [*Ice-flower*] to fetch some asafoetida – we call it *anj*; in Persian it's *hin* or *row*. They loaded the horses and brought them back. The sun had just about set when three people came down from Sar-jangal, friends of ours. They said, 'We can't go any further, can we stay here?' I said, 'Of course, you're very welcome.' I told the women, 'Cook some meat for them, quickly, our guests are hungry, they say they haven't eaten anything.'

Now, a dervish on a white donkey had travelled with us all the way since Neymadân. Wherever we pitched camp, he'd stop nearby. We fed him, and in effect he was with us. We never once asked each other, 'Where are you from?' That evening I called out to him, 'Come and eat!' but he said, 'No, bring it to me outside.' I said, 'But it's raining, come inside.' I forced him to come and join us.

We all sat down to the broth, took the meat out and put it on the plates, and just had taken a couple of mouthfuls, when there was a noise of stones cracking, like gunfire, and the ground started shaking. What on earth could it be? The dervish suddenly bounded out of the tent and – by God's power – called to me, 'Hey!' – he didn't know my name – 'Hey, it's a flash-flood! For God's sake, get the kids out of the tent!'

We got out just as the flood arrived, bringing rocks as big as houses. O God, what were we to do? I held a Koran in front of the water, and I told the dervish, 'You know God better, speak on the Koran and make the water turn back!' Then, by God and the Prophet, this water went back up again from down below! Up and up it went, until it turned round again – but it kept away from our tent.

We stayed there several days while floods came from all directions. If you tried to go out you'd sink into mud up to your waist. On one side, the camels couldn't move; on the other, the sheep were lost. We were stuck! Finally, thank God, the floods stopped, the weather turned fine for a few days, and the ground dried out. We set off again and pitched camp at Chaman-e-kalân [*Big-meadow*]. Then on we went up to the place where we camped last year. There we struck camp in the middle of the night, reached the foot of the pass at dawn, and went up onto the snow. When you and I were there last year there was hardly any snow, but that year it was deep, all over those steep slopes. So we dug into it with axes and shovels, put rocks on it and built up a path, zig-zagging up to the top of the pass, then down the other side the same way. Luckily we had some Bakhtyâri with us; they're very powerful guys, big and strong, and it was they who took shovel and pick and carved out the path.[2] Without them we couldn't have done it; we wouldn't have got the camels up, even in ten days. I was just one family, and we were just two men, Allah-dâd and me.

When we got down the other side, the sheep's feet were all swollen from foot-and-mouth. We sent them with a few people over to Pordel's place on the mountain, while we went on down below and pitched camp at the graveyard where we camped together last year. The sheep just couldn't walk, and we slaughtered three or four. We went on and camped above Siâh-cheshma, at Qodughak, then we sent the camels back to bring the sheep up in gunnysacks. That year, foot-and-mouth killed more than thirty of our sheep. Their feet were so bad their hooves fell off. It got some of them in the stomach. We spent about forty days there, while the survivors recovered. Two or three were still lame, but we got them back to Sar-e-pol.

[2] Readers familiar with the early film *Grass* (Cooper and Schoedsack 1925) will be reminded of scenes where the Iranian Bakhtyâri nomads carved their way up the snow-bound slopes of Zardeh-Kuh. The Bakhtyâri of Sar-e-pol may be related to those of western Iran, but I know of no evidence for this.

Maryam recalls the same flash-flood, and some others.

One year when I went to Siâh-band ... there's a place in the Kâshân valley where there are two meadows by the river, one big and one small, and on one side there's a deep gully, and on the other lots of trees – have you seen it? That year we camped right there: our family, and Allah-dâd and his family. One or two lambs had been born, and I'd earlier cooked the meat; we'd eaten and all were now asleep. Tumân, his mother Nâzu, my small children and me; and Allah-dâd. Nobody else in this room was there then, only Baya-khân and me. I was tired, and fast asleep.

All at once rain came down the mountain and began pelting *tak-tak* on the tents. One side of our tent was up and open, the other side was down. Suddenly the floodwater arrived, sweeping mud and rocks along with it – Baya-khân remembers. The floodwater roared, *shur-shur*, the rain beat on the rocks, *tak-tak-tak*, like when you hammer in the tent-pegs. The storm knocked over the tent poles and everything. Everyone got up, Khâni-âghâ, Tumân, Nâzu, Allah-dâd's old mother-in-law Mahâla. The camels took fright; they lit a lamp to stop them panicking and stampeding into the river, and drove them all up the gully. We had a dervish travelling with us; he took a Koran and held it up before the water and compelled it to avoid our tent – by God it's true, Baya-khân saw it – by the Day of Resurrection, the waters parted, the mud stopped in front of the tent, the rocks flew aside. If it hadn't been for the dervish, the flood would have swept Tumân and me and all my sons away.

There we were, lying in the mud in the gully. Early in the morning people started arriving: people from my father's family: the camel-trains of my brothers Pordel, Kohandel and Haji Khoshdel. Seeing that our tent had been knocked over and we were stranded there, they asked, 'What happened? Why on earth did you camp there? Thank God, you were really lucky the flood didn't wash you away!' My brothers went on; then we packed up our tent, found the camels and loaded them, then followed my brothers and camped with them at Qabr-e-chopân – you've been there? When we'd pitched camp, I told them the story, how the water had come upon us.

We all got up early the following night and trekked over the Dangak pass. While my brothers went on to their summer pastures on top of the ridge, we camped down by the Adira mosque, and spent a few days there while other camel-trains passed. We slaughtered a sheep and did a sacrificial distribution at grandfather Shir's shrine. We waited for our flocks to arrive, then we milked them and in the morning we went on to our summer campsite, which was then at Dara-ye-Kamar. We separated the lambs from the ewes, and the next night we got out the butter-churns and prepared them by dampening them. My mother-in-law and I milked the ewes; we filled a huge cauldron with milk, 20 or 30 maunds. Then we churned the butter, and we made so much ghee that there was even enough for the dogs.

Once when I was newly married there was a thunderstorm in the steppe. The clouds opened and rain poured down. That night I took our large silken quilt and spread it over my [grand]father-in-law Haji Zabtu; poor man, he was very ill. As I did this, there was a thunderclap. Haji Zabtu cried, 'It's a flash-flood, get out!'

I sent the women up the ridge behind Dur-khân's place. They all ran – Moshkendi, Durkhâni, and many others. A cousin of mine came and with a servant's help we got my father-in-law up the ridge. We had many fresh lambskins in our tent; I stuffed as many as I could into a sack. I collected all our things – I had nothing of my own, no children, there was just Tumân and me – and carried them up the hill. Children were crying and women wailing, calling me, so I ran up to join them, before a great rushing torrent came down by our tent.

All the household stuff we'd taken to the top of the ridge got thoroughly wet. I'd left the tent and joined them, when I saw Salim Zuri's wife Lâl-bibi blithely riding along on top of my tent. The tent had collapsed into the muddy water and was being swept away, with that crazy woman riding on top of it. I called out to Nâzu, 'It's taken our tent, with a woman riding on top!'

That night, all our fine quilts, felts, pillows went with the flood. If Bibikuh were sitting here, she'd tell you the same story! Haji Mahmad's household lost wool and skins, and his wife's fine chest; two necklaces and other jewellery, all were swept away. You know the well below our place? His tent stopped there; the rest were carried right down to Tabu's place, into that large pit.

Another flood happened in Boghawi. After Nawruz, people set off for the mountains. We did two or three stages and came to Boghawi. All the families were there in the same place: ours, Ghâfur's, Afzal's. Some had put up shelters only, not tents. That evening, some had already cooked a meal, others hadn't, when a sudden fierce gust of wind blew down some people's tents, while others secured theirs. A thunderstorm broke and the rain just pelted down. Everyone huddled together and cried in fright; the children wailed, 'A flood's fallen on us!' Then a flash-flood did come, and it would have swept people, camels, everything away. But Seyyed Jamâl Âghâ – you didn't know him, he was our mullah – went outside, taking a Koran with him; he held it out in front of the flood, and the power of almighty God parted those waters, which passed either side, leaving us dry in the middle. The clouds disappeared and sky was blue once more.

You know that big gully in Boghawi? It was full of debris brought down by the flood. The next day we dried the tents under the sun, with all the bedding, the camels and the people. When everything was dry, we moved off again and climbed up the ridge above Boghawi, stopping on top of Gazak where there are some wells. We spent the night up there – we were exhausted.

Home

The Piruzai, as mâldâr, *still practise semi-nomadic migrations, but they have always had a definite sense of 'home', as Baya-khân makes clear.*

There was a sparrow in a cage. It was very unhappy, and as it fluttered up and down in the cage it sang, 'There's no place like home!'[3] Someone said, 'Let's free the poor sparrow and see where its home is, that it's always singing about.' So he followed the sparrow for several days until they came to a stream. In the middle of the river was a reed, and the sparrow alighted on the reed, and happily it sang 'No place like home!' as it played in

---

[3] *khpël watan bëlbël watan*; 'One's own home is brilliant/like a nightingale.'

the water then settled back on its reed. Its home was now the stream, and it preferred the reed above anything else.

Our homeland (*watan*) used to be in Kandahar, where elderly people like uncles Haji Ghâfur and Haji Wahâb and Aunt Saduzi lived before they came here. For us, Konjek is the best place to be. Wherever your father was born, or you yourself, that's your home. As soon as you've properly understood where your home is, and you've grown up and played with the other kids there, then that place never leaves your mind.

When we go to the mountains, we're unhappy; we miss this place, our home. When we come back down to Kâshân, it's better than the mountains; then when we get to Esmeydân we look forward to getting to Kachan; and when we reach Kachan, then we're almost home. When we get to Chenâr, we spend several nights there and we already feel at home. Wherever we go, we prefer home. Even if you feed us meat and rice, we won't stop thinking of home.

The Pastoral Year

The Piruzai flocks produce lambs, lambskins, wool and milk. The main production season is late winter and spring. In spring and early summer, women process milk into dried whey and ghee, storing both for later consumption. People say they once had such a surplus of ghee that they could sell it at great profit; nowadays, for various reasons, production is lower, and all needed for domestic consumption and for distribution among relatives who have no ewes.

Men shear the winter fleeces in spring for sale on the market for local carpet-making. In autumn, they cull the oldest animals, usually selling them to non-Pashtun villagers in need of meat for the winter. Cash income from sales of Karakul lambskins, Arabi lambs and spring wool goes towards household supplies or ceremonial expenses. Brideprices ideally include large numbers of live sheep.

The narrators, all expert shepherds, are the brothers Pâdshâh, Darwiza and Baya-khân.

Mating and lambing

In May 1971, on the spring trek, Baya-khân talks about mating practices.

Right now the rams are with the ewes, but they don't mate. A few may, but most ewes aren't ready until later, during the return trek, when we separate the rams and take them down with the camel-train, along with the lame and thin lambs. We take special care of the rams, fatten them up nicely; some people let them in as soon as they're home, in August, so that the foetus grows early, but mostly we put the rams with the ewes in early October.

A few ewes lamb twice a year. Hazâragi ewes have rich mountain grass and fodder, and good water and air, so they often lamb twice. Sometimes we buy a goat in the mountains, with a kid, and it has another when we get home. That's what Hazâragi ewes can do. But our sheep very rarely do.

In August 1972, after the disastrous winter, Pâdshâh tells more.

Most ewes come to the ram in September or October. Some come in November and December, along with the snows. The ones that didn't get pregnant come again in December or January, when there's just a little snow. It doesn't happen in spring; the rams aren't thinking about the ewes in spring. If a ewe approaches, the ram may tup her, but not like in autumn.

Sometimes they come in summer, like now in late August. In fact the ewes are ready for the rams from late June, but the real high point is mid-September to early October; then, when a ewe sees the ram, she'll bleat, *baaa*. If she just smells the ram . . . if the ewes are lying here, and the ram is driven by, they'll leap up after him – you can tell they're ready for him.

We have a special custom for when we put the ram among the ewes. While the shepherds slaughter an animal, the owners cook the special fatty layered bread we call *ghërey* and bring it along with sweets, melons and watermelons to distribute. As they let the ram out, they wallop him hard on the head with a watermelon, breaking it on his horns; some people do it with a melon, but most use a watermelon, because by autumn there aren't many melons left. We call it the ram's sacrifice. Then the shepherds eat the animal they've killed out there in the steppe, it's their sacrifice.

Also, when we bring a ram out of the yard, if we want more ewe-lambs than rams, our Afghan custom is to put a little girl astride him; but if you want more rams, then you put a boy on him – just for a few moments, that's all! We do it every year. Last year they did it at Haji Ghâfur's place; they were looking after our rams, as there was no grass here. This year we have no rams; we had one, but we sold him before you came. Our herding partners have three.

Only a very few of last year's lambs will come to ram this year; for example, there's a couple of ours that will, if we look after them and they're very fat. The others won't, but next year they will for sure, so long as they aren't sick for some reason.

At mating time we keep Arabi and Karakuli separate all the time, whether grazing, watering at the well, sleeping, night-grazing. Different people tend them. This lasts six to eight weeks, then they join together again. In late autumn a few Arabi ewes will come to ram again, those that didn't get pregnant the first time round, perhaps one in ten.

You can tell whether a ewe's pregnant forty days after tupping. If I'm with the ewes, I know which ones the ram's tupped. We don't separate them, just keep an eye on them. Most ewes that have been tupped come to the ram again, a week or two later. Some ewes come only once, others twice or even more. But ewes that come four times, even twenty times, won't give birth; they're too old, or perhaps they're barren. If they're thin, they haven't the energy to go to the ram. Any creature – human or animal – that's fit and has plenty to eat can find the energy.

When lambing's finished, the shepherd counts the ewes that have stayed dry. With very fat sheep, hardly any stay barren, perhaps 3 or 4 per cent. But if they're really very thin, then many remain dry, 20 per cent. Some ewes have twins, some triplets, but most of them just one. Generally you get the same number of twins as barren ewes. The shepherd counts the twins with the dry ones, so in effect all 500 have lambed.

Lambs are born in late winter to early spring. Males are commonly slaughtered or sold in the first year; ewe-lambs join the flock from their first autumn, though they do not mate and lamb until their second season.

August 1971 in Konjek. Darwiza, in his early twenties, starts military service in two months, so he has stayed at home this summer. The most experienced shepherd among the brothers, he tells us about his work.

You can tell when a ewe's about to give birth, because she'll lie down in the sheepfold. Moaning and bleating and groaning, she'll get up and lie down here and make an effort to push; then she'll get up again, lie down over there and try once more.

If the shepherd's asleep he'll wake up. When he's awake he'll come and pick up the lamb and help it to suckle. If it's in the sheepfold, he'll leave the lamb there, but if it's somewhere else, or if it's time for him to take the sheep night-grazing, he'll take the lamb home to its owner and leave it in a room or a pen.

Once the mother's seen and smelled her lamb and licked it just two or three times, if you take it to the owner's house overnight, when you bring it back in the morning the mother will recognize it, even among ten other lambs. If ten or twenty ewes have lambed, each will recognize her lamb. Very rarely, a mother rejects her own lamb and goes around bleating and sniffing from one lamb to the next. In that case we tie her two front legs together and put her lamb under her, then she'll accept it for sure. For a whole day, we keep the ewe focused on her lamb, and put them out together.

We slaughter the male lambs and leave the females. If the ewe gives birth at night out in the steppe, the owner won't know; the shepherd's responsible. On the day you engage the shepherd, you tell him: 'You and God know what you're doing, whether you eat them or steal them or bring them to us; you're responsible, we leave it to you and God.' If it's twins and one dies, it's his responsibility. The shepherd will kill the males right there; he'll also kill the occasional ewe-lamb if it has a really good grey skin. A nice ewe-lamb with a black skin he'll save, since, he says, when this ewe gets fat, we'll decorate her and dye her red and blue, she'll be very nice to look at.

A two- or three-week-old lamb with a weak, thin mother will have difficulty surviving. If it's a ewe-lamb, which we don't want to kill, we'll take it to a fatter ewe just at the moment she's giving birth; we don't let her see her real lamb – we remove it for slaughter – but show her the other one, wipe its tail over her nose, tie its feet and put it in front of her, and she'll accept it as her own and you can let them out together. However, this ewe's beestings may not suit it at all – the first three days' milk, the beestings (*tandi*), is yellow and the ewe's own lamb will thrive on it; after three days, until the end of the year, the milk is whiter in colour. But with another lamb, in warm weather, the beestings milk will harden in its stomach into cheese and make it ill or even kill it. You should draw all the beestings from the ewe's teats during the first three days, then you can bring the lamb and it can drink the later milk fine. Meanwhile, let it suckle another ewe.

You can get a ewe to suckle a goat's kid. If she's given birth to a male lamb – which we remove for slaughter – and there's a kid that's hungry or its mother's sick or dead, we bring the kid, tie its feet, rub its bottom, and put under the ewe, and she'll happily accept the kid and suckle it. The kid will thrive on ewe's milk and get really fat! Some people even get a nanny-goat to suckle a lamb; goat's milk really suits the lamb and will fatten it well! And you can put a lamb to a cow whose calf has died. The cow will accept the lamb; it'll grow so fat that after a year it'll be as big as a ram!

That's what we do when the ewes lamb out in the steppe. The shepherd sends his assistant; or one of the owner's sons takes food and water out to the shepherd and collects the lamb. Every few days they bring all the newborn lambs back home, with the carcasses or skins of those the shepherd's slaughtered. If he's cooked and eaten the carcass out there, that's okay, but if not, he'll send it home.

In spring, as shearing time approaches, the ewes may shed wool if they've grazed well. The shepherd can cut off some wool and exchange it with a passing peddler for raisins, pomegranates and other things; his boss won't object. We shear the sheep in early May. This spring wool is for making sacks, blankets and things, not felt. People sell it for cash or credit.

The shepherd may divide the herd into two: in one, wethers go with ewes that have lambed, including those with lambs; in the other, any ewes that are still pregnant. Every day one or two or more give birth; he'll slaughter the males, but keep the ewe-lambs at home. The traders won't buy the skin of a male lamb that's the wrong colour, or its wool fell off the day it was born, coming out by hand like this. Some people castrate such a lamb on the first day and let it out to graze with its mother, and then its tail will grow, which is good when it's slaughtered. If you don't kill it, and leave it intact, it'll grow into a nice large ram.

We don't let the lambs out to graze for forty days after they're born. It's not a question of teeth; some two- or three-week-old lambs are capable of eating grass. It's to prevent the Evil Eye. This is the custom among all *mâldârs*, whether Afghan, Arab, Uzbek, Hazâra, Turkmen.

But some people don't separate the lambs from their mothers. As soon as a lamb's born, they put it out with the mother, and they go around together day and night. We call this *barapay*. The lamb gets much fatter than one kept in the house; it'll be full of meat and fat. Like a lamb born before the winter, it'll survive much better.

If you keep a lamb inside for a few days, it won't be able to keep up with its mother, and you don't let it out to graze until forty days are up. A newborn suckling lamb that hasn't eaten grass doesn't make proper droppings, only a little loose dung, which you must collect every day, putting straw under the lamb to keep it dry. If it suckles well for three days, it'll soon get plump, compared to a newborn lamb that you take from its mother.

There's a plant we call *morchagol*, with bright yellow flowers; lots of them come up in early spring. A very sick ewe that eats some *morchagol* may die, but a ewe that's getting stronger may well benefit from it: first she'll have an attack of diarrhoea, then she'll get better and put on weight every day. Another tonic for a ewe is two or three eggs in their shells, put straight into her mouth, to be chewed and swallowed.

There are two kinds of diarrhoea, black and green. If a ewe has black diarrhoea, she'll die; but green diarrhoea's good. Some people get sheep pills from the bazaar, yellow or red ones. Sometimes they work, sometimes not. Last year Haji Wahâb and Jomajân fetched a government doctor, who gave some of their sheep injections; they all died.

Lambs and spring grazing

Baya-khân and Pâdshâh add further details to Darwiza's account.

(*Baya-khân*) – After a ewe gives birth, unless we kill the lamb for its skin, we keep it at home, in the hut or the tent, as you saw. For the first week or so, we allow the lamb to suckle its mother twice, once in the morning and again in the evening. After a week, when it gets bigger, it suckles only once a day. When its first forty days are over, it's grown up and understands about grass; we'll let it out into the steppe and it'll start to graze. A small boy will tend it until it gets used to grazing. Near the time to head for the mountains, we'll cut its ear with a mark. Everybody does this.

(*Pâdshâh*) – When the ewes are lambing, the shepherds sleep among them, as new lambs are born every night. In spring, when the owners come out with their families to camp in the pastures, some of them interfere with the shepherd's decisions, telling him where to take the sheep: 'I saw some nice grass in such a place,' and so on. The rest leave it to the shepherd to graze them as he thinks fit – after all, the shepherd's a partner in whatever's in the ewes' bellies, it's in his interest just as much as the owner's to do his best for the sheep, even if he sometimes makes mistakes.

Darwiza continues, on herding practices on the spring trek.

At spring migration time, days are longer and nights shorter. Keep the sheep on the move. At night, if there's cultivation ahead or thieves or wolves about, don't do night-grazing. It's better to do a short stage, driving them gently on until you get there; in hot weather the sheep hate to be hurried.

When there's a bottleneck, with too many herds, or cultivation beside the track, people drive their sheep on. You concentrate on the lead-goat, and someone else pushes the herd from behind, to get them through. At a bridge over a river, one person must take each end of the bridge and let the sheep over one or two at a time. If you let the sheep force their way past you, they'll start jumping into the river, and they're liable to throw themselves from the bridge too – they'll all drown. So, hold the sheep back, let them pass over one by one.

Hard work in the mountains

In mid-summer, after the lambs are weaned and the milking over, men shear the ewes and older lambs again, and women process the wool into domestic felts, though some may be bartered for fruit and other mountain produce. Darwiza again.

When you reach the mountains, and your sheep are exhausted from the trek, if you take them straight to graze on the *byetsa* plants and let them sleep there, they'll all go blind, and never grow fat. Graze them first on *mâst-pechak*, *shir-khowla* or *komâla* for a few days;[4] then you can take them to the *byetsa* and graze them there, day and night, and they won't go blind; they'll fatten up nicely.

---

[4] We were unable to identify these plants. Dictionaries are not helpful. Doubtless Breckle and Rafiqpoor (2010), reviewed by Clark (2012), has answers, but I have been unable to trace a copy.

To fatten the sheep the shepherd must move them several times during the night. Once they've come up from the water, we don't let them down onto level ground again but keep them grazing until morning without sleeping, however rough the ground is. If the ones higher up get full and lie down, then the ones below move on, and once they do, the others will get up and start grazing again, and so on, so that both those above and those below keep moving on. The poor shepherd too is up all night. He may tell his *mozdur*, 'Come and take over at such-and-such a time, I'll need a rest.' The *mozdur* may promise to come, but if he doesn't turn up the shepherd must stay out until dawn, to come back and find the *mozdur* asleep with the donkey and the dogs.

The sheep'll be happy if the shepherd can graze them well for a week like this; just short moves from place to place. They'll quickly fill up and want to rest. Just move a few of them from behind, they'll graze on for a few steps before resting again, and they'll be full. All night they won't move more than a hundred metres. In the half-light just before prayer-time he should keep them moving, until about seven or eight o'clock, driving them up to the top of the ridge to graze on the softness up there, then putting them to rest. At noon move them on again – it's time for 'hot-grazing' [*garmchar*].

In the mountains that's what really puts the fat on, the hot-grazing. Move them off at noon for a good graze, graze them as much as you can until they're nice and full; then rest them until evening, then graze them again, then by morning they'll be so happy they'll put on bellies like this, sweating all over their flanks. They'll be blissfully content, as though they'd been bathed in oil.

Pâdshâh.

When we arrive at the summer camp, we separate the lambs from the milking ewes and put them with the barren ewes, though some keep them with the milking ewes for a few more days. The shepherd and his *mozdur* go with the milking ewes; another *mozdur*, if you have one, or a small boy, tends the rest. Meanwhile, the women work hard; they put out the long rope for milking; they milk the sheep in the morning, and they make butter. They heat the milk, and churn it in the skin at night. They keep milking for about forty-five days. Then we shear the lambs, and ewe and lamb no longer recognize each other.

Baya-khân.

When the milk dries up, we shear the ewes too. We give them different fancy cuts: *shâbâzi, du-kamari, kamar-kal, shopra-kal, ghajari.* [*See Fig. 9*] When the wool's good and not greasy, we do *ghajari* and *shâbâzi.* A shepherd gives a really nice animal the *kamar-kal,* colours it to his taste, in blue and red, or some aniline dye; the owner's happy, and so's the shepherd: 'Our sheep are fat, our rivals will be jealous.' A ewe looks very good, larger, if you don't shear it; some shepherds won't shear a fine animal at all, just colour it. If the fancy takes him, the shepherd may do *du-kamari.* It's up to him: he'll get bored if he does them all the same style.

For an animal that's not fat, he'll do a complete cut, *shopra-kal*; if he did *kamar-kal*, or coloured it, people would laugh and say, 'His sheep are thin, yet he shamelessly colours it or does a *kamar-kal!*'

Roughly sketched during the summer shearing, 1971.
Shopra-kal (not shown) is a complete cut. Nobody could
explain the name *farânsawi*

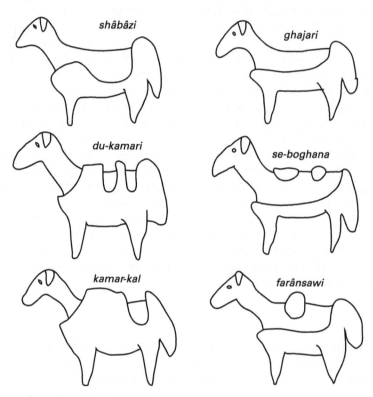

Figure 9 Sheep-shearing cuts.

The different cuts and colours have no other meaning: they look good. Another cut for setting off a nice ewe, like *du-kamari* and *kamar-kal*, is *se-boghana*. The shepherd first colours the sides, then he puts indigo on the back. Then he does the two humps, like the back, in indigo [*nili*] and the rest in red. People use different dyes; some use green too, but most people use indigo on sheep. The red is from 'red-earth' [*khâk-e-sorkh*, ferrous oxide], which we buy from Hotaki traders who come to Esmeydân and Cherâs nomad bazaars. They also bring indigo, but there's plenty of that in Sar-e-pol bazaar. If they've no indigo, some people use aniline dyes: red, green, pink, there are all kinds. Aniline dyes soon wash off, but indigo lasts.

As for shears, we usually buy them in Sar-e-pol bazaar, though you can get them in the mountains. Some are steel, some iron, but steel is best. We've bought good ones for 30 to 40 rupees; 25 for small ones. The best are 100 or 150, even 200. Good steel shears last ten to fifteen years; others seven to eight years. When we get to the mountains, we send them to Ustâ Khân-Ali in Adira for sharpening. He doesn't have a wheel every year, but this year he brought a good one. For the spring shearing, we take the shears to Sar-e-pol bazaar to be sharpened by craftsmen, experts who'll do them very well for 5 to 10 rupees.

We use the summer wool for felt. For the smaller felts, *nitsey*, two or three women work together inside the tents, beat the wool, lay it out, pour warm water on it; after pressing, wet it again with warm water, and two men stretch it. They make patterns in different colours. Then gradually we get on the move again, and come down to Kâshân; some people make *krâst*, the larger felts, there or further down in Tarpaj or Chenâr.

After shearing we put lambs and ewes together again. Some people separate them for two months; they keep the fertile ewes up here in the mountains until mating time, sending the rams, thin lambs and ewes down earlier with the camel-train. If mating took place in the mountains or on the trek, the ewes lamb in early winter, even late autumn.

Some people make yoghourt in spring and eat it, but it's not important. In the mountains the milk has much more fat than in spring. Women put the milk on the fire to heat, but not to boil; it cooks without boiling; they taste it to see whether it's cooked or still raw. When it's cooked they take it off, stir it with a spoon while it cools, put in some rennet, and it turns into yoghourt. Some of it we eat, the rest they put in the churn. They shake the churn and it makes butterfat and buttermilk. Women differ in their churning skills! Some aren't much good at it, they can't churn properly; they keep churning, but they don't make much butter. Others are experts. Women also make various cheeses, including dried whey, *krut*. The shepherds eat a lot of dried cheese; it's very strong.

One night in mid-summer, when milking's over, we make ghee, clarified butter. We remove the milking-rope pegs and collect some of the earth the pegs were in – for blessing. Then we fix the milking-rope up around the inside of the tent, and hang things from it like shears, shepherd's sandals, camel-hobbles, and plants that are common in the mountains, like *shir-khowla, usmâl, kâzubân, tërkh, ganda-bâghâl*. This is a custom we've always had; we do it because we hope it'll bring good luck.

Then we take a cauldron and put the earth from the pegs on the lid; around the cauldron we tie a horse's bridle – horses are lucky; on top we put a pair of shears and a piece of bread; some people put a Koran. We believe the jinns are afraid of the bread and the Koran, and won't be able to take any of the ghee. That's why we do all that!

Making ghee's a really tricky job. No more than two women can be present, and ordinary people like us stay away. When the butter's melted, it suddenly comes to the boil. It's very bad; it dislikes hearing voices; it can boil over, spill into the fire, catch fire and burn down the tent and everything. One year this happened to a Breti; his tent burned down. Once it nearly happened to my stepmother; the fat boiled over, but we quickly threw the churn-skin over the cauldron and took it off the fire. Pâkiza was shattered! She said, 'When we took the cauldron off, for a whole hour my heart was like this, all over the place, I was so worried the tent would catch fire.' We poured off some of the ghee, then put the cauldron back on the griddle to boil it up again. The churn-skin was ruined. I washed my hands and kicked the cauldron; then we finished the clarifying.

When the ghee's made, we measure it out in maunds [*8 seers, 56 kg*]. Some people say, 'We made twenty maunds!' Others say, ten. If you've got many ewes, you can make twenty. We eat it on migration and back in the Valley; it should last until spring, but some years people run out. Then, to serve their guests they'll have to buy more animal ghee, or vegetable ghee, or even sesame oil. We keep a few kilos until spring for the sheep; if a ewe aborts and catches cold, we give her some ghee, mixed with mulberry or melon syrup; that'll clean out her womb.

You can also get ghee when drying meat (*landi*). Everybody keeps two or three old ewes or rams, or buys one in town; you fatten them up for a month or two on barley, corn, lucerne, then slaughter them in spring and dry the meat – and make 10 to 15 kilos of ghee. Some people kill one or two animals for food during Ramazan, and they'll keep some ghee for later. The ghee is excellent, rich and good with bread, especially during Ramazan nights.

In the mountains, if you graze the sheep in daytime then put them to sleep, they'll keep on grazing at night; the shepherd won't have to drive them on constantly, like in spring. If he did, they wouldn't get fat. At nightfall you settle them on the slopes – you've seen them – for an hour or two but no more; they'll move and you'll have to settle them again on the slopes, keeping on until they reach their resting place. A smart shepherd keeps ahead of the herd and prevents them moving too far, throwing stones if necessary. Mountain grasses are rich but bitter; there's plenty of *shir-khowla* – after they've eaten a little, their mouths get sore and they can't eat any more. So they graze for an hour or so, then they need to rest for an hour before moving on to graze some more.

Pâdshâh.

In the mountains the shepherds work night and day to fatten the sheep. They compete to have the best-looking sheep around. But grazing methods are different from the steppe, where they take the sheep out only once at night. When they arrive in the mountains, they move the sheep several times between dusk and dawn. Later, when the *shir-khowla* turns yellow, you reduce that to two or three times, and that continues after shearing until some of the wool has regrown. Once the caravans have set off down from the mountains, the pasture dries up and there's not much left, so it's only one night-grazing until everyone's back home again.

We use the mountain pastures like this: we assess all the hollows, say there are eight of them, and we reckon that half, or perhaps only two or three, have good strong grazing that'll fatten the sheep, while in the others the grazing may be plentiful, but less fattening. The shepherd can take them to the richer hollows every night, since it's fattening them, and the plants are tall – you've seen them – they don't get trampled. If the sheep graze in one such place for ten days, even a month, they soon get fit, and the pasture doesn't get spoiled. They aren't like the steppe pastures, which get trampled, dirty and covered in droppings. Sheep much prefer to eat grass that isn't trodden down. If they graze the steppe pasture for two nights, it gets trampled, rotten and smelly, and they won't eat it on the third.

Autumn and winter

Between September and early May the flocks are tended in the steppe pastures. To the north, the steppe is sandy, with little vegetation; to the south, undulating loess hills provide good grazing from late autumn until spring, then stay hot, dry and dusty from late spring until the autumn rains. Scattered wells yield mostly brackish water, unfit for humans but drinkable by animals. Pastures near the Valley are public state land, but in practice they are divided among the Pashtun mâldâr, who seized them on arrival in the north. In each pasture there is a campsite, usually with walled sheepfolds, where the flocks sleep and leave their dung, later collected for fuel. Other stabling and shelters are constructed for newborn lambs and for transport camels. In most campsites, besides the tents, there are one or two mud huts with doors and windows and timber roofing. Finally, there are often one or more stacks of hay, mown in summer after the flocks have gone.

The winter months pass in a series of Forties (chella). The actual reckoning appears to vary according to region and altitude. In Sar-e-pol, from 21 December to 31 January is Black Forty (tora-chella), also known as Big Forty (chella-ye-bozorg). February coincides with Red Forty (srë-chella). Then most of March (until Nawruz on the 21st) is White or Little Forty. The mâldâr sometimes also reckon the Migration Forty, the last month or so before winter sets in. At different times in late summer 1971, the brothers Pâdshâh, Darwiza and Baya-khân tell how the sheep are grazed over the winter.

Pâdshâh.

After the shearing, while the caravans trek home, some shepherds keep the sheep in Siâh-band for forty days more. You leave supplies with them, and you can leave further supplies of flour and stuff along the route at friends' houses, asking them: 'When our herd arrives, please hand over the flour.' You tell the shepherd to turn up at particular places and times to collect the supplies.

They bring the sheep back along the same trail they came, stopping a night or two wherever there are nice meadows for them to graze, like Spina-kala, Ghozba-khâna, Shorshorak. Then one or two nights at Dahana-ye-Tarpaj; the schedule's up to the shepherd.

Darwiza.

Returning from the mountains, bring the sheep down gently, don't let them realize they're on migration; just make sure you get them water and grass. If they come down easily, when autumn arrives they won't suffer here, so long as there's a good well and you water them at the wellhead.

Baya-khân.

In autumn, when everyone's back, we herd the animals together. People sell any surplus male lambs or infertile ewes. It's better to lighten the herd; in winter, grazing's in short supply, and it's hard for the sheep to get enough to eat. If they're too many, they won't get full.

Down here, at first you can take them a long way to graze at night. The shepherd leads them, the *mozdur* drives them on from behind. In the dark the shepherd whistles and the sheep follow. When they're full, the sheep don't mind, they can rest wherever they are. But by the end of autumn you keep them in the sheepfold, or somewhere they won't catch cold.

Winter begins with Black Forty, followed by Red Forty, which begins in early February and lasts until early March. In Red Forty the earth reddens; people say that an ember falls from the sky to the ground, the earth warms up and grass soon starts to grow. Then comes White Forty: spring is white, yoghourt and everything are plentiful, and sheep that have survived won't die. There are only these three Forties: Black, Red and White. During the Forties, people think the stars are fighting; that is, the moon and that bright star, you've seen it? When they pass each other, people say they're fighting with each other, so it'll snow.

After the snow comes *khâklewa*, when rain covers the ground with new grass. If you graze the sheep well during *khâklewa*, they'll soon fatten up come the spring. You should move them out near midnight. The more they graze, the better; fresh new grass tempts them, they'll graze the whole night. Some people keep them grazing and don't bring them back to the fold until nearly sunrise. Then they'll sleep as soon as you bring them in and settle them down; for example, if you bring them in at six o'clock, they'll sleep until it's good and light, and you needn't move them again until ten or eleven.

Khâklewa lasts a month or more, it varies with the year, depending on how early the grass comes up. Some years, when there's little snow and much rain, it comes in the Black Forty. One year the rains came in late autumn, early winter; there was little snow, the sheep filled up with green grass as early as Black Forty, and sometimes we brought them here to the Valley to water them. There was plenty of rain that year; it was good weather, some days it rained, followed by several days of warmth. The sheep were full of green grass by the end of January. In other years there's more snow in Black Forty; then it gradually melts, and *khâklewa* comes in Red Forty.

In the steppe, saltwort [*shura*] and other salty grasses like *dawdawak* and *siâbak* aren't much good for the sheep. Saltwort is like porridge; if you eat it, you soon get hungry again. The others all turn to piss in the stomach. What's good for the sheep is lucerne, what we call *tâla* or *shpushtak* – *nokhodak* in Persian. *Kondali* is good too. *Khoshkyâr*, *tâla*, *worbushak*, *shkarey*, *kharwarak*, these are very good for sheep; they're stronger, like bread, after which you don't get hungry so quickly.[5]

Darwiza.

During the three months of autumn we cut hay, bring it in and stack it beside the sheepfold. When the time comes, we'll have four or five stacks for the sheep to eat. In a tough year, with deep snow, they'll finish off all the hay, and we'll have to get straw from the village – that's hard work, really rough on the camels, which get sore backs or go lame; and people suffer too. In the village we spend the days stuffing sacks with straw. Straw costs 200 to 250 rupees for a big gunnysack in the autumn; in a hard winter it'll reach 500, or 200 to 300 for a smaller sack – if you can find it. We give straw and alfalfa to the stronger ewes, but we put aside the weaker ones and feed them barley, and perhaps make *ârdâwa* dough-balls for them, or even give them bread. Some ewes die, some survive. If they die, perhaps their unborn lambs will be worth something for the skins, but with many there's nothing we can use apart from the wool and the guts.

---

[5] Apart from saltwort and lucerne, plants not yet identified.

From September onwards, the sheep are *inâr*, watered every other day. Now graze them at night and bring them back during the day. This 'water-grazing' fattens them in autumn. In the morning, after watering them, drive them onto the farmland, where they can eat chaff and stubble; when they're nice and full, put them to sleep for a few hours. After you've put them to sleep at midday, as the sun gradually goes down and the shadows shift, don't move them. If a shadow falls on their bodies, they may start to move of their own accord and they may scatter. God grant they'll stay asleep until dusk. That's one thing; another is, it's not good to shout loudly at them, '*hey!*' and '*pshi!*' or to turn them sharply round. They don't like the noise, they'll piss at once and they won't graze or shake themselves – their fleeces will remain tight like felt.

When they're properly rested, wake them and you'll see the difference: as they get up, they shake themselves two or three times, and their wool sparkles. They're really in good shape. At dusk, move them onto some grass, and graze them well until late evening, then rest them, don't let them move; in case they move by themselves, put a *mish-band* (ewe-string) on: tie one end of a small string round the neck of one of the ewes, and the other end to your foot, so that when they move they'll wake you too. Then around midnight wake them, drive them out to graze and don't let them rest. Drive them through the night until near dawn; let them rest for an hour, then drive them on. On a watering day, take them to the well first. If it's an *inâr* day, don't let them sleep again until late morning. This way, they'll get nice and fat. If the shepherd takes this sort of trouble, they'll have a happy time.

The sheep start moving on their own, slowly, one by one; once they move they'll be fine and wander round the hollow. When they're all up, drive them into another hollow, let them graze there, then drive them into yet another. Eventually let them rest a little; then bring them home, the shepherd in front and the *mozdur* driving them on from behind. However far it is, don't force them, drive them gently, allowing them to graze on the way; gently, gently, then around three in the morning let them sleep for an hour. At four, when they've ruminated a little, move them on, don't let them rest again, drive them the rest of the night until dawn. At dawn graze them towards the water. Water them at the well, move them on and let them graze a little, then bring them back to sleep. After sunrise, take them to the steppe to graze, but don't move them, if they've had some good night-grazing. The *mozdur* stays back, cooks some food, waters the dog, and unloads the donkey, rubbing down its back and attending to any sores. Then he takes food and water out to the shepherd, who's asleep among the sheep.

As the cold weather sets in, after sunrise fill the sheep up well. If there's snow in the sheepfold, shovel it aside and collect the sheep droppings. When you've swept up all the snow, spread the droppings over the ground to dry it properly. In the evening, when the sheep are full it's best to let them sleep; don't move them until eight or nine o'clock, even ten if it's cold. Why? Because they're dry underneath, and if you move them, they'll piss at once; then, if you take them a short distance away to some fodder you've put down, in the time they take to eat the fodder their piss will have frozen solid. If they return and lie down on this frozen piss, they'll promptly catch cold and they'll either die or miscarry; neither owner nor shepherd will profit from them. The *mozdur*, though, couldn't care less if the lot die, he'll still get his food, his sandals, and his pay.

From January until early March the nights are still long, but by March the ground is warming up from underneath, and the winter cold loses its bite: it's *khâklewa* time. Remove the sheep from the fold, it's better to put them to rest somewhere else, because they like the smell of grass; when it's time for night-grazing they'll graze well if they're allowed to move when they want. But when you take the sheep out night-grazing, if there's just a light frost, don't let them lie down, no matter how drowsy they may be; keep them moving and grazing until morning. Look behind, look ahead, and if you see just one ewe lie down in the sheepfold, go straight over and rouse it; let it lie on that frozen ground for just 5 minutes and it'll catch cold and miscarry or die. Also, during *khâklewa*, the grass may be sharp and cut them inside, and they'll leak a little blood; just like when you're given an injection or some good medicine, if it's doing you good you too will leak blood from your anus.

Night-grazing in *khâklewa* time will get the sheep into excellent condition. If their stomachs are full, they'll get very fat. As the grasses grow tall and strong, but before they start to dry up, if you graze them properly their bellies will expand again and get good and fat.

Gol-Ahmad explains the difference between awi *and* inâr.

Some people make their sheep *awi*, which means watering them every day. In spring, we water the sheep *inâr*, every other day; if you do that, they get good and plump, their flesh doesn't melt away. It's up to the shepherd. During the migration we water them every day; once we arrive in the summer pastures, every other day again – and we give them salt every other day. After two weeks we give them salt every three days; after that, every four days, then every five days. When we get home, we water them every other day; when the rains come, we water every third day, then in winter snow and rain we water only once a week. As it gets warmer and drier, then every other day.

In August 1971, before the bad winter, Pâdshâh is cynical about the whole business.

Nine months of the year we struggle to tend and fatten the sheep – and horses, donkeys, camels and cattle too – to get them all in good condition. Then after all this trouble and effort, three months of winter come and strip them of their meat; some die, some abort their lambs.

Shepherding Contracts

Employees

*Each herd is tended by a hired shepherd and his assistant (*mozdur, dombâlawân*). Their employers are responsible for keeping them supplied, but sometimes they are out of contact for several days. The shepherd's job is to graze the animals properly, to fatten them over the spring and summer, and to keep them that way in autumn so that they survive the winter rigours well enough to throw good lambs with good skins.*

Darwiza has worked as a shepherd, for his father, who didn't pay him, and for his uncle Ghâfur, who paid him his dues.

The shepherd leads the herd and the *mozdur* brings up the rear. From the day he's taken on, the shepherd's responsible for the herd. He must answer for any animal lost or dead. The owner will ask, 'Why, how did it die?' If it's lost, he'll ask, 'What have you done with it? Was it stolen? Did a wolf eat it? Did you let it go lame? Did you sell it?' The shepherd answers, not the *mozdur*.

The shepherd's due is 10 per cent. Suppose there are 500 ewes, and all 500 give birth and not one dies or remains dry; they bear 250 ewe-lambs and 250 males. He gets 25 of the ewe-lambs; we slaughter all 250 males, and give him 10 per cent of the cash received for each skin. Until he's done the full twelve months, the shepherd gets nothing from his employers except a felt cloak, a pair of sandals and his food. Two people – shepherd and *mozdur* – and one dog get half a seer of flour per day, or cooked bread if they're near camp.

A *mozdur*'s paid 500 rupees a month, 6,000 a year. For twelve months the employers provide him with sandals, water-skin, donkey, a blanket for the donkey and barley if needed. The day you engage him, you give him 2,000 rupees, telling him to spend it on something for his home. After six months, with winter approaching, you give him a cloak, two suits of clothes and a turban, and another 2,000 rupees. When the year's over, you pay him the rest and release him. If you engage him for just six months, you give him a felt cloak, one set of clothes, and his sandals and food. Some people take a *mozdur* on a monthly basis, at 300 rupees. Some *mozdur*s will work for 200, even for 100; last year it was 300, this year it's risen to 500; but you can still find them for 300.

Suppose all the sheep die and the lambskins are no good. The owners will be unable to pay the shepherd, and he'll get nothing at all. But the *mozdur*'s payment won't vary. Even if the herd's wiped out, the *mozdur* gets his due. If only five sheep remain alive and he stays with them, you must pay him the cash, food, sandals, cloak, two suits of clothes – whatever you agreed.

But if God favours his work, a shepherd can make more in one year than a *mozdur* can make in ten. If all the ewes bear lambs, and the skins come out right, he'll make a huge profit. Our mullahs tell us that God will provide for a shepherd so long as he says his five daily prayers without omissions, tells no lies, does no trickery or deceit, doesn't graze animals on other people's wheat or barley – that's morally wrong, since the farmer's worked hard too, and he'll say, 'Hey! Damn your house!' If the shepherd avoids these evils, after two or three years God will grant him whatever his heart wants; he'll be well contented.

Baya-khân hasn't yet been formally employed as a shepherd, but he often herds for his father and uncles and knows the business well.

A good shepherd grazes the animals until they're fat enough to stand the winter snows. If they're fat, some of it'll melt away, but it won't matter if they go hungry some days. If they're thin, then just two snowfalls will kill them; their flesh won't stay on their bodies. It's vital that the sheep are fat for the winter. A good shepherd is proud of his fat sheep; he'll contrast them to your thin ones: 'Why didn't you graze them properly? Your sheep are so thin: were you dead or asleep?' If the whole herd is fat, well cared for, nicely coloured, then people reckon he's a good shepherd and want to hire him. Some people keep a good shepherd for several years, renewing his contract every year.

The shepherd isn't happy until the rams have been put in; after that, he's a partner in whatever the ewes have in their bellies. His income depends on the lambs. If the ewes survive the year and give birth, he gets his share of ewe-lambs, and cash for the males, so he's happy. The *mozdur* gets his money whether the sheep live or die, but the shepherd gets nothing if they die. He has no interest in the wool, except enough for a *kepanak*, the felt cloak a shepherd wears at night, which is part of his due. Some people give a seer of wool after the women have carded it with rods, but most give more – whatever was agreed the first day of the contract. Others give *barak* cloth or ready-made felt. It's up to the shepherd; he may ask for the cash equivalent, say 300 rupees. You agree all these details – wool, felt or cloth – on the day of the contract. Some people also give the *mozdur* wool, but only half as much.

If the shepherd needs something, he'll ask, and he'll get it. He doesn't share in the wool or the milk products, and he doesn't get cash wages; he gets his tenth only when all the ewes have given birth, the ewe-lambs are grown up, and the owners have sold the skins. If the skins fetch 10,000 rupees, you give him 1,000; if they fetch 1 lac, you give him 10,000. That's shepherding.

When a young man works for his father, he may or may not take his due. Haji Jallât's sons, Musa for example, take their due, as they've separated from their father. My brother Darwiza took nothing from our father, who was paying his brideprice for him; but when he worked for uncle Haji Ghâfur, he took his due. Generally, a boy won't take his due as a shepherd from his father when they still live together. After they're separated, he'll take his due, unless of course his father's poor and hungry, then he'll help him even if they're separated.

Pâdshâh, eldest son while Khâni-âghâ is away, is often in charge of the flock (particularly, as we shall hear, during the 1971–72 winter) and deputizes for his father as employer.

Right now we have two shepherds with the sheep. Instead of a *mozdur* there's my brother Nasib [*Tumân and Maryam's sixth son*], who's a shepherd, but we give him a *mozdur*'s wages. When he gets tired of the work, we won't force him to continue, we'll take on another *mozdur*; perhaps we'll send Baya-khân, or one of those Arabs, or someone else. *Mozdurs* like Nasib get anything between 250 and 400 a month. Nasib will put the money into his own pocket; nobody else has a claim on it. Our father could take Nasib's wages from him if he wanted, but he doesn't. After all, Nasib's grown up now, he won't throw it away or lose it; he can spend it by himself, on clothes and such.

As for the main shepherd, we engage him in early spring. We write down the day he was hired; his contract ends the same day next year. A good shepherd who gets on with his boss will work up to a month extra for nothing, before taking his leave and going home. When all the skins have been sold, he'll come and collect his skin-money; later he'll collect one in ten of the ewe-lambs.

If the wife of any of his employers has a baby son who survives at least a month or two, the shepherd will bring the father a piece of clothing, like a jacket, a nice *jallak* cloak or a nice waistcoat. In return, the father gives the shepherd a *pituki*, an extra payment, of an adult ewe, or perhaps a lamb or a kid, or a donkey foal or even a camel calf. If God lets the baby live, people say, 'This shepherd brings such good luck.' This is the custom in Afghanistan. People point to a woman whose babies all died until they hired this shepherd, and with his good luck God gave her a boy who grew up. If it's a daughter, they won't give him a thing!

Karim from Kachan tells his story, halfway along the spring migration. He complains – joking, but with justification – that his employer, Gol-Ahmad, was negligent in preparing for the trek.

This is the seventh year I've worked for Gol-Ahmad: one year as shepherd, and six years as *mozdur* or house-servant. One year I stayed in the village with Haji Ghâfur, while Gol-Ahmad went to the mountains. Two of my brothers worked for Dur-khân [*Tumân's brother*] for three years, and two years for Jân-Mahmad [*Ghâfur's brother*].

Last year I was a shepherd; this year I'm a house-servant, for six months at 250 rupees. My boss Gol-Ahmad stayed in Konjek, telling me to go to the mountains with his brothers Joma-khân and Ajab-khân. Then he kept Joma-khân back and sent Ajab-khân with me. Ajab-khân and I came together up here to Târikak, where we got a letter from Haji Tumân telling us to go ask Mirzâ Hoseyn for some flour. Mirzâ Hoseyn refused. Ajab-khân and I begged him, 'Please give us a little flour,' but he wouldn't give us any, nor fodder for the camels. We were left high and dry. Our boss has twelve transport camels, and thirteen mouths to feed in the house. And Gol-Ahmad is a very difficult person. Only Baya-khân is a good uncle to us; so is young Sepahi. The others are difficult. All day we tend the camels; at night we load and move with them. Now Gol-Ahmad's arrived, and he's upset with us. His stepmother, aunt Keshmir, rows with us all day long, fighting and crying. In the mountains she exhausts herself at night loading the animals, then fights with us all day. She asks us, 'Are you dead or alive? You sleep all night while people are loading around you, why don't you get up?' Last night we slept peacefully, then in the morning the women came and said, 'We can't manage the camels', and told us to get on with it. Finally I went to uncle Abdol's house, filled the kettle and brewed some tea for myself. That's how these people oppress us!

Partners

Usually several owners join their flocks into a herd of around 500 ewes and a few goats, tended by a shepherd and a mozdur; *the employers share the expenses, as Darwiza explains.*

The shepherd and the *mozdur* take their dues from all their employers, divided according to their holdings of sheep; the same with the supplies and any other expenses, for example renting pasture or a stubble-field. In winter, when the sheep are out in the steppe, the partners take turns to go out to them, whatever the weather, snow or rain. If it's your turn, it's up to you to provide water, bread, tea, etc., or you take the shepherd some ghee or meat, whatever he's due, for all the days of your turn. The turns last not just the winter but the whole year, as long as we're partners. If you aren't happy with us, you can decide to split, it's up to you. You can take your sheep to join someone else, or graze them alone, or your boy does, or you take on a *mozdur* to graze them, and you don't take turns with anyone – it's up to you and your sheep. But if you stay with us, we expect you to take your turn; and when your turn comes, you're obliged to get on your horse or donkey or camel and take out the flour, the bread, the water and so on.

The turns are reckoned this way: a herd of 500 sheep makes a cycle of 25 days, one for every 20 sheep; with a herd of 600 sheep, the cycle is 30 days. Say there are 500 sheep, with five partners, one with 200 sheep, one 100, one 50, one 70, one 80. The one with 200 has to do most. For ten days he'll provide food for both shepherd and *mozdur*, as well as water-skin, donkey, ropes and the rest; with flour at half a seer a day, he'll give five seers for those ten days. The dog's food is also up to him, and he must provide whatever the shepherd and the *mozdur* ask for. The partner with 100 sheep does five days: the one with fifty does three days once, two the next time; when it's two days, he'll give one seer of flour, and when his three-day turn comes round, he'll give one-and-a-half seers.

Pâdshâh gives some examples – speaking after the winter losses of 1971–72.

In 1970–71 we [*Tumân and family*] were herding partners with uncles Dur-khân and Akhtar. If we're three partners, we discuss the best arrangement: who should take their family to the steppe with the animals for the winter, who should stay at home in the village. It depends who has people available – sons, *mozdur*s – and who has draft animals. The one who goes out doesn't expect to be compensated by the others for his trouble, all he asks is that they should bring drinking water from the Valley, that when it's their turn they should be ready to send out a horse or camel or donkey. If the partner out in the steppe has his own draft animal, he'll just ask you to make sure the water's delivered. After all, he doesn't have to watch the animals all the time; it's the shepherd who takes them out to graze. He's there just to watch for thieves and predators.

For the last five or six years, my family's been the one to be with the animals from autumn until spring. The others stay in the village, then they come and join us in spring.

Our sheep are now joined with Haji Ghâfur's; this will continue until Nawruz, when we'll hire a new shepherd. Our shepherd is Samad Nurzai. His wife's our maternal uncle Kohandel's daughter. They live in Khârkash, near Pâkiza's father Mullah Jabbâr.

We – Haji Ghâfur, Jân-Mahmad, Dur-khân – employ Samad and Nasib jointly. We don't pay Samad a penny; all we give him is a pair of sandals, a *kepanak* cloak, and his food. The partners share all the costs. We price everything, e.g. 100, 200, 500 rupees for the *kepanak*, and we calculate everybody's share according to the number of sheep they have, then collect the money to buy the felt and the *barak* cloth, and stitch the *barak* onto the felt to make a *kepanak*.

Baya-khân gives more detail on the complex partnership arrangements.

Our shepherd works with the whole herd, no matter whose sheep they are. With shearing, for example, he does whoever's sheep are being shorn that day. It's like this: the shepherd works mostly for the person who has most sheep, but that's just because of the relative numbers; or the *mozdur* does the others. It makes no difference; nobody says, 'Why hasn't the shepherd come to me?' The partner with most sheep is headman, *sar-kheyl*, and has first call on the shepherd's labour.

Suppose there are two brothers, living separately, each with 100 sheep; but only one of them takes all 200 sheep to the mountains and does all the work; the other brother will provide all the expenses for three to four months: some cash, the flour, salt, sandals and clothes for the shepherd. For example, when uncle Akhtar went on military service, and his brother Dur-khân refused to go to the mountains, for two years I took their sheep. I did all the work, they paid my expenses, and we reckoned up afterwards.

Each partner contributes according to how many sheep he has. For example, four families jointly herd 500 or 600 sheep; each has 150 to 160 sheep, or 50, or whatever, but we calculate one day's expenses of flour and other supplies for every 20 sheep. Dogs aren't counted; but the donkey is. Suppose we're in the mountains, and I'm the headman, the one with most sheep, but I have no donkey, then if you have a donkey I'll ask to borrow it. A headman doesn't really worry about the donkey . . . In all my life as far as I recall, I don't think we ever asked our partners, Akhtar or Jân-Mahmad, for a donkey! My father always provided. As for dogs, anyone with a spare dog sends it with the herd – who cares! But with the flour, for every 20 sheep you give one day's supply of flour, at half a seer per day. If you have 100 sheep, you'll give the shepherd five days' worth of flour, that is 2½ seer, and this'll be enough for them and the dogs.

When they go to the mountains, some days when it's raining the shepherds can't cook or bake bread because the fuel's damp or they're tired, so if the ewes have milk they make some cheese. Also, they draw some milk and mix some flour into it to make what we call *ârdâwa*; just a little flour makes a whole pot of *ârdâwa*, enough to fill them. If they're running out of flour, they're far from the employers or a village, and they've no money, then they'll make one seer of flour last several days, making *ârdâwa* every day.

In October, when it gets cooler, the sheep are *inâr*, which means they're watered only every other day. One day the shepherds bring the herd near the village to water, collect cooked bread from the employers and take flour and water back to the steppe for the next day. For example, today you drive the sheep out to the steppe; early in the morning the *mozdur* will fetch the flour, then he'll go to the sheepfold, collect some dung-fuel, make a fire and cook a *kumâch* loaf – you've seen the shepherd's *kumâch*? They dampen the flour in a pan, or a cloth if they have one, then they knead the dough, extra well, to make a nice loaf. They have no proper *tâwa* griddle, they just beat the fire with a stick to break up the embers, then place the dough under them. If they don't break up the embers, the *kumâch* burns. If they cook it well, it comes out nice and sweet.

6

For the Animals

Camel Care

The Piruzai keep one-humped dromedaries and a few two-humped Bactrians, and breed the hybrid[1] when they can. Some camels have personal names.
   Baya-khân is a camel expert. One day on the trek he talks about camel care.

There are three kinds of camels, *râsta*, with one hump, *arri*, with two, and *maya*, a hybrid. A male *râsta* is called *luk*, a female *ârwânâ*.

The *maya* hybrid's an excellent animal, very strong. If there's mud on the track, it'll bend its legs and go down on its knees. A good one can carry a load of fifty or sixty seer. A one-hump *râsta*'s good too, it can carry forty or fifty seer, but the *maya*'s stronger. The two-humped *arri*'s kept for breeding. If you take a good, pure-bred *ârwânâ* – a one-hump cow – a nice red one, with a fine hump, to an *arri* bull, it'll bear an excellent *maya* calf, worth 10,000 rupees. If you mate an *ârwânâ* with a *maya* bull, it'll bear what we call a *du-raga*, a mongrel. It's not as good as a proper *maya*, but it's still very powerful, with huge thick thighs.

Some people start loading a camel when it's two years old, but it's better to wait until it's three or four. If you load a calf too early, it'll burn out, it won't grow to full size; but if you wait, it'll get strong, with good bones, and it won't mind being loaded. A camel will carry loads for ten to fifteen years, twenty if you look after it properly.

Up here in the mountains, camels thrive on thorns. There are three kinds that they eat: *gag*, *shishnak* and *krap*. They eat other plants too, like *shir-khowla*, *gheyghân* and *komâla*, but they much prefer the thorns. When we go down into valleys like Kâshân, there are meadows with tall grasses; they like that. But in Kâshân there are also bushes that they like to browse. Further north, on the Reg-row mountains as far as the Kachan valley they'll find thorns again.

In Kachan there won't be much for them to eat, except wheat-stubble, so we take them further down to a place called Awparân, where there's a spring and another kind of thorns, and other plants the camels like; we stay there a few days and let them wander around freely. Further down again, at Malek, Dehmana and Poshta, the camels eat *zuz*, another thorny plant, which is plentiful all the way to Sar-e-pol and stays green from spring right through to winter.

---

[1] See R. Tapper (2013).

If your camel's thin, or you're particularly fond of it, you'll keep it at home and feed it *ârdâwa*: damp straw, mixed into barley flour. Or you'll give it dried alfalfa, if you have some.

In the mountains a camel's liable to get rheumatism, which can kill it. On the way down, it might get *baghal-gir*, a kind of fever; then you must bind its feet tight and lay it down with several blankets on top, to sweat out the fever.

Sometimes camels go crazy. Did you see that calf in spring? It just took off. Dur-khân and I grabbed it and branded it with a pair of hot shears. I don't think you saw us when we did that. Anyway, we were lucky, the calf recovered.

A camel can also get a cough; its nose goes funny, and it won't graze for some days. You pour some pepper on it; some people use powdered sugar. A cough can kill a camel, it's really dangerous.

If your camel falls – and they often do, in the mountains – and breaks a leg, then you'll have to slaughter it, there's nothing else for it. If it's a minor wound, you can put heavy oil or butterfat on it, but if it breaks a leg in the mountains, you must kill it. An adult camel's leg won't recover quickly; the animal's heavy and it'll put all its weight on the other legs, and stop using the broken one. It's not like a sheep, which is lighter and can recover quickly from a broken leg.

In the village next summer, after the bad winter, Baya-khân enumerates the camels owned by his family and his close relatives – tracing the animals' origins and genealogical connections.

Uncle Akhtar has seven camels left this year. Only one died, the lame one. He has an old black *ârwânâ*, you may have noticed it; he bought it early one winter for cash from the Alizais of Kaltar, along with another *ârwânâ*. They were both *maji*, that is, they hadn't given birth before, but the Alizai owner had mated them both, and they calved in the spring. We called this one Black-Camel; the other one we called Ding, because whenever it saw green grass it would head straight there and nothing would stop it. Ding had one calf; all the others came from Black-Camel.

Black-Camel has calved every other year. When it calved that first spring, it had a female, which is now grown up. The next year it didn't give birth, but Akhtar mated it again, and the following year it bore a little *luk*, which he sold for six to seven thousand rupees to Ghâfur – the fellow you visited today – but it died a few years ago.

Next was another male, a plump *luk*, which Akhtar sold to Nâder-shâh for 3,500 rupees. Then this last spring it produced another female. Meanwhile, its firstborn gave birth, first to a female, three years ago, and then this last spring another female.

Female camels are very good. We used not to have any at all. When we separated from Big-Haji, the only camel we had was a big white *luk* that we called Kâbuley, a powerful animal that could carry anything, up to 50 seer, and moved so fast that nobody could catch it. When you loaded it, one of its ears hung down like this. It was quite a camel. Everyone wanted it. But it grew old, and finally someone gave it the 'Eye' and it went night-blind. I don't know who did it, we never found out. It was all right during the day, but at night it couldn't see the path. It was a real nuisance when we returned from the mountains, on the night moves it was always falling. We managed to get it down to where we lived then, up by the mill. In those days our friend Haji Châri of Chârbâgh used to have a contraption for pressing sesame seeds and making oil-cake (*konjâra*). When our camel went night-blind, my father said, 'Take it there'. It was very fond of oil-cake. My father gave it to Haji Châri to fatten it up for slaughter in a public sacrifice. He fed it oil-cake for three weeks, then one night, without anybody noticing, it fell into a pit and died.

We got another of our camels, a female, when my aunt Âwâs married Dâdollah; his father Abdollah gave it in her brideprice. The *luk* that died this winter – the one you used on migration last year – was that female's offspring. At Nawruz, in the green grass of the spring camp, the camels are well-fed and the calves don't notice whether it's wet or dry. A big *luk* knows if a female's pregnant and won't do anything; if it's not, the *luk* will mate by force. But a calf that's newly developed, like a fresh boy, can't see anything with its eyes ... Well, some calves were chasing this female over the hills, and I think it must have tripped or something, anyway it went lame without anyone noticing. We fetched Akhtar Bâdi; people said he was an expert, good with camels. He came to the spring camp, took the camel and branded its leg. Then he made a wooden stake and passed it through the flesh of its leg, like so, then bandaged it. He said, 'I know what I'm doing'. But the camel didn't recover, so we slaughtered it.

It had some other calves, apart from the one that died this winter. One was a *luk*, which we lent to Habib and crowd, but they made its back sore, and it wouldn't heal. It was very badly scarred below the hump, where the saddle rests. The wound kept opening again, from inside. We'd dry it, clean it and everything, then in the morning it opened up again, like a spring. Whatever medicine we applied, it didn't get better. It survived for a few years but didn't improve; so three years ago we took it to the mountains, with a light load. We thought, with all the steep climbs, we shouldn't overload it or it'd get worse. We took good care of it, giving it hay and *ardâwa*, and by the time we got to the mountains it was nice and fat. Then somebody told us to give it some broth – if a sheep dies haram,[2] we put it into a large cauldron, fat and bones, tail and all, and cook it into a fatty broth. They said, 'This camel's lungs have gone bad, but it'll get better if you give it some broth.' I said, 'No, the camel's nice and fat now.' However, just then a sheep died haram, so we took it and put it in a large cauldron and cooked it for a long time – there's plenty of fuel in the mountains. All the meat was reduced to liquid. When the broth had cooled, we stirred it, removed the bones and fetched the camel, and several people pulled it over, somebody opened its mouth, and we poured the stuff in. Then we let it loose with the other camels.

Well, what can I say? The broth didn't go down at all well. The camel worsened daily, and even lost the flesh it had put on. We moved camp down to the shearing site. The camel was on its feet, but it looked so weak, you could see it would never make it back to Sar-e-pol. Then two Hazâra Seyyeds came up from Adira village and said, 'Sell us the camel; we're several people together, we'll buy it.' We said, 'The two of you won't be able to take it, go and fetch some more. When we're gone from the mountains, look after it, feed it thorns and wait until winter, and then you can sacrifice it.' We were trying to trick them. One of them was a friend of Pâdshâh's – ask him! This Seyyed, called

---

[2] I.e. dies without having its throat slit to make it halal; so its meat cannot be eaten.

Shâhmusâ, said, 'Pâdshâh's our friend, we gave him rice, and he came back, you remember?' We told him we were off homewards in four or five days. Shâhmusâ returned to the village, then came back with some others, one called Ustâ Khârali and a couple of others whose names I forget. They looked at the camel, and asked the price. We agreed on 1,200 rupees, and told them: 'Pay us next year in wheat or something.'

Off they went with the camel. After just one night, they changed their minds and sent it back. A wind got up, and they let the camel go, without sending anyone with it. It was still some days before we planned to migrate. Now you may have noticed that when it's time for the return migration, the camels are eager to go; they remember home, just as we do. Why? Because in the mountains when they're busy eating thorns, after a while the thorns get tough, and they start thinking of all the nice sweet and salty grasses of the steppe.

That evening the camel came back into camp. We saw it, but we said, 'Leave it, they didn't bring it themselves, next year when we come we'll say we didn't see it.' So next morning we set off, but the camel had fallen down and couldn't move, so we left it behind, sending them word that their camel had stayed on the campsite, but there was no longer anybody there. When they heard, they brought the camel back; it stayed alive for a few days, then died. The following year they pleaded with us, and finally we took only four or five hundred rupees, letting them off the rest of the price; the hell with it. So that's how that camel died.

That was all some years ago. We had no female camels left. In those days Uncle Mowzoddin had so many camels that there was no room for them all in his compound. His camels were famous in the village, nobody had better camels than his. His *ârwânâs* were really good, with fat humps. Khâni-âghâ bought this very *ârwânâ* from him for 3,500. He'd mated it to that white *luk* and that first year it bore this big red camel; it was in the daytime, in the hollow behind our hut. We brought the calf and its mother back; we put a little fat in the calf's mouth, and marked it, in case it got lost, by clipping one of its ears.

A year later the *ârwânâ* mated again, and next spring it had another calf, this time in the hollow behind Big-Haji's sheepfold. Pâdshâh and I went and brought it over the hill to our place. We took turns carrying it on our backs. It was a very good calf. For three days after a camel's born, if it hears the voice of a woman who's wearing a charm against jinns, it'll be badly affected. This calf had heard some woman, I believe, and within four or five days the poor thing died. We laid it down for two or three days as though it were still alive, and its mother grazed nearby; then we skinned it and put the skin on a donkey, and that poor *ârwânâ* would spend the whole day going around after the donkey, sniffing at it.

Camels are terrible things. Have you ever seen a camel whose calf has died? One year in the mountains another of our camels lost her calf; she gave such a bellow – she wouldn't graze, all she did, all day long, was rush about in all directions, wherever her calf had been, sniffing, bellowing, moaning. These camels have a rough life, they get very sad.

Our *ârwânâ* was really fertile. The next year it produced that *maji* – you've seen it, another red female. The year after that, it aborted a calf in winter, just ten days short of its time. The following year we took it to Haji Molk's, to mate with his *arri*, the white two-humper he'd bought for 12,000 rupees from the Âqcha Kabulis. It had hair this long. We took our *ârwânâ* to their spring camp; they kept them together for a couple of days, until they mated. There's no fee for such services; some people don't give anything, but others do. If you take your female to mate, it's luck whether it's successful or not.

Our *ârwânâ* bore a white *maya* hybrid calf. When it was a year old, in late winter, the mother was mated again, to another *arri*, a dark-red bull belonging to Alo Baluch. My father had sent word and we took her over early, before breakfast. Alo Boy said that somebody else had brought their cow over the previous night, and it had mated successfully; maybe the bull wouldn't do it again. Luckily the bull managed to mate again, and last year, while you were here, the *ârwânâ* had a female *maya* calf. We went to the mountains and came back, then, after you'd left us, out there in the spring camp a snake bit that calf. Its leg swelled up; it was so stiff, it couldn't get up. I was there with the sheep, along with Mirzâ-khân's son Alâoddin. That night, around this time, we slaughtered the calf and skinned it. The leg was full of pus, quite uneatable. But the rest of the meat was nice and tender, and it was very fat. When I'd finished skinning the camel, it was time to move the sheep. I was very tired and hadn't slept. Alâoddin and I drove the sheep down Jar-qoduq [*Well-hollow*] and into Jar-e-Ghwâ [*Cow-hollow*] but before we knew it a wolf had grabbed a nice fat ewe and taken it off over the hill. In the morning we saw the vultures gathered round; it was such a fat ewe, it had a bell on its neck and a huge tail.

We have two other camels. One – Fat-Lips – we got from Abdol-Hamid, the Uzbek from Buyna-qara. Do you remember the mare we used to have, the red one we took there? We sold it to him for two camels. It was very agile: the Hazâras of Chamâq, the other side of Chârbâgh, used to play buzkashi on it. A Chârbâgh Hazâra bought it from them, then we bought it from him for 7,000. One year when we still had it, the mare got pregnant, and gave birth to a foal in the spring pastures. Two years later, Abdol-Hamid was very keen to buy the mare, so we sold it to him. In the spring Khâni-âghâ took it to his house and brought back the two camels.

Abdol-Hamid tended the mare, and wouldn't let it be ridden, then he took it to Ghawsoddin Khân and Seyfoddin Khân,[3] and got it pregnant by Kharpuz, one of their fine stallions. It gave birth to a very strong foal. The next winter, as they were gradually breaking the foal in – before it had been ridden – someone offered over 8,000 for it. It was a big-boned animal; at just one year old, it was as big as a full-grown horse. Then, just before the end of winter, my brother Darwiza went to Buyna-qara; Abdol-Hamid handed him the foal and said, 'Put it out to graze in the steppe and fatten it up; take care, we're very fond of it!'

Darwiza drove the foal back by stages. At the end of winter, if they've been ridden hard, animals get very thin and light-bodied. Well, when they got to Behsud the foal couldn't go on. They stayed the night there. I don't know whether anyone gave it straw, whether it ate enough or not. Pâdshâh went and got it to Haji Kabir's place, then they brought it on here. When it arrived, it wouldn't eat straw or anything. People said, 'Try some fresh grass, that'll be better.' There were also some barley-shoots ready at that

---

[3] Aymâq khans of Sangchârak.

time, but it wouldn't eat those either, even when we fed it by hand. In the evening they said, 'The foal's hungry but its heart's frozen, perhaps it'll get better if its mouth gets warm; let's cook up some *ârdâwa*, and put it in its mouth.' But that evening, as we were eating, we looked into the cowshed and saw the horse lying there with its mouth open, dead.

We were really upset, because this foal belonged to a friend who'd entrusted it to our care, and then this happened. Haji was very angry with Darwiza for rushing it home too quickly.

Big-Haji [*Haji Ghâfur*] has eight camels now. You remember Crook-mouth, the *ârwânâ* with the cut lip? She too came from Abdol-Hamid. The Kabulis have many camels. One spring, on their way up to the mountains, they pitched camp at Langar-e-Shâh-Abdollah. One of them had this calf, Crook-mouth, which couldn't walk. He asked his friend, Abdol-Hamid of Buyna-qara, 'I have a camel calf that won't walk, would you like to buy it?' Abdol-Hamid bought it for 70 rupees; he didn't notice until afterwards that one of its lips was wormy, but when he did, he put some medicine on and it got better. He didn't migrate to the mountains, but there was plenty of grass and alfalfa at his place, so he fed the calf well and it grew up.

The first year we got Crook-mouth from him, it came with a small male calf, which died; then it gave birth to another, a female. Now you know how, when we hold a wedding for a young man, his new wife won't enter the house until we've 'untied her feet', for example by giving her a present and bringing her some food; that's our custom. So, when we brought Joma-khân's wife home that spring, Big-Haji gave her Crook-mouth's new foal, 'for the veil' (*paruney*). Some of the women didn't approve of this, but they couldn't say anything, Haji just gave it without asking them, to untie her feet. The foal died last winter.

Long ago Big-Haji got two *ârwânâ* in town from Haji Mullah Hâfez – a relative of Hâshem here – who was friends in those days with both Big-Haji and my father. In spring he'd come out with his flocks and his cattle, and pitch camp in a hollow near us. He was a very honest man. We bought those *ârwânâ* from him: one *ârwânâ* and later another *maji*, and I believe there was also a *luk* that Big-Haji bought. The *ârwânâ* calved several times.

Big-Haji had another *ârwânâ*, which bore good *luks*; but they died. Another *ârwânâ* would bear every year, like a ewe; good strong calves, including one of our present *luks*. Another good *luk* that she bore was called Wild-one. You know that bearded Sufi Niâzi? He was very drawn to it, every year he asked my father to sell it. In those days camels were cheap, four to five thousand, but he offered nine to ten thousand. It was a very good *luk* – but it was stolen. Another of her *luks* went crazy.

Most of Big-Haji's camels come from Haji Mullah Hâfez's camel. Now all his *luks* have died. All his remaining camels are *ârwânâs*. One of them he bought from Khalifa-Patih for 4,000 rupees. He still has the one we gave him. He got another camel, a little black one, from Khalifa-Patih, when Mumin was marrying Gol-Mahmad. He gave it to her free; they still have it.

They got one of their camels from the Arabs, a very nice one that died the year before last. Another they called One-ear, because one of our camels attacked it and bit off its ear; it died last year. Another calf also died.

Big-Haji's sons are useless. When they go to the mountains, they don't look after their camels, they don't graze them properly. Once you've pitched camp, if you care for your animals you send them out to graze. If there's nothing for them to graze, you go into the hills to look for fodder, or fetch straw or other fodder from a friend in a local village. But some people, like Ajab-khân, don't care; they say; 'We're tired, let's rest; why should we work, what difference will it make?' Ajab-khân and the women are as bad as each other. He's crazy like his mother, Keshmir.

Sometimes they move two stages at once: one year, after they'd struck camp at Cherâs, they went on down beyond Esmeydân, all the way to Kâshân. We normally take two stages to do that – last year, if you remember, we camped by the pond at Mordâr-Hawz – but they did it in one. In a hurry not to get left behind, they'd packed their stuff any old how, and as we left we called to them that they'd overloaded one camel. Arriving in the campsite, they settled their loaded camels and sat for a while without unloading them, then, seeing us pitching our tents, they got their camels up again and went on to Esmeydân. The women wouldn't dismount when going up or down steep slopes; their camels were exhausted and hungry – they hadn't fed them enough in the evening – and now they were overloaded, all of them suffering cramps and covered in sores, on their ribs, flanks, everywhere.

They had a very strong horse that they used on migration. When you pitch camp, you remove the horse's saddle. If you don't uncover a horse's back and rub it down, it'll wear out; the skin will fall off. But these people, once they'd set out for the mountains, didn't once unsaddle that horse until they got to Dangak pass. They just didn't care. The poor horse remained saddled day and night, and finally its back swelled up. When we got to Dangak, it stopped at the bottom; Ajab-khân stayed by it, terrified it'd die. Finally, in the afternoon, he gave the horse some hay, and got it over the pass; but next morning it died.

One of Jân-Mahmad's camels was the white *ârwânâ* he got from Boghawi, with a two-year-old male calf, which the Star struck and killed [*see p. 114*]. Another was from the *ârwânâ* that Big-Haji got from Haji Mullah Hâfez. When Jân-Mahmad's son Tuti was small, they took him to Big-Haji, who said, 'Whatever's in my camel's belly this year, it's his.' In spring, the camel bore a little she-calf, and Big-Haji told everyone it belonged to Tuti. When it was four years old, they took Tuti's *ârwânâ* to Haji Molk's *arri* for mating, and it gave birth to the white *maya* calf they have now.

When his daughter Talâk married Haji Molk's son Gollu, Jân-Mahmad got three camels. There was the young *luk* you saw; and before the wedding Haji Molk gave an *ârwânâ*, together with its little male calf. The year before last it gave birth to another calf, which he still has; but the *ârwânâ* wasn't much good, it was past it. Jân-Mahmad would have preferred skins, or donkeys. He got many skins in that brideprice; they completed it by paying 500 rupees one day, 1,000 the next, and so on.

Those were Jân-Mahmad's camels. As for Shir, he used to have an *ârwânâ* that we called Short-tail. She seemed to be sterile but after ten years she finally bore a black *luk*, which grew up but died. Shir also bought a white *ârwânâ* from Jamâloddin for 4,500 rupees, a mongrel, with a *maya* hybrid father and an *ârwânâ* mother. It had a large frame and strong thighs; it was very fast – that was the camel that went crazy, you remember? It came running up from below, but people gathered round and stopped it;

we hit it on the hump, knocked it over and jumped onto it. Dur-khân and I branded it all over the nose, and then, thank God, it got a little better, but it's still crazy. One of our camels was like that when small; we branded it too, and it survived – though it died this spring.

That mongrel *ârwânâ* is a *maji*: this year it'll mate for the first time. Shir had another *ârwânâ* that died; it had a calf that died at one year old, then a hybrid male calf, which he has now. And he has another *luk*, left from another of his camels. Some time ago he bought another *luk* from Jamâloddin for 4,500 rupees, but it died two years ago. Now Shir has just these three camels, two of them male, the other female.

As for Gol, that year when there were so many dust storms and flash-floods, he'd hobbled one of his camels, so when the storms and rain and floods came from up above, they swept that camel away. Big-Haji gave him a camel when his daughter Mumin married Gol's brother Gol-Mahmad. Gol had another *ârwânâ*, a *maya* hybrid. The year before you came, he was camping with Big-Haji; one day when his *ârwânâ* was above Haji's sheepfold, all the young male calves gathered around and beat it to death. The shepherd told Gol. His sons went and saw that the camel had died haram.

Gol has another hybrid female, from one of his own camels that died of old age. One year his family went to the mountains, but he kept the *maya* back because it was pregnant and he wanted it to calve down here, where there's plenty of grass and it can graze peacefully – it's a pain in the neck when a calf's born on migration. The camel gave birth here during the summer, but it wouldn't let the calf come near. Several people helped rope the *maya* up tight, but they couldn't hold it; it just hated its calf, bellowed loudly whenever it smelled it coming, and bit it whenever it came near her udder. The calf couldn't get any milk; it lived briefly, then died of hunger.

That mother's the only female Gol has left. He drove it to join the Baluch camels until the nomads came back from Siâh-band. He bought another male calf for 3,500 last year, at the very end, when there was no straw. It was a terrible time. At first people put out plenty of straw for the sheep – they couldn't know how much snow was coming. When the first snow fell, lots of straw got left underneath. It snowed for several days. In early March, as the snow melted, there was no straw left, but the sheep started to get full by grazing. Sheep eat quickly, but not camels; they have large front teeth and they can't eat so fast, so they stayed hungry and had to be fed hay and straw. At that time, anyone with a camel went out to the sheepfolds to find what had been left under the snow by the sheep, who wouldn't eat it. We lent Gol-Mahmad a large sack, and he happily swept up the leavings from our sheepfold. Then he drove the camel back home, beating it as they went down the main valley, this side of the little pass. He was so happy to have found the straw that he drove the camel at a run, even though it was tired and overloaded. When they got over the main valley, the camel suddenly collapsed from hunger and exhaustion. Now a camel says, 'My master can load me with 50 seers, and I'll carry it all day long on a level road; but on hilly tracks he shouldn't ride me or load me; I mind the hills very much.' This camel was very thin; all winter it had been working, some days it ate its fill, some days it went hungry. Everybody was that way this year. Only perhaps ten people in the village kept their camels full. Camels were so thin at the end of winter they couldn't carry even ten seers. If a person or an animal loses weight, his strength goes too, and he can't breathe. That's what happened with this camel: it ran out of breath. Gol-Mahmad had pushed it too hard. In the morning he went back and found that the camel had died haram; he skinned it and left the rest for the dogs.

This year many camels died. When we went to fetch straw, we saw camels lying here, there, everywhere, all because of hunger. If you care for a camel, don't let it go hungry; give it cotton-cake, for example, then it won't mind working for twelve months in the year. Now the Turkmens take their camels to the salt-pans – you know how far away that is – and to Sar-e-pol and Sangchârak. That's what camels are like.

A camel eats as much straw as six or seven sheep, but you feed it only twice a day: if you give it enough in the morning, it'll be fine until evening; then if you fill it again, it'll be happy until next morning. Sheep eat less than camels, but they're always hungry, curse them; you must feed them early in the morning, at midday, again in the afternoon, and then give them 'night-grazing'.

Some horses eat a lot, some not so much. Cows can't endure hunger, they soon go under; so do donkeys. Sheep are more tolerant; if the ground's clear, and you feed them a little, move them and graze them at night, they'll get by. Donkeys are different; they can manage on almost anything in the way of grazing, they soon fill up. We have a saying, 'what the donkey's eyes see, and its eye-teeth taste, can't easily be cleaned',[4] that is, if a donkey sees just the smallest bit of green grass, it'll get stuck in its eye-teeth – sheep don't have any such long teeth.

Goats are more like sheep. But sheep won't climb hills. For example, at the beginning of *khâklewa*, when the fresh grass is appearing, if you put a herd on a hillside, the sheep won't go to the top, it's too high, they'll go round the side; but the goats will leave them and go straight to the top. The grass on top is like a meadow, because the sheep don't go there. Goats are only happy on the hilltops, so they get full quicker than sheep.

Sheep's droppings are very good. Sheep are excellent, pure animals, better than cows, donkeys, better than any other animal, everything about them is halal. When a ewe gives birth, within half an hour the lamb is walking around after its mother. It gets clean and dry without making a human dirty. Lambs are well behaved. Goats aren't the same, they're rather dirty. Male kids are devils, you may have noticed; at only twenty days old they're already sniffing the females – I've often seen them; they can tell the females, so we call them devils. That's goats for you. Lambs don't do that.

An Old Wolf's Tale

Late one August evening Baya-khân tells this tale; only Pâdshâh and ourselves are present.

There was an old wolf, which was thin and hungry. Whenever a flock of sheep came by, he couldn't get near, the dogs would chase him off. He was a greybeard, really past it.

One day he was following a flock at a distance, hoping to catch some straggling lamb or kid, but afraid that, even if he managed to get one, the dogs would be too much for him and he wouldn't get a meal. He kept well behind, as far as Pâr-khân's house

---

[4] '*Che pë stergo mâlumezhi pë nuse no walukezhi, dë khrë shë ma-pâkezhi.*'

from here, just sniffing the air to keep in touch with the flock; and there, lying on the trail, he spotted a little kid. As he seized the kid by the neck, it gasped – in those days, all the animals could speak – 'Don't kill me, just wait five minutes, I've some nice songs to sing you; in your father's time, I'd sing some very fine songs.' The wolf opened his mouth, and the kid bleated as loud as it could. The shepherd heard it; 'That's one of the kids, it must have fallen behind!' and he called the dogs. They went and chased the wolf and rescued the kid, and the shepherd took it back into the flock.

The wolf went off, saying to himself, 'Curse my stupidity, how could this kid ever have sung my father a song?' He came to a place like our spring campsite, and there he saw a donkey. He loped down to the donkey and said, 'I'm going to eat you' – in those days, everything could speak. The donkey said, 'Don't eat me, wait a few minutes; your father played a lot of buzkashi on my back; I was his buzkashi horse.' The wolf asked, 'How did my father get to ride you?' The donkey explained, 'He'd put one hind leg this side, the other that side, and his two forelegs here on either side, then he'd shut his eyes, and we'd gallop off all over those valleys and hills playing buzkashi.'

Without thinking, the wolf mounted the donkey, who told him, 'Don't open your eyes; if you do, you'll fall off; your father was a great buzkash, he kept his eyes closed when he was riding me.' He closed his eyes, and the donkey galloped off home to his people. As he arrived, a boy cried out, 'A wolf, a wolf!' and when the wolf opened his eyes he found himself in the middle of a camp. He leaped off the donkey, but the camp dogs came after him, and the men beat him, and it was only with the greatest difficulty that he managed to escape.

Exhausted, he sat on top of a hill to rest. After a while he moved on, and came across a camel, a big hybrid. He told the camel, 'I'm going to eat you.' The camel replied, 'Why bother to eat me? My meat will barely last you a few days. In the foxhole under my feet are your father's land deeds. He left them with us a long time ago, then he disappeared and we don't know where he went. Take your deeds, then you can decide whether it's worth eating me or not.'

The wolf said, 'Okay, give me the deeds.' The camel had put a foot on the mouth of the foxhole, and it repeated, 'They're under my foot.' 'How can I get them, then?' 'Come here where I'm standing; I'll raise my leg, you put your head in and fetch your father's deeds.'

As the wolf put his head in the hole, the camel stomped on him so hard that he couldn't get out – camels are very strong. The wolf shat himself trying to get free, until he finally managed to escape, and limped off.

He headed for a high hill and lay there, quite done in. 'Curse me, what made me fall for the kid's trick, when it promised to sing me a song, and got away? And what made me believe that donkey's story about my father playing buzkashi, which led to such a beating in that camp? And as for the story about my father and some land deeds ...'

As he was reflecting on his stupidity, down below he saw a flock; and suddenly a couple of dogs saw him and attacked. The wolf was unable to get up, the shepherd arrived, beat him and killed him.

That was the old wolf's tale!

Wolves and thieves

Wolves are indeed a constant danger, winter and summer. Many mornings we awoke to hear there had been wolves around that night, though we never saw one alive. Shepherds have dogs, not for herding but to defend the herd; they also use slings, stones and long heavy cudgels, rarely firearms.

Pâdshâh pairs wolves and thieves as the shepherds' main enemies.

The shepherd keeps count along the trek, stage by stage. He'll know when a thief or a wolf comes at night. 'The wolf eats, the thief steals.' Some thieves ambush the shepherd, tie him up, beat him or kill him before stealing the sheep. They know the owner's too far away to call for help. It's a day or two before the owner hears; he'll go after them, and may catch them; more likely they'll disappear without trace.

Darwiza details the tactics to follow when enemies threaten.

Dogs quickly get thirsty, you must water them several times a day: early morning, midday, afternoon, and again in the evening. If – God forbid – a wolf gets into the herd, the dogs will chase it around once or twice, but in warm weather they'll soon get thirsty and come straight back. The *mozdur* must fill his bowl with water and give it to them. If you don't give a dog water, it'll stand there, its mouth hanging open, panting from thirst, and it won't chase the wolves.

If you're on your own, with no *mozdur* and no dog, and a wolf cuts out a couple of sheep right in front of you, you must forget them and gather the rest together. If you leave the herd to rescue those two, other wolves will come and split the rest of the herd into two or three, and by morning they'll have ripped up the lot. The owner will be ruined. So, don't even try to find out what happened to those two, just gather the rest and stand with them.

When the shepherd's moving the herd from one hollow over to the next, once the leading animals have reached the ridge he must hold them there to allow the ones behind to catch up; then he should let the front ones down into the new hollow, while the *mozdur* hurries the stragglers over, keeping them together in a bunch. That's because, when the sheep are grazing on the ridge, as the leaders are going down and the others are still behind, a thief will choose just this moment to cut some out, whether from above or below, and neither shepherd nor *mozdur* will know.

The same with a wolf. If half the sheep are on one side of the ridge and half on the other, he's such a crafty bugger, he'll cut them in half on the ridge. He'll get some from both the shepherd and the *mozdur*: with two hundred sheep on each side, he'll grab one before the shepherd sees him and drag it off just a short distance, then before the shepherd can get there, he'll go back and rip open several more. The shepherd must let the wolf have the first, he mustn't abandon the others. But if the dog and the *mozdur* are there when a wolf comes, and the sheep are packed close together, the shepherd should stand fast above the sheep, not below, and stop them breaking away; he should keep the herd together and the *mozdur* can take his dogs after the wolf and rescue the sheep.

Say the wolf's ripped the sheep open and it's lifeless when you get there; slaughter it at once. Our mullahs say that if it just kicks one foot, it's halal. If its limbs aren't moving, yet blood is flowing, kick it the moment you arrive and slaughter it at once – it's halal. The wolf may have started devouring the tail, stomach, liver, guts – why, in five minutes a wolf can eat a lot – no matter, the sheep could still be breathing; look at the heart, and if it's so much as fluttering, slaughter it, and it'll be halal, not haram. Once the heart's gone, the sheep's life goes too, and it'll be haram.

That's how a wolf eats a sheep. As for thieves, if one comes when the sheep are asleep, he'll sit up on the ridge, while the shepherd and *mozdur* are both asleep. The sheep sense the thief's presence at once, and they'll gradually move up from below to get closer to him. They'll shake themselves, their feet, their ears, look around, and off they'll go, right up to him; then he'll take the sheep down, one by one, bind their feet together, come back to get another, and so on. If he knows that the shepherd's still there asleep and not about to come after him, he'll divide the herd and take half. To prevent all this, a smart shepherd will tie 'ewe-strings' (*mish-band*) – one end to the shepherd's arm, like this, the other round a sheep's neck – both above and below the herd.

For us, death and sleep are the same; if a fellow's tired and goes to sleep, he's not aware of anything. But these sheep never sleep. When a sheep's lying down, you can't tell whether it's asleep or dead. As it chews the cud it breathes from here – it might well be asleep; but it moves its eyes round and hardly closes them at all, so you'd think it was awake. Not one of the sheep in the herd is really asleep; if one moves, then the other 500 all know at once and follow it. Wherever the front ones go, the back ones follow. You need a good lead-goat, which'll respond when the shepherd calls 'Cha!' and threatens it. If there's a cliff, or a chasm – like the ones you saw at Sang-e-solâkh – once the sheep head for it, whatever you do, however many shots you fire at them, they won't turn back, they'll hurl themselves off the edge, every single one. Even if the shepherd stands in front of them, urging them back, they'll trample him down or knock him over the edge.

Baya-khân earlier praised sheep as 'excellent, pure animals'; now he declares them to be 'very bad', and tells a story of how a thief got treated.

Sheep are very bad. One year in the mountains, several of our sheep hurt their feet on the rocks and went lame. One grey ewe was so cut up that Khâni-âghâ said it couldn't go on. The Hazâra Seyyeds wanted to buy it, for payment next year. In those days sheep were cheap, but we sold it to them for 800 rupees, on credit. Why should I lie, these sheep are very bad things. The Seyyeds' house was just down below – you've met them. We sold it to Mullah Ahmad-shâh – you didn't meet him, he died. He took it home, and two or three days later he let it out on the slopes to graze on *byetsa* and stuff. But this ewe, I swear, set off on its own and came right back to our campsite. We were surprised to see it; didn't it like that place? So we wouldn't give it back, even if they paid us 5,000 rupees next year. 'It came back all by itself,' we said, 'So we'll take it home; if it gets there, fine, but if it dies en route, we'll eat it.'

We brought it back gently, sometimes driving it along, sometimes tying it on the back of a camel. In those days we used to come right over by Lataband, it's only in the last few years that we've been coming via Sukhta. When we got down to Suzma-qala, the ewe was with the rams; but it strayed, and someone from the village took it off and killed it.

That evening we saw that the ewe was missing. Khâni-âghâ declared, 'There's only one way of finding it,' and he mounted his horse saying he was going to the village to get it back. He's a real expert at such things, very smart, I'm not joking. When he got to the village, he didn't say, 'I've lost a sheep.' He went around asking, 'Has any one got a sheep's head, I need the *kalamang*' – bone-marrow or brain, which we use for fevers. He asked everywhere, and finally a woman produced a sheep's head for him. When he saw it, he seized the householder, saying, 'This sheep was mine! You've killed my sheep, and now twenty of our sheep have been stolen, give them back or we'll get you for this!' The village elders brought the thief to our camp – we were several families – and pleaded with us, 'Please, just take one sheep, forget about the others and let him go!'

Now the law here is as follows: a sheep has twelve bones, and when you catch a thief, according to the sharia and the Book [*Koran*], one stolen sheep becomes twelve sheep, one for each bone; that's the tradition, the custom in Afghanistan.

So when the thief said, 'Your sheep was lame, I'm really sorry, my face is black, I'll give you another sheep for it,' we replied, 'No, you must give us twelve sheep, we shan't let you off; besides, many of our sheep are lost, it's not just the one.' He pleaded: 'I'm so sorry, I did a really bad thing, my face is black, I have nothing, take the one sheep; your sheep was lame, I'll give you a healthy one.' We repeated: 'No, according to sharia it's one sheep for each bone, twelve sheep for one sheep; and there are probably twenty of our lost sheep here, we'll take 140 or 150 sheep from you.'

Finally our relatives and the elders said, 'Let him go, he's apologized. So we went and took a healthy black sheep from him, and let him off the rest.'

The tick man

Ticks (gang) *are another enemy. Baya-khân tells what they do and how to get rid of them.*

If you don't renew the mud-plaster on the sheepfold walls, it'll peel off; then next year, if it's warm, it'll produce ticks. Ticks don't stick to smooth daub. Some people smoke out the sheepfold every year. They build a fire of sheep droppings, smoking under the walls; the ticks don't like smoke, so they come down and run away, migrate somewhere else. People do this smoking only if they know it's going to be a warm year, otherwise they leave it. We don't do it ourselves, because open sheepfolds like ours don't get many ticks. It's only when people build roofs over the sheep, or put them in huts, that they're liable to get ticks. If there's no roof, they stay cool.

If your sheepfold's covered and you don't smoke it, ticks will attack your sheep in autumn and winter. They know where the sheep are and go straight for them; they're crazy for sheep's blood. They land on the sheep's head, dive into their wool and drink the blood, that's all they want; they suck it out and swell up. In two or three weeks they can drain a sheep's blood and knock it off its feet. Sheep or humans, we depend on blood; without blood, we're finished.

If you find out in time, you can get rid of them. Find a *gangi*, a tick man, in Neymadân or Chârbâgh. Send someone by horse or donkey to offer him two or three hundred rupees. He'll hold back: 'I want more money.' Promise whatever he wants, and bring him to the flock. He'll take off his turban, wave it around and run among the herd, crying three times, 'Ticks drop off!' The ticks will open their mouths and drop off, all by themselves. If he's not a proper *gangi*, it won't work. Some people decide the *gangi*'s too far away, so they go among the sheep and kill the ticks by hand.

When a mother bears a son, she may decide to make him *gangi*. The women fetch forty ticks from the sheep, and every night for forty nights they kill one inside the infant's mouth, and the blood enters his stomach. There's another way of doing it. They put the forty ticks in a glass with forty raisins; they'll eat the raisins, then they'll start eating each other, until there's only one left, which has eaten all forty raisins; they kill this one in the boy's mouth, and he'll become *gangi*.

When a *gangi* grows up, and someone's flock is tick-infested, they send for him. I've seen them do it. One year when I was small, they brought an Arab *gangi* to do it – I don't recall whether it was our flock or Haji Ghâfur's – and the ticks just fell off. And we have this lad here, who says his name is Gangi – that's what they call him, but he's a bit crazy, I don't know if he's a real *gangi*; if he were, the ticks would run away. But I've never seen an Afghan *gangi*; Arabs do it, not Afghans.

The Tale of Nokhodak

Baya-khân tells the tale of Nokhodak ('Little-pea', i.e. Tom Thumb).

Once upon a time there was a poor cowherd. He grazed the cattle, but the poor chap had no children, nothing but his wife. If there was any food left, he'd put it in his pocket as he drove the cows out to graze in the steppe. Some mornings, there was no food and he left home hungry. Some days he stayed hungry and thirsty. His wife couldn't go out to the steppe, so there was nobody to bring him food and water. He was out alone in the steppe until evening.

One day his wife went to collect some cow-dung for fuel. She lifted up one cowpat, and underneath she saw a tiny child. She asked him, 'Who are you and where did you come from?' He was called Nokhodak, Little-pea, because he was small as a pea. He told her where he was from: 'I came with a cow, but the cow pissed on me, and I got stuck under this.'

The cowherd's wife was very happy. 'God hasn't given me any children of my own, I'll take him as my child.' So she adopted Nokhodak. In the evening the cowherd came home, and she told him, 'Look at the child I've found!' and he was very pleased. They had a little welcome party. Nokhodak said, 'I'll stay with you and be your child.'

Every day, after the cowherd took the cattle out to the steppe, Nokhodak's mother would bake some bread and then fasten some around the boy's waist. She kept one of the cows back for him, he took hold of its tail, and it would lead him out to take bread and water to the cowherd, who was now very happy: 'God's been kind to me; he gave me a son, who brings me bread and water.'

A long time passed, and every day Nokhodak brought him his bread. Then one day, as he took the cow's tail, suddenly the cow pissed and the poor little boy once more got left behind. When the cowherd came home that evening his wife said, 'Nokhodak took you your bread, what have you done with him?' He said, 'I haven't seen him.' She said,

'Dear God, our son's lost, perhaps a wolf or something has eaten him.' They searched high and low for their son.

Some girls were out gathering droppings for fuel. One girl, picking a piece to put in her bag, also put Nokhodak in. He said nothing. The girls put their bags down, and went further afield to find more droppings. When they were out of sight, Nokhodak collected all the bags, and headed for the cowherd's house, carrying the five or six bags of fuel-droppings with him.

When he got home, he unloaded the bags. His mother was delighted: he'd come back, and he'd brought all these bags of fuel. She asked him, 'What happened to you, where've you been?' He told his story: how he'd been under the cow and its urine; how the girls had come and so on. 'I brought all these droppings from those girls.'

Nokhodak went back to taking the bread and water out to his father, helped by the cow. Then one day a wolf came upon Nokhodak and ate him, but in such a way that it didn't actually touch him with its teeth, as Nokhodak rolled himself up and went straight down into the wolf's stomach like a pill. From then on, whenever the wolf approached a flock, Nokhodak would shout, 'Hey shepherd, the wolf's come!' This was a real problem for the wolf, but it couldn't do anything, since Nokhodak was in its stomach! Every time it got near a flock, Nokhodak called out to the shepherd, who set the dogs on it. The poor wolf was really distressed and grew very thin and tired.

The wolf said to Nokhodak, 'Why are you doing this to me? If I'd known, I'd have chewed you up properly. Now you've got me really angry with your shouting to the shepherds.'

Anyway, the wolf couldn't get near a flock, the dogs always chased it away. Its life was miserable and it grew thinner and thinner. One day, it approached a flock, and Nokhodak called out as usual, 'The wolf's come!' The shepherd's dogs were very strong, they knocked the wolf down, killed it, and ripped open its stomach. The shepherd got Nokhodak out and was delighted, 'God's given me a son!' and Nokhodak said, 'I'll be your son now.'

They lived together for some time, then the shepherd fell ill. Nokhodak said, 'Dad, no matter, I'll go out with the sheep for a few days instead of you.' The shepherd stayed at home. Little Nokhodak took a huge stick, put it over his shoulder and started talking big; he led the flock, making the right noises so that the sheep followed him.

One day a herd of the padishah's camels passed in front of the shepherd's flock. One of the camels was a great man-eating hybrid, which the padishah was very fond of, giving it special care and attention. This camel came up and ate Nokhodak, swallowing him whole like a pill. From inside the camel's stomach Nokhodak called out, 'The camel's eaten me, the camel's eaten me!'

Meanwhile the shepherd moaned, 'I've lost my son, and I'm not well myself.' He asked everywhere, then he came to a village where some people said, 'There was this camel, and something inside its stomach was calling out, "I'm Nokhodak and the camel's eaten me!"' The shepherd collected several thousand rupees, saying, 'I'll go and buy the camel, kill it and rescue my son, so he can come back and look after my sheep.'

He found the camel and asked whose it was; they showed him the camel's owner, who was asking six thousand rupees for a camel worth four thousand; but he bought it, for the sake of his son. He brought the camel home and killed it, and found Nokhodak in its guts and took him out.

The shepherd went back to bed and sent Nokhodak out with the sheep. Soon the shepherd recovered ... and my story's come to an end.

Expedition to the Salt-pan

In the Dasht-e-Leyli, known as 'the other steppe', there is a major salt-pan, Kân-Bâbâ, which supplies the whole region and beyond. The mâldâr *of Sar-e-pol send annual expeditions to the pan to fetch salt for their animals. (See Map C; Favre 2003)*

   Baya-khân narrates his first expedition.

Every year in September or October we go to the salt-pans over towards Andkhoy. We leave on the tenth or twelfth day of the moon, because then it's light all night long, so the camels can see the way. We take food and water and melons. Watermelons are very good, the more you take the better, because there's no water out there in the desert. We also take straw for the camels.

I went the year before last [*1970*]. It was my first time, though Pâdshâh and others had told me about it. They said, 'Don't go, it's very hard work getting salt. It's like rock, it'll cut your hands. You won't be able to lift it.' I said, 'We'll see! Anyway, you won't stop me, I'm going!' So I went, and I did a good job of lifting and loading the salt. If you're tough and willing, you can manage it easily; not if you're weak and lacking energy.

Five or ten people go together, each with several camels. I went with Mahd-Rahim's son Akhtar, Mahd-Amin's son Shirgol, Rawu's son Nasrak, Khoday-râm's son Gol, Haji Wahâb's son Habib and one of his hired hands, my uncle Akhtar, and Jomajân's son Zâher-shâh. I took four camels, Uncle Akhtar one, the other Akhtar two, Zâher-shâh two, Shirgol three, Nasrak three, Habib five, and Gol took two for his cousin Dust-Mahmad.

We started early in the morning, heading towards Seyyedâbâd. We passed Seyyed-Mâmur's cafe at Emâm-Sâheb, where there's a hill as you pass the khans' graveyard. After the hill we turned west, across the river and into the steppe. There are no tracks. I hadn't been before so I didn't know the way, but Habib and the others knew.

We drove the camels on all morning, without rest. We kept them going, munching a little bread as we rode along. At noon we stopped, a little short of Turkmen-Well, where there were some Afghan camps. The camels were very tired. We'd have let them out into the steppe, but there was very little grazing there, so we laid out some straw. They ate a few mouthfuls, while we had our own food. We remounted – we'd left them saddled – and went on to Turkmen-Well, which has brackish water. There was a *mâldâr* there with his two flocks, an Afghan from Akhtarkheyl, I can't remember his name; he kindly lent us his bucket and pulley to water our thirsty camels. Off we went again, to our friend Gol-âghâ's place, up on a hill. Habib went in, and Gol-âghâ's wife came out with him. She asked each of us to bring her back a little salt. Some people agreed, others said nothing.

We set off again, and the rest of the day we just drove on through the Dasht-e-Leyli. It really is God's desert. By nightfall the camels were tired and we were hungry. At nine we stopped at Choghân. We stopped there in a hollow; we gave the camels some straw and we ate too. We left their saddles on once more, and at ten we started off again. It was bright moonlight, and on we drove, right through the night.

Around nine in the morning we came to the edge of the plateau, and there before us was the salt-pan. Have you seen it? It's a vast expanse of salt that would take you a day to get round by car. Imagine the whole Valley between Konjek here and the other side, then up to Sar-e-pol, Âktâsh and Haji Mahd-Omar's place; imagine all that land made of salt.

Before we went on to the salt-pan, we let the camels loose to graze for a while, as there'd be no grass near the salt. When we arrived, five of us went to see the Salt-Boss. It's not a real Company, but there's a Boss in charge of the salt, and all the salt passes under his pen. He writes down every sale. We chose Uncle Akhtar as our leader, to deal with the Boss. When he goes to the Boss, he has the people under him recorded as his group, like a village headman; he says, 'We're so many people, and we have so many camels, 30 or 40.' Each person reckons how much salt they want, according to what their camels can carry. Some camels can take more than 30 seer of salt, some only twenty. For example, if you had two really good camels that could each carry 35 seer, then you could take 70 seer.

Salt was very cheap, just under 5 rupees a seer. We gave the money to Akhtar, saying exactly how much we each wanted, and he handed it to the Boss. Here in the village salt was 10 rupees, but some years, if there's lots of rain, like this year, and the roads are blocked, the price goes up to twenty.

The Boss says, 'This year we're taking salt from the eastern side.' Or he may say, 'We'll take it from the Seyyedâbâd side, or the Chârbâgh side.' They rotate, so that salt is allowed to form in the water; each sector gets its turn every three years.

There are five or six trucks there, with one or two hundred workers, who get 20 to 30 rupees a day from the government. The salt is under water. Some of the workers dig up huge blocks with their picks, weighing 5 to 10 seers. Others pile the blocks up, so that the bottom ones remain in the water but the others get dry. The Boss tells everyone to help themselves to salt and bring it to the scales, along with their camels, and he'll weigh out the salt and give it to them.

We fetched our camels, and sat them down in the water. The workers had built up several piles of salt blocks. We went in pairs, collected blocks and put them on our camels; they didn't like it and wouldn't stay still, but we loaded them and took them to the scales, great wooden ones that could weigh 25 seers at a time, so that if you wanted to load 25 seers on your camel you could weigh it all at once.

We took turns doing the weighing. When we'd weighed some blocks we set them aside, each man's pile separately. As I was inexperienced, I took my turn first. A pair of us could carry only one block at a time. Some people had the bigger saddlebags, others the smaller ones; we secured each one with two ropes. First we fixed the saddle firmly, then we loaded the saddlebag, then we put ropes under the saddlebag – salt is like rock and would tear – and finally we fastened the ropes so that they took the strain.

The scales give you more than you ask for; for example, if you want 25 seers you get two extra; after all, there's plenty of salt. There's so much salt lying there, as though it's taken over the whole country. Some people steal it and cart it off by camel. In the old days, people didn't bother weighing the salt, they'd tell the Boss, 'I've two camels, here's 300 rupees, I'll go and help myself and load them, don't you bother.' You could get a lot of salt free. You'd bring one huge powerful camel, settle it down beside the salt – and hide the other one out of sight. You'd pay 100 rupees to load 50 or 60 seers onto the big camel; then you'd load half on the other camel – one couldn't possibly carry 50 seers all the way home.

Nowadays they've cottoned on, they know all the tricks, and they weigh out the salt. And there are many workers loading the trucks. The trucks go all over the salt – which is hard, so they don't sink in – and bring the salt to the Boss's hut for the winter. All round his hut there are huge stacks of salt blocks, like walls or buildings.

Around there you find a grass called soapwort – you remember, we brought some from the mountains, women use it to wash their hair. There's also a lot of the reddish broom that we saw in Belanghor, and all sorts of other grasses. Anyway, some of these workers make hay from these grasses, red broom and saltwort; they pile it all on top of the salt, and then they pack earth onto it like daub. If they don't, winter rains and snows wash the salt away; but with the piles covered like this, water won't get inside however much it rains.

If you go in autumn when it's dry, you get salt straight from the pan, but in winter the salt in the pan dissolves in the rain. When people come for salt in winter, they take it from these covered piles, starting at one end. Many people go there throughout the winter, like the Turkmen caravaneers. They look after their camels well, feeding them cotton-cake and *ârdâwa* dough-balls, and use them twelve months in the year for carrying salt. People also take salt by truck to Sheberghân and Sar-e-pol. You can hire a truck for 1,500 or 2,000 rupees.

We started work there at nine in the morning, and we were in and around the salt-pan until three or four in the afternoon before we were finished. Then we left the pan and headed back into the desert. I didn't know the way and the others managed to lose it as soon as we got up onto the plateau. As you've seen, it's very flat, and it's very difficult to find the tracks. There's no broad trail for the camels. To go round by the main road would take at least a week. On the short cut across the steppe, some people get lost, but in the end they find their way.

When we got lost, Habib said, 'This way,' Gol said, 'That way' – Gol was experienced too – and Akhtar said, 'No, that way.' They argued, and finally Gol said he'd recognized the track; Habib disagreed, but Gol said, 'If I lead you astray, do what you like to me; but I'm sure it's this way.' Off we went, and Gol turned out to be right. Around ten in the evening we got back to Dasht-e-Leyli. We went down into it, and as we were all very tired, we stopped, ate some food and gave the camels some straw. After two hours' rest we set off again.

When we got to Turkmen-Well we stopped to pick up the straw we'd left with the camp there. In late afternoon, when we'd nearly reached Dara-ye-band, we decided to stop again; there was plenty of grass and the camels were very tired. We let them loose, and they ate their fill. We put some straw out for them in the evening, but they wouldn't eat it.

It got very cloudy, and during the night it began to rain. Everyone was afraid our salt would dissolve. 'Let's get going again, hurry down to the Valley and find a house or a hut where we can protect the salt.' So we set off at midnight, and well before dawn we came down into the Valley. The first canal was full of water, and it was very dark. We dragged the camels over, but one of Nasrak's fell in. We got together to help it up, but some 5 to 6 seers of the salt were gone. Nasrak moaned that his salt had dissolved and his camel had fallen and got very wet, but we reloaded his camel for him and said, 'Forget the salt, be thankful your camel didn't go lame!'

Off we went again, and around six o'clock we got to Emâm-Sâheb, where there are shops and a cafe. Some of us stopped for tea and bought some corn and melons to eat on the road.

And so we came home, via Seyyedâbâd and the Arab villages, arriving here around ten or eleven in the morning. We unloaded the salt, put some of it in the hut, some in the house. Some people's feet were very swollen, so they put grease on them, and also on their hands, cut by the salt. As for the camels, they were very tired and we didn't take off their blankets or saddles for three days; if you bare their backs when they're tired, their skin will swell up.

Some people fetch salt for sale, for profit. As I said, there you pay less than 5 rupees a seer; here in the village you can sell it for 10, or 15 in an expensive year. Everybody needs salt, for household use and for the sheep and camels. Some take 20 to 30 seers of salt when they go to the mountains, for the sheep and camels, as we did last year. We give it to the animals, and to our friends there.

There's no other salt place in northern Afghanistan. People who live in the mountains greatly value salt; there's none there, and they can't come to the salt-pans themselves, they're too busy with farm work. It's too far for them, several nights on the road. They have no camels, and donkeys are no good for this job. *Mâldârs* like the Kamuzai take salt up there by camel. Down here, they can usually get salt at 7 to 8 rupees a seer, ten at most. They take it up to places like Cherâs and barter it for an equal weight of wheat, which is worth 50 rupees or more, or for double the weight of barley. That's the kind of profit they can make. But the thing about salt is that it's as heavy as rock; if you load camels or donkeys with it, they get exhausted and thin. It's very bad for the animals – and also very hard on a man's hands.

Last year [1971] nobody from this village went for salt. It was such a bad year, there was no grass, and everybody was busy collecting hay and stuff. This year perhaps people will go; the summer crops have been excellent, so you can take lots of watermelons. There's plenty of grass in the steppe so you won't need to take straw for the camels.

A Terrible Winter

1971 is the second year of drought in northern Afghanistan, affecting both pastures and crops. Many Piruzai suffer sheep losses, and many who previously went to the mountains do not bother to do so, or send only an unmarried son with the flocks, sleeping with friends or relatives, in a small canvas tent, or even out in the open. Of the 177 households of the Piruzai core lineages, 124 (70 per cent) go, in whole or in part, out to the spring pastures, where they form 43 camps; only 35 households (21 per cent), accompanied by young supervisors from nine others, trek to the mountains.

Two years of poor harvests mean grain is scarce and very expensive; in some parts of Afghanistan people have to eat their seed corn. Winter 1971–72 (between our visits) is severe, and the result is famine and starvation, especially in Ghor and the north-west. Sar-e-pol is much less affected than areas to the south and west, and most Piruzai are able to sow crops (a good harvest follows in 1972), but available winter fodder is soon exhausted, and sudden late snows inflict catastrophic flock losses. Many households abandon pastoralism, some perhaps for good. Few families join the remaining animals in the spring pastures, and none go to the mountains that summer.

We record three separate accounts of the winter, on different occasions.

Piruzai economic difficulties are well illustrated by Baya-khân's account of his attempts to keep the family flocks supplied with fodder during the snows.

Last winter was terrible. We had such a hard time. In the autumn, it became clear that it was going to be a bad winter. There was no grass left in the steppe where the sheep were grazing, it was all dust, just like the tracks. Then for two nights there was a foul dust storm. The first night, a whirlwind came from downriver. You couldn't see your hand in front of your face. In the morning when we went out to the steppe to look for the animals, they were all over the place – and so were the wolves. Everywhere you went, you'd see four or five flocks all mixed up, but in little groups; and the wolves had got several animals and torn them to pieces. Several flocks from here, like Gollu's and ours, were jumbled together; one bunch was here, another over there. We separated them and found that many animals were lost. The next night was windy again, but it was better, moonlit. Those two nights, the wind uprooted what little grass was left in the ground, swept it off and buried it in a pile of dust at the bottom of the hill.

I saw all this myself. I was with the sheep for a while in autumn, just before winter. Grass had fallen into the mouse-holes; I spent the whole day digging it out with a stick, ahead of the sheep. Then the sheep learned to dig in the holes themselves with their feet. This year the sheep fought the dust. When they start doing that, if they bite on the earth when there's no grass, they soon age: their teeth get blunt and fall out.

Our sheep ate through three haystacks out in the steppe, and lots of straw here. We made one haystack in the autumn, and we had two left over from before. Ten or twelve years ago we took three or four *jeribs* of land in pawn from Seyyed Mahmud Âghâ's brother Seyyed Mahbub, in return for thirty sheep and a radio. Last year he bought some sheep when they were cheap, so he came to redeem the land: 'Come and get your sheep.' If he hadn't given us the sheep we'd have taken 1,000 rupees each from him. So off we went to get this villain's thirty damned sheep, skinny as foxes. Winter hadn't set in, but we thought, 'Even if it's a bad one, we have the haystacks.' We kept these thirty apart from the others, put them on some good stubble, and watched over them. Then we let them onto the haystack and they ate like cows, they were so hungry; they were at it day and night and they got through pretty near a whole stack. Because they were so thin, we gave them hay and masses of barley, hoping they'd recover in time for winter. But all but two of them died. If it wasn't for them, our straw would've lasted through the last snow, and we wouldn't have lost so many sheep.

Without those three haystacks, all the sheep would've perished in one night. If we'd sold those thirty sheep in autumn, there'd have been enough hay for at least

2,000 sheep. We thought all of ours would survive, but when that snow came in February, we'd finished our haystacks, so the sheep went hungry for two days, then they started dying; every night 10, 20, 30 of them. We couldn't even slaughter them, we had to throw them out. We sheared them and looked in their bellies, and if there was a lamb foetus, we took it out for the skin, and threw the rest away. The carcasses stacked up.

That was the sort of a year it was. None of our animals died at first, but later they went hungry. Once a sheep 'falls from its stomach', it'll drop dead.

In other years, the new grass is up by late February and the sheep and camels are grazing their fill. This year it wasn't until late March. At first you could find fodder here, at a price. But in late February it ran out completely. My job was to find straw and take it to the sheep.

We went out to the steppe by the lower road, past our graveyard. We reached the sheep after dusk, unloaded the straw, then, without anything to eat or drink, turned the camels round and got back home late, after people had gone to sleep.

My trousers were frozen stiff. It was so cold, you couldn't raise your arms from your sides. When we went by night to places like the main valley, we could hear wolves howling out in the snow. Once, on our way back, we were with some Omarzai, and one of them fell behind; we saw some wolves on top of a ridge and we said, 'Watch out that fellow doesn't get eaten!' We watched, but he didn't make it.

One day, quite early on, my father bought some sesame straw when it was still quite cheap, two gunnysacks at 500 rupees, and Seyyed-shâh[/*Golusar*] and I set off with them for the steppe. We took the good red camel. It was very windy, and that day there was water on the ground; the sun had melted some of the ice, but it was still frozen underneath. As we passed the Ludins, my camel – loaded with a huge gunnysack – tumbled into a deep ditch. I prayed to all the pirs that it wouldn't be injured, that it wouldn't die. Thank God it didn't fall far. I untied the load, fetched a shovel from Mir-Ahmad's house, and made a path for the camel. Then Seyyed-shâh found that we couldn't lift the camel's load. It was very cold, and the sack was huge. Then two men appeared, Haji Najibollah and another, and they helped reload the camel.

We brought the stuff back home. In the morning I loaded it again, to take it out to the sheep. It was snowing hard, snow up to the knees. After a certain point, your feet go to sleep. If you walk in the snow all day, you don't know whether they're your feet or somebody else's, but they don't get any colder. Afterwards, when you thaw out, your feet itch and ache terribly.

Once I went to fetch thorns in Ghajar; another time I went for straw with my father, Akhtar and Seyyed-shâh. They'd turn the camels over to me, and I'd take them out to the steppe. Every day I'd come back, then I had to go off again for more straw. One afternoon I came back from the sheep, but by noon they'd already eaten the stuff I'd taken. My father said, 'I know you're tired, but the sheep have nothing to eat tomorrow; be so good as to go to Haji Molk's' – he'd promised my father two gunnysacks of straw. It was late afternoon, the sun was down. 'You'll get back in time to sleep, so go and fetch the straw and take it to the sheep early in the morning.'

It was dark before I reached Haji Molk's straw-shed. He'd promised us some good straw, but he didn't even fill a small sack for us, let alone the extra one I brought; and it was only leftovers and thorns. I left for home late in the evening, and got back at midnight. In the morning I took off again for the steppe.

That was how I'd fetch and carry the straw. One day the sheep were very hungry, they hadn't eaten the previous day, and in the morning there was nothing. My father had gone to Sheberghân for straw. Here in the village I found a half-full small sack for 800 rupees; I took it on horseback to the sheep and came home. My father got back the next day. I took the camels to the road to fetch the straw he'd brought; I packed it up and took it off to the sheep.

Once again we ran out of straw. My father told me to go to Sheberghân to get some. I went to Sheberghân by truck twice, and three times by camel.

The first time, when I got there, it was too expensive, so I went on to Balkh, and then to Mazâr-e-Sharif, and straw was expensive there too. I returned to Balkh: this side of it is a village called Piâz-kâr, where I got some straw for 55 rupees a seer; there they have the Mazâr seer, twice the amount of one of our Kabul seers [7 kg], so in effect I got the straw at 27½ rupees a seer. I filled my sacks with straw, put them on a truck, and got back to Sheberghân at dusk the second day. There were no more trucks leaving for Sar-e-pol then, so I had to stay the night. At noon the next day I found a truck and loaded the straw. By mid-afternoon we'd reached just above Karim-khân's place, when we found the road blocked by twenty or twenty-five trucks, all loaded with straw or flour. A tractor came and dragged one or two out of the way. Some trucks got through, others were stuck. We stayed there until late evening, hungry, thirsty and cold. They finally cleared the road by ten. We got to Shâh-Mahmad Khân's teahouse in Seyyedâbâd at two in the morning, very thirsty. We stopped the driver, got out and entered the teahouse. Our food was frozen; we had 4 or 5 days' food left, but we were hungry so we ate it. We drove off again until we stopped level with the village, opposite the graveyard. It was bitterly cold, but the people here didn't know I'd arrived, so I slept there on top of the straw. That night some Bakhtyâris had arrived before me with some straw, and they'd made a fire. I warmed myself at their fire; in the morning I sent someone to fetch camels for the straw.

I spent the day here at home, but the next day my father said again: 'The straw's finished, off you go.' So off I went to Sheberghân again. I bought straw at 25 rupees the basket-load, which I thought was cheap; I got a good bundle. That day, though, it was late, and there were no more trucks. The next day I put my load on a truck, but it was dark before I got back. They brought the camels to the road, and we loaded them and took them home.

A couple of days later the straw ran out once more. What can you do if you have several hundred sheep, ten camels, and five or six cows? We just kept them going for a few days by giving each one a mere handful at a time; they were neither starving nor satisfied. We couldn't go to Sheberghân by truck any more, as our money was running out, so my father told me to go by camel. Those camels were our salvation. If it hadn't been for them we'd have been done for. In fact, it was quicker to go to Sheberghân on foot, with the camels, than by truck.

Three times I went by camel. This first time I was with Seyyed-shâh's brother Delâwar, who's lame and can't walk; he rode a donkey, while I had neither horse nor donkey – our one horse was busy here carrying straw – so I walked with my camel. When we got to the graveyard it was snowing hard, with a bitter north wind. Delâwar said: 'We can't go on in this snow, we'll die! I'm going home.' I answered: 'I'm going on even if it kills me; we can't go home, there's no straw or anything there for the animals; if you let the animals starve you might as well kill yourself. Go home if you want, but I'm going on into the steppe. I'll take my chances with the wolves.'

Delâwar stayed with me, and on we went. He let me ride a few paces, and sometimes on that first trip I rode my camel for a short distance. When we got to Sheberghân, we found some baskets of straw at 35 rupees; it cost 1,000 rupees to fill one sack, a light camel-load. We spent the night, then at nine in the morning we set off home, driving our camels on without stopping. We'd bought four pounds of cotton-cake, which we gave the camels along with a little straw. We stayed on the road up to the halfway point, just before the Pakhizai settlement, then we cut across to the steppe at the graveyard.

After we got home, it wasn't two days before the animals got hungry again. However tired I was, if the animals were hungry it was no good sitting around, so the next day my father sent me off again. This time there were more of us: Madu, me, Parwiz's son Dust (who was going for Jomajân), Jomajân's servant, and Rawu's son Nasrak. In the morning, after some tea, we set off. We reached Sheberghân late in the evening. Next morning we bought straw for 30 rupees a basket – cheaper than last time. For a good camel-load – two sacks – we paid 1,500 rupees. We loaded the camels and got home around ten or eleven at night.

We slept for a couple of nights; then the straw ran out once more, so off we went again. Three times I went with this same camel; the others couldn't have made it, they were quite done in. The third time, I found some straw, filled the sacks and left them at a teahouse for the night. At nine or ten in the morning I gave the camel a little straw and cotton-cake and ate some bread myself, then we set off. By the time we got to Karim-khân's place, my feet had swollen so much in my boots that they were like this. There was nothing for it, I had to go on. When I got home my feet were so swollen that I couldn't walk for several days. All my toenails turned black and fell off, and new ones started. When I put my feet near the fire they hurt so much; they didn't like the fire, they burned.

One day the camels were hungry. They went around the compound bellowing. My father wasn't there, so I broke up the cowshed, which was made of dry straw and grasses. Any other year, the camels would have rejected such stuff, but these camels jumped on it!

Anyone who had straw made a pile of money. People would come and beg him. He'd behave as though he were on a mountaintop. He'd sit up there, and he wouldn't come down. However much you begged, he wouldn't give you any, even for ready cash. As for getting straw on credit, not a hope! People went from house to house with money in their pockets, but the straw was finished. That was the sort of year it was.

Haji Wahâb [*Khâni-âghâ's father-in-law*] sold lots of straw. He's a smart guy, he knows the world – he dreams it at night! He knew what kind of winter was coming. They worked hard to fill their straw-shed; they collected 300 to 400 loads. When people ran out of straw, they went to Haji Wahâb and his daughter-in-law Nanawor and begged them. Women went to Nanawor, men too. She took 100 rupees from one, 200 from another; she sold the straw off, by stealth. Later it snowed, and the Kohestâni people brought their flocks down. Haji Wahâb is a hard man, and he sold them straw at 200 rupees a seer. In that snow, the Kohestânis were forced to pay, they'd nowhere else to go.

One day Habib [*Nanawor's husband*] gave us a sack of straw. My father sent me to fetch it, and Habib said, 'Wait until my father's gone out; hide behind the compound, walk around.' But Haji Wahâb wouldn't leave the straw; he spent the whole day watching over it, in case his family gave it away. When he came this way round the compound wall, I went the other way, and vice versa, to stop him seeing me. Finally, when his father went to the mosque, Habib sneaked a sack-full for me. It was rotten yellow straw, leavings, but we were so happy to get it.

We got some straw from Mullah Jabbâr [*Pâkiza's father*]. He had only a cow and a bull to feed. We went two or three times – Pâkiza went twice. Twice he gave us a sack of straw worth 700 or 800 rupees – in the end you couldn't get such a sack for 2,000 rupees. Akhtar and I went to Mullah Jabbâr's house one cold early morning. We filled a sack with straw. We jumped on it, to get more in, and he kept saying, 'That's plenty, don't jump on it,' but we finished off his straw! We got some 2,500 to 3,000 rupees worth of his straw, and he gave some to others until he had nothing left. He'd also sold some for 10,000 rupees.

When my father was up there, Haji Kabir Alizai gave him two sacks of straw. Early in the morning he sent Haji Kabir's man on horseback to get us. A heavy snow had fallen that night and the road hadn't been cleared, so we took the camels. The snow filled my shoes. I loaded the straw and took it straight out to the sheep, without coming home. I got back late in the evening.

Haji Ghâfur didn't have to buy any straw this year. Once he gave us some. He farmed his own land and brought in his own straw and grain, and he never ran out of straw. In early winter, after the Migration Forty, his sheep were grazing with ours on the set-aside. When the grass finished, he sent his sheep up to Kuh-e-Naw. Not one of our sheep had yet died, and they were nice and fat; and if they'd gone too, they wouldn't have died later. But Haji Ghâfur's sheep were kept too long on Kuh-e-Naw, until January. On the way down they all caught a chill, and when they got back they started dying, two a day, five, ten; about a hundred of them died, before any of ours. They never went hungry, they died of cold. If a sheep catches cold, its tail freezes solid, so that even if you melt it, it won't make fat. In our case, it wasn't cold, it was hunger.

Nobody else sent their sheep to Kuh-e-Naw. At the same time, though, or a little later, but before the snow came, others in the village – Haji Wahâb, Gollu, Mahd-Omar – sent their sheep up to Mirzâ-Walang, where the locals set aside meadows for sale; it's like Kohestân, with trees and bushes. They spent a few weeks there. Gollu lost a few sheep; Rawu and Mahd-Omar didn't lose any. Haji Wahâb lost a few, but he still had a sizeable flock left. Everyone lost sheep, except those three or four families. As for Jomajân, his dead ewes had lambs with skins worth something, so that whenever he lost one he'd open its belly and the proceeds of the foetus paid for a replacement.

Mahd-Omar lost none at all, and he never bought any fodder. But one snowy night, when his shepherds were asleep, the sheep moved away. There's a gully near Mullah Jabbâr's camp; the dumb sheep fell in – sixteen fell on top of each other and died. The shepherd didn't know; when he awoke and found them, he managed to slaughter two or three but the rest died haram. So Mahd-Omar lost a few, but not from hunger or cold. Perhaps he lost some twenty-five or thirty in all. This year, if somebody lost half of his flock, people thought that was nothing. It was a terrible winter.

Mâldârs in the western steppe had two or three flocks each. They say there was a rich man with two flocks, and one night there was a blizzard and both flocks were buried in the snow; they all perished, including the shepherd. In the morning the owner went and nothing was left of them.

The Mahmudkheyl over there had sixteen or seventeen flocks. They took them to the area of the Kân-Bâbâ salt-pans. A blizzard started and one or two from each family went to bring the flocks home. As they were driving them home, the blizzard got worse. Sheep can't go into the wind, it hurts their eyes. Well, those flocks were annihilated, all in one place. Barely fifty animals were left.

Cows died this year too. Do you think their stomachs were full enough to keep them alive? The Hazâras lost many cows. Two of our camels died; one was Crook-mouth, you saw her last year, the female with the cut mouth that was suckling her calf. She starved, then faded away day by day. We slaughtered her on the veranda over there. The carcass stayed there four or five days, there was nobody available to skin it or take it away. My father was away, so was I. Pâdshâh and Nasib were out in the steppe-camp, and 'Sheykh' Kala-khân is not the sort of guy to do any work, you know; he came out, then quickly went back indoors saying it was too cold! Once I was free I collected a few guys and we skinned the camel. Seyyed-Gholâm's house ate some of the meat, and Pâkiza took some and cooked it one night. But people were too busy to care for meat. This year my father and I were so tired and miserable about the sheep, we just cried. Don't ask any more.

It was a terrible winter. My bones shiver when I think of it. The sheep died, but that wasn't as bad as the endless labour, which really got us down. We went hungry; many a morning we went without breakfast. You couldn't go out in the snow, but we had to go and work. This year people didn't think of their stomachs. Everybody asked about straw or thorns. If you went to Sar-e-pol or Sheberghân and saw someone carrying straw, you asked where he got it from, how much for. That was the talk; not who'd run out of flour and was hungry. People worried about the hunger of the camels, the sheep, the horses. One of our camels aborted its calf from hunger; and our mare aborted its foal.

Anybody who ran out of straw had to find some cash. You'd beg off your friends. If you had credit some place, you went there, otherwise you had to take a loan on interest. For example, you might get 10,000 rupees for 12,000 after a month. My father went to Chârbâgh and got 10,000 for, I think, 13,000 after three months. He had a friend there called Haji Jafar, so he went and said, 'I'm doing my son's circumcision ceremony; you're my friend, one day I could help you; can you lend me 10,000 rupees?' So he gave my father the money, making a profit of 3,000: 1,000 a month. If my father'd said he wanted the money for straw, he wouldn't have given it. That money too ran out. My father went there once more, but found that they wouldn't lend money at less than 100 per cent per month.

This is called *sud*, usury. *Sud's* very bad. *Salam*, pre-selling, is different; for example, when wheat is 50 rupees a seer, you pre-sell the coming harvest at 25 a seer; then, even if wheat rises to 100, you still have to pay him back the agreed amount of wheat. *Sud's* just cash. In other years, people would loan 1,000 rupees at 100, even 50 a month . . . but this year they wouldn't loan 1,000 rupees at 300. If you make a deal with a usurer, borrowing 10,000 over three months, he'll never press you to repay, he's happy to wait; if you pay him within three months, Okay, but if you're a month late, he'll demand more money. But he won't ask for his money back, he's happy to let his money grow.

The Hazâras of Chârbâgh are rich. The poor folk from the western steppe came and pawned their rifles, pistols, carpets. They brought good Sefiri and Malakhi guns worth thirty to fifty thousand rupees, and pawned them with the Hazâras for 10,000. They'd contract for three or four months, or perhaps until autumn; for example, 'We agree today that you take my gun in pawn for 10,000 rupees, and if I don't redeem it within three months, it becomes yours, whatever it's worth.' You'd get a gun worth 50,000 for just 10,000. That's how the Hazâras made so much profit this year.

One day, when the government was distributing cotton-cake at 25 rupees, my father wasn't around so Seyyed-shâh and I went to Sar-e-pol to get some. We spent two nights in town. We hired a horse-cart for 150 rupees, then I went to Tâj-Mahmad Khân and said, 'My father isn't around, please help us get some cotton-cake; our sheep are hungry and our straw and barley are finished.' He sent someone with us to the godown (*godâm*), and they sold us 70 seers. By then it was already noon, so Seyyed-shâh and I and the carter loaded the cart and set off home in the snow. After we passed Big-Haji's house, the track got muddy. At every canal, we unloaded the twelve sacks and carried them over the canal on our backs, then reloaded them on the other side. When we got to the canal by Mullah Jabbâr's house, the horse slipped on the frozen ground, fell and broke some teeth and was bleeding. The carter cried: 'Curse the day when I agreed to come, I was going to make a little money, but look what's happened to my horse!' Well, we got home around this time of night, wheeled the cart inside the compound and unloaded the cotton-cake onto the veranda here. We brought the carter in; we'd got so wet on the way, the poor guy was frozen stiff. At home they'd made some curd-soup, and he wolfed it down. In the morning we said goodbye, and off he went.

The animals were so thin, we gave them only a little of the cotton-cake, but several seers went every day. To get cotton-cake we rode to town on horseback, camels couldn't go fast enough. We took two horses; one was Haji Kabir's mare – which Richard borrowed last year. After our straw finished we sent it back. At the end of winter, people said: 'Ah, now the horses can graze their fill', so they let the horses out. Haji Kabir sent the mare out with that useless son of his; he wasn't thinking, and let the horse go hungry for several days, and it died. But our own black mare is very strong and healthy, look at it. It was ridden all day, to and from the mill, by us, Dur-khân, Seyyed-Gholâm. One day that bastard Seyyed-Gholâm took it and didn't give it any barley until late afternoon. If you do that to a pregnant mare, she'll get mouth-sores and abort her foal. He brought her back that evening, without having fed her, and next morning she aborted.

It was a very bad winter. It makes me shiver just to think of it. My toenails all fell off, and my feet swelled up. I put salt on them. It was very hard.

Pâdshâh and his wife Pâkhâl stayed out in the steppe with the sheep and the shepherds. Pâdshâh had to supervise the animals as they succumbed to the cold and hunger.

In autumn, after you left, Nasib and I went out to the steppe-camp to make hay. Pâkhâl was with us, but at first there was nobody else. Niâzak, the Arab *mozdur*, was grazing the sheep. Nasib would go out at night with Dastgir the shepherd, and every other day he'd come to the Valley for water. We continued haymaking like this right through the autumn.

Then late one afternoon at the end of November, a violent whirlwind came from the north and filled the air with dust. You couldn't tell whether the sun had set or not. People wouldn't go outside, for fear of falling into a well or a ditch. The sheep couldn't see their way, and all the flocks in the steppe scattered, no matter what the shepherds did. We could hear shepherds calling from all directions, but the flocks simply wouldn't stay put. Pâkhâl, Nasib, my young son Pastuk and a couple of Dur-khân's men helped me round up some 60 Arabi, and we tried to shoo them by hand into the trees, over the wall into the sheepfold. It was really hard; I couldn't keep a lantern alight. Finally we got those sheep in. I posted people around, to keep them from getting out.

I took the lantern and went over to Haji Tabu's flock, below Dur-khân's house, where the track goes down. The wind had spooked the sheep. They wouldn't keep still however much you yelled and whistled at them. They scattered, one bunch heading for the wells. But that night you couldn't see a thing, neither wolf nor dog. I spent the whole night wandering around looking for sheep. I went off to Rishmin's camp, and there were our two shepherds, Dastgir and Niâz, both fast asleep, along with their dog, but no sheep in sight, not one! We had 630-odd sheep, and there weren't six of them left! They'd no idea what had happened to them. I said, 'Up you get, let's go find those sheep!' So I sent them off in different directions. We found five in one place, ten there, twenty here, forty there, and brought them back to reunite them with the ones in the sheepfold. Dastgir brought in some, Niâzak others, and I brought in some more. When we got back, forty more sheep came after us of their own accord! Others were mixed up with Big-Haji's flock, or Gollu's or Tabu's, or with the Nâmanzais. Everybody's went everywhere, you couldn't tell. What a night it was! In the morning both my eyes were red and sore, full of dust.

At last the wind died, and people rode out from the villages. We drove all the flocks back to the Valley, and everybody began sorting out their own sheep. When they'd put their own flocks back together again, some found they'd lost twenty, some just two or three, or none. But many had perished.

Soon it rained and some grass came up. We had a set-aside meadow and plenty of grass, and our sheep got nice and fat. Elsewhere there wasn't a single blade of grass, and the sheep were very thin. People came to look at ours, and said, 'What nice fat sheep!' If you'd seen them, Richard: their colour, their tails, their backs! I'd dyed them in different patterns, so nicely you'd have wanted to take pictures. Nasib and Dastgir took care of the Arabi sheep, and put an Arabi ram among them.

Then one January day the first winter snow fell. When it had melted, I came here and suddenly I had a premonition; I told my father, 'You must buy straw; this year we'll run out and the sheep will die of hunger.' Somehow the words came out of my mouth. Haji smiled and said, 'Out there are three haystacks, and we have plenty of straw here in the village; we don't need any more.' I said, 'Okay, but I've warned you!'

I returned to the steppe. A week hadn't passed when the snow set in. It snowed at least every other day, and it settled thickly. When it began, we had some seventy newborn lambs, together with the thirty thin sheep we got from that Seyyed Mahmud

Âghâ. The lambs were tiny and I didn't want them to catch cold. We made a shelter, put them inside, and fed them special barley and cotton-cake, and some of them a little bread, to ensure they survived the winter, for their skins. I kept feeding them grass and stuff; and the snow kept falling. It got very cold, my feet swelled up – Nasib and I were as bad as each other. I had an Uzbek *mozdur* from Sayyâd; his feet were even worse, poor chap. None of us could walk properly.

After the hay finished, every day Baya-khân would bring some more. When he brought four sacks, I'd open one and pour it out, but there were hundreds of animals and they couldn't get enough – sheep eat a lot, you know. At dusk, we gave them the next sack. In the evening we gave them barley and cotton-cake. I knew very well that one sack at a time was too little. They were like a man with a large stomach, who can't get enough to eat. I kept sending to Haji for more, but all that came was a camel loaded with two sacks of hay, or two sacks of straw, or a donkey-load of thorns. Two camel-loads would have been okay, but one wasn't enough. So Baya-khân rode all over the place, to Chârbâgh, to Behsud; he bought thorns for six or seven thousand [*rupees*] from Seyyedâbâd, from the village, from Mullah Jabbâr. We got some from everybody, from Big-Haji, from Haji Molk, from the whole village.

My arms got as green as grass. I picked up one ewe, another one fell. Eventually I couldn't pick them up any longer. Then one day, the straw didn't come. Every day my father would send Baya-khân and Akhtar off, with cash, but now they couldn't find straw anywhere. In the end he told them, 'If you can't find a sack of straw for 10,000 rupees this evening, I'll have to go and get a truck-load from Sheberghân.' So Baya-khân and Akhtar went off, but they couldn't find any. They weren't like my father; everyone has his own weight.

I was out with the sheep and knew nothing of this. I didn't know that Baya-khân hadn't sent any straw. By midday nothing had arrived, and the sheep were left high and dry. I went over to Big-Haji's place; his son Joma-khân was there with his mother Keshmir and his sister-in-law Negâr, and they had some straw. I pleaded with them; I bared my head and said, 'By this cap and turban, my straw hasn't come; give me some, or my sheep will be dead by morning!' Richard, I begged them, but Joma-khân swore that he couldn't give me any straw. Finally I used force. I knew they had some sweepings left, so I grabbed Joma-khân and said, 'Kill me, but I'm bringing my sheep onto that straw, where your sheep have already eaten.' I brought them, but Negâr got up to prevent them, and so did Keshmir and Joma-khân. I said, 'I'll kill myself, or I'll break you into little pieces – let my sheep in!' Finally he put down a little straw for them; the sheep got something to eat, better than nothing.

The following afternoon, our father sent Kala-khân with a camel-load of straw, in the big gunnysacks one buys in Sheberghân. This was enough for 24 hours. In the evening I laid out the straw in forty or fifty little piles, then I went to fetch the sheep, led by the *serka* billy-goat. The ewes with late lambs in their stomachs came to the straw and ate some, but half the ewes – those with larger and heavier lambs inside them – just stayed put, so hungry that they couldn't get up. Meanwhile the weather had turned very cold; man and beast were freezing. The sheep just lay there. As I passed behind Jân-Mahmad's hut, I cried; why should I lie? I was so angry, I swore at everybody, Akhtar, Baya-khân, my father and everybody.

Don't ask me any more. That's how it was with the sheep. I told Pâkhâl, 'Take all the flour we have and make chapatis, give the sheep one each, and perhaps their stomachs will warm up and they'll feel better.' But whether I gave them bread or cotton-cake, the sheep were done for. That night I didn't sleep. I got up to move the sheep; I was really worried they'd all go. I tried to pick them up, one after another. In the middle of the night I found some leftover straw, put it down in the sheepfold, and set the sheep onto it. Those that had eaten that afternoon, they ate now too. The others were still unable to eat: I offered it to them in bowls or pots, or on a cloth; some ate a little, but some ate nothing, they were done for. That one night I slaughtered 25 ewes. I took out their lambs, some so big, some so small, some with two or even three. All I did was open their stomachs; there was nobody around to shear them or skin them. I had nothing to eat that evening or the next morning.

In the following days we slaughtered 10 or 20 sheep a day; never did I kill fewer than five or ten. All I did was cut the throats, when I could; many of them were haram. I filled the hut with the carcasses. There was nobody to skin or butcher them. I took the foetuses from their stomachs, and put them in sacks, along with the guts. I piled the wool alongside the carcasses, like a haystack.

Nasib and I worked on throughout the winter. I'd get up three or four times a night to dry out the sheepfold, then go back to sleep. I'd clear the sheepfold floor and then make patties of the new dung, for fuel. But despite all my hard work, my feet – ask Pâkhâl – froze stiff as sticks. I couldn't come near the fire; if I stretched out my hands towards it, it was as though I'd cut them open. At mealtimes I'd tuck them under my arms for half an hour, then later, when I'd got a bit warmer, I could put them over the fire.

So it went on until mid-March, the end of winter. One day I climbed the big hill behind the sheepfold. I looked around, feeling so miserable I wanted to throw myself down into a gully. I saw the sheep, their necks all bent from hunger and suffering, their udders so small and shrivelled. I couldn't bear to look at them, and I didn't want to go home. My heart was really in my boots. I was so tired, I just wanted to disappear.

What can I say? Thank God those days came to an end. At last the snow melted, and the remaining sheep got enough to eat. After an evening meal we had a quick nap, then got up to herd the sheep again; I took them out with the *mozdur*. All night we kept them moving, from hollow to hollow, grazing continuously until dawn. Before the sun was up we brought them back. For three weeks we struggled on that way, grazing the sheep night and day, going without sleep. We reckoned that if we could get through this hard time, things would be okay, these 100 sheep would be saved, otherwise …

Well, during those three weeks, the sheep did find themselves; they put on weight, they recovered their strength, and I realized they'd be all right. However, all the ewes aborted their lambs. I gave the dogs the really immature foetuses. I sent about a hundred to my father, those with just a little wool, lambskin-wise. I sold a few to passers-by. For a month or two in spring, I acted as shepherd myself, with the survivors. They'd suffered a lot, not one of them had been able to walk. In the winter I gave them all sorts of pills and herbal medicines, but whatever I did, Richard, it was no use. During the forty to fifty days I was with the few survivors, they put on weight, but then the bastards lost their wool. As soon as they got back into condition, it fell off by itself.

So it all came to an end. There'd been 650 sheep in the flock when they went to the mountains; about twenty died or were lost or sold, so they brought back some 630 for the autumn – after you left. We took them out to the steppe, and counted them there. Our own animals, including the lambs, and those belonging to my brothers Darwiza and Khâni-âghâ, came to 380 or 390 head. Uncles Dur-khân and Akhtar I think had sixty. Rishmin had 150 – he was still with us. Then there were thirty belonging to Ahad the Arab, whose house you visited the other day. I asked the shepherd how many had died, and so on, then we counted them, and the total came to 630. That included last year's lambs; we count the lambs from autumn onwards; we had 73, three of them male; now there are only sixteen or seventeen left.

When I counted the ewes in spring, there were altogether 107 left, including Khâni-âghâ's and the others. Forty of them were Arabi: we'd had sixty Arabi ewes that were mated; nobody else had any. Only twenty of them died, I think they were better than the Karakuli, most of which died.

Uncle Dur-khân had twenty-seven left; he sold a couple in spring, and a few more when they came down here in June; then he sold nine to Jomajân for 9,000 rupees; so he has a dozen left.

Rishmin had 150 sheep, large and small. Fifty died in the winter. In spring he bought fifty replacements, so he now has as many as last year. And his skins came out all right; he put the ram in in late September, while we waited until mid-October; it made all the difference. He did have some Arabi, but he put them to a Karakuli ram; this year skins sold very well, and Arabi skins sold as well as Karakuli, there was little difference in price.

Big-Haji has about 110 sheep left, I believe. Last year, he had 350-odd, including about 290 ewes and about 60 of last year's lambs. Jân-Mahmad had 113. He didn't starve them; he had plenty of grass and straw, and not that many sheep. They were in Haji Ghâfur's flock, but he separated them out in early autumn. He wouldn't join anybody else; all winter he grazed them himself, in the steppe. His family went too. He has some forty-five sheep left, including rams; the rest died.

So we really lost a lot of sheep. If there'd been straw, if my father could have sent it from Sheberghân, if these lads could have found it here ... There was plenty of straw but the owners wouldn't sell, the bastards. They said, 'What about my cow, my donkey, it'll die.' They were scared, they kept looking at the sky to see if it was raining, while they kept tight hold of their straw. We couldn't take it by force! After my father left for Kabul, the sheep died of hunger. We lost the lot. We slaughtered some of them, Richard, they were so plump. We cooked their meat in their fat. Their stomachs had gone quite dry, there was no grass inside them; their guts were thin and transparent, as though you'd blown air through them. When a sheep's fat, see how big its guts are. We gathered up their guts, and there was hardly anything in them, not a scrap of hay or straw.

Oh God, the troubles we saw. One day I asked Abdol to give us some straw, and then in the afternoon I took up a stick and went off towards the Valley. As I came down to Mullah Hâfez's sheepfold I met Kala-khân coming up from below. I swore at him, 'What happened to you? If you don't get some straw to the sheep right now, they'll die!' But the sheep wouldn't eat the straw he brought, which our father had bought in Balkh. Balkh straw is very chunky: they thresh it with horses, which don't do it properly; you need oxen with a proper threshing-board. The sheep were already weak and they couldn't eat this chunky straw, so they died.

That winter we sat with the kids in one room – the one with the door, where you slept. We cooked in there. We put the sheep in the other room and another hut we'd put up outside. I'd go out in the snow and look at the sheep: 'See, that one's done for, it can't get up.' I'd hoist it on my back, and bring it into the hut, hoping it would get warm. All the same, in just a few days they died. We brought in some more, and they died too; and so on. It was better outside; a few of the sheep actually improved. Once you bring a sheep inside, you can wash your hands of it. There's a saying, left from old times. *Che pë kur de krë, pë gur de krë*; 'What you bring into the house, you bury.'

Pâkhâl tells Nancy how she was mistreated by Tumân's half-brother Dur-khân and his family.

This winter I suffered so much. There were several snowfalls before the sheep started dying. During the first they were fit and well. They survived the second, when the ground was white everywhere. Then it snowed for three days and nights – that was when I had my daughter. The morning after the birth, it got warmer; a nice clear day, and much of the snow melted. Then Akhtar arrived with camels and a horse, loaded with thorns and straw. They unloaded them here. I was lying down, still unwell, but he was hungry, so he ate some dry bread before going off again.

Gol-Ahmad's family – his wife Negâr and his mother Keshmir – arrived the day after the birth.[5] They brought a horse loaded with dry firewood, and a sack full of dried dung. That night their *mozdur* Mir-Hamza [*son of Ghaws and Shâhpari*] came over, saying, 'Pâkhâl, Negâr wants a few sticks.' I said, 'We don't even have enough sticks to heat our own pot.' But Dur-khân said, 'I'll get them some.' While we were still asleep, he came and said, 'Pâkhâl, give us some fuel.' I said, 'I haven't got any to spare; I've got just a little, here in the hut; but I'm unwell, I can't go out to get more, please don't take it.' As I lay there, Dur-khân grabbed most of it, leaving only a scrap. Even what he took wasn't enough for a proper fire, so – still early in the morning – he came back with his kettle and said, 'Get up, Pâkhâl and boil this for me.' I said I was unwell. He repeated, 'Up you get,' so I had to get up, boil his water, make some dough and cook some bread – Dur-khân's family had brought the flour. Then his daughter Golapruz came and said, 'Sister-in-law, all our clothes are wet, our place is wet, give me some dry fuel.' So I got up and gave her two dung cakes.

The night this daughter of mine was born, four of our sheep died, but the dying hadn't really begun for us, unlike other people. The next night, after Akhtar left, it clouded over; and five sheep died. The following day was cloudy, and it wasn't warm. I was still lying by the brazier; my feet, my back, all my body was aching from the cold. Baya-khân arrived and said that morning he'd been to Seyyedâbâd, and he hadn't yet eaten anything. I said, I'm not well, and there's no flour; I haven't cooked this morning. So Eyjab [*Abdol-Mahmad's wife*] cooked some bread for me, and I gave him a piece. He ate it and left.

That night ten of our sheep died. Next morning Baya-khân came again. It was sleeting. There were clouds, sleet and wind. Baya-khân said that Kala-khân and Manân

---

[5] Pâkhâl tells more of her birthing in Chapter 12.

were just coming, bringing the new ewe-lambs from the village. Their father had said, 'It's spring, time to take them off to the steppe.' I said, 'But the ground isn't black yet, there's no hay here, they'll get covered in snow, and they'll go hungry. Let them wait until the snow's gone and they can go grazing on the hillsides and eat the new green grass.'

We had little bread left ourselves. Baya-khân didn't bring any, saying it was coming with Kala-khân and Manân, and he went back, leaving us hungry. Eyjab had cooked some corn bread; she came and said, 'Pâkhâl, you're hungry!' I said, 'It doesn't matter, we've got no flour left, what can I eat?' She said, 'Have some of this corn bread.' She gave me a few mouthfuls, and she brought some tea.

After Baya-khân had gone home, the snow started to settle; the ground was soon quite white. Although I was still unwell, I went out to look for fuel, but there wasn't any. I went up that hollow near our hut and swept it. It was snowing as I swept. This was just two days after I'd given birth. Everything was snow-covered. Pâdshâh shouted from the sheepfold, 'What are you doing? Go back in!' I told him the fuel had run out. He was always busy with the sheep, and they were hungry. I filled a blanket with sweepings, took them back to our little room, and fed the fire in the corner.

Around noon, Kala-khân and Manân arrived with the lambs, which they put in Uncle Dur-khân's hut. They complained of the cold and the snow. I told them I couldn't go out to get fuel; my legs ached, my back ached, I just couldn't go. So Kala-khân went himself and got some dung cakes, and they warmed themselves by the fire. Then Kala-khân said he was hungry. I said, 'You may well be hungry, but there's no food. Eat some of the bread you've brought with you, and leave me the rest.' Kala-khân said nothing.

That night they fed all the sheep and put them in the sheepfold or the hut. Then they came in to eat: Manân, Kala-khân, Nasib, Mir-Hamza, Pâdshâh, and my two sons. They'd been out since breakfast and were tired and hungry. I cut up the two sheep they'd slaughtered that day, put the meat in a cauldron and cooked it on the fire; the cauldron was full but they ate the lot, and I gave them a piece of bread each.

The snow really started that day. We slaughtered 50 sheep, and put the carcasses into Pâkiza's hut, filling it to the door. I could only cut open four or five to look for lambs with good skins. I tried to get Kala-khân and Manân to help cut open the sheep's bellies, but they refused. We didn't even shear them. We threw the remains out into that yard behind the hut.

In the morning, as we'd run out of flour, I asked Pâdshâh what I should cook, and he said Abdol's house too had very little left. I beat the sack, and got a bit of flour out, enough to cook one piece of bread per person. But as I was cooking, Kala-khân and Manân fled, saying, 'We're not staying here; we'll die!' Even though the snow was up to their knees, they abandoned us.

Then Baya-khân arrived with more hay. I cried to him, 'The sheep are dying and we'll die here too! Our hut's small, and there's no fire, we're hungry and thirsty, there's nothing here, and I'm unwell.' Baya-khân said, 'Keep calm, sister, you won't die. I'll tell my father and get him to send some sweets and things.' I said, 'He won't send anything, I'm going to die here, I want to go to the village.' He said, 'Don't go, your sons are here; there's all this snow.' So I sat and cried, I was so worn out. In the daytime I was never finished with housework, and at night I was feverish. At night we took the sheep into our tiny hut. I went to sleep with sheep on my bed.

The snow fell for three days and nights, and from then on each night at least twenty sheep died, sometimes forty or fifty. When we cut them open, the foetuses were very undeveloped. One morning early – Pâdshâh was still asleep – I went to get the sheep in the tent back on their feet. I found four of them had died. I cut open their bellies, and there was one skin that was excellent. It was one of Khâni-âghâ's sheep. As I was skinning it, a man came up, and Kala-khân sold it to him for 1,000 rupees. Later he sold it on for 1,200. That same day, Abdol got a good skin too. When Abdol's and Haji Ghâfur's sheep died, their foetuses were very large; when our own died, they'd been hungry and there was only a tiny shrivelled foetus in their bellies.

One day we took our sheep to Haji Ghâfur's sheepfold and pleaded with the shepherd to give us some fodder. We said, 'Haji has plenty, and he won't mind our Haji having some.' He refused. One of their sheep had died much earlier and they'd thrown the foetus out; our sheep were so hungry, they ate it like a carrot. There was nothing else. They hadn't brought any straw. Nasib and I cried so much, Nancy. We thought we'd all die of hunger and cold that night. But as the sun went down, I saw the black mare coming from below. It was Kala-khân; I called Nasib, 'Kala-khân's come! Come and help cover up the straw, otherwise the birds will eat it.' Our valley was full of crows, so hungry they'd peck out the eyes of the sheep, which couldn't get up. Look at our sheep now, some of them have eyes missing. Two of our sheep were attacked like this, but they're still alive.

One day Ridigol came. After three days, he went out to that hollow behind our hut to tend the lame ewes, then suddenly he ran off. I called out, 'Ridigol, where are you going?' I told Nasib he was heading home to the village, and Nasib rushed off after him. He saw someone coming up from below on foot – it was Akhtar – and called out, 'Hey, Uncle, stop him!' Akhtar stopped Ridigol, but he cried and cried, 'I want to go home!' Nasib wanted to beat him, but Akhtar stopped it. Ridigol refused to stay; they let him go.

It was after Ridigol went that those two ewes had their eyes pecked out. He'd been looking after the sheep, and this happened after he went. He was only concerned about his own troubles.

Then there were just Pâdshâh, Nasib and me, and Pastuk – the poor lad suffered a lot this year. Oh Nancy, I start crying when I think about it! In the afternoon, I sent him to stop the sheep getting over the barrier. As he sat there he got cold, and when he got back his feet were frozen into his boots; they wouldn't come off. When we finally got them off, he cried, and so did I, I couldn't stop.

That night I slept. The next morning there were dead sheep lying everywhere. We piled the carcasses into the yard, and one day when it got warmer we took them out – Pâdshâh was also at home – and cut them up. My hands smelled foul, and I felt dreadful. I was so worn out, nobody suffered like me.

At last the snow melted. The ground became black and then green. Dur-khân's family came to join us. They brought nothing with them, no wood or fuel, nothing. I swept up some droppings in the sheepfold. Baya-khân arrived and asked what I was doing; I explained that I was collecting what fuel was left. There was quite a lot, but I was too tired to bring it all back in, so I just brought a little bucket full, leaving the rest piled up. Then Dur-khân's family arrived and his daughter Golapruz came and took half my fuel. I'd swept it up, but she took it. I called out to her, 'Why are you taking my fuel? I'm sick and I have two small sons,' but she wouldn't give it back. I'd put some fuel in our tent, but she took that as well.

Nancy, I'm falling asleep …

One night at the end of winter, the rain and snow beat down on our hut. Dur-khân's hut was riddled with holes; there were places you could put your hand through, and only Dur-khân, Koreysh and Golapruz were sleeping there. They sent their other three daughters and their son Amânollah to sleep with us. In our hut, the room with the sheep was full of holes too, but our sleeping room had no holes – except the doorway. Neither Pâdshâh nor Nasib was there, they were both out with the sheep. Mir-Hamza had gone, because our flour had finished and he complained of hunger. He said, 'If you can't give me food, what else can you give me?' We had nothing to give him, so we had to let him go. Baya-khân in the village wasn't free to go and fetch flour.

The ground was still covered in snow. That's why Pâdshâh was out with the sheep. I spent the night alone with Dur-khân's son and daughters. But Nancy, I didn't sleep a wink. You remember the veranda outside? Well, all of a sudden the whole thing collapsed! I got such a fright.

Then the wall of the little room in Big-Haji's hut fell in. Negâr rushed out, scared to death. Negâr had no children with her – her daughter Boghak was in the Valley – whereas my baby girl was born out there. Negâr and Keshmir went out to their sheepfold to sleep in the tent. Their shepherd Samad asked, 'Ah sister, what are you doing here?' She said, 'My hut has fallen in.' He said, 'You can't sleep here in the tent, it's very damp and full of sheep; I'll take you over to Pâdshâh's and you can sleep there.' There was no man in that household; the men had gone to the Valley. Negâr cried out to Pâdshâh that her hut had fallen in. She had a blanket, a felt and a pillow on her head. Pâdshâh said, 'Our hut's gone too, and there are sheep in the tent.' 'Where can I go?' 'You'll be all right here, don't worry!' She told me, 'I'm alive but my hut's fallen down.' She complained that she hadn't slept all night. The whole night she was crying that her hut had fallen down. She didn't have Boghak with her, but there she was, complaining that she had nothing but misery. I said, 'What's the matter with you? You're still dry!' The suffering was all mine.

7

Land: A Golden Tent-Peg

The Value of Land

In Chapter 1, I described how the Piruzai acquired some irrigated lands in the Sar-e-pol valley soon after their arrival.

By 1970, most Piruzai own some land, inherited from one of the original purchasers, or bought or otherwise acquired. As holdings must be divided among heirs, they have become highly fragmented, and individuals commonly own several widely separated plots of different quality. Deeds are crucial to ownership, but both officially and locally the situation is vague, expensive and open to manipulation; there appears to be land-grabbing at all levels.

Pâdshâh/Tumân articulates the common view of the benefits of land.

Land is more productive than anything else. Sheep are trouble, from one spring to the next, and bring little gain; sometimes they all die. But land produces wheat, barley, melons, sesame, corn, and makes a good return.

But Pâdshâh/Parwiz notes that the mâldâr *only recently realized the value of land.*

At first we didn't care about it, we were *mâldâr*, busy grazing our sheep and camels, watering them and collecting hay, and we didn't cultivate the steppe. The Hazâras have been doing that for ten or twenty years, now there's nowhere left uncultivated. They farmed Afghan lands as well as their own; the Afghans who farm now learned from the Hazâras and Uzbeks. It's only about ten years since Afghans realized about land, first irrigated, then, only a few years ago, we learned about farming in the steppe.

Baya-khân compares Afghan and Hazâra abilities as farmers.

Hazâras like land. They plough well and work hard. They don't have much, maybe 4–5 *jeribs*, 10–20 at most, but that'll feed a household for a year. They spread plenty of manure on a small plot, and it gives them good crops. They grow melons and corn; they tend them until ripe, then take them to market and sell them for cash: 10,000 to 15,000 rupees from one melon-patch.

We Afghans own much more land than Hazâras, but don't take the same kind of trouble. We don't know how to work it properly. We Piruzai have enough or more than enough land for all. Most of us have land; some have rather more, a few have none at all. If you average it out and include all the poor and landless, I think it'd come to about twenty *jeribs* per household.

Gol-Ahmad tells how Piruzai pastoralists gradually became farmers too.

When we arrived in Turkistan, people cared nothing for land. We were vagrants, my father says, not settled like now. For ten years we moved around: a year or two at Emâm-Sâheb, a year or two here, and a year or two at the nearby steppe-edge. We traded and did other kinds of work. Now we're here, it's our homeland, we can't move away. He says, we'd go to Qataghan to buy rice; one famine year, we traded rice to buy that mill and the land from Abdor-Rahmân Âkhondzâda Hotaki, as in the deeds you've seen.

Dâd-Mahmad came a few years earlier, sharecropped for some years for people in Emâm-Sâheb and Emâm-Jafar, and soon realized the sweetness of the land, while we didn't. He and Karim-dâd and the Khârkashi people now have lots of land; they saw the potential of landowning and farming. Afzal and Karim-dâd bought the land from Tahsildâr's son. After the purchase, Karim-dâd, Afzal, Dâd-Mahmad and others went to Mecca. Then Tahsildâr denied selling it and refused to hand over the deeds. My father went to Mazâr to see Re'is Abdol-Ghâfur Khân, and gave him some money; he got the deeds, finished the business and returned. If you ask me, most of the money spent on this land and canal came from my father. Originally they paid four to five thousand for the Khârkash and Soltân-Ghajar canals. Our canal is Soltân-Ghajar; Hazâras own half of it.

Every year things progressed, until today one *jerib* fetches 10,000 to 20,000 rupees. A certain Jabbâr Kâboli told my father, 'Now this one canal has 3,000 to 4,000 *jeribs* of land, worth altogether 4,000 rupees; but one day you'll see one *jerib* worth 10,000.' My father says, 'When I heard this, first I bought the mill, then the land at Khâm-rabât, then some land in Sangchârak.' Other people did the same. Haji Afzal himself bought some land in Sheberghân. 'In those days,' he says, 'this was such a god-forsaken wilderness, you couldn't get through. We only had tents, nobody thought about houses.' There was no village, we all camped here together, thirty to forty families; now we've become many. Haji Afzal was the first to build a house; then it became the fashion.

Both these villages are called Khârkash. The other village is officially registered as Afghan Konjek. But now people call our village Konjek and the other one Khârkash. At first, our Konjek people, my ancestors, were wealthy; the Khârkash people had nothing, they were hungry. Now they've done well. When we got our land, we had lots of money, but nobody wanted land. We bought the land as partners. We said, 'If you want more, help yourself.' They said, 'We don't need it.' We said, 'No, take some more.' They started with nothing but ended up with more than us.

When people saw the profits, they all came and pressed for some. Some time after the land purchase, Amir's group [*from the Upper Quarter*] moved to Qataghan, one after the other, saying, 'We don't need land.' But later they returned and demanded their land back. There was quite a fight; in the end, people did *qawmi*. The place was run by warlords; the government was weak and people paid it no heed. Then Wazir Mahmad-gol Khân came and said the land should be divided according to need. Now wolves and sheep eat together. Amir's people got their land back.

I tried to track down the original land deeds. All known copies seemed to be on loan to somebody involved in one of the current land disputes. Haji Tumân tells of one such dispute.

We have a deed from 1305 [*1926*], the time of Amir Amânollah, before Wazir Mahmad-gol Khân. But my copy is much newer than that, you can read every letter. It's with Khoday-râm, or perhaps Rawu's son Nasiroddin. Khalifa-Patih had a dispute with them – they took it to court. Khalifa-Patih gave Rawu 22 *jerib*s, but Rawu denied it. At the time Rawu had a deed; when he was a child, his father [*Haji Abdol-Nabi*] promised him 36 *jerib*s of the land in the deed. When he grew up, Rawu realized what he'd been promised and thought, 'It must be part of that belonging to my cousins Khalifa-Patih, Khoday-râm, Dust-Mahmad, Shâdi; I'll take the deed and get my share.' [*See Fig. 10*]

But we said, 'That's not your land; it's your father's. If he'd meant it for you he'd have officially registered it in your name.' He got very upset with us: 'Give me the land, it's mine, in my name.' He showed us where it said, 'Rawu 36 *jerib*s'. We said, 'Where did you get this from? Your father may have put those 36 *jerib*s in your name, but he didn't register it, so it's not a proper document. You were small when your father did that; why are you now oppressing these poor people?' His brothers said, 'Did you buy it alone? Where did you get it? Father may have put your name on the deed, but it's not yours alone. If you'd bought it from someone else, they'd have officially transferred ownership and given you a deed.' My land, for example, is in Haji Ghâfur's name, but we all use it, there's no problem. 'Give up this pointless dispute; it's bad for a Muslim to do this to people.'

He persisted and went to court; they summoned us, and asked, 'Whose is the land?' We said, 'The land in his name is his father's inheritance, and it belongs to him and his five brothers and nobody else.' So the judge decided against Rawu: 'That land isn't just

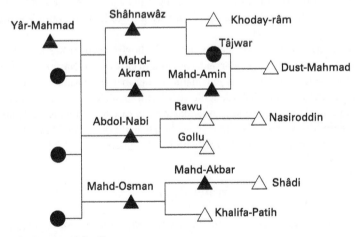

Figure 10 Rawu and family.

yours; everyone from the village community says so. If it had been registered, there'd have been a plot in your name. Do as your father intended, and share the land with your brothers. There are these 36 *jerib*s, and some 70-odd others, making 112 *jerib*s in all; you're six brothers, divide it into six, each will get eighteen or so. That's the way to do it, there's no need for you or anyone else to suffer or do anything unlawful, or you'll face consequences.' He still wouldn't agree. Finally the poor man fell sick; last spring he died, still full of anger and resentment.

Pâdshâh talks further of Seyyed-shâh and his brother Jamâloddin, who has no land in Konjek but has a small house built on someone else's land. (See Fig. 3)

The house Jamâloddin lived in last year belonged to Shir. He and Seyyed-shâh have no land here; they're both Shir's *hamsaya*. Without land or relatives here, they can't claim to be important. They don't say, 'I'm on your land, so I'll be your servant,' but Shir may ask Seyyed-shâh to send someone to help. Or my father may say, 'All my sons are out, send someone to help.'

Jamâloddin built a room this year on Mir-Hamza and Shâhpari's land. It's in the same compound, on the west side; Shâhpari's on the east. They cook and eat separately. There's a third room in the middle, where they sit and talk during the day. Jamâloddin would help Shâhpari, but she doesn't really need it. They don't pay rent, they don't give her any flour or food, everyone provides their own. We don't have renting among us, or anywhere in Afghanistan except the cities.

Jamâloddin has land in Hazhdah-nahr; more than Seyyed-shâh. His father-in-law's there; he has land, and he's from Wardak too – his son's educated, with good connections with government as well as in the steppe. Jamâloddin plans to go and live with them, safe from trouble with the police.

And in Chenâr, we're partners with Jamâloddin and Seyyed-shâh in a little vineyard on the riverbank, with some 600 to 700 vines. You went there, I think. He's with his cousin Nasrak. Haji Ghâfur, their maternal uncle, gave it to Nasrak as a present on his son's birth – that's one of our customs. Some people give a jacket or a belt; in those days Big-Haji was wealthy and extravagant, so he gave a share in a vineyard! We got our share of it in payment of a debt.

Jamâloddin has a wife, two daughters and a baby boy. His cousin Nasrak is the boss, though he's younger and not yet married. Jamâloddin gave one of Nasrak's sisters in an exchange for a wife for himself. Seyyed-shâh's brother married Nasrak's mother, while Nasrak's engaged to Seyyed-shâh's daughter, who's still small. Now Nasrak has authority over Jamâloddin, who's keen to keep Nasrak sweet, in case he demands his rights and abandons them. That's why Jamâloddin allows him to make decisions. They eat together if they're both at home, and the wife eats with her daughters.

Water Rights

The Sar-e-pol river feeds some forty canals, twenty of them between Sar-e-pol town and the Sheberghân district frontier. These canals take water for eight days in each 18-day cycle; the other ten days go to Sheberghân. Each canal irrigates the lands of one or more villages according to a complex schedule.[1] *Every plot of land comes with a specified number of hours of water from a particular canal, in each cycle. In Khârkash and Konjek, one* joft *(ploughland: 44* jeribs, *a* jerib *being 0.2 hectares) gets eight hours of water.*

Haji Tumân provides some context.

The good lands down in Âqcha and Hazhdah-nahr produce excellent thorns, while our Sar-e-pol lands are barren of grass and thorns. There are no thorns in these parts except in Konjek here; not around town, nor in Boghawi. In Sheberghân city itself there's not much, but better than here. But over towards Salmazân, at Khoja-Gugerdak, the thorns are really good.

Sar-e-pol is also unlucky with water. Sheberghân takes water from the river for ten days, Sar-e-pol for only eight. Sheberghân also has underground springs, in case the river runs dry. Âqcha gets water from the Balkhâb river through Hazhdah-nahr; most years it stays full, though last year [*1971*] it did dry up. It comes down to Balkhâb, then Ak-Kopruk, Kishindi, Buyna-Qara, then out to Cheshma-ye-shafâ, the Emâm-Bokri bridge, and then to the eighteen big canals of Hazhdah-nahr. Âqcha gets the last of the water; there's not much left. Last year Âqcha didn't have one day of water; the poor Muslims stayed quite dry. They couldn't grow summer crops, and whoever sowed wheat or barley didn't get their seed back. This year, thank God, there's plenty of water, the seed bore well. There were many flash-floods. The rivers were full of floodwater from the mountains, the lands were inundated, the ponds filled. When the floods receded and the fallow fields dried up in April, they ploughed them again; all the rainfed crops came up abundantly: melons, watermelons, sesame, beans, and a lot of corn.

Baya-khân gives some details on the canals.

[*When our ancestors arrived*] the old canals were ruined, and the land was wild. Gradually people built new canals. There were no clocks, so they reckoned time by *kotorey*, a bowl with a hole, made by a needle; they put it in water, and it filled after an hour, so your time was, for example, two *kotorey*.

Welayat Canal divides into Khârkash and Soltân-Ghajar Canals above Khârkash village, by the Uzbek lands. Originally the sluice-gate wasn't concreted; they'd just put a piece of wood in the middle to divide the water. If someone came with just a thorn, a chip or some mud, he could divert the flow to one side. It was concreted last year, after you left. I don't know how much the bricks and concrete cost, but I'd guess 3,000 to 4,000 rupees. Everyone with shares in the canal contributed. Now the water's divided exactly in half, and it can't be fiddled, unless you put a spade or something in the works – but nobody dares do that. Half the water goes to Khârkash and half to the Hazâras of Ghajar, the Ludins and us. Four days and nights are for Ghajar, then four days and nights it comes down here to Konjek, where it's divided by turns. [*See Map J*]

Most of our land is with Ghajar Canal, and gets water only after the Hazâras have had their four days and nights. We also have land near Khârkash, and take water for it

---

[1]   Thomas et al. (2013) give detailed analysis of the system, based on research in 2012.

from Khârkash Canal. The law says if your land's above mine, you get water first. This year our melons are down below, and get water last; but water's plentiful now.

Yesterday I showed you the new canal; we wanted to dig it in early winter, but the Hazâras refused. The Afghan leaders, like Nâder-shâh and Haji Tumân, conferred and decided to separate our water from the Hazâras at that junction, where the canal divides into two, one half of which is ours. 'Let's dig a new canal; we'll take half the water and concrete the sluice-gate so that our water's clearly separated from the Hazâras.' They started digging, then it rained and snowed. Work stopped, as everyone was busy with the sheep.

Another concreted canal was coming to our upper lands. The water wasn't ours, and we didn't want it to cross our lands, but Nâder-shâh and others in Khârkash called Haji Tumân: 'Let's draw the canal here, and the community will give you two-and-a-half hours of water.' Haji said, 'But our lands are above that canal; the water won't reach, they'll stay dry.' The community pressed him to accept the two-and-a-half hours. So he said, 'To hell with those lands of ours, it's better that the community should benefit; let the canal pass.' Then the bad winter came, the canal wasn't dug, and people were busy with the sheep. We'll see what happens this year, when winter approaches.

Baya-khân and Pâdshâh together talk about what can be done with water rights.

Gholâm-Ahmad Khân has land and water rights up above, near the head of Behsud Canal, and his water passes by Haji Ghâfur's land. But some of his land is down below. You know our rainfed melons? The land this side of it, with all the thorns, belongs to Gholâm-Ahmad Khân. He can't use Behsud Canal there, as it's below his land, so he takes water from Behsud Canal above, puts it in Khâm-rabât Canal, then takes it off onto his land down below, by the mill here. So he has rights in both Behsud and Khâm-rabât Canals.

It's possible, and legal, but rare, to put your water into a neighbouring canal. For example, I could have land here, but water rights in Qerâghu; or rights in Welayat Canal, but land in Emâm-Jafar, and take my water from the river down at Emâm-Jafar. That's what Anârgol has done with Shir's land here; he took Shir's water and irrigated some land up there. Or, depending on where we're doing summer crops, we can take our water from either canal.

It doesn't matter where you take your water, it's delivered from any convenient canal, wherever's convenient to you. For example, I've a plot of wheat here and another there, and six hours of water; in spring I can put three hours of water on each. It's organized at the canal-head: you let the water-master know what your plans are. They're likely to change every year. In a dry summer, like last year, the water often doesn't get down here, and the summer crops dry up.

Say there are two canals, Welayat on this side, Khâm-rabât on that, and one year everybody on Khâm-rabât Canal cultivates, but few on Welayat do, so Welayat has a surplus of water; whatever happens, they won't give any to Khâm-rabât without payment. If irrigation water's not needed, you sell it. After they've finished watering their wheat, some people sell an hour or so of water for the summer crops. Nobody gives it free; some do it like sharecropping (*keshtagari*), claiming a half-share in the crop, but most people sell for cash, and have no further claim until the autumn. The buyer gets complete control of that water, every cycle, until the cotton and corn are ready and it's time to water the new wheat. In November, the water reverts to its owner. Someone short of money may also sell water in winter.

Water's sold by the hour. You have five hours, say; someone whose corn is dry and hasn't enough water will buy an hour of yours. You can sell it in advance, if you need cash, but it'll be cheap, 250–500 rupees. In a dry year, an hour costs at least 900 rupees. If you give it to pay a debt, like Shahâboddin, who promised it in payment for some straw in winter, it'll be 700 to 800.

Shâhpari has one hour of water; she used it for her winter wheat and barley, but she sold it for the summer – she always does. Haji bought it for five seers of wheat. She was hungry and wheat was 120 rupees and hard to find. Actually, he didn't give wheat; he paid her 600 rupees cash.

In spring, water's abundant, everyone has plenty; you give any extra to me, and vice versa, it doesn't matter. In March, people don't water their grain crops much: there are three days and nights – nobody knows which – when watering your wheat and barley will ruin them. Some people don't worry, others are scared of ruining their crops. Water's plentiful, but it's used for melons, sesame, corn, cotton, beans, not white crops. From April, water's no longer free, people sell it.

Canal water also runs a number of mills; Seyyed-shâh/Soleymân explains how these operate.

The last two years we've rented Haji Ghâfur's mill for 80 seers of wheat. The other mill, down below, went for 70 seer. We operated it ourselves; the owner provides a new millstone, which he buys in Sar-e-pol, though we pay for transport. Stones used to be cheap, about 700 rupees, but they'd last only one or two years. For some years now, stones have come from Jalalabad; they cost 8,000 to 12,000, including transport, and should last eight to ten years – that's why they're so expensive. If the mill's in good order, with new stones, it should grind 240 seers a day. The operator used to get one seer in twenty; this year it's down to one in thirty.

Inheritance

Rules of inheritance – with land the most valuable part of an estate – are complicated by every father's duty (passed on to his heirs) to see all his sons married, as Pâdshâh explains.

Two sisters get as much as one brother. Sisters don't take their shares, but give them to their brothers. A sister gives her share to a favourite brother, or she might divide it between them. If there are four brothers and two sisters, each sister may give a quarter of her share to each brother; then everyone's heart is happy. She'll never take it to her husband, that's not our custom. Uzbeks and Fârsibâns may take their wives' inheritances, but we never do. People would laugh at such a thing. If someone has no sons, only a daughter, she'll inherit but give her share to her father or mother. For example, Haji

Ghâfur's wife Bibiwor has no sons, but three daughters, all married. When he dies, Bibiwor will take her daughters' shares and her own, and it's up to her whether to keep them for herself or to pass them to her sons-in-law or her stepsons. But she's not her daughters' agent, unless they make her so. If they do, she can use or dispose of their property without anyone complaining. If two daughters are happy to give Bibiwor their shares, but one refuses and gives hers to her husband or [*her half-brother*] Gol-Ahmad, then she can do so.

If only a daughter remains after both parents die, she'll get something, but the land will go to her paternal uncle or closest relative. She has authority over the property while she remains in her house, unmarried. If she's sole heir and stays with her uncle, she can eat and wear what she likes. Once she's married, her uncle takes over. If she wants to take her share to her husband, the mullahs will get together to decide, from the Book, what she owns, and she can take it to her husband. That's possible. Otherwise, her paternal uncles have prior claim, and it's divided among them. If she has no uncle, it'll go to her nearest or most senior relative; then remoter cousins like Shir, Shahâboddin, Wazir. If absolutely no relative can be found, you can fetch a man from somewhere and declare him to be your relative, and then he'll inherit.

Baya-khân adds details.

If he wants, a father can give a separated son his share while he's alive; he marks off the land and gives him his share. But some fathers say, 'You've no rights to this while I'm alive.' Some do, some don't. While his father's alive, a young man has no legal rights, according to our Book; he can't say anything; the only claim he has is enough wealth to get married. Then it's up to the father whether to turn him out or let him stay. After the father dies, the sons and daughters squabble as they divide up the land, and everyone takes their share.

When someone dies leaving property, the sons divide it and they do a sacrifice. Rawu had two wives and six sons and they all ate together; they weren't separated, they had *entepâk* (family solidarity). When he died, a mullah came and divided their land between the sons. The share of Rawu's small daughter by his wife Morghak went to her two full-brothers. Then they did the sacrifice; the mullah brought the Book – without a mullah the sacrificial distribution wouldn't be accepted. Mayoddin-jân did it, but any mullah will do.

A wife can't sell her trousseau (*kur*); she has no authority to do so, it's under her husband's control. If he's well off, he won't sell any of it, but if he's poor, he might sell a felt or a bolster, to help with expenses. When a girl leaves home, she has no animals; but if her father's rich he may give her a camel at her wedding, or a sewing-machine, or a radio – and these belong to her.

Some examples where women's shares are disputed.

(*Pâdshâh*) – It's several years since Dâdollah's family came from Sheberghân with their sheep. First they stopped where Khalifa-Patih's just built himself a house. They looked around for a while, then Dâdollah's mother Bibiwor's four brothers, Golusar, Mahd-

Amin, Mahd-Hanifa and Sâleh, gave them this place. First they lived there in a tent, then they built themselves what's become a large house. Dâdollah calls the house-plot his own, his mother's inheritance, her one-eighth; but Mahd-Amin and Golusar say it's theirs, their sister Bibiwor's inheritance belongs to them.

Bibiwor's sister, Neshtar, did take her share; she owns the ground of her house. Now her half-sister Hazâragi wants her own place too, the place where she's living. She's built a hut. She won't move, even though her sons are causing trouble – thievery here and there. Now she insists that since her sisters have received their inheritance, so should she. 'I'm staying, I'm going to build a house.' If she goes to court, it'll find for her, and the affair will worsen.

(*Baya-khân*) – Hazâragi got her house-plot from Mahd-Hanifa, her full-brother. She stayed in his compound for a year or two, but it didn't work. She said, 'I want my share of land.' Mahd-Hanifa was forced to give her a place to build. She said, 'That's enough for me, I can make my home here.' So she built her own hut, where she lives with her sons.

Pâdshâh/Parwiz's uncle Heydar made a will.

The oldest of Heydar's sons is Masâdek; then comes Sarwar, then Khâni-âghâ – they're all separate. All the little daughters are with Khâni-âghâ. When Heydar was dying, he divided his property. He willed that: 'My daughter Nik-morgh be exchanged for a wife for Masâdek; my daughter Mayagak for Sarwar; and Maysundar for Khâni-âghâ. The other daughter is for her mother: she can marry her off for brideprice, or whatever she wants.'

Sarwar already had a wife. Heydar said, 'Sarwar still has rights in my property,' so he gave him Mayagak, to marry off for brideprice or to exchange for another wife – it's up to him. Heydar's widow Borey lives with Khâni-âghâ, even though she's not his own mother; it's entirely her business how her own daughter's married, but if she goes for brideprice, Khâni-âghâ will get it.

Heydar's will was written down properly, before a mullah. A good Muslim divides his property while he's alive, to make things easier for his family. It's the proper, clean thing to do. If you don't do it, you'll suffer punishment in the grave. But I don't know anyone else who wrote such a will. My father didn't have anything except land. Before he died he told us, 'One-eighth of the land, those gardens, goes to my two wives, half each – that's what I owe them. As for the rest, it's up to you to divide it among yourselves.'

8

On the Farm

The Tale of the Ox, the Donkey and the Hen

Baya-khân tells how some farm animals, abandoned by their Afghan nomad owners, grow some corn and outwit the wild beasts, but then succumb to the Afghans when they return.

There was an Afghan camp out in the steppe. It was spring, and they soon migrated to the mountains, leaving behind a bony ox, a skinny donkey and a hen. There was a canal nearby, full of water, but all the people had gone. The animals discussed what to do. They decided to sow some corn. The donkey said, 'I'll irrigate the land.' He got up and struck the canal bank several times with his foot and let the water onto a plot of land; when it was nicely irrigated he stopped the water again. After a few days the soil was dry enough for ploughing, and the ox came and ploughed it. Then the hen came and sowed the corn seed, and they smoothed down the soil.

Soon the corn shoots came up. It was the donkey's turn again, to give the crop some water, so the donkey broke open the canal bank again and let the water onto the corn, and he also went and made sure, with his feet, that the water reached each of the shoots.

Time passed and the corn formed ears. Then one day a wolf, a fox and a jackal arrived and asked the hen and the donkey and the ox, 'Give us a few ears of corn to eat.' They gave them ten or fifteen ears each. The visitors ate them and left.

The corn ripened, and the hen started eating the grain, while the donkey and the ox ate the stalks and leaves. They all grew fat, and strutted around their little patch like panthers, though there was nobody else to see them.

Shortly after, the wolf said to the fox and the jackal, 'Let's go visit the ox and the donkey, and if they won't give us any more corn, we'll just eat them. They're too weak to stop us!' The wolf was the leader; he twirled his moustache and really fancied himself.

They came to the donkey and the ox and sat down. They exchanged greetings. Then the wolf arrogantly demanded some corn; he thought he was so much better and stronger than them. The ox refused: 'Let's see if you're strong enough to take it!' he said. 'But we want some corn,' said the wolf, and jumped up and headed for the crop. The ox rushed after it. The jackal leaped up, followed by the donkey, and the fox leaped up, followed by the hen.

There was a long battle. The wolf got its head stuck up the ox's backside; the ox shook its haunches so that the wolf's body was beaten black and blue and the wolf was frightened for its life; with great difficulty it freed itself and fled, pursued by the ox. The jackal fled, pursued by the donkey; and the fox fled, pursued by the hen. Up and down the hills they chased them. Finally they came back to settle by their corn; there they stayed for two or three months, eating their corn crop.

The Afghans returned from the mountains and cried: 'Look at that corn! Look at the donkey, the hen and the ox, how fat they are!' and they fell on the poor animals, fighting over them, everyone claiming they were his. 'You're worse than wolves, damn you! You abandoned us here in the steppe, now we don't belong to anybody; you've no claim on us.'

Well, the people stopped and, after some discussion, slaughtered the poor ox and ate the meat. They caught the donkey and put it to work fetching and carrying people and their flour to the mill – this was their winter quarters. As for the hen, they'd brought a few roosters down from the mountains, and they mated one of them with the hen. That's the end of the story.

Farming in Sar-e-pol

Fields are normally cultivated on a two-year rotation. The main crops are either 'white' – winter-sown wheat and barley; 'green' – summer crops such as melons, sesame, flax, beans, corn, alfalfa, tomatoes; or dry-farmed – wheat, melons, sesame and other crops. In good years cotton is widely cultivated as a summer cash crop, while, in years with a poor wheat harvest, corn is favoured. The basis of the Piruzai diet, as in most of the region, is wheat bread and animal ghee, supplemented by rice and meat on festive occasions, and more often for the wealthy. The poor, particularly in lean years, replace wheat with low-quality rice, corn or millet; and ghee with sesame or linseed oil. Fruit (apricots, grapes, melons) is much eaten in season, but vegetables are incidental and not highly regarded.

During our time in the villages, both after the return migration in summer 1971, and in summer 1972 when nobody went to the mountains, the 'white' crops had been harvested and were being threshed and winnowed. I learned much about cultivation, both by tramping the fields with village experts, and by recording (when they had spare moments) accounts of how farming was done.

'White' crops

Seyyed-shâh/Golusar compares wheat and barley.

We say that men are like wheat and women are like barley. Barley ripens quickly, like a woman. Wheat, whether winter or spring sown, takes longer. People grow barley more on irrigated and wheat on rainfed land. On irrigated land, if you sow ten seers of barley, with God's help it'll make 500; if you sow ten seers of wheat you'll get 150 at most. But ten seers of rainfed wheat, with God's help, will make 500.

This year [1972] there's more wheat than barley. In years when the soil isn't so hard, people grow lots of barley. This year people had to leave half their lands 'black'. For example, I got some barley seed and planned to sow it where Haji Tumân had melons last summer, but the earth was covered in snow and the soil was too hard to plough. When we could finally plough, it was too late for grain, so we sowed melons again. Now I don't know if Haji's letting me sharecrop it or not!

In other years, most land was planted with either barley or wheat. This year, with so much land still black, people decided to do melons. They ploughed, sowed melon and watermelon seeds, and ... well, God gave us nice melons and watermelons. This year's melon land will be wheat next year – there should be more wheat than barley. The year after, barley will be the main crop. You grow barley, then wheat, then barley, and so on. Where Haji's grown barley this year, it was chickpeas last year. After harvesting the peas, he sowed 70-odd seers of barley. It made 700 seers. If he'd sown earlier, like the wheat that others were sowing, he'd have got 1,400 seers.

Baya-khân describes how to grow the main crop, wheat.

Everybody ploughs as much as possible; every run increases the crop. The more you plough, the harder you work the land, the better the yield. If you plough twenty times, the soil will be excellent. With wheat, the earlier you start the better, in October or November. If you plough first in October, then the wheat'll have its full nine months, and it'll be outstanding, so long as it doesn't go thirsty. It depends on the land. Some land gets no water until November or December. As soon as the water reaches your land, you're ready to plough and sow.

The first watering breaks down the soil. The land's uneven, so you make sure the water covers it. The next watering's much easier, you just let the water flow down the channels, and the soil absorbs it. Once it's soaked down onto the seeds, next time it'll go of its own accord; the seeds settle down, and there won't be any left dry; so long as the canal doesn't dry up.

You sow well-ploughed land straight after watering; plough the seed in, and go over it with the smoothing-board – you've seen a wooden smoothing-board? Land that's been left to thorns is watered before ploughing; the next cycle it's watered again, seeded, then ploughed twice more; in a dry year, water it every 18-day cycle, and it'll crop well. In a rainy year it needs less water.

Manure helps: it stops the soil drying out, strengthens it and increases the crop, but few people can afford it. They might do it if they've only a little land. We Afghans sometimes spread manure for melons, but not much. You can put it down for wheat or barley too. Those Wardaks who live below us manure their land. When those so-and-sos first arrived they hadn't a thing, not even a chicken. In Logar, or wherever they came from, they had no land, or it was all stony; they'd fetch soil from a hillside, spread it over the stones and then sow wheat on top. Now they have this land here, they spread manure all over it, and it yields huge crops. Visit their place, you'll see they have twenty-five cows and twenty to thirty Qataghani sheep, the large Arabi kind; and this year they'll get at least 1,000 seer of wheat; not counting 400–500 seer of barley, not to mention melons and corn.

If someone gets a good wheat crop, he'll calculate how much to keep for seed. Say his crop was 300 seers, and he wants to sow 100, then he'll keep that 100 back and eat the rest. If he hasn't got enough, he'll buy from somewhere like Qoshtepa, or he'll ask around; he may hear of someone who has good wheat and wants to sell, so he'll buy from him. If he has enough, he'll sow his own 100 seers, and if they run short of wheat to eat he'll go to town, or buy some in the village. Some Afghans go up to Sangchârak or as far as Kachan, where they have debtors. Up there grain is cheaper by 5–10 rupees because there aren't many buyers and it's too far to bring to bring it to town themselves, so people go there with camels to buy it, saving themselves some money. Or you can get government 'bald-ear' seed, which came just two years ago. The ears are bald, without awns. You can sow it in March, and it'll still ripen in time.

Barley's sown in autumn. It grows quicker than wheat, and it'll ripen early, in June; but if you sow early, you harvest in late May. Both Afghans and Hazâras say: *ney Sawr bi-sar, ney Jawzâ bi-deraw*, 'No May without ears, no June without harvest' – in April–May even wheat produces ears, while the barley's cut for sure by June.

Pâdshâh summarizes crop rotation.

With crop rotation, wherever we grew barley this year will be wheat next year. After wheat, you should do barley. If you sow a second crop of wheat, it'll crop, but very poorly. It's better to rotate, in alternate years. If you fallow the land, then grow 'green crops', the following year it will be very strong and make excellent wheat, as the government does when it uses chemical fertilizer, or if you spread cow, sheep, horse or donkey manure. Ploughing and fallowing has the same effect as fertilizer. You should plough the land four or five times. The sun beats it, burns into it and strengthens it. And after the harvest, during the winter you can let the animals onto it, until Nawruz.

Shoot- and stubble-grazing

For many people with well-watered land, there's profit in selling fields of grain shoots for animal grazing, as Baya-khân explains.

After breaking up the soil with the first water, some people sell the shoots. In years when there's been little hay mown, shoots fetch a high price. When lambs are both many and thin – not like this year, but when everybody has lots of lambs – you approach a landowner and bargain with him over his wheat-field. You pay 2,000 rupees; a good field may go for 4,000 or 5,000, but a big stockowner, with many lambs, won't mind paying that.

Say I sell you my field for 2,000. We fix how long you're going to let your 50–100 lambs graze on the shoots. At first, one or two may get sick, even die, but after a week the rest will get nice and fat. After several weeks, when your lambs have quite finished the shoots, you've no more claim to the field, and you must remove them.

Then the landowner irrigates it once more, and the next crop of shoots will emerge, better than the first; if he doesn't want it himself, someone else, or the same person, will buy it for another 2,000, and graze animals on it again. We only let the sheep onto the field if it's dry and they can't ruin the shoots by trampling them. And we don't graze sheep on rainfed wheat because the soil's too soft; the animals would uproot the shoots.

You can let cattle and donkeys wander in the field right up until February; it doesn't matter how much they eat. On strong soil, where melons have been grown, people let animals graze until early March; on weaker soil, they stop them in mid-February.

After animals have grazed a wheat-field, the shoots never mature. Wheat and barley shoots both form these nodes. Once they've formed nodes and the animals have bitten them off, that's it. After that, the wheat's just like wild grass; it won't produce ears. But the owner can sell the field three times over, once a month during the winter, if there's not too much rain and snow covering the ground. So they continue to let the animals onto it until early March.

There's much profit in this shoot-grazing. Near the year's end, in February and March, when straw and hay are finished, many people get permission from the owner of a wheat-field to reap it like alfalfa with a scythe or a sickle, and bring the shoots home in the evening, for the donkeys or camels. If you have cattle, you can let them graze it during the day; but not camels, because they have great heavy feet and trample the remaining wheat – yes, like elephants! The shoots are good for the animals; they get very fat.

Shoot-grazing is excellent; you just sow the grain once and then you can go on grazing it until March, so long as the land's good and strong, ploughed and manured. The more it's grazed the better it gets. If your land is strong, and you sow your wheat early, and if you haven't grazed it, the stalks will get too tall; before the ears fill out, they'll be unable to bear their own weight and they'll fall over. If you've grazed it, the stalks will stay upright – unless of course there's a storm.

This practice is rare in our village, though, because our land is at the end of the canals and gets little water. Places above, like Chârbâgh and Behsud, do it much more; Behsud does it from early on, so does Qerâghu. When we had a lot of animals, we'd take them to Behsud and Chârbâgh for shoot-grazing, once or twice, until we found shoots to graze down here, then we brought them back. It's better here, where the land is stronger, more fertile; it only lacks water. Much-watered land gets weak.

After the wheat and barley harvests, animals can graze the stubble and also any ears left on the ground – the gleaners can't collect them all, and the stalks are very fresh. Wheat takes 8–9 months to ripen. For seven months while the animals haven't been in it, various weeds have grown up; when the harvest's over, these make very good grazing for the sheep.

Here, stubble-fields are open to all. When the harvest's in, anyone can take their animals there; landowners won't complain so long as they keep them off the piles of grain and straw. Some claim the right to put their own animals on their stubble first, but after that it's free. In Sheberghân and Chârpaykâl, though, stubble remains the owner's preserve, they won't let anybody else onto it, or they sell it. The price varies widely, from a few hundred to several thousand rupees, depending on both the area and the amount of grass and stubble. Some stubble-fields are large but have little grass, so they go cheap. What matters is the amount of grass.

'Green' crops

Baya-khân describes how best to grow the 'green' crops.

After the barley harvest and threshing, you can plough and then sow beans, corn or melons. Melons increase fertility. If there's plenty of water, some people just irrigate the land, plough it and then let it lie fallow; the sun will burn the clods, and if you sow wheat there, it'll crop very well next year. It doesn't matter whether you plant melons, or just plough and fallow.

After the wheat harvest in July it's too late to plant melons or beans or anything. Most people give the land some water, if there's enough, and leave it until autumn, then sow barley for next year. But if you've done melons or corn this summer on land that was barley, or left it fallow, in the autumn you'll sow wheat, not barley, and it'll crop very well.

With irrigated melons, you plough three or four times. Some people manure the land to strengthen it. Then you build up mounds, make a hole on top, put in some manure – sheep, cow or horse dung – then a little soil, put in the seed and cover it with soil. It'll sprout within a week. When the plant starts to spread, water it. It's hard work! After a few weeks, loosen the earth at the bottom of the plant, add some more and tamp it down – that's very useful. Water the plants every cycle; keep them free of thorns, grass and weeds, and they'll grow quickly and crop well.

For a good crop of rainfed melons, plough several times in March and April. The more you plough and break up the clods, the better the crop: up to seven times. Then cast the seed in the bottom of the furrows. Some people do sesame and melons together; after ploughing, you sow sesame in the furrows and then board it. Sesame seed is small and weak, if it goes too deep into the earth it won't germinate; if it's on top, with just a little soil covering, it'll soon grow. Then if you want to plant watermelons, plough again and sow the seed at the bottom of the furrows.

Sesame can be irrigated but most people do it rainfed. Sow in May and it'll ripen in September or October. You don't cut it, you drag it out by the roots. Pile it up in a cleared space, and leave it about a week to dry. Some people load it straight onto donkeys and camels, take it home and dry it on the roof. When the seedpods are dried they open, so you hold the stalks by the roots and beat the pods by hand, so that the seeds fall out. The stalks are used for fuel. The leaves are very bitter; they're okay for animals to eat, especially camels, but not for sheep.

You gather the sesame seeds and take them home. If you have a farmhand, first he takes his sixth. Some people take their seeds to a press to make sesame oil; the Baluch, the Turkmen have presses. Ten seers of seeds make 5 seers of oil; the rest is oil-cake, for fodder. The press-owner takes 10–15 rupees per seer of seeds. Other people take their seeds to sell in the bazaar.

Sesame seeds are very pricey this year; they reached 200 to 250 a seer. Sesame seed imported from Bangladesh was cheaper at 180, but people didn't sow it as much as local sesame, which is better.

You sow cotton in May, on land that's rested since a previous year's wheat crop. You plough four or five times in March and April; if it's dry, give it some water to dampen it – not too much – then plough again and sow the cotton. Then you pick in October; but you can leave it until November or December, sometimes even until the first snow – cotton goes on flowering and cropping until the winter cold strikes, when the leaves fall off, leaving only the stalks. Some of the bolls freeze; if you collect them and put them on the roof under the sun, they'll open up and you can pick the cotton. In December, after the cotton, sow wheat and it'll crop very well.

We do more cotton in years when wheat is cheap and plentiful. For three or four years now, people haven't grown much cotton. This year people didn't because it was such a bad winter. In a hungry year like this, people grow corn and melons rather than cotton. If you sow corn in July, it ripens by September; so people say, *Asad ya berasad ya narasad:* if you sow in Asad [*23 July to 22 August*], in a warm year it'll ripen, otherwise it won't. Cotton is hard work, while corn lasts longer.

Seyyed-shâh/Golusar adds, on cotton.

Cotton makes a profit for the [*State*] Company. The price has varied a lot, from 50 to 500 rupees a seer; this year it's about 100, but nobody's grown it. When people are hungry, they don't grow cotton. The Prime Minister announced that since people are hungry this year they shouldn't grow cotton; let them grow corn, make sure their families have enough to eat. This year there's lots of corn. Haji too has sown it – for example, over behind Jân-Mahmad's house, where the barley was. He's harvested some; more has just ripened.

Baya-khân runs through all the other summer crops that are grown locally.

Sar-e-pol townspeople grow masses of carrots, so do people in Boghawi, and some in Angut. They're sown in little furrows in July, and they're ready in November. They pull them up, wash them and sell them in the city. Peddlers also bring them to the villages and exchange them for barley. When they first arrive, they go for 20 rupees a seer, or weight-for-weight with wheat, but later they get very cheap, down to 2 rupees.

You can sow turnips, chives, onions in March and April. For onions you make small paddies and stamp the earth down, or beat it with a spade, until it's as hard as stone. You broadcast about a pound of seeds, then cover them with manure – sheep, cattle or horse dung – to keep away the ants, which really like onion seeds. Or you can spread ash, which is black like the onion seeds, so the ants can't make them out. The harder you beat the earth, the bigger the onions.

We grow alfalfa for the cattle. You buy seed in the bazaar for about 10 rupees a pound. In March, after ploughing well, you build ridges to form paddies, then fill them with water; when they're waterlogged you scatter 5–6 pounds or half a seer of seed in the water. After reaping the alfalfa, you make sheaves, collect them and tie them into bundles. We count the bundles; for example, we have 2,000 bundles this year. In winter we give it to the animals, as well as straw.

Vines do grow here; Mullah Fakhroddin has planted them; and there are a few in Khârkash village. The Baluch of Qoshtepa have many vineyards, so do the Hazâras of Âktâsh. They don't need much water, not like other crops; but it's good to water a new vineyard every cycle. New vines don't produce grapes for three years. Once they're producing, water them in winter and don't bother afterwards, though water won't hurt them. You draw furrows, take the little vines and bury them on the edge of the ditches. Then you grow crops of melons, watermelons, tomatoes or leaks; some do Indian hemp or corn. After three years the vine will produce a few grapes, which you remove. In the fourth year it'll give a proper crop, and the fifth year will be very good. In late November, when the leaves have fallen and winter approaches, you bury the vines underground so that the frost won't get them; then uncover them again in March. It was very cold this year, and any vines left unburied dried up; the old wood dried, but a new vine grew from the root.

People sow lots of flax, both irrigated and rainfed. It doesn't grow very big. When it's gathered in, we get the oxen to trample it, then the farmhands take pitchforks and winnow it, but not like other crops: the larger straws stick in the fork and can be separated from the smaller chaff, which falls to the ground so that you can then winnow and sieve it. When it's clean, you divide the crop. Cattle will eat the flax straw, but it's best for camels. The seeds are only for linseed oil, and the cake that comes out in the mill. Linseed oil-cake, like sesame cake, is good for cows and sheep.

Once people grew sunflowers; now not so much. When they first appeared people sowed them a lot. People eat sunflower oil too. They also make oil from melon seeds.

Chickpeas are excellent; people sow them on rainfed land, in March or April, and harvest them in June. You reap them by hand, not with a scythe; then you collect them and thresh them. You do the same with grass peas; their stalks are very useful. Some people eat chickpeas at home; others sell them in town to shopkeepers, who roast them with raisins.

Some people grow asafoetida. It goes for 2,500–3,000 rupees a seer and the sap is exported to India where the soil is full of worms, so when they irrigate they put asafoetida at the mouth of the canals; the worms hate it, they disappear or die.

Rainfed farming

Pâdshâh and Baya-khân comment on rainfed farming in the steppe.

Rainfed wheat can crop twice or three times as much, and it makes excellent wheat. All depends on rain. In a good rainy year like this one, rainfed wheat is like irrigated: it doesn't go thirsty, and it gives an excellent crop: sow 10 seers, and you'll get 200 or 300. There was lots of snow in winter, and many flash-floods in spring; the land was thoroughly soaked, not just the surface. Every week or two we had rain, and the wheat came up good and true. Last year people in the western steppe sowed summer crops, and they failed; you couldn't see any sesame in Khâmushli; but when that land gets plenty of snow and rain, like this last winter, whatever you sow – melons, sesame – won't go thirsty.

In the steppe, as in the Valley, we sow wheat in November, December or even as late as January. Some people sow earlier and it can turn out well. At Neymadân, for instance, they sow wheat straight after their melon crop. First, they plant melons and watermelons on a ploughed field; they'll all reach their best, ripe and sweet, by October, if they keep them until then. In early October the landowner harvests them and divides them among his sharecroppers. Right after the harvest, he just scatters 15 seers of wheat seed down among the earth clods, without ploughing: instead, he lets camels and other animals range over the land, eating up the stubble and stalks, raising the dust and trampling the soil, which being unirrigated is very soft and crumbly. The seed stays underneath; the more it's trampled, the better. When the rain comes in late autumn, the seed absorbs the moisture and sprouts. This autumn wheat is very special. It ripens in 8–9 months, at just the same time as the wheat that's sown in November or December. That's one way of farming rainfed land.

The Tale of Secret and Satan

Baya-khân tells how Secret tricked Satan when they grew some crops together.

Secret and Satan were partners. They decided to do some farming, so they sowed a crop of wheat. Secret asked Satan, 'Do you want the tops or the bottoms? The ears or the roots?' Satan thought for a bit, then said, 'The roots.' The crop ripened, they reaped it and piled up the harvest. Satan came and saw that Secret had taken all the grain, and there were no roots left, just a little straw.

Next the two of them sowed some onions. Secret asked Satan again, 'Do you want the tops or the bottoms?' This time Satan said, 'The tops.' The onions ripened, Secret cut off the tops and gave them to Satan, and took the bottoms himself, and his onions filled a whole storeroom.

Next they sowed corn. Secret asked Satan, 'Which do you want, the tops and the bottoms, or the middles?' Satan thought to himself, 'Well, I thought I was the smart one, but he's been so smart, he got the best of the onions and the best of the wheat!' so he said, 'I'll take the tops and the bottoms.'

The corn grew. As you know, it produces ears half way up the stalk; Secret gave Satan the tops and the bottoms, and kept the corn ears all for himself – and that's the way Secret fooled Satan.

Farming Contracts

A Piruzai landowner adopts one of several possible arrangements for cultivating his valley land. If they have the labour, he and his family will work the land themselves. If not, he can hire a farmhand, find a sharecropper, or even rent his land to another farmer for cash or part of the crop.

Farmhands and sharecroppers

Baya-khân explains the different contracts and dues.

Most people in our villages either do their own farming or take on a farmhand. A landowner with his own oxen, seed and enough people in his family won't need to employ help, and he'll get the entire crop, both grain and straw. He only has to pay the dues of the water-master and the reapers.

A farmhand [*dehqân*] works for the entire year, starting when the wheat's sown. He drives the yoke of oxen, brings them home, waters them, puts on their blankets, cleans their place, sweeps up their dung, makes dough-balls – he grinds barley into flour, 4–5 pounds per animal, then dampens some straw, tamps it down and mixes it into the flour: the oxen really like it, and it gives them the stamina to work all day.

That's the farmhand's job. He gets one-sixth of the crop, and he lives with you and eats your food. You give him a few hundred rupees pocket-money, to spend as he likes, on clothes, flour for his family, whatever. You also give him *bugarey*, a small plot quite separate from yours, and 5–10 seers of seed to sow, depending on how big it is. He uses your animals for ploughing and threshing; when his grain's ripe, he harvests it himself, threshes it and takes it off. Ten seers could yield 100 or 120 seers of wheat, all for himself: you've no right to it. This is custom, tradition, not an obligation. It makes no difference if the farmhand's an Uzbek or a Hazâra. Every landowner does it, unless they've only a very little land. If you can't afford *bugarey*, you make it clear when you engage him; in that case you'll pay him wages for ploughing; from 200 to 700 rupees, depending how much land there is.

When you engage a farmhand, you agree everything at the start. You say, for example, 'For one year you'll drive my oxen, plough and look after my wheat, and I'll feed you and give you ten seers *bugarey*.' These farming contracts – like shepherding ones – are nothing to do with government. If you break the contract and fail to give him his share, he'll go to an elder and declare, 'By God, he's eaten my share!' He'll do that first, because it's best to get the matter settled here, rather than going to the trouble of a government complaint. But if he doesn't get satisfaction here, he'll go and register a complaint; the government will question both sides, and if the employer's to blame they'll give the farmhand his share. But nobody would eat the farmhand's share; I suppose it's just possible, among our 400 to 500 families . . .

If you've a lot of land, you entrust it to a sharecropper [*keshtagar*]: a Hazâra or an Afghan. A sharecropper who provides seed and oxen will do all the work and get half the crop. He'll water the land, let it dry out for four or five days, then plough it. He may take on a farmhand to drive the yoke and so on, to work for him through the white and green crops, until cotton-picking time.

If you supply half the seed, then your sharecropper gets only a quarter of the crop. If you provide all the seed and the oxen, then he's just a farmhand, and he'll get a sixth of grain and straw.

Heydar's son Sarwar – our water-master [*arbâb*] – has little land himself, only a small paddock near his house, but he has a yoke of oxen, so he farms other people's land. He'll plough your land, sow 100 seers of seed and irrigate it. He also hires a farmhand, and when all's threshed and ready, first he takes out the farmhand's share, then he halves the rest with you. It's a good deal for him. For example, 100 seer of seed, God willing, will bear 1,000 seer: the farmhand's share comes out first – 150–200 seers – leaving 800 seer; you get 400 and Sarwar 400. It's the same 'halves' arrangement with the straw, and also with the green crops.

This year Sarwar sharecrops only for Kolagey – I showed you their huge wheat pile, near here, by Jân-Mahmad's land. But he also grew rainfed melons and corn on Rishmin's land, which had been inundated by a flash-flood. He also farmed wheat in the paddock near his house, which he shares with his brothers Masâdek and Khâni-âghâ.

When the reapers [*derowgar*] have finished the wheat, the farmhand collects the sheaves and carries them to the threshing ground. He may hire an assistant to bring in the sheaves and help with threshing. Some rope the sheaves onto their backs; others make a wooden frame, heap the sheaves onto it, and get a yoke of oxen to drag it to the threshing floor, where they unload it and pile it up with pitchforks. After they've brought it all in, they hitch the oxen to a thresher [*chapar*]. Have you seen one? It's made of mulberry branches, with a kind of sticky blue thorns; you dry it out for a week, then stick clods of mud onto it. There are two guys: one drives the oxen, the other stirs the straw with an iron pitchfork, to help the threshing, cutting up the straw.

When they've threshed the whole pile, they form it into a long mound, facing the wind. There it stays for a week or two; then they winnow it, to separate the grain from the chaff. The landowner will help, or the farmhand gets another assistant. One of them winnows like this, the other stands by and sweeps the grain with a thorn broom, piling up separately the husks and chaff. When there's a good wind, good big grains fall down to one side and thin, undeveloped grains fall further away. They winnow it once more; then they sieve it to clean it. The chaff stays in the sieve and the grain falls onto the pile. Then they bring the oxen to trample the chaff and straw that are left; they cover their mouths to stop them eating it, and someone drives them from behind, holding a wooden bowl to collect any dung, which would spoil it.

If I've planted melons or corn, as soon as the young melons emerge, I'll hire a warden [*qorukhmâl*]. During the day he sits out there in the shelter. His job's to keep animals and children away. If an adult comes, he tells them to keep to the path and not to walk through the corn or the melons. On the day the crop's divided, he'll get a twentieth, whatever the crop, corn, sesame, melons or anything else. He can eat as much as he likes, if it's ripe, for free.

Crop division is the same for barley and wheat. On the day the grain's cleaned, the landowner brings a mullah, like Mayoddin-jân or Mowlawi, to bless the crop and supervise the division. The landowner and the sharecropper draw a line round the pile, then measure out the grain with the sieve, counting as they go. First we take out the farmhand's share: one sieve in six. Two separate piles form. From a 600-seer crop, 100 go to the farmhand, 500 to landowner and sharecropper. If the farmhand has an assistant, he'll pay him out of his sixth at the crop division.

As for the reapers, you let them know the harvest pile's ready. Some people take out the reapers' dues first, before the measuring and division of the pile; otherwise their dues come from the landowner's share, not the sharecropper's or the farmhand's. You fixed their due with them on the first day, one in four, for example; if you sowed 40 seers, they get ten seers of the crop. The reapers divide it among themselves. Formerly, with barley, the reapers got the amount of seed sown; if 20 seers were sown, they got 20 seers of the crop. With wheat, they got half the seed sown. But recently, as grain prices have risen, the reapers' share's down to a third or a quarter of the seed sown. It's the same on rainfed land. Besides, this year there were so many people without work, available as reapers. When the good years return and prices fall, the reapers' share will be as before.

The mullah gets his tithe from the landowner's share, not from the farmhand's or the sharecropper's. For example, when you saw us dividing our barley, one-tenth went from our share, not from [*the sharecropper*] Haji Qâsem's. The recorder's and water-master's dues also come from the landowner. The recorder [*zâbet*] gets just one sieve from the pile. His job's just to put his seal on the piles, to prevent theft; also, when the crops are unripe, he goes around to ensure people don't let animals onto them. The water-master gets 25 seers per *joft*.

A sharecropper can also farm rainfed wheat, and he'll get a third or a quarter of the crop. If you just take a farmhand, he gets one-sixth. It's not such hard work, because once the seed's sown, there's no watering or anything to be done. On rainfed land, the farmhand ploughs and so on; but it's different with the reapers. With irrigated crops, if you've sown 100 seer, you give the fraction you agreed, as we said before: half, a quarter or a third. But from the rainfed wheat harvest, the reaper gets the same amount as was sown; that's what we do, but it varies: some people give the whole amount, some a third, some a half. Here, at the end of the canals, where most land is rainfed, people give the reapers less. In a rainy year, it comes to the same.

Pawning, renting and selling land

If a landowner needs cash to pay off a debt, or anticipates major expenses, he can pawn some or all of his land for a sum well below market value, giving up rights to cultivation and produce until he pays back the same sum – with the serious risk he may never be able to do so. Baya-khân explains.

Pawning [*gerow*] land works like this. If you're short of cash, you go to a wealthy man; if he hears you want to pawn some land, he may come to you. He'll pay you 10,000 to 50,000, depending on the amount of land. Once he's given you cash, you lose your rights to the land; it belongs to him, he'll cultivate it and take the produce, for up to ten years. But once you pay back the money, you resume ownership; the land's yours again. It's not only land, orchards or vineyards; you can pawn a watch, a radio, a gun, and redeem it in the same fashion.

You can also rent out some of your land; for example, for 400–500 seers of wheat. The landowner has nothing to do with cultivation; the tenant does the sowing, watering and so on, then at the crop division the owner will take the amount they agreed, plus half or a third of the straw.

Anârgol and Âdamjân have no land of their own. They rented Shir's land, with six hours of water, for 400 seers of wheat. In spring, they irrigated the wheat on Shir's land down here. The water belongs here, but when they'd finished watering the wheat they used the water rented from Shir to irrigate Haji Molk's land above – the corn that you saw. They shared the seed half-and-half with Haji Molk, and they'll halve the harvest too. The land remains Haji Molk's.

Jân-Mahmad did it too this year: our Hazâra sharecropper rented that bit of his land near our harvest pile, after the harvest, for 300 seers. But renting land this way is unusual.

It's a matter of luck whether sharecropping or renting is a better deal. In a good year, with plenty of rain, like this year, Shir's land yields 1,000 seer; a sharecropper would get 500. Shir has another harvest pile, from government wheat – people call it 'bald-ear' wheat, because it has no awns on the ears; it ripens very quickly. They sowed in April, and it was ripe in three months. We sow ordinary wheat in March. He piled it at night; it must have made 100–200 seers.

That plot by the pond where Mowzoddin planted melons – you must have seen it – actually belongs to Golusar. Nobody wanted it, because the canal water didn't reach it; it just lay there. Then Mowzoddin came and levelled it, brought water from the Ghajar Canal, and cultivated it. Now he's been growing crops there for some years. Golusar said, 'That's my land, look at the deeds; I want it back.' Golusar will get five elders together to prove his claim. Nobody did anything with that land until Mowzoddin developed it. Golusar says, 'okay, he's worked my land, but now he's been eating the produce – wheat, melons and so on – for ten years without giving me my share.'

Selling land is complex and sensitive, not least because, first, neighbouring plot-holders (known as shapp*) have a legally recognized first option, and secondly, Piruzai will try to stop any of the original holding going out of the sub-tribe permanently. Pâdshâh, Seyyed-shâh/Golusar and Pâdshâh/Parwiz together outline the process.*

If I want to sell some land, and you want to buy it, I must consult my neighbour, to prevent him complaining afterwards. He has first option. If he doesn't want to buy, or hasn't the money, then I can do as I like. But if he wants it, then he must match the price another buyer's offering. He'll try to raise money by selling household goods and so on. If he can't, he'll have no right to complain.

Once a sale's agreed, and the deeds exchanged, the parties decide the terms. So if the deed states it's 11 *jeribs*, they must agree on the actual boundaries. None of these lands have been measured for a long time. If a government surveyor came, there'd be many discrepancies; extra land would emerge, and the owners would lose it.

For such an agreement, it's important for a mullah, or five witnesses, to be present, to make it correct by sharia. An agreement without a mullah or five witnesses is only customary law, which is no good; troublemakers might say, 'Where are your witnesses?' A mullah's a big witness. When it's done according to sharia, you must stick to the agreement. Land deeds are sharia. A customary law document is when you get a scribe to write a note saying, for example, 'I've bought your land, or taken it in pawn.' This kind of document's no good these days; the previous owner could deny it and get his land back, or sell it to someone else.

Farmlands here fetch different prices and rents according to distance from the canal-head. There are three grades, upper, lower and middle. Thus, Haji has three plots of land; one is upper, by Haji Ghâfur's, close to the canal-head. The second is middle, second-class, in Khârkash. The third is down here near our village; it's the worst grade.

Land in town is expensive. For a shop, it's 20,000–25,000 rupees a *jerib*. When you come to Kohna-Bâzâr it's not quite so good, and even less so in Chârbâgh; then down to Khârkash, where a *jerib* is 9,000–10,000; here in Konjek it's about 6,000. All depends on the water.

Dry land in the steppe is plentiful, worth no more than 500–1,000. With pastures, you can rent the grazing rights just by a verbal agreement, for so many thousand rupees, or an animal for slaughter, or a horse.

Farming Up-country

The Piruzai are familiar with the different farming practices of villagers along their migration route, from the Hazâras in Lâl-o-Sar-jangal and Kâshân, to the Aymâqs of Cherâs, Gholduri and Kachan, to the Uzbeks and others of Sangchârak.

In the mountains

Baya-khân has observed how the mountain villagers manage to grow crops.

The Hazâras of Sar-jangal – you saw them last year – have 6 or 7 months of winter. Their wheat's like ours, but it doesn't grow so tall; when it's ready, some reap by hand, some with a scythe. They don't make piles in the fields, they collect the crop in huge cloths, throwing the sheaves on the cloth, beating it down and loading it on cows and donkeys. They take it home, pile it up there, then thresh it and take it inside. Their barley's different from ours: it's reddish and very like wheat. They also grow beans and potatoes.

In July they cut their fodder crops: with their long, hard, snowy winters, they need lots of fodder. They make huge piles of *kowda, gheyghân, khowla* and other shrubs for the winter. Their houses – you've seen them – have only one entrance; there's a room for people, another for sheep, and another for cattle, with mangers for the animals. Their winter life is very hard; all day long they're shovelling snow off the roof in case it falls in. The snow stops them leaving the village; all they can do is sleep.

In a hungry year, they eat *tosla*, a grass that only grows on sand and rocks on high mountain slopes; it has long thin leaves – like the fox-tail lilies you saw – and dark blue flowers. They collect it in sacks and bring it home by donkey or cow. First they boil it in water to leach out the dirt and bitterness, then they dry it in the sun. When it's dry, they boil it with milk and tie it up tight in a big cloth. To eat, they throw some into a pot and boil it down in water, with a little ghee if they have any. When the kids, large or small, cry from hunger, you give them a handful to eat with buttermilk. In a year when they've no money or can't find flour, this grass lasts them until the new harvest.

Hazâras also eat spinach and saltwort as green vegetables. Some eat *matsotsak*, which you find in the sand: it has flowers, and comes out bright orange like a carrot; you eat it with milk or cooked under the fire. They also eat *kharpati* leaves: they make a milky juice when you pick them. Then there are two kinds of *komâla*: one that sheep eat, the other, which we call Hazâra *komâla*, makes very thin stalks like wild celery, which you've seen; the stalks taste good, like celery. If they've no grain, this is how Hazâra people manage until the new harvest.

People in Cherâs and Gholduri dig a pit in the ground outside their house, and put a sort of basket in it, leaving a small opening. They keep back enough wheat for the winter – between 100 and 500 seers – and mill it; then they bury the rest in the pit, filling it through the opening and sealing it with mud. At ploughing time, they open the pit and take out some grain, sow some, and mill the rest for flour. Sometimes we *mâldârs* leave wheat with them, stored in their pit; next spring, when we return, they give it back to us.

From Kachan downwards, people have special storerooms just for wheat. We used to have one, near uncle Jân-Mahmad's old house, but it decayed and fell apart. Now everyone brings their wheat inside in sacks; you build a wall and pile the sacks up behind it, then put flax straw on top and plaster it over with mud. Whenever you want some, you open it up. You put wheat from this harvest in, then in February or March you take some out and make flour to take to the spring camp. It'll keep for a year or two; longer, if you pile straw on top. But if you keep it too long it collects tiny insects.

In Kachan and Sangchârak

Karim the shepherd tells how his Kachani people farm.

You won't find anywhere as nice as Kachan. We grow barley, wheat and apricots; our meadows produce hay – so do the mountainsides, though they're too far away for us to mow it and bring it down. People migrate up to the ridges for 20–25 days, then they move over to Michiluk, then to Qaghzâr, then Kuri, staying several weeks; then everyone comes down to the orchards. Every family has apricot trees. You can find everything in Kachan. But winters are very hard; three to six months of snow. You spend all day sweeping the roof, it's hard work. People suffer from lack of water, and from ice. [*See Map D*]

Kachani people work very hard, farming on the mountainsides. They gather the harvest; for two or three days they thresh and then winnow it, load it on donkeys, bring it down and take it to their creditors and the *mâldâr*, who buy the wheat for 200 or 250 rupees a seer, then sell it for 1,000!

If someone has a pair of oxen, and four plots of land, he's okay. Otherwise poverty forces them to do something else for a living. We don't have such things. There are some very wealthy Kachani Boys. In our village there's Abdol-Momin, who has 12 yoke of oxen, 500 Arabi sheep, five cow-skins full of cash. They're three brothers. One year he beat and killed his uncle and father-in-law; he got twelve years in jail, but he bought his way out. He acts like a khan. If there's a fight, a quarrel, or a robbery, people come to him first. If he resolves the matter, it's over; if not, they'll they go to the *hâkem*.

Seyyed-shâh/Soleymân and Baya-khân talk about changes in farming in Kachan and Sangchârak.

(*Seyyed-shâh*) – Cultivation in the Sangchârak valleys has expanded. When we pitched camp before, our mares and camels could wander to graze. For every *jerib* of cultivated land, ten *jeribs* went uncultivated. Land didn't have the value it does now.

(*Baya-khân*) – We also have land in Sangchârak and up in the mountains, not to mention the rainfed steppe-land. For example, we're three to four households, and we all share in land here and near Big-Haji's place up there, and we have irrigated and rainfed lands up in Kachan, Dehmana, Kataqala, Buinaqara, Langar and Chayrak. In former years the Red-Gorge, right down to Dehmana at the end of Kachan, was uncultivated meadows and trees; you could lose your way. People didn't care about land; you just scattered a few seeds and it cropped well. Then land became sweet, so people picked out the stones, dug it up with spades, and cultivated it; they'd collect meadow grasses by hand and pile them elsewhere. But for some years now, whatever's sown hasn't cropped so well, and people have gone hungry.

Pâdshâh describes farming in Sangchârak, near the vineyards his father Tumân owns.

Our soil in Konjek's ordinary, earth-coloured, but some Sangchârak land has a strong reddish colour. Lots of red land's rainfed, but it's hard to find irrigated red land – there are many disputes over access to such land. People won't sell for 20,000 rupees a *jerib*. It's fantastically fertile, if you grow corn or wheat, but particularly the vines are first class: the grapes are extraordinary, better than others in Sangchârak. Plant vines on a plot the size of this compound, and they'll bear more grapes than you could eat.

There's some red land as you turn the corner towards Buyna-qara – you know, near Wahâb's house? That's good red land, or so the local Uzbeks say; they've lived on it for seven generations, so they know. Since we bought fields and vineyards there, they've been telling us that red earth gives two seers to every one from ordinary lands. Some say it's ten times as fertile. I don't know what it has that makes it this way. I've seen the lands they point out, and they bear so heavily, some years the peach tree branches are so heavily laden, they have to prop them up with poles. And the frost doesn't affect the trees there: almonds, apples, apricots, mulberries.

The Sangchârak subsoil's sandy and damp; the water-table's close to the surface, not like here in Konjek and Khârkash, where the water's deep down. There, if you dig a well, you hit water at once. It's close to both the mountain slopes and the river. It has rocks in it, which retain the heat; that's why it's so damp. Irrigated land in Sangchârak won't grow good wheat unless it's ploughed. Two things grow well in that damp soil: reeds and bamboo. If they leave it for a year without ploughing, next year for sure it'll be green with reeds. Reeds with deep, thick roots grow along the canals. The roots take hold and the soil hardens; you can plough it, but it's very tiring for man and beast. That's why they plough it first. They break it up, cutting the roots, then the sun does its work and burns them; they dry up and the soil softens. If they didn't do this, the land would be thick with reeds. Once I brought some seedlings here to plant in our pond, hoping they'd sprout, because when they do, they're there for good. But they got buried in the mud.

On rainfed land, shortly after they've harvested melons or sesame and removed the greenery for the animals to eat, they plough long, widely separated furrows, then fill their shirt-tails with 60–80 kg of wheat seed and sow it. This'll be nine-month autumn wheat. The first rain or snow, it'll sprout immediately. It's excellent wheat, the best in Sangchârak.

On thorn-covered land – *tuk*, as they call it – which they didn't plough at first, they grow another kind of wheat. They plough once, then after a second run they board it; after one more run they sow the wheat. This too will be good, but not quite as good as on melon land.

They sow barley in mid-January, in the middle of the Black Forty. Once the Forties are over they plough and sow flax. When the land gets 'black', it starts warming from underneath. If the seeds sprout then, it doesn't matter if the weather turns cold. Flax is very small when it first sprouts; as spring advances, in March and April, it'll be very good. Flax sown up to the end of March will be excellent. In some places it'll reach a metre or more in height, and bear so heavily that a single stalk makes a bush like this – in good soil; it depends on the soil.

With the flax and barley harvested, it's time to prepare for next year's wheat. Once the land's ready, everyone sends out his farmhand. If the lands are some distance away, all the farmhands gather somewhere like a sheepfold and spend the night there, in case of thieves. They take their own supplies: rice, fat or meat if they have any, but most just take bread or flour and some cooking-pots, and when their flour runs out their boss will bring more from the Valley, or they'll go and fetch it themselves. The farmhands plough night and day, and stay until everyone's finished. If the land's close to the Valley, they can stay at home and get up early to go out on a daily basis, even coming back at midday and going out again in the afternoon. Then they sow wheat on the ploughed land.

As for land where wheat was harvested, they just plough it once, then leave it. Land that's wheat this year will be sesame next, and the following year they'll let the sun beat down on it. Land that's weak should be ploughed and left fallow, to burn in the sun; it gets very thirsty and gains strength, as if you'd put sheep dung on it. You know when you put dung on alfalfa, how big it grows? When the sun beats down, ploughed land gets very hot and strong and burns like embers. If you leave land in the sun unploughed, it stays cold and weak underneath.

Baya-khân tells how Sangchârak people grow Indian hemp.

It's very hard work. You plant seedlings or bushes. There are male and female plants; the males don't crop but when they get big they produce a large white flower; then you uproot the males and leave the females to grow. It's some years before the bushes are big enough to gather; then you hang them up at home and the dust settles on them. When they're dried, you take the leaves and wash them. You collect the seeds in a soft cloth, and roast them in a griddle on the fire, rolling them around and keeping them over the flames until they're cooked. You can press the seeds for the oil: it's edible – I've had it with rice; it's very good, very strong, particularly for curing rheumatism. Every year I used to get severe pains in my arm and leg joints; I had some of this hashish oil, and it cured them.

The seeds are cheap. Hashish itself fetches 2,000 or 2,500 rupees a seer, though tourists buy it for 4,000–5,000. Once this year it got very dear, then cheap again. When a large amount is exported to some other country, the price here goes up. We have one or two seers in our house now, from last year's crop. We sold 3–4 seers to a Sheberghâni, at 2,500.

Some people won't cultivate hemp. Religiously, it's highly illicit. It's not good to grow: it ruins the soil, curses it for 40 years, so the sheykhs and *mowlawis* say. You can plant wheat or some other crop after Indian hemp, but the soil has lost its bounty. No other crop has the same effect.

Of course, gambling and pederasty are also illicit.

(R) – But you can't grow those! [*laughter*].

Vineyards in Sangchârak

Several Pashtun mâldâr, *including Haji Tumân, Haji Ghâfur and Seyyed-shâh/Soleymân, bought vineyards in Sangchârak from the local Uzbeks. They tend to get local farmers to sharecrop their vines; recently, as Seyyed-shâh told us earlier, locals have started to withhold the Pashtun owners' shares, finding ways of keeping all the produce for themselves. Ensuing legal cases don't always go the way of the* mâldâr. *In August 1971, while we are camped in Chârkent, Seyyed-shâh, Chârgol and I interview an unnamed local gardener (G) on growing grapes and other local crops.*

(*Seyyed-shâh*) – When do you plant vines?

(*G*) – In May–June.

(*Seyyed-shâh*) – Do you dig holes for them?

(*G*) – Yes, we dig a spade-depth into the soil, plant the vine, cover it and water it, then mark the place; that's it!

(*R*) – How often do you water it?

(*G*) – Four times before winter, the last one in December.

(*Seyyed-shâh*) – How many years before it bears grapes?

(*G*) – If you work it well, it'll bear grapes in the fourth year. You should keep the soil under the vine moist, water well by the stalk, keep the roots damp, but not too damp, don't let the leaves burn.

(*R*) – So a new vineyard makes grapes in the fourth year; how many years before the vines go bad?

(*G*) – A vineyard, *enshallah*, lasts 80 to 100 years, if the owner works it well. Otherwise, 20 to 30 years.

(*R*) – How old is the oldest vineyard here, for example?

(*G*) – About fifty years.

(*R*) – Good. If a vineyard has 1,000 vines, how much will it produce in a good year like this?

(*G*) – Listen: If the owner's careful, 1,000 vines will produce 50 big seers of grapes [*2.5–3 tons*].

(*R*) – How much does one big seer [*56 kg*] fetch?

(*G*) – 600 rupees, this year.

(*R*) – How much was it last year?

(*Seyyed-shâh*) – Last year it was 600 too. The year before, it was 800.

(*G*) – No, that's wrong!

(*Seyyed-shâh*) – Last year it was cheap, 600. This year, right now, the price is still 600. They'll fix it around January, probably it'll reach 800. Last year there was no agreement.

(*R*) – What determines the price? In a good year, does the price go up or down, or what?

(*Seyyed-shâh*) – It's a government matter; whatever they agreed with America, USSR, Germany. It's international. We grow too many to eat ourselves! Some people sell 10,000–20,000 big seers [*up to 1,000 tons*] to the traders. Tell us, how do you make Sayegi, dried green raisins? Do you make them from these same grapes?

(*G*) – No. My friend, they take 20 to 30 days to dry.

(*Seyyed-shâh*) – Tell us what happens: first you cut them, then what do you do?

(*G*) – Do you mean, how do we make the drying-racks, how do we tie them up? How we make *khorda* . . . what do we call them? Yes, Sayegi—

(*Seyyed-shâh*) – Richard, he can't talk properly! Listen to me.

(*R*) – But he was doing fine!

(*Seyyed-shâh*) – No, he keeps getting stuck! What he's trying to say is that when they make Sayegi . . .

(*G*) – . . . We tie the grapes up, and hang them in bunches, in pairs; perhaps eight or ten at a time.

(*Seyyed-shâh*) – That's it! Carry on.

(*G*) – If there's a lot hung up, they make 2 or 3 big seers [*110–170 kg*], and we'll sell them for about 100–120 rupees a Kabul seer [*7 kg*]. We only sell them if the price is good.

(*Seyyed-shâh*) – How many varieties of raisins are there? How many are grown in the Sangchârak district?

(*G*) – Khalili; Tayefi; Alamân-tayeri-Jushi; Black-Grape; White-Grape; Hosseini; Sugar-Grape. That's it.

(*Seyyed-shâh*) – Which ones ripen quickest?

(*G*) – The Khalili ripens quickly.

(*R*) – Do you grow all these varieties in the same place? Or does one place, here for instance, specialize in one variety, such as Hosseini?

(*Seyyed-shâh*) – No, they're found everywhere. When you plant a vineyard, you go and take a cutting from a good vine; what you plant is the dry wood. Only when it bears fruit do you know the variety.

(*G*) – When we take a cutting, we ask the owner what kind of vine it is. He'll tell us, Shur-Qara – that's another variety – Khalili, Alamân-tayeri-Jushi, Tayefi, Sugar-Grape.

(*Chârgol*) – What's this one? You're the gardener; tell us what it is.

(*G*) – This one? [*He eats it*] It's . . . I've forgotten the name.

(*R*) – It doesn't matter; the grape won't be on the tape! Now, these kinds of grapes, they're found in all parts of Sangchârak district? In Chârkent, in Chayrak . . . but not above here? Not above Malek?

(*G*) – They're found in every province . . .

(*Seyyed-shâh*) – Not much above Malek: some in Dehmana and the lower Kachan valley. From Malek downwards every variety's grown; in all Seven Valleys, including Sangchârak district centre.

(*R*) – What about below Suzma-qala, in Sar-e-pol district?

(*Seyyed-shâh*) – Yes, but not like here in Sangchârak district.

(*R*) – Have people here always grown grapes like this, or did they grow them differently before?

(*Seyyed-shâh*) – God knows what was here before. We Afghans weren't here, this land belonged to others. There were vines when our grandfathers arrived; we didn't know what they were, but gradually we all acquired vineyards, we learned from each other, and the area became full of vineyards. Now, in the whole of Afghanistan there's no place like Sangchârak for grapes.

(*Chârgol*) – What about Arghandâb in Kandahar?

(*Seyyed-shâh*) – Yes, there's Arghandâb; but there's nowhere like Sangchârak for grapes. Dawlatâbâd in Maymana has grapes, but not like those of Sangchârak. What about peaches, how many varieties are there? Tell us about peach trees.

(*G*) – They bear after 2 to 3 years. They last for 5 to 6 years, depending on how well they're tended; they might last for ten years before they dry up. In strong soil, if you keep the roots properly watered, they'll keep bearing fruit for a few years more.

(*Seyyed-shâh*) – What about apricots?

(*G*) – Apricot trees bear after 10 years. They last 100 years.

(*Seyyed-shâh*) – What about walnuts?

(*G*) – A walnut tree lives for 1,000 years.

(*Seyyed-shâh*) – How is it planted? Does it have a seed? Where do you find a seed?

(*G*) – You get the seed from the nut itself. It bears nuts after 20 years. The walnut tree never ages, it lives for a long time, and it bears nuts from top to bottom ...

(*N*) – What about corn?

(*R*) – How do you cultivate it, water it?

(*G*) – We sow corn in June. We plough the land again and again, and water it as many times as you want. If you and your team don't get tired, the soil will benefit the more you water it.

(*Seyyed-shâh*) – Would you do it ten times?

(*G*) – Ten times would be good. If you sow 1,000 seer, it would be good to water it ten times. Sow the seed, smooth the earth, water it until the green shoots appear, then cut the water.

(*Seyyed-shâh*) – So how many times do you water until it ripens?

(*G*) – Four times, sometimes five. Not more.

(*Seyyed-shâh*) – When we do corn there, it gets eight waters.

(*G*) – It depends where you are. If you've lots of water, no schedule to observe, there's no problem.

(*R*) – You mentioned this before; there's no irrigation schedule in this valley, so far?

(*G*) – Not this year.

(*R*) – Does your water reach Sar-e-pol or not?

(*Seyyed-shâh*) – In a rainy year, when there's lots of water, it reaches Sar-e-pol. In a dry year like this one, we need our water, and Sar-e-pol has no rights in it; it won't even reach Suzma-qala, which gets its water from another direction. They have no rights in our water; if they get some, it's from friendship, they can't take it by force.

(*R*) – So water just runs in the canals all year long?

(*Seyyed-shâh*) – It's free, all year long, nobody interferes with anybody else; use it for one day, or ten days, whenever you want. We have plenty of water, it's land we're short of here; and our people can't work it properly. To make this land and water fertile, you start with fertilizer; then plough it properly, several times. Once or twice isn't enough. The land loses its strength. These people in Chârkent are lazy and feckless. The people of Chârbâgh in Sar-e-pol are hard-working, zealous: their land yields 20,000–30,000 rupees per *jerib*, When Chârkent people cultivate the land belonging to us Afghans, one *jerib* won't give 2 seer [*100 kg*]; but when Shir-Mahmad ploughs one *jerib* of his own land and sows barley – it's not even one *jerib*, it's only 15 *beswa* – it produces 20 seer [*1 ton*] of barley.

(R) – What was that you said, *beswa*? How many *beswa* in a *jerib*?

(Seyyed-shâh) – Twenty. His land was 15 *beswa* [*0.15 ha*]. He grew barley and it yielded 20 Sangchârak seers. Then he manured it and sowed corn, which'll make at least 40 seer.

(R) – How much corn seed do you sow on a *jerib*?

(Seyyed-shâh) – Half a Kabul seer [*3.5 kg*], not more. Sow thinly; if you sow liberally the land won't produce so much.

(G) – Over-sow, and it won't ripen properly.

(Seyyed-shâh) – If the land's good, and you cultivate it well, half a seer of corn seed will make 50 seer, perhaps even 200 or 300 seer.

9

Other Business

Work for the Landless

Piruzai who own no land, and cannot find work as herdsmen or farmhands, make a living as casual labourers, reapers or household servants, or by local or long-distance trade.

1971: after two drought years, times are hard; staple crops reach record prices. Pâdshâh and his family are relatively well off, but he is very familiar with the situation of the landless.

We Afghans of Khârkash and Konjek used to hire Uzbeks or Hazâras – especially Hazâra casual labourers – as farmhands. Nowadays, we don't take non-Afghans so often; mostly, we hire other Kandahari Afghans, poor men, for example, with no home and usually no family, who come from Maymana and other places. Such a man will join your family, eat with you, sleep in your home and work for you. If he has a wife and kids, or a brother, you'll give them a room and he'll stay with you as your *hamsaya*, 'client'. With no animals or land whatsoever, he comes out of poverty, and he'll work for you as a farmhand, his brother will work for someone else, his son will take your camels out grazing, and so on. If they work hard, they'll make a living that way for several years, fill their stomachs. With luck, they'll manage to acquire a couple of goats, a few sheep, or a cow, look after them, get milk to drink. Or they'll get a yoke of oxen, and farm your land as sharecroppers. That's what a farmhand aims at; if he works hard, he'll make good, and with luck he won't go short.

Some people hire relatives or fellow-villagers as farmhands; but it's not a good idea, because if it goes wrong it's difficult for either of you to complain. But a stranger, you don't know who he is; if you hire him as a farmhand, you can threaten him, beat him and so on, without hesitation, for the first year or two. After that he becomes familiar, even a friend – like you!

What's the best work for a poor stranger? It depends what God gives. In a good year, when there's plenty of hay and the winter's not too cold, a shepherd working with the sheep can do better than a farmhand. In a dry year like this [1971], every farmhand here in the irrigated lands of Khârkash, Konjek, Behsud has done better than a shepherd. Prices are good: a one-sixth share of straw fetches 2,000–3,000 rupees, wheat's 80 a seer, beans, sesame, melons are 15–20 rupees. The farmhand knows his takings; he puts them safely into the storeroom. But there's little hay or other fodder. God knows what'll happen next winter and spring, how the shepherds will manage.

After the hard winter, the 1972 harvests are good, but prices remain very high until the crops are in. Pâdshâh discusses other strategies for making a living.

Someone with surplus grain brings it home and puts it in the storeroom. When the wheat price rises, he'll sell it to you, me and the poor, on credit until spring. If the market price now is 50 rupees, he'll give it at 90 or 100, to be paid in spring. Some people do *qawmi* and charge 10 or 20 less. Others sell their surplus in town at the market price – if they're short of cash, have someone going on military service, or got into a fight or some other kind of trouble and need money. Or perhaps they're planning a wedding and need to put together a son's brideprice or a daughter's trousseau. Perhaps they're collecting money to go on Hajj. They may simply want to go into trade.

A poor man with no wheat will try to find some in the village. If he finds someone who'll sell at the market price, he'll pay; otherwise he'll have to buy on credit at an inflated price. If he can't buy here for credit or cash, he'll try another village, or go to Sar-e-pol or Sheberghân. Many people buy from the bazaar. If wheat's too expensive, they buy poor-quality rice; whatever they can afford.

This year wheat reached 120 rupees a seer, nearly half as much again as poor rice, which was a bargain at 80 to 90. Some buy bean or barley flour, or they take barley or millet or corn to mill for flour. If they've a cow, they buy a seer or two of rice and at night they can eat milk-rice-pudding, and in daytime, *shola*: rice cooked in ghee. They manage somehow until the next harvest ripens.

There's a kind of cumin that grows in irrigated wheat. The owner of a wheat-field may take me on as warden, allowing me to collect the cumin. I'll keep people off the wheat and pick the cumin again and again, giving him his share; then I'll sell my share and make enough to buy rice, flour and barley to feed the kids and keep the family going a little longer.

After the cumin, it's time for the barley harvest, and I can reap it for you. If you've sown 100 seers, you give me half that, 50 seers, out of the harvest; though if barley prices are high, you'll give me only a quarter, 25 seers. When I'm engaged as a reaper, I look at the field and reckon whether I can do it all myself; if not, I take a partner and we share the proceeds. Then my wife and kids, young and old, will come and collect the gleanings, and that'll keep them going for a while.

When the wheat's ready for harvest, we can reap that too, and get half or a quarter of the seed sown. In the mountains beyond Kachan they give the reapers the same amount as the seed sown. In a bad year like the last two, they give a quarter or a half, but they also feed you every day, give you water, bread, fat, rice and tea and a good animal for slaughter. It's up to you what to do with the animal and the bread, but you can live on what they give you. You can eat the meat at once if you want, or just a little every day. They'll also bring you tea, sugar and such things to consume there, and milk if they have any. That's what the people in the mountains do.

Few people from round here go to the mountains to reap. Boghawi's closer to the mountains; people above Boghawi go up and reap until mid-October.

The farmers tell the reapers when to return: after the wheat is threshed and winnowed. They bring camels or donkeys to fetch their share; it might be 5 maund [*nearly 300 kg*], which will feed the family for the winter.

Some people trade in animals. Others supply oxen for ploughing and threshing, and get a sieve-full of wheat every month for that. That's how they get by.

Some people take two sticks [*defence against dogs*] and go begging. If you can't find work, this is easy and you'll get 2–3 rupees, or some flour, barley, corn or sesame from each home. These last two years there have been many beggars around here; many people were really destitute; but now, thank God, there are very few.

Last year six lads went to Lataband, this side of Suzma-qala. Wherever they went nobody would give them work. The farmers didn't like the look of them, and thought that if they hired them as reapers they might kill or steal. On their way back the rascals were caught stealing some wheat; everything they had was taken from them, including their clothes, and they got a severe beating!

These days Afghanistan has become smart. A clever guy reckons whether you're up to working; he'll ask for your ID card [*tazkira*], and if you have one, he'll hire you as a servant or farmhand. If not, however well you're dressed, he won't take you on; he'll be afraid that one night you'll steal his cows, his camels, his sheep or something from his home; how can he find you if you don't have ID? People are very careful now. Before, it didn't matter. If you came from England, someone would take you on as a servant. If I went to England, somebody would hire me!

Mâkhân pawned his land and hasn't been able to redeem it. He's a gambler and a spendthrift – may the Koran strike him. If he saw something in a shop he'd pay 20 rupees over the price; that's where his money went. He makes a living: he gets regular brideprice payments for his two daughters, both engaged. He also does building work. He'll plaster a room with mud and daub for 500 or 1,000 rupees, depending on the size. He's probably made 4,000 to 5,000 rupees that way. Two people can be partners, share the work and the payment. Also, you know that his sister Golla married Haji Nâder Nâmanzai? He was very wealthy, but he died. Mâkhân would go to his sister's house and she'd secretly give him stuff: 5 maunds of flour, or barley, a skin, a couple of hundred rupees, clothes.

In Mâkhân's house there's just himself, his wife, his sons and daughters. He has no sheep, but one cow, I believe, for milk. He's closest to his uncle Mowzoddin and his brother-in-law Akhtar, but they can't help him; their sheep have died, they haven't much land left, they're in poor shape too.

Mowzoddin has a large family, and there's never enough to eat. This year in particular was hard for them; they went hungry and thirsty. In spring, they'd go and weed the wheat and barley fields. They also collected cumin. People also paid them over the odds for skins and animals; for example they'd pay 1,100 or 1,200 rupees for one worth 1,000. Anyway, they did various jobs, and managed to survive until the barley harvest; then they went to collect the gleanings, for their evening fare.

Mowzoddin does have land, several plots: one down below, where they did rainfed melons; one near the pond by the steppe, where they grew squash and then wheat; and one here near Akhtar, which was wheat too – their harvest pile is still standing. His sons do the farming, with their own oxen; if they're all busy, his daughters, even his wife, watch over their crops. He had forty-odd sheep, but he had to sell the few that survived the winter. Apart from the oxen, he has half-a-dozen goats. He recently married one daughter to Mahd-Amin's son [*a non-Durrani*], over at Haji Shamsoddin's. Nobody here would give much for her, so when Mahd-Amin made a good offer, Mowzoddin accepted, out of hunger and poverty. He ignored what people said; 'I'm hungry, and since you won't offer enough, I must take what I can get for her.'

A few years before I married Pâkhâl, her brother Payz married my sister Zeytun. Then they separated from his father, Mahd-Amin. But a year later poor Zeytun died, God bless her,[1] leaving their three kids with his mother, Nik-morgh; one was newborn, and it too died after a few months.

Payz doesn't yet have any land or animals. His youngest brother Mahmad-mir is away on military service; when he marries, Mahd-Amin will divide the land among the brothers, after setting aside enough for his Hajj. After he dies, everything else will be divided among the brothers and sisters; the brothers will separate, and the sisters will decide which brothers should get their shares.

Until then, Payz has nothing. He reaps, he earns 30 to 40 rupees a day winnowing or making mud-bricks, collecting dung-cakes, digging out a well for 50 or 60 rupees, fetching hay from the steppe. He's never been a farmhand, but he does herd people's sheep and camels. The important thing is that he manages to provide enough for his two kids and himself. He won't remarry just yet; when his daughter grows up, he'll exchange her for a wife for himself, or give her to someone for brideprice, which he'll use to get a wife.

One hamsaya – *a 'poor stranger' – worked for a while as a cobbler, as Baya-khân recalls.*

When we were in the mountains last summer, Joma-khân Nurzai came here with his wife, small son and three daughters. He begged to be allowed to stay. Dur-khân gave them a room in Jân-Mahmad's old compound; the rest had been pulled down, but Jân-Mahmad had plenty of roof-beams and left this room intact. Joma-khân had nothing: no sheep, no donkey. He was Dur-khân's *hamsaya*. He worked as a cobbler: he'd make and mend shoes, shepherd's sandals, milk-churns and well-buckets. At that time there wasn't anyone else in the village that did this. Dur-khân gave him a room because he was a poor stranger: that's what a *hamsaya* is. He didn't work for him, though he may have mended his shoes free. He's related to Din-Mahmad Nurzai; they and Âghâ-Mahmad are all related. This spring, Din-Mahmad sent camels to fetch them, and they moved to Dara-ye-band.

Several villagers have tried their hand at shopkeeping. Pâdshâh himself currently has a small shop in his house, though he doesn't mention that here.

Madu's son Amiroddin has a shop; that's all he does. He makes enough to fill his belly – what else is necessary? He collects wheat, barley, flax, cotton, corn; some farmhands steal wheat or melons and sell them to him cheap, and he sells them on. His wife's mother, Malek, brings her daughter bread, wheat and flour – she doesn't want her to starve.

Dâdollah is Pâr-khân's sharecropper; his brother Paydak is their farmhand – he ploughs very well, he's the brother who understands the land. Another brother,

---

[1] *Khodâ biâmorza,* 'God forgive her'.

Shâhzâda, collects lambskins in spring. The fourth brother, Dirty Golak, has had a shop for many years. Many people won't buy from him, but he makes a profit somehow – no one keeps a shop if they don't make a profit. He sells stuff to the mountain Aymâqs who bring their sheep down here in spring. So do the other shopkeepers; there's lots of business at that time of year. The barley and wheat harvests are also good times for business; so's winter, when people eat a lot of sesame halva for the warmth.

Cowherds

One community job, herding the village cows, is religiously favoured. As their due, the cowherds receive a share of the harvest, and daily bread known as khoja-khedri, *after Khoja-Khedr.*[2] *Seyyed-shâh/Golusar explains.*

I've never been a cowherd myself. When we were small, Nazar Kachi and his son were community cowherds, *gurwân*; Fârsibân people say *pâdawân*. There are two of them. If you had a yoke of oxen, for each ox he looked after he got a seer of wheat at harvest-time. In those days, too, for the cattle, they collected bread as *khoja-khedri*, not cash. They'd come to each house and call, 'God bless you, send out the *khoja-khedri!*' One piece of bread in the evening when the cows come in, another at noon, whether you had one cow or three. The evening bread lasted until next midday; they didn't eat any in the morning.

The mullahs say that *khoja-khedri* bread is ultra-halal, so pure that there's not the slightest flaw in it. With ordinary bread, you don't know you're not paying stolen money for it: for example, if I've borrowed money from Richard and failed to repay it on time, this could lead to problems, and the possibility that any bread I buy with it may be haram. But *khoja-khedri* bread's spotless. He stands in the sun, tends the cattle, takes them to water at the river or the canal; he has a hard time in the mud and the dirt; if you give him bread, it's really halal, it brings you merit.

A farmhand's bread's halal too. He works twelve months in the year. So long as he doesn't steal: for example, if you give him 20 seer of wheat to sow and he sows only ten and skims the rest, then neither the land, nor you, nor the farmhand will prosper; the blessing's gone. If he hides or sells 10 seers of seed, who knows but God? The cowherd's bread is much cleaner than the farmhand's.

When Nazar Kachi died, his job went to Haji Tumân's maternal uncle, Ghaws. He herded the community cattle for several years, taking them out to the steppe with his wife Shâhpari and bringing back their dung. Ghaws would take the cattle right up to Kand-e-Jabbâr. Shâhpari would collect some milk, yoghourt and raw *pataka* cheese from Haji or Shir, and take it to eat with Ghaws, in a *katëw* cauldron – it's like an iron bucket, but made of hardened mud, with an opening as big as this; it's clean, and if you put ghee or anything else in it, it'll last for ten days or more. Normal metal cauldrons corrode, and turn milk or yoghourt bad in a couple of days.

Ghaws [*see pp. 337–39*] died about twelve years ago. After his death his sons Darwiza and Mir-Hamza went on for some years; they tended our cattle, took them out to graze

---

[2] The 'Green Saint'; see www.khidr.org; Krasnowolska (2009); and *Wikipedia*, s.v. 'Khidr'.

in the steppe. They'd go out with their mother Shâhpari, as far as Ali-Mahmad's hollow – where we saw the sesame crop, that day we went to the steppe together. They played ball, while Shâhpari collected dung and loaded it on the donkey. They got *khoja-khedri*. Then after a few years they said, 'Give us cash instead.' So people paid, at first two-and-a-half rupees, then 5 rupees, per cow per month; thus for three cows, they got 15 rupees a month, 30 for two months. They halved the takings. Then Darwiza died, and for two years Mir-Hamza herded cattle on his own, until he became Shir's farmhand.

After Mir-Hamza, the cattle passed to Beydu and his sons, who looked after them and took them to the steppe along with thirty sheep belonging to Akhtar the shopkeeper. Once, a wolf got among the sheep and ripped open their throats, one after the other. When it had finished with them, there was nothing he could do to save the sheep, so he had to slaughter them. He prepared their skins and sold them. Beydu herded the cattle very well for about five years, until his death. Then, his sons fooled around and didn't do it seriously; each wanted to be boss. This year, they saw that gleaning was more profitable, so they dropped the herding and became farm-workers. If they drive a yoke of oxen over your harvest pile, you give them half a seer of wheat for every day.

Kamaroddin's son Ali-khân took over the cattle, together with Gholâm-Mahmad, Rangin's son. But Ali-khân saw that his father had a load of barley: 'Why am I herding cattle? Look, my father's got all that barley, go and eat it!' So Ali-khân dropped out. Now Gholâm-Mahmad looks after the cattle, together with Mahd-Hanifa's son Atâollah. They're partners; they get 10 rupees a month for each cow or calf or donkey, which they divide in half. They get paid every month, if they want.

The Tale of Soltânyâr

Haji Tumân tells the tale of Soltânyâr the cowherd, who became a very rich merchant.

According to the old books, there was once a wealthy merchant, who had no male relatives – no father, sons or brothers – and spent his life trading. In God's due time he died, leaving his mother and his pregnant wife. Some months later she gave birth to a son. The boy had no father, no male relatives to support him; all he had was his mother and his grandmother. As God willed, his mother died, leaving him alone with his grandmother.

In due course, the grandmother lost all the wealth her son had left. The boy, Soltânyâr, grew up, and when he was old enough to work, she told him, 'There's nothing left, you must go to work as a cowherd. Off you go.'

What else could he do? All day long he tended the cattle out in the steppe; towards evening, as he headed home, he collected firewood, loaded it on his back and delivered it to his old granny, then he went round the houses to collect pieces of bread, *khoja-khedri*, the cowherd's due.

One day, Soltânyâr took the cows out to the steppe as usual, to a place where there were some nice bushes, which he started to dig up for fuel. As he was pulling one up, in the roots of the bush he saw a jewelled ornament, a *churi*, black with tarnish. He picked it up, took a piece of cloth and rubbed it hard until he'd cleaned just a corner of it. It shone like daylight; it was clearly some *churi*! He put it back, covered it up, left the cows there and came straight back to his old grandma.

'Grandma, he said, 'I was digging up a bush, and I found a *churi*; I cleaned a corner and it shone so brightly, like daylight; what shall I do with it?'

'Phooey',[3] she said, 'You little rascal, you'll get us into trouble with the government, with the padishah, digging up treasure like that; leave it, don't dig it up again!'

Disappointed, the boy went back and dug out the *churi* once more, cleaned another corner, then buried it again. By then it was evening, so he went home with the cattle and the firewood. From then on, every day he went and cleaned a little more of the *churi*, and within a week he'd polished it so nicely that its brightness blinded him like sunlight; he could hardly look at it. During the day, he'd come and dig it up to have a look; then in the evening he'd just bury it again.

One day he was out with the cattle when he saw a caravan passing down below, on its way to another country. He went to meet the caravan and asked for the leader. When they'd pointed him out, the boy went up to the caravan leader and kissed his hand. The leader asked him who he was, whose son he was. He said, 'I'm Soltânyâr, son of Merchant so-and-so, but my parents are both dead, and all my family wealth has gone, so I look after these cattle and do odd jobs; during the day I graze the cattle and in the evening I collect *khoja-khedri*; every house gives me a piece of bread. That's how I make a living.'

Hearing this, the caravan leader embraced the boy and told him, 'Your father and I used to trade together in the old days; I was a small merchant, he was very big. Any wealth I got was thanks to my contact with him.' The boy was glad to hear this, and asked him where he was going. 'I'm taking a hundred camel-loads of goods to another country, where I hope to sell them: cloth, guns, all sorts of things.'

The boy said, 'If I entrust something to you, can you deliver it?' 'Of course?' 'Let the caravan go on, but please wait here a moment, I'll be right back.' He ran off, dug up the *churi* and polished it, so that when he handed it over it shone like the day.

The merchant had never seen anything like it. 'What shall I do with it?' he asked.

'Take it off to that country, and tell the padishah, "A young man called Soltânyâr has sent you a present." Perhaps he'll give you something in return, like a ceremonial robe; or perhaps he'll let you off the taxes' – taxes were very heavy in those days. The merchant was excited to take such a rare object; he put it in his saddlebag, gave the boy some cash, 20 rupees or so, and went on his way.

He journeyed on, day and night, watching, resting, watering his camels. After forty days and nights, he reached his destination. The padishah heard that a certain merchant had arrived who some time before had failed to pay his taxes, so he sent men after him at once. 'We must deal with him.'

The merchant was drinking tea when seven of the padishah's men arrived. He got up, found a nice tray and put the *churi* on it under seven silken cloths; he took it, borne by one of his servants, to the castle, where he greeted the padishah. As they lifted the silken cloths, the whole castle lit up and shone like the day.

---

[3] She says, 'Ay, I'll fuck your father's mouth'. Tumân's tale is full of obscene or blasphemous phrases, which are normal; but literal translations give the wrong impression, so I keep only a few, where they seem to fit.

The padishah asked, 'What's this?' He answered, 'A person called Soltânyâr from a certain country has sent you this as a present.'

The padishah looked at it and thought, 'There's no way we could make such a thing in my country; if we put everyone to work, we couldn't produce anything to equal it in value.' He was delighted with the merchant and told him, 'You're lucky; I was so angry with you, I was about to confiscate all your camels and goods and put you in prison. But now, I won't take any taxes from you; go and buy what you want, but let me know when you're about to leave.'

The merchant was overjoyed. He'd owed 1 or 2 lacs of rupees in taxes. Instead, he sold all his goods at excellent prices and stocked up with other goods. He prepared to load his camels, but first he went back to the padishah, saying 'Sir, I leave tomorrow morning either before or after first prayers, so I'm informing you as you instructed.'

The padishah looked all round and couldn't find anything. So he loaded seven mules with gold and silver and gave it to the merchant, saying, 'I've nothing else to give that young man who sent the ornament. Please greet him warmly from me and tell him, "This isn't a suitable present, but as you sent me one, here's mine; I hope you like it."'

The merchant told himself, 'If he sends such a present back, the boy will be very happy!' He said, 'Thank you very much,' took his leave of the padishah and departed with the mules. Early next morning he loaded his camels and left.

He returned the same way, *hala–hala–hala–hala*, forty days and nights on the road, until he arrived back at Soltânyâr's place. There he saw him sitting with his cows, which were grazing along the roadside. He called out, 'We're back!' The boy kissed his hand and greeted him. He said, 'Dear boy, we took your *churi* and delivered it, and the padishah gave us seven mules loaded with gold and silver for you; what shall we do with them?' Soltânyâr replied, 'Mr Merchant, be kind enough to wait while I ask my grandma what to do; I can't do anything without consulting her.'

Off he went to his old grandma and told her, 'That *churi* I told you about, I cleaned it until it shone like the sun, and I gave it to a merchant; he took it off to a certain padishah as a present, and he sent seven mule-loads of gold and silver; what shall we do with them?'

'Curses on you and your father!' she said, 'Who do you think you are? You gave the *churi* to a merchant, who took it to a padishah, who sent you gold? Thanks to you, we'll be outcasts!' She beat him until he cried, and he ran back to the merchant.

The merchant asked, 'What happened to you?' He answered, 'My old grandma beat me and told me not to bring the stuff home, what shall I do? Where are you going from here?' He said, 'I'll rest at home for a few days, then I'm off to another country with all these goods to sell.'

Soltânyâr said, 'You're going to that country? Then please take these seven mule-loads and give them to the padishah, saying "Soltânyâr heard that you lost some of your wealth, so he's sent this as a present to help you and your country." He'll be pleased with you.'

'That's a good idea.' The merchant took another 20 rupees from his pocket and gave them to the boy, then set off again. After a few days on the road he arrived at his own home, where he rested for a week while his camels recovered their strength; then he set off for the other country.

He journeyed for a month or so, *hala–hala–hala–hala*, until he arrived. Once inside the city, he stopped and spent the night, then in the morning he loaded the mules and came to the padishah's castle; at the gate he asked the stewards, 'Let me see the padishah.'

They said, 'Where are you from?' 'I'm a merchant from a certain country.' They reported to the padishah, who said, 'Let the fellow in.'

The merchant came in and greeted the padishah. 'Where have you come from?' 'From a certain country where a young man called Soltânyâr, who's a good man and very rich, heard that your city was raided and your wealth gone, so he sent seven mule-loads of gold and silver to help you.'

The padishah thanked him profusely, called his treasurer and said, 'Put the stuff in the treasury.' He told the merchant, 'Please go round the city and dispose of your goods as you please, I won't take a penny in taxes or duties from you; and let me know the day before you plan to leave.'

So the merchant went and sold his goods well, at such good prices that he made a huge profit, and he was delighted to have no taxes to pay. The afternoon before his caravan was ready to depart, he came to the castle. The padishah gave him a nice reception, with food and entertainment, and kept him for the night. In the morning he told the merchant, 'Our country was plundered and our property stolen; I've nothing left, but I looked in my stable, and there are ten nice horses, never ridden and never broken, they just stay and eat at the manger.' He gave the merchant all the horses, with their golden saddles, silver bridles and complete trappings, together with ten grooms, the only ones who could control them.

In the morning the merchant set off; somehow he attached the horses to the caravan, with two men to each horse, one holding the reins on either side. Each horse was worth a crore of rupees, but they were crazy, unbreakable by any man, and such trouble that he soon regretted all the profit he'd made. He went home and spent a couple of nights, but the horses wouldn't rest, so they travelled the remaining distance – like between here and Sar-e-pol or Chârbâgh – until they got back to Soltânyâr, who was sitting looking after his cows.

When the boy saw him he came and kissed his hand. The merchant said, 'You rascal, forget about the profit I made, you caused me enormous trouble!' 'What happened?' 'I took that gold and silver and gave it to the padishah, and he gave me ten horses that are completely uncontrollable; men have to stand guard over them all day, and when we're on the road two men are needed for each horse. What shall I do with them?'

Soltânyâr said, 'Wait here a moment while I consult my old grandma.' Off he went to his grandma and told her how he'd sent all that wealth to a certain padishah, who responded with the ten horses; 'What shall I do with them?' Now Soltânyâr was a baldy; he had no hair on his head. His grandma hit him on the head until it bled. She said, 'Horses, you bastard? What do we want with horses? Don't you dare bring them home! What if the padishah hears about it? You're a cowherd, we're poor people, what do we know of padishahs and horses? You must be mad if you want to bring horses here! Let them go! If you bring them here I'll throttle you!'

He returned to the merchant and told him what she'd said. 'What shall we do? The old woman hit me. Where are you heading now?' The merchant said, 'I'm going back to the country where you sent the *churi*.' Soltânyâr said, 'Take those horses then, and say: "Soltânyâr said he could find nothing else to send you, so he just sent these ten horses," and he'll be pleased with you.'

The merchant saw that all his trouble and effort might be worthwhile; every cloud has a silver lining. 'Fine,' he said; 'Whatever the trouble, another twenty days makes no difference.' He took a few rupees from his pocket again, gave them to the boy, said goodbye and went off with his caravan.

This time he covered two stages in one, *hala–hala–hala–hala*, and in twenty days he arrived at that country. The cry went up, 'The caravan's come, the merchant's come and he has some wild horses!' He pitched his tents, drank his tea and gave instructions for the horses to be taken straight to the padishah. He informed the steward that he wanted to see the padishah. The padishah said, 'Bring him up.' There was a great reception.

The merchant said, 'Soltânyâr has sent these horses as a present for you.' The padishah was delighted, on the one hand, since there were no such horses in his country. But on the other hand, he was distressed because Soltânyâr had sent a present that he couldn't match in his country. 'I sent him back gold and silver, and now he's responded with ten horses, worth a crore each. This man must have a motive.'

He ordered food for the merchant and told him, 'Whenever you want to leave, let me know in advance. Now go freely round the city, whatever you want to buy and sell, it's up to you, I'll take no taxes.' The merchant went off and did his business. When the padishah came home that evening he was dejected; he sat down and wiped his face with a silk hanky. He had a very nice and able daughter; she said, 'Dad, why are you so downcast today? Is everything all right?' He said, 'The reason I'm upset, daughter, is this; you know that *churi* that's so bright that we need no lamps in our apartments? How I couldn't find anything to send in return except seven mule-loads of gold? Well, the fellow's now sent me ten horses, each worth a crore of rupees. What does he want from me!'

His daughter said, 'I know what he wants.' 'Tell me, dear daughter, what is it?' 'He wants me,' she said. The padishah was very happy: 'God bless you, that was my thought too, but I couldn't tell you.' He was relieved, and prepared to give his daughter to the fellow. She too was delighted.

The padishah sat in his castle for two or three days. Then, when the merchant came to say, 'Tomorrow I'm off again,' the padishah said, 'Don't leave tomorrow; stay here another week.' 'Why?' 'Because I'm giving my daughter to Soltânyâr, and I want to hold the wedding send-off.'

So they held a fantastic party: they made one street of *kabâb* meat, one street of halva sweets, one street of pilaw and *chelaw* rice, one street of *shurwa* broth, and everyone who came could eat pilaw, or if he wanted, *chelaw*; or any kind of cooked meat. The celebrations went on for seven days and nights, then the padishah loaded a hundred camels with gold and such stuff, with a hundred retainers and a hundred maidservants, and a regiment of soldiers, all to accompany the bride and the merchant on their way to Soltânyâr, this baldy cowherd!

After they'd been on the road for a few days, the merchant thought to himself, 'You fool, what have you done? What will the princess do when she discovers she's marrying this baldy? She'll kill you!' He was distraught. In the end there was nothing for it; he stopped the caravan and sent word to the princess's attendant, 'I must come and see Bibi.' The princess herself was riding in a *kajawa* pannier. She said, 'Let him in.' The merchant greeted her and she said, 'You're like a father to me; what's the matter?' He said, 'The problem is our retinue; we don't need all those people, send them back; I've enough men for us all.' She agreed, 'Fine, whatever you think is right.' So he released the hundred retainers, the hundred maidservants, and the hundred camels loaded with gold and stuff.

They went on, *hala–hala–hala–hala*, until they were about as far away as Âqcha from here, and the merchant found a really nice place with plenty of water and plenty of grazing for the camels; he unloaded them and pitched the tents. He appointed a man to oversee the campsite, while he went off to find Soltânyâr. He found the baldy sitting there with his herd, counting his lice. Soltânyâr came up to greet him, but he said, 'Away, you rascal, we've had a disaster!' 'What's up, sir?' 'I've brought you a princess, and look at you! What shall I do with you! I wish I'd never started this.'

The boy said, 'Just wait there a moment, while I consult the old lady.' He came to his grandma and told her the story: 'I sent off those horses to that padishah, and he sent me his daughter.' 'Oh, you idiot!' she said, 'Now you're going to marry a princess? Curses on you and your father, you hypocrite baldy, we're done for!' and she started throwing stones at him.

But baldy Soltânyâr was now angry. He suddenly remembered that there was a sword from his father's time that he'd put somewhere in the hut. He went and got it, and he dragged the old woman out, saying 'I've had enough of this! What a life you've forced me to lead! Death is better than this.' He cut off her head. There was a river nearby, as big as the Oxus or the Helmand, and he said, 'I'll throw myself into that river, let the merchant do what he wants with the princess.'

He rushed towards the water, crying *bismillah!*, but he stopped short of the very edge – life is sweet after all, and the current was so powerful that there was no chance of getting out. He backed off, as far as from here to the door, then once again ran towards the river, and once again his courage failed him. But the third time he closed his eyes, and *zoom*, threw himself into the river.

By the power of almighty God, Khoja-Khedr – I don't know what you call him – picked him up from the bottom, and said, 'What's up, why throw yourself into the water and try to kill yourself?'

He replied, 'By God, such things have happened that I had to do it; look at my bald head, I've no clothes, no land, nothing; if that princess comes, where can I put her? It's better for me to die.'

'My son, close your eyes,' said Khoja-Khedr; 'Then just say "God is Great!" and see what God gives you.'

Soltânyâr closed his eyes and said, "Allahu Akbar!" When he opened his eyes again, he saw, pitched on the riverbank, one hundred tents, each of them worth a crore of rupees, black, white, red, green, with splendid furnishings inside and gorgeous coverings outside; he found that he himself had become a dashing young man, with a full head of hair, and awesome clothes; God had given him a perfect appearance, so brilliant in fact that you couldn't look at him. There he sat; God had granted his wish.

A fellow was passing by, and he beckoned to him. 'Yes, sir, what do you want?' 'Go to such-and-such a place, you'll see a man there on horseback, tell him to come here. Are you a servant?' 'Yes.' 'How much do you earn?' 'Ten rupees a month.' 'I'll give you twenty to work for me.'

The servant went off and fetched the merchant, who saw the tents, and recognized Soltânyâr and was astonished at what had happened to him. Soltânyâr asked him to fetch the princess, so he happily spurred his horse off to his campsite, collected the princess and the caravan and all.

After a few nights on the road, *hala–hala–hala*, around midday the princess, who was riding ahead in her *kajawa*, made out in the distance the dazzling sight of the hundred tents. She called out, 'Stop the caravan, let me look at this through the telescope.' They stopped, she looked through her telescope and saw, seated inside one tent, a young man unlike any other on this earth. She was astounded and called the merchant; 'Is this what you've brought me to? He'll never even accept me as his servant.'

He said, 'Hey, Bibi, it was you he wanted when he sent those horses and things; it was all for you!' He took the caravan ahead and unloaded by the tents. And they held a wedding reception for seven days and nights; he left them there to their lovemaking.

He gave me a nag to ride home on, but it went lame on the road, so I left it and came on foot, and here I am to tell you the tale!

Trade and Exchange

The mâldâr *always regard trade as an honourable addition to their pastoralism. It involves: (a) attending the famous 'Kabuli' nomad bazaars in the mountains, usually as customers, but also selling livestock and their produce; (b) highly profitable barter with villagers along the migration routes; (c) trading expeditions of various kinds, usually taking goods up to the mountains for sale, to acquire cheap grain; and (d) professional trade in livestock.*

Nomad bazaars

During the first half of the twentieth century, several large nomad bazaars convened in summer in the central mountains: Pashtun trader nomads from the east set up large tented camps, selling cloth, guns and other wares brought from India and Pakistan to the locals and to pastoral nomads from south, west, and north.[4] In late July 1971, as our train passed through Esmeydân, we visited the small camp of traders there; and in July 1972 as we drove from Herat to Kabul, we visited the traders camped outside Kâsi/Chaghcharân, the provincial centre of Ghor (see Maps C, D). Both camps were clearly mere shadows of what they had once been, as described here.

(*Haji Tumân*) – The nomad bazaar of Âbol in Ghor – the one that now goes to Kâsi – used to be in Lâl-o-Kermân. It was a huge bazaar; people came from Kandahar, Herat, Bâdghis, Maymana, Turkistan, Qataghan, with livestock, carpets and camels to trade with the Kabulis, who brought cloth, guns, ammunition and things from the east.

---

[4]   See Ferdinand (2006), Frederiksen (1995).

(*Gol-Ahmad*) – When we arrived in Turkistan, my father says, rams were 12 rupees, wethers eight. He took them to the Kabuli traders in Sar-jangal and Lâl-o-Kermân, and exchanged a ram for three bolts of cloth, different kinds: one called *Patu*, another *Dust-Mahmadwâlâ*, another *Sherchab-jim*. A ram he'd bought for 12 rupees went for twenty; a wether bought for eight went for fifteen – double the price.

(*Baya-khân*) – When skins were cheap, after the ewes lambed in spring we'd sell the better skins and take the others to the mountains, including poor skins entrusted to us by those who stayed behind. On the return trek, we'd stop by the tents of the Tâghâr and Niâzi Kabuli traders who came to Esmeydân, near Teymur-shâh Khân's place. They put up their tents there in the huge meadow, where the horses can eat their fill. Anyone with skins to sell took them to the Kabulis, who'd pay with cloth or cash. You could buy many different kinds of cloth: silk, chintz, linen and so on. The Kabulis knew nothing about skins, good or bad; they were happy to have any of them. They'd offer 200–300 rupees for a skin worth 20–30 here in the Valley.

These days, few traders come to the Esmeydân bazaar. Before, when the Afghans went there, they'd buy 20, 50, even 100 metres of cloth; but this year [*1971*] nobody bought much. They also sell cloth to the local Aymâqs. There are more traders at the Cherâs bazaar, but none of us goes there unless we have business. I've never been, though I've seen the market-place there.

In Pashtu we call Sar-e-pol town 'Bazaar'. Since there are more tents than elsewhere at those Kabuli markets in the mountains, they're like towns, so we call them 'Bazaar-places'. If the Esmeydân bazaar is like Sar-e-pol, then the larger one at Cherâs is like Sheberghân, comparatively.

(*Seyyed-shâh/Soleymân*) – The Kabuli traders first camped in Cherâs, then Esmeydân, and finally they came down here to Chârkent in Sangchârak, where they pitched their tents, some sixty to seventy of them, over on that hillside. They sold cloth on credit: they gave it in September and then came for payment the following September or October. Once they'd pitched their tents, they set about collecting their money.

The Uzbeks here gave no trouble; if they couldn't pay, the Kabulis would 'pigeon' them: strap their legs to their necks and hang them up, send someone else to fetch the money, then release them. Nobody dared complain to the government. But they wouldn't treat us Afghans like that; rather, they sold us stuff at half-price. At first they took only cash; they weren't interested in land, at any price. They kept a written record: we'd sit down together and they'd write down what we owed.

It's several years since the Kabulis last came. They grew weak and the takings fell. Finally, just Sufi and Nâder-khân came. Sufi got on with people, and caused no disputes. Others still go to Cherâs and Esmeydân and sell their goods there, then they go home. Now they're happy to take land in pawn; vineyards too. If we Afghans buy from them, we know when they'll come to be paid: in April, after our lambskin sales. Times have gone bad.

Trade on the trek

Trade with local villagers along the migration route is more complicated, and – particularly where cash or cash values are involved – liable to be very profitable for the mâldâr. *Each mâldâr family, and sometimes each individual, forms their own trading contacts with individual villagers. Contacts (âshnay) are often women. Baya-khân explains.*

Haji and others would buy cloth at the nomad bazaar in Esmeydân for 12–13 rupees a metre. When we got down to Kachan, local Aymâqs would come and buy it at 25–35 rupees, on credit. Next year we'd go and collect the money.

On our way down from Siâh-band, we stay four or five days in Kachan, letting the camels roam up on the mountains; we go and check on them every other day. Our contacts, who bought cloth or sheep from us, now bring firewood and a sack of fodder from their gardens for our horses, which we tether by the tents. Kachani women also bring soapwort and *jâmashu*, which are abundant there. *Jâmashu* is good for getting dirt out of clothes and wool; soapwort is what Afghans use for washing their hair – it cleans the dirt right out. Kachanis are crazy for wool and sheepskins, as they have few sheep themselves. We offer them whatever we can spare; they give *jâmashu* for an equal weight of wool. They make lambskin bags for storage, for raisins, flour and so on. They stretch the skin and salt it and it comes out very nice for rolling dough for bread. Shepherds and travellers keep their flour supplies in those bags.

They also bring *goldâru*, a plant that grows on both dry and irrigated land, with white flowers that smell very nice. Women pick the flowers when they're seeding, dry them, pound them with a stone, then sieve the powder through a fine cloth, discarding the stalks. *Goldâru* powder is a delicious pot-herb; it really sweetens a broth. Afghan *mâldâr*s eat it a lot; our women barter wool for it, weight-for-weight or two-for-one. And apricots are plentiful at this time; they'll give twice or more times the weight of the wool.

Pâdshâh tells of some other bartered goods and exchanges.

When Kachani women come to our tents, they bring raisins and apricots, which are plentiful there, and a herb they call *ostugh* – we call it *wuslan*. They barter these for wool, wool-scraps, camel's wool, or ghee or *krut*, some meat if you have it; or some old shoes or slippers. They don't usually want animals; sometimes a man asks his wife to look out for a donkey, or an old sheep.

Our trading contacts bring us bowls of noodle *âsh*, or apricots; or a bowl or a spoon as a present for our daughter, or a *chigh* – a cane-work screen for drying *krut*. Our women cook meat or pilaw for them, or give them something as a present, such as a small felt blanket, or a chicken, for our contact's daughter.

Baya-khân tells how the mountain villagers, in Cherâs, Kâshân and Kachan, face grain shortage. Loans, advances and 'interest' are carefully negotiated among themselves and with the mâldâr, to whom they often end up deeply in debt.

In Cherâs the crops ripen late: barley in September, wheat in October or November. Kâshân and Esmeydân are warmer, so they harvest barley in July or August. In a year when grain's scarce and the Aymâqs of Cherâs run out, they go to their Hazâra contacts in Esmeydân and Kâshân after the barley harvest and ask for an advance, *taqawi*, of, say, a 10-seer donkey-load. They say, 'If you want barley back, I'll bring it after our harvest, since you've been good to me; if you want cash at the market rate, I'll bring cash.' It's difficult to get such an advance unless you have contacts.

For the Cherâs Aymâqs, it's closer to go over to Kâshân. The people of Gholduri, Târikak, Supak, Kachan, Chenâr and Sangchârak come down to Sar-e-pol; many of them did this year, and got barley advances from us Afghans. If a Kachani contact comes to your threshing ground, and you have 100–200 seers of barley, you can give him 10 seers; usually he'll return the same amount, but you can ask for the market rate, or even for wheat. Wheat's more expensive, so they give one seer of wheat for two of barley. Khoday-râm's son Gholâm gave Kachanis around 100 seers of barley this year at 50 rupees, and in October he'll go and get his money.

When we go to the mountains we also give cash advances for wheat. Aymâqs and Hazâras come to the tents and say, 'I'm stuck for cash; give me some, and next year I'll give you wheat.' So if wheat is 50 rupees a seer, you give him cash for wheat at twenty or twenty-five; or he'll take your cash for wheat at 50 rupees when the going rate's 100. He'll say, 'Come and get your wheat in autumn after we've threshed,' or he'll give you the wheat next year when you come to the mountains. If he hasn't got your wheat, he'll give your money back at the market rate, and if he hasn't enough cash, you take a sheep or something instead, to release him from the debt. This isn't *taqawi*; people call it *pishkhur*; it's a kind of pre-selling [*salam*].

Kachanis from Tagawboy and Alâr, like the Hazâras of Esmeydân and Kâshân, don't keep camels. Donkeys do all their work, so they'll pay well for a strong donkey. In Tagawboy, there's plenty of land; and people are impatient. When you camp in Kachan on the trek down, if you have a fine donkey every day twenty people will offer to buy it, on credit. Someone offers you 2,000 rupees for a donkey worth 1,000. You give him the donkey; he promises to pay 500 next spring in cash, or wheat at the market price, or other goods to make up the 500 he owes; another 500 the next trek down, in wheat or barley at the market price; another 500 in autumn at 'spare-camel' [*shotor-kotal*] time, as the Aymâqs say, when the Afghans go to collect their wheat and call in their debts. 'I'll pay the last 500 next spring, when I've sold my skins and stuff.'

Last year on the way down, at Ghozba-khâna in Kâshân, we sold two sheep at 1,300 rupees the pair, and a sick lamb that couldn't move further, for 150; so they owe us 1,450 rupees. They said, 'We'll pay half when you come next spring. If you want wheat, we'll give it at the cheaper autumn rate; we'll pay the other 725 rupees in August on your way down.' Nobody went to Kâshân this year – how could we know it'd be such a disastrous winter? We'll collect next year, if we're alive.

The Afghans put these people deep into debt. They offer too much for our animals, and they're very keen on credit, they just don't care. If you have such a contact-debtor in Kachan or Kâshân, he'll also give you hay when you go there. He welcomes you, hoping you'll give him a donkey another day, or let him postpone his debt if he can't pay. If he pleads that he's got nothing to give, you take a goat or something, cheap. Some people are happy to do that; but a harsh creditor will force him to pay on time: 'You agreed to pay my 500 rupees now!' If he can't pay, the creditor will increase the value of the debt: say wheat is 50 rupees a seer; he'll demand wheat in payment at

25 rupees, and the 500 rupee debt becomes 20 seers of wheat, to be paid in autumn, after the threshing. That's what a harsh creditor does, he saddles the poor guy with an increasing debt.

If a Kachani owes you money, both Afghans and Fârsibâns have a saying: 'Let my debt be with a crow, let the crow stay alive.' So long as he's alive, he'll pay you off every time you visit, little by little: some straw, some hay, some bread, a few rupees.

Trade for a living

Many Pashtun mâldârs *in Sar-e-pol have no land, so finding wheat flour, their staple, is a major concern for them, often met by trade, as Baya-khân explains.*

Kamuzai and Nâmanzai *mâldârs* have no farmland in Sar-e-pol. Sometimes they buy wheat from the villages, but usually they go to town, where prices are fair and they can find rainfed wheat, which makes better bread. Of course, a poor man makes do with irrigated wheat, or rice or barley; you buy what you can afford.

Many Kamuzais go to Cherâs to buy wheat in advance. On the spring trek the camels are loaded with household stuff, so they can't take goods for sale; but they take cash. Cherâs people need cash, so they'll sell you wheat cheaply for cash in advance. Kamuzais buy 50–100 seers at a time; then in autumn, after the return trek, and when the Cherâs crops are in, they take the camels back up, loaded with salt, rice, tea, soap, matches, melons.

They buy soap here for 5 or 6 rupees, and sell it there for 10 or 12. Matches, bought for 10 rupees here, fetch 20 there. They buy poor-quality rice here for 60 rupees and barter it for twice or even three times the weight in wheat, making a huge profit. Cherâs people don't worry about quality; they say, 'The town's much too far for us to go ourselves; it takes several days, we and our donkeys get so tired; when rice or melons come here, forget the price, we're happy to buy at home!'

Melons sell very well in Cherâs, but particularly in the Gholduri and Qerghaytu gorges, where there isn't enough sun to grow them. People there, men and women, go mad for melons, and they'll give double the weight in barley, or an equal weight of wheat. Those who've been to the mountains before have contacts in several villages there, so, when they get down through Sang-e-Solâkh, they take their melons to each village; everybody gathers, calling, 'Hey, the melons have come!' A camel-load of 30 seers of melons, bought for 300 rupees here, becomes 30 seers of wheat, worth 2,000–3,000 rupees! Some people take grapes. If you've given cash in advance, when you get there your wheat's ready waiting, and you can take it once it's threshed. Then you go from village to village and sell the melons and rice.

Mountain people buy supplies for several months. Things get very expensive there as winter approaches, because the snow stops them coming down. It's a very hard road. Those ranges that you and I crossed last spring and summer, in winter are snowed in so deeply that a bear can't survive the cold. So if you take things there as winter approaches, people buy a lot. Many traders take camel-loads of rice and stuff. If you take 30 seers of rice, you can bring back 70–80 seers of wheat.

When all your goods are sold, you collect your wheat, not forgetting any paid for in advance, put it in sacks and take them to a contact's house. You load as much as you can on your camels, and leave the rest with your contact, with the sacks sewn shut, to be collected and milled later: 'Please keep this until spring, when we come to the mountains.' Then you take the loaded camels slowly home, to Khâmushli if you're Kamuzai. If you reckon that 40–50 seers will be enough for you, you sell the rest. Then in spring you return to your Aymâq contact in Cherâs, retrieve your wheat, mill it and use it while in the summer pastures.

This trade is very profitable. Many people do it: Kamuzai, Nâmanzai, Baluch. From our village, some years Mahd-Amin's son takes melons up to Qerghaytu. *Mâldârs* from the other steppe too go trading, up a different road: Qurchi, Nawâ-ye-Khawâl, Qala-ye-shahr. They take melons, rice, matches and soap. Those places are far from town, people will buy anything, 'It's very difficult for me go to town, it'll take a week or two, I'll get tired, so will my donkey.'

The Kâshâni mountain people are poor and weak; they're frightened, particularly of my father. He used to 'hit' them. One year, Haji Molk had a problem with debtors there: one was my father's contact Akbar, headman of Ghozba-khâna; another was Wâli-Mahmad. My father dragged them along and said, 'By God, I'll take you to Sar-e-pol!' In those days they'd never been to town, and knew nothing of official ways; they were scared of government. If they saw a soldier, they were terrified. The government didn't control them, they were wild men, like outlaws. Now it's a little better, since the *alâqadârî*'s closer; so are the towns. People are smarter; the *alâqadâr* visits, sends commissions. Times have changed.

In October or November, after their autumn shearing, Kachanis and Uzbeks spin the wool and weave *chakman* cloth. Spring wool will do too. One woman weaves; there isn't enough room at the loom for two, unless they put down a special seat. They cut the cloth down, put it in hot water and stir it vigorously, spread it on a kilim, then rub and squeeze it with their feet. This should disperse the colour and give the cloth a nap, which it doesn't have at first. People won't pay much if there's no nap; the more nap the better. When the nap's gone, holes appear and it won't keep you so warm. They sell the cloth in town, or use it to pay off a debt. It goes for 300 to 500 rupees a metre – not as much as the *barak* cloth of the Sar-jangal Hazâras, who have a different kind of sheep; their *barak* comes out reddish, and it's very warm. Kachani *chakman* isn't so good; it's black, sometimes grey. The *chakman* made by people in Gholduri and Sopak is better, but it's still not red. People this side of Cherâs often bring cloth to Sar-e-pol and Sangchârak for sale. Occasionally the Sar-jangal people bring their *barak* too, but most take it to Kabul, which is easier to get to via Lâl.

Livestock trading

Some Piruzai make a living from trading livestock. Baya-khân has the story.

Livestock traders go to the mountains to buy goats, sheep, cows or donkeys. Here, buyers are plentiful and prices are high; if you've an animal to sell, and nobody in the village wants it, take it to town and you'll find a buyer immediately. In the mountains, far from town, buyers are few and animals cheap; that's why traders go there. They can buy an animal there for 150 rupees that'll fetch 200 here. They go in groups, pooling their money and buying animals jointly. There's a definite risk of robbers, who may catch you asleep, beat you and take your money. If they're many, they may kill you and throw your body into a river, or hide it under some rocks, and take your cash and your animals. Robbers don't care, they're that bad! Most traders are very wary, and take a rifle or a handgun. One or two can't go alone; they'd be too nervous out in the open during the day, and they'd be too frightened to travel at night, so four or five go in a band, and robbers won't bother them.

They spend several days on the road, heading to the mountains via Kachan, to Peghola, Esmeydân, Balkhâb, or Taykhoj, places far from town. If they make profitable purchases in Kachan, they leave them in the care of a local contact, saying, 'We're going on, we'll collect them on the way down.' Or one of them stays behind. The others go via Zeynadir to Alâr, to look for bargains there too; at Sehpay they go up and over to Kâshân and the Balkhâb river, to Peghola valley and other places, some even as far as Sar-jangal, snapping up any sheep, cows, horses that are cheap there and expensive here. Other traders go the other way, via Gholduri and Sâlrizi to Cherâs.

They may spend weeks, even a month, going round the villages until they've spent all their cash on sheep or other livestock. Then they return, driving the animals slowly, letting them graze and keep fit. In Sar-e-pol, they herd their purchases into the *ganj*, the place near the Garage where animals go for sale. If they find Sar-e-pol prices are too low, they hand them over to a couple of drovers – many Arabs do this – who'll drive them on foot, for 1 or 2 rupees an animal, to Âqcha, where they'll fetch a better price. Once the animals are sold, the trading partners all sit down together, reckon up and share out the takings equally. If they've made a loss, they share this too.

In every village, five or ten people do such livestock trading in the mountains. In our village, for example, Nazir's brother Wazir; Musajân's brother; Dâdollah's brother Shâhzâda; Jomagey, son of Âdam-khân; Amir and his brother Nâder. This year, all of them went.

Jomagey has a little land, not enough to live on; his brothers farm it for him. He has a horse; he buys sheep in Sar-e-pol and takes them to Sheberghân, Âqcha or Balkh; or he goes to the mountains and buys sheep in Sar-jangal, where they're very cheap, and brings them down here for sale.

The brothers Kajir, Nazir and Wazir have no sheep; all of them trade in animals and their products. Kajir's family live with his uncle and father-in-law Khalifa-Patih, but he spent all last winter in town. If you bring some sheep from town, Kajir will drive them to Sheberghân or Âqcha for you for 50 or 100 rupees. People get him to carry a cowhide or a sheepskin for a couple of rupees. That's the sort of work he does; he's very poor. Wazir and Nazir used to make a living trading skins and so forth. Now Wazir buys and sells animals. He borrows cash and goes to the mountains to buy them; when they're sold in Sar-e-pol and Sheberghân, he repays the lender, taking half the profit.

Some people go by truck to buy wool yarn in Maymana, where it's cheap because there are more sheep there than anywhere else in Afghanistan. This year they all died. Others go to Maymana to buy goat hair for tent-cloth; it was 400 rupees a seer there when it was 500 or 550 here.

Sar-e-pol Hazâras don't often go to the mountains to trade in animals; rather they trade here in their woven goods, rugs and so on. But some Kachanis do bring animals to trade. It's mostly Afghans who do such trade, because they're not scared like Hazâras and Kachanis. If you look around here, you'll see that Uzbeks stick to their own neighbourhoods. Other people don't venture far away like the Afghans. Don't you remember the traders who came up to the mountains last year to collect skins? Hazâras wouldn't do that for a lac of rupees! Though actually, that year one Hazâra from Chârbâgh, a friend of ours, did come. There were two of them; they didn't bring cash, they brought *chapân* cloaks – like yours – which they'd bought here very cheaply, for 100 or 150 rupees each. Those people of Kohestân and Sar-jangal are dumb; they've never been to town, they haven't seen what it's like. The Hazâra traders also brought iron ploughshares, which fetch a lot in the mountains, as do spades; and ginned cotton, which goes for an equal weight of ghee, as there's absolutely no cotton there and they need it for their bedding.

The skin trade

Shortly before we left in September 1972, as we sat with Baya-khân, Chârgol and Seyyed-shâh/Golusar, the conversation turned to the trade in karakul lambskins.

(R) – Are there any other lambskin traders like Mir-Ahmad who come from town?

(*Baya-khân*) – We have an arrangement with Mir-Ahmad. He's a friend and comes every year.

(*Chârgol*) – We trust him.

(*Baya-khân*) – Haji collects everybody's skins to sell him.

(*Seyyed-shâh*) – Some Turkmen traders also come.

(*Chârgol*) – Haji gives Mir-Ahmad his own skins and takes him to other places he trusts, to get their skins for him too, whether he has cash or not. They trust him.

(R) – Who else comes to this village? Who does Haji Wahâb trade with, for example?

(*Baya-khân*) – Haji Wahâb sells his skins to Mullah Qarâr.

(R) – From the Qoshtepa Baluch? Has he got a shop in town like Mir-Ahmad?

(*Baya-khân, Seyyed-shâh*) – No.

(R) – Then what does he do with skins he's bought? How does he sell them on?

(*Baya-khân, Seyyed-shâh*) – He sells to the big traders in town, the Turkmens.

(*Chârgol*) – And they'll pass them on to other traders . . .

(*Baya-khân*) – . . . and make a profit in their turn.

(*Chârgol*) – All the skins end up with Haji Mahmad-Gol.

(R) – Mir-Ahmad showed me his permit to trade in skins. Do the others have such permits?

(*Seyyed-shâh*) – They all do.

(*Chârgol*) – Your backer advances you cash to buy skins at 400 rupees; if you buy them for less, at 350, even 390, you keep the difference. But they won't give you what they're worth, as they expect a profit themselves. They do pretty well! They have big sacks of cash.

(R) – But nobody else with a shop in Sar-e-pol comes here, like Mir-Ahmad?

(*Baya-khân*) – Once they did. Yaqub used to come from town, but he hasn't been for years. Mullah Hâfez's son Abdol-Ahad came too.

(N) – Yaqub's Uzbek too?

(*Baya-khân*) – Yes. His shop's near Mir-Ahmad's. All he does is trade skins, nothing else.

(*R*) – So these last two years only Mir-Ahmad came?

(*Baya-khân*) – This year, even Mir-Ahmad didn't come. There was no straw; there were no skins.

(*Chârgol*) – Forget this year; poor Haji was sitting here all broken up, out of straw, his sheep dying; I brought him a few sacks from home. Everybody helped as much as they could.

Debt

Debt is a sensitive issue, given the religious ban on charging 'interest'. Some people make a living lending money. Pâdshâh refers to his uncle Jân-Mahmad's son-in-law Abdor-Rahmân.

Abdor-Rahmân came from Kandahar as a mere boy; he had nothing to eat, so he worked as a cowherd, then as a farmhand. He saved some money and started trading by fore-buying lambskins, wool, sesame, flax, wheat, barley, on *salam*, a kind of usury. In winter he'd give cash advances for lambskins; if they were priced at 500 rupees, he forebought them for 150 or 200. People give advances for wool, sesame, cotton, beans, everything. A boy might steal a skin from his father or brother, and Abdor-Rahmân would pay him for it. Suddenly Abdor-Rahmân was a wealthy man. He's come a long way!

Baya-khân continues.

Abdor-Rahmân had nothing to start with. He was a farmhand; he himself did the farming, while his two stepsons were cowherds. This went on for a long time, then he began to make money. He used to give cash advances for wheat, and also he'd give advances for lambskins at 200 or 300 rupees; in spring he'd collect the skins and sell them for 600 or more. Now look at him. That's how he made money, in effect by usury. These days some people make a lot of money that way.

According to the mullahs, our Book says *sud*, usury, is very bad; you'll suffer dearly for it in the other world. Hazâras do *sud* a lot; few Afghans will, they don't like it. *Sud* is if I give you 10 rupees one month, then you give me eleven back. It's much the same thing as *salam*, which is when you come to me begging for cash, and I pay you 20 rupees in advance for a seer of wheat, at a time when the price is fifty; after all, nobody gives money for free. Next year, I come to you and say, 'Give me my wheat, or the market price in cash'. You plead with me, 'I can't find any wheat, and I'm hungry; please excuse me until next year.' But the market price has now risen to 100 rupees, so that's what you owe me; but you can pay in wheat at 50 – for delivery the following year; so that one seer of wheat becomes two. That's *sud*.

This winter, when Afghans ran out of cash, they'd go to the Chârbâgh Hazâras. Haji went there and borrowed 10,000 rupees, for 11,200 after one month. Many people from our steppe came to Behsud and Chârbâgh, desperate for straw and barley for their livestock. They'd run out of cash, as well as straw. Cash was in such demand in Chârbâgh that it went for a hundred per cent per month: in one month, one rupee became two. Meanwhile the poor souls from the western steppe brought in Sefiri guns worth 50,000, and good Malakhi guns worth 30,000 to 50,000, and pawned them for 5,000 to 10,000.

The Hazâras gave them the cash, saying, 'You have until autumn; if you haven't paid back the 5,000 rupees by then, your 50,000-rupee gun is mine.'

Pâdshâh distinguishes terms.

Taqawi, an advance, is different from *por*, a loan; so is *sud*, usury. Some people do *taqawi*: I give you 100 seers, and you give me 100 seers back in a year's time. Few people do this now. In the old days, people were much simpler, they weren't so profit-oriented. Now, everyone wants to make money out of everyone else. Or they want to buy cheap and sell dear, or get a commission on everything they do. Only very close relatives do *taqawi* these days: if a relative advances you some wheat, if he's doing *qawmi*, in the new year you'll return the same amount. Otherwise, when you arrange the advance you'll make sure to fix exactly how much extra to pay – that's *sud*.

Por is, for example, when you come to me and say, 'I haven't any flour, I'm going to the mill,' and I give you a seer or whatever you need. It's a loan, because you say, 'When I've got my harvest in, I'll give it back to you.' Or when I go to the mountains and buy cloth, or dyes, or a tent, from a Kabuli trader; I may give him skins or a camel or a mare, but if I've no cash or anything else, then I'll buy these things on credit, and next spring I'll pay the Kabuli in cash. As I come down from the mountains, I may sell the stuff myself in Kachan, Dehmana or Chenâr, for credit. If I bought for 15 rupees, I'll certainly sell for 20, to be paid next spring, and make 5 rupees profit. We write the debt down, and fix the time for payment, with the names of witnesses.

If you need a few cups of rice because you have guests, our custom here is to borrow it – that's *por*. If I run out of sugar, I ask you for some, to be returned when I next go to the shops, that's *por* too. Technically I suppose it's *taqawi*, but people don't call such little things *taqawi*. It's the same if I have some guests and need to borrow some tea. I'll say, 'Lend me a *tâk* of tea' – a *tâk* is enough for one teapot. Some people simply lend me the tea but others ask for money. In town, nobody gives you credit unless you're a regular, a contact. If a shopkeeper gave everyone credit he'd soon be finished!

Going to market

Talking with Pâdshâh, Baya-khân and Kala-khân about going to market.

(R) – How long does it take to get to the bazaar?
    (Baya-khân) – How long does it take by car?
    (R) – One hour.
    (Pâdshâh) – Then it takes three hours by camel.
    (N) – How long by camel to Sheberghân?
    (Pâdshâh, Baya-khân, Kala-khân, after discussion) – Seven or eight hours by fast camel.
    (Baya-khân) – In the winter I left at 8:00 am and arrived about 7:00 pm.
    (R) – If you go to Sar-e-pol by camel, which caravansaray do you go to?
    (Kala-khân) – Our friend Eslam.
    (Pâdshâh) – Any *saray* you want. Nobody says, 'Why didn't you come to my saray?' It's up to you; tether your animal anywhere.

(R) – What do they charge per night?

(Pâdshâh, Baya-khân) – Two rupees for a camel or horse, one for a donkey or a sheep; it's the same just to take the animals inside for five minutes.

(R) – Do they give any straw?

(Pâdshâh) – No, you must buy fodder yourself in the bazaar.

(Kala-khân) – They also take 5 rupees per person.

(Pâdshâh) – Normally it's 2 rupees per person per night, but in winter, for a good place with nice bedding, it'll be 4 or 5.

(Kala-khân) – In Mazâr they take 10 rupees.

Rising prices

In another conversation, with Pâdshâh and Pâdshâh/Parwiz, we discuss how prices of grain and livestock have changed in recent years.

(R) – Last year [*1971*] sheep went for only 200 rupees. What about previous years?

(Pâdshâh) – It's a long time since sheep were as cheap as last year. Long ago, when our fathers were young, before I was born and when this Pâdshâh was a boy, sheep were very cheap; and so was grain. Sheep prices have increased. Last year they were 200 or 300, but in previous years they were rather better, 350 to 400. Our elders have never seen sheep reach 1,000 rupees. If you had a fine, fat animal, you'd never have got more than 500 for it in the city, more likely 300 to 400.

(R) – What about wheat? Last year it was up to 120 a seer.

(Pâdshâh) – And the year before. But before that it was 20–25 rupees in Sangchârak. I remember well; I took camels to Chârkent myself, and bought wheat at 20. Then two years ago it got very expensive, 120 or 130.

(R) – Eight or nine years ago wasn't there another hard winter, with lots of snow?

(Pâdshâh) – Yes, many years ago there was another 'ewe-killer', almost as disastrous as this one.

(R) – What price was grain that year?

(Pâdshâh) – Grain was cheap, 30 to 40. Until two years ago, it was never more than 45; probably it didn't even reach 50. The regular price was 20 rupees; if someone bought it for 25 or 30 we'd complain that he paid too much – except in spring when grain ran short and it rose to 30 or 35.

(R) – Wasn't it even cheaper fifteen years ago: 10 or 15 rupees?

(Pâdshâh/Parwiz) – Twenty years ago I remember collecting ears of wheat for 1 rupee a seer, taking them to sell in the bazaar for 3 *qerân* [*1½ rupees*], making 1 *qerân* profit.

(R) – So the rate was 3 *qerân* or 2–3 rupees; didn't people complain when it got to 15 to 20?

(Pâdshâh/Parwiz) – No, people said nothing. The price rose gradually, perhaps by one rupee a year; people didn't really notice to complain about it. For the last eight or ten years, as I recall, it was steady at 20 to 25, rising to 30 to 35 in spring.

(Pâdshâh) – I'll tell you why wheat prices have increased; first, the population has increased; secondly, people are trying harder to make money. The reason wheat is

scarce is that most people plant other things like cucumbers and leeks, hoping to make some money. Some years ago they planted a lot of cotton, and the wheat ran short. Some people do well, but the poor and unemployed don't benefit; people who work make money. For example the Hazâras of Chârbâgh make money on their kilims; most of them put their energy into growing stuff like cucumbers and leeks; they also do special things like opium, or trading.

(R) – They don't farm wheat then?

(Pâdshâh) – No, they're out to make a profit. That's why grain's so expensive.

The Zuris

Konjek villagers are concerned about the family of Nazar Zuri, an 'alien' rogue who trades for a living. His son Nabi has perpetrated a fraud. Baya-khân and others tell the story.

Nazar was one of the Zuris who came early from Kandahar, like Anwar and Mahmad-Lâl. There were many of them, and all but Nazar went to Aliâbâd in Qataghan, where they got some land.

Nazar had nothing here, though he once had a few sheep. His only work was herding, farming and harvesting for other people. He knows a lot about donkey's teeth, and he used to go to town, buy donkeys and take them up to Kachan, where he sold them at a profit; he was a donkey-trader. But now he's a much-reduced old man. He stays at home, he hasn't worked for years. His wife's dead; she was Zuri too, so were his daughters-in-law. He had another wife, who died without leaving any children. He had no in-laws here. People wouldn't give him their daughters: 'He's Zuri, he's not one of us; if we gave him a girl, he might up sticks and take her far away.' Zuris aren't Durrani, they're a sort of Fârsibân.

He has four sons. The eldest, Nabi, was a shepherd, the younger ones worked here as servants or farmhands. His second son Musagey went to Qataghan and got engaged to Anwar Zuri's daughter; when he'd paid some of the brideprice, he worked as a farmhand for his father-in-law and others, to pay off the rest. After a few years another son, Shâhwâli, went there to work as a farmhand; and last year the youngest son went.

The only son left here is Nabi. Last year he came to the mountains to trade. On the way back, at Cherâs, he bought 30,000 rupees-worth of cloth from the Niâzi traders, and they wrote down what he owed; payment was due after Jashn, around now [*late August*], when the Kabulis come to collect.

Every autumn he used to go to Kachan on horseback, taking rice and melons for sale; then in spring, when the Kachanis brought their animals down here, he'd go to his partners and say, 'Give me your lambskins to sell, and I'll give you the money when you go – and we'll all be very happy.' Once or twice they gave him skins, and Nabi sold them at a good profit and gave them their money, so the Kachanis, poor people, reckoned they could trust him: 'He gave us our money, let's give him lots more skins.' So they gave him 40 or 50 skins, worth 25,000 rupees; he said, 'I'll sell them and give you your money in a few days, after I've taken my 5 rupees commission.'

He left the skins with Sâleh – you know Sâleh-bey – then they got together and bolted with the skins. For two months they were thieving in Qataghan, Konduz, Pol-e-

Khomri, Maymana and Andkhoy, and they never came back. All spring the poor Kachanis chased after them; they went to Sheberghân to look for them, without success; they came here cursing and crying, 'Damn his house! He's taken our money, our home's far from town, our families are hungry, we must get them flour and tea.'

Then one evening he came and told his wife, 'Pack everything up, we're leaving, I'm bringing a truck at midnight.' Sâleh's family noticed that their bedding and stuff was all packed, and realized that they were planning to flit that night. They told Dâdollah – Nabi owed him money – who told Abdor-Rahmân, whose nephew Joma was engaged to Nabi's daughter. They'd paid off the brideprice and were just waiting for Nabi to return before holding the wedding; now they suspected Nabi was going to steal his daughter away, hoping to be able to demand another 10,000–20,000 rupees before he let her go – that's the kind of trick he played.

Dâdollah told Joma and his elder brother Hâshem. He put Hâshem at the entrance of the alley beside the mosque: he was to watch there until morning, to make sure that Nabi's family didn't sneak past with their stuff. Then Joma went to his in-laws, saying he'd come to *bâzi* [*see Chapter 10*]. They said, 'It's not convenient; come some other night,' but he insisted, 'I'm coming now, I'm not going away.' So they put him to sleep under two rugs. Poor chap, he was tired, he'd been working at the harvest, and soon he was sound asleep.

Nabi brought Nazir Kachi Sheykhanzai's son to help shift the stuff to the road. Nazir used to live here – now he's with the Malekis; one of his daughters is married to Nabi, another to his brother.

Hâshem didn't see them arrive. They managed to load the household stuff without waking Joma; but as they started off, Hâshem woke up and grabbed the horse's reins saying, 'By God, you're going nowhere!' Nabi drew a pistol on him and threatened to shoot, just to frighten him off. Hâshem said, 'Shoot me ten times, I won't let you pass!' and held the reins tightly. People heard their struggle, until Dâdollah seized Nabi, took him to his house and set a guard over him until morning.

Nabi also owed Wazir money; he'd bought the horse from him and hadn't paid for it, so Wazir went in the morning and took his horse back. Nabi was forced to pay 500 or 600 rupees to Dâdollah; Abdor-Rahmân took his daughter and completed the marriage with Joma, without a wedding party.

He was a shameless bastard. He had numerous creditors: Kabulis, Kachanis, Pashtuns, to the tune of 85,000 rupees. That's why he hid, and tried to take his family off by stealth – including his engaged daughter. But they stopped him. The Kachanis heard he was around and came after him.

But two or three days later, Nabi escaped and ran off once more. He disappeared for a couple of weeks, then another night he came back to his house saying, 'I'm bringing a truck, we're moving tomorrow.' This time they managed to get all their stuff to the truck, and off they went to Qataghan.

A trip to Qataghan

Like Nabi Zuri, people in trouble among the Piruzai frequently seek refuge in Qataghan, the former north-eastern province that included the current provinces of Baghlân, Konduz and Takhâr, closely related to the neighbouring Badakhshân. (See Map A) Indeed, many Pashtuns settled there during the early twentieth century. Two years ago, Seyyed-shâh/Golusar was in trouble with his own family (though he denies it) and sought refuge in Qataghan with his relative Haji Amir (see pp. 101–2).

Qataghan's a depressing place. I went there, around Jashn-time. When I got to Sheberghân the celebrations were finished. I spent the night at Mazâr; the next morning we left at eight, then stopped at Tashkurghân. I asked the road to Dasht-e-Mir-Alam, and they showed me. I asked, 'Do trucks go that way or not?' They said, 'No, they go to Qârizi, then turn off to Konduz.'

So from there I went to Aybak, to Samangân. When I got there I stopped with some Tâjiks, my father's maternal uncles; I went to the house of Haji Mahd-Karim, who had only one hand. In his house he had two wives, but no children. He had a really impressive table radio; he also had a charpoy, which he put outside in the open. He told me, 'Come and sit down.' We sat on the charpoy and talked. He asked me, 'Where are you from?' I said, 'From Sar-e-pol.' He said, 'Where in Sar-e-pol? Are you from Haji Ghâfur's village?' I said I was. He said, 'Haji Ghâfur had a nephew, who was a boy then [*he meant Tumân*]; does he have any sons?' 'Yes,' I said, 'He has many sons.' Then he asked me, 'Where are you going?' I said, 'I'm going to Haji Amir's house; he's crazy.' He said, 'He's in Kalân-qodukh.' I asked, 'How long to get there?' He said, 'If you start early in the morning, you'll arrive by nightfall.' So I said, 'But I'm a stranger here.' He said, 'I'll find you someone.'

I spent the night there and he found me a guide; after breakfast, he loaded the camels and drove them on. *Hala–hala–hala–hala*, the road never gets shorter. It's a real desert, just like the Dasht-e-Leyli, sand in all directions. I fell into a ditch, and I swore that if God ever got me home I'd never come this way again.

At dusk we arrived at Kalân-qodukh, Haji Amir's place. He asked, 'Why've you come?' I said, 'I want to be a servant here.' He said, 'I bet you've left home after a quarrel; I'm not going to hire you. Stay in my house, eat with us, wear our clothes, but we won't make you a servant. Then I'll take you back home.' I said, 'There's been no quarrel.' But he wouldn't change his mind.

I spent a week there. Haji Amir sent his nephew Ajab-khân to the house of one Haji Jahângir to collect 400 rupees: 'This is my nephew, give it to him and see this lad onto a truck.' He collected 1,600 rupees, gave them to me and had me escorted back to Aybak, where I got a truck. I thought, 'I'll never come back to Qataghan; it's a very bad place.'

One day when I was there, a mountain covered in pistachio trees caught fire. Some Turkmens were there collecting nuts, and fourteen camels and their loads were burned there among the pistachios. Trucks couldn't get there because of the sand. Some people brought small water-skins, but ... The ground itself was burning and the fire stopped them reaching the other trees.

The nuts hung down in bunches, like grapes; there must have been 30 kg on each tree. They'd collect them and take them off to trade among themselves. There was a boy, a very smart lad who could write – he'd studied in high school for several years. He went and bought seven lacs-worth of pistachios; they were cheap, 50 rupees for a seer of good nuts. He hired some trucks, loaded them with nuts, brought them to Aybak and sold them in the market, at 150 rupees. He probably made seven lacs profit.

Women too were selling them; they said, 'Won't you buy a seer or half a seer of pistachios? I need some money.' Every house had a flock of sheep, even two. Where did they get so much money? They had such guns, all of them carbines, no, Bolsheviks, Five-shots. The elders tell us how the Five-shots first appeared, in the Saqawi years [*1929*]; how the bullets reached the target so fast. When we have a gun we hang it from a peg on the wall; but they just threw them down in the dirt.

The Tale of the Fox and the Miller

Baya-khân's tale of the smart fox and the stupid miller is a variant on the classic 'Puss-in-Boots' fairytale.[5] In Baya-khân's telling, there is a possible anti-Hazâra subtext: several references to Hazâra dialect, some unintelligible phrases: is the fox a cunning Hazâra agent? Or the miller a stupid Hazâra?

Once, long ago, there was a miller, who had nothing but his mill. He milled people's grain, and took the fee they paid. One night as usual he piled up some clods in the entrance – in those days, mills didn't have doors – and went home. In the morning he found that an animal, a dog or something, had licked up all the flour left around the millstone. He thought, 'This won't do, it'll eat up all my flour.' So he went and fetched a large trap and set it at the mill entrance.

In fact, a fox had taken to coming after the miller left; it'd lick all round the mill, then leave. That night the fox came again and started licking around, then suddenly it trod on the trap, which went *krap!* and caught its foot fast, and it couldn't move.

In the morning the miller found the fox, whose eyes were yellow. The miller said, 'By God I'll kill you, you rascal!' The fox answered – in those days, all creatures could speak – 'Why kill me? All you'll get is my skin, which won't fetch more than 30 rupees in the market. But if you let me live, I promise I'll get you the daughter of Girzang Pâdishâh.'

The miller thought to himself, 'Well, it seems tame enough, let's release it and see whether it's lying or telling the truth.' So he released the fox, as it had made a promise. In those days, all creatures not only could speak, they kept their promises.

The fox twirled its tail and headed off to Girzang Pâdishâh's castle. When it arrived, the padishah was drinking and playing knucklebones, as padishahs do. He looked down and cried out, 'There's a fox!' The fox called up to him, 'Haven't you seen a fox before?' It calmly walked through the gate into the castle and greeted the padishah, 'Salaam, how are you?' and sat down on a carpet.

Girzang Pâdishâh was frightened: 'What sort of fox is this, that can speak?' He asked it, 'Where have you come from? How are things, what's up?' The fox said, 'Gurzang Pâdishâh commissioned me to come and ask for your daughter's hand.' The padishah thought a bit, then said, 'Let me go and ask the family.' They brought pilaw and *chelaw* for the fox, which ate its fill; meanwhile it talked itself up, lying about its country and so on. The padishah went to consult his wife and family, saying: 'Look, this Gurzang

---

[5] For essentially the same story, recorded in eastern Turkey, see Sakaoğlu (1969).

Pâdishâh commissioned a talking fox to ask for my daughter; he must be stronger than us.' His wife and sons instantly agreed, and they put together the scarves for the betrothal *târ* [*see p. 262*] knotted one of them and tied it to the fox's neck, and gave the *târ* to the fox.

The fox twirled its tail, and half an hour later it was back with the miller. The fox told the miller he was now Gurzang Pâdishâh. 'I've got Girzang Pâdishâh's daughter for you; take those clothes off and if you have some decent ones put them on.' So Gurzang Pâdishâh went and took off his old clothes, which were full of lice, and found some new ones.

Two or three years passed, while he went on milling, then one day the fox came and said, 'Put your best clothes on, we're going to your wedding.' They headed off and when they got near Girzang Pâdishâh's country, the fox told the miller, 'You sit here, I'll go to the padishah.' And it put him in a rocky place, well out of sight.

The fox ran into the city. When they told the padishah that a fox had come, he said, 'Haven't you seen a fox before?' The fox entered the castle and went and sat down, looking really miserable. The padishah said, 'Hey fox, what's happened? Last time you were so happy.'

The fox – lying of course – said, 'We were planning to arrive this evening. We set off in a huge procession, with so many people, drummers and pipers, and an army with horses and baggage. Then last night there was a storm, and a flash-flood carried off the whole of Gurzang Pâdishâh's army; I told the padishah to grab my tail, and somehow he managed to scramble out of the water; but everyone else was swept away, all those people, the whole procession, none of them are left except Gurzang Pâdishâh and me.'

The padishah was distressed to hear that so many people had perished. The fox went on, 'Gurzang Pâdishâh's clothes and his turban were torn to shreds last night. Please give him some new clothes; I'll take him the clothes and get him dressed. And he's in a bad way from the water; bring a horse, and some servants to help with it, and we'll put him on it.'

They found some robes – belonging to the padishah's son – and the fox took them straight to the miller and said, 'Be quick, damn you, jump into that canal and throw your clothes into the water.' It took the miller's clothes off and gave him the nice princely robes to put on.

They'd brought a horse with grooms holding the reins on both sides; but it was a buzkashi horse, spirited and hard to control. The miller looked at it and said, 'Foxy, I can't ride, that horse'll throw me!' The fox swore at him, 'Pull yourself together, I've told them you're a padishah, you can't be scared of a horse. I'll tell the servants, "Hold on to the horse, my master's all done in from the flood last night, he can't hold on by himself, make sure it doesn't throw him."' He put his master on the horse. The poor miller was terrified, he'd never ridden before; but the grooms on either side held the reins tight and restrained the horse.

They arrived at Girzang Pâdishâh's castle, where people came to welcome the padishah's new son-in-law. They'd prepared a nice room for him, and they settled him on the rugs and there was music and conversation. He was still down in the mouth – after all, he was just a miller and didn't know what to say! But when people asked why he was so miserable, the fox said, 'Wouldn't you be miserable if you'd lost an army, a people, a kingdom, and you were the only one left?'

When evening came, the fox whispered to the miller, 'Hey, Gurzang Pâdishâh: at dinner they'll put seven different dishes in front of you; you'll be full if you take just one spoonful from each dish, don't take more. This is the royal court, people stay up talking beyond midnight. If you eat too much you'll have to go out to the toilet, and that'd be very bad manners among all these princes and viziers. So, go easy on the food!'

After prayers, the meal arrived, seven courses: pilaw, *shurwa, shirbrenj* and so on. As each one came, he took one spoonful: the stews, the rice ... but when some dhal came – we call it *patey*, it's made from lentils and millers love it! – the fool grabbed the dish and plonked it in front of himself. The fox winked at him, clicked its teeth, and finally nudged him to stop. Ignoring it, the miller shovelled the stuff in, and soon emptied the dish. The fox was furious: 'He's ruining things!'

The atmosphere in the room grew heavy. The miller stayed morose; he had no conversation, he was only a miller after all, so when people asked questions, the fox answered for him; it was very skilled at conversation, saying, 'My master's depressed, he's mourning his lost army, his people; it's best not to talk to him.'

Around ten o'clock the miller whispered to the fox, who was sitting beside him, 'I have to go to the toilet.' The fox whispered, 'You idiot, why did you eat so much, when I told you not to? You can't go out in front of all these people! You'll have to hold it in.' He said, 'No, I really have to go.' The fox said, 'Just hang on a little longer, people will soon be leaving.'

Well, to cut a long story short, the miller badly messed his pants. The fox was deeply embarrassed. The padishah noticed and asked, 'Hey foxy, what's up, why are you upset?' The fox told him, 'My master has two little brothers, and in the evening he sits one of them on each of his knees; they were left at home and he's missing them.' The padishah immediately called for one of his little sons to be cleaned up and dressed in fresh clothes; and also one of the vizier's sons. Servants went and found the boys, washed them and perfumed them and dressed them nicely in new clothes and new turbans; they were brought into the guest room and placed on the miller's knees.

The miller looked askance at them; the fox whispered to him, 'Damn you, kiss these kids, play with them!' Meanwhile it put its foot inside the miller's pants and managed to move the shit from the miller's pants into those of the boys. Then the fox suddenly leaped up. The padishah asked, 'What's up?' The fox said, 'The boys have messed their pants, and it's gone all over my master!'

Well, with that the party broke up; the padishah and the viziers rose and left. The fox said to the miller, 'Throw yourself into this millstream!' So the miller jumped into a millstream; his dirty clothes went down the stream, and they brought him some new princely robes, which he put on. Then he went to spend the night with the padishah's daughter.

The following morning they started the wedding ceremonies, which lasted several days. The first morning, they brought out the bride, displayed all her clothes and trousseau and loaded it all onto mules, and Girzang Pâdishâh gave Gurzang Pâdishâh five mule-loads of gold and silver. He also gave him forty retainers, and forty maidservants for his daughter. He bid them farewell with the firing of guns.

Now the miller had no house, and he wondered, 'Where shall I take all these people and all this stuff?' The fox told Girzang Pâdishâh, 'Twenty women and twenty men are enough for us, take the other twenty of each back.' It headed off into the steppe, telling Gurzang Pâdishâh, 'I'll go ahead, you follow me with your wife and her trousseau and all the stuff.'

The fox soon came back to tell him, 'There's a large castle ahead, which belongs to a *div*; there's a canal that waters the *div*'s land; he has a whole canal's worth of land.' The fox told the miller all this privately, nobody else heard; he added, 'When we approach the castle, have them fire twenty guns; when we're in front of the gate, another twenty guns, and once we're inside, another twenty guns. The *div* has lots of gold and silver, rooms full of it, and storerooms full of grain – think how much land that canal can irrigate. When the *div* asks me, "Fox, what's up?" I'll answer, "The padishah's army's come and he's sworn to leave nothing alive, fox or *div*!"'

The fox went ahead, and as they approached the *div*'s castle the miller's men fired twenty guns; when they were at the gate, they fired twenty more, and once they were inside, they fired another twenty. The *div* asked the fox, 'What's up, foxy?' The fox answered, 'The padishah's come with his army and he's sworn to kill us, *div*s, foxes, wolves and all.' The *div* cried, 'Where can I hide?' Beside his house the *div* had a huge pile of wood for the winter; the fox said, 'You'd better hide there under the woodpile; keep absolutely quiet or he'll find you and kill you!' The *div* was very strong, so he hoisted the whole pile onto his shoulders and then lay down underneath it.

The army and the wedding procession came inside and camped right there. They opened the doors of the rooms. The fox found some kerosene and told the men to pour it over the woodpile, while the *div*, who'd been told to keep quiet or he'd be killed, didn't utter a word. The fox struck a match, and burned the *div* to death right there.

Now the fox took over the castle and the canal, all in its own name, and became a padishah in its own right! After some time, the miller sent back all the retainers and maidservants, 'Enough, we don't need you, go home!' Only the miller, the princess and the fox remained. After some time, the fox pretended to be ill; 'I'll test the miller and see whether he'll look after me, after all the things I've done for him.' Two or three times the miller looked after it well, but one day he got up and said to his wife, 'Enough of this fox, why's he just lying here claiming to be ill, let's take him by the feet and throw him out.' At this, the fox leaped up, 'You shitty miller, you were a poor miller, you had nothing, and I got you the princess; by God I'll go to the padishah and complain!' Hearing this – 'Is he just a miller, really?' – the miller's wife put on her chador and headed back towards her father's house, and the fox himself headed off into the steppe.

The stupid miller was left alone, thinking, 'God's truth, I must go after the fox, I'll never get my wife back without him.' He came and kissed the fox's feet and hands, 'For God's sake, get my wife back, I can't do it without you, I'm really sorry, I'll look after you properly, give you anything you want to eat.' His wife had already gone a long way, as far as Chârbâgh from here, when suddenly the fox came up to her, twirling its tail: 'Where are you going? I was just having a tiff with my master, when you up and left!' And he managed to turn her round, and brought her home.

Time passed, and the fox really did get ill and died. They gave him a proper burial. They gave me a nice shawl, but when I came to the village the dogs grabbed it from me, and here I am with this story for you.

Plate 1 Sar-e-pol town and river; August 1972.

Plate 2 The steppe east of Sar-e-pol valley, looking south-east; April 1971.

Plate 3 Tumân and Maygol, his youngest daughter; Chenâr, September 1972.

Plate 4 Gol-Ahmad and Tumân; Konjek, August 1971.

Plate 5 Maryam milking; spring camp, April 1971.

Plate 6 Bâdâm and her children;
spring camp, April 1971.

Plate 7 Neshtar, the 'headwoman';
Konjek, May 1971.

244

Plate 8 Darwiza and nephew; Konjek, September 1971.

Plate 9 Pâdshâh and Pâkhâl; Konjek, September 1971.

245

Plate 10 Baya-khân, Tâjak, Sepâhi, Darwiza, Kala-khân and lead-goat; spring camp, March 1971.

Plate 11 Abdor-Rahmân collects fleeces for market; spring camp, April 1971.

Plate 12 Pâkiza makes bread; spring camp, May 1971.

Plate 13 Jamâl boils whey for *krut*; Dangak camp, June 1971.

Plate 14 Rishmin and Tumân buy eggs from Aymâq villager; Sarghân, May 1971.

Plate 15 Climbing up Dangak pass; May 1971.

248

Plate 16 Women roll a *krâst* felt; Kâshân, July 1971.

Plate 17 Piruzai camp; Boghawi, August 1971.

Plate 18 Negâr and Gol-Ahmad; Chenâr, August 1971.

Plate 19 Manân, Chârgol, Richard, Kala-khân; Chenâr, August 1972.

Plate 20 Division of Tumân's barley crop: the sharecropper, Tumân and Mayoddin-jân Âghâ; Konjek, August 1972.

Plate 21 Baya-khân and Nancy in a melon field, July 1972.

Plate 22 Pâdshâh, son of Parwiz;
Konjek, August 1971.

Plate 23 Seyyed-shâh, son of Golusar;
Konjek, August 1972.

Plate 24 Students (*tâlebân*) of Mayoddin-jân Âghâ; Konjek, August 1972.

Plate 25 Girls singing; Haji Molk spring camp, March 1971.

Plate 26 Women dance at wedding; Haji Ghâfur spring camp, May 1971.

10

The Marriage Market

The Tale of Jallât Khân and Shamayel

This tale is a classic; Baya-khân's version follows fairly closely the Pashtu one published by Nuri (n.d. 1: 152–65), which Tumân may have read aloud to him.

Once upon a time there was a poor woman, who had nothing but her two sons. The elder son made a living for them by going out every day to gather firewood on the hillsides. He'd dig up shrubs with his shovel, take them to town and sell them for a few rupees.

One day, as he raised his shovel to dig out a bush, he saw that a bird had built its nest in the roots, and in the nest there was an egg. It was a strange wild bird, not like these normal birds; a phoenix [*simorgh*], I think. That evening he took the egg home to his mother: 'I found a nest today, and in it was this egg; tomorrow I'll take it to town.'

The egg turned out to be very valuable. Next day, he took it to town to sell and showed it to all the merchants, but they all recognized it as a phoenix egg and said it was worth more than they could pay. They directed him to a certain rich merchant, who could probably afford to buy it.

He went to the rich merchant, who examined the egg and asked him, 'How much do you want for it?' He said, 'What will you give me?' The merchant said, '3,000 rupees', and the deal was done.

The boy continued going to the hills to cut firewood, but one day he laid a trap for the bird. A few days later, he found the bird caught in the trap. He brought it home, looked after it well, and it laid an egg every day. From then on he had an arrangement with the rich merchant; whenever the bird laid an egg, he took it to town the following day. He sold each one to the merchant for 3,000 rupees, and soon collected a lot of money.

Then his mother said, 'This fellow who buys your eggs for 3,000 rupees, he must be a good man; we should invite him here for a meal.' He said, 'Fine, I'll invite him to be our guest.' The next time he went to sell an egg and got his 3,000 rupees, he said to the merchant, 'My mother told me to invite you one evening to our house; every day I eat your food; you're now a good friend, please come and visit us, let's get to know each other better.'

The merchant said, 'The only way I'll be your guest is if you kill that phoenix, cook it, and refrain from eating any of the meat yourselves. If you agree to that, I'll come and be your guest; otherwise, I won't come.'

He went home that evening and told his mother what the merchant had said; that he wouldn't come unless they cooked the bird in front of him and refrained from eating any of it themselves. His mother, 'Fine, we'll kill it, what does it matter? Let him come.'

So he brought the rich merchant home, and they killed the phoenix. The merchant reminded him, 'Don't touch the meat until I've eaten first.' They agreed. They cut the carcass into pieces and put them in the pot. The mother stood over the pot to make sure the boys didn't take some meat and anger the merchant. But once she had to go to fetch salt or something, and both sons came, lifted the lid off the pot, and put a spoon in; one of them ate the bird's head, the other its heart.

At dinner, they washed the merchant's hands, put all the meat on a plate and served it to him. He searched through the meat and couldn't find either the head or the heart. He sent the plate back, saying, 'I don't need this meat. What I wanted was the heart and the head.'

He was really annoyed, and the mother was very angry with her sons and beat them severely. They both ran away, and kept running until, exhausted, they came to a willow tree by a pool of cool water fed by a spring. There they lay down and slept. Then one of them got up; he looked at his brother, who'd drunk some of the water and was dead to the world. He said to himself, 'Poor boy, let him sleep.' Then he looked closer and said, 'But he's not breathing! He's not asleep, he's dead!'

He thought, 'I must wash my brother's body, put it in a shroud, dig a grave and bury him, but I can't do this by myself, I need a mullah and people to help.' He looked around but there was no village, no sign of anybody. He went off, in search of someone who could help.

Then a parrot and a mynah bird arrived and settled in the willow. The parrot said to the mynah – in former times, these birds could speak – 'Mynah, this poor boy's in trouble.' The mynah replied, 'Parrot, he's very much in trouble, I don't know the remedy, but let's find a cure and make him better.' The parrot said, 'If you take some leaves from this very tree, squeeze them and pour the juice into his mouth, he'll recover at once.' The boy still lay there unconscious, unaware of any of this. So the parrot and the mynah took some leaves and mashed them with their feet, and some juice fell into the boy's mouth. He woke up, looked around and could see no sign of his brother or anybody else in that wilderness; so he too ran off.

His brother, who'd gone off earlier, came to a country where the padishah had just died. All the people of the country, including the poorest cowherd and cameleer, had been summoned and were gathered to choose a new padishah. In olden days, when a padishah died, the people would choose as padishah the person on whose head a hawk alighted. They sent the hawk up and it circled around. At this point, the boy arrived and wondered what was going on, what all these people were doing.

Now these boys had eaten the heart and the head. This meant that both of them would become padishahs – and that was the reason the merchant had been so keen to get the heart and the head, and why he'd rejected the rest of the meat.

The boy arrived and joined the gathering. After circling around, the hawk settled on his head. People said, 'Why didn't the hawk settle on one of us? Where's this nobody from? He's just a cowherd from the desert, who's he that the hawk should settle on him?

It's made a mistake!' They sent the hawk up again, but again it settled on the boy. Some people said, 'Okay, let's make him padishah', others said, 'No, impossible.' They sent the hawk up a third time, and once more it settled on him; so they made him padishah, and called him Khunkâr Pâdishâh. They took him to the capital and installed him on the throne.

The other boy went to another country, and there too the padishah had just died. He came and joined the crowds; and there too they sent up a hawk, which circled round and settled on him too. People said the hawk had made a mistake, he couldn't be padishah, but here too the hawk settled on him a second and then a third time, so they made him padishah, calling him Shâh-Selim Pâdishâh.

Shâh-Selim Pâdishâh married and had seven sons. Khunkâr Pâdishâh had a daughter and named her Shamayel. The two brothers were unaware of each other's fate. The first thought the second had died, that God had taken him; the second thought the same about the first. Neither knew the other had become padishah in another country.

One day Shâh-Selim Pâdishâh's six older sons went out hunting; the youngest, Jallât Khân, was too small and stayed at home. The six princes climbed a hill and looked around; there was no sign of deer or anything, so they came down, and there in front of her house was an old biddy. As they came up, she greeted them, 'My sons, my chickens, what's up, where are you going?' They answered, 'We're going hunting.' The old biddy said, 'In that case, why don't you go after Shamayel, Khunkâr Pâdishâh's daughter; you'll like her, she's fantastically beautiful, like a fairy; but there are some tasks to be completed to win her.'

So, instead of going home, the princes headed for that country, where they found that Shamayel's father had indeed set her suitors a number of tasks. First, a *div*, in the form of an iron bar, was in love with her. 'Whoever wants my daughter must split this iron bar with a wooden axe. A second task involves a fierce buffalo, also in love with Shamayel; the task is to milk the buffalo and take the milk to the top of a certain tall tree and down again without spilling it. The third task is a roomful of millet and sesame seeds, which must be sorted into separate piles by dawn. Whoever wants my daughter must complete all these tasks.'

The princes asked for the padishah's castle, and people showed them the way. They greeted the padishah, who was standing in front of the bar. He said, 'How are you? Why have you come?' The brothers said, 'We came hoping to win your daughter; let us attempt the tasks.' Of course, they hadn't recognized each other as uncle and nephews. The padishah said, 'But you're a bunch of nice young men, please don't do it. You know that if you fail to split the bar, there's a man with a sword standing there and he'll cut your head straight off. I've already had many suitors killed this way.'

But the older brother got up, took the axe and struck the bar. Nothing happened, so the executioner struck off his head. The others . . . to cut a long story short, five brothers failed and were executed, only the sixth was left. What can I say, he too tried to split the bar with the wooden axe, but nothing happened and he too was killed.

After Shâh-Selim Pâdishâh heard that his six older sons had been killed, he made sure that his youngest son, Jallât Khân, who'd stayed at home, grew up unaware that he'd lost his older brothers. Jallât Khân would play jacks in the street with the old biddy's bald son. Usually he won, but if the baldy won, then Jallât Khân snatched the bones back from him, and they'd fight. The baldy would go back to his mother, crying, and she'd say, 'Baldy, if he does this once more, ask him, "Don't you know that a padishah has killed your six brothers? If you're a real man, why don't you do something about it?"'

One day the biddy's son was playing jacks again with Jallât Khân, and he won. When Jallât Khân hit him, he said, 'Jallât Khân, you're stronger than me, you can beat me, but what sort of a man are you? Your six brothers have been killed, why don't you go and avenge them?'

Jallât Khân was very upset by this; he threw down the jacks in front of the biddy's son, and he went and asked other people about his brothers. They said, 'Yes, that's right, you had six brothers, and Khunkâr Pâdishâh killed them.'

Jallât Khân went home and said to his mother, 'Please make me some popcorn, I'd really like some.' So his mother put a griddle on the fire, and when she'd made some popcorn she called her son and said, 'Son, bring a tin or a plate.' Jallât Khân said, 'No, give it to me in your hands, I want to eat from them.' She put some in her cupped hands. He took her hands and held them tight together. She said, 'For God's sake, let go my hands, they're burning!' He said, 'I won't let go until you tell me: did I have some brothers?' She said, 'No, you didn't.' He pressed her until her hands were badly burned, then she admitted, 'Yes, you had six brothers; they went to Khunkâr Pâdishâh, who'd set tasks for winning his daughter; they went there, and he killed them.'

On hearing this, without taking leave of his parents Jallât Khân headed straight off to Khunkâr Pâdishâh's country. As he passed a thick, impenetrable forest, he saw a long-haired dervish seated by the road. This dervish was a close Friend of God; he'd made his home in the forest, where he could avoid men's voices, say his five daily prayers, and recite God's names.

He greeted the dervish and asked for a blessing. The dervish – whose hair fell to the ground – didn't raise his head, so he sang to him: 'Long-haired dervish, give me a nice blessing, I've a difficult journey to Khunkâr Pâdishâh's country, where they've killed my brothers.' The dervish raised his head and cleared his hair from his face. Jallât Khân kissed his hand. The dervish asked, 'You say you're off to another country where they killed your brothers: did you get permission from your parents?' Jallât Khân said, 'No, I didn't.' 'Did you say goodbye to them?' 'No, I didn't.' So the dervish said, 'Go home and say goodbye to them properly, then come back and I'll bless you properly.'

He went home and apologized to his parents, who said, 'Why are you going there, you can't do anything, you'll just get yourself killed too. Everything you need is here: wealth and comfort, a wife to marry.' He replied, 'No, I won't stay here. He's killed my six brothers, let him kill me too, I'll be the seventh; either that, or I'll bring back that woman. He's a good padishah, he'll be fair and just.'

He took leave of his parents and came once again to the dervish, kissed his face and hand. The dervish asked, 'Did you take leave of your parents?' He said he had. The dervish said, 'Good', patted him three times on the back, blessed him and gave him a letter to Mullah Miru, who'd once studied with him, and was now Khunkâr Pâdishâh's mullah. 'Take this letter and tell Mullah Miru, "Dervish greets you warmly," and he'll take good care of you and do whatever you want. He used to be my murid, and studied a lot with me.'

He took the letter and set off again for Khunkâr Pâdishâh's country. He was nearly there when he saw a farmer watering a plot of land and, as he did so, drowning large numbers of ants. Jallât Khân asked him, 'Why are you doing this? It isn't right to drown all those ants.' He answered, 'What do you mean? I'm watering the land, then I'll plough and sow a few pounds of seeds, to grow a few pounds of wheat for us to eat; why should I worry about ants?' Jallât Khân said, 'How big a harvest do you get from this plot?' The farmer said, '100 to 200 pounds.' Jallât Khân said, 'If it's 200 pounds, I'll give you the price of 300 pounds of wheat; now cut the water off.' The farmer cut off the water and drained the plot, and Jallât Khân gave him the money, telling him, 'Don't cultivate or water this plot this year.'

Now the ants have a padishah too. The padishah, Mandoshâh, came and greeted Jallât Khân and said, 'Come, tonight you're our guest.' Jallât Khân said, 'No, I have to go.' The padishah said, 'No, you must stay the night with us, eat our food, then you can go on.' The ants brought Jallât Khân and sat him down, and brought him a grasshopper leg to eat. Jallât Khân said, 'Thank you for your hospitality and generosity, it's enough, but I can't eat it.' He left the grasshopper leg – how could he eat such a thing? Then the ant-padishah gave him one of his whiskers – you've probably noticed that ants have whiskers – and told him, 'Whenever you're in a tight spot and we might be able to help you, then strike a match and set light to this hair, and we'll be there for you in an instant.'

When he reached Khunkâr Padishah's country, he found his way to Mullah Miru's house. He greeted Mullah Miru and gave him the letter. Mullah Miru read it, kissed it, then embraced Jallât Khân, and from then on took good care of him. Jallât Khân became his student, and studied so well that every day he learned all he'd been taught. He grew into a fine young man.

One day there was a death and Mullah Miru went to officiate, telling his wife, 'I'm going out today for the funeral, so I'll be late coming home. Jallât Khân's in the mosque, please send him some food.'

He went off, and his wife prepared some *shurwa* and told her daughter, 'Take it to the *tâleb*, Jallât Khân.' Now Jallât Khân had never been in their house, as he lived in the mosque and took his food there, so the women hadn't seen him before. When the daughter came with his food, he was reading, with his head down. As soon as she saw him, she was smitten: 'What a nice young man, I'd like him for a husband!' When he raised his head, the girl instantly fell into a dead faint. Her mother wondered what had happened to her, and came and saw her lying there unconscious; then she looked at Jallât Khân and she fainted on top of her daughter! Jallât Khân was so good-looking, they both fell for him.

Jallât Khân got up at once, 'What will Mullah Miru think when he finds both these women like this?' He recited a prayer over them – he'd studied so hard, he was now a proper mullah. They both recovered, but next time they sent someone else with his food. The daughter was now in love with Jallât Khân, and he became very upset, 'It's a bad business. Mullah Miru must think I've done something to his daughter.' Of course, Mullah Miru did think, 'There's something going on between them, secretly.'

But Jallât Khân wasn't interested in her, his heart was set on Shamayel, the padishah's daughter. He was so upset by what had happened that one day he left the house thinking, 'This girl won't leave me alone; I must go and live somewhere else.' He came to the house of an old biddy, put his hand in his pocket and gave her twenty gold pieces – he'd brought a lot of gold with him. The biddy was thrilled, and she adopted Jallât Khân as her third son. She had two other sons, Mamandey and Samandey; both were skilled carpenters who made all the doorways, boxes and wooden objects throughout the country. Jallât Khân lived and worked with them, and became even better than them at carpentry, a real master.

The old biddy was one of Shamayel's many maidservants. Every evening Shamayel would summon her to come and chat, entertain her and tell stories. Khunkâr Padishah had a garden with all kinds of flowers, and every afternoon Shamayel told the biddy, 'Go and make three posies and bring them to me.'

One afternoon when the biddy was picking flowers to make the posies, Jallât Khân asked her, 'Mother, why are you making these posies?' She said, 'I'm making them to take to Shamayel; she likes to see them in the evening, all these different flowers, and they smell so nice.' Jallât Khân said, 'I'll make a posy too.' She said, 'No you don't, she'll guess it was made by a man, and she'll be angry with me.' 'No, I'll make one, and if she asks who made it, tell her, "I have a bald granddaughter, she made it."'

Jallât Khân made a beautiful posy; when the biddy took the posies that evening, Shamayel exclaimed, 'What a nice posy! Biddy, every day you bring me three posies and none of them are any good, but this one's perfect, who made it?' The biddy said she'd made it herself; Shamayel said, 'No you didn't, someone else did, who was it?' The biddy said, 'I have a bald granddaughter, she made it.' Shamayel said, 'Tomorrow evening, bring your granddaughter.'

The biddy was frightened: 'I've told her a lie, I have no granddaughter; if she finds out, she'll have my guts!' She came home very upset, and sat down. Jallât Khân asked her, 'Biddy, why are you so down? What happened?' She told him that Shamayel had asked her to bring her granddaughter; 'But I have no granddaughter, she'll have my guts if she finds out.' Jallât Khân put his hand in his pocket again and gave her 50 gold pieces, saying, 'Don't worry yourself, I'll come with you and take care of it.'

Next day they made more posies, and in the evening Jallât Khân put on women's clothes, with a chador on his head. The biddy gave him instructions. Now you must have noticed how a man starts walking with his right foot first, while a woman starts with the left. The biddy told Jallât Khân, 'Start with your left foot, so that Shamayel doesn't suspect anything.'

They went in, exchanged greetings and sat down. The biddy whispered to Jallât Khân, 'I've brought you in, now it's up to you.' Shamayel told the biddy's granddaughter, 'Come and sit next to me.' As the 'granddaughter' sat down by her, Shamayel took his leg and put it over hers, thinking, 'If this is a man, he'll keep his leg there, while if it's a woman, she'll ask me to put my leg over hers.' Shamayel placed her leg under his, and it stayed there, but he said to himself, 'My leg's very heavy, she must be tired of it,' so he removed it – Jallât Khân was very smart guy, he was behaving like a woman, to stop Shamayel suspecting.

After the biddy and Jallât Khân had visited Shamayel together like that for several nights, Jallât Khân went and built a fantastic toy lion out of wood, with wheels, and a secret place inside with a hidden door so that nobody would guess that someone might be sitting inside. The padishah heard that Mamandey and Samandey had made a lion that was fun to play with, and he sent word to them, 'I'm bored, let me see your lion.' Jallât Khân got inside and fastened the door tightly behind him; there were no hinges or knobs – nobody could tell it was there.

Samandey and Mamandey took the lion to the padishah, who was delighted and played with it. Shamayel heard that he'd got a lion and was playing with it, so she sent her maidservants to her father, 'Send me the lion, I'm very bored.' He sent it, with Jallât Khân still inside. After Shamayel and her maids had had dinner, they had great fun playing with the lion, jumping on top of it, pushing it around, until they were all exhausted and it was time for bed. At midnight, when they'd gone off to sleep, Jallât Khân opened the door and came to Shamayel's room. It was brightly lit by two lamps, at her head and her feet. Seven shawls were spread over her. He took the lamp from her head and put it at her feet, replacing it with the lamp from her feet; he drew back her shawls and kissed her face, then he got up and shut himself back inside the wooden lion.

In the morning, Shamayel – who was tender-skinned – found her face burning, and when she looked in the mirror she saw that it was red. She also noticed that the lamps had been swapped around. She was upset to realize that somebody had been with her.

Mamandey and Samandey asked the padishah to send the lion back: 'You've played with it for long enough.' The padishah returned it. Shamayel realized that the lion was in some way connected to the biddy and her granddaughter; she guessed that the 'granddaughter' was a man, but she liked him very much and wanted to have a secret assignation with him, so she asked the biddy, 'Come tonight to talk to me and tell me stories.' The biddy once more prepared three posies, one of them made by Jallât Khân, and took them to Shamayel. After they exchanged greetings, Shamayel looked at the posies and said, 'You didn't make one of them,' and the biddy said, 'It was my granddaughter, the baldy, who made it.' So she said, 'Tomorrow night, bring the baldy.'

The following night, the biddy was scared: 'If she finds out, she'll have my guts.' She didn't know that Jallât Khân and Shamayel had already connected. So she instructed Jallât Khân once again: 'Make sure you put your left foot first; if you put your right one first, she'll be suspicious.' She took him along, and they talked together for a while; then Shamayel told the biddy, 'When you go, leave your granddaughter with me; I'm bored, we'll continue to talk.' After the biddy'd gone, she told her maids, 'I'm very tired and I'm going to sleep until noon. If anybody disturbs me, I'll cut off her head.' So she kicked all the maids out into another room and locked the door.

Now Shamayel told Jallât Khân, 'I've found you out, you're a man; but I won't have any other man for my husband.' Jallât Khân was very happy, and he told her who he was. She kept him with her for a whole week; during the day Jallât Khân wore women's clothes and they talked together in her apartments; then they spent the nights together, without anyone else knowing what was going on.

Eventually he said, 'This is great, but what shall I do about completing those tasks? I could give 5 or 10 lacs of rupees, but he won't give you for a cash brideprice.'

As we said earlier, Khunkâr Padishah had set certain tasks for his daughter's suitors. The first was to split the iron bar with a wooden axe. The second was to milk the fierce buffalo that was in love with Shamayel, take the milk up and down that tree without spilling it. The third was to separate a roomful of millet and sesame into different piles in the space of one night, without a single grain out of place. Jallât Khân said, 'These three tasks are very hard, how can I do them?'

The padishah had a huge palace, with a penthouse on top; during the day Shamayel went up to the penthouse, at night she came down to a different set of rooms. She gave Jallât Khân a hair from her head and said, 'Put this in your pocket. I'll be up there in the penthouse, which has a little window. Keep looking up there, and the moment I show myself, wind the hair round the iron bar and strike the bar – it's a *div* that's in love with me. Until you see me, hold back, don't strike, whatever anybody says; just keep your arm up, saying you're about to strike; the moment I show myself, say *bismillah* and strike at once, and the bar will split in two.

'That's one task. Next is the buffalo, which won't allow anyone near; if anyone does approach, it'll trample them underfoot and tear them to pieces. Take this bandana and wave it in the wind; it has my scent and the buffalo will smell it and come of its own accord; it's in love with me, and it'll ignore you; just take a bowl and milk it.' Then she gave him a ring saying, 'Put this ring into the milk, and it'll turn into cheese; then you can climb up that tree and down again, and the milk won't spill' – plain milk would spill if you climbed a tree with it, while cheese is solid!

She went on, 'I've solved two of the tasks for you. What shall we do about the third?' Jallât Khân said, 'I'll separate the millet and sesame myself.' Shamayel said, 'Okay, the third task's up to you, with or without God's help.'

Jallât Khân went home, having arranged with Shamayel, 'Tomorrow morning I'll attempt the iron bar, remember to show yourself at the little window in the penthouse.'

In the morning he came and presented himself to the padishah in front of the iron bar. The padishah said, 'You're a nice young man, I've no wish for you to die; don't waste your effort on these tasks, you can't do them, you'll just end up losing your head.' Jallât Khân answered, 'No, my six brothers have tried and failed, I'm the seventh, perhaps I'll succeed.'

The padishah said again, 'Don't do it!' And the executioner standing there with his sword in his hand said, 'You're a nice young man, forget it, you'll never succeed.' He answered, 'God has decided my fate; whether I live or die, I'm going to try.'

He looked up at the penthouse, but there was no sign of Shamayel. 'Where is she?' he thought; 'I hope she hasn't gone to sleep!' People said, 'Why are you just standing there? Go on, strike, it's someone else's turn!' He said, 'Wait, I'm just summoning my strength.' He kept looking up, while raising his arm to strike, but there was still no sign of Shamayel at the penthouse window. He looked and looked – then suddenly, there she was. He took the hair from his pocket, wound it around the iron bar, raised the wooden axe, shouted *yallah!*, struck the iron bar – and it split in two.

Immediately, people fired their guns and shouted, 'Someone's completed the first task!'

Now for the second task. Jallât Khân took out the bandana that Shamayel had given him, and held it up into the wind. The buffalo was a vicious beast; if it met a donkey, a cow, or a man, it'd kill them without hesitation. Now it saw Jallât Khân and wanted to kill him. When he waved the bandana, it charged at him; but then it smelled the bandana, with Shamayel's scent on it. As the buffalo was busy sniffing at the bandana, Jallât Khân milked it into a bowl, then threw in Shamayel's ring and the milk turned to cheese in an instant. He climbed the tree with the bowl and climbed down again, without spilling a drop – it was cheese after all, which doesn't spill like milk.

So once again there was gunfire, because the second task had been completed. But the padishah was very angry that Jallât Khân had completed the first two tasks and was determined to chop his head off himself if he failed the third. He'd no idea that Jallât Khân was his own nephew.

For the third task, Jallât Khân remembered Mandoshâh, the ant-padishah, who'd given him a whisker and said, 'Whenever you need my help, burn it and smoke it, and we'll be at your service.' Jallât Khân took the whisker from his pocket and set fire to it, and instantly a vast army of ants appeared. Mandoshâh said, 'What are your orders?' Jallât Khân said, 'This, my third task: to separate all this millet and sesame before dawn. If it's not done by morning, Khunkâr Padishah will chop my head off!'

Mandoshâh told him not to worry; 'We'll get it done in half an hour.' The army of ants entered the room, and by midnight they'd separated the millet on one side, and the sesame seeds on the other – you've probably noticed how they collect grain from the fields, they're a real whizz at that, those ants. In the morning the padishah and the people came to see whether the grains had been separated or not. When they entered the room, they saw two piles of millet and sesame. They searched them thoroughly for a single grain out of place, but they were completely separated.

There followed great celebrations and merry-making. The padishah gave Jallât Khân his daughter in marriage, and handed him the throne for forty days. When he was padishah, Jallât Khân ordered them to take out Khunkâr's eyes, which they did – he still didn't know he was his uncle.

After his eyes had been removed, Khunkâr was still alive. At last he asked Jallât Khân, 'Where are you from? Who's your father?' Jallât Khân him the whole story: 'My father is Shâh-Selim Padishah. He told me that he came from another country, but his mother was angry with him, so he fled to his present country, where by God's will he became padishah.' He added, 'When he fled his country, he was with his brother. They came to a tree, and he, Shâh-Selim, lay deeply asleep under this tree. His brother saw him and thought he wasn't breathing, that he was dead, and went off to find people to help arrange the funeral. When he awoke, there was no trace of his brother. Then the parrot and mynah came …' – he told Khunkâr the whole story, just as I've told you already.

Now Khunkâr realized who he was: 'By God, you're my nephew!' and he wept and embraced him. Jallât Khân also wept and was so sorry for what he'd done. Khunkâr said, 'I didn't know you, and I killed your six brothers earlier – I should have given my daughter to one of you long ago. How complicated everything became, and what trouble was caused!' They sent word to Shâh-Selim Padishah, and the brothers were reunited in sorrow and joy.

And that's the end of my story, and if you're happy with it, so am I.

Getting Married

This is the central subject of Nancy's Bartered Brides; *she analyses the complex procedures, the lengthy negotiations, the colourful ceremonies, the multiple interested parties and the huge expenses of brideprice, trousseau and feasting involved in most marriages.*

The main narrators are Tumân's sons Pâdshâh (married seven years ago) and Baya-khân (next in line to get engaged). Each talked alone and independently. Other narrators are the widow and women's leader Neshtar, often with her eldest son Abdollah; her nephew Seyyed-shâh/Golusar; and her cousin Pâdshâh/Parwiz.

Engagement

Engagement (known variously as târ, fâteha, kozda, wëkrey) is considered irrevocable. There is no equivalent of 'fiancée' or 'fiancé'; once engaged, the couple are referred to as 'husband' (merë) and 'wife' (mayna); perhaps still 'boy' (hâlëk) and 'girl' (njëlëy); or 'bride' (nâwey) and 'groom' (zum).

Baya-khân – who's looking out for a wife himself – narrates.

Everyone chooses freely: a close relative, someone from the village, someone from far away, no relation at all – if you fancy her, and can afford her. Everyone will be after a beautiful girl. If she's plain, a poor man will take her, but if she has a rich father, people ignore her looks and only consider his wealth: 'If my father throws us out, then we can go to my father-in-law, he's got lots of land and sheep, he'll look after us!' A plain girl's behaviour is important: can she cook rice properly, for example. If they need a woman around the house, they'll consider how industrious she is, how well she can manage, and don't bother about her looks. If a plain woman has a pleasant personality and works hard, they'll take for her those qualities. But if she's pretty, they'll marry her without worrying about her work. A rich man can marry a pretty woman, and she'll sit idly beside her husband while servants do the work; or he'll get her a co-wife.

We have a saying: 'Even a sewing needle won't go without a husband.' So long as she has a hole, like the eye of a needle, every girl will get married one day. Since you've been here, have you found any woman who's remained unmarried? I never have. If a girl's ugly and lazy, it would be shameful for her father to go round asking people to take her. Some may do it, but the fact is that here, however ugly a girl is, someone will marry her. Occasionally a girl says, with her father's approval, 'I don't want a husband, I'll stay here.' Like Bulbul, the blind girl in uncle Khoshdel's house. Nobody'll marry a blind girl. If a girl's plain, it doesn't matter so long as she can see. But what can you do with a blind girl? She's no use, she can't work properly. Bulbul hasn't married, and says she doesn't want to. Her father will look after her.

When Gorey asked for Mowzoddin's daughter, in truth, the girl didn't want him; she's young and he's old, and that's very bad. Several times this year she said, 'I won't have him, I'll call out some other man.' Despite my father's threats, she refused to marry Gorey: 'I'm young, he's a greybeard, it's not right.' The women of their house said she'd call someone out, but she hasn't yet.

If a girl calls out someone's name, he must marry her. His honour's at stake; he'll die rather than let anyone else have her; it'd be cowardly not to stand up for her. And after all, she comes free – there'll be no brideprice. They're betrothed according to sharia. You can go to the government and get it registered. But it doesn't happen often. Once a Bakhtyâri girl called out Seyf-khân's son. He took the poor girl to the bazaar and spent some nights with her; but the poor chap had no money and no *qawm* to support him, and there was a dispute for a year or two. They paid bribes and got her back. If he'd had *qawmi* support, they couldn't have taken her from him. She had no ID; when he took her to the judge to do the nikah contract, he asked for her ID card number. She said, 'I haven't got one.' The judge said, 'Take her back to her father.'

When you've chosen a girl, your father sends some greybeards and a mullah to her father, who'll serve them a meal. After the meal, and some tea, the delegation make their proposal; the mullah recites the *fâteha*, and the visitors say, 'We've been sent to ask for your daughter.' If the father approves, he'll consult his brother and his father – if they live together – and his wife, saying, 'So-and-so's sent a delegation asking for our daughter; what do you think? If you're happy, let's give her.' They discuss it. If they agree, he'll come back and tell the visitors. But if they don't, he'll say, 'Sorry, we couldn't agree; my wife, or my son, didn't like the idea. We can't give her.' The visitors go home disappointed. Sometimes the father pays no heed to what his brother or his wife says, and just gives her. Nobody can stop him if he does.

Neshtar

There are three stages to marriage: *târ, khoshey* and *toy.* The *târ* or *wëkrey* is when they give the girl to the boy. A poor man does only the *târ*, not the *khoshey*; while a wealthy man does both, and after the *khoshey* he has a big *toy*, with lots of entertainment and music.

At the *târ* they recite the *fâteha*, they give scarves, they say *Allahu-Akbar*. After that, she belongs to him. If her father's wealthy, many men gather, and he gives lots of scarves, ten, twenty or more. They put the scarves in the turban of the groom's brother or nephew, and send him off, then they fire their guns and celebrate.

Seyyed-shâh/Golusar

In earlier days, old people tell us, we were simple. If Richard had a daughter, someone would just say, 'Give her to me!' Richard would answer, 'Why not?' 'Give me a *târ*, a thread.' Then Richard would tear a strip off his turban right there, give it to him and name a brideprice. Just like that. There was no praying. When the groom had produced the brideprice, he'd hold the wedding and take her.

The brideprice was fixed; he'd ask, say, 20,000 rupees and that was it. People weren't so money-grabbing. There was lots of wealth. He'd ask 5,000 for the girl, and he'd get goods worth 100,000 today. A sheep was one rupee, 1 *qerân* [½ *rupee*], 3 *qerân*. My grandfather said, 'I was a servant for one *qerân* a month!' People were that simple. Money had *barakat*. Now nobody will be a servant for 500 rupees.

Pâdshâh/Parwiz

If you went to town with 1 rupee, you could buy a horse-load of cloth: damask, silk, whatever you wanted. Sheep were plentiful, everything was abundant. People would be amazed if anyone paid 20,000 for a wife. 'What sort of woman can this be?'

Nowadays it's tough. If you take a sack-full of cash you can't get a horse-load of cloth. The population has increased, and brideprices are expensive. A girl who can't even wipe her own nose fetches 50,000 and 100 sheep; or 30,000 and 80 sheep. For example, when I got uncle Mahd-Amin's daughter for my brother, I gave 85 sheep and 50,000 for her.

Pâdshâh/Tumân wants to give the complete picture.

First, a man needs a wife. We get a wife in the following way. If my parents are alive, then my father, my mother, my sisters, my aunts, my uncles, my cousins, everybody will look round for a good-looking girl for me. She should be pretty, well-behaved, good-tempered, hard-working, and chaste; a good, modest girl – not like Rangin's daughter.

When we have a girl in mind, first my father sends his own wife or sister to inspect her, to see whether she has any faults, whether she's cheeky, plain, lazy. This is done very discreetly, as her family won't like it if they suspect someone's come to look their daughter over. After this discreet inspection, we wait for a month or so, then we send another special secret envoy, an independent woman, asking her too to take a good look at the girl, her manners, her looks, her character, her family. She'll report back; if she approves of the girl and her family, a few days later we'll send some more women – for example my sister, my mother, an aunt – to see the girl.

If that goes well, then we send a formal delegation of five village elders – you, my father, Haji Ghâfur, for example – to our prospective in-laws; you also take a mullah. As they approach the house on horseback, some women will come out and sprinkle water in their path, three or four times. This is for blessing: 'Let our daughter be a blessing to them, may God let her grow old with them!' It's an invocation passed down from the ancestors, over many generations. Those women aren't from the in-laws' family, but their own sisters-in-law, neighbours or some other relative. The visitors tip them, though it's up to you whether to tip; it's the same for everybody, my father, my brother. It's a matter of reputation; people will remark on who gave how much to the water-sprinklers. Such a thing is important for us Afghans! When Manân and Gol-Ahmad were engaged to each other's sisters that spring, you saw how it was Nâder-shâh Khân, not my father, who tipped the sprinkler. Sometimes you'll see a man give something and his father won't say anything. It's a matter of each individual's own self-esteem. My father can't force me to give something because I'm with him; he'll give something if I don't.

Anyway, when the elders arrive, boys come out and take care of the horses. The hosts serve tea, then rice or meat-broth. After the meal, you make your proposal. 'Give your daughter to our son' – you name him. The girl's father may agree, but his brother may object: 'No, we won't give her out of the family.' If this happens, then the delegates and all the girl's family will try to win him round, so that everybody's happy.

Then they discuss brideprice. It'll be either 100 sheep and 50,000 rupees; or 80 sheep and 40,000, or 90 sheep and 45,000. There should be twice as many sheep as the cash amount in thousands.

When they've agreed the brideprice, they do the *târ*. The bride's side provide a *târ*: a long white cloth, or some nice scarves with lace embroidery, like on Nancy's veil, on a tray, covering some sweets. They set the tray before the mullah, who holds up the scarves, recites a homily and some verses, then asks the daughter's representative – father, brother, uncle or some other close relative – 'Richard, is your daughter's name such-and-such?' You respond, 'Yes.' He also asks her father's and grandfather's names. Then he asks the boy's side: 'What's your son's name?' 'His name's Baya-khân,' and so on.

Then he says, 'Richard, do you give your daughter Shahzâd (let's say), your only daughter of this name, to Baya-khân, Tumân's only son of this name?' You say, 'I gave her to him, I give her, I've given her.' Then he asks the boy's father, 'Do you take Richard's only daughter named Shahzâd for your only son named Baya-khân?' He says, 'I took her, I take her, I've taken her.' They repeat these words three times before the seated gathering.

The mullah hands the *târ* to the groom's side; he says two or three more *takbirs*, and it's done, there's no going back. It's most important that a mullah should be there, to make it *shar'i* [*sharia-compliant*]; without a mullah, it's just *orpi* [*customary*], and things can go wrong. Without a mullah and five proper witnesses, people can cause trouble later: 'Where are your witnesses?' A mullah's a powerful witness.

Immediately after the *târ*, people leave the room and fire their guns, as often as they like: once, ten or a hundred times; it's important for there to be gunfire. Then they depart; but before they go, they put down some cash: a few thousand rupees, 10,000 to 20,000 if they're wealthy. They count this first payment right there. And they agree a date for the *khoshey* ceremony: a few days later, maybe a couple of months. The boy's father asks the girl's father to be ready to host the *khoshey* party on such-and-such a day. Now you may have agreed to this, but one of his brothers may say: 'I wasn't allowed to object earlier. All right, you've given her, but I won't agree to a *khoshey*. Aren't you ashamed at the idea? He gave you money, why don't you give me some?' It's a matter of placating him; it may take a month or two, even a year, before he comes round; anyway, people will pressure him to withdraw his objections.

Meanwhile at home, after the men leave, the groom's mother gathers the women, and they sing. When the men bring the scarves, they hang them on those sticks and the women come and comment; some like them, others complain: 'These women were lazy, or clumsy, the scarves are no good!' They're women, after all; each says different things!

The women sing songs until evening; they're fed rice, then raisins and sweets and so on. As the women leave, the groom's sister or aunt, someone especially close, distributes the scarves, tearing them in half if there aren't enough. His mother keeps some back, to be given later to the daughters-in-law. That's the end of that.

Baya-khân's version.

Once the girl's family agrees to give her, they discuss the brideprice. Girls go for 100 sheep, 50,000 rupees; others for 80 sheep and 40,000 rupees. A very wealthy man will give as much as one lac cash and 150 sheep for some women in Afghanistan. On the first day they'll hand over 10,000 to 20,000 cash, or maybe only 2,000 to 5,000; it depends how well off they are. They'll give as much as they can – they want to pay it off as soon as possible.

When they've agreed the brideprice, the bride's family bring a tray with the *târ*: on the tray are sweets, covered by some scarves – always an odd number, never even: one scarf is all right, but some people, for prestige, give three or five, or as many as seven, of different colours; most people prefer white ones. Each scarf has a strip of fine lace embroidery or gold thread. Inside they put rock sugar – they say, 'God make the girl and boy sweet together like this' – wheat, to make their land fertile, and cloves – they have a nice, strong smell – to make them nice to each other. Some women put in a black raisin, or a sheep dropping, pierced by a needle; this is to make the bride hard-working, so that the husband doesn't scold her.

The mullah holds the scarves up in his hand, like this. Then he recites a homily; he asks the girl's father, 'Have you given this girl to this man's son?' He replies, 'Yes, I've given her to this man's son.' He asks the boy's father, 'Have you accepted?' and he answers 'I've accepted, I accept, and it's accepted.' They both say it, three times each. Then people say *Allahu-Akbar*, and they distribute the sweets. They also announce the brideprice, for example 100 sheep and 50,000 rupees, so that it's publicly witnessed and no one can deny it later. There are perhaps fifteen or twenty witnesses.

They take the scarves and tie them to a boy's turban – the groom's brother or cousin. Then the visitors distribute the sweets, come out and fire their guns, and off they all go, back to the groom's father's house. When they arrive, the women are gathered, singing songs. They hang up the scarves, tied to a stick or something; everyone throws sweets or raisins or sugar-lumps at the scarves, and the small children scrabble for them. If they really want to be remembered, they serve the women guests rice. When they've eaten, the women disperse.

Marrying relatives

Like other Muslims, Pashtuns allow marriage of first cousins; unusually among Muslims, it is not a preference. However, most people prefer to marry into a family that they already know or are related to. Baya-khân expresses his opinion.

Some men like to take a brother's daughter for their son – his first cousin – but he has no claim on her; it doesn't matter if she marries someone else. But if you ask your brother for his daughter for your son, he's unlikely to turn you down. He thinks, 'She'll be with my nephew, we'll be together, we'll stay friends for ever.' An uncle won't ask much brideprice. It's up to the boy; if he doesn't want her, he can marry someone else. But sometimes his father will force him to take her, and he won't be able to object.

If you want a maternal cousin, fine; a maternal uncle too won't take much brideprice. Paternal and maternal uncles are the same – it depends how well you get on with them. If your father's dead and you're poor, or times are bad, you'll probably go to your paternal uncle first for help. Other relatives are unlikely to lend you anything: 'You'll lose it, how will I get it back?' I suppose people aren't as close to a paternal as a maternal uncle. If your maternal uncle's a good man, you could be lifelong friends. But it varies a lot; some prefer their paternal uncle, others dislike him and marry their maternal uncle's daughter.

Pâdshâh, already married to a distant cousin, broadens the perspective.

People say: 'You can't do better than your own ewe's lamb', which means that no girl's as good as one from your own people. Strangers won't give you a good girl; they'll give you one who's jinn-possessed, crazy or stupid, or a flirt who smiles at everybody – you know the kind! She's unlikely to make a good wife. A good woman won't leave her own village. If her own people won't marry her, they'll pass her off on someone from the wilds, or another tribe. If you take a bad animal to market, once it's sold, they can't return it. How could they know? It's the same with women.

If you want a good girl from a distant tribe, you'll need a lot of money. They'll ask double the rate. But such a wife will be more respected than one from your own family. If she's from Sheberghân, Maymana, Sar-e-pol or somewhere far away, she'll have no family here; she'll be on her own and people will quickly take to her. If she's good-looking, behaves modestly and works hard, we'll all treat her well; we'll make allowances for the fact that she's a stranger, far from home. Of course, if she's a bad woman, we'll scold her, beat her, curse her, even if she's from far away!

It's commendable to marry a woman who already knows your family; why give a daughter or a niece to a stranger from another tribe? We have a saying: 'If charity is the norm at home, who needs a mosque?' With an insider, if someone scolds her or beats her, it has no consequences, it's a family matter; however much you scold her, it's commendable that she's in her own house. When you marry a cousin, her children will be fully members of the family. If you bring a stranger into the family, her children will be yours, but one strand in their heredity will be unknown, possibly warped.

Pâdshâh/Parwiz explains the importance of 'sworn' brothers and sisters.

When you have a 'sworn' sister or brother,[1] you call them just 'sister', *khur*, or 'brother', *wrur*. There's no special way of entering such a relationship, it's just something that's said. If I tell you you're my sister, it'll last a hundred years. If we're both pure in heart, then we'll help each other in the other world, more than brothers or sisters by the same father. So long as the brother–sister feeling's in the heart, so long as we're true and not dishonestly motivated, then in the other world we're the same as our own siblings. But if one person has sinful intentions, it'll be bad for them in the other world.

The Book says 'sworn' brothers and sisters can help each other in the next world, after they die. If you and I are 'sworn' brother and sister, and we die, then if I've fallen somewhat short in my piety, you can come and say, 'You're my brother', and take some merit from your own store of piety to make up what I'm missing. Or the other way round. We each compete to make sure that God forgives the other, if we're 'sworn' brother and sister. Actual brothers and sisters are no use to each other in that world; each wants to make the most of their own share of piety, and they don't care for each other.

Nothing will come between 'sworn' brothers and sisters, even if their respective families are hostile. If your people don't like me, then I'll come to you and say, 'Sister,

---

[1] Persian: *Barâdar/khâhar-khând*; Pashtu: *wrur/khur-balâli* – literally 'invited/mentioned brother/sister'.

what's the matter?' If your people want to kill me – or the other way – then we'll communicate secretly; you'll tell me, 'Brother, don't come by day, they'll kill you.' If your people find out that I'm with you – 'Pâdshâh's here!' – you'll quickly get up and say, 'Who says? He isn't here.' You lock the door and hide me; after all, you're my sister. I'll do the same for you, my 'sworn' sister, if I can. That's what happened with Paroddin after he shot Soleymân-shâh [*see p. 86*]; his 'sworn' sister Pastu, Hazâr-khân's mother, hid him.

Pâdshâh/Parwiz, Neshtar and Seyyed-shâh discuss some of the complications of marrying relatives.

(*Seyyed-shâh*) – With us, it's fine for to ask your brother for his daughter for your son. It doesn't matter if they grew up in the same household, so long as they haven't had the same milk.

(*Neshtar*) – If either's been suckled by the other's mother, then in the Book they're like brother and sister and completely forbidden to each other. Sometimes two close paternal cousins have lived in the same household since they were small. When they're grown up, the boy's father may say, 'I'll get your cousin for your wife.' The boy may say, 'But she's like my sister, I won't have her.' His heart won't let him marry her, and whatever the father says won't make any difference.

You can't marry two sisters at the same time. But you and your brother can marry two sisters. My sons did just that!

(*Pâdshâh/Parwiz*) – If I'm 'sworn-brother' with someone, like Seyyed-shâh, then my wife becomes his sister, and forbidden to him; and his wife Khâsak becomes, by God, even closer than my own sister. So, whenever I come I can ask Khâsak to make me tea; and I pay no attention, and lie down here, just like with my real sister or mother. But if someone does this with evil intent in his heart, it's worse than anything; it's like incest with his own mother. So if you call someone sister, and you have other intentions in your heart, that's *lewâtat*, which is the same as *zenâ*.[2]

(*Seyyed-shâh*) – Your wife's sister's forbidden to you; they'd be sisters-in-law as well as sisters, and that would make things very difficult. *Nârawâ*, forbidden, is the same as *zenâ*. If brother and sister, or mother and son, or father and daughter sleep together, that's both *zenâ* and *nârawâ*; the man should be killed, God will send the killer to heaven. And it's *zenâ* if a woman sleeps with her brother-in-law in her husband's absence, e.g. on military service.

(*Neshtar*) – That does happen, occasionally. It's not so terrible.

(*Pâdshâh/Parwiz*) – No, it's utterly forbidden. After all, the bastard's taken his own sister-in-law and fucked her!

(*Seyyed-shâh*) – It's even worse than *zenâ*. She should be like his sister.

(*Neshtar*) – If the husband dies, his brother's an heir, and he may marry his sister-in-law.

(*Pâdshâh/Parwiz*) – It's not *rawâ* for this woman to go to anyone besides her brother-in-law. She has no right. But if he doesn't take her, he can give her permission to marry wherever she wants.

[2] This is a popular understanding of Islamic law regarding forbidden sexual relations.

(*Neshtar*) – Our people say in Pashtu, *marg haqq, mirâs halâl*; once the husband dies, his legacy is permitted to his heirs.

Exchange marriage (*mëkhi*)

A common form of marriage, though it is morally dubious, is the direct exchange, commonly of a son and a daughter from each of two families. Nancy has analysed direct exchange in detail (N. Tapper 1981). Baya-khân explains.

Some people do exchange marriages; they give daughters to each other's sons, but it's not really a good thing. For example, if one husband beats his wife and her brother hears about it, he'll say, 'Why did he beat my sister?' and he'll beat his wife in turn. If he won't let your sister go home for a visit, you'll do the same to his sister; or if one bride goes home for two nights, and the other stays for four or five, the first will complain that it's not fair. It can escalate. Exchange marriage is such a bad thing! If you marry for brideprice, it makes no difference if you beat her or not; she's not so dependent on what her brother does.

There's no money involved in an exchange. For example, my father this year promised his daughter Khurak to Haji Ghâfur's son Gol-Ahmad, in exchange for Golak [*for his son Manân*], with no brideprice involved. The boy takes some cash when he goes to *bâzi* [*see below*], otherwise nothing. At the *târ* in Khâni-âghâ's tent, the mullah asked my father, 'How much do you want?' He said, 'Three lacs,' and the mullah prayed over 3 lacs, what we call an 'open price'; so my father has the right to claim 3 lacs from Haji Ghâfur. But he won't, they're close family after all, first cousins.

Someone with many sons and daughters may try to do exchanges, to save on brideprice; or he may marry the girls elsewhere, to bring in brideprices to pay for wives for his sons. But few people do exchanges. It's better not to do it. The brothers-in-law compete with each other; it can lead to disputes and violence.

Mahd-Omar isn't a poor man, but he has six daughters and doesn't see why he should pay for wives for his sons, so he does exchanges for them. If the couples do quarrel, it won't be serious. If he himself gets angry, he has the authority as father-in-law, so his son-in-law comes to kiss his hand and apologize, and they're reconciled. It's that kind of thing.

Pâdshâh and his wife Pâkhâl were married in an exchange with his sister Zeytun and Pâkhâl's brother Payz; but he speaks here in hypothetical terms.

If I've given my sister to someone and married his sister myself, after the weddings I might lose my temper one day and hit my wife for some reason – it can happen! – or curse her parents. Then the gossips – Afghanistan's full of gossips; when I'm not there, he'll tell you what I said, and when you're gone he'll tell me what you said – the gossips might go sneakily and tell her father's family, 'Your poor daughter's suffering; whenever I go there they're quarrelling, he's beating her. Don't you care what happens to her? You've given your daughter away – What's the matter with you?' If they're sensible, they know that my sister's blameless; everyone's responsible only for their own mistakes. But if her husband's stupid, he'll find some fault with her work and take it out on her, for his own sister's beating. She cries, 'Why beat me? For God's sake, I've done nothing wrong!'

That's why people say exchange marriage is bad; if one husband beats his wife, the other feels compelled to beat his own, or at least to scold her. People used to do exchange marriages, but now they've become smarter, they avoid it for this very reason, to prevent quarrels. Instead, they give their daughters for brideprice.

In-laws (*khish*)

As Baya-khân notes, when a father considers a spouse for his son or daughter, whatever a candidate's personal 'qualifications', it is the in-laws' status and the potential of relationship with them that counts for most.

For some people, it's important to have a wealthy father-in-law, even if his daughter's not much good. They think, 'If my father ever turns me out, I can go and live with my father-in-law; he's wealthy, he'll look after me.'

A girl who's unhappily married to a greybeard can't return to her father. Occasionally a man gives his daughter to a wealthy old man against her wishes; but not if he's really old, only someone like my father, perhaps. But nobody listens to the girl. A father never consults his daughter: 'Do you like so-and-so?' And she'll never say who she wants to marry. If she cries and says, 'I won't marry that man!' too bad; if her father wants to give her, there's nothing she can do.

But he won't give his daughter to a bad family; he'll look into it. 'Bad' means they have no property; if he sees that they haven't got much in the household, he won't give her. Generally, a rich man gives his daughter to a rich man, and a poor man takes a poor man's daughter. If a poor man's daughter's really beautiful, a rich man may want her, and he'll be happy to give her: 'I can go and live beside him, and I'll do well there.' He won't get as much brideprice as a rich father would, but if he has another daughter, he'll get a higher brideprice for her; instead of 30,000 or 40,000 rupees, he might ask for 150 sheep and 1 lac, or 100 sheep and 50,000 rupees.

Pâdshâh says in-laws can be better than family.

When we marry, we see our in-laws regularly; we have very warm relations with them – I don't know if it's the same with you people. We say in Pashtu, 'Affinity's rope is long' [*tanaw dë khishey wuzhd*]; this means, once you and I are in-laws, our relationship is forever. However much we quarrel, even if there's a killing, we'll be on bad terms for a month or two, even a year, but eventually we'll be reconciled because of our relationship. My daughter, or my sister, lives with you; I need to visit her or fetch her home for a visit.

Relationships with in-laws can be better than family, all things considered. If your own family behave properly, do right by you, deal with you openly, that's best. But if they treat you badly, it can be worse than anything a stranger can do to you. Strangers will make peace, but family quarrels can go on forever. With our own family, one day we quarrel about a camel, the next over some hay, the next over some water, or a shepherd. That's how it goes: we're always up and down with each other.

Strangers aren't partners in your land, your sheep, your pastures; their lands are elsewhere, they take their water from another canal – so there's nothing for you to quarrel about, nothing to spoil warm relations between in-laws. If two in-laws quarrel about a camel, they soon make peace. It lasts a few months at most; or some big man, like Richard or Haji, brings us together: 'Why are you upset with each other? There's no feud between you. If you're upset today, in ten years you'll have made it up by yourselves, so why don't you make it up now?' The elders scold us and take me to your place – or the other way round – and there'll be a reconciliation feast.

Brideprice

Most marriages involve brideprice (Pashtu: wĕlwar, Persian/Uzbeki: kâlin), a payment of sheep and cash (but possibly including other items) from the groom's father to the bride's. Brideprices in 1971–72 commonly amounted to an ordinary worker's income for several years. In most families, household productive activities are geared towards making payments on the next marriage. It is clearly a huge investment, and the risks are considerable, as Nancy shows in Bartered Brides.

Baya-khân outlines the requirements.

Brideprice is the Afghan custom. We don't get wives for free, but for money: you can pay it off in sheep, cash, camels, a gun, anything. The money isn't about compensating the father for the loss of his daughter's labour. Whatever he gets, he'll spend on her trousseau. He'll send her to her husband with up to 60,000 rupees-worth of clothes and household goods: ten to fifteen outfits, ten veils, four or five bolsters, bedding bags, large and small storage-sacks, saddlebags, black felts, carpets, a sewing-machine, tea-pots, etc. All he'll keep will be a few sheep and some cash.

For a close relative, from the same village, perhaps he won't take so much; he'll put a high price on her, what we call an 'open price', say two lacs, but he won't take it all. He'll say, 'It's not important, we're relatives.'

When brothers live in the same household, they're partners and they share the brideprices paid for any of their daughters. A father doesn't say, 'She's my daughter, I'll keep it all.' But if they're in separate households, he'll keep his daughter's brideprice; his brothers have no claim. Similarly, if the bride's father lives separately from his own father – like Khâni-âghâ for example – the brideprice goes only to him, his father has no claim. But he may give his father some, if he chooses.

As for the boy's father, he has to find the brideprice himself, his relatives won't help him. Except that, at the end, when he's finished paying and is preparing for the wedding, often the groom will go round the village, or the camps, and ask his friends and relatives for *nimawri*. They'll give him a sheep or a goat, or some cash: 1,000 rupees if they can afford it, but only 100 if they're poor. It varies a lot. When he comes round, it's entirely up to us whether we give anything. It might all come to a few thousand rupees, at most 10,000. With this, he'll buy rice and ghee for the wedding.

The brideprice must be paid up before the wedding. Well, the bride's father has the right to demand it all, but some take pity. If they're cousins or from closely related families, as I said, some people will let the groom off a few thousand rupees, or perhaps some of the sheep. They may have agreed on 50,000 rupees and 100 sheep, for example, but it's up to the bride's father how much he takes. God willing, he'll let the groom off the last 10,000 rupees or so; and if the groom's handed over 70 or 80 sheep, he may let him off the last twenty. Some do, some don't. But if he's delivered the whole lot, he has the right to get one sheep back; we call it *sarwandárey*, 'for the milking-rope.' He'll get that one sheep, no more. As for the cash, he'll pay it all and get none of it back; particularly if they're from a different sub-tribe.

Some people give the sheep stated in the brideprice, but if you have no sheep, you give just cash, at an agreed rate. When Abdor-Rahmân married Jân-Mahmad's daughter, they agreed on 80 or 90 ewes – I think – and that he'd give 600 rupees per ewe. But you'll give sheep if you have them. You don't give lambs or old sheep, but young ewes; not the best or the worst, but middling ones. Then it depends on the going rate. In years when the best are worth 1,000 rupees, and second-rate ones 600 to 700, they'll give cash at the 600 to 700 rate. With a high brideprice, one or one-and-a-half lacs, they may rate the sheep at 1,000 rupees even if their real value is only 600. So people who have sheep may well give only sheep. But some people have no sheep, so they can't.

For relatives, too, they write down a high rate for the sheep, for example 1,000 rupees; or they rate at 10,000 rupees something worth only 5,000 to 6,000, for example a good camel – not a hybrid, though. So the brideprice is inflated, for relatives. But if they're not relatives, the bride's father may well keep to the market value, no concessions.

Pâdshâh/Parwiz adds.

If you're getting my daughter for 60 sheep, you don't give them all at once. I'll send someone over; you count out the sheep I'm due and he'll bring them to me. I'll send back two or three as *sarwandarey*. The debt's paid. When the sheep arrive at my home, there's no ceremony; I'm happy to see them of course, but I'll just put them with my own animals. I'll remember which ones came in the brideprice, for sure. We know the history of every sheep, just as we do with the camels.

Some people don't give *sarwandarey*; it's entirely up to the bride's father. Mahd-Amin didn't give me one *sarwandarey* [*when he gave a daughter to Pâdshâh's younger brother Sarwar*]. I didn't say a word – I had no right to it, I had to accept his decision. It didn't matter. If he'd given it, very good; people would talk of it.

Pâdshâh/Tumân explains the difference between 'open' (mosamma) and 'fixed' (kotara) brideprices.

An 'open' brideprice means it isn't fixed on the first day in front of the mullahs: whatever the bride's father asks for, whether 1,000 rupees or ten lacs, the groom can't refuse. He has to satisfy his father-in-law. Nowadays people are much sharper and smarter, they always fix things on the first day: 'Fix your daughter's brideprice; for example, if you want sheep at 500 or 1,000, fix it now.' But with an open brideprice, you can take whatever you want.

When Haji Molk got Talâk for his son Gollu, he agreed to an open brideprice. Jân-Mahmad promised Talâk when she was very small, and Haji Molk gave something

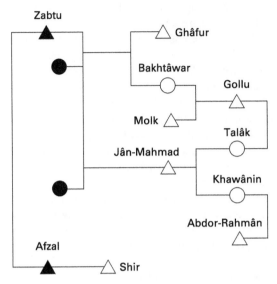

Figure 11 Ghâfur and Molk.

every year, not one great lump sum. Jân-Mahmad kept things to himself; nobody knows what he got, but altogether, including some 40 sheep and everything, he must have taken 90,000 rupees, perhaps a lac. Haji Molk couldn't say, 'This is what we fixed on the first day,' because nothing was fixed. But for the sake of kinship, Jân-Mahmad probably took only 80,000 to 90,000, including the sheep; he must have paid 50,000 to 60,000 for the trousseau: clothes, rugs, carpets, bedding, felts and so on. [*See Fig. 11*]

When he gave Khawânin to Abdor-Rahmân, Jân-Mahmad took much the same as for Talâk, 80,000 to 90,000 including sheep and other things. But Abdor-Rahmân is no relative, so it cost him more than it did Haji Molk; and Jân-Mahmad gave much less back in the trousseau.

Haji Ghâfur's close to us; Shir and the others are further; Haji Molk and the Khârkashis are further still, and Abdor-Rahmân is further away from us than they are. The further away someone is, the more the brideprice. For example, Mowzoddin gave his daughter Potsaki to Mahd-Amin Ghiljai for a high brideprice. He wouldn't have got as much for her within the village. You ask less from your relatives than from a stranger; 'You're family,' you say, 'and if family means nothing on a day like this, when will it mean anything? One day, you'll help me out.'

Akhtar gave his daughter Fâtema to Rawu's son Râmoddin ten years ago when she was tiny. They agreed a brideprice of 35,000 rupees. If Rawu'd paid it when it was agreed, Akhtar would have accepted it, but now she's nearly grown up, he won't any longer. If it had been fixed before a mullah and five respected elders, it would still be 35,000; but since it was done before a bunch of youths, without a proper religious ceremony, the agreement's invalid. Akhtar can ask whatever he likes. It's up to him. Best if he accepts the 35,000; but he's saying, 'There were no Hajis, mullahs or elders to witness it; a boy's word isn't enough. I want 80 sheep and 40,000.' He'll make a huge fuss, and eventually he'll get 50,000 to 60,000.

Rawu got that girl when she was very small. If she turns out well, fine, and if the brideprice was fixed, it'll stay the same, even if she turns out plain-looking. You can't tell how a small girl will turn out; it's only when she's grown up that you know whether she's pretty or plain. I expect it's the same with you. Grown women with good qualities – light-skinned, a pretty nose, hard-working – fetch high prices. It'll be less if she turns out bad; her father will worry, 'What shall we do with her, she's too dark, her nose is unattractive, her eyes are bad.' If she's good-looking, even if her family's poor she'll fetch a good price. As for the daughter of a Haji or a rich man, however plain or lazy she is, someone will pay a lot. If a relative doesn't take her, someone from far away will, from Pakhizai, Nâmanzai, Baluch.

No women are as expensive as ours, in these two villages of Khârkash. Torkheyl and Pakhizai women are expensive too, but not as much as here. Out in the western steppe, when they still had all those sheep, their women were even more expensive than ours: 100 sheep. But this year all their sheep died, and nobody will take their women.

Neshtar resumes her account of the procedures.

That first day, when they're giving the *târ*, they'll decide on the brideprice: 30,000 rupees, 40,000, 1 lac, 2 lacs. The groom will pay it off gradually, according to his means: one day he'll give 20,000, another day 10,000, another day 1,000 – whatever he can afford.

The brideprice is higher for a beautiful girl; also, if the young man's fallen in love, the brideprice will be tough. If the fathers are brothers, even if the couple are in love, it'll be much less. But when their families are far apart, the brideprice will be tougher and higher. If a boy's in love with his maternal uncle's daughter, and his uncle likes him, he'll take less brideprice; but if he's a hard man, he'll take a lot. But that's true of paternal uncles too.

The girl's father may dislike the boy and demand a huge brideprice; but if he later sees he's a good boy, he'll let him off some of it. If he sees, 'Our bridegroom's poor, he hasn't got much,' he'll let him off several thousand rupees. But if he doesn't like him, he'll take it all!

If the brideprice was fixed at, say, 1 lac of rupees, and the boy later goes off and becomes a thief, the brideprice won't go up. Whatever he does, they gave their word. Even if he gets sick or goes mad, it's the same; the deal they agreed on the day of the betrothal can't be changed.

With her son Abdollah's help, Neshtar continues.

At the *târ*, when they agree the brideprice, they also fix the rate for the sheep. Brideprice for a nice girl is 100 sheep and 50,000 rupees. If the girl's father wishes, he may let them off a bit, but he may take it all. Her family will prepare good clothes for her, nice dresses, felts and rugs, bedding and pillows, then the boy's father fetches rice and ghee and musicians for the wedding.

If they agree 50,000 rupees cash, it can be paid in animals or anything you like, so long as the bride's father is satisfied. He may let you give wheat and barley, camels, wool, rugs, guns ... anything he's willing to take. If he's happy with the boy, he'll raise the values of any animals, take a camel worth 2,000 for 5,000, for example. Last year sheep were worth 200, this year they're 1,000, so now they try to pay off the cash in high-value sheep.

Baya-khân has more to say on the difficulties of paying off the brideprice.

A boy may go and work for his father-in-law before the nikah, if he's nearby. The father-in-law will call on him to help bringing in his hay, daubing his house or watering his sheep. There's nothing wrong with going to help like that, staying over a couple of nights. But it would be wrong to go and live there, like a woman after she's been married. We laugh at someone who goes to live with his father-in-law: 'Other men marry their wives, this man's wife has married him!' Afghans find this ridiculous. If he likes his son-in-law, after he's married the girl and worked for him for some years, he'll let them go wherever they want. But if they don't get on, he'll tell him angrily, 'I've let you off 40 or 50,000, I've fed you, and you haven't worked here enough; you must stay and work some more. Go home to your father for a couple of nights if you want, but you must come back.'

It's up to the father-in-law whether he reduces the brideprice; if he likes him, then maybe he'll let him off some of it, saying, 'She's my daughter; if I take all my son-in-law's wealth, what will my daughter have to eat in future?'

It isn't our custom to say, 'Hurry up and pay the money.' A bride here's like a pawn-pledge to be redeemed. You don't force it. The only force is when the groom comes and says, 'Give me my bride.' Then her father can say, 'There's still 10,000 left to pay!' Even if it's untrue he can demand it. But he'd never go himself and ask for payment. It's up to the boy to plead with him to release her, perhaps to be excused the last few thousand rupees. The girl's father will never plead with him. Why? Because the girl's father doesn't care, while the groom does – people laugh at him if he doesn't hold the wedding and his bride stays in her father's house.

Suppose a man has several sons and only 100 or 150 sheep; after finding wives for two or three sons, he'll have no sheep left. Then his other sons must go and work as shepherds, herdsmen, farmhands, labourers. They'll manage somehow, but they won't be able to afford rich men's daughters. They'll find wives at 40,000 or 50,000 rupees, and work to pay off the brideprice gradually.

A wealthy man with no sons may take another wife. But even if his first wife has borne sons, he may marry as many as four, or three, even five. An ordinary man with a wife who hasn't born children won't take another wife while she's still alive. It's all a matter of wealth. We have a saying, 'A man leaves wives, a dog [*i.e. miser*] leaves wealth' [*dë merë shëza patezhi, dë spi dunya*].

Going to bâzi

Once the best part of the brideprice has been paid, traditionally there is a further ceremony, the khoshey, *when – so long as they are old enough – they can begin* bâzî. Bâzi *is a courtship ritual the Piruzai greatly enjoy. If the two families get on well, the groom is expected to visit his bride at night in her father's home, supposedly by stealth. Then they can whisper, pet and sleep together well before the marriage ceremonies are completed and the bride is brought to her husband's home.*

Headwoman Neshtar explains.

Some months after the *târ* they do the *khoshey*, which is when the groom starts going to *bâzi*. The boy's father must prepare rice and meat to feed all the women and girls, who wear their best clothes, play the drum, sing and dance. The men go off to the bride's family, who cook some 10 maunds of rice. By then the father's received much of the brideprice, so he too takes a lot of trouble and expense.

Then ten or twenty fellows, good boys and men, take the groom to his in-laws; their hosts henna their hands and serve them rice, and the guests throw money in the tray; in return the hosts give them nice scarves, hats, turbans, cloaks; then they go home, leaving the groom behind. They henna his hands and they lead him to the sleeping place, and he sleeps with his wife. When he gets up in the morning he puts a few hundred rupees under the mattress. The woman who collects the bedding gets the money – it could be his bride's mother, her sister, whoever. He only pays on the first night; after that, he goes alone – and it's free! He goes for three nights, and after that whenever he wants.

Baya-khân is unmarried, but has been in parties taking grooms to bâzi.

After a few months, they do a *khoshey* for the boy. Men and women gather; the men ride over to the bride's place. Their hosts feed them and present them with scarves and a *bëni*, which is like a clothes-bag, but made from two or three metres of brightly coloured cotton or silk cloth, red or green. They fill it with sweets and raisins, which they take home to the groom's mother, who distributes the sweets.

Then they take the boy to *bâzi*. *Bâzi* – in Persian they say *kangalbâzi* – is when he goes to visit his wife at her father's house. His father invites some of the boy's close friends and relatives; they gather and take him off to the in-laws, who cook rice and meat for them. Her father doesn't know; if he does, he keeps quiet about it, but since he might object, they say nothing too. Her mother does know, but she doesn't say anything; she lets them in. The guests arrive and sit down; a boy washes their hands, and they give him 10 or 20 rupees – up to 50 if they're well off – to thank him for the hand-wash; they've brought cash with them. After they've eaten, they throw down cash in the food-tray: 20, 50 rupees, maybe a few hundred, according to their self-worth. The bride's father or mother takes it, and in return they give the young people presents; a silk cloak (if they're wealthy), a hat, a turban, a belt, a bag, a knife-sheath, a scarf. Around nine or ten o'clock the guests take their leave. The groom stays and talks for a while, then they make up a bed in a separate place; his wife joins him, and they sleep together. Their feet have been untied.[3] During

---

[3] The Pashtu is *pshe-ye khlâse kawël*, which I have translated as 'untying the feet'; the Shahsevan in Iran have an identical phrase, *ayagh-açti*. But since both *psha* in Pashtu and *ayagh* in Turkish can mean either foot or leg, the translation should perhaps be 'untying the legs', to clarify a possible sexual allusion.

that first night, the groom puts some money under the bed – we call it bed-money [*jaypuli*]: 1,000 rupees if he's rich, otherwise a few hundred. In the morning, whoever makes up the bed collects the money.

The first night, when they 'untie their feet', his close friends accompany him. After that, he goes alone. He goes to *bâzi* at least three nights, that's our custom; then it's up to him whether to continue. The mother's very fond of her son-in-law; she looks after him, some nights she feeds him pilaw, eggs; she gives him whatever she has in her house. She spoils him for her daughter's sake. Some husbands are good, some are witless! She doesn't want him to reprimand her daughter for her mother's failure to be good to him.

Not everybody does a *khoshey*; it doesn't matter. But the groom's always taken by some friends to the first night of *bâzi*, and they exchange money and presents as I said.

Pâdshâh, unlike Baya-khân, is married; he tells more of what happens at the first bâzi:

For the *khoshey*, the boy's father buys rice, carrots, raisins, onions; he hires a cook, slaughters an ox or a couple of goats or sheep and invites all the village women. In the morning they come to the boy's house; someone plays a drum, and all day long they sing songs; they have a meal, eat their fill.

As for the men, the boy's father's relatives set off at nine or ten in the morning for the in-laws' place. All their food is at the bride's father's expense: rice, bread, tea, sweets and so on. They have fun: they dance *atan*, play buzkashi, shoot at targets, whatever people want to do. In the afternoon the girl's family put together ten to twenty scarves, in two bunches – you saw this in the spring – and put them on a large tray like yours, heaped with sweets, with the scarves on top. People come and sit down, in a room like this. They bring the tray before the mullah, and then they repeat the threefold formula of the *târ*: 'Richard, have you given your daughter to this man's son, Pâdshâh?' You reply, 'I gave her, I give her, I've given her,' and so on. Then they distribute the sweets, take the scarves and attach them to the turbans of two boys, brothers or cousins or other close relatives of the groom; one bunch of scarves for each – or all of them into just one boy's turban.

Then they make two special cloth bags that we call *bëni*, one red and one green, and fill them to the brim with sweets and raisins. We fix straps onto them, and the two boys hang them over their shoulders. We put cash or scarves or something in the opening of each one, then close it. They take these two *bëni* home to the groom's mother; if she's dead, his stepmother, sister or sister-in-law. They hang up the scarves, and women come to admire them. When they're all gathered, they throw things over the scarves: sweets, apricots, raisins, sugar-lumps, even coins, whatever takes their fancy. There's lots of joking and horseplay among the women – they have a good time. Then late in the afternoon they take their leave and go home.

That evening, the boy's family sit down and discuss the first night of *bâzi*. It should be the next Wednesday, Thursday, Saturday, Sunday, or Monday – absolutely never a Tuesday or Friday. Most people choose Wednesday or Thursday. First, we send someone – a shepherd, a workman, one of our sons – to the in-laws to say, 'We've paid this much money, this many sheep; now we'd like to bring our boy to *bâzi* with your daughter, on such-and-such an evening.' They may agree, they may not, but eventually they'll have to give in. They'll say either, 'This Wednesday's inconvenient, wait until next week, or the one after;' or just, 'Do bring him.'

When the agreed Wednesday comes, they send word at midday, 'We're definitely bringing him this evening.' The girl's family go to town and buy a cloak, a turban, a scarf, a bag or a belt; they fill a saddlebag full of sweets, henna for colouring the hands, and other things. The groom too buys some things, such as a hat, some clothes or a cloak. He goes round his close relatives and invites them to come with him that evening: someone from each family. If they can't go themselves, a son or a sister will.

Off we go, ten or twenty people, to the in-laws, who've cooked plenty of rice and meat. We arrive and sit down; someone goes round washing our hands, and we each give them some money: five, ten, up to 500 rupees – he won't tell you how much to pay, it's up to you, your own self-esteem. After the hand-washing's over, they bring the rice, one platter for every two or three people. When they've eaten, again everyone throws some money onto the platter, according to his self-esteem.

The girl's mother collects the money after the platters are removed, then fills a large bowl with a paste of the henna they bought in town. A boy – perhaps your nephew – goes round with the henna; he'll take your hand and redden it, and you'll give him a few rupees, whatever you want, according to your self-esteem. If you give me nothing I'll never complain, but it's customary to give something. If you don't, other people will remark, 'Richard didn't even give 2 rupees!' If you're embarrassed, or think you're too old for it, you just put a little finger into the henna, to redden it for good luck – that's what it's about. Often, youths get their hands reddened right up to the elbow. It varies; some do everything, some just a little finger. Any woman who came with you, as well as her hand she'll have her foot hennaed up to here. After reddening your hands, if you're his uncle he'll give you a nice present, a cloak, a turban, a cap or a bag. He goes round everybody, and gives especially nice presents to close relatives, and lesser ones to more distant people.

When that's done, all these people take their leave; only the groom stays, and the in-laws sit and chat with him. Then the women come in, his wife's sisters and cousins: his sisters-in-law [*khoshlicha*], while he's their brother-in-law [*âkhshey*]. They all chat with him for twenty minutes or half an hour. They tease the young man, who's on his own; he's very shy. They say things like, 'Brother-in-law, don't be so shy! Why didn't you come a few days earlier, so we could get to know each other better?' During all this, the girl's father is sitting right there, not participating; he may say something, but he just sits there with his rosary or whatever. Then, as they're chatting, a senior woman gets up and says, 'We've spent the whole evening chatting, let him have a few minutes to talk with his wife, to get to know her! Up we get!' The others may answer, 'Just give us give five more minutes to talk with our brother-in-law. We didn't see him during the day, now he's here but he'll soon be going, let's get to know him!' But they soon get up and leave.

Now however many rooms the girl's father has in his house, one or ten, in the room where the groom's been left his mother-in-law now lays out a fine bed, a mattress, nice pillows and quilt. The father, brothers and the rest have all gone, but she stays with him for a few minutes' chat, then she leaves too. She may leave the lamp on when she goes, or she may turn it out – meanwhile the bride's sitting there in a corner, shy and modest.

As her mother leaves, she hands the girl over to him. They go to bed. What they do is entirely up to them: whether they play around, or sleep; perhaps they talk all night.

Very early in the morning – the time we start off during the migration, before dawn when it's still dark – the groom gets up. As he does, he puts some money under the mattress: between 100 and 2,000 rupees, it's up to his self-respect how much. After the sun's up, a woman comes to pack the bedding and collect the money; not the bride's mother: she'll tell another daughter, daughter-in-law or sister-in-law to do it. Then, after everyone's baked bread and had breakfast, all the women of the family gather to see how much the groom's left, and to discuss what he was like. If he left a lot, they say, 'Bravo, what a man!' But if he didn't leave much, they say, 'He's mean, he has no authority in his own family', that sort of thing. Then they distribute most of the money: ten or twenty rupees to each women present, for example; everybody gets something. So the groom must bring small change with him: it can't be in 500 or 1,000-rupee notes! But it could be hundreds, which they'll manage to break somehow. Best if he can bring tens, twenties, fifties.

The groom comes again the next night, and the third night. Then his father-in-law gives him a turban, a cap, some boots, a waistcoat, or a nice silk cloak like yours and mine. He puts it on and comes home; everyone asks, 'Who gave you this?' Of course they all know it was his in-laws.

The wedding – and after

When the brideprice is fully paid, the groom can demand a wedding – to bring the bride to his house. The bride's family hosts the biggest feast of all, paid for by the groom's side. Pâdshâh again.

The groom goes to *bâzi* for a year or two. When he's finished paying all the sheep and cash, his father-in-law asks, 'Please wait a month, we haven't yet put together her trousseau.' So you wait a month, then you press him: 'Hurry up and get ready so that we can have the wedding; Ramazan is coming – for example – when there are no weddings; or winter's approaching. On such-and-such a day (any day but Tuesday or Friday) we're definitely going to have the wedding.'

When the time's up, the girl's father lets them know he's ready. Then the groom goes round his relatives – not his in-laws – to ask for *nimawri*. Some, like his maternal uncle, may well give him a sheep, a goat, a kid or a lamb; perhaps a horse, a donkey, or two sheep and so on. Other relatives give a seer of barley, two of wheat, three of corn, or 50, 100, 200 rupees in cash.

When he's collected all the *nimawri*, they make arrangements for the wedding. His father takes everything he's collected – cash, animals, grain – and calculates whether they've got enough for the wedding. If so, he won't sell the animals; he'll put the sheep with his own flock, tie up any camel, donkey or horse at home, and put the grain in the storeroom. But if he reckons they don't have enough for the wedding expenses, that they'll run short, he'll take the *nimawri* animals – sheep, goats, donkey or whatever – and the cash, plus some of his own, and go to town on market-day to sell the animals and buy rice. He reckons how many guests there'll be, and how much rice is needed: say

80 seers. He buys second-grade rice, not the best; and for 80 seers of rice he buys 3 seers of carrots, 10 of onions, 10 of raisins, 15 or 16 of ghee. He takes all his purchases home, then lets his in-laws know, 'On such-and-such a day we're having the wedding.' Further, he slaughters an ox, a calf, a sheep or a goat, and hires a professional cook to do meat and rice.

Before the wedding, the groom's women send a 'bridal shower', as Neshtar says.

Before every wedding there's a *push*. It's compulsory, clothes needed for the bride. At the *push*, women put together three, five, maybe six suits of clothes – like when we took them from Jomadâr for Magar – perhaps up to twenty outfits; it's for the girl's reputation: 'See how many outfits she's been given!' When the bride's family receive the *push*, they give caps to the women who brought it; or a chador, or a chemise. In return they give money: 20 rupees, 100, 200, according to their means; it goes to the girl's mother, stepmother or sister-in-law; they take it for their own work, it's nothing to do with the men.

Pâdshâh describes the wedding day itself, and the 'blessed business' (kâr-e-kheyr) at its centre.

The day before the wedding, the groom's father loads all the stuff – fuel, rice, ghee, carrots – onto separate camels to form a train of some ten beasts. When we pack the camels, we put a stick into each load and wiggle it around so that the load looks bigger; and we tie some scarves to it, white and green, different colours, so they stand out on each camel. Some young boys – the groom's brothers, cousins, or other close relatives – accompany the camels; plus a special person who can unload the camels and then stand guard over the rice and stuff, in case the in-laws steal it – they don't want an embarrassing incident the following day!

When the brothers enter the in-laws' home, everyone comes and takes one of the scarves. They probably brought lots of them; they can't ask for them back now, it would be shameful. The rice guardian stays; the others take the camels home.

Once they're back, the groom's father immediately sends them out again with invitations: one rides off to Sar-e-pol, one to Haji Mahd-Omar's, one to Âktâsh, to Khoshtepa, Seyyedâbâd, Emâm-Sâheb, Upper and Lower Khârkash, the Malekis, the Hazâras and so on; to every village, every elder, every headman – all depends on what he can afford. In each invitation he writes: 'Please come to our wedding party tomorrow at such-and-such o'clock.' He also sends someone to hire drummers and pipers; one, two or three pairs, whatever he can afford. He may also send for dancing boys. Many different musicians come; it's a party, after all! A drummer charges between one and three thousand rupees, it's very variable.

The drummer arrives during the afternoon. Anyone who hears the drum says, 'Hey, it's so-and-so's wedding, let's go!' That evening there's music and dancing; some people sing, some play instruments, everyone's free to do what they're good at! The host cooks a large cauldron or two of rice, to feed these people as well as the musicians, and they serve tea, sweets and everything.

And that night, the wedding eve, five companions take the groom for his last *bâzi*. The in-laws feed them rice, redden their hands again, and receive money from them – they don't ask for it, but it's customary to give. Early next morning, the groom goes home, where the wedding's about to begin. Some grooms help with preparations; others are shy and go into hiding.

In the morning the guests are served tea, then they go out into the open again to dance; people do whatever they want. Then around eight or nine o'clock everyone sets off for the bride's place. Men and women go separately. They shouldn't mix, but it doesn't matter which go first, it's up to the elders and the groom's father. When they arrive, the women gather near the bride's home to dance and sing, while the men stay out in the open. There'll be lots of horses and people, and traders come to sell things. There's probably buzkashi. Of course, you do get a lot of fighting in the buzkashi: if someone grabs your reins or something, trying to seize the calf, then you fight back; you beat each other with whips. The police don't come. If there's a fight, the greybeards or the khans knock heads together. They warn you, and you make it up. The fighting doesn't get murderous. It could happen that someone's trampled to death under a horse's hooves. At my wedding four or five people got broken ribs that way.

They feed the men rice, and when they've eaten they feed the women. Once the women have finished, people gather at the bride's home. They lay a kilim outside, and bring out the trousseau [*kur*], piece by piece. Some fellows stand there in line; one of them receives each piece as it's handed out of the house or the tent, and the others pile them up for display.

When that's done, the mullah calls *Allahu-Akbar* over it several times, then he dresses the groom, who puts a scarf inside his cap and hands it to the mullah, who puts it in his pocket. As they dress him in his new clothes, he ties his old turban round his waist and hands his old belt and waistcoat to his brother or some other relative to take home; if he has an old cloak, he gives this too to his brother to take home. Once the mullah's finished dressing the groom, he calls *Allahu-Akbar* again. The groom kisses the beard of his father-in-law, who pats him on the back three times, like this, saying *bismillah*. Then he kisses the hands of some other elders and Hajis, and they embrace him, saying, 'God grant that you grow old together.'

Inside, the bride's brother parts her hair with an iron spindle. It's customary for a brother to do this; if she has none, then a cousin or other close male relative, though a woman could do it if there's no man available. Meanwhile, they bring up the camels and load them with the trousseau. They guide the bride past the hearth, out of her home, in front of the Hajis. Her close relatives – mother, sisters, father and brothers, uncle, cousins, all help put her on one of the loaded camels. She has a white chador over her head, hiding all her body. A woman brings a bowl of water, and three times the bride stretches her hand out from the chador and flicks water over her own head, like this – I'm telling it well, aren't I?

(R) – Very well!

She's crying, so they comfort her and give her courage: 'Hold this rope tightly, or this one, be brave, don't be frightened, don't worry, they're not strangers, we're all one family, and in ten days or so we'll come and bring you home!' When she's settled on the camel, her brother or her uncle lead it off by the halter. A close kinswoman – her mother, her sister or an uncle's wife – accompanies her to the groom's place.

Neshtar tells what happens when the bride arrives in her new home.

When the bride arrives, her mother or brother takes her by the hand and puts a quilt and a shawl down at her feet; she stops and before she enters the house, they call her husband, '*Ha lewâri, ha lewâri*! Hey, brother-in-law! the new bride wants a veil, what'll you give her?' He gives her a camel, a horse, a cow, or a ewe. This animal's hers; it's her decision whether to eat it, sell it, or wear it, nobody else, neither her husband nor her father-in-law nor her brother-in-law can interfere. If it's a ewe, all the wool, lambs, skins and so on belong to her, nobody else. Indeed, a woman who looks after such an animal, and doesn't squander it, could build up a flock of 100 sheep.

That night the boy's father brings a mullah and some elders, feeds them rice and meat; and they do the *nekâh*. Each side chooses a representative: the girl takes one, and the boy another one. They can be anyone who's present, it doesn't matter. They bargain over the bride's dower, her *mahr*; the mullah makes the wife an equal partner in her husband's hearth; she becomes equally responsible for providing food and everything, and will share in good and bad times.

The *mahr* is a few thousand rupees. It doesn't matter how closely related they are; and it makes no difference whether she's pretty or plain. The husband doesn't pay anything then, it becomes a debt; he owes it to his wife, nobody else. She has the right to claim it, and to spend it on clothes, a nose-jewel, a bracelet, a chador or a scarf; or she can buy a ewe for lambing. Except, as the couple sleep together that night, he may ask her, 'Let me off the *mahr*.' If she's a good woman she will, but she doesn't have to. If they're dear to each other, like you and Richard, she'll let him off. Most women do, if they're sensible. Only stupid women refuse: 'By God, I'll never let you off! You owe me this money; if you don't treat me well, I'll demand it!' She can keep him in debt, and he must pay if she asks. He can only plead: 'Please release me, don't keep me in debt like this; you're my wife, anything I have we'll spend together.'

After the nikah the elders leave, and the couple sleep together. For three days she remains covered; they make a space by the bed, where they lay out a shawl and she sits on this 'throne'. Her feet are 'tied'. She doesn't have to get up and do any work. As she sits there, women – it's nothing to do with men – come from all the other families to see what she's like, then they go home to report, that the new bride is nice, good-looking and so on.

On the third day, women cook *ghërey*, three-layered fatty bread with sugar sprinkled on top, and bring raisins and melons, whatever they have, and they joke and sing, then they raise the bride, remove the throne, beat the quilt. The bride sits on a rug; she's free, her feet are untied.

There's more: the community women take turns to invite the bride to their place – to untie her feet. They feed her, give her presents: necklace, scarf, chemise, makeup bottle, sometimes cash, saying this is her 'veil', *paruney/porëney*. Everyone should invite her, until she's got to know them; from then on, she can go round the houses by herself, just like other women. If someone doesn't invite her for *paruney*, she won't go to that house for years afterwards; they haven't untied her feet.

Baya-khân's version . . .

On the wedding day, the bride has a veil over her head, a transparent white nylon affair. When she arrives at her new home, she won't go in; it's our custom for the husband to promise her a camel, a horse, a sheep, or something else, before she'll come in and sit down. They put the animal in her name; like any that her father gave her, it's hers. If she wants, she'll give it to her husband on the first day; but she doesn't have to, he has no right to it, or to the offspring if it gives birth. She can sell it if she wants; but if they get along, she'll let her husband sell it.

After she's arrived, all the women come to meet her, but she tries to keep her face hidden by holding her veil like this. For three days she just sits there on a mattress, unseen by the men – her father- and brothers-in-law. If it's a house, she's in a separate room; in a tent, they hang up a tarpaulin or curtain to one side. The women all come to see her – her own relatives, but also strangers; many come on the first day. Her mother, sister, mother-in-law push her hand aside to uncover her face, so that others can see it.

On the third morning they remove the mattress, and all her male in-laws get to see her face. She starts work: making bread, doing the housework and so on. She works alongside her mother-in-law, who continues to work, unless she's very old; she won't say, 'We paid so much brideprice for this bride, let her work so that I can take it easy!' That's not on, a mother-in-law can't behave like that!

Some time after the bride's gone, her brother goes or sends his cousin to visit. When he arrives, the groom's family kill a lamb or a goat, chop up the meat and cook it in a pot. They bake chapatti, wrap each piece of meat separately in a chapatti, pile it all on a cloth, and put it in a saddlebag. The bride puts on new clothes, and any gold jewellery or bracelets she has; if she has some gold she puts it on her neck or arms; she does her hair, oils it; then she comes home. When she arrives, everyone gathers, and the word goes round, 'So-and-so's daughter's come!' Her uncles and other close relatives distribute the meat to men, women and children. They also hand round sweets and raisins, whatever she's brought.

She stays there up to a month, then the groom or his brother comes to fetch her. Her father slaughters a lamb, a kid or a full-grown sheep – if he kills an adult sheep to make a name for himself, people remember it. They cook the meat, wrap it in chapatti, and also make fatty bread, and the groom's party take it home and distribute it.

. . . and Pâdshâh's.

She doesn't know her way around in her new home. She's too shy to say, 'I'm thirsty,' or 'I need to go outside.' They put up a curtain for her to sit behind, for three days, while visitors stay the other side. If it's a tent, they hang the curtain up like this; if it's a room in a house, they nail it up. During those three days, the groom sleeps with her at night but during the daytime he stays away, joining the crowd of women visitors, sitting quietly and chatting with them.

On the third day the local women come round, bringing whatever's in season – walnuts, raisins, melons, watermelons, cucumbers, pomegranates – but there must be some fatty bread. They remove the mattress the bride's been sitting on, with a *bismillah*.

She joins them on the felt or kilim where they're sitting, and they chatter away as they distribute the fatty bread, sweets and other goodies they've brought, especially among the children, big and small.

After that, the bride gets up and pours water for her parents-in-law, for washing or drinking. Then she starts work by baking bread, in the oven or on the griddle, depending what she knows. She cooks meat-broth and rice. She goes with other women to fetch water from the pond; if there's a well, a man draws the water while she holds the water-bag open, fills it up and takes it home. Gradually she takes on the housework, sweeping and so on. For some days, until she knows her in-laws, she keeps her face covered in front of them. But she gets used to things. She stops worrying about the dogs and goes about her work by herself.

Then she'll have her first baby; it could be only a few days later, a month, or a year or more. Some women give birth on the very day of their wedding! But a bride mustn't have a baby before the wedding. Her mother privately tells the groom, 'You've put my daughter in the family way – may your household be full of wheat – so hold the wedding without delay!' In that situation, the groom is forced to bring forward the wedding, whether or not he can afford it. It would be very shameful if she had the baby too early. People would say, 'Look, that idiot's daughter couldn't wait, she gave birth too soon!' If a woman manages to hold off getting pregnant, all her relatives, her mother and the rest, are happy, especially when she gives birth after the wedding – then we're all pleased with her, 'Excellent! The boy went to *bâzi*, nothing happened, then later she gave birth.'

Neshtar's role as 'headwoman' mainly involves organizing women's parties, especially at weddings.

Whenever there's a wedding, I'm the one to be informed. If there's a wedding over in Khârkash, they send someone with an invitation, saying, 'Give it to Neshtar, she'll get the women together and bring them to the party.' That's why I went there for Chârgol's bride's 'Coming Out' ceremony. Others like the Baluch also send me invitations; I've had several.

The last few years I've done it rather less. I used to sing a lot, and all these women and girls were under my authority. Haji Ghâfur and Haji Tumân and the others would say, for example, that no women may go to Khârkash unless Neshtar goes too. I went in front, and the women followed. So when Tumân says, 'She's the headman [*qariyadâr*],' that's what he means.

But as I say, I've rather lost interest in those matters. Now everyone's their own boss. If there's a wedding in Khârkash, they'll find a senior woman to go. Perhaps I will. A formal invitation doesn't come, but I still go. If women want to have a party and I say, 'It's not a good idea', the men will stop it. If I approve it, it'll go ahead. Parties are still my responsibility, throughout the community. The girls come and beg, 'Please, let's have our party tomorrow,' or in a few days' time. Also, it's up to me how long the party lasts; one day or twenty, it's my decision.

If there's a discussion, for example whether and how to do a particular ceremony – as in Chârgol's case – this too is my business. If I'm not there, they still have to do it.

Somebody will insist that I go along. If there's a ceremony that's part of a wedding – like Jomadâr's, you were there – I'll tell them how to do it.

When people are sending a delegation to propose marriage to a girl, somewhere I have some influence, then the boy'll come and ask me to get her for him. I'll definitely make sure the proposal arrives – and succeeds. And if they ask me to go and inspect a girl, I'll go – along with a man. If it's far away, like the Alizais of Kaltar, they'll send a horse for me. We call these delegations *maraka*. If I approve of the girl, I'll tell them, 'She's a nice girl, you should take her.' Then the men'll put together another *maraka*, a big one.

If the proposal's accepted, the groom gives me a nice *châdri*, or a fine jacket. That's the honourable thing to do: 'You've taken trouble for me, so take this *châdri*, it's yours.' And if I take the women to Khârkash for a party like Chârgol's, for sure they'll give me something. At Chârgol's, his sister Pâkiza told her relatives, 'Give her a cap.' If Pâkiza hadn't been there, the party would've been under my authority. Pâkiza said she'd take charge herself, so I said 'Fine, it doesn't bother me!' She said, 'They'll still give you a cap.' I said, 'I already have one!' But that's how it is, they'll certainly give something. I started doing this when I was widowed, over twenty years ago. I don't know if anybody did it before me.

Irregularities

There are many instances where people break the rules (the case of the runaway Kimyâ was perhaps the most extreme), and there are further rules for what happens when a marriage ends in death or divorce.

Jumping the gun

One of the commonest irregularities is when a bride becomes pregnant before her wedding. Speaking in spring 1971, Baya-khân gives some examples from his own family.

Sometimes a woman gets pregnant in her father's home. Then her father 'ties her feet' again; he tells the groom's father, 'Your son's dishonoured me, I'm not giving my daughter.' He'll have to pay extra before he can hold the wedding: 10,000 to 20,000 rupees, that's the custom. We call it *bâbirey*. Uncle Jân-Mahmad's wife Shekar was that way. My father says, 'We had to give her father Masâdek a 10,000-rupee gun before he let her go.'

With my brother Khâni-âghâ and Bâdâm, though, she gave birth three or four nights after the wedding! Her father Haji Wahâb knew, but he was close family [*his wife Saduzi is Khâni-âghâ's aunt*], so it didn't matter. Shekar's father Masâdek's more distant. Jân-Mahmad's own daughter Talâk was pregnant before her wedding, but it wasn't known until several nights after.

Bâdâm died suddenly in summer 1971, leaving her three infants in the care of Pâdshâh's mother Maryam and wife Pâkhâl. A year later, Khâni-âghâ is still away on military service and still doesn't know what's happened. The third brother, Darwiza, is himself halfway through his service; engaged some years earlier to a second cousin, Haji Afzal's daughter Sawur, he expects to marry on his return. However, after he left in autumn 1971, Sawur was rumoured to be pregnant, and people wondered what would happen. Now it appears that she wasn't pregnant, or that, if she was, she's had an abortion. Nonetheless, it's planned to hold the wedding in Darwiza's absence, so that Sawur can come and help look after the orphans. Shir, her brother and family head, returns (with Khâni-âghâ) from military service in a few weeks. Pâdshâh talks of the family's dilemma and plans.

When Shir returns, he'll sort the matter out, and we'll hold Sawur's wedding. We'll do the nikah with a gun, because Darwiza's away. To get him home earlier, we'd have to bribe his commanding officer, who might not agree. The gun's a thing, it can't speak, but we'll make it Darwiza's representative. Our mullahs say that the Book allows this. Everybody'll come for the nikah; they'll pray and treat the gun as though it were Darwiza himself.

Many people have done this. For example, they did it for Rawu's son Nasrak, while he was on military service. The usual reason is that the bride got pregnant while still in her father's house; they must make sure she doesn't give birth there. Nasrak's wife was pregnant; now her baby's a big lad, he goes out tending the animals. Sawur isn't pregnant; if she had been, we'd have held the wedding earlier. The reason we're marrying her now is so that she can come and look after Khâni-âghâ's orphans.

A father won't know his daughter's pregnant. Her mother knows – women know these things – but her father's a stranger. He's away, in town and everywhere, so he never notices if his daughter's belly swells. He doesn't ask, he doesn't even think about it. If he finds out, it's because some woman – his wife, his sister, some other relative – tells him privately: 'So-and-so's dishonoured you, he's done this to your daughter.' Usually, if the mother knows her daughter's pregnant, she'll say nothing, for shame and for fear of her husband. She'll go and tell the boy's father: 'My daughter's in the family way, my husband mustn't know, you must have the wedding at once!' If they manage to have a quick wedding, they can prevent the father finding out.

Some fathers, if they do find out, pretend they don't know. Others get angry, shout at their wife and daughter – 'Why'd you do this?' Then he demands extra brideprice, which we call *bâbirey*. He says, 'You've dishonoured me in front of the tribe by doing this with my daughter.' That's why he takes *bâbirey*. On the wedding day, when the groom's side arrive, carrying guns worth 20,000 to 30,000, or nice hybrid camels, he simply grabs a nice gun from someone's shoulder, or a camel; or he demands money. Nasrak's father-in-law did find out, and he took eighteen sheep as *bâbirey*. It's a sensitive matter.

Elopements; infidelities

In May 1971, before Kimyâ elopes, Baya-khân broaches the subject of sexual misbehaviour.

If a husband hurts his wife, beats her, stabs her, breaks her arm, her leg or her head, her brother won't let him get away with it, he'll lodge a formal complaint. He might go to the headman, or to my father, who'll compel them to sort it out. If a woman's attacked, wounded or killed by a thief, or a stranger, then both her husband and her brothers will take action; or rather the husband must, but her father and brothers will be behind him. In fact they'll hold the husband responsible for her death. If they don't know who the killer was, they'll seize the husband, saying, 'You've taken my daughter/sister and killed her.' But if they catch the fellow who did it, husband and father and brothers will all take action.

A girl's father doesn't worry that she might run off with someone else. It would be very shameful [*'eyb*] for an Afghan girl to run away. It doesn't happen here. I've never heard of an Afghan married woman who eloped with another man. People would laugh: 'What a slut! She left her husband, the shameless bitch!' This would shame her father.

It can happen that someone secretly makes an assignation with a girl and they elope; that's the end of it. If they catch them, or get hold of his father or brother or somebody, they'll demand something from them, for brideprice or whatever; but if not, she's gone, lost. Among us Afghans such an act is very shameful. If a girl elopes, everyone laughs at her father, 'His daughter was so shameless, she didn't care for her father's or her mother's honour, she ran off with somebody.'

But a man who sees a married woman misbehaving with another man may kill both the man and the woman. If the government hears, it won't ask any questions; they did something bad and both of them are gone. It's the husband's responsibility. Some husbands, if they find out, just beat her. There are all kinds of men, some are cuckolds, they say nothing even if they know someone is doing bad things with their wife. But if her brothers hear about it, they'll beat her, or scold her for doing such a thing. She's dishonoured the family.

A few months later, after Kimyâ's elopement but before he goes on military service (and before he gets Sawur pregnant?) Darwiza sets out the rules of married life.

With us, if two brothers live together and, God forbid, one of them dies, the other should marry his widow. If he doesn't, and she elopes with some other man, then they'll take three women from him, saying, 'You've dishonoured us, taking our woman.' That's our custom; it's happened before and it'll happen again.

Also, once a woman's engaged, nobody else can ask for her. If someone does take such a woman, he must give three women: one to replace her, one for her dishonour, one for the meeting of people who impose the fine, as a deterrent. Otherwise, a married woman might say, 'I don't like my husband, I want that man.' If they don't fine him, someone else will do the same thing. This is very shameful for us, people would taunt us, 'Look, so-and-so's wife has gone!' One day you might quarrel with someone, and he might say, 'What sort of a man are you? How come your brother's widow ran off, why haven't you fetched her back?' If you said that about someone, he'd have no alternative but to kill you on the spot, or you must kill him. That's the custom for us Afghans. But for Fârsibâns it doesn't matter.

Once an Afghan's married, no other man should even look at his wife. He can speak to her, as we're talking now, but no way can he – forgive me – sleep with her or do something bad like that. If he does, he'll pay for it heavily. It's not good, not the custom for Afghans. It may be different for Fârsibâns, I don't know about that; but I'm sure they don't approve either.

If you saw a married woman in a room with another man – it often happens, I've seen it myself, a man and a woman in a room doing such things – if it happened, God forbid, in this very room, then if you killed them right here, neither the government nor God in the next world would call you to account, our mullahs say. God would say, 'Such misdeeds shouldn't happen.' It's provided for in our Book; everything our Book says is true, none of it's lies, that's well known.

If you saw these two people doing such things right here, and stopped them, but you weren't strong enough to kill them, then, once they set foot outside the room if they both suddenly repent in their hearts, saying, 'Oh God, what a bad thing we've done!' then, if you kill them there outside, their blood's on your hands. They'll both be martyrs, God won't call them to account, a shrine will be built above them, and God will cure anyone who comes and who's jinn-possessed or sick in some way. But if you caught them here, still in each other's arms, and killed them on the spot, their death would be no different from the death of a donkey; whatever punishment you inflict on them in this world, God will inflict ten or twenty times as much in that world, saying, 'You called yourself Muslims, accepted Islam; why did you do such things?' That's what our Book tells us.

However, if somebody else saw your wife in a room with another man, it's not really for him to kill them: it should be her husband, father, brother or mother, nobody else. He should lock the door, leaving them inside, then tell the parents; they'll have no alternative but to kill the pair, whether by stoning or with a knife or a gun; or by starving them to death. If someone saw them from a distance doing such a thing, and saw that the man had got away, and if he kept his mouth shut and said nothing, then it doesn't matter. But once he starts talking about it – 'So-and-so's wife was doing such things with that fellow' – the woman's relatives – her husband, father-in-law, or brother – will demand damages from the man who was with her: one, two or three woman, as a deterrent, to prevent him doing such a thing again another day. 'You've shamed me, doing such things with my wife.' Afghans absolutely disapprove of such things.

People are always spreading lies, 'X's wife is doing this with Y,' or 'A's daughter is doing this with B's son, C's sister with D's brother.' Well, it may be so, but if nobody sees them, it doesn't matter. After all, not all women do such things; perhaps only one in a hundred or even a thousand. If someone comes up to you and says, 'Hey, I saw your wife with another man,' and it's a lie, it doesn't matter. But it does matter; your heart does burn a little, you look into your heart; and you have to look behind you all the time, for a month, a year, two years, and if anything does happen you'll catch them. If they're in love, how can they keep apart? And if it's true, and that man really saw them and was able to lock them inside, and shout out, 'Hey, you didn't believe me, now look!' then, one way or another, you'll catch them together, day or night, and kill them.

In August 1972, Seyyed-shâh/Golusar tells a story.

My uncle told me a story about Borjân [*from Lineage A, Khârkash*]. Once long ago, he said, we were trekking to the mountains and we met a Shinwâri train; we had donkeys, they had camels; wherever they stopped, we stopped too. Among the Shinwâris was a girl like a flower. She captured our hearts. We decided to follow her everywhere. Whenever her father moved, we too loaded our donkeys and followed. And we stopped in the same place.

With them was a fine young Shinwâri. Her parents said, 'This young man and that girl, they go well together.' Her father gave her to him. Now one evening they'd camped at the Dehmana graveyard; the young man came to *bâzi*, riding a nice mare, with a gun on his shoulder and a bandolier round his neck. As he dismounted, the girl threw herself down saying, 'I'm unwell.' His mother-in-law said, 'She's ill, not this evening.' 'What else can I do?' He remounted and rode off.

The girl, this bitch, had a servant, and she'd made a date with him that night; 'You and I will sleep together.' Shinwâris have lots of camels; everyone has 50 or 100, some 200. They made a bed among the camels and lay down together, and so they made the night into morning.

At dawn, as they were loading the camels, he was snatching kisses from the girl. Over here, Borjân saw them and lit up like a fire: 'Look at that! That fellow's with the girl, the other poor chap's gone!'

The caravan set off. Along the way (my uncle said), we told them, 'We're going back to look for some things; we'll catch up later.' We spotted a coin necklace; it must have fallen off when she was making out with that fellow. We picked it up and took it with us.

Meanwhile, the girl told her mother, 'Mum, I've left my necklace back there.' The mother told her son-in-law, 'Go and fetch it.'

That girl's days were numbered. The young man galloped off on his mare. He met our people, who asked, 'Where are you going?' 'Back to the campsite, something got left behind.' 'What was it?' 'Something belonging to a woman.' 'What?' 'A coin necklace.' 'We've found it, but we need to tell you a story; it's up to you whether you believe us.' 'What do you mean?'

As they returned together to the caravan, they said: 'Was she your wife?' 'Yes.' 'Do you remember last night you came to *bâzi*, but she lay down and said she was sick?' – they'd been close enough to hear it – 'Well, when you'd gone, she got up, laid a place among the camels, and slept there with the servant; that's where she lost the necklace, and that's where we found it.'

He looked at them, 'Why are you lying? Do you want me to kill my wife?' They said, 'Come with us and see for yourself.' One of the girl's camel-loads had slipped, and she was readjusting it. Kabulis never string many camels together, only two or three at a time; mostly they drive them freely. As they were fixing the load the servant was kissing the girl – and her husband saw her. He was livid: 'You shameless bitch, you dare give your face while I'm alive! What would happen if I died?' He had a good Malakhi gun and he galloped off to fetch it; he loaded it. She'd got back on the camel, but he shot her off it. Then he shot the servant twice, then three more times.

The girl's mother reproached Borjân, 'You son-of-a-bitch, you've shamed us, may your Kandahari house catch fire! You made him kill my daughter!'

Pâdshâh/Parwiz and Seyyed-shâh comment on recent developments.

(*Pâdshâh/Parwiz*) – Three years ago the government made it possible for a woman to choose her own husband. Now, if an unmarried girl makes an assignation with a lad, goes off to his house at night, and next day declares to the government, 'This boy's my husband,' the judge will immediately do her nikah. They'll have a sweet-distribution, and that's the end of it. They did it by themselves. Several educated girls around here have done it. But I think they've repealed that law, for fear that all the girls would go off. Imagine, if it should become 'democracy', or whatever it's called, and a woman could pick and choose, or reject her husband and go to another – we can't have that! But they revoked that law. It's not going to happen again in Afghanistan.

(*Seyyed-shâh*) – In Boghawi there was a Moghol boy who had an affair with another Moghol's wife. She left her husband, who was still alive, went to that boy and declared, 'This is my husband!' They took the matter to court, and that boy got the woman. She had her first husband's son in her belly; when it was born she sent it to him, saying, 'This is your son, do what you like with him.' This happened four years ago.

There are a lot of bad women! But, thank God, there aren't any such women in our village. As for other women, I don't know what's wrong with their men, are they weak? They can't hold them back. Women are just like a motorcar that you have to keep firm control of, when it gets hot.

Parwiz and Shamayel

Pâdshâh/Parwiz continues, with both pride and humour, relating the deeds of his father.

My father was one of a kind. He had a bay horse with no equal in Afghanistan. He was very fond of it; he'd take it tent-pegging [*neyza-bäzi*] at Shamsoddin's place.[4] Shamsoddin had a daughter called Shamayel, who was already engaged; her husband had done the *târ*, but hadn't been to *bâzi*. My father went to their *târ* party for the tent-pegging. His horse went so fast that its hind legs scraped its forelegs; one leg bled, so he wrapped it in silk handkerchiefs – in those days they were cheap – and took it to Shamsoddin's pond to water it. But the horse was so proud that it wouldn't bend down to drink.

Shamayel happened to be looking down from the glassed-in second-floor balcony. Seeing how the horse wouldn't stoop to drink, she took a bucket and went down to the pond. She told Parwiz to water his horse with the bucket, which he did, without thinking. Then she called out to him, 'They've given me a husband today, but I'll only marry you! Everyone else is my brother.'

Well, that evening he went and hid behind her house, waiting for her. He asked her, 'What will you do tomorrow when your husband shows up?' She said, 'Let them cut off my head; you're the only husband for me.' So they made an agreement, and my father came home. He went to Haji Shamsoddin: 'Your daughter doesn't want that husband; she wants to marry me, she'll divorce him.' He replied, 'Off with you, I'll never give her to you!'

---

[4]   Haji Shamsoddin, a wealthy Ghiljai who lives nearby in Khâm-rabât village.

My father was very proud. Shamsoddin was rich; he loaded his gun and took two men after my father into the steppe: 'I'll kill him!' When they saw Parwiz, they galloped after him, but he got the drop on them and said, 'I swear I'll kill you unless you give me the *târ* for your daughter.'

Haji Ghâfur was passing with his flock; he rescued Shamsoddin from Parwiz, saying, 'Give him your daughter, you fool, or he really will kill you!' So he tore his turban and gave Parwiz a strip as *târ*, saying, 'I'll give you my daughter; go and release her from that man.' Then my father went after her husband; he was going to kill him, but people gathered and pleaded with him, so they went to the government, where he forced the husband to throw down the three stones [*see p. 297*]. He was a wealthy man; he'd paid several thousand rupees in advance for the girl, but my father gave him 50,000 to free her.

Everyone knew he'd had her freed by force. After ten days Parwiz came back to Shamsoddin and said, 'I've freed your daughter; now I'm going to free the brideprice.' But Shamsoddin said, 'I want more brideprice from you.' So what happened? That night he went, tied up his horse near the girl's house, climbed the wall and went to her. He said, 'I've released you, what shall we do now?' She said, 'If you've released me, I'll marry no one but you, even if the world becomes infidel.'

Shamsoddin's brother Mahd-Amin had said, 'I refuse to let Parwiz have the girl!' and put a guard over her. One evening – my father had gone home – the husband, who was a relative, came round. Mahd-Amin locked the compound gates behind him – big gates like Haji Tumân's – and told him, 'Go in to that woman, she's yours.' She was upstairs, quite alone, but saw what was happening through the windows. She called, 'Don't let him up!' The man was furious, took up his loaded gun and fired up at her; the window broke and she was showered with glass. She came out and started to chase him, but he ran away; she shouted, 'You won't escape me alive!' Hearing this, her uncle Mahd-Amin came and held a Koran before her, saying, 'Look at the Koran!' She grabbed it and hit him in the stomach with it: 'Piss off, you bastard! How dare you send a stranger to me like that!'

Next evening my father went to Mahd-Amin and said, 'Why'd you do such a crazy thing, you idiot? I should send ten bullets through your backside! Am I dead, that you dare send people to my wife!' Mahd-Amin swore he hadn't done anything. So in the morning Parwiz collected some people here and went and took Shamayel by force. He brought her here, and they did the marriage contract.

It was spring migration time. When they got to Gol-e-yakh, past Kâshân, Shamayel died. She'd been 'Koran-struck'; she'd lost her temper, struck the man with the Koran, so the Koran struck her. My father had fallen in love with her, but they had only a month together. After she died, he made a coffin and brought her back to this graveyard. He wandered about, mad with grief; but finally he got another wife from Âktâsh, Dust-Mahmad's mother Golak. When she arrived, he returned to sanity.

This was all a long time ago; I was very small, perhaps a little bigger than Khâsak's son here. Later we made it up with Haji Shamsoddin. After Shamayel died, all his sons would bring their wives to our house. While my father was alive we all visited each other, but since he died they haven't come, and we haven't gone there. If I go there, they cry out, 'Hey, nephew, where are you going?' She left no children, nothing. It lasted just a month.

Madu

Pâdshâh/Parwiz tells another tale of scandal, involving his father's half-brother Madu.

About twenty-five years ago my uncle Madu abducted a Ludin woman, Keshmishân. She was engaged to a boy, but he'd died. Her brothers-in-law wouldn't take her. Then she got to know uncle Madu. She'd go to the pond and there they arranged things. Madu said, 'Come one evening and we'll elope.' In those days he was very fit – it's just as well his arm's broken now!

So he brought her one night to his house, which was right here, you know the old compound? In the morning her people created a hoo-hah because the girl had been abducted. My father said, 'My brother's taken her; there's nothing you can do about it.' Our people stood firm against them, and they couldn't do anything.

Unable to get her back by force, her people went to Kabul and petitioned the government. They brought government orders from Kabul, but my father got them revoked. The orders stated that the person who had taken the woman must return her, and must himself be taken to Kabul and jailed. Ten times they brought an order, and he had them all revoked and didn't return the woman.

Then mullahs brought Korans and made peace between us. Once they'd made peace, my father couldn't go against the Koran, so he gave them one of our girl-cousins and 50,000 rupees cash; another 50,000 went on dealing with the government, so altogether he probably spent about a lac. They released the girl to him, but after a year she died, childless – she'd been cursed.

We had lots of fights – our people are like this, very feisty; but in those fights, that feistiness, we got left behind. Madu abducted another girl, Jamâl, daughter of Hazâr-khân Kamuzai. She'd been promised to another man. When Madu took her, the other guy went to court; but Hazâr-khân promised him another daughter, releasing Jamâl. Madu paid Hazâr-khân a proper brideprice, 40,000 rupees. Nancy, you may have seen the woman Hazâr-khân promised the other guy, she's still around, a tall well-built figure. She's been engaged, but not yet delivered to her husband; she's just sitting there. Now her brother tells me, 'We'll give her if you give us your daughter in return: do an exchange with us.' I say, 'But this girl's engaged, you've already promised her to someone in Kandahar.' They say, 'No, we've released her.' That's a lie, they haven't released her, it's still in dispute. That poor girl will soon be an old woman! Two or three years from now, she'll be past it.

The pimp

Shortly before we leave in late summer 1972, we learn about some goings-on in Konjek that we already suspect. Our Uzbek cook Hâshem has hinted at such affairs, not just in Konjek but also in Khârkash, which is close to his family village, Beshqapı – though he has not mentioned that almost certainly similar things happen among the Uzbeks. Baya-khân, Pâdshâh and his wife Pâkhâl have been bursting to tell us of this scandal, which involves some of their relatives. We knew the people mentioned well (they include some of our narrators). Here alone, I use the same pseudonyms (except for the narrators) as Nancy does in Bartered Brides, *adding a few more as necessary. (See Fig. 12)*

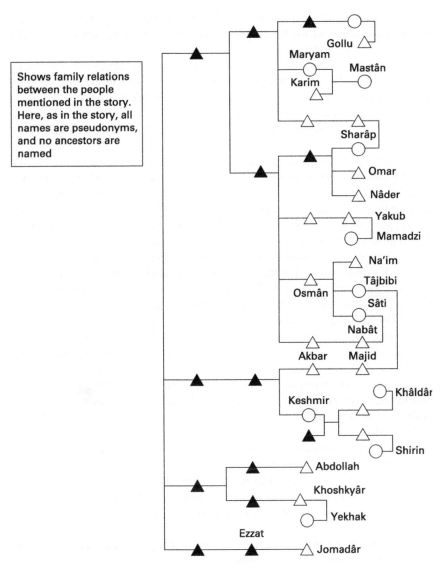

Figure 12 The pimp.

Baya-khân and Pâkhâl open the story, joined later by Pâdshâh.

(Baya-khân) – My cousin Majid is a pimp [*mordagaw*]; we know he is.

    (Pâkhâl) – Pâdshâh says, before you go, he'll tell you about this on tape.

    (Baya-khân) – He fetches women for Ezzat's sons. He's a pimp. I'm not joking, it's not only me saying it, everybody knows. Ask Pâdshâh, ask anyone. He's not a good man.

    (R) – Don't people complain?

(*Baya-khân*) – Well, some people say things to him; but if the girl's guardian won't say anything, what can we do? People say he's now got Karim's daughter Mastân involved.

(*Pâkhâl*) – And Nabât's wife Sâti [*Majid's sister-in-law*]; and Yakub's wife [*Mamadzi*].

(*Baya-khân*) – He used to take Sâti; and Sharâp; and Mastân; he fixed Mamadzi up with the son of Khoshdel Nâmanzai, Mullah Abdol-Manân's brother. Majid's a pimp, he'd take money from them and spend it.

(*R*) – Don't people say, if so-and-so lets his daughter do this, my name will be bad too?

(*Baya-khân*) – If the girl's guardian's a poor man, he won't say anything. Nabât's young, people don't listen to him, and don't care what he says. As for Mastân, her father Karim's not here, her uncles have gone, and now her mother [*Maryam*]'s gone, so she's her own household head. Other women can't stop her from going around; she'll just say, 'I'm going to such-and-such a house.' If he's going to arrange an assignation, Majid doesn't go himself, he sends [*his wife*] Tâjbibi to fetch the woman. People take no notice – who worries about a woman? 'They're women, they've probably got something to discuss.' A woman sent by her husband to another man to fix him up with another woman is a go-between, *ruybâr*. She takes messages and makes assignations. Some women don't agree, they angrily reject it; they don't try her again.

(*R*) – What does Majid's father Akbar say?

(*Pâkhâl*) – Nancy, we don't go to Akbar's house now; they're very bad.

(*Baya-khân*) – Akbar strongly disapproves. He used to be a wealthy man, and so fond of Majid, he cried so much when he went on military service. But Majid went bad: he played cards, lent money on usury, and finally Akbar had to pay all his debts. Majid used his father's name as surety for his debts, and his debtors called them in. That's why he's now turned him out.

(*N*) – What about Sharâp? She's got two brothers.

(*Baya-khân*) – He used to take Sharâp to his house too. Tâjbibi arranged it, they're first cousins. But now she's gone to her husband.

(*N*) – But Sharâp's brother Omar's someone to be reckoned with.

(*Baya-khân*) – In truth, Sharâp paid no attention to what Omar or Nâder said. She said, 'It's none of your business!' But there are other women who intervene . . .

Pâdshâh comes in; he expostulates about our not believing him and about our visiting pimps like Majid who tell us lies. 'Ask anybody.'

(*Baya-khân*) – Majid has hooked Jomadâr, and brings women to him there. Sometimes his wife brings them, as *ruybâr*. Nobody notices when women go from house to house, so she brings them together. If there's no one else at home, she puts them in the room and locks the door. Then the man – God knows, men are stronger than women – covers her mouth, and what can she do? If the woman is unwilling, they make her agreeable, or Majid lets her go. The men give him cash, wheat, other stuff; it's his trade.

(*Pâdshâh*) – Apart from his wife, there are Keshmir's daughters-in-law Khâldâr and Shirin; and Nabât's wife. I know them well. I won't lie, or keep them secret, Baya-khân won't tell you them all! How many women is that? Four. Then there was the wife of

Yakub, who's migrated and gone. Then Maryam's daughter [*Mastân*]. That's five or six women, servants of Majid and his wife, who are their bosses. He takes money and gives them half.

(*R*) – How much does he get?

(*Pâdshâh*) – All sorts of things; we call it a bribe [*muk*].

(*Baya-khân*) – It's a fee for bringing them together.

(*Pâdshâh*) – Then on market-day he buys a pound or two of meat and a few pounds of rice, and that evening they have a fine meal. Every evening his pot's on the stove, his 'friends' bring him things to put in it. Baya-khân went there this spring, but Haji told him off. Majid isn't a man, he's like a cow. As we say: when someone goes to his house it's like a match, his roots catch fire, he's tarnished, his whole body's defiled. Majid's a pimp. What can we do? It's his trade.

(*Baya-khân*) – He secretly winnowed some of his poor father-in-law Osmân's wheat, sold it and bought clothes, melons, grapes and other things.

(*Pâdshâh*) – He did the winnowing at night, and got 40 or 50 seer, then he took it round the shops and merchants. So Osmân's wheat disappeared. And those clothes they wear—

(*Baya-khân*) – Osmân's son Na'im told me the other day, 'By God, we know perfectly well that Majid's taken our wheat.'

(*Pâdshâh*) – You know Keshmir? Now I'm not under compulsion to tell you this story, no government commission! But I tell you freely that one midday her daughter-in-law Khâldâr took a man – by God I'm not joking; ask anybody, did she or not?

(*N*) – Who was the man?

(*Pâdshâh*) – Abdollah. I'll name the people involved, it's not far, I won't pretend it was somebody from Kabul; and her other daughter-in-law Shirin was with Gollu, he was fucking her. Keshmir as a woman didn't have the power to act alone; one day she brought Pâkhâl's brother Payz, and locked him in the room, saying, 'Hide in here, we'll get them when they come.' Keshmir is Pâkhâl's aunt, that's why she's angry!

(*Pâkhâl*) – Nancy, Khoshkyâr's wife Yekhak came—

(*Pâdshâh*) – Abdollah had sent Yekhak: 'Tell them I'm coming at noon'; it was by appointment.

(*Baya-khân*) – She was acting as go-between.

(*Pâdshâh*) – Keshmir got suspicious. Khâldâr told Yekhak, 'That's fine, tell him to come at noon.' Keshmir found out, and hid Payz in that room. When Abdollah came, he'd hardly got inside the room – you've seen it – when Keshmir and Payz seized him. I was there too; they hit him with sticks and their fists, they tore his clothes; they beat him up for some five minutes. He was ashamed, he said nothing, and fled. [*Pâkhâl tries to say he's lying*] Don't say, 'He's lying!' I'm telling the truth! By God, if I'm lying, may the world fall in. Ask anywhere else. Richard, there are two hundred houses, here and Khârkash, right? Why don't I tell you it's some other family? I'm telling you straight, what really happened.

(*R*) – Does it happen in Khârkash too?

(*Pâdshâh*) – Don't ask. It does happen, but not so openly that everybody knows about it; it's hidden. A few people know, but not everybody, not the whole community. In this case, every farmhand, herdsman, cowherd, shepherd, camel-herd knows Majid's business. With only two weeks left, Nancy, I didn't want to tell you not to go there, Richard might have got upset; but it's not a good house.

(*Baya-khân*) – When I came there today, didn't I say, 'Let's go home'? I wanted to take you away, but you were taping, so I didn't push it.

(*Pâdshâh*) – You're the most intelligent woman in Afghanistan, I swear; don't you see how his eyes are those of a pimp? Wild and shameless. When he goes out, he lets anybody go with his wife. He knows they'll be finished at such-and-such a time, then he comes back and makes himself known.

(*N*) – Don't the elders say anything?

(*Baya-khân*) – Some do; but his eyes are like locusts, he doesn't listen to anybody ...

(*Pâdshâh*) – Haji's chastised him many times; his father and others have beaten him with sticks, kicked him; he swears on the Koran that he won't do it any more, but a week later he's doing it again. Once someone is addicted, that's it. Does this happen in your place too?

(*R*) – Yes, but if it happened in some village, I guess they'd turn such a fellow out.

(*Pâdshâh*) – Well, in Afghanistan ... I'm not joking, I wouldn't lie; if you don't believe me—

(*R*) – We do!

(*Pâdshâh*) – I'd say it in front of Haji, Osmân, or his father; I'd say it in front of Majid himself, with all of us sitting there. If they deny it, then forget it, erase the tape!

(*N*) – Why shouldn't we believe you? These things happen!

(*Pâdshâh*) – I get nothing for telling you.

Endings

Widowhood

Baya-khân sets out what should happen when a marriage is ended by the death of one spouse.

If the bride dies after the *târ* but before her wedding, and the boy's paid brideprice and gone to *bâzi*, he can take back half what he's paid. If he hasn't yet been to *bâzi*, then he gets back everything he's paid. He doesn't have the right to ask for another girl. Her father may be willing to give another daughter in her place, but that's up to him. Should the wife die a year after the wedding, without producing any children, that's the end of it; her husband can't ask for a replacement. But all her trousseau belongs to him; her clothes and things stay with him; her parents have no right to anything.

When a husband dies before the wedding, his brothers, as his heirs, have first claim on his widow. She'll go to the oldest unmarried brother, who might take her for his son, or give her to a cousin. If she has no children, she has no choice; he'll take her if he wants to. She's their inheritance, as we say. They'll never give her to anyone else, though if her husband had no close family she may go elsewhere, taking all her personal stuff, but not the carpets and things she brought.

But a widow with children can choose. Her in-laws will ask her if she wants to remarry, but they won't press her. She can say, 'I won't remarry; I'll stay with my children.' If they're very small, she'll probably stay with them, raise them and look after their property. She can remarry if she wants to, and take her small children with her. Her brothers-in-law have the first claim, but they won't marry her if she objects. If she wants to marry someone else, not a family member, they'll take some brideprice from him; not as much as for a new bride; something like 15,000 to 30,000, in sheep or cash. When a widow remarries, they do the nikah contract, but there's no wedding party.

A widow who remarries elsewhere can take all her trousseau things with her; but any animals and property like that belong to her sons and must stay behind with them. If she has only daughters, she'll take them with her, and she'll keep her trousseau for them. When they marry, if they're all closely related, any brideprice will stay with the family, otherwise her new husband may get the brideprices for his stepdaughters. Her brother may take them in; but their brideprices should go to their dead father's family.

Neshtar, Pâdshâh/Parwiz and Seyyed-shâh add some details.

If a man dies, his father can't marry his widow; it's forbidden; it'd be like marrying his own daughter. Also, if a widow has a daughter, you can't marry them both, that'd be forbidden too.

Suppose Seyyed-shâh married this widow – her husband had no close relatives to claim her – and her unmarried daughter came too; this girl would be Seyyed-shâh's daughter, and he'd eventually marry her off and receive brideprice for her.

However, if I'm a widower with an unmarried son, and there's this widow with a daughter; then I could marry the widow, and my son could marry the daughter. The son and daughter are unrelated – she's somebody else's daughter, right? She's not permitted for you, but she is for your son.

Divorce

The rules about divorce are simpler: it shouldn't happen. But of course there are exceptions, as Baya-khân admits.

Afghans don't divorce their wives, however bad they may be. Someone who did would be mocked for the rest of his life by his relatives and others, and if his son or grandson got in a fight, they'd taunt him, 'You're the son of so-and-so who divorced his wife because he couldn't control her!' It never happens among Afghans. A Hazâra, once his wife displeases him, will divorce her on the spot, and marry another.

But anything's possible! For a divorce, five elders bring three stones and gather in the wife's father's home; the husband just throws them down in front of them: that means divorce. The elders witness it, so he can't deny it later. They tell him he no longer has any right to the divorced woman. She stays in her father's house; later she'll marry someone else.

It's not good to give a married man three of anything; it's like threatening divorce. If someone offers us three sweets, for example, we say, 'Don't, my wife will be divorced!' Give one, two, four or five, that's fine!

Seyyed-shâh tells what happened to Teymur.

When his father Khântamâ died, Teymur was a child; his grandfather Abdollah raised him, alongside his uncle Dâdollah. Khântamâ was wealthy and left Teymur several hundred sheep and other property. Soon after Dâdollah's daughter Wolesmir was born, Abdollah betrothed her to Teymur. That was about twenty years ago. There were witnesses, Khalifa-Patih, Majlun and others; they celebrated, they fired their guns, the women had a party, they distributed sweets and coins. [*See Fig. 13*]

While Wolesmir grew up, Teymur worked as a herdsman and farmhand; but soon all his inheritance was gone, since he gave Dâdollah his earnings, and anything else he could find, as brideprice for Wolesmir. When she was sixteen, Teymur said to Dâdollah, 'Let me come to *bâzi*.' Dâdollah said, 'No, by God.' We all went on military service, and while we were away, Pâr-khân came to Dâdollah with a proposal for Wolesmir, promising 80,000 in brideprice. Dâdollah told Pâr-khân he was agreeable. Neither Teymur nor Wolesmir got a say, it was Dâdollah's idea. He'd just got engaged to Gollu's daughter Malâl, and he thought, 'If I get some wealth from Pâr-khân, I can give it to Gollu and get my own wife sooner.'

But people like Parwiz, Tumân, Haji Ghâfur and Mowlawi said that Pâr-khân's marriage would be quite wrong. If Teymur were forced to divorce his wife so that she could marry someone else, that marriage would be like a man sleeping with his own sister or mother. Of course, if he divorced her willingly, the new marriage would be religiously correct. Pâr-khân and Dâdollah both said, 'We'll make it correct.'

But Teymur wouldn't divorce Wolesmir. He went everywhere, to Nâder-shâh and Mullah Jabbâr, crying, 'They're giving my wife to someone else!' Dâdollah threatened to kill Teymur if he didn't divorce her, and promised him another daughter, Tânak, instead. Teymur gave in, and Dâdollah gave Wolesmir to Pâr-khân; the wedding was two years later. Then last year Teymur went to Haji Tumân and the rest: 'Give me my wife, so I can go and find work somewhere.' Dâdollah said, 'My daughter's still small; let's do the contract, then when she's grown up you can take her wherever you want.' They did the contract last year, after you left; but now Tânak rejects Teymur; he follows her around, but she won't sleep with him. Dâdollah backs her up. Haji told Teymur, 'Don't worry, I'll sort it out.' But he's worried he'll lose this wife too.

Meanwhile Pâr-khân and Wolesmir are cursed; she hasn't borne any children. As they say, God is strong, his servant isn't; but you didn't fear God, you feared his servant!

Neshtar recounts another case, that of Habib.

Gollu promised his daughter Karâr to his cousin Anwar's son Habibollah, when they were both very small. But after Anwar died Habib went crazy [*lewâney*]. A thoughtless lad, he just wandered around idly. Time passed and he made no effort to finish paying the brideprice. So Gollu decided, 'This boy will never grow up, he'll never be able to look after my daughter, he'll abandon her;' and he gave Karâr to Habib's paternal cousin Dust-Mahmad.

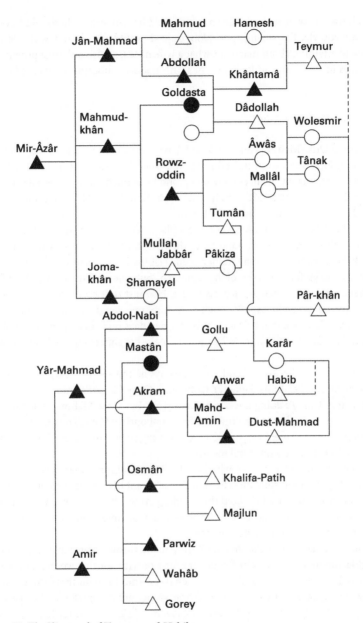

Figure 13 The 'divorces' of Teymur and Habib.

First Habib had to divorce her, officially. He couldn't just do it by himself; it wouldn't be correct according to the Book, and Karâr's marriage to Dust-Mahmad would be unlawful. It was done last year in front of Mowlawi Golzâr. Habib was forced to do it; Gollu threatened to beat him until he agreed. Habib worked for Gollu, but in private Gollu abused him, and now Habib's disappeared.

Habib was crazy; if he hadn't been, why would he run away? He should have said, 'Whatever you do, I'm staying put.' Nobody else would give him a wife. He didn't understand anything about marriage, what a wife needs; a husband must provide food and clothes for his wife and look after her. This good-for-nothing, how could he look after her?

Baya-khân continues the story.

They say that Dust-Mahmad and Karâr will have their wedding in a few days, after the harvest's in. First she was promised to Habib, when his father Anwar was still alive. Anwar was rather crazy; he had a few sheep, and he worked for his paternal uncle Haji Abdol-Nabi, looking after his camels and so on. Haji Abdol-Nabi betrothed his son Gollu's daughter Karâr to Anwar's son Habib.

Haji Abdol-Nabi's sons aren't good people. They're bullies; they'll lean heavily on anyone who's too scared to stand up to them. Gollu and his sons used to hit Habib and kick him around. Since his father died, Habib's been crazy too. He'll work for you for five days for the sake of his stomach, but one unfriendly word and he'll take offence; he won't even ask for his wages, he'll just quit and move elsewhere, for another five days. Gollu said, 'I won't give him my daughter, he's crazy; he can't look after her. If I give her, he'll stay at home five days and then spend a year in the steppe, and Karâr will go hungry. Why should I make her suffer? I'll give her to someone else.'

Gorey said, 'Give her to me,' and for some days he pressed his case; though he was also asking for Mowzoddin's daughter. Gollu said, 'Okay, I'll give her to you,' and people started saying, 'Gorey's doing it today or tomorrow.' But Dust-Mahmad told Gollu, 'By God, if you won't give her to Habib, then I have first option; Habib's my paternal cousin, his property comes to me. Everyone knows he's crazy, so give her to me. If you won't, I'll register a complaint; you must kill me first.'

The mullahs and elders reproached Gollu: 'Dust-Mahmad does have first option. You can only give her to someone else if he doesn't want her.' So Dust-Mahmad got her, a few years back, and soon he'll hold the wedding. Anwar had already paid most of the brideprice, some 20,000 rupees and 40 sheep; at that time women were cheap and Karâr is very plain, as you must have seen.

Habib was crazy, but he did divorce Karâr; he did throw down three stones. People brought Habib here: 'Curse your father, you can't provide for this women or anything else; you're here for five days and there for ten days.' They brought three stones for him to throw down, before fifty or so elders. These stones are in our Book. They gave him one at a time, telling him to say, 'I release this woman.' He said it three times, throwing down the three stones; then she was free.

But Seyyed-shâh and Pâdshâh/Parwiz say that Habib is still around, and he has not divorced Karâr properly.

Gollu eventually gave his daughter to Dust-Mahmad. When the mullah came, Gollu said, 'We've agreed 60,000 rupees and 80 sheep,' but secretly he'd agreed to accept somewhat less. Even though they'd agreed a fixed amount, it turned into an 'open' brideprice: they had a quarrel, and Gollu's now taken a lot of sheep from the poor man, and almost 60,000 in cash, plus a camel and a nice gun.

The point is, Karâr's real husband Habib's still alive and hasn't properly divorced her. Gollu took her from him by force. Unless her husband divorces her properly, her marriage to Dust-Mahmad won't be correct: she'll be committing adultery. Karâr wasn't married to Habib, but she was engaged, and if they marry her to someone else without his consent, it'll never be correct.

Habib's around; at the moment he's Haji Wahâb's servant. But he won't come. Karâr's wedding is in five days. There's no chance it'll be stopped; people would laugh. So they'll do the contract, but in our eyes it won't be right. But if they have children, it won't matter – they won't be bastards, they'll be Dust-Mahmad's! They'll bring the mullahs, Mayoddin-jân or Mowlawi, or Mullah Abdorrahim, to do the nikah. We'll see if they say anything about the contract; they'll fetch Habib from wherever he is, like a dog, and make him throw the three stones down, to make the contract lawful; but it won't be right.

Baya-khân tells three further stories where plans are frustrated.

Neshtar hasn't yet tried to find a wife for Alâoddin. She did say, 'I'll get Nazir's daughter Mandakak for him,' but so far as I know she hasn't sent any elders. I don't think they'll give her. They say she's a good girl: 'We're poor, so we'll marry her somewhere else for money and some sheep.' Maybe they'll give Alâoddin the younger daughter.

Some people say Gol's going to marry Mandakak; he was certainly round there a lot. Even Nazir's brother Wazir told me: 'Gol's given us 60,000 for her; we can't give her anywhere else.' I think he'll marry her when he returns from military service. People talk. Nobody knows whether he really gave the money, but Wazir says: 'When Gol returns, if all goes well, we'll give her to him; until then, we won't give her anywhere else. When Nazir and I went on military service,' he said, 'Gol looked after our house well, so we'll wait for him; he has first refusal.' If Gol changes his mind, they'll return his money and give her elsewhere. There hasn't been a proper *târ*, with five witnesses; it's just hearsay, 'He'll take her.' But if he'd done the *târ*, then people would laugh at them. Some people say Gol's already slept with the girl, but he hasn't. He's fallen in love with her and wants to marry her. He used to go there often, but his wife Khândân was furious when he said he'd take a second wife, and she gave him hell.

Seyyed-Gholâm from Torkheyl claimed Seyyed-shâh[/*Soleymân*] had promised him Durkhak. They had a violent argument, and Seyyed-Gholâm threatened to burn down his haystack. When Seyyed-shâh's brother or his herdsman took the camels out to the steppe, he'd beat them up; he caused no end of trouble. Seyyed-shâh had a huge haystack near his bread-oven, 40 to 50 camel-loads brought in from the steppe, and one night this guy came and set it alight. That year, Pâkiza and I had stayed at home; we'd made our beds up on the platform, and were asleep there. When we lifted up the blankets, we saw a bright light. I said, 'Something's going on,' and climbed onto the roof. I saw a huge blaze. The bastard who'd lit the fire, this Seyyed-Gholâm, had disappeared. [*See Figs 3, 6*]

Poor Seyyed-shâh was one lone family. That bastard Seyyed-Gholâm's really a crook, nobody could catch him. He'd wander around the steppe with a gun on his shoulder, from hill to hill, stalking Seyyed-shâh's camels; he'd fight the guys who were with them. Once Seyyed-shâh's brother Kamâloddin was collecting hay out in the steppe, with Shir's brothers, Shahâboddin's son Madat, Jamâloddin and others. Seyyed-Gholâm started a fight, and drew a pistol on Kamâloddin, but the others grabbed him and told Kamâloddin to return to the Valley to prevent a serious incident. Back in the Valley he told everyone what had happened, and that night we all took our guns and went out to get Seyyed-Gholâm, to arrest him and deliver him to the government, but we couldn't find him.

Eventually the elders got together and said, 'This man's a crook, he doesn't care if one of you dies; if you don't give him the girl, one day this bastard will do something terrible.' My father wouldn't have allowed it, but he was in Kabul at the time. So Seyyed-shâh had no alternative. He said, 'Whatever happens, I'm not giving him Durkhak; he can have the younger one, Latak.' They were engaged last summer. Seyyed-shâh hasn't yet received any brideprice. In fact Seyyed-Gholâm's in jail. After Sâtu was killed that spring, Seyyed-Gholâm was arrested and jailed for twelve years, in Sheberghân. Seyyed-shâh can't release his daughter and marry her to someone else. How could he? Afghans don't do such things. She won't be free unless Seyyed-Gholâm dies. She'll be 'asleep' for twelve years; once he's freed he'll gradually pay off her brideprice.

They say Masâdek's son Anârgol's *narmâda*, half-male, half-female. [*See Fig. 14*] I haven't seen it myself, but some people saw him when he was small. It's not good to talk about it. He's not a pederast [*bacha-bâz*], but if he gets a wife, he can't father children. Do you understand? People here wouldn't give him a wife. But he's engaged to Gol-khân Nâmanzai's daughter; he hasn't yet had the wedding, he just took the *târ*, nothing else. This poor guy Gol-khân came here hungry; he's married to Khalifa-Hakim's daughter, and this year he came and stopped near Khalifa-Hakim's son Nazar-shâh. They fixed the brideprice at 50 sheep and 30,000 rupees. It's cheap, but Gol-khân was poor and had nothing when he came here. The girl's all right, but she's still young; you

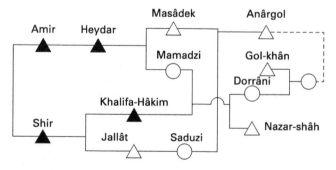

Figure 14 Anârgol.

can't tell what she's like until she reaches puberty; she might be pretty as a child, then lose her looks when she's a woman.

We don't know what will happen with them. If she stands up and says, 'He's impotent, he can't have children,' then she has the right to take another husband. It's up to her. She might go to Gol-khân, or she might go to the government herself and say, 'I can't have children; he's a woman and I'm a woman.' It's a bad business; the government won't like it; they'll say, 'Get a husband from somewhere else, anywhere.' In Chârbâgh, our friend Haji Châri, a Hazâra, gave a daughter to another Hazâra who was like this; he managed to free his daughter and give her to someone else.

The Tale of Sheykh Shâdi

Haji Tumân clearly enjoys telling the tale of Sheykh Shâdi, and the moral lesson to be drawn from it – as in his earlier tale of the girl who eloped with the Turkmen.

Although it did not occur to me at the time, Sheykh Shâdi and Khoja Hâfez must be the Persian poets (familiar to Tumân) Sa'di (1210–91 CE) and Hâfez (1315–89 CE). Though both were born in Shiraz, their lives did not actually overlap.

Sheykh Shâdi lived for a hundred years, and he spent them womanizing. At first he was very upright. Then one day, on the way to the bazaar, reciting poetry, he met Khoja Hâfez, coming from the other direction. As they passed, he said to Hâfez, 'May your love not be thorn-free'; to which Hâfez responded, 'May your wife not be shame-free.' In effect, each cursed the other. With this curse, once he reached puberty Shâdi started on his women. He took ninety-nine wives, and none of them were any good, because Hâfez had cursed him. All his wives turned out to be shameless. He didn't kill them, he divorced them, all ninety-nine.

After he'd divorced his ninety-ninth wife, Shâdi was visiting a nice, clean, upright house. Sitting in the guest-room, Shâdi said to his host, 'Your wife's pregnant; if God sends you a daughter, give her to me.' The fellow said, 'But only God knows whether there's a boy or a girl in her womb; and you're such an elderly man, why do you want my daughter?' Shâdi pressed him: 'I've had so many wives, and they've all turned out shameless; if God gives you a daughter, with your permission I'll take her up a mountain, I'll care for her, raise her properly and maybe my luck will turn.' He begged and pleaded with the fellow, who finally said, 'You win: if God gives me a daughter, she's yours.'

As they were talking, a maidservant came and announced, 'Sir, God's given you a daughter.' So he told her, 'Take the baby, feed her some ghee, fill her on her mother's milk, bathe her well in warm water – not hot, because her skin's tender – then bind her in nice clothes and bring her to me, so I can give her to this man.'

The servant went to the wife's room and told her, 'The master's given these orders, what shall we do?' She said, 'That's fine, whatever he says.' She took the baby girl, bathed her well, filled her with her mother's milk, swaddled her in nice clothes and brought her to her father, who handed her over to Shâdi. 'Here's my daughter, do with her as you will.'

Shâdi took her and wrapped her in the folds of his cloak. He carried her carefully up to the top of a mountain. There he built a house and put her inside, together with a goat, and fed her on goat's milk. He looked after the baby by himself; there was absolutely nobody else, just the two of them. He'd put her to sleep, then go off to town to buy bread, rice, tea and such things. After a few days he'd come back, make sure the girl was sleeping peacefully, then sleep for an hour or two before returning to town.

The girl grew, she started walking; and eventually she was grown up, 15 or 16 years old. Shâdi went to town every day. Then one day he said, 'My girl, today I shan't go; we'll make a *shurwa* broth together.' She said, 'Fine.' So he showed her how to make *shurwa*. She cooked the *shurwa*, and at noon she brought it and they ate together.

A fly came and settled on the *shurwa*. The girl flicked it away, saying, 'If I catch you, I'll shove the handle of this ladle up your arse!' Shâdi was shocked. 'Why did you say that? Look how small the fly is, and look at the size of the handle; if you put it in, it'll die!' She replied, 'Hey, it's fresh young skin, it won't hurt!' So after they'd eaten, Shâdi took out his thing and did his business with the girl. She had a good time, and they got to know each other very well.

One day the girl said to him, 'You brought me here and planted me on this mountain, and I seem to have no family. I'm sitting here idle, let me learn something, bring me something to do.' Shâdi went to town, looked around and ended up buying several pounds of wool. She asked, 'What shall I do with it?' so he showed her how to spin. She spun all the wool into thread, then took the thread, doubled it, tripled it and then spun it again into very strong yarn, winding it into a huge ball.

One morning, when Shâdi had gone, she took the yarn and, holding firmly onto one end, let the ball roll down the mountain; down it went, down and down, God knows where. What happened to it? A cowherd, a strapping, swarthy lad, was turning his cattle into a side-valley when he saw this ball of yarn bouncing along. It had started huge, but now it was very small. He went after the ball until it ran out, then returned, gathering the yarn as he came and rolling it up into a new ball. On and on he went; he'd already made three or four large balls of yarn when he found himself at the foot of the mountain. As he stood there, the girl was watching from above. She called out, 'Can you see the way?' He replied, 'What way? You're sitting up there, how should I know what way you mean?' She said, 'Up here, this way!' *Hala–hala–hala;* this fellow came up and joined her, and they made love and got to know each other very well. After that he came almost every day; she knew which days Shâdi would come, so the fellow took a break on those days.

Shâdi normally didn't examine the path up the mountain. But one afternoon, as he was coming up, he noticed a footprint in the dust; he looked further, and found another. He wondered, 'Whose footprints can these be?' When he got there, he looked around and couldn't see anybody. But then he looked up, and saw that someone had spat on a roof beam, and some spittle was still there.

So he asked the girl, 'Did you spit there?' She said, 'Yes.' He said, 'Were you lying down, sitting or standing?' She said, 'I was lying down.' He told her 'Spit!' She spat, and it stayed dribbling from her lips – you know how women can't spit properly! So he said, 'Sit up and spit!' Which she did, and the spit fell on her neck. So he said, 'It seems you must have been standing when you spat. Now stand up and spit.' But even then her spit didn't make it.

Shâdi was shocked. He said, 'Girl, you've been up to something, I don't know what, but I'm going to find out.' In the morning he told her, 'I'm going out, I'm not coming back today, and I won't be back without letting you know.'

He set off downhill, but then turned, crept back up behind the house and climbed carefully onto the roof. There he sat until the middle of the morning, when he saw a herd of cows at the bottom of the mountain. The cowherd left the herd and climbed up the path to the house, where the girl fed him eggs and ghee, lots of good things to eat; and then off they went and slept together. As they were at it, the fellow cried, 'With my plough and your soft earth, we'll harvest a ton!'

At this, Shâdi, who was watching from above, pulled down his trousers and cried, 'If the seed were mine, one ton would make a thousand tons!' The fellow was dumbfounded, sat up and pulled on his trousers, and the girl quickly hid him in a trunk and locked it while Shâdi got down from the roof. Shâdi came in. He looked everywhere and couldn't see the fellow, but soon guessed he was in the trunk. He told the girl, 'Open the trunk at once!' She said, 'I've lost the key.' He replied, 'If the key's lost, I'll take the trunk and sell it.' 'Take it then,' she said. So he got a rope, tied the trunk firmly on his back, and left.

Off he went with the trunk, down the mountain and into the valley, *hala–hala–hala*. He looked around, and saw some nomads camped beside a stream. There were several tents in one place, and a single tent a little apart. He stopped near the single tent. A woman came out and called to him, 'Brother, you can't stay here; my husband's away, and I've nobody to bring you food. Why don't you go over to the other tents; there are men there, and they'll bring you food.'

Shâdi said, 'By God, woman, I think you're hiding something, but I'm tired, I can't go any further.' They started to quarrel; the woman told him to go away and he refused. Eventually the woman pulled down the entrance-flap of her tent. Inside, she was busy carding a huge pile of goat hair, for tent-cloth. As Shâdi watched he saw a fellow come and sneak into her tent; then they clearly had a good time together. While they were at it, suddenly she heard her husband's voice. The woman was dismayed; 'How the hell did this happen? What shall I do?' She took the fellow and hid him in the pile of goat hair.

As the man came in, his wife said, pointing to Shâdi, 'That bastard arrived today, and although I told him repeatedly not to stay, he dug himself in and he's spent the day laughing and playing around. He wouldn't let me get on with my work.'

This man was a cuckold. Cuckolds are very bad; they do just what their wives tell them. He seized a club, came out of the house and said, 'Damn you, how dare you come and treat my wife like that? Why did you camp here? You should have gone over there.'

Shâdi said, 'By God, don't be like that, I'm just a traveller.' The husband said, 'None of that, you bastard!' He raised his club and said, 'Let's see what's in your trunk,' and he smashed it to pieces, releasing the cowherd, who ran over to the tent and jumped into the pile of goat hair. Shâdi came and hit the pile – and out leapt the two men, one from this end of the pile, one from the other! The husband was flabbergasted: 'You bastard, what have you been up to?'

Shâdi said, 'Look, it's you who's a stupid cuckold, to do what your wife said. This fellow in the trunk was my wife's lover. As for the other one, I could tell your wife was up to no good when she attacked me at the beginning, and that's why I didn't go away. Then I saw that fellow arrive and they got down to making love, and when she heard your voice, she hid him under the pile of goat hair. That's what it's all about. I divorced my wife; off you go, you do the right thing too.' The fellow came and said sorry: 'If you divorced your wife, I'll divorce mine.'

And Sheykh Shâdi said, 'I repent, I'll never marry again,' and he went and lived in the mosque for the rest of his days.

11

Family Matters

A Tale of Three Brothers

Baya-khân tells a story with an obvious family moral – a sort of Cinderella for men.

Once there was a padishah with three sons, two by his wife and one by a servant-girl. He loved the first two dearly, clothed them nicely and looked after them well, but he didn't like the third, insulted him as a servant's son, put him to work and so on.

After some time, the padishah became ill and said to his two favourites, 'When I die, sit by my grave for three nights until dawn and pray for me.' As for the other son, 'That bastard' he said, 'He's a no-good son of a servant, he'd never do that for me.' His two favourite sons would be his heirs. 'Just watch at my grave for three nights, that's all I ask.'

The padishah died. The two favourite sons said, 'The padishah's dead, he's left us all his wealth. As for watching for three nights over his grave, forget it!' The servant's son came and said to them, 'Brothers, don't be like that, our father willed that we should do it, it's only three nights after all; we can take a night each.' They laughed at him: 'Piss off, little boy! We're not doing it. If you want to, that's your business.'

Well, night fell, and the boy took a sword, went out to his father's grave, and sat down a little distance away. He couldn't sleep; his father had willed that he shouldn't, and he felt bound by his father's will; it's only for three nights after all, he told himself.

In the middle of the night he saw a man in white clothes and a white turban, riding a spirited white horse; he dismounted, struck a peg into the ground by the grave, and tethered his horse, then started to dig up the padishah's body. The boy said *bismillah*!, took his sword, struck this fellow and cut off his head. In the morning, this son of a servant-girl mounted the horse, rode it back and locked it up in one of his own rooms; he kept it there and fed it raisins and sweets – it was a very nice horse, it wouldn't eat stuff like straw.

The next afternoon the boy didn't tell his brothers what had happened, that he'd killed a man and brought back his horse. He said, 'Brothers, last night I went to the grave, tonight one of you should go, and tomorrow night the other one, to fulfil the three nights, as our father asked for in his will.' They refused. So that night again he took his sword, went to the grave and sat down out of sight. Then he saw a man, all in black, on a black horse, who dismounted by the grave, tethered his horse and started digging up the padishah's grave. The boy struck him with his sword and killed him too; he took his horse and rode it home to the village.

The third afternoon he said, 'Brothers, I've done two nights; our father didn't like me, but he was very fond of you, you two should go and do the third night, as he willed.' They said, 'No way, we're not going.' Night fell, he took his sword once more, and this time it was a man in brown, with brown clothes and turban, and his horse was a bay. The boy killed him too, and rode his horse home in the morning.

Now there was another padishah living nearby, who had three daughters. He set a test for their suitors. He had seven ditches dug, and anybody who wanted could try to jump over them on horseback; he'd give one of his daughters free to any man who succeeded, but anyone who failed would have his head chopped off.

The two favourite sons saddled their horses to go and try. The servant-girl's son appealed to them, 'Brothers, let me have a horse too, so I can go and watch.' They brushed him off, 'No, you can't have a horse!' The two brothers rode off to the other country, which was about as far away as Chârbâgh. The other boy went straight to his room, put on white clothes and took out the white horse, and galloped off like the wind, very soon passing the others and leaving them behind. When he got to the padishah's ditches, he had no difficulty jumping over them, and he took one of the princesses and mounted her behind him. Nobody recognized him. His brothers hadn't made it beyond Khârkash when he passed them on his way back with his princess. They saw him and cried, 'That man's already got a princess, and look what sort of a man he is, and what sort of a horse he has!' and they turned back. He got home well before them and locked the horse back in its room, and also hid his new wife in another room.

Next morning, the brothers saddled their horses again; 'One princess has gone, let's go and try for the others.' The servant-girl's son came again, begging them, 'Brothers, let me have a horse so I can come too.' Once again they swore at him and refused: 'What can you do, there's no way you could get a wife before us!' So they rode off again. When they were gone, he put on black clothes and turban and got out the black horse; again he rode like the wind; again he jumped his horse over the ditches, and he won the second princess, mounted her behind him and rode home with her; and again he came stealthily home, locked up his horse, and put his new wife in another room. When his brothers got back, he said, 'Well, haven't you brought a wife home yet? Who did get her?' They said, 'Two days running now we've set off and before we've even got there some bastard has ridden past with the princess; we didn't recognize him, we've no idea who he was.'

The third morning, they saddled their horses once more, and once more he asked them for a horse and they refused, and this time he took out the bay, and rode like the wind to the neighbouring country. When he got there, he jumped the ditches, put the third princess behind him, brought her back and put her in another room. When his brothers got home, he asked them, 'Brothers, who got the princess this time?' They said, 'Somebody got there before us again, he passed us, we don't know who it was, but his horse was like the wind.' They were really upset at the whole thing, they'd headed for that country three days in a row, but each day, before they'd even arrived somebody else had won the princess.

Two or three days passed, then he told them what had happened. 'My brothers, just as our father willed, I went and spent three nights at his grave. Each night, a man came; the first night, the man in white, and I killed him; the second night, the man in black, and I killed him too; and the third night, the man in brown. I'm the one who did as our father willed, and I'm the one who won all the princesses. You were our father's favourites, but you paid no attention to his will.'

Then he gave the oldest princess to his elder brother, and the next princess to the other brother, and kept the third princess for himself. His brothers were full of remorse that he'd been the only one to fulfil their father's will, and had spent all three nights at the grave. 'We give up this country,' they said, 'You'll be padishah, you're our superior, we're your juniors, we'll do whatever you tell us.'

And they went that way and I came this way to tell you the story!

Family Solidarity and Break-down

Piruzai place great store on family solidarity (entepâk)*. It is very clear that large families that manage to stay together are much better off. The greatest fear is family ruin (Pashtu:* kur-speri, *Persian:* khâna-kharâbi)*, meaning the break-up of a joint household, commonly as a result of the death of the male or female head and the failure of the survivors to stay together. It is a common curse to wish such ruin on someone. Pâdshâh tells how his own family and his nearest relatives struggle to maintain their* entepâk.

We have a saying: 'A family with *entepâk* won't be ruined.' *Entepâk* means this: here, for example, ten men and women live in the same house; the women serve the house; the men, perhaps six of the ten, go out, one as herdsman, one as farmhand, one as peddler, one as shopkeeper, one as labourer, one works their own land; when they come home in the evening, each one brings something. If someone says 'Bring a stick,' six sticks appear. But if these six become separate houses, the divided family is ruined. One couple on their own are stuck; the man can't leave his wife and go out to work; they have friends and enemies, it won't do. But if we're six men in one place, four can go away to work for several months, and there are still two to guard the house against thieves, etc. That's why *entepâk* is important.

However many there are in the house, if the women are on good terms there's no need to separate. *Entepâk* works if the women are getting on; after all, the men are always out in the steppe or in town or elsewhere, they don't quarrel. But if two or three women fight over bread or water, or one hits another's child, they won't stay together more than a year or two. Women's quarrelling becomes a headache; it hurts the ears! If you come home and hear that the women have been fighting, it's upsetting. Your wife says, 'That woman hit my child! Come on, let's separate, we'll have our own food and water, nobody will interfere with us.'

When his wife Bâdâm was still alive, my elder brother Khâni-âghâ wanted to separate from our father. Haji asked me: 'Tell your brother not to go; it's not necessary, there's no point; let's all stay together in one place.' So I took Khâni-âghâ aside and told him, 'Don't go; our food is yours; anything we have, you have.' He answered, 'No, I must get out.' The reason was that Bâdâm (God rest her) wanted to be alone, to have less work to do: 'Why should I work so hard? I can't serve Haji as required; with so many guests coming, I get tired. I want to look after my own kids, my own husband, that's enough for me. I'll cook five or ten pieces of bread, enough to last the day.' Khâni-âghâ said, 'I'll be on my own, I'll get my own sheep, camels, and so on; we'll manage.' He was determined to go. Haji asked me to approach him again, but it was no use. [*See Fig. 15*]

Everyone was leaving the spring camp to return to the village – I was off to Siâh-band. That very day, as we loaded the camels, Bâdâm picked out her own clothes and things and packed them onto separate camels. I called Khâni-âghâ, 'What are you doing? Don't go, stay with Haji.' But he wouldn't listen to us, only to Bâdâm. They went to uncle Jân-Mahmad's old house – you've seen it – and stopped there with him, in a separate room. Haji and I were both upset, but we said nothing.

I went to Siâh-band. Darwiza was with me – he was our shepherd. When we got back, Khâni-âghâ was still with Jân-Mahmad, but Bâdâm asked Darwiza to join them, to help out and keep Khâni-âghâ company. Our mother also asked him to go. So Darwiza set aside the sheep he'd earned as shepherd, branded them, and went to join Khâni-âghâ, right up until he went on military service [*autumn 1970*]. But after poor Bâdâm died [*summer 1971*], they had nobody to cook for them, so they re-joined us. Now my brothers and I are all together again, with our mother; thank God, we're numerous. But my mother and my stepmother Pâkiza cook at separate hearths. My mother looks after Bâdâm's orphaned kids; they squabble a lot. Everyone has their own bedding, but the rest is joint: barley, wheat, sheep, anything else that turns up.

That winter [*1970–71*], before Haji left for Mecca, he called his children – he summoned me from the steppe where I was camped – and said: 'I'm going on Hajj; it's a very long way; who knows if I'll get back alive; we go by aeroplane, danger and death are present, and we are mere mortals. These sheep, half go to you, half to Pâkiza's sons.' I said, 'But I can't act for my brother while he's on military service. Please, let's get some elders, a mullah, the Koran, sit together and do it according to the Book. If we just divide it up on this kilim, the minute we finish, nobody will believe us: Khâni-âghâ won't, nor will any mullah, we'll have wasted our time. Mowlawi will ask me, "Were you their agent?" and they'll say, "Since when were you our agent?" If I'm not their agent, it won't work.'

So the matter rested. Haji said, 'Okay: I just wanted to settle my affairs before going on Hajj. But I'll only be away a month or two, and if I get back alive, we'll stay together.' After he'd gone, we realized there were too many of us, so we separated our flour supplies, and Pâkiza's family cooked separately, like now, until Haji returned, after which we all joined together again.

But this year our food's separate again: my mother, my brothers and me, from Pâkiza and her sons, and we'll never be joint again. We haven't yet divided the sheep or the land, these things are still to be done. We're waiting for five elders and a mullah to come and sit down and ask everybody, Haji and the others, what they want, to determine what everybody is entitled to; what to divide among the brothers, what among the sisters. We don't yet know how it'll turn out.

Darwiza has his own sheep, but they aren't for his brideprice; that's Haji's responsibility. Darwiza has the right to 50,000 rupees, 1 lac, or whatever the price is, from Haji's wealth, before it's divided. But he has no further rights. When Haji found wives for all his sons, except only little Ridigol and Kayum, he'll set aside what's necessary to get them wives, and divide the rest among all the brothers and sisters.

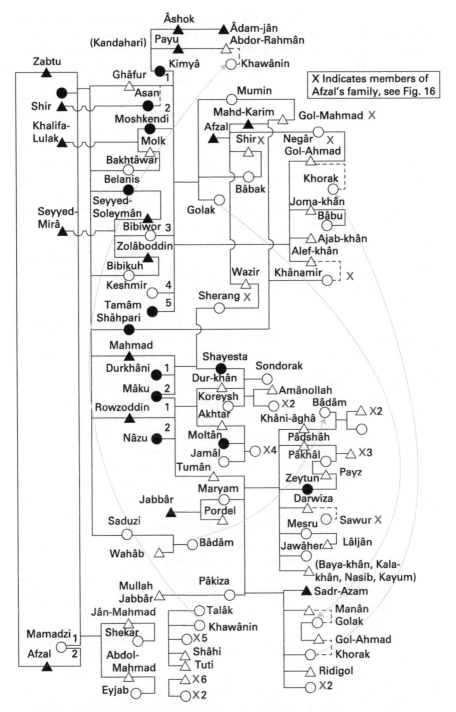

Figure 15 Zabtu's family: marriages, inheritance matters.

Even if I separate completely from Haji, with my own land, sheep and so on, as long as he lives he'll still be head of our family. Whatever he says, nobody will question him. If he gives away something from my house, such as a couple of sheep, I can't object; after all, he's our elder, our father. The most he'll take is a camel or something, but what's that? He raised me, worked for me. If, one day, he sees that his son's destitute, he'll give me something.

As for Haji Ghâfur's family: in spring, his wife Keshmir, her sons Gol-Ahmad and Ajab-khân and Gol-Ahmad's wife Negâr go to the spring camp; their food, cooking and eating are quite separate from Haji and his other wife Bibiwor, who stay in the village; but they're really dependent on them to send supplies, and have to accept what they're given. They do get the right amount of flour, but quite possibly they miss out on other things. In a good spring, with plenty of grass and milk, the rest of Haji's family go to the spring camp too. They leave a farmhand to look after the irrigation; a servant or a neighbour keeps an eye on the house to prevent theft or break-in. When they're all together, they share the food and cooking, but when it's ready they eat separately. Bibiwor and her daughter Golak eat together with Haji, Joma-khân and his wife. Gol-Ahmad, Negâr, Ajab-khân and Keshmir eat together, along with their employees – Mir-Hamza and the rest – and usually the youngest son, Alef-khân; though he eats where he wants. They eat separately because they're so many; also, Negâr and Bibiwor don't get on.

In Dur-khân and Akhtar's house, Akhtar was angry with Dur-khân and wanted to separate from him. He asked our Haji several times to divide all the flocks and lands: 'We won't stay with Dur-khân any more.' Dur-khân owed him some money. At that time grain was dear; he asked for the money several times, but Dur-khân didn't send him a skin or anything to sell. Both he and his wife Jamâl were really annoyed with Dur-khân and Koreysh. But my father scolded Akhtar, and warned him and Dur-khân: 'You're two brothers, from one mother, you've no-one else. Dur-khân has one son, the rest are girls, and when they're grown up they'll marry and leave. You must stay together.'

They accepted his words and stayed together until now. The only time they were apart was in the spring camp, and when Akhtar went to the mountains; then they separated food, water and everything and didn't interfere with each other's spending. Akhtar was free to spend as he liked, without Dur-khân or Koreysh questioning him; and so was Dur-khân. They were apart until October, after Jashn. After Akhtar and Jamâl came back, they joined their food together again. But this spring again Jamâl wanted to separate. She announced this several times: 'I'm not staying with Koreysh and the others, I've had enough.' Relations between them were terrible. Haji warned them again: 'There's just you two brothers; keep together.'

In Jân-Mahmad and Abdol's house, if they're together they cook and eat together, but for the migration they separate. Their mother Mamadzi eats apart. She doesn't lift a finger herself, her daughters-in-law Eyjab and Shekar cook for her: one makes bread, the other broth, for example. She doesn't leave her own room, and they send over a separate bowl, broth or pilaw or rice-pudding, or melon or watermelon; or only dry bread with tea – we call that 'dry bread' however much candy or sugar you give with it. Whatever they cook, Mamadzi's food is separate. She does leave her room, but she doesn't go into theirs to socialize; they'd never stop her from coming in, but she won't go.

As Haji Ghâfur's stepmother, Mamadzi did have rights to a share of his land and animals, but she lost those rights when she remarried [*to Haji Afzal*]. Now she has rights to a share of her stepson Shir's property, if she wants it. If she went to a mullah, he'd give it to her; if he didn't, she could go to court, and the government would give it. But this isn't our Afghan custom; people would laugh and say, 'She must be hungry.' If she'd stayed with her own sons, they'd have shared everything, but now she has no rights in their property. If she separated from Jân-Mahmad she wouldn't get a penny. But they give her food and clothing and make sure she lacks for nothing.

As you know, although Jân-Mahmad's older, Abdol's actually household head; he and his wife Eyjab are in control, not Mamadzi. Abdol told Jân-Mahmad, 'You understand nothing; people are always tricking you; you can't bring anything home; you have too many sons and daughters; if you get hold of any money you go and spend it all in the bazaar in one day. Even ten lacs, you'd lose it in ten days. So I won't accept your authority. I'll be responsible for buying and looking after everything.' They quarrelled, and wanted to separate, but our Haji wouldn't allow it; he reproached them both. Several times Jân-Mahmad came out to the spring camp this year, and asked Haji to divide the flock in two; but he wouldn't, and told them to keep the household together.

But they will split up. I'll tell you the truth, from the clean bottom of my heart: it's because Abdol's wife Eyjab's a harridan. If Jân-Mahmad's daughter won't do as she asks, she attacks her. If Jân-Mahmad's son Shâhi won't work for her, she scolds him, saying, 'My sons work, but you just sit there lazily like your father. My husband and sons bring things, and you eat them. We'll separate.' Most of the time Jân-Mahmad and his wife Shekar say nothing. Finally, when she's completely worn them out, they'll be forced to ask someone, a big Haji, or an influential woman, 'Please go to Abdol and get our share, we want to be shot of them.'

The brideprices that Jân-Mahmad gets for his daughters may be used to get wives for Abdol's sons. For example, Jân-Mahmad's now got Bajar engaged, and he'll be receiving her brideprice; if Jân-Mahmad agrees, Abdol may use it for a wife for his son – but he has absolutely no right to ask for it. If they're on good brotherly terms again, and partners in the household, he'll agree. If he doesn't, people will consider them separated, and they'll soon divide the land, the sheep and camels. If Jân-Mahmad doesn't give him something from the brideprice, like a sheep, a camel or a radio, you can be sure they'll separate everything. Then neither will have rights over the other; both men and women will become heads of their own households. Their mother will have to decide which son to go with. If Abdol quarrels with her, she'll go with Jân-Mahmad, or vice versa.

Haji Afzal's sons were Haji Bahâoddin, Mahd-Karim, Nur-Mahmad, all deceased; and Shahâboddin, Kamaroddin, Wazir, Shir, Kolakhtiâr and Nik. When he was alive, he separated Mahd-Karim, next Nur-Mahmad, then Haji Bahâoddin, Shahâboddin, then Kamaroddin, then Wazir. He gave them their shares in everything, during his lifetime. The full-brothers Shir, Kolakhtiâr and Nik were young when their father died; they still live in his house. Haji Afzal owned all the land on which the houses from here to Mowzoddin's and Shahâboddin's were built; now Shir does. When Afzal died, his surviving widow, Mamadzi, went back to her son Jân-Mahmad. Gol-Ahmad's wife Negâr is Mamadzi's daughter by Afzal – she's Jân-Mahmad's half-sister. [*See Fig. 16*]

Mahd-Karim's sons Gol-Mahmad and Soltân-Mahmad live in the same house as their uncle Kamaroddin, but their water, bread, land, camels, sheep, everything, are

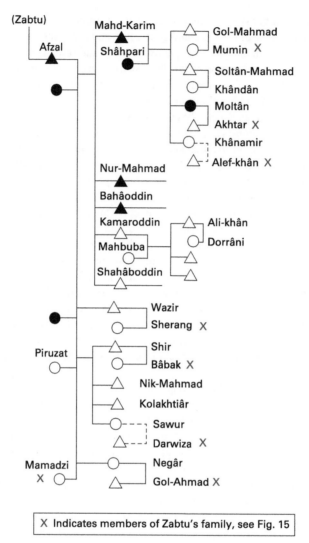

Figure 16 Afzal's family: inheritance matters.

separate. Whatever Kamaroddin decides – to kill himself, or jump down a well – they have no right to interfere, and vice versa. However, if Soltân-Mahmad wants a wife for his son, for example, he'll consult everyone – his uncles, my father – saying, 'I want to take Richard's daughter, is that okay with you? The brideprice is one lac (or whatever), what do you think?' If the uncles and the rest are happy, the affair can go ahead; if not, it can't be done.

There's no need for a wall between Gol-Mahmad and Kamaroddin; their compound's large, each has his own camel place, cow place, horse place, donkey place. They all have separate rooms where they live and eat. They're not animals, to get mixed up.

Sometimes Soltân-Mahmad's and Gol-Mahmad's wives quarrel, and they cook separately; but now they're joint. The other day they had a big fight and separated; and it'll probably happen again. When they separate, people come and scold them, saying, 'People are laughing at you for squabbling while Soltân-Mahmad's away on military service; put up with it and behave until he gets back.' They agree to get along for a little while, and they say things are okay, but you can't see what's in their hearts.

Ali's split from his father Kamaroddin; his mother Mahbuba fought with his wife Dorrâni, and beat her with a stick, without reason. Poor Dorrâni is a good woman, no trouble to anyone, but this bitch[1] Mahbuba shouted and beat her all the time. She was crazy. If Kamaroddin said anything, she'd hit him. She'd beat Ali, shout at him. Everyone told him, 'Get out, we'll help you!' He had to leave.

Kamaroddin has some land, but little else. Ali has nothing, and no right to demand anything; but when Kamaroddin dies, his sons will divide the land and livestock. Ali will bring a mullah and force them to give him his share. One reason he can't take anything now is that Kamaroddin must set aside enough for wives for his two younger sons – they have first claim on their father's property. Ali will force them to divide whatever's left after that.

Hearth and home

One index of family solidarity is the number of hearths in the household. Baya-khân explains this, and describes some common family rituals.

The hearth's very important for us, because both bread and rice are cooked over it. *Negharey* in Pashtu means both the hearth-place and the iron tripod on which the pots and griddle sit. The night of the marriage contract ceremony, they give the wife a quarter share in the hearth. The other night though, that silly man Shahâboddin didn't do it, he rushed the whole thing. He's really stupid, don't pay attention; Mullah Abdorrahim wasn't much good either. I asked them why they hadn't done the hearth ceremony; they said it was too late.

Everybody knows how many hearths there are in a household, whether they're separate or not; but even when they're joint, each family has a hearth in their own room, which they use for cold times like in winter; or they have separate hearths, one for cauldrons of rice and stews, and another for bread. Some women make a hearth out on the veranda.

When a household divides, to help dig the new hearth they bring an older woman from a large household, or a midwife who helps women give birth. They ask her, 'Come and help make a new household for us; help dig out the hearth.' She won't get paid, only perhaps a present of a scarf or veil, but she won't refuse to come. All she has to do is a few spade-strokes around the edge; they'll finish it themselves. They recite a prayer, asking God to send blessing and good fortune. When a new household forms, women

---

[1] Pâdshâh actually used the very common expletive *pedar-na'lat*, 'cursed-father'.

neighbours and friends often bring fruit like melons, watermelons, raisins and mulberries, and hold a party to wish the new household blessings and good luck.

Once they've made a new hearth, they've no further interest in the old hearth. If the man or his son gets a new wife, then she gets a quarter share in the new hearth, not the old one.

If someone passes a black cauldron between two other people, they say, 'Why did you do that?' It's something Afghan people avoid: it's a bad thing to do, it'll make their hearts black towards each other, and they won't make up. If women have to get a cauldron past two seated people, they'll make sure to lift it high over their heads.

Another thing we don't like is hitting the top of a kettle with your hand – which kids sometimes do. They say it'll bring the house seven misfortunes. Another is whistling inside the house; all Afghans dislike it, we say that this too will bring seven misfortunes on the house. If you must, go and whistle outside, in the steppe, not in the house. Songs and singing are fine, just not whistling. Also, we don't like people cutting toenails inside the house; fingernails don't matter. Other things are bad in the house: some boys take a piece of wood, shave the head, put a thread on the end and they wave it around – we don't like that. Then there's the spinning-top that boys make; they take a piece of wood, tie a thread around it, pull it, and it makes a big noise; it's bad to see one inside the house.

Es'hâqzai people have a custom: after midday we don't give anybody salt, however hard they beg for it. We say that the household's *barakat* would go with the salt. If we're forced to give it, we dampen it first. This custom has stayed with us from long ago. We can give salt before noon, but afterwards we cover the salt and don't give it to anybody. Our group of four or five houses have this custom: us, Haji Ghâfur and Jân-Mahmad, Haji Afzal and his crowd. I don't know about the rest of the village, or other villages. Some give salt, but not if they see Haji and the others coming. A woman who's aware of things won't give it; a thoughtless woman will. We value salt very highly.

Haji Zabtu's Family

In Bartered Brides, *Nancy shows how statistical analyses of 'types' of marriage (for example, how many marriages are between close cousins, how many between different villages, and so on) is less revealing than tracing how each marriage is unique and yet forms part of a family history with all the changing relations between different families, as well as ethnic and other considerations.*

First we hear the marriage stories of Haji Zabtu's descendants, a group of five households; the stories tell of the challenge and gradual takeover of authority by Tumân from his uncle Ghâfur, Zabtu's eldest son, the oldest member of the family, a wealthy but declining patriarch. (See Fig. 15)

Ghâfur's wives

Gol-Ahmad, in his father Ghâfur's presence, tells about his marriages. Ghâfur has had five wives, only one of whom has borne him sons. He was once engaged to Asan from the Upper Quarter, but managed to get out of it (see p. 101 where Gol-Ahmad tells of the

*village rift this caused). Here Gol-Ahmad jokes as though the marriage took place, but his
father denies it.*

Father gave 2,000 rupees for his first wife, 7,000 for his second, 10,000 for his third,
30,000 for his fourth, 40,000 for his fifth, and for his sixth—
    (*Haji Ghâfur*) – What sixth wife?!
    That's how it was. When he married Khalifa-Lulak's daughter Moshkendi for 7,000
rupees, people were amazed. It was like paying seven lacs today. How would he pay it off?
The year after he became engaged to Moshkendi, he went to the mountains; our summer
camp was at Tell-e-Khoshk, a black hill this side of Kermân, you may have noticed the
shrine there. 'We had 500 or 600 wethers,' he said, 'and one night I dreamt that a stream of
red gold passed through my house. In the morning I saw a trader with some donkeys. I
bought cloth from him for 5 to 6 rupees, and sold it on for 12.' He said, 'I swear, I sold 100
bolts to the Hazâras for 3 or 4 sheep each, and all at once I had a whole flock. Khalifa-
Lulak had nothing but 60 sheep, including lambs; I gave him 100 bolts.' From that day
when God favoured him until today, he's done well; he became a capitalist! So he went on
until he'd finished paying, and he married Moshkendi. But she bore him no sons.
    Then he married a widow [*Tamâm*]; she too bore no sons. Then my stepmother
Bibiwor, and she bore no sons. Then my mother Keshmir, who at last gave him four
sons.
    Father's first wife Kimyâ's brother Âshok came from Kandahar, with his son,
Âdamjân. Payu's son Abdor-Rahmân Kandahâri is his cousin. Payu and Âshok would
come to visit us in Michiluk, in the mountains above Kachan, father said. Then Kimyâ
died. He gave them two mares, and they went back to Kandahar. After our feud with the
Khârkashis, father didn't go to the mountains again until the year he went on Hajj.
After that, our people became stronger, and we went again.

Bâbu and Joma-khân

*Ghâfur's quest for male descendants continues. Gol-Ahmad himself has been married to
Negâr, daughter of Zabtu's brother Haji Afzal, for many years; but her only surviving child
is a girl, Boghak. In spring 1971, after a prolonged dispute with Tumân, Ghâfur agreed to
give his youngest daughter Golak to Tumân for Abdol-Manân, his eldest son by his second
wife, in exchange for Manân's eldest sister Khurak, aged about nine, who was to be a
second wife for Gol-Ahmad; the weddings would not be held until the girls grew up.*
    Baya-khân and Kala-khân tell how Ghâfur got a wife for his second son Joma-khân.

For Joma-khân, Haji Ghâfur first wanted Zeyn Nâmanzai's daughter; then there was a
daughter of Bâbujân Wardak from Chenâr. Neither worked out. They also failed to get
Haji Khoshdel's daughter, though they didn't actually get a delegation together to ask
for her.
    Then Zarin, a Tâjik from Sheberghân, saw that Haji Ghâfur was very wealthy, and a
good man, so he came and said, 'I trust your family; take my daughter for your son.' His
boss, Mahd-Hoseyn Khân, sent a supporting letter. Zarin came several times, and
eventually Haji agreed and gave him the ring on his hand as a token. Then he took Pâr-

khân, Shir and Seyyed-shâh with him, and they brought back the scarves. He gave 40,000 rupees, and then – in one day – 50 sheep; that makes 90,000. It's cheap for such a fine girl – but Zarin would have given her for free.

On the wedding day they really gave a large trousseau [*kâlâh, clothes*]; and Haji Ghâfur distributed lots of cash. There were many people there. Joma-khân was very nervous. He kissed the elders' hands: Zarin, Haji, then Mahd-Hoseyn Khân's brother Rashid Khân. They dressed him, and he left. They sent the camels, with the women and a few men, through the steppe via Cheshma-ye-shirin; they put Bâbu in Mahd-Hoseyn's jeep, which came by road. We young men took our guns and came by car too.

Afghans much prefer a distant wedding. There's more fun and games; people enjoy themselves. It took two days to get to Zarin's place; we spent the night at Emâm-Jafar, setting two guards to protect the women.

Zarin never took the full brideprice; he got 50 sheep and some cash, but not the full amount. If someone gives you his daughter 'free', it isn't free, and you'll certainly give something for her. Haji Ghâfur paid from a sense of honour. Zarin approached Haji himself, 'Take my daughter.' It's not Afghan custom to press your daughter on someone; people laugh and say, 'The girl's fallen from him into that house because she's so heavy.'

Haji Ghâfur was well known, he had a great reputation. Long ago he gave three camel-loads of tea to Re'is Abdol-Ghâfur Khân, free. He was really wealthy then; he had so much that whenever someone in our village got involved with government, Haji Ghâfur would pay his expenses himself. Whoever came to visit, he wouldn't let them go without something. But Zarin didn't know his sons were so dumb. When he came, he'd say to Joma-khân, 'Take my rosary and show it to them, while I'm here, and they'll let you sleep with my daughter.' Joma-khân didn't go, Zarin was joking. He's a very jokey fellow.

Mumin, Khânamir

In another exchange, Ghâfur gave his daughter Mumin to Mahd-Karim's son Gol-Mahmad, and Mahd-Karim gave his daughter Moltân to Haji Ghâfur's nephew Akhtar; the second couple, being older, married first. Darwiza tells what happened next.

We said, let Mumin and Gol-Mahmad grow up, then we'll hold their wedding. But Moltân died, and Haji Ghâfur said, 'I'm not giving you Mumin,' and her mother Bibiwor too refused to give her. Then Mahd-Karim's wife Shâhpari told Haji Ghâfur – her brother – 'I'll give you my other daughter Khânamir for your son.' So she engaged Khânamir to Haji's [*third*] son, Ajab-khân. Several times she assured them: 'We'll have your boy's wedding, once you've given us Mumin.' So Haji allowed Mumin's wedding.

When Ajab-khân grew up, Haji sent a delegation to Shâhpari to ask for Khânamir; but she said, 'I never promised her – God forbid!' Haji pressed her, so did we all, the whole village, saying, 'No, you simply must give her.' She refused: 'No, it's forbidden; Ajab-khân suckled at my breast.' Eventually she gave Khânamir to Ajab-khân's brother, Alef-khân; and Haji had to give them some money too, or sheep or land. Now they're satisfied, and they'll hold the wedding in a few days. Don't go.

Haji gave 7,000 rupees for her; and we've got two women in exchange for Mumin! Mumin's such a good woman. But Khânamir's unhappy: 'I'm older than my husband. If my in-laws shout at me – Gol-Ahmad, Bibiwor, Keshmir, Joma-khân, Ajab-khân – my husband Alef-khân isn't big enough to stand up to them and say, "Why are you attacking my wife?"' If Khânamir comes here and sees Mumin working, making a bolster, a sack or a camel-saddle, she'll stop her, saying, 'I'm not getting married! My husband's too young; what does he know of women?' Now she cries all day long. Thank God, Mumin's had three children; two of them died, but the third's alive, a daughter as big as Khânamir; before Khânamir's married, Mumin will have another child.

Khawânin and Abdor-Rahmân

Ghâfur's two younger half-brothers Jân-Mahmad and Abdol-Mahmad have seven daughters and two sons, and six sons and two daughters respectively, of which only Jân-Mahmad's eldest daughter Talâk is married (to her father's sister Bakhtâwar's son Gollu). They all form a single household, with Abdol the head. Jân-Mahmad's second daughter Khawânin recently became engaged to Abdor-Rahmân Kandahâri, a former hamsaya who has become wealthy through shady dealings (see p. 230).

Pâdshâh gives the background.

First, Shir wanted Jân-Mahmad's daughter Khawânin for his brother Nik-Mahmad. There wasn't really a proposal, he just told Jân-Mahmad or his wife, 'If you agree, I'll send a proper delegation, and we'll give our brother Kolakhtiâr's daughter to your son – the older one Shâhi, or Tuti, whichever you want.' But it didn't happen. They didn't want Kolakhtiâr's daughter.

Nobody else asked for Khawânin, until Abdor-Rahmân Kandahâri. He pressed Haji, my father: 'I really like your family; I want us to become related. Find me a girl from one of your three houses, either one of your own daughters, or Dur-khân's, or Jân-Mahmad's.' He promised Haji this radio, if he gave a girl. The very day they did Khawânin's *fâteha*, Abdor-Rahmân sent a boy to Haji with the radio, as a present for getting him the girl.

Haji had to get Jân-Mahmad's agreement, or it wouldn't have worked. His wife Shekar was furious; 'Abdor-Rahmân already has two wives, I won't give my daughter as a co-wife!' She went up and down cursing and crying for her daughter, but it was no use; Haji insisted. Abdol was angry too and absolutely refused to approve, but Haji threatened to beat him and he ran away.

Abdor-Rahmân's very wealthy. He worked very hard for his wealth, but it's all from usury, which is unacceptable among us. Our Book rejects it; there's nothing worse in this world and it's very bad in the other. He'll be below unbelievers, donkeys and dogs. He'll bark like a dog, or have people riding him like a donkey. That's why Abdol was unhappy; 'Forget him, he's a no-good usurer.'

Tumân and Maryam

Our host Tumân has three wives. He received his first wife Maryam in the late 1930s immediately after the feud, when they were both children. Her brother Pordel had killed Tumân's father Rowzoddin. This is how Maryam, now in her mid-forties, likes to remember the early days of her marriage.

My father Haji Jabbâr died in Mecca. Haji Zabtu, who'd been with him, called me, 'Maryam, come sit by me and I'll tell you about your father. I took good care of him; I brought doctors, they cut him open and took several buckets of water out of his stomach. They sat by his sickbed and gave him a little milk, and he drank it and got better; but he died of hunger. He said to me, "My daughter"' – he meant me – '"has seen a lot of trouble, I'll give her to [*your son*] Ghâfur."' That's what my father Haji Jabbâr said; but it wasn't to be, and I was given to Tumân.

Poor Zabtu himself died when we were about to start the spring trek. He was such a good man. I haven't seen anyone like him, apart from Afzal and Ghâfur. He was so sick, and he suffered so much from his illness. People gave him every kind of medicine they could think of; we gave him some baby swallows to eat – the black ones that fly around – but he didn't get better. We held his funeral and buried him in the graveyard here; you've seen it. Many people gathered for the funeral distribution. His daughters and wives wept. After that I worked for them, I put up their tent for them. His widow Mamadzi was on her own, so I went and looked after her, cleaned and swept her house. His daughter Bibikuh and I did; and I cleaned my own house and cooked.

When Tumân married me, he always stayed by my side. He'd follow me wherever I went. His uncle Haji Mahmad and a servant put me on a camel and took me to my brothers' house. I spent ten days there, then they fetched me back. When Tumân saw me coming, he cried, 'Ah, my wife's back,' and rushed to meet me, and very soon he was sitting beside me again. I looked at him and laughed and asked what he thought he was doing, sitting by my side. All the women gathered round me. My mothers-in-law were all there, Dur-khân's mother Mâku, Tumân's mother Nâzu, Jân-Mahmad's mother Mamadzi, and Haji Mahmad's wife Durkhâni. Then Ghâfur's wives Moshkendi, Tamâm and Keshmir, and his sisters Bakhtâwar and Bibikuh and Belanis, all these women gathered round when I returned. Moshkendi was my uncle Haji Khalifa-Lulak's daughter [*from Khârkash*]; what a woman she was – like a flower! She was a big woman. She sat down with me and we laughed and laughed.

We had a really good get-together. My brother slaughtered a sheep and I brought the meat with me, wrapped in pieces of bread. That's our custom. When we bring a bride home, we slaughter a sheep and bake bread and wrap each joint separately in bread. We also take the head, tie up the mouth, cook it nicely, wrap it in bread, and put it on top of the stack. That was what I'd brought. They give the head to the grandfather. Haji Zabtu had died, so it went to Haji Ghâfur. There were several houses: Haji Mahmad, Ghâfur, Tumân, and Allah-dâd – he was our guest at the time. We gave each house one piece of meat and one joint.

In those times, rice was plentiful and very cheap. Zabtu's wife Mamadzi kept our rice. One day shortly after my wedding I went to get some from her. She was a nasty woman! Being newly married, I was very shy. As I opened the rice sack, I looked round and saw people sitting there, and I was embarrassed as I got the rice out, so I didn't notice that some grains got into the huge bracelets I was wearing. As I lifted the bowl up to my shoulder, a few grains fell out. I picked up a few that spilled, but I didn't bother about the rest; I didn't think it mattered.

I went home, cooked the rice and made rice-pudding. When I'd gone, Mamadzi asked her husband, 'Haji, did you see the bride?' 'What's she done?' 'Didn't you see, she took some rice and didn't look what she was doing, so the rice spilled, and now the ants have taken it all away. She's such a stupid woman, she doesn't know anything.'

In the morning Ghâfur's wife Moshkendi came and told us what Mamadzi had said. She asked me, 'Cousin, weren't you looking?' I said, 'Why, what happened?' She said, 'When you fetched the rice, some got into your bangles, then it fell out and the ants took it and hid it in their nests.' I said, 'I saw it; just two or three grains fell; show me the ants!' She said, 'How silly Mamadzi is!' Haji Zabtu was such a good man, God rest him. He said, 'Hey Mâmuk, don't be silly, don't talk that way, she's just a girl, she doesn't understand. What is it, after all? It isn't gold!'

Two years after my wedding God gave me my first son, Khâni-âghâ, three days after we had Bibiwor's wedding to Ghâfur. We were in their tent eating supper; I had mine, then Khâni-âghâ was born. Moshkendi got up with a gun and fired it into the night all by herself, again and again! Haji Mahmad also fired his gun; everybody came from all around, Haji Afzal and the rest, and fired their guns. Everyone was happy, their hearts were full. For two or three days we had such a party, so many guns, such a *nashra* [*see* p. 368]. It was like a wedding party, when Khâni-âghâ was born. He was so dear to everyone, they said, 'May he survive!'

Then my daughter Mesru was born, then after her, Pâdshâh; then my sons Darwiza, Baya-khân, Nasib, Kala-khân, Kayum, and my daughters Zeytun and Jawâher. God has given me these sons and daughters. Thank God, we've been free of poverty and worry. Thank God, they've grown up and they all work hard, and every year there's plenty of ghee and meat, enough even for the dogs.

Mâku remarries

Maryam tells what happened to her father-in-law Rowzoddin's widow, Mâku.

There were lots of my relatives already camped up there. I went to visit two uncles of mine, Khân and his brother Atâ-Mahmad, Koreysh's father. I took my cousin Haji Molk's sister Moshkendi with me. We went to Atâ-Mahmad and Khân's tent. Khân's two wives, Hazâr-khân's sister Sabru and Surat-khân's sister Gug, were there. So was Atâ-Mahmad's wife Bibi, Haji Malek-Mahmad's sister. We sat there and they brought us a bowl of roast corn. Gug and Sabru were chatting away. [*See Fig. 17*]

Also there was Dur-khân's mother Mâku, Kamaroddin's wife Mahbuba's sister. Moshkendi mentioned that Mâku wanted to remarry. Sabru said, 'Why don't you marry your brother-in-law Ghâfur?' Mâku answered, 'I don't want to.' 'Why not? Is he blind or lame?' She said, 'I won't marry him, he has no shame', and instantly Sabru and Mâku started to quarrel. The food remained uneaten. Khân suddenly got up and started beating his wife Sabru with a stick, hard, as if she were a donkey; he hit her again and again. Eventually she lost consciousness, muttering something like, 'What's happened to my nose-jewel?'

Moshkendi and I just sat there agape. We hadn't eaten; we just said our prayers and went home hungry. It was late afternoon and we were to move in the morning, down the other side of the ridge where we'd camped. We saw a boy driving the lambs home – it was Rawu – we asked him, 'What happened to Sabru?' He said, 'She's all right,

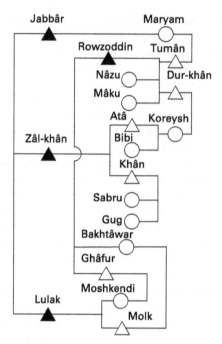

Figure 17 Maryam and Mâku.

nothing's wrong with her.' This was the woman who'd cried out that she was dying as we sat there! Next morning, we were afraid she'd fall off her camel, but their camel-train passed by as we were still loading, and we saw Sabru riding hers, seated spryly on a nice cloth spread. She always put on a show like that. This was the woman who asked Dur-khân's mother why she didn't marry Ghâfur!

Well, when we got to Siâh-band, Mâku married Ghâfur's brother Haji Mahmad. Poor Mahmad was a sickly little man. Mâku didn't want to marry him either. She said things like, 'He has a big red bum, I won't marry him.' So Ghâfur said, 'That woman's shameless, I won't marry her.'

So Haji Mahmad had to marry Mâku. Two years later she bore a fine son. Then she conceived again before her first son was a year old, and bore another son. People said, 'That widow already had Dur-khân and Akhtar, now she's borne two more sons.' But after the second birth, by God's command the poor woman started to have problems; she got sicker and sicker, then died.

She was a really good woman, Mâku. She lived in Haji Mahmad's household for only three years. His other wife, Durkhâni, was a good woman too. But after her third daughter was born, she died too. Haji Mahmad himself was ill; his face was covered in boils. There were no doctors in those days. For several days after she died, Haji Mahmad would ask, 'Where's my wife?' They said, 'She's just given birth, she's lying in.' The poor man didn't know what had happened to him: that his wife had died and his household was ruined. His stepmother Mamadzi and her daughter Malek looked after him. A few days later he died too, leaving only his daughters Shayesta, Sherang and Jannat. His household was finished. His brother Ghâfur inherited everything. They took his clothes and household stuff to the bazaar, to the house of Mullah Hâfez, an Uzbek, a good pious man. As for his property, he was very wealthy: he had many camels, two flocks of sheep, horses, cows; Ghâfur took the lot. His daughters came to us, but then they went to live with Ghâfur. Dur-khân and Akhtar, Mâku's sons by Rowzoddin, came to us.

Haji Mahmad's two wives quarrelled fiercely all day long. It started when Durkhâni hit one of Mâku's sons, who was just a toddler. It seems he'd done a poo somewhere, and Durkhâni picked him up and hit him hard; the boy gasped for breath a few times, then died. People say it was because she hit the child that Durkhâni herself died, Haji Mahmad died, the household fell apart – it was God's punishment. Jân-Mahmad's mother Mamadzi saw it all happen. Durkhâni was a co-wife, like me and Pâkiza. Mâku's other new son survived, to be looked after by his stepmother Durkhâni – as it were by Pâkiza; may God not let it happen to us.

After all this, Ghâfur married Keshmir. My cousin Moshkendi had died, and his only other wife was Bibiwor. He had married Gol-e-Alam's widow Tamâm, and after a year she conceived, but on the trek back from the mountains, before her baby was born, she caught typhoid and died. His wives Tamâm and Moshkendi, his sister Belanis and her husband Soleymân, they all died. Belanis was pregnant, but the baby in her womb melted away; she lived for about two years and then she died. It was the end of that family; only Ghâfur and his nephew, my husband Tumân, remained.

This last comment is exaggerated: Ghâfur's half-brothers Jân-Mahmad and Abdol-Mahmad, and Tumân and his half-brothers Dur-khân and Akhtar, all have large and thriving families.

Tumân and Pâkiza

The story of how Tumân won and married his second wife, Pâkiza, is legendary among the Piruzai. Neshtar tells how it happened.

Pâkiza's brideprice was fixed, 1 lac. In those days such an amount was unheard of; the highest brideprice was 30,000 to 40,000. Pâkiza was a fine girl, as you can see; at parties and in gatherings, she put on a good show. Tumân fell for her, and went after her, and a year later he married her. Jân-Mahmad led the delegation for him; Mullah Jabbâr asked for 70,000, and he agreed. They went there and were fed; then, when the scarves were in the middle, Jân-Mahmad asked, 'How much?' They said, 'We want an "open" brideprice.' Jân-Mahmad and the delegation said, 'Impossible!' Mullah Jabbâr insisted, but they refused. They argued back and forth; finally Mullah Jabbâr said, 'I want 1 lac for my daughter. It's up to you; if you agree, go ahead; blessings on the food you've eaten. But I won't give her for a penny less than 1 lac.' The scarves were already before them; so they had to agree.

After Pâkiza had gone for 1 lac, everybody demanded 1 lac for brideprice. She's the one who raised all the brideprices around here.

Ghâfur helped Tumân, his nephew, who was like a son to him. They shared their wealth. Their land, their flocks, their camels, were all joint, and there was harmony in their family. When Tumân lived for several years up above in that compound on Ghâfur's land, things were fine. But when their sons grew up, the harmony was broken. The sons made things difficult. Before that, Tumân would have stood in the fire for Ghâfur, he'd have done anything he asked. If he said stand, he stood, if he said sit, he sat. He was small when his own father died, and Ghâfur had raised him well. Tumân's sons too would do whatever Ghâfur asked, like their father. Things changed when Pâkiza's firstborn son Sadr-e-Azam died. Tumân's heart went black, and this came between them.

Pâdshâh/Parwiz and Seyyed-shâh add an important detail – Tumân's rivalry with Nâder-shâh.

Tumân paid 1 lac for Pâkiza. First his uncle Jân-Mahmad had agreed 25,000, fixed, with Mullah Jabbâr. But then some people started making mischief: they said that Nâder-shâh was also interested in the girl. They were childhood rivals. Nâder-shâh would have given 70,000 to 80,000; Tumân said, 'I'll give a lac for her'.

Anyway, Jân-Mahmad took the delegation to Mullah Jabbâr, who angrily rejected them: 'If you want her, give me a lac, otherwise go away!' Everyone was very embarrassed, and they had to agree. In those days Tumân was very wealthy, he had no trouble finding 1 lac. He was joint with his uncle Haji Ghâfur, who told him, 'Go on, I'll give a lac; if he wants 2 lacs, I'll give two.' So Mullah Jabbâr took a lac from him. At that time nobody had given one lac for a wife; for one lac you could get several wives. But Tumân was in love with Pâkiza, so he gave it.

One evening in August 1972, Maryam talks to Nancy at length about her co-wife. Pâkiza and Tumân have been married now for nearly twenty years; they are demonstrative, loving and clearly fond of each other. Pâkiza lost her first three children, but now has two healthy young sons and three daughters. Since Pâkiza's marriage, Maryam, despite her many sons, has had little influence in the household or the community. Her closest relationship – one of constant bickering – is with her second son Pâdshâh's wife, Pâkhâl – who is also present this evening. Maryam speaks reasonable Persian, larded with Pashtu words and phrases. She has much to say and the words tumble out of her, so her stories are not always easy to follow, and Pâkhâl frequently corrects or contradicts her on facts and dates. Though she understandably resents Pâkiza, Maryam's humanity and sympathy show through. (See Fig. 18)

After we'd held Dur-khân and Koreysh's wedding [*see pp. 88–90*], the *mâldâr* went to the mountains. When we got back, I was pregnant with my [*fifth*] son Kala-khân. My husband was engaged to Pâkiza, and was about to fetch her.

Tumân said, 'Everyone take their own stuff and move out, we won't be all together any more.' This wasn't because of a quarrel. He said there were too many of us together; we should divide the household, do *wêsh*, as we say. 'If we separate, it'll be more comfortable for everyone when Pâkiza comes.'

Kala-khân was born. Then Tumân held Pâkiza's wedding and brought her home, and we divided the household. For a year after we left Tumân's house, his mother Nâzu and I lived with her stepson Dur-khân and her brother-in-law Jân-Mahmad. There were only Dur-khân and his wife Koreysh, Jân-Mahmad and his wife Shekar; Dur-

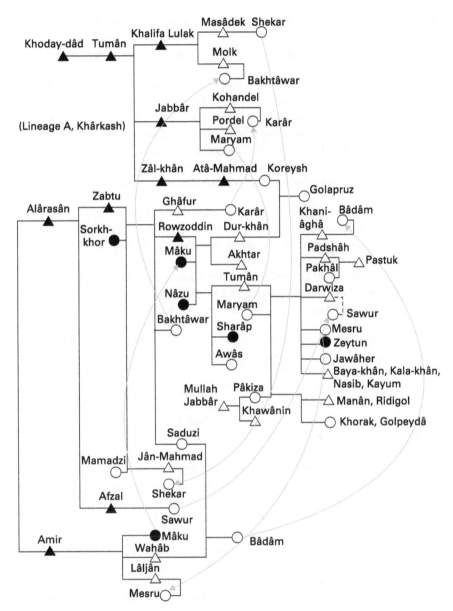

Figure 18 Maryam's family.

khân's brother Akhtar wasn't yet married. I went with Nâzu; we drove one camel, and Shekar and Koreysh drove another. I took a huge skin full of ghee with me. There was a large sack of *krut*, we divided it and took half each.

Before their wedding, Tumân would go to *bâzi* with Pâkiza every night. Nâzu was very fond of me, and she said, 'Tumân, dear, you shouldn't go every night, you're hurting poor Maryam. You have one beautiful wife, what do you want with another? Don't go there.'

But he said, 'Why shouldn't I go? Maryam is at home now, you come and sit with her.'

His mother answered, 'Then I won't stay in your house; how can you talk like this, before you've even brought your new wife? Why are you so mean to Maryam? How dare you talk that way about a woman who's dear to me? Why do you go there every night? Don't you already have a fine wife? Sleep with her, don't go to the other one!'

I said nothing myself, not a word; I thought, 'Let him go, it doesn't matter.'

She said, 'Why should he go, he's bringing you a co-wife, it'll be so hard on you.' She told him, 'Don't you know how upset Maryam will be when you go and sleep with that woman?'

So it was for my sake that his mother left his house and went to Jân-Mahmad's. She owned ten ewes, so she took them with her. She also had a large saddlebag, two big black felts, two big bolsters, a sack, a donkey saddlebag; she collected all her clothes and things and took them with her.

Nâzu and I lived with Jân-Mahmad for two years, in that compound by the mill at Kal-qeshlâq; it's Haji Ghâfur [*Tumân's uncle*]'s house now, but it was ours first. That was before Pâkhâl's wedding, but my daughter, dear Zeytun, God rest her, was married. My sons were still small.

When Pâkiza was about to have her first baby, she was in her father's house. They sent her back to have the baby; they mounted Khawânin [*her half-brother*] behind her on the horse, and she held another boy in front of her.

We were watching for her. When I saw her, riding the horse so awkwardly, an arm and a leg on each side, I couldn't help laughing, 'Why are you riding like that?' She said nothing, she was so embarrassed, and she was ready to give birth!

We dismounted her and all the boys asked what was up. I said, 'Your stepmother's ill! Come on out, leave room for the girls.'

So the boys came out, and I took Pâkiza in. I held her here, like this, as we hold a woman in childbirth. After an hour or so, the baby still hadn't come, so I told her, 'Pâkiza, I've done this for an hour, just hang on, I'm going to fetch some cloths and water and things.'

My son Nasib – he was still as small as little Pastuk here – said, 'Mum, you must be tired, get up, I'll hold her!'

I got up and went to fetch some cloths. As I went to fetch the water I couldn't help laughing, that Nasib offered to hold his stepmother! She laughed herself and said, 'Dear boy, what are you thinking of?' Pâkiza had brought Sija's wife with her – from Kal-qeshlâq, where we lived then, you know. I fetched water, washed out the cloths and things and brought them; and the baby was born.

It was a boy. I said, 'There's another one.'

She cried, 'Another one? Where is it then?'

I said, 'Honestly, there's another baby still inside you.' Lots of people were sitting there; the women were on one side with me and Sija's wife, and the men on the other, with Sija and Tumân.

After an hour she gave birth to the twin, a fine big baby. I'd thought, 'It can't be twins, it must be triplets!' Pâkiza was crying, 'Where is it? Why did you say there was another one?' I said, 'It's come, you've done it!' Sija's wife said, 'In God's name, what a huge baby!' The baby was born, it grew, but it cried all night long.

Ten days later, Tumân brought home two or three *chambarkash* melons – you know, the big ones – that Sija's household had given us. Sija was there, and Pâkhâl's father Mahd-Amin, and Tumân, and my sons. I spread the cloth, and everyone gathered round. We were one household again – me and Pâkiza – inside our large tent. I cut up the melons.

Pâkiza was rather tired. I melted some sesame butter – I'd never seen such fine sesame – and gave it to her with some bread. Suddenly she said, 'I don't want bread, give me some melon.'

I said, 'Don't eat it, it'll kill you!'

Tumân, who'd brought the melons, cut off a tiny slice for one of the babies. He said, 'What's the matter? I gave the morsel to the child, do you want to eat the lot?'

Pâkiza ate the melon; why, what got into her? Nancy, she absolutely refused to eat the bread and butter, but she ate the whole melon, such a large one. If only she were sitting here while I tell the story! She wouldn't listen to anybody. She's a very silly woman.

I laid beds for Mahd-Amin and Tumân, then I put the children to bed. Only my sons Baya-khân and Nasib were there; Kayum wasn't yet born, nor was my daughter Jawâher. I told Pâkiza, 'Come and sleep next to me; I'll look after one baby, you do the other.'

She said, 'I'm not coming near you, I'll sleep by myself, and I'll look after both babies.' She was in a temper, and she was fed up with her husband Tumân, who was asleep over there. That night, they slept apart.

When everybody was fast asleep, Pâkiza suddenly cried out. 'O God, I'm dying!'

I said, 'What's up?'

'My stomach aches, it feels like it's split in two!'

I said, 'I told you not to eat all that melon.' Well, all night long, while her stomach was performing, I was up cuddling both crying babies, right through till morning. Tumân stayed fast asleep, dead to the world.

At dawn, at first prayer, Pâkiza vomited. All that melon and stuff came up – by God, I swear it was a whole bowlful. Such a foul, sour smell it made, you had to hold your nose. I took the bowl with everything in it out and threw it to the dogs.

She cried out, 'O God, fetch my parents, Maryam's killed me!' Her mother died long ago, the year after my own mother died. But I rubbed her stomach for her, like this. I've been really good to my co-wife! She's not been good to me, though.

Pâkhâl's father Mahd-Amin – he'd spent the night there – was awake; he asked, 'Maryam, what's up?'

I said, 'She's got a really bad stomach.'

Then Tumân woke and called, 'Hey girl!' – he used to call me 'girl' – 'what's up?'

I told him, 'Pâkiza's got a belly-ache. I told her, "Don't eat melon, it's bad for you."'

He swore at her, 'You stupid woman! She told you not to eat it, but you went ahead.' He sent a boy – 'Quick, my wife's dying' – who brought a huge goat and they quickly slaughtered it and skinned it. I put the intestines on her stomach.

When I'd done that, she got better. You could feel that her stomach had split, it had made another stomach; a sort of lump, like a baby's head; a swelling like a stone. She said, 'O God, what a mistake I made! O my father and my mother, I nearly died!' But once Tumân had slaughtered that goat, her stomach settled down.

She might have died! I was thinking, 'What shall I do with the babies? God, don't put this burden on me!' The babies were crying; she hadn't fed them or attended to them at all.

Tumân said, 'This won't do, she can't manage these babies unless my mother comes to help.' So he sent Pâdshâh to fetch Nâzu from Jân-Mahmad's house where she was living.

So Nâzu came back and looked after one baby, and Pâkiza the other. A year went by, the twins grew; they were sitting up. Then whooping cough came. It was spring, lambing time . . . Pâkiza went off to her brother Khawânin's, and there one of the twins caught whooping cough, and he died.

She and Nâzu had cared for it; it was such a fine baby – both twins were so beautiful. She cried so much; so did I, and Nâzu, we all cried. The second baby escaped the whooping cough, but a few months later he died of smallpox. Pâkiza's twins died, one after the other.

Then she had another baby; it was born, but it had died in her stomach. It had arms and legs, but no proper head; just a little nose, and ears, and places for eyes. A jinn had struck it over and over again in the womb, and broken it.

The night Pâkiza gave birth, Nâzu called out, 'Maryam, come and see, she's borne a monster!' Nâzu was frightened: after the twins died, this is what Pâkiza produced.

When I saw it, I said, 'There's no God but Allah and Mohammad is His Prophet – what is this monster? It's like a puppy-dog!'

Pâkiza was upset: 'Why do you say such things?' I said, 'We were afraid; thank God it's dead.' I covered it in a cloth and put it aside – it was night, you can't go to the graveyard at night. I made a fire for Pâkiza. At dawn, we gave it a proper funeral. Pâkiza took the baby to the graveyard to bury it; it had a little shroud and everything.

We went to the mountains. Poor Pâkiza was left desolate, alone; she had nothing left, no son, no daughter, all her children had died. When we got back, she was pregnant with Abdol-Manân, while I was expecting Kayum. It was winter, and raining, when Manân was born. I was her midwife. She said, 'You sit with me, I don't want anybody else.' I sat with her, and held her waist, and Manân was born. Everybody gathered, they fired their guns; we had a *nashra* ceremony, distributed sweets; I made some nice clothes and gave them to Manân.

Five months after Manân, my youngest son Kayum was born; and a couple of years later, as winter came, Pâkiza's second son Ridigol was born. Again his mother said, 'I don't want anyone else, you come and sit with me, okay?' Ridigol-khân was born: I called his father, and they all had a party, fired the guns, and Pâkiza was finally happy. We bore these two sons together. Pâkiza's two boys grew up well. She's also had three daughters, one after the other. First, her daughter Khurak was born. I wasn't there for that birth, Nâzu was the midwife, with Koreysh and another woman.

When Khurak was a couple of years old, Pâkiza went to the mountains with Tumân – I stayed in this house with Koreysh and Shekar [*Maryam's sisters-in-law*]. Right at the foot of the Dangak pass, Pâkiza gave birth to her second daughter, Golpeydâ.

When the twins died, Tumân cried so much. Poor Nâzu went back to Jân-Mahmad's; I said, 'Tumân, call your mother back.' So a few days later Tumân fetched her back: 'Mother, your home is here.' I begged her to stay, so did Pâkiza – all her children dead and gone, she melted Nâzu's heart. She came back, and cried again when she saw Pâkiza. Then Pâkiza had those two sons, one after the other; they brought her happiness at last. We looked after them so well.

Nâzu saw Pâkiza's two new sons before she died. Her own daughter Sharâp died. She hadn't been so upset when her brother Ghaws died. I asked her, 'Nâzu, do you miss your brother most, or your daughter?'

She said, 'My daughter! My own blonde girl!' – Sharâp had blonde hair. When she died, Nâzu fell ill again, and died herself; her heart was broken. It was in the autumn, when we let the rams among the ewes, that's when Nâzu died. She was such a good woman. I was very close to her, unlike Pâkiza.

We'd all go to the mountains; but after Manân was born, Pâkiza stayed in the village in summer. I said, 'Why don't you go with Tumân? Thank God, you're newly married, while I'm an old woman.'

She said, 'Let him go, I'm staying.' She wouldn't go, so I went. She stayed at home, either with her father, or in Haji Ghâfur's house. After we got Pâdshâh [*her second son*] married, for several years Pâkhâl and I went; we churned the butter, made the ghee and *krut*, pressed the felts. You know that big black felt? Pâkhâl and I made that, and I gave it to Pâkiza.

She wouldn't go, even though she was now recovered. Now she hardly does any work; she wants more children. She doesn't make felt, her husband provides. Pâkhâl or I do the work, we can never get Pâkiza to do anything.

When she first came, Pâkiza had nothing; no camels, no cows, no sheep. She was so poor. My house had everything; I collected so much ghee, I filled many bowls for her. I cooked a small lamb in ghee; I put the raw carcass into the pot, cooked the meat, and my eldest Khâni-âghâ – he was small then – took it to Pâkiza, and they ate it there.

Then Tumân said, 'She hasn't got any wool; give her some.' He didn't tell his mother or Koreysh; he did it by stealth. He said, 'Pick out some really good wool, I'll take it to Pâkiza so she can make some bags, sacks and things for her own place.' So I got out some wool, and he filled a huge sack with it and took it over at night.

(*Pâkhâl*) – We went to the mountains, otherwise we wouldn't have had it to give. Now see what Pâkiza does; when she goes to the mountains she brings us nothing! [*Pâkiza came with us on the trek in 1971*]

(*Maryam*) – Now she's the favourite. I used to be so dear to Tumân, but now I'm used up, and she's number one. Now she collects lots of wool, but she doesn't spin it herself; she's got plenty of money, so she pays women to spin it for her.

(*Pâkhâl*) – She simply gets Haji to bring her wool and pays other women to spin it. She has money. If my nails should fall off, do you think Pâdshâh would give me any money?

(*Maryam*) – Pâdshâh would give it to you, he has brothers, he can get anything. But Tumân's the headman, everybody gives him things. I could pay for spinning too, but I don't want to, so I do it myself. Pâkiza says, 'I have sons, I have to find them wives, pay for their weddings, and have a good time.' But she has no money worries; she just goes and spends it, getting people to make her clothes and things.

(*Pâkhâl*) – She doesn't make clothes herself. She bought a sewing-machine, then she gave it to Golapruz [*Tumân's niece*] to make clothes for her; she pays for it, and Haji helps her.

(*Maryam*) – Now Pâkiza's in control. Wherever I went with Tumân, he used to say, 'Don't bother to get up, Awâs [*Tumân's sister*] and Mesru [*Maryam's eldest daughter*] will do the work.' Now every day he says, 'Pâkiza's my favourite. You were once, but now you're worn out and she's young.'

And I say, 'When did I suddenly get worn out? How can you say I'm worn out and she's young? A young woman can never do what an older woman does; older women do things their way, younger women do it differently. In what way is she better than me? Nothing! All our community are my relatives, but Pâkiza's a stranger, her people are barely two or three families – we don't even know where they're from, by God.'

Pâkiza's father Mullah Jabbâr was born without relatives. They say a woman left him in a mosque when he was a baby as small as Spin here. Another woman nursed him, and he grew up, became a youth and married. Pâkiza's from his seed.

Now you know. If Pâkhâl hadn't mentioned it, I wouldn't have told you. She's what our people call *armuni*, born the wrong side of the blanket. Everyone calls them *masjedi*, 'mosque-children'. But now they've exchanged women with this house and that. Now she's Tumân's favourite, and he tells me, 'I don't need you any more.' In effect he's turned me out. Now they've gone up to [*Tumân's vineyards in*] Chenâr, and there he is, nicely settled with his wife.

I've seen so much in my life. We got my brother Kohandel married to Haji Ghâfur's daughter Karâr. She was a good woman. Kohandel came to *bâzi* with Karâr, and two or three years later we had their wedding, out in the steppe. There were drums and pipes, we brought lots of sheep, and they served so much rice that everybody ate like dogs and the cauldrons were still full. My mother brought one skin container full of ghee, at least a maund – I'll bet no one ever brought so much ghee.

Then Kohandel took another wife. They all slept in one place. Those two poor women had such a hard time, and for some years they had terrible quarrels.

Pâkiza and I have never quarrelled, I can't be bothered; I never raise my voice against her. I don't care if he sleeps with her. But Karâr was in trouble all her life; she drove my brother mad, threatening to kill herself. She scolded her husband, threw her co-wife's things around, and when her stepson wanted to go to sleep she'd pick him up and throw him around. They all slept in one place, and when a man takes a second wife, he shouldn't do such a thing. When a man takes a second wife, that's what he can expect.

Khâni-âghâ and Bâdâm

Khâni-âghâ, Tumân's eldest son, was the second to marry – a few years after Pâdshâh. Bâdâm and Khâni-âghâ were very close; but their marriage ended tragically in 1971 with her death while he was away on military service.

Baya-khân tells how they married.

My father kept saying, 'I'm going to get a wife for Khâni-âghâ'. Aunt Saduzi used to come here a lot, and she said, 'You're my nephew, take my daughter Bâdâm; she's a nice girl. I'll sneak some money off my husband and I'll pay half the brideprice myself; I'll give it to you and you give it to him.' She got hold of about 5,000 and said, 'I'll give you more.' My father was happy with this. Every day Saduzi would come, saying, 'Nephew, take this money for your son; whatever you need, I'll give it.' In spring he gathered some people like Rishmin and Mâmuk, and went off to Haji Wahâb's for the *târ*. There was only a small brideprice: 50 sheep, and he was let off five, so he only paid 45. Then about 30,000 to 35,000 cash, that's all. Haji Wahâb was generous, because they were close. And poor Bâdâm brought a really good trousseau, lots of stuff.

Neshtar divulges the ill-kept secret that the wedding was rushed because of Bâdâm's pregnancy.

When Khâni-âghâ married Bâdâm, her brideprice was 40,000, fixed. At the wedding, the girl had a baby in her belly. Haji Wahâb demanded *bâbirey*; they had to give a nice gun, worth 18,000. Everybody was gathered, Haji Tabu, Dâdollah and the rest, and the party was in full swing. Haji Wahâb just sat there and said, 'There's no wedding unless you give me that gun; or so many thousand rupees.' Anyway, they brought the gun and said, 'Let her go.' This is called *bâbirey*, a premium payment. It was a pledge, in effect: he kept the gun until and unless they paid him the money. Haji Wahâb had the gun for ten years. Then two years ago Tumân collected 14,000 rupees, handed it to Haji Wahâb in a public gathering, and got his gun back.

Pâdshâh/Parwiz and Seyyed-shâh/Golusar give another version of the brideprice.

Bâdâm's brideprice was 100 sheep and 40,000 rupees. No, sorry, it was 60,000, fixed. Then there was the 16,000-rupee gun, for *bâbirey*! This was compensation. Suppose you give a daughter to Tumân's son and, God forbid, the girl's belly gets full; then he must give you whatever you ask for, 50,000 or 1 lac. It's not done in front of a mullah. But if you fear God, you'll only take 10,000 to 20,000.

On the wedding day Haji Wahâb seized that gun from his shoulder. Tumân bought it from the Kabulis for 7,000 long ago, when the first 'double' guns appeared. The year before last, Tumân collected the elders, fed them and said to Wahâb, 'Please give back my gun; I'll give you whatever you want.' The elders persuaded Wahâb to let him off 5,000, so he gave 14,000 cash and got it back.

Pâdshâh and Pâkhâl

Pâdshâh, Tumân's second son, was the first to marry; it was initially arranged by Ghâfur following Tumân's suspected misconduct with someone in Mahd-Amin's family.

Mahd-Amin's sister Neshtar explains how subsequent events involved Ghâfur's relations with Tumân, and also the intervention of the late senior elder, Haji Abdol-Nabi.

Tumân got Pâkhâl for his second son Pâdshâh by giving his daughter Zeytun to my brother Mahd-Amin's son, Payz-Mahmad. At first it wasn't an exchange. There was a problem, there'd been some bad feeling between our families, and as a result Zeytun was given to Payz, free. But it wasn't Tumân who'd given her, it was his uncle Haji Ghâfur. Tumân had no authority over his own sons and daughters. Ghâfur got Zeytun engaged, and her father Tumân resented his uncle's behaviour.

People went and 'untied her feet' and Payz started going to *bâzi*. Then my brother Mahd-Amin said, 'I'm going to hold my son's wedding;' but Ghâfur refused. Then Haji Abdol-Nabi, who was fine in those days, said, 'It's not good for Tumân's daughter to go for nothing. People's hearts should be settled.' So he arranged to give Mahd-Amin's daughter Pâkhâl in exchange.

Mahd-Amin was furious. Haji Abdol-Nabi sent for me – we were in the steppe. He was sitting in the mosque; he said, 'Tell your brother to stop sulking. We're all related, the quarrel's over, he should give the girl to Tumân's son.' I said, 'He won't listen to me,' but he said, 'Yes, he will. Bring him round, persuade him that it's the right thing to do.'

I went back to the steppe and talked at length with Mahd-Amin. I said, 'What Haji Abdol-Nabi says is right; give your little daughter to Tumân's son, because his daughter's coming to your son. You have other daughters. It's time to end this quarrel.' My brother wouldn't come round. I talked with him for three days, and finally he relented. He's a good brother; he does listen to me. When I'd calmed him down and he'd agreed, I let Haji Abdol-Nabi know; so he called Mahd-Amin to his house here; they gave the scarves, fired the guns and all was done. Once these two younger ones were engaged, we held the wedding for the older ones. All ended well.

Pâdshâh can only talk about the unprecedented scale of his wedding – his father Tumân was making a political statement.

For my wedding, huge crowds came from town and beyond, from as far downriver as Chârpaykâl and as far up as Boghawi. There were three drum-and-pipe duos. My father bought 80 seers of rice, and killed an ox. We put up a guest tent, and my, what a lot of pilaw we cooked. We served food all day until evening, again at night, then again in the morning. He invited the khans from down below, and they all came. Nobody had done such a wedding before in Khârkash, Kal-qeshlâq, Qoshtepa or the Malekis. Ask anybody. It was a huge wedding. There were so many people we didn't know who they were, friend or family.

Pâkhâl tells Nancy the story of her marriage.

I was married very young. My exchange partner, my brother Payz's wife Zeytun, was rather older, and she had her wedding party two years before me. Two years later, she had a baby girl. When she was known to be pregnant, they held my wedding. But I was still a girl, not a woman. My periods hadn't started. It was an outstanding wedding party, better than any other that's been held in this village. They bought 100 seers of good rice. People came from Sheberghân, from Boghawi, from all over. It was before winter started.

After my wedding we spent three months here in the village, then we moved out to the steppe and spent a couple of months there before we migrated up to Siâh-band. There were just my brothers-in-law Khâni-âghâ, Nasib, Kala-khân, Darwiza, my father-in-law Tumân, his wife Pâkiza, and me; my husband Pâdshâh stayed behind, so did Baya-khân, with their mother. We did *mâldâri*. That year I made lots of ghee and *krut* – I was exhausted by nightfall! I was just a young girl.

The season passed and we came down from the mountains. They said Pâdshâh would come up to meet us, but he didn't. I was disappointed! I was happy to be married – it's good to have a husband. When we got down to Chenâr, Pâkiza said, 'Let her go home to see her husband', but Tumân said, 'What's the point; send a boy to tell him to come up and join his wife.' I got home before them – in those days we lived up where Gol-Ahmad lives now – and unloaded, but by evening Pâdshâh still wasn't home himself. Next morning the rest of our camel-train, Pâkiza and the others, arrived from Chenâr. The day passed, it was afternoon and I was cooking – even though I was small – when Pâdshâh arrived at last. We had that night together, and the next day I came here to Konjek, to my father's house. When I arrived, my mother and I both cried for joy. I found that my sister-in-law Zeytun had had a baby girl. She was tiny – like mine here, perhaps a little smaller. She was such a good girl, like a flower. While I was there, they took Zeytun to her father's place – Tumân's. She spent three nights there, then my brother Payz brought her back, and Pâdshâh came to fetch me.

On the way back, Pâdshâh and I had a fight, a bad one! He said, 'You shouldn't have spent six nights away!' I said, 'You fetched me too early!' He said, 'This year I stayed at home and you went to the mountains. When you got back you spent just one night with us, then went to your father's. Should I have left you there?' I said, 'Why shouldn't I go to my father's house?' Anyway, when we got home I found that Tumân's mother Nâzu was sick, very sick indeed, as she had been all summer.

Then my father's household went out to the steppe. After a month or so, Payz came, along with our mother's brother, who was on a visit from his home in Sheberghân. Tumân wasn't at home, he'd gone to town; Pâdshâh wasn't around either, he'd gone on a trading expedition to the mountains. But Khâni-âghâ was there. Payz asked to take me to their camp, but Khâni-âghâ wouldn't let me go: 'We need her right now – Haji's mother's very ill.' I said, 'I'd really like to go.' Nâzu told Khâni-âghâ, 'The girl's homesick, let her go for a few days.'

So I went out to my father's camp in the steppe. My mother was there too, and I spent some days there with them. Then Pâdshâh got back from the mountains with the camels. My youngest brother Shir went to the mill by their house and Pâdshâh told him, 'Tell your sister, "Come back; we agreed that you wouldn't go, and I'd bring you all sorts of things; but you went; since you weren't here, others have taken all the things I brought you. If you'd stayed, nothing would have happened to them!"' Shir told me this. I'd waited for Pâdshâh for two or three months in the summer and he never came. Now he comes back and he wants me there at once!

Well, a few nights later Tumân sent word that his mother had died. He asked my father to come. We rode down to the Valley; I was mounted behind my brother. Crowds gathered for the funeral – the house was packed full of women; after all, it was Haji's mother who'd died. We slaughtered lambs, we cooked meat and rice, with raisins, barley, walnuts, sugar; many people came, and we had a huge distribution feast; it went on for days. She was a good woman, Nancy.

Tumân and Sarwar

Tumân acquired his third wife inadvertently. He used to visit an Uzbek friend in Buyna-qara village in Chenâr when passing on migration or spending time there in the vineyards. After his friend died, Tumân continued to visit the family; but the Uzbeks found this shocking and forced Tumân to marry the widow, Sarwar, to whom he had 'given a bad name'.

Maryam clearly took to her, not least as a possible ally against her rival Pâkiza. Her youngest son Kayum is also present.

When my husband Tumân brought his Uzbek wife Sarwar from Chenâr, we'd come back from the mountains and gone to the steppe. Tumân himself was in the Valley; I was out in the steppe with my co-wife Pâkiza and my daughters-in-law Bâdâm and Pâkhâl. We'd put up a large tent. One day, Tumân came, and said. 'Come, I've done the wedding. Sarwar's arrived. We've brought her from Chenâr.' He'd taken Shahâboddin, Tabu, Mahd-Amin – lots of people. Tumân put his new wife on horseback, and held the horse tight to stop her falling off. Everyone came for the arrival of Tumân's wedding procession. Many guns were fired. They brought her all the way down to Haji Ghâfur's house – he was living in this house at the time; we were living up in Kal-qeshlâq, where he is today.

She spent a few months here. Everyone invited her to 'untie her feet'; she was taken to Nâder-shâh's, Rishmin's, Haji Molk's. When a woman's newly married, everybody invites her. Her new in-laws and relatives give her food, clothes, a sheep, a camel, cash.

(*Kayum*) – Nâder-shâh gave her 500 rupees; Rishmin gave 250; Haji Molk gave a sheep.

(*Maryam*) – Everybody took Sarwar, Tumân's new wife, into their homes. I was out in the steppe at the time. Shahâboddin and Tumân both came to fetch me, but I said 'I'm not coming.' Tumân said, 'She's newly married, you must come. Pâkiza's there, and it would be good if you're there too.' After a month, I did; I struck the tent and loaded the camels, and came to the house. I had one room, Pâkiza another, and Sarwar another.

Sarwar was a very good woman – a really classy lady. She was so dear to Tumân that he ignored Pâkiza, and everyone saw her sitting with Tumân. She'd talk with everybody, saints and sinners [*pir-o-faqir*]; such a kind woman. Kayum here saw it too.

(*Kayum*) – She was good-natured.

(*Maryam*) – We were all happy with her, me and Pâkiza and the rest. Then one day she said, 'If only God would give me a son or a daughter, I'd have a proper share in this house.'

Later, we shall hear Maryam tell how she accompanied Sarwar on pilgrimage to Mazâr, to ask for the shrine's intervention; but Sarwar never had a child by Tumân. She knew no Pashtu, was unhappy in her new home, and after a year or so she returned to Buyna-qara to live with her son (married with children) by her previous marriage. The separation is permanent, virtually a divorce, but Sarwar is still spoken of as Tumân's wife, and he still visits her once or twice a year.

Darwiza and Sawur

When Tumân's third son, Darwiza, went on military service in autumn 1971, he had been going to bâzi with his bride, Sawur, for some time. It seemed she was pregnant, and that there would have to be a quick marriage 'with a gun' (see p. 286). There was no baby, but it has been decided to hold the wedding in Darwiza's absence anyway, so that Sawur can come and help care for Bâdâm's orphans. But there are further complications, involving relations between Tumân and his uncle Ghâfur, and between Ghâfur and Sawur's brother Shir, due back from military service in 1972. Ghâfur had promised his daughter Bâbak to Sadr-e-Azam, Tumân's eldest son by Pâkiza; when Sadr-e-Azam died, Tumân wanted Bâbak to be transferred to Darwiza, but Bâbak's mother Bibiwor refused, as did Pâkiza – both claiming that Darwiza's mother Maryam was 'dirty', and that if there were a transfer it should be to another of Pâkiza's sons, the infant Manân. Ghâfur proceeded to marry Bâbak to Shir, whose first wife had just died. Tumân was furious and cut relations with his uncle; who eventually sought to make peace by arranging the marriage of Shir's sister to Darwiza, and his own daughter Golak to Manân. But Shir was annoyed at Ghâfur's actions, and challenged the brideprice.

For the complete story, see Bartered Brides, *(N. Tapper 1991: 269–72. Pâdshâh summarizes.*

Finding a wife for my brother Darwiza? That's a long story; a delicate matter.

(N) – To do with Bâbak not being given?

Yes, that's it: you know all about it! Many years ago we did the *fâteha* and *târ* for Sawur. For three years he didn't go to *bâzi*, and things went quiet. Then we took him; and then a year ago he went on military service. The day he went to *bâzi*, Haji sent Shir, her oldest brother, 30 sheep and 10,000 to 12,000 rupees. They said, 'We agreed 80 sheep, so now 50 sheep are left.' But we said that it was 50 sheep originally, so there are only twenty left. That's the problem; we'll see what happens. Witnesses at the *târ* heard only that Haji Ghâfur's daughter Bâbak was engaged to Shir, his daughter Golak to my brother Manân, and Shir's sister Sawur to Darwiza; so all of them were mixed up. Then Shir got a little greedy, that's why we've still got a problem. When Shir comes back from military service, the matter will be resolved, and we'll hold Darwiza's wedding.

A bride for Baya-khân

Baya-khân is not yet engaged, but during our stay there is an active search (in which we participate) for a suitable bride, much to everyone's amusement. Everybody wants Haji Tumân as in-law, so there are many possibilities, but in 1972 Tumân has no spare cash or animals; and he has been thoroughly spooked by the Kimyâ elopement. Baya-khân himself has certain girls in mind, but is unwilling to discuss them. He makes his preference known by visiting his favourite, the daughter of Mullah Pakhroddin (who is also in favour of the match); and this is the subject of jokes as Pâdshâh tries to summarize the situation; Baya-khân, Kala-khân (who's next after Baya-khân) and Seyyed-shâh/Golusar participate.

As for getting a wife for Baya-khân, the problem is that we've run out of sheep! Nothing's left. Wherever there's a girl, if Haji sends a delegation, they'll give her right away. Everybody in these villages wants Baya-khân! No really, I'm not joking! Rishmin and his crowd are eager to have him. Anyone who approaches them on Baya-khân's behalf will be accepted. Mullah Pakhroddin too would be delighted: the house beyond the âghâ's, where Bârân comes from.

[*Kala-khân and the others keep joking; they won't let Pâdshâh talk*]

Mullah Pakhroddin has told all his farmhands and neighbours, men and women, 'If Haji will have us as in-laws, I'll give Baya-khân whichever daughter he wants, an older one or a younger one; then we'll become Haji's relatives – he's a very good man. I won't give to my own people, I'll give to him.'

Mâmuk too would be happy to give whichever of his sisters Haji approves of. And Pâr-khân has a daughter; he'll give her if Haji approaches him. The point is, it's up to Haji.

Mâmuk's sister Manakey was willing to marry Baya-khân, and he was happy too; but she went to Kadujân. The women discussed the matter at a party; they talked the way women do, saying 'He's a nice chap, I'll take him for a husband.' Pâkhâl heard them. Older women are too senior to talk that way. It's the kind of talk that goes on between close friends; everyone talks with their own crowd at a party; there are many women and they gather in small groups, or they go off behind a wall while the other women are singing. Pâkhâl was talking with Manakey herself and her sister Angurak. Pâkhâl is 'sworn-sister' with another sister, Galugak, Kuk's wife. But Haji didn't like these women [*they're all closely related to Kimyâ*]. 'One night they'll run away, and the shame would last forever.' Can't you see Baya-khân being deserted?

Golapruz and Soleymân-shâh

Golapruz is one of many daughters of Tumân's half-brother Dur-khân. This is another example of an early engagement that fails because: (a) one of the parents dies; and (b) one of the offspring proves inadequate.

Neshtar, Soleymân-shâh's paternal aunt, explains.

Let me tell the story of Soleymân-shâh and Golapruz. First, God gave Dur-khân no sons, only daughters. Soleymân-shâh's mother Sharâp was Dur-khân's sister. She said, 'Brother, why are you so upset?' Her husband Golusar said the same. Dur-khân said, 'What on earth shall I do with all these girls?' Sharâp said, 'Our sons are your sons.' Dur-khân said, 'I'll give you my baby daughter Golapruz,' and she said, 'We accept.'

After that, Dur-khân's uncle Jân-Mahmad gave the *wëkrey/târ*. They said the prayers, fired several guns and the deal was done. Time passed. Sharâp told us Soleymân-shâh would fetch his wife when she grew up. We made her all the right clothes, and took them as *push* to Dur-khân, and the affair was settled.

Now everything's gone wrong. Sharâp's dead, and Dur-khân's changed his mind. If his sister were still alive, his heart would still be settled. Now he says: 'Who gives his daughter for 3,000 rupees?' That's what was fixed, soon after she was born. Now we'll see what happens. People change.

Pâdshâh elaborates.

When Golusar's wife Sharâp was alive, she went to her brother Dur-khân and said, 'Give your daughter Golapruz to my son Soleymân-shâh.' They were both tiny. He didn't want to upset his sister, so he agreed; they had a *târ*, with sweets, scarves and so on. It was just Jân-Mahmad who did the prayers, with only Golusar and junior people present; so it was a verbal agreement, there'd been no real mullah. Golusar gave them a goat; he says he gave it as brideprice, but Dur-khân says, 'No, I bought it.' At that time a wife cost 25,000 to 30,000; a good one, 30,000 to 35,000. Since then, Golusar's given nothing more, and the girl's grown up, so's his son.

Then one day a delegation came to Dur-khân; it was Pâr-khân, who said, 'Give Golapruz to me, and I'll give my daughter to your brother Akhtar.' Akhtar had a wife, but he too had no sons, only daughters. Anyway, they turned him down. When they heard about it, Golusar brought his brother Mahd-Amin to Haji Tumân, saying, 'What's going on, my son's still alive!' Dur-khân too came to Tumân with Akhtar and said, 'What are you doing? You can do what you like to me, but I shan't let this girl go, she's engaged to Soleymân-shâh.' Pâr-khân gave up his suit.

Another time, Manakey sent a delegation; he too was put off. The same happened with Shâh-Mahmad Khân from Seyyedâbâd; Golusar sent and warned him that it wasn't on. Another suitor was Mullah Ahmad-shâh from Khârkash. Several people have tried, but the matter's unresolved.

The other day Golusar came to me and said, 'Tell your father we've a vineyard up there in Chenâr, with 1,000 or 1,200 vines; he can have them, and I'll also throw in my little daughter Sayrak, Soleymân-shâh's half-sister; but tell Haji that I'll kill myself before allowing Golapruz to marry anyone else.'

I haven't yet told Haji; I haven't found the right opportunity to speak about such a matter. With luck it'll be resolved. You too could try and help. The problem is, Golapruz doesn't want to marry Soleymân-shâh: she thinks he's good-for-nothing, he won't do anything by himself. 'What can I do with such a lazy fellow?' We tell her he's her first cousin; he may be poor, but he's a good man. She says she wants a real man; a fine young man, with a thick neck and a big chest! She says, 'I'll accept anyone my father chooses, except him.' But it's not her decision; it's up to her mother Koreysh and her father Dur-khân, nobody else; not even Akhtar.

Ghaws and Family

This is the sad story of Tumân's mother's brother Mahd-Ghaws and his family. He started off well, with plenty of animals and land, but fell into a downward spiral, due to bad luck and some bad planning. His eldest son died of smallpox; one daughter died of scrofula; another daughter drowned in a flash-flood; Mir-Hamza, the surviving son, is regarded as 'simple-minded', unable or unwilling to adjust, or to resist his land-grabbing cousins, despite efforts by his remaining half-sister. (See Fig. 19)

Baya-khân starts the story.

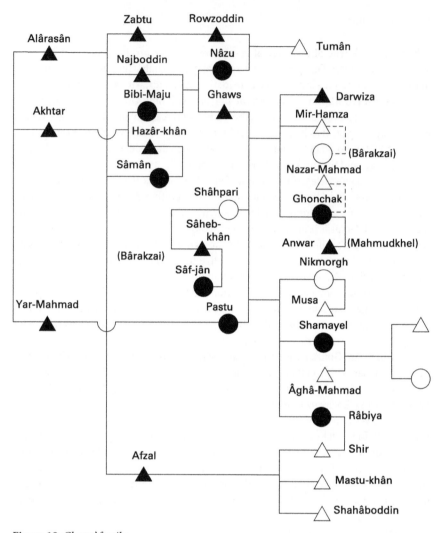

Figure 19 Ghaws' family.

Ghaws gave his daughter Ghonchak to Nazar-Mahmad; I think the bastard came to *bâzi* just one night, then divorced her. Did you meet Sâf-jân last year? She died this spring. She was the widow of Sâheb-khân, Ghonchak's mother Shâhpari's brother. People said that although Nazar-Mahmad was engaged to Ghonchak, he had an affair with Sâf-jân, and forgot about his bride. For some years he sat around, neither coming to *bâzi* nor paying any brideprice. Shâhpari and others got people together and told him, 'This won't do; give us our brideprice and take your wife, or we'll give her somewhere else.' Then, people say, Sâf-jân told Nazar-Mahmad, 'Why do you want this woman? Divorce her and I'll look after you.' He was involved with Sâf-jân, and she pushed him off the Right Path. So five elders got together and Nazar-Mahmad threw down the stones and divorced Ghonchak.

After that, Anwar Mahmudkheyl came from Qataghan with 35 Arabi wethers. In the spring Haji took his sheep with our flock; at the end of spring he told Haji he wanted to marry Ghonchak: 'I'll give these animals and 10,000 rupees.' So Anwar gave 35 wethers and some cash; he went to *bâzi* for a month or two, then one evening people gathered and they did the nikah; they didn't have a wedding party. Some say Nazar-Mahmad had been to *bâzi* once or twice, secretly; others say not. Poor Anwar was an old man, he didn't care whether she'd done *bâzi* or not. He just needed a wife to cook for him, and nobody else would give him one. But less than two years after the wedding poor Ghonchak died; a little later Anwar died too. Ghonchak died about four years ago, of scrofula (*khanâzel*): she had swellings like Bakhtak, Seyyed-shâh's daughter. They're terrible; they throw up lumps like melons, but if you remove one, the next year another will appear.

Pâdshâh introduces Mir-Hamza.

Someone with a large household but few sons will hire a house-servant (*kur-mozdur*). Haji Ghâfur, for example, has sons, but they're not up to working, so this year he took on Ghaws' son Mir-Hamza. Last year he was our servant; Pâkiza and her sons were in the mountains with you; I was here alone, so I hired Mir-Hamza and showed him what to do. Smart people can do the work without needing their boss to tell them how, but Mir-Hamza's a bit slow; you have to help him along.

Mir-Hamza and his mother Shâhpari eat at home when they have food; otherwise they come to us, or to Shir, Jân-Mahmad, Dur-khân, Wazir, wherever they can find it. Some people give Shâhpari flour. If she goes to Nâder-shâh's house she'll get flour, she can't bring cooked food all that way.

Mir-Hamza is saving cash to pay his brideprice; nobody will help him. He sold 5½ *jerib* of land to Mastu for 3,000 rupees a *jerib* – cheap, but it was some years ago, and there's no water there. He's nearly finished paying the brideprice, there's not much left. He still has another 5½ *jerib* up at Khârkash, near his uncle's.

Baya-khân adds more on Mir-Hamza.

Mir-Hamza is Ghaws and Shâhpari's son. Their elder son Darwiza died about nine years ago. Since he was buried, people fetch dust from his grave and scatter it among the sheep; it cures their diseases. He was a very good lad, smart and capable. If he'd been here he'd have hung on to their land, worked hard, and so on.

Mir-Hamza's rather simple; he'll work for you as a servant, but he can't help himself, he can't work his own land; he insults everyone, even small children. He can't look after his mother or anyone, even himself; he doesn't dress properly, can't tie his turban. He won't work properly, he just sits there like a stomach.

Mir-Hamza has 11 *jeribs* of very fertile land up beyond the hill, near Mullah Jabbâr, and an hour of water registered in his name. Sixty *jeribs* of land are registered in the deeds in Ghaws' name. Somehow, it's now shrunk to 5½ *jeribs*; his cousins Mastuk, Shir,

Shahâboddin and crowd have grabbed the rest. Pâdshâh[/*Parwiz*] sharecropped Mir-Hamza's land. He sowed some 25 seers of wheat and reaped 370, an excellent crop. Now Pâdshâh's done melons there, but Mir-Hamza sold half-an-hour of water to us, and half-an-hour to Jân-Mahmad.

Seyyed-shâh/Golusar has more on the family.

Ghaws was very fond of his other wife, Pastu. She had many chickens and we used to go there and steal her chicks. When Ghaws died, Pastu and her son-in-law Musa demanded her daughter Nik-morgh's share of the inheritance, which Shâhpari and Mir-Hamza had taken over and sold to Mastu, giving Musa thirteen goats and a radio as compensation.

Mir-Hamza now works as Gol-Ahmad's house-servant. He's engaged to a Bârakzai girl, but he can't afford to fetch her from her father's house. He's dependent on Shir. Right now, Shahâboddin's using land that belongs to Mir-Hamza; in the deeds, Shahâboddin has a right to 5½ *jerib*s at most. I saw Mir-Hamza there the other day with Pâdshâh, bringing in their beans and straw; I told him, 'You idiot, you've 60 *jerib*s in your father's name. Sell 10 *jerib*s and take the case to court, and you'll find 50 *jerib*s will fall into your hands.'

Mir-Hamza's half-sister Nik-morgh declared that she'll take them to court. Nobody can deny that she has a claim. The other day she came again and said, 'I'll fight for my rights. All I've had is a cow and some goats. Where's my land? The deeds show 60 *jerib*s in my father's name, but there's only 10 *jerib*s to be seen. We've one brother, Mir-Hamza, and we're two sisters; Shamayel married Âghâ-Mahmad Nurzai. We'll divide the land in half: 30 *jerib*s to Mir-Hamza, 30 to us. From our 30, 15 go to Âghâ-Mahmad and I'll keep 15 for myself.'

If they go to court, the judge will give them their rights. Now Haji and the rest are trying to calm them down, saying, 'Sure you've got a right, we'll sort it out.' Haji knows what to do, it's up to him. Someone who's illiterate might as well be blind. If you can read and write just a little, you can find the road and go a long way.

Baya-khân tells the tale of Mir-Hamza's brother-in-law, Âghâ-Mahmad Nurzai.

Âghâ-Mahmad Nurzai came here 30 to 35 years ago. He has no land. He married Mir-Hamza's sister Shamayel when her parents Ghaws and Pastu were alive. I was very small at the time. That year when there were many flash-floods in the steppe, one of them swept Shamayel away, poor woman, with all her belongings. We sent Seyyed-shâh to find her, along with some others from the village. They found her all the way down at Cheshma-ye-shirin – when someone's died in the river, it throws them up again. The floodwaters threw up her trousseau in one place, the lambs in another and her tent in another. They brought her back and buried her in this graveyard. It was a terrible year.

When Shamayel was alive, Âghâ-Mahmad was wealthy: he had 250 to 300 sheep, and a nice fat horse that he kept for buzkashi. But after she died, he lost the lot. She left him with a son and a daughter, now in their twenties. A year after she died, he married his daughter to Din-Mahmad's son, and for a year or two there was no woman in the house. A household without a woman to keep things together can't manage, it's ruined. They say, 'Man fetches with a shovel, woman sweeps with a broom' [*mard mira kat-e pâru, zan mizana kat-e jâru*].

Then he got Karim Nurzai's daughter for his son – I think he gave 100 or 120 sheep in brideprice. After he'd paid for the wedding and other cash expenses, his sheep were gone. Last year he had two sheep and two goats, and he sold them at the end of spring. Then he had only five or six camels left. They became his living. This year, when he got hungry, he'd sell a camel for 4,000 to buy flour. His horse died of hunger, and so did two camels. He sold a camel to Jân-Mahmad's Arab sharecropper. In the winter the Arab gave him a load of hay, to be paid for in spring. When he heard that Âghâ-Mahmad was strapped for cash, he demanded payment; Âghâ-Mahmad said he had no money, so he sold him a camel to pay for the hay.

Another camel was stolen the other day in the steppe, along with Mowzoddin's. There's been no trace of them. They went after them, but a good thief will have taken them non-stop into the western steppe towards Maymana; or east to Mazâr. Âghâ-Mahmad has one camel left, the rest are finished.

His son's a piece of work. If there's flour or anything in the house, he steals it and sells it to shopkeepers and traders – I've seen it with my own eyes. He steals his own wife's coins and sells them. And he's heavily in debt, having taken money from people in advance for cumin and wheat. He owes money all over the place. Now he's disappeared; he's living somewhere, working as a labourer. People didn't want him around. Once he came back for a few days; he slept in that hut day and night – I saw him. His father said, 'If his creditors see him, they'll grab him, they won't leave him alone.' He stayed a few nights and then went off again.

His father calls him *harâmi*, someone who doesn't belong to his father but goes around with his mother. He steals things his poor father's collected, and sells them at half-price; if flour's 100 rupees he sells it for 50. When his mother was alive, she didn't let him thieve so much. His wife says nothing. Âghâ-Mahmad is a man of the desert; he'd go out to fetch thorns for the camels while his son lazed around the house. What should one do with a son who doesn't look after his father or obey him? If you sour your father's heart, it can't be good.

Neshtar tells the story of the flood that carried off Ghaws' daughter Shamayel.

It was about ten years ago, in May, just after the shearing. The weather was very warm. In our tent there were only me, my daughter-in-law, and Mowzoddin; Seyyed-shâh had gone to the village along with all my sons. About midday, suddenly there was a violent wind. I sent the women to secure the tent. With the wind came hailstones, as big as rocks – those white hailstones that can kill a man; they piled up against Wazir's tent like a wall and stayed there for three days.

Shamayel's family were asleep when the flood came. Her husband shouted, 'Hey, stupid, get up, get out!' But she didn't, and when the flood arrived, it wrapped her in the tent and swept her away. Nobody did anything that night, but early in the morning her children came to their uncle Shir's place; they cried and cried, 'Our mother's gone!' Their uncles Shir, Kala-khân, Komaydân, Gol, all rode off to find her. When they came upon her, only one foot was showing, the rest of her was hidden under the hail; but her clothes had been torn to pieces; only her overshirt remained, the rest was lying around in shreds. Even her nose-jewel had fallen out. She was naked, indecent. There were no women with them, so Shir took off his coat and put it over her to cover her properly, and took her home to her mother; then they buried her in our graveyard.

Golshâh Taymani

Neshtar continues the story of her brother Rangin's widow Golshâh Taymani (See pp. 55f. and Fig. 4). She marries Rangin's nephew Bâlu, but he and his mother Badri badly mistreat Golshâh's children by Rangin, and she takes them to safety among her other in-laws.

Rangin's brothers were Mahd-Amin, Sâleh, Golusar and Mahd-Hanifa. When he died, his widow Golshâh passed to Sâleh, who was on military service. Sâleh came on leave and found Mahd-Amin sitting with Golusar in his house. Sâleh said, 'The widow's young; marry her to anybody you like.' Golusar said, 'She's like our sister, she shouldn't marry one of us.' Mahd-Amin said the same. Sâleh said, 'Then either let my son Bâlu have her, or one of Mahd-Amin's sons, whichever one wants her.' So they said, 'Okay, we'll arrange it.'

Sâleh told her, 'Marry my son; go and tell my brothers that you'll marry Bâlu.' She said, 'Okay.' The next day she went to Golusar's house, washed her hair, combed and braided it; she didn't ask Golusar, but she went to Mahd-Amin and told him she'd marry Bâlu. Mahd-Amin said, 'Fine, go ahead'. But nobody knew anything about it. I was her sister-in-law; she should have come to me first to say, 'I've worn your clothes, I'll go with you;' or to her brothers-in-law, Mahd-Amin or Golusar, to say, 'I've eaten your food, I'll go wherever you go; but I won't remarry.' But she acted without consulting anybody.

That night several people passed by, saying, 'Nikah, nikah!' My daughter-in-law Shamayel said, 'Mum, people are calling out nikah; it looks like Rangin's widow's getting married.' I said, 'But I haven't heard anything about it.' In the morning, after I'd got up and said my prayers, I saw that Rangin's house had moved; they'd dismantled the beams, the doors, all the timber, packed their clothes and loaded everything on the camels; they'd taken Golshâh, her daughter, her two sons, the tent, the lot, to Sâleh's house. Mahd-Amin said, 'It's okay, Sâleh will take care of the children, he's their uncle.' But then Sâleh went back to his military service.

Sâleh's wife Badri – daughter of Delbar Pakhizai – is a very bad woman, with a foul tongue, really dirty. None of our people, neither my brothers nor their sons, like that family. In spring, we moved out to our campsite; we were sitting on a kilim laid in the middle of the camp. Golshâh's young son Gholâm-Ayâr was scratching himself on his bottom. I asked him, 'Son, what's the problem?' I wondered if he had boils. Badri said, 'Yes, he does.' 'What kind of boils?' She said, 'Like this.' She built up the fire, and her son

Miru took the child, held him over the fire and burned his bottom all over. Miru wasn't that young, a teenager. His mother told him to take the child and hold him over the fire. He held him by the head and the poor orphan got all burned. After that, he wouldn't come home any more.

Golshâh asked, 'What happened?' 'He'd got some boils,' Badri answered, 'and if anyone says anything, I'll kill them.' She said the same to Golshâh's other children, Bibiwor and her older brother Gholâm-Mahmad, who now looks after the cows.

Then one morning Bibiwor went out into the steppe with some girl-cousins: Golusar's twin daughters Saduzi and Mamadzi, and Mahd-Amin's daughter Bibiyakh, who married Sarwar. They'd gone up a hillside to collect dung-fuel, when Bibiwor burst out crying and said, 'I'm never going back to Sâleh's house!' They asked why. 'Because that woman burned my brother and beats my brothers, my mother and me!'

Bibiwor went back with them to Mahd-Amin's. When she didn't come home, her mother and brother went out looking for her. Bâlu and Miru and their mother too looked for her. All the while Bibiwor was sitting in Mahd-Amin's tent. In the afternoon Mahd-Amin asked Bâlu what they were looking for. He said, 'Bibiwor's gone, where is she?' 'She's in my place.' Bâlu called, 'Come out, Bibiwor!' Mahd-Amin said, 'She's staying here. You behaved badly, hitting the orphans and so on; it won't do.' Bâlu went mad; he took up a stick and attacked Mahd-Amin.

That evening Bibiwor's mother Golshâh came. 'If you enter that tent,' Bâlu said, 'I'll be damned if you continue as my wife.' Golshâh said to Mahd-Amin, 'Brother, give me my daughter so I can take her home.' He refused; he said, 'You've let the orphans be beaten, and they've suffered so much; I won't let you have her.'

Early next morning Bâlu said, 'Where did you spend the night, in the tent or in the steppe? You aren't my wife. I hereby repudiate this woman.' And he went off round to our cousins Mowzoddin and Akhtar, saying, 'The woman did this, and ran off, and cried, and took the girl to Mahd-Amin.' Akhtar and Mowzoddin came and pleaded with Mahd-Amin, but he wasn't moved. Then they fetched Tumân, Tabu, Jomajân, Lâljân and all Haji Ghâfur's crowd, everybody. They said, 'Give him the woman, Sâleh will soon be back from the military.' Mahd-Amin said, 'No; I'm keeping them all until he does come back, in four months.'

But eventually he said to Akhtar, the senior cousin, 'You be our representative and tell them, "If you promise not to beat this poor boy and girl, not to shout at them, you can take them until Sâleh returns."' So he handed the kids back to Bâlu, and Akhtar got some medicine from the bazaar; they put fat on the burns, and the boy got better.

A few months later, at this time of year, when the *mâldârs* came back, Golshâh once more suffered at Badri's hands. She beat her and her kids, threw one child into a horse-trough and shut him in there for a day and night; he could have died of hunger. In the evening Golshâh took all her children over to Mahd-Amin and said, 'I'm not going back, they'll kill me.' Next morning she left for Sar-e-pol, to lodge an official complaint; Mahd-Amin followed her to Khârkash, where he got Nâder-shâh to take her and her kids in. 'Stay here until Sâleh comes, then his son will either marry you properly or release you.' Golshâh and her kids didn't really understand what happened.

When Sâleh returned, he went with Mahd-Amin and Rawu to Nâder-shâh to get his daughter-in-law back. They rebuked him: 'Look what your son and your wife have done.' He said, 'It's nothing to do with me, I was on military service.' They said, 'Take your daughter-in-law home, but her children will go to Mahd-Amin's house, and they should receive their property.' They'd inherited a lot of stuff from Rangin.

Mahd-Amin took the orphans to his own house and looked after them. But Sâleh and Bâlu grabbed all their property, tent, animals, cash, the lot. The kids managed to take a couple of blankets. Golshâh tried to claim her widow's eighth share but Badri lost her temper again: 'Go and find your eighth!' They fetched Mowlawi to resolve the argument. Golshâh got eight sheep and one cow, and some household stuff, which she took off to her kids. Mahd-Amin's family looked after her children like their own and gave them nice clothes; then he gave his own daughter Khurak to Rangin's son Gholâm-Mahmad, and took Bibiwor for his own son Shir-Mahmad. He resolved the matter of Rangin's inheritance within his own household.

Golshâh's now like a maidservant in Sâleh's house; she washes the clothes, cooks the food, sweeps, collects dung, fetches water.

Baya-khân tells the same story.

Rangin had no full-brothers or sisters, so when he died his estate went to his half-brothers like Mahd-Amin and Sâleh. Sâleh's son Bâlu took his widow Golshâh. Mahd-Amin said, 'I'll care for the orphans until they're grown up, then I'll marry Bibiwor to my own son Shir.' He kept Bibiwor for two or three years, then married her to Shir; he also engaged Khurak, his own small daughter by Bakhtâwar, to Rangin's son Gholâm-Mahmad. This was a direct exchange.

For a few years Shir went to *bâzi* with Bibiwor but, poor man, he couldn't afford a proper wedding. Finally he did it, in the spring campsite, with his own and Mowzoddin's few tents; he bought a couple of seers of rice and invited some women who sang songs, then early in the afternoon they did the contract. There wasn't much of a trousseau.

Bibiwor was much older than Khurak, so Shir agreed to pay Gholâm-Mahmad a 20,000-rupee premium [*sar*], but that poor lad is too young to claim it; what does a boy know of such matters? He's in their hands. Perhaps when he and his fiancée grow up and he hears what his rights are, he'll confront them and get his money. I don't know what happened to Rangin's land; if he had any, Mahd-Amin probably passed it to the sons long ago. But if he registered it in his own name, with deeds and witnesses, there's nothing they can do about it. If he didn't register it properly, when these boys grow up they should be able to get the land from him, if they go to the government.

Gorey's Deceit

Summer 1972 sees the apparent climaxes of two long-running stories, both involving once-wealthy men in difficulties. Gorey is beset by marital misfortunes, Mowzoddin by an irresponsible brother. Matters for both are aggravated by daughters' extramarital affairs.

Haji Amir's son Gorey, an ageing widower, is third of four brothers. The eldest, Parwiz, and the youngest, Heydar, are both dead. The second, Haji Wahâb, married Saduzi, Haji

Ghâfur's sister and Haji Tumân's aunt; he heads a large, thriving household. Each of Gorey's brothers fathered several sons; he has only one, Kala-khân. Gorey is desperate for another wife and more sons. Baya-khân and others narrate his constantly thwarted efforts, and his eventual resort to trickery. (See Fig. 20)

Baya-khân begins the story.

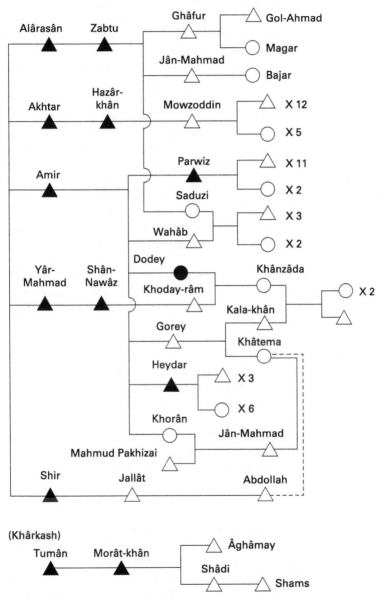

Figure 20 The story of Gorey.

Haji Wahâb doesn't have much land. He bought some from his brother Gorey, here and up above. Gorey and Kala-khân have a joint household; they eat together. Gorey's wife died; Kala-khân's wife Khânzâda is daughter of Khoday-râm and Gorey's sister Dodey. Gorey is old; Kala-khân is household head and tells him what to do. Kala-khân has a yoke of oxen and does sharecropping. He also has a little land of his own, right here, which he cultivates; this year he did sesame and melons. They don't hire anyone, but do all their own work; Gorey helps sometimes, but Kala-khân does most of it.

Over ten years ago – I'll tell you the truth – Gorey's daughter Khâtema, who wasn't engaged to anybody, had an affair with Haji Jallât's son Abdollah. One day Madu's son, Amiroddin – their house was in the old compound here – saw them together in the storeroom, so he took a stick and started beating Abdollah, who fought back but couldn't say anything because he'd been caught in the act. They made a lot of noise, and other people heard it. A few days later Khâtema said, 'I'm going to call out for Abdollah!'

But Gorey took his daughter away, by deception: 'Come, girl, we're going to my sister's' – she's married to Mahmud Pakhizai – and off they went. Gorey told Mahmud, 'I've got this problem: take my daughter or she'll run away or call out for that boy; they'll go to the judge, and she'll declare, "This is my husband"; he'll give them a certificate, and I'll be unable to stop them – and I won't get my hands on any brideprice for her.' Mahmud agreed to take Khâtema for his son Jân-Mahmad, because they were close cousins, and Jân-Mahmad had often told him, 'I want to marry that girl.' They did the nikah right there. Mahmud didn't have much cash, but he gave 50 sheep and 20,000 rupees. Gorey didn't mention that Khâtema had already been with Abdollah; if Mahmud found out later, he kept quiet; it would've been wrong to say anything.

People didn't seize Abdollah for going with Gorey's daughter. With us, if a girl elopes with a Hazâra, it's very bad; but if she goes with an Afghan, then five elders gather and get the boy's sister for the girl's brother or some other paternal relative. Or they pay compensation, like a brideprice, and restore relations again. It's like this: if he'd taken the girl from her house, if she'd fled far from home, then compensation would be paid. In this case, Amiroddin saw them right there, in the storeroom; but she hadn't actually declared, 'Abdollah's my husband', or fled to his house. If she'd gone to his house, they couldn't have brought her back; and if they'd taken the matter to the government, the judge would've said, 'She went willingly, they're certainly husband and wife,' and everyone would've accepted it. That's how it is with us. In this case, they'd just been meeting secretly when they were caught. That's why Gorey took her away. He couldn't tell Abdollah to marry his daughter, because she denied being seen with him. People said they were having an affair but she said, 'That's a lie; they're dishonouring me!'

Pâdshâh.

Gorey asked Haji Ghâfur for his daughter Magar. He sent a proper delegation, he tried really hard: 'Give her to me, she's ugly and smelly, nobody else will take her.' But Gol-Ahmad turned him down: 'He's an old man, I won't give him my young sister.' Gorey also sent a delegation to Jân-Mahmad for his daughter Bajal; he said, 'Give her to me, her mouth is crooked, young men don't like her.' But Jân-Mahmad rejected him because of his age and his shamelessness.

Gorey was also after Mowzoddin's daughter. They have this dispute. You know that rainfed melon-patch that Gorey has? Well, previously it was wheat. After the sheaves were stacked, one night he was sleeping on top of the pile, when somebody came and stole one of his sheaves. He ran after them, but fell into a canal. He says he lost one of his teeth, but it's a lie, it fell out long ago! He's kept it in his pocket for an opportunity like this. In the morning he grabbed Mowzoddin and said, 'Last night your son stole my wheat, punched me in the mouth, and knocked out my tooth! I'm going to make a complaint! You'll have to give me your daughter.'

Mowzoddin didn't take him seriously and said, 'Okay, off you go then.' Gorey complained to the elders, but they said, 'What you're doing to poor Mowzoddin is unfair. You say he stole from you and knocked your tooth out, but that's nonsense, you're lying. We won't take this any further.' Gorey got angry and went to town to file a formal complaint with Tâj-Mahmad Khân. He gave the khan a few thousand; the khan asked Mowzoddin, 'What are you offering?' He took money from both of them, and sent them away. A waste of time! It's all nonsense; Gorey's harassing him.

Our government takes teeth very seriously! Let me take out a tooth then grab hold of Richard to get him to find me a woman! Listen carefully: don't fight with the people of Afghanistan; if you do, and you knock out someone's tooth, you'll have to find him a wife!

Now Gorey says, 'Mowzoddin promised me his daughter on the first day, and now he denies it and won't give her.' The dispute continues today. They say – I haven't seen it myself – that Mowzoddin has agreed. Gorey will give his granddaughter to Mowzoddin's son, in exchange for Mowzoddin's daughter for himself. They'll hold the weddings together. You could say he got a wife because of the tooth, since nobody would've given him a girl otherwise. Gorey's an old man.

At Mowzoddin and Gorey's *fâteha*, when they gave Kala-khân's daughter to Mowzoddin's son, the mullah declared that if one girl died before the wedding, the brideprice for the other should be 'open', in sharia terms, that is, whatever they want. Actually it's fixed: Gorey's given Mowzoddin 15,000 for his daughter. If the other girl should die, Gorey has the right to just take Mowzoddin's daughter. If she dies, then Mowzoddin has the right to get Kala-khân's daughter without further ado.

Baya-khân and others.

Earlier this year, Gorey asked Shams for his sister: 'Give her to me this year for a small brideprice.' It looked like he would. Yesterday Kala-khân was here, you remember, and he said: 'We'd agreed it with Shams and Âghâmay. We went to the bazaar and bought supplies for the *târ*, ten seers of rice, two seers of ghee, raisins. When we got home, we thought, "The girl's sickly, nobody else'll marry her; he won't take much brideprice."' They'd even arranged the scarves.

But it wasn't fated to be. People in the village were saying, 'He's taken the rice: he'll get her today or tomorrow.' But they couldn't agree on the brideprice. It was all done privately between Gorey and Âghâmay. When Gorey took it all over, Âghâmay said, 'We want 50 sheep and 30,000 rupees; how much are you offering?' Gorey replied, 'I'll give you 40 sheep and 20,000, and I'll pay in instalments, not all at once; or I'll give you five *jeribs* of land, if you let your sister go right now.' Then they both backed down; so they ate their own rice. Meanwhile Gorey arranged to marry Mowzoddin's daughter.

Gorey had a harvest pile where he now has melons. He saw that Mowzoddin was poor, but he thought, 'Who'd give his daughter to a greybeard? The only way I'll get her is if I trick him.'

He'd removed one of his teeth earlier, or it was loose and he took it out now. He made a trail by dropping wheat grains from the pile all the way to Mowzoddin's house. Then in the morning, he told someone, 'Last night thieves came; it was Mowzoddin's sons; they attacked me, knocked out one of my teeth, and stole my wheat.' The elders assembled and told Mowzoddin, 'Give him your daughter.' He refused point-blank. So Gorey went to Sar-e-pol and made a complaint to Tâj-Mahmad Khân. Now the khan took 10,000 rupees from Mowzoddin, saying, 'Don't worry, I won't let them take your daughter.'

The dispute continued. The elders tried to persuade Mowzoddin, 'Give him your daughter and take his granddaughter for your son, and he'll pay you something too.' But whatever they said, he refused. In spring Gorey even went to Kabul and made a complaint at the ministry, saying, 'He knocked out my tooth, he promised me the girl, but he wouldn't give her.' In the sharia, if your tooth's knocked out, you have a right to seven women and seven pregnant she-camels. That's how noble teeth are! So when Gorey complained, they asked him to stop. They couldn't agree, so he started filing petitions – he showed us. Then the elders said, 'We'll force Mowzoddin to give the girl.' He said, 'Over my dead body! It's nobody's business but mine whether I give her. I'll kill my son and say that Gorey did it. That's the only way I'll get myself out of this mess!'

Eventually Haji Tumân fixed the deal, otherwise Mowzoddin would never have agreed; he arranged for Gorey to give his son's daughter to Mowzoddin's son, with a premium of 15,000 rupees. Gorey managed to collect 7,000 cash; then he had to pawn some land for 5,000. He brought Haji 12,000 in cash and a young camel; then that day they did the *fâteha*, said the prayers and gave the *târ*, right here – we were all there.

It was an awkward, bad-tempered business, and there's still much bad feeling between them. If Mowzoddin had been happy with the deal, he'd have been more accommodating; he wouldn't have taken the premium, or he'd have allowed Gorey to give it gradually. Gorey's relatives wouldn't help him. Only Haji Wahâb gave him 2,000 rupees, but it was a loan, he'll have to give it back. Sarwar also lent him 500.

In truth, the girl wasn't willing; she's young and he's old, and that's very bad. She didn't want him, and several times this year she said, 'I'm not going to have such an old man, it's quite wrong; I'll call out for some other man.' Haji Tumân put a lot of pressure on her. She didn't call for another man, though Haji Wahâb's women said she would.

Mowzoddin's Misfortunes

Mowzoddin's troubles didn't begin with Gorey's trickery; he was brought down by the behaviour of members of his family, in particular squabbling sons, an uninhibited daughter, and a gambling nephew, not to mention his own incompetence with property.
Seyyed-shâh/Golusar explains.

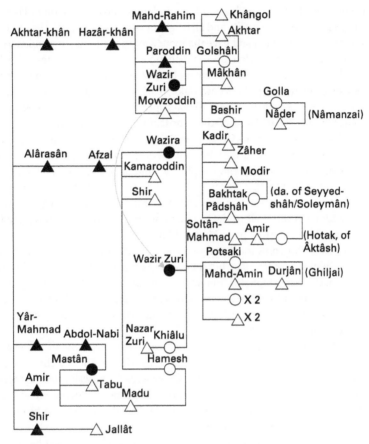

Figure 21 Mowzoddin's story.

Paroddin was a very powerful man, nobody finer than him in the village. His compound was by Akhtar-Mahmad's pond; his tent was separate. In summer, when people came from the mountains, he pitched his tent and didn't go into his house, which he kept locked up. He had 15 or 16 camels. He married his daughter Golshâh to her cousin Akhtar-Mahmad, and Golla to Haji Nâder Nâmanzai. [*See Fig. 21*]

Once, Paroddin killed a soldier, at the Dehmana gorge entrance. He spent ten days in jail, then Haji Afzal bought his release. In those days we didn't have these silk *chapâns*; people wore *kepanak,* felt cloaks. Haji Afzal took along money hidden in the folds of his *kepanak*, and got Paroddin released.

Paroddin would go around wearing his bandolier, with his gun on his shoulder; Jallât was afraid of him and did his bidding. He died long ago – when I was about one. My mother told me about him. He was older than Mowzoddin, but the oldest of the three brothers was Mahd-Rahim. He'd engaged his son Mâkhân to Mowzoddin's daughter. When he died, he left Mâkhân 150 sheep, thirteen camels, one Malakhi gun, one horse, and 22 *jeribs* of land. Sometimes a bad man can father a good son; how is it that a good man can father such a good-for-nothing gambler? This idiot Mâkhân now sold 80 sheep to people on credit, and all he got in return was an IOU. His camels went the same way; he sold them and gave the money to Abdor-Rahmân Kandahâri, who'd lent him money on interest. He'd lost so much money gambling, right here with Abdor-Rahmân. If you said to him, 'Hey Mâkhân, I really like you!' he'd give you 500 rupees, and you'd owe him nothing. That's how Mâkhân lost his home and his father's name. He had a fine black tent, worth at least 10,000 rupees; he sold that for 2,000 to Akhtar [*Dur-khân's brother*]'s wife Jamâl's father. The tent went to Kandahar.

Now Mâkhân's sold his land. He sold his 22 *jerib*s ten times over. Twice he sold them to his uncle Mowzoddin, and then he sold them to Abdor-Rahmân, so Mowzoddin took some of his own money and bought the land back from Abdor-Rahmân; next Mâkhân sold the land to Haji Nâder. Mowzoddin was going to buy it back from Haji Nâder, but it didn't work. Mâkhân gave Haji Nâder the deeds for those gardens.

Mowzoddin was very well-to-do; he had hundreds of sheep. First he suffered at the hands of that Mâkhân, then poor Mowzoddin went to Kachan. The Kachanis asked him, 'Mowzoddin-boy, how much are your sheep?' '1,000 rupees; take them.' Now they owe Mowzoddin at least four lacs; but they won't pay up. First he lost Paroddin's wealth, then his own. If it weren't for Haji Tumân, Shir and his brothers would have got hold of it. If Paroddin were still alive, he'd never have let this happen. Now, Mowzoddin and his crowd are pushed around by Jallât and Tabu and their people. They have nobody to stand up for them, except Haji.

Mowzoddin married Kamaroddin's sister Wazira, Paroddin's widow Wazir, and also Nazar Zuri's daughter Khiâlu. But since his sons Mullah Kadir, Zâher, Modir, and Pâdshâh grew up, they've caused him a lot of trouble; each one wants to be independent. In his household you can find at least twenty-four people, including the women; but they don't cooperate or share the food. Now Mullah Kadir wants to head his own household; if he gets some cash, he gives it to his own wife, buys some clothes or hides it in Qâri Azim's shop. If Pâdshâh finds something, he sends it to his father-in-law-to-be in Âktâsh. If Modir does, he takes it to his father-in-law Seyyed-shâh's house.

(*Baya-khân*) – Four years ago, Seyyed-shâh[/*Soleymân*] offered his daughter Bakhtak to my father, Haji: 'I like your family, I'll give her to you, for any of your sons; if you want her, you have first option.' But Haji turned him down. Bakhtak has these swellings on her throat; it's scrofula (*khanâzel*), a terrible disease, the swellings never go away, it could kill her; it certainly disfigures her. I think that's why Haji wouldn't take her. If he had, Seyyed-shâh wouldn't have asked much for her, mainly because Haji's headman; and besides, Seyyed-shâh has land up there in Chenâr, and so do we, and if it wasn't for Haji's support the people there would have thrown Seyyed-shâh out long ago. So he was hoping to keep Haji's support and friendship by giving his daughter to him cheaply.

In the same year, Mowzoddin got his son Modir engaged to Bakhtak for 40,000 rupees and 80 sheep. Uncle Mowzoddin hasn't paid much yet, perhaps 25 sheep; most of it's still due, 20,000 rupees and 55 sheep. Poor man, he has nothing, he can't afford to pay any more. Some people laugh at him: 'How many years since he got that girl for his son? Why hasn't he fetched the bride yet? He's very slow: can't he pay off the brideprice?' Seyyed-shâh would never go to him and say, 'Give me my brideprice!' – it would be shameful.

(*Pâdshâh*) – Mowzoddin's engaged his son Modir to Seyyed-shâh's daughter Bakhtak. So far he's given no more than twenty sheep. The entire brideprice was, I think, 80 sheep and 40,000 rupees. That's low for such a fine girl, but nobody wanted her because of her scrofula; also, Seyyed-shâh's just one house, they've no relatives here. If he had relatives and backing, and a good daughter, people would pay a lot for her. Seyyed-shâh would've given her to someone else, if they'd asked; however he's given her to Mowzoddin, and become in-laws with him.

The wedding of Mowzoddin's daughter Potsaki to Mahd-Amin Ghiljai's son Durjân was definitely second-class. The reason he gave her was that nobody would pay as much as that man offered. The brideprice was set at 1 lac, and he got about 90,000 altogether, including sheep, a cow, and 200 to 300 seers of wheat and barley. His relatives would've given much less; Mahd-Amin was a stranger, and Mowzoddin didn't let him off one single *qerân*.

Actually, he gave her to a stranger because he had to. Potsaki's a good girl, tall; but there was an affair: people whispered that she'd been with Neshtar's son. That's why none of us wanted her. She'd 'passed through the water, to the other side.' It was voluntary on both sides – just like you two liked each other when you were studying in University. But she didn't intend to marry him. Mowzoddin's young son, a small child, saw them and told his parents, 'He's doing things with my sister!' When this happens, the community doesn't interfere, it's up to the girl's father and relatives whether they do anything. Some people keep it hidden, never let the matter out.

(Baya-khân) – Mowzoddin's daughter Potsaki was married in early winter, ten days before Ramazan. It was a small wedding; people from Mahd-Amin's village went, some men from Rishmin's and the Baluches by the steppe, and a few from Khârkash; but nobody from our village.

Mowzoddin's son Pâdshâh's engaged to the daughter of Haji Soltân-Mahmad's son Amirak. Pâdshâh's also called Nâder; some people call him Garg and Pêk, because he lost his hair and went bald. Now he's better. He used to have such swellings on his head, we treated it with the dye we use on sheep; his head smelled and people laughed at him. They had the *fâteha* last autumn, after Pâdshâh returned from military service. Mowzoddin had just received some sheep and some cash from Mahd-Amin for Potsaki. He should have finished paying off the brideprice he owed for Modir's wife Bakhtak, but Mowzoddin's such a thoughtless man, as soon as Pâdshâh was back, he got him engaged too, giving 25 sheep and 5,000 rupees on the first day. People laugh: one girl's still in her father's house, yet he's taken on another. If he were a man, he'd have done the first girl's wedding before taking on another! If I get engaged to twenty girls and can't pay brideprice for any of them, what's the use?

(*Pâdshâh*) – Mowzoddin's son Pâdshâh – he'll hit you if you call him Gargey! – is engaged to a Kabuli, Haji Soltân-Mahmad's granddaughter. They did the *fâteha* recently; the brideprice is 70,000 to 80,000; he's given 25 sheep and 3,000 rupees. Haji Soltân-Mahmad came to Mowzoddin and said: 'Your son Pâdshâh can come and work for me, and I'll take no money from you. I'll give her right now, do the nikah, and he can live here with us.' But Mowzoddin wouldn't let his son do this. He said, 'Take your proper dues and then we'll come and fetch the bride.' If he sent Pâdshâh to work for his father-in-law, some people might poke fun and say: 'Others marry off their daughters, but you've married off your son! He works for them, but what kind of Afghans are they? They're Fârsibâns! They're our rivals, it's not a good idea.' But other people don't worry about it; it's no big deal.

Finally, Mowzoddin was responsible when his brother Paroddin's widow, Wazir, began an affair with his distant cousin Madu – whose affairs have featured before (p. 292).
Pâkhâl tells the story.

Mowzoddin's brother Paroddin was a good man with a neck as thick as this [*demonstrates*]. Barely a week after he died, his widow, Wazir Zuri, smiled at Madu as he passed. We asked, 'Wazir, why are you smiling?' She said, 'Nothing.' She was a bad woman. Then one night Madu came. Mowzoddin's wife, Wazira, saw him and told her husband: 'A man's come and Wazir's hidden him in her hut' – which was all on its own. Wazira and Mowzoddin lit a lamp, to go see who'd come, and they found them both sitting together. All the men gathered around, seized Madu and beat him. Meanwhile, without their noticing, Wazir got away, with her little daughter at her breast. She fled straight to Madu's house; she slipped in the ditch behind his house, and her daughter fell into the water, but she got her out again – the poor little thing was all dripping wet. When she got inside, Madu's wife Hamesh, said: 'You shameless slut, you dirty cunt, get out! Don't you dare enter my house!' But she said nothing and just came in.

When they let Madu go, he crawled off without looking behind. They took the lamp and looked for Wazir, but she'd disappeared. 'Where is she? We've looked in all the houses, everywhere. She's gone!' When Madu got home, he found her sitting in his house: 'So what if they've beaten me, thank God the woman's here!'

That same night, all our men – Mowzoddin, my father and the others – went to see Haji Abdol-Nabi. They told him what happened: 'The woman escaped while we were beating Madu.' Haji Abdol-Nabi's wife Mastân was Madu's half-sister, so they sent her to his house – and there she found Wazir: 'Filthy cunt, what are you doing here? You'd better come with me.' She answered, 'No way! This is my husband.' Mastân retorted, 'You dirty bitch, do you want men to be killed on your account?' She still refused to go. So Mastân returned. 'She won't come'. Then both Haji Abdol-nabi and his wife went, saying, 'Come to us; you don't need to go back to Mowzoddin.' So that very night they brought Wazir to their house. She stayed there for a month, then Mowzoddin came and they did the nikah there at Haji Abdol-nabi's house. But she didn't go to Mowzoddin's house for a whole year – she was scared they'd kill her.

12

Religion, Life, Death, Disease

Religious Practices

These accounts represent ordinary villagers' beliefs and practices; they should not be taken as statements of 'orthodoxy' or 'orthopraxy'.

Mosques and *tâlebs*

Every local community has its mosque, built by communal effort and paid for by wealthier men, who also see to the hiring of a mullah, or finance the training of one of their own, to officiate and to lead prayers. Senior men of the community attend the mosque for at least the last two prayers of the day, and the midday prayer on Fridays; and all men attend the most important religious events of the year there – the Greater Id, as well as the month of prayer and fasting at Ramazan that concludes in the Lesser Id – before going off to join secular festivities elsewhere. The mosque is also men's main communal meeting-place, where they take important decisions, air and resolve disputes. Mullahs, and other religious figures such as âghâs, descendants of the Prophet, are expected to make peace among disputants.

Pâdshâh enumerates the Konjek mosques.

We built this lower mosque ourselves about twenty years ago. Our previous mosque, built by Haji Afzal and Haji Zabtu, was larger, and different. We pulled it down, and brought a builder from town for the new one, which we built by communal effort: Haji Ghâfur, Haji Bahâoddin, Shir-Mahmad, everyone from Khoday-râm downwards gave a beam, and money for the plaster-work.

The Upper-Quarter people started their new mosque about a month ago. They'd had their old one – did you see it? – since Haji Amir's time. Tabu, Madu and the others on the edge of the steppe have no mosque. They're partners in the upper mosque, and they come there on both Ids, if they can, if it's not raining or snowing or too muddy or cold. Otherwise, they all go to Rishmin's little mosque, with Mullah Sharâpoddin; they go even though they're not partners there. Sharâpoddin is a good mullah, but he doesn't have *tâleb* students like Mayoddin-jân. They go to him throughout Ramazan. If the weather's really so bad that they can't even go there, then they pray at home.

Kala-khân stays in Konjek and studies, seriously, in the mosque with Mayoddin-jân Âghâ, the village mullah and son of respected Sufi Mowlawi Golzâr. He is nicknamed 'Sheykh'; he

has some knowledge of religious and moral affairs, but knows little of farming or herding.
Probably he will emerge as the family mullah. He summarizes his study programme.

Among us, when a boy starts his lessons, first they give him a bookstand, then, after he's
learned how to pray properly, a Koran. When he's studied that, there are the Five Books;
when he's studied them, there are *Tofangsaya*, then *Zeleykhâ*, then *Hâpez*, then *Shâr-e-
soâlât*, then *Qodri*, then *Qand*, then *Mokhtasar*, then *Shâr-e-liâz*, then *Mostakhlâs*, then
either *Sarp* or *Edahi*.[1] If he doesn't study them, he can't be called Muslim. People say, 'If
you don't pray, if you don't say the creed, then people will beat you with clubs and expel
you from the community.'

First, I went to the Alizai village and studied with their mullah; that's where I got my
bookstand. When the *mâldâr* went to the mountains, half our family came here to Haji
Ghâfur's house in Konjek, and I was able to study in the mosque for a year. Then for two
years I had to go to the mountains – I didn't want to, I cried a lot, but they gave me 100
rupees, so I went. There was no mullah up there and I couldn't study at all; I had to
work. When we came back, I studied here again with Mullah Mayoddin-jân Âghâ.
There were other *tâlebs*, Mullah Dâdollah, Mullah Gol-Mahmad, Mullah Râmdel,
Mullah Rostam, I studied with them all. When we all moved here, I studied with Mullah
Sharâpoddin, who lives with Rishmin; and in summer with Mayoddin-jân.

We have five daily prayer-times; Sobh, Pishin, Digar, Shâm, Khoftan. In winter,
during Ramazan, we do *tarawi* prayers at night. Before we pray, we must do our *târat*
ablutions: we wash our mouth, then nose, then face, then hands, then feet, then we're
ready to pray. If there's no water, for instance in the steppe, where water's far away, we
do *tayammom*, the dry ablution. Sometimes there's water at a spring, but for fear of
wolves we do *tayammom*, not *târat*, before our prayers.

When I've studied all that, studied the *Sarp*, I'll have graduated and I'll become a
mullah. I'll go round and collect *mollâ'i* donations. Some go to places like Peshawar,
Qataghan, Bokhara, to study further and become a good, powerful mullah. Then they
come back and collect *mollâ'i* and zakat.

The Hajj

In early 1971, Tumân made the pilgrimage to Mecca, accompanying his paternal aunt,
Bakhtâwar, wife of Haji Molk, a respected Khârkash elder, and the first Piruzai woman to
make the Hajj. In his precise, laconic account, recorded early in our stay, he does not refer
to her; he also fails to mention that all her money was stolen while they were in Mecca. He
gives no hint of his emotional and spiritual experience – this contrasts sharply with his
later, much more graphic narrative of the pursuit of Kimyâ (pp. 59f.).[2]

---

[1]   Unfortunately, we did not check Kala-khân's account with a local mullah. Some of these books are
      among the fifteen listed by Pierre Centlivres (1972: 60) as the 6 to 10-year-long syllabus in the
      traditional schools of the town of Tâshqurghân in the 1960s. As for the Five Books, Centlivres mentions
      only *Chârketab* (Four Books), as 'sorte de catéchisme'. Perhaps they include the scriptures: Torah, Zabur
      (Psalms), Injil (Gospel), Koran.

[2]   Bakhtâwar was much more forthcoming – and humorous – about her Hajj experience, but unfortunately
      we never taped her. Compare also the standard Hajj guides, some of which Tumân had read.

Bismillahirrahmanirrahim. This year I performed the duty of Hajj. We went to Sheberghân and made an application, and it was accepted. We got our passports, came home, collected our money, and set off for Kabul. In Kabul we handed over 20,880 rupees at the Kabul Bank. Next morning we travelled to Kandahar. We stayed there four days, then at 12:30 we went to Kandahar International Airport and boarded a plane. We boarded at 8:00 in the morning, and at eight in the evening we arrived at Jedda itself, and passed the night there. We left at 1:30 the next day for Mecca, Beyt-ash-Sharif.

At Mecca we did the *tawâf-e-qodum* circumambulations and we did [*the* sa'i *between*] Safâ and Marwa, then we went and purified ourselves and put on our [*ihrâm*] clothes. We spent eighteen days there. After eighteen days we went to Mina and spent the night there; after morning prayers we left for Arafat. There we did the second and third prayers together. At sunset we left, and arrived by night at Muzdalifa, where we did the two evening prayers together and then the next morning prayers. After prayers we came and stoned the first Devil. From there we went to Ushukuri, the Sacrifice place, and there we bought a kid for 850 rupees. We slaughtered it, then we came and purified ourselves and put on our clothes. Then we boarded the bus and came back to Mecca, where we did more *tawâf*; then we did Safâ and Marwa. We set off once more for Mina, spent the night, then in the morning we stoned the Devils, all three of them, seven stones each. Then we returned to Mecca, and spent six more nights there; we came Friday eve, then we left and came by night and arrived at Madina. We spent ten days in Madina. On the 11th we left again for Jedda, and we spent seven more days there before our plane arrived and it was our turn to fly.

That evening we boarded the plane; the plane flew through the night and the next morning at prayer-time we arrived at Kandahar; after spending the day there, next morning we travelled to Kabul. After five days in Kabul, we left, and arrived in Mazâr in the evening. Next day we left Mazâr at noon, and arrived home that evening, *bismillah, Allahu-akbar*.

Fasting and alms

Like other events in the religious lunar calendar, the fasting month of Ramazan and the two Ids are eleven days earlier every solar year. The Lesser Id (Kuchney Akhtar) at the end of Ramazan is the occasion for giving the annual alms-tax. Forty days later, the 10th of Dhul-Hijja, the Greater Id (Loy Akhtar) is the Feast of Sacrifice, and the culmination of the Hajj.
   Baya-khân talks about the Ramazan fast.

As the years go round, Ramazan falls during migration, or in winter, or in milking season. Even when it's in summer, when people are so busy, they must fast. But people vary; some don't fast, but most do. Shepherds out in the steppe don't fast. 'We're tired,' they say, 'going around all day and night, we can't fast.' And they don't pray. It's very hard for them to go all day without food or water. If you fast, you must take nothing the whole day, our mullahs say; no water, no cigarettes, no *naswâr* snuff; it'd be a great sin. After the evening prayer is called, between 5:00 and 7:00, you can eat. Then you eat *sahari*, between 1:00 and 3:00 in the middle of the night. You fill up, as you can't eat again until the next evening. It's like that for a month. The women see the food as they prepare it, but they can't eat.

Pâdshâh elaborates the rules.

During Ramazan, when people fast during the day, they still work. Well, some people don't, like the khans, who have hired workers, or townspeople who don't have much daily work. A townsman with a cow, a horse or a donkey, he too has labourers to work for him, while he sits back. But, apart from elders like Haji or someone with junior relatives to do his work, we Afghans have to work, women and men. You work to feed yourself; in snow or heat, you still have to work when fasting. You can't say, 'My son's tired and needn't fast.' Or, 'You're fasting, stop working for a month.' That won't do. However thirsty or hungry you are, you can't just stop working.

Some people are allowed to eat during the fast. If you're travelling to Kandahar or Kabul, you may eat until you get back home. But if you're going to nearby places like Sheberghân, Mazâr or Sangchârak, less than a day's journey by car, it's not permitted to stop fasting. One day's car journey is three days by camel, that's what counts. If you drove your camel for three days, you'd cover a lot of ground. Some say that a pregnant woman needn't fast, but that's wrong: she too must fast; but a woman who's just given birth has a delicate condition, and she doesn't have to fast until it passes. But any days she misses for this reason she must make up afterwards.

If someone deliberately breaks his fast, he must either fast for sixty extra days or feed sixty destitute people with plates of rice or bread and water; or he must free a slave; then he'll be forgiven. Fasting is very difficult, in our Book!

The 19th of Ramazan is the Night of Power. This night some people stay up until the dawn call to prayer; Fârsibâns do it a lot, Afghans not so much. They go out and look around, to see if Khoja Khedr [*see p. 215*] has come. You can make a wish to Generous God: first bless our property, secondly give us limitless wealth; you ask Him to grant your heart's desire. Then if you see Khedr that night, and make whatever request is in your heart, in the morning the whole lot will come true for you.

This happens on the 19th, also on the 27th and the 29th, I believe. For sure Khedr will appear on one of these three nights, somewhere in the world. I don't know how long he stays, a few minutes, half an hour, but no more; then he'll smartly disappear. Not everyone sees him. He doesn't show himself to everybody, no indeed, only to someone who doesn't lie, doesn't fornicate, doesn't steal, doesn't commit other sins, doesn't do unjust or deceitful things, but says his five prayers, speaks truth and justice. Such a person will get to see him. But I don't believe you could find such a pure and just person anywhere in Afghanistan these days.

That night, if you go out for a pee or a walk, you may suddenly find that it's very bright, like daylight; and you may see a horse in the yard behaving like a sheep, chewing the cud. Meanwhile, everything looks towards Mecca; a tree will be upside down, resting on its branches with its roots up in the air. All this happens while Khedr is there. When he's gone, everything immediately goes back to normal. Once there was a woman who saw all this; she left the house at night – of course, being a woman she wasn't very bright, and she didn't know what she was seeing. She thought, 'What a strange tree, and how bright and leafy this grass is!' and she tethered a calf to it by the horns, without thinking of making a wish. But the tree was upside down! When she got up in the morning, there was her calf, up in the branches, hanged by the neck, dead. Then she realized what had happened and what she'd missed.

After the fast's over, everybody must pay *sar-saya* [*zakat; 'head-shade'*]: from ten to twenty rupees, depending on the price of wheat. This should go to the poor, but people give it to the mullahs, who have no salary. This *sar-saya* is useful after we die: in the other world, in the Plain of Mahshar, the sun will come down to earth like a spear, unbearably hot; everything in heaven and earth will boil. All the peoples will stand there on the Plain in the sun's heat. Then all the *sar-saya* you've paid, the extra Ramazan prayers you've performed, will shelter you from the heat, like an awning or a punkah.

Kala-khân knows the zakat rules.

The zakat charity tax works like this: if you've a flock of 40 sheep or more, you give one; over 100, you give two; over 200, you give three; over 300, you give four, over 400, five, and so on, one more for every hundred more sheep. On every 5 camels we give one sheep; on 10 camels, 2 sheep, on 15 camels, 3 sheep, on 20 camels, 4 sheep. If we have 25 camels, we give one camel-calf, a one-year-old, weaned from its mother. On 61 camels, you give one large camel, like yours. On donkeys, nothing; we only use them for trading. From every grain harvest we give *ushr*, a tenth of the grain.

We deliver the zakat and *ushr* to Mayoddin-jân Âghâ, here in the village. He distributes it among the poor and deprived. He's our mullah, our prayer-leader, he teaches us prayers and so on. Every village chooses its own mullah, its sheykh.

Pâdshâh adds.

If the mullah has no shepherd, he'll sell the sheep. You can buy back any animals you've given as zakat; otherwise, he'll sell them to someone else, or take them to the bazaar.

The Ids

Pâdshâh describes the formalities of the two Ids.

The day of Id is blessed throughout Islam; a day for good and bad. On the first morning everyone from the village, young and old, goes to the mosque. In this village, people from Khoday-râm's house downwards come to this mosque; those beyond Khoday-râm go to the upper mosque. Shepherds can't go to the mosque, as they're out with the flocks. Camel-herds, cowherds and donkey-wallahs wait until they've eaten their Id meal before letting their animals out. People who don't have such work stay around for the fun and games.

On this day, what the angels have written down comes to the Creator's attention. His investigators, sitting beside him like secretaries, bring it all before him, the bad and the good. On this very day – whether the Greater Id [*of Sacrifice*] or the Lesser Id [*after*

Ramazan], you should remove bitterness from your heart. Especially on the Greater Id, people settle disputes. Even if someone's killed your son, or you've killed his, don't even think about it on that day; greet him and ask him how he is. For example, if Richard and I have quarrelled over a camel, a sheep, some pasture, or a government fine, tax or whatever, we may avoid each other for many months. People will try to reconcile us, but if nobody's succeeded before Id, then that very day, in the mosque, we'll remove the bitterness from our hearts, greet each other, embrace and kiss on the face. There's no need for an intermediary. We have a saying, 'A real King will release all the prisoners from jail.' They should be given a free pardon on the Id.

Do you remember our dispute last year with Tabu and the Upper Quarter? [*see pp. 101f*] It went on and on. Sometimes they came to my father themselves, or sent delegates to seek reconciliation: 'Don't be angry with us, we didn't mean what we said,' and so on. But Haji said 'No, impossible; what's ours is ours, what's yours is yours, we're finished with you, we're no longer *qawmi* relatives.' When government wheat came to town, they went to get some, but the government wouldn't give them any; they only distribute the wheat to villagers with their headman present. So they came and pleaded with Haji to come; but he wouldn't, as he was still angry with them. People begged him. He made it up with some, but absolutely not with others. On the Lesser Id, at the end of Ramazan [*25 December 1971*], some of them came to visit, but Haji only made up with the juniors, not the seniors. Then on the Greater Id [*30 January 1972*], he was reconciled with the rest – though he's still not speaking to Lâljân. Now Tabu comes visiting, and so do Pâdshâh and others from the Upper Quarter. When they have problems they come to my father. Whatever it is, especially government matters, they're helpless on their own. That's why they all came and made up on the day of Id.

On the twelfth of the month Rabi-ol-awal [*the Prophet's birthday*], we do the 'Twelfth', *dwalasey*, sacrifice. Everyone slaughters an animal; if you can afford it, you kill an ox, a goat or a kid, a sheep, some people a chicken; some people cook rice, or Uzbek *chaplak*; others make *ghërey* – you know, fatty layered bread. Even the poor will try to do a sacrifice, if they have anything at all; they'll cook four pounds of cracked wheat, which substitutes for something big like an animal. It's a sacrifice, so you give it to the poor; you take it to the mosque, where large numbers of poor people gather that day to eat it. If there are no poor people, you give it to a neighbour. The sacrificial meal is eaten by the destitute, who have nothing in the house for the children, no ghee, no flour. How can they sacrifice? If they cook something, and others eat it, what will their children eat? For them it's merit enough to do their five daily prayers.

Baya-khân and others describe Id visiting.

On the day of Id people are very happy, it's a celebration. We have egg-fighting, wrestling, buzkashi; and there are other shows to watch. The night before, some people bring henna and dye their hands, and put on new clothes if they have them. Women prepare special dishes of rice and meat, milk-rice, pilaw, or *shurwa*, or they cook *ghërey*, fatty three-layered bread, and so on – potluck. This happens on both Ids.

They take the food to the mosque; after the mullah's led the morning prayer, he delivers a sermon and a homily about the other world, to lighten people's hearts, to calm them, bring them closer to God; so that they don't steal, do or say bad things to each other. The mullah speaks very loudly, so that everyone can hear, and with passion – he weeps. This goes on until seven or eight in the morning. As soon as he's finished, everybody turns to greet everybody else. You kiss the mullah and all your seniors on the hand, and your equals and juniors on the face.

After greetings and congratulations, everyone sits – anywhere, inside the mosque or outside, in the open, in front of all the food. They eat, and when they're full everyone goes visiting other peoples' houses. We visit all our close maternal and paternal relatives and in-laws. They expect you to visit. If you don't go, they're upset. It's a holiday, no excuses! Men and women, all go visiting.

If you arrive at someone's house to find they're not at home, perhaps because they've gone to your house, it doesn't matter, it's enough that you entered their house. You greet the women too; if she's elderly, you kiss her hand and she kisses your face; men and women the same. A new husband visits his father- and mother-in-law, kisses their hands, and greets his brothers-in-law – for Pâdshâh, it would be Pâkhâl's brother Payz. You shake hands with everyone, house by house.

When we're finished greeting all our own people here, we'll go visiting in the Upper Quarter only if we've a close relative there, like a married sister; not otherwise. For example, we go to Haji Wahâb's house: our cousin Jannat is married there, and our aunt Saduzi. As for Khârkash, I went this year to my maternal uncles Haji Khoshdel, Mullah Jabbâr and their families; if I didn't go, they'd complain. In Khârkash I also visited Haji Molk's house and Nâder-shâh's.

When you visit a house, they serve tea, meat, bread, pilaw, sweets. Some people buy raisins, carrots, mulberries to serve. Some give eggs, as they make people very happy. People serve whatever they can afford. That's the custom on the day of Id. You sit for a while, and then you go on. Eventually you go off to the parties.

Id and Jashn parties

For many years up to our arrival, both Ids fell in the colder and wetter months, when the weather and the slowdown in agricultural activity made mass feasting and games such as buzkashi feasible. The other big celebration, the secular Jashn-e-Istiqlal, Independence Day, commemorating the 1919 Treaty of Rawalpindi, falls on 19 August.

Baya-khân talks of the festivities – men from Konjek and many other villages converge on the Nazarzai khans' party in Seyyedâbâd.

For the Id parties, men and boys go to Shâh-Mahmad Khân's place in Seyyedâbâd. Don't you know Shâh-Mahmad Khân? He's our nephew [*son of Âghâ-Mahmad Khân and Tumân's aunt (also called Tumân)*]. There's buzkashi, pipes and drums, wrestling, gas-lamps, cards. Mind you, buzkashi isn't possible in late autumn and early winter: the ground's too hard. Horse-owners won't let them run, they'd be ruined. After the first dew, they'll walk them round – slowly, because they're full. Only after two or three dews does the ground get soft enough for buzkashi.

Many shops and stalls come from town. They slaughter two or three calves a day for the buzkashi. There are tea-tents, cauldrons of rice, melons. Shâh-Mahmad Khân feeds everybody who goes – not in daytime, when everyone buys his own food, but in the evening. Whoever's there, fifty people or five hundred, they go to his house, or his uncle's. He'll give your horse barley and straw, and he'll give you meat and rice or meat-broth; and in the morning, tea with milk.

Seyyedâbâd's where the party is. In our village nothing happens. People who live nearby come home at night, others stay there. Those Id nights, it's a real party: they play *dambura* and other instruments; they've great songs on tape. Last year [1970] there was a Jughi woman who danced for Shâh-Mahmad Khân. Every night there are dancing-boys (*bacha-bâzi*); he's a great one for them.

That's where men go. Some go to Emâm-Sâheb, but it's rather too far away. The party lasts at least three days, depending on the weather; if it's warm, up to seven days.

Women's parties are separate. Our women gather by the pond on the edge of the steppe. Several hundred gather there, some from far away. The women's elders get the others together: 'Let's go to this or that village.' Neshtar's our women's elder; she was a great singer in her time. There's always a good party, lots of women; they have several dancing groups, and several places where they sing. There are sideshows and stalls selling all sorts of things. Stallholders come from this village and others; there are peddlers from the Hazâras and other places; Afghan shopkeepers go too. Men give cash to their children, their wives and sisters, who ask, 'We're going to the show, give us some money or we'll go hungry.'

Women from Khârkash gather by their own village. They're just one village; their Hazâra and Uzbek neighbours don't join them. Some of them come here, as our party's much better. Here, many more gather, from five villages: from Rishmin's, ours, the Ludins, Shamsoddin's, sometimes the Baluches. Women from Qoshtepa go to Seyyedâbâd, where they have a party for women too, up on the hilltop at Mariba, you know it? Some years they come here. But Hazâras don't come here, nor do Uzbeks or Arabs. A few Arabs who live there by the hill go to the Seyyedâbâd party, but they don't come to ours; they might come, but not to sing, just to watch the women's show.

Hazâras don't put on their own shows. The men go to Seyyedâbâd, but the women don't have a show; they go round to congratulate each other, but they don't have parties.

If we're in the mountains at the time of Id, we can't have a show, it wouldn't work: there are just five or ten families in one place, two or three in another. But in Sar-e-pol valley the showgrounds are well known, and all the women and small children go.

Pâdshâh on buzkashi and other games.

Both Ids are three-day festivals. The first morning's in the mosque, then there are celebrations and games. Boys paint boiled eggs in coloured patterns, then fight with them, to see which will break; there's much merry-making, and things to see and do. The women party over on the steppe-edge; the men go to Seyyedâbâd and spend the first day there.

Last Id was before the proper snow started; there'd just been a little rain. For three days the women had a good show. These last two years of hunger there's been no buzkashi, but usually there's buzkashi at Seyyedâbâd or here. In previous years, there was buzkashi every Friday, in Seyyedâbâd or here, by the Baluches, at Kal-qeshlâq, or at Chârbâgh.

For buzkashi, every village makes up a team; it's not done by tribe or sub-tribe. For example, on one side Seyyedâbâd, on the other Khârkash and us – our two villages combine for such an occasion. Sometimes all villages from Seyyedâbâd to Zakâ, Haji Qayum's place, are on one side, and Behsud, Chârbâgh, the Malekis, the Baluch and so on up to Sar-e-pol are on ours. There'll be only two teams. If there are too many people, then it's not done by village. An elder, or some khans, Hajis or headmen, stand in the middle and they divide people into teams. When the two teams have formed, they have a blessing and start to play.

Jashn is much bigger than Id, but it takes place in town. There are good shows there too, but there's no buzkashi and such stuff, that's for the winter months. For Jashn there's cinema, women singers come from Kabul, other performers, lights, lottery tickets. There's wrestling too, as well as the *atan* national dance, performed by Wardaks and other Afghans. The governors – the *wâli* in Sheberghân, the *hâkem* in Sar-e-pol – come to the shows on the first day; they sit and watch the marches and parades. In Sheberghân, if somebody has a fine camel, horse or dog, he dresses it up, decorates it and parades it past the *wâli*; if the *wâli* likes it he'll give it a prize.

Sometimes there's tent-pegging before the *wâli* in Sheberghân. You strike a peg into the ground, then you take a wooden spear, with a very sharp iron point, and you gallop up on horseback, aiming to spear the peg. It takes a lot of skill. Some people are really good at it, they spear the peg right out of the ground, and people clap loudly. Shâh-Mahmad Khân did it last year; he's also a fine buzkashi rider.

More on buzkashi, from Baya-khân.

For buzkashi, to mark the goal they dig a circular trench, or pile a ridge of hay, with open space in the middle. They fight for the goat or the calf, and try to throw it down into the goal; inside the line, it's good; outside, it's not. If it falls outside the goal, or somebody else gets it, then there's a general tussle – it's buzkashi! – everyone trying to drag it their way. When someone scores a goal, the horse's owner gets the kudos, so he gives the rider 50 to 200 rupees. So does the game-sponsor – he pays the rider for the sake of his own name.

Jughis are reckless of their lives. They'll kill themselves for 10 rupees, those people! They're very hungry, but they're also fanatical buzkashi players, they fight for the goat without caring whether they get their heads and arms broken and bloody. The horse's owner gives his Jughi rider money to encourage him to play harder and to enhance the horse's fame. Some horses are worth a fortune; if a horse is strong, fast and nimble, and has scored a lot of goals, the owner won't sell it for 50,000 rupees.

Some mullahs

Mowlawi Golzâr is a learned and respected mullah, who lives in Konjek. He is also a Sufi pir, though few villagers are his murids. Many villagers, as we shall hear later, are murids of other pirs, particularly of the Naqshbandiyya and Qâderiyya brotherhoods.

Pâdshâh, with Kala-khân, introduces Mowlawi and his family.

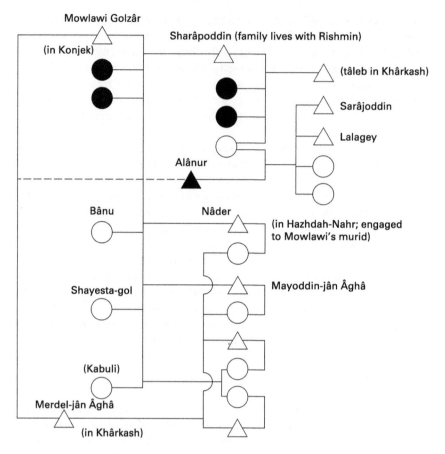

Figure 22 Mowlawi Golzâr's family.

Mowlawi's family are all pirs. They're originally from Band-e-Teymur[3] in Kandahar, where they have relatives. They're Es'hâqzai, Piruzai – our distant relatives. Mowlawi has murids everywhere: Qataghan, Hazhdah-nahr; he goes every year to see his murids, and brings back 100 seers of top-grade rice, and cash. His son Mayoddin-jân Âghâ goes too. His *langar* ('lodge') is very honourable; everybody gives to them. [*See Fig. 22*]

Mowlawi has three wives alive; two others are dead. He has three sons. Sharâpoddin, the oldest, separated from his father a few years ago, when he married. He owns nothing himself; he isn't entitled to anything that people give Mowlawi. He has his own murids, and he also gets something from those of both Mowlawi and Mayoddin-jân. He's had three wives: two are dead, one alive; and two sons and one daughter. This wife has two

[3]   This is also the birthplace of (a) Nur-Ali-jân Âghâ, whom we shall meet later, and (b) Mullah Akhtar Mansur Es'hâqzai, Mullah Omar's immediate successor as Amir of the Taliban. See Gopal (2014: 103–16).

sons and two daughters from her previous husband, Mowlawi's kinsman Alânur. We don't know where she's from herself; not from Khârkash.

Mayoddin-jân lives with his father; his wife is daughter of Mowlawi's brother Merdel-jân Âghâ, they have a small son. Mowlawi's youngest son Nâder is in Hazhdah-nahr; he has two wives; the first is another daughter of Merdel-jân; Mowlawi arranged the second one, but they haven't yet had the wedding; she's daughter of his murid, Mullah Karam, who gave her free.

Mowlawi's family is closer related to Nâder-shâh than to us. Merdel-jân Âghâ lives in Khârkash; he has two daughters married to Mowlawi's sons, and two sons married to Mowlawi's daughters.

In Mowlawi's household, food is cooked in one place, but they eat in three separate places. Mowlawi eats with his Kabuli wife; Mayoddin eats with his mother Shayesta-gol; and Bânu eats with her own son Nâder. Bânu's the oldest; Shayesta-gol's second; and the Kabuli's third. Bânu is senior wife, but Mowlawi's favourite is the Kabuli.

Their house – with the yard, gardens and pond – is on land that Haji Afzal gave free, for God. They have two servants: Tuy-Mamad from Kachan, who works for God and asks no wages, and the Arab house-servant, a murid, who gets clothes and things. They eat separately.

Mowlawi has some farmland. He bought some rainfed land in Neymadân, not much, 10 to 15 *jeribs*. The Arabs there are his murids, they farm it for him; they plough it, thresh the crop, winnow and clean the grain and bring it to him, by camel or donkey. Whatever the crop – barley, wheat, melons – they bring it here. Sometimes they send the straw, or they store it there, or he gives them permission to sell it. They don't sharecrop, they work for free; some take a share, but most don't; they just take the farmhand's share, but not the rest, because he's their pir.

He also recently bought some irrigated land in Hazhdah-nahr, at Pashm-kala, below Emâm-Sâheb. Mayoddin-jân Âghâ's just gone there to bring in the harvest. It's farmed by Mowlawi's murid, Mullah Karam. Mayoddin says it's 50 *jeribs*, but I don't know whether that's correct. He must have bought the land; nobody gives so much land away. The most anyone would give would be 2,000 rupees, or 20 seers of wheat, or 10 of rice. The absolute maximum, from someone who's really wealthy and really keen on helping, is 100 seers of wheat. People might give a cow, a sheep or two, a horse, a good *chapân* cloak, and so on, but never such a large amount of land.

Mowlawi Golzâr has a cow and a horse, and two or three donkeys, but no sheep. He can't keep sheep, because if you gave him 100 he'd slaughter one a day for meat until they were finished. If he kept the sheep he receives he'd have a whole flock within a year. People give them for God's sake, and he kills them in God's name. His family and guests eat them. There's never a day without guests, from Kandahar, Qataghan, Hazhdah-nahr. They aren't *tâlebân*, they're murids.

Mowlawi's eldest son Sharâpoddin has no servants. His sons Sarâjoddin and Lalagey work for him; they collect dung for fuel and fodder for the animals. He has some fifteen sheep, left by his wife's previous husband Alânur. They're with Rishmin; last year they were with us. Last year there were about twenty-five, the rest died. Then this winter or spring a thief came, ripped open the bellies of four or five and removed the unborn lambs – for the skins, the *takir*. They say Sharâpoddin's own son – not one of Alânur's orphans – gave them to the thief, because his father doesn't look after them properly. Now he's a *tâleb* in Khârkash, that boy.

Baya-khân tells how Khalifa-Patih deceived the mountain Aymâqs into believing him a holy man.

Khalifa-Patih's first wife Fâtema is an Aymâq from Târikak. Khalifa-Patih used to go to the mountains on horseback; he had a beard and a rosary in his hands. Up to Kachan, people knew who he was, but beyond Kachan the Aymâqs were naive and called him *khalifa* [*deputy pir*]. He went up as far as Târikak; he was very much revered up there; he'd act the *khalifa*, write nonsense amulets and chant charms for them. All day long his beads were in his hand. He made himself out to be a great sheykh. He'd go and sit down; they'd put a footstool for him, and people covered his horse and fed it barley. They'd give him horses, goats, wheat. That was Khalifa-Patih's line of work!

Then the Târikak Aymâqs gave him this girl Fâtema. 'This *khalifa*,' they said, 'this sheykh is a good man, let's give him a girl.' He gave a brideprice for her, but not much, less than 10,000 rupees. After he'd married her, for a couple of years he did really well. He came and went and collected a lot of money and stuff. He even got an Aymâq wife, Archagol, for his nephew Shâdi too.

For some years Fâtema and Archagol didn't realize the truth. But those Aymâqs started coming down, and saw that Khalifa-Patih wasn't treated so respectfully here as he was up there. He didn't write amulets, and they realized that he didn't know how to do them properly. He'd write all over the paper, fold it and tell them, 'Don't open it, keep it covered in green, white or black cloth; if your shoulder hurts, put it there and it'll get better.' They saw that he wasn't a *khalifa*; he'd lied to them, he was a nobody. 'We've been tricked! He knows nothing!' Now he's completely lost their respect.

In truth, in those days Khalifa-Patih did go around with Mowlawi Golzâr. Wherever Mowlawi went, people called Patih his deputy, *khalifa*, saying, 'He's with Mowlawi, he must be a holy man himself.' He got a certificate from Hazrat-seb [*see pp. 431–32*]; he used to have a good reputation, but now it's gone.

Childbirth and Infancy

Reproduction of the family through the birth of children, especially sons, is a vital concern to all Piruzai, and the main purpose of marriage – which, as we have heard, is the chief focus of economic activity and rivalry between families. But the dangers of childbirth in the absence of medical care mean that perinatal, infant and maternal mortality are extremely high.

Piruzai attribute most such deaths to attack or possession by jinns, and they have various practices to prevent or remedy jinn attack.

Birth

Maryam, Tumân's first wife, explains to Nancy her role as midwife, and what the job involves.

When a woman gives birth, neighbours come and sit with her. Women from further away don't come yet. I squeeze the umbilical cord slowly, to expel the air, then cut it with a knife. I don't tie up the end; it'll fall off by itself. If the mother's smart, and wants to cut the cord herself, she smoothes and squeezes it first. It doesn't matter whether you cut it yourself or get me to do it for you; if somebody else says she'll do it, tell her to go and wash properly first. Some do, some don't. When I've cut cords, I swear I've never washed properly!

If the mother has a jinn, on the day of the birth I wrap the afterbirth (*numna*) in a rag and put it by the baby. You can leave it there, removing it after the fortieth day. In hot weather, to stop it smelling bad, grind some salt and put salty water onto the afterbirth, then wrap it again in the rag and put it back with the baby. Some people bury it underground, some throw it into a canal or a river, but that's not a good idea, because people drink the water. Better to bury it. Or you can make it into a charm: when it starts to smell, salt it well then wrap it in a small rag and sew this amulet inside the swaddling clothes next to the baby's heart. Keep it there, tightly bound, until the baby starts to move.

We wrap the newborn, put it in a cradle, then lay the mother down. Another woman sits on her stomach and asks: 'Am I heavier or are you?' She says it several times, until the mother says: 'You're heavier!' It doesn't matter whether it's a grown woman or a young girl who rides on the mother – but she mustn't be jinn-possessed. A boy can't do it. It's our custom, something our ancestors did long ago, and they told us about it.

After the birth, we apply kohl to all the women's eyes, including the mother, then put her back to sleep. Any childless women there will ask the new mother to dream of a child, to see whether God will give them one. Whatever she dreams, people take it as a kind of omen.

The first three days, women come and cook *leyti*. They put a big pot of water on the fire and add turmeric, pepper, brown and white sugar, and mulberry syrup. They give a little to the new mother, take some round to Haji Tumân's and to Mowlawi's, and send bowls of it to every house in the community. In return, some people put coins in the bowl, others knucklebones, some a couple of beads, some just water. The women collect all these things and give them to the mother; she puts the beads on the baby's arm or leg.

We also cook some fatty bread, *kumâch*, for the mother. The first day, she drinks a cup or two of water with the bread. After that she won't drink any more water; otherwise, for those first three days, we just give her ghee. On the first and second days, some mothers drink tea.

As for the newborn baby, on the first day we give it just a little ghee, to calm its heart. When the afterbirth comes out, we say the baby's water's now passed and it'll no longer get kidney stones. Do your people get kidney stones? This happens when a woman's given birth; if she doesn't eject the afterbirth quickly, or the baby's water doesn't pass, then it'll get a kidney stone, and its stomach will go bad; when a boy grows up and becomes a young man, these stones are found inside him.

If you hear that a woman's giving birth, fetch any women who's badly jinn-possessed, and sit her down by the mother – but not until the afterbirth is out, otherwise it would kill the mother or her baby at once. When the baby's born, bind it, lay the mother down, and from that morning don't let any other possessed woman or a man in the house;

they'll kill the baby; the new mother will be possessed, she won't recognize her baby and it'll die; or her next baby will die. If a woman's clean and has no amulets, they welcome her and ask her to sit down; she may come and go. A woman who comes with an amulet on her head or her shoulder will kill the baby.

Pâkhâl has told us of the privations she suffered out in the steppe in early 1972; among these was having to deliver her own baby daughter; she and the baby survived.

One day I felt slightly unwell and I knew my time had come. It was snowing, and there wasn't any bread. In the evening we had a meal; I cooked only *kurcha*, which we normally make from a little flour and fat to give the sheep – but we were so hungry we cooked it up and ate it ourselves, then everyone went to sleep. I went outside; after I came back in I sat there in the dark, in pain. Pâdshâh brought in some dung-cakes and made a fire, saying, 'You sit here by the fire, I'm going to sleep.' So I sat by the fire, in the dark; I had no lamp, they'd taken it out with the sheep. As I sat there, Nancy, a fox got in among the chickens, and took one. Pâdshâh woke up and went after it; he came back in with a chicken, but the fox escaped. I said, 'Pâdshâh, bring the lamp, I'm in labour.' He wouldn't give me the lamp; he said, 'I can't spare the lamp, I need it out with the sheep. Get up, you're a human being, not an animal. If the ewes fall down, they can't get up by themselves, they'll lie there and die.'

I did go to bed, but I woke up as my pains began. I went into labour around midnight. The baby came in the early hours. No one was around when it happened. Nancy, the birth was awful; having my daughter was worse than the boys, which was bad enough.

I gave birth and did the ritual ablution, then I woke Pâdshâh. He went and got some fuel and made up the fire. I called Nasib, who was out in the sheepfold: 'Nasib, please come in!' He asked what had happened; Pâdshâh said, 'Your sister-in-law's had a baby daughter.' I asked him to go and fetch Abdol's wife, Eyjab. When she arrived, Eyjab cried, 'Hey, Pâkhâl, has your baby come?' Pâdshâh said 'Yes, thank God.' I'd been really desperate, I didn't think it would end, and I didn't know what to do. I was so relieved it was over, and I told Eyjab. She was very happy for me, for the birth of my daughter. I didn't say anything more; I was exhausted. Eyjab said, 'Thank God it's over, sister!' She found some rags and swaddled the baby; then she put together a brazier and I lay down beside it; she brought fire for the brazier, and covered it and me with a blanket. I lay there and went to sleep, and she went home.

In the morning, she cooked bread for herself and for me. Then around noon she cooked some broth for me – only a little, since there was no ghee. I ate half of it; half I put aside for the evening, when I had it cold. Then I slept again, and next morning I had some bread and tea. The tea was very bitter – out there in the steppe we had no sugar, nothing sweet of any kind. Eyjab came and said, 'Have you been drinking tea?' I said I had. 'Why? You should have had some ghee, tea isn't good for you.' I said, 'Aunt Eyjab, we have no ghee, it's finished.'

In the evening when Pâdshâh came, Eyjab said, 'Your wife's drinking tea, which isn't good for her; give her something else.' That afternoon I went out to the sheepfold to collect some droppings and firewood. Eyjab was outside and saw me; she scolded me, 'What are you doing out there? You're not a child, you're a grown woman, you should know better! Isn't there anybody to care for you, that you have to come out and collect fuel?' I said, 'What can I do? I don't have anybody.' That night Eyjab cooked some fatty bread for me and brought it over. She said, 'Have some of this with your tea; tea on its own is no good for you.' Nancy, I ate it, I was very hungry. The bread was rather dry, and the tea was bitter, but I was starving.

Baya-khân talks more formally about what happens at a birth.

If a girl younger than twenty is having her first baby, she doesn't know much about it, so an older woman, who does know, comes and sits behind her, holding her round the waist. When the baby's been born, the older woman takes it and wraps it in swaddling clothes. They give it ghee, and look after it. Then the woman who held the mother's waist – the midwife – will press the baby's father or grandfather, 'What'll you give me for my hard work, I'm exhausted!' He'll give her a chador, or a suit of clothes. We always give the midwife something, it's the custom.

Not every older woman can be a midwife; when someone's having a baby, women like my mother Maryam, or aunt Bibikuh, or aunt Neshtar, experienced women like that will go to help. Sometimes two or three women go, sometimes only one. Apart from the midwife, it's good for other women to be present at the birth. They send the men out. Girls and small boys are all right, but they won't allow older boys, who understand what's happening. When a woman's giving birth, she cries and shrieks, and they don't want the kids running out and telling everyone about it, what she said, how she cried and so on; that's why they don't let them stay there!

On the first day the women go round the camp and tell the others, 'So-and-so's had a baby, please come.' If a woman with a jinn or one who's crazy comes on the first day, says a few words, and the baby hears her voice then, it'll be all right; it won't matter if she comes to the house every day after that. But if she didn't come that first day, and the baby hears her voice afterwards, her jinn will work straight into the baby's body. Also, if a possessed woman comes and shakes her skirt over a newborn baby, it'll die.

Possessed woman generally don't have babies; or they don't survive. Sometimes the jinn kills the baby in her womb; if she does give birth, the baby may survive a month or two, but then the jinn will kick it and kill it. If the child survives, the jinn will possess it.

We don't tell people far away about the baby, only people close by. If a woman from far away comes to your house, and your house is next to ours, tell her not to speak loudly. Suppose I'm possessed, and I come to ask you for something; or you're my sister; it's important not to raise our voices, but to talk softly so that the baby doesn't hear. People take care of the baby; they'll look out, and if they see a possessed woman coming, they'll keep it inside with its mother. It's like that for forty days. After that, it doesn't matter if it hears a possessed woman's voice, or anyone else's.

For the first three days the mother stays inside, lying down. She can get up, but she won't go out. They say it's not good for a new mother to go outside, she may get rheumatism. They grind some sugar, mix in ghee and flour, to make what we call *leyti*, which is quite like the halwa that you make. They make a lot of it; the fat and sugar – brown, white and rock sugar – make it very sweet. It's for the new mother, but they also distribute some among the relatives, and the women in the camp. Each woman puts a little money, a rupee or two, or a bead into the bowl; if she doesn't have anything, she pours some water into it. Everybody likes *leyti*.

Sometimes the father sees his new baby on the first day. He'll come to see what it looks like! Some men don't bother, they come later. It doesn't matter when the father comes.

Nashra **and** tsalweshti

Piruzai hold two ceremonies for sons – not daughters: nashra *three days after birth, and* tsalweshti *after forty days. Baya-khân tells us.*

We do *nashra* for a firstborn son. On the third day, the boy's father goes to town to buy sweets, oleaster (*senjed*), apricots, raisins and other things. They fetch a mullah: 'We're doing *nashra* for our baby.' The mullah stands up in front, and behind him stand all the *tâlebs*, big or small, who are studying with him in his mosque. *Nashra's* a book, so the mullah chants from the book, and all the boys say *Allahu-amin*. After he's finished the chant he sits down; they bring fruit and the mullah distributes it. Then the mullah and the *tâlebs* press the baby's father for some money. If he's rich he'll give the mullah 100 to 300 rupees, others give 20 to 50. He'll also give from 5 to 50 rupees to each *tâleb*.

After forty days, the mother brings her new son to her father's house for the *tsalweshti*, 'fortieth'. Her father's family will be delighted and full of love for the baby; his maternal uncle, or grandfather if he's alive, will give the boy some animal: a lamb, a ewe, a foal, or a camel's calf; or he might give some clothes, even – if he's a wealthy notable – a gun. This gift belongs to the boy, but as he's a baby, they give it to his parents to keep until he grows up. They can't sell it or give it away.

On the day of *tsalweshti* the village women and the relatives come round. Some bring fatty bread, others raisins, sweets, fruit. The women bake three large *kumâch* loaves with milk and sugar, so that God will make the boy sweet to us when he grows up. They set the loaves up, one on each side and one on top, like a bridge. Two women sit opposite each other and pass the baby three times through the loaf-bridge: suppose I'm one of the women, I pass it once to you, and you take it, that makes once; then you pass it back to me, that makes twice; then I pass it to you once more, that makes three times: finished. Most people do it three times, they like that number best – though some do it seven times. After that, they take the fatty bread, the raisins, walnuts and sweets, everything they've brought, and distribute them among the women and children.

People don't do *tsalweshti* for daughters – they don't care so much for girls, they prefer boys. But we do it for every son, however many there are, and not just the firstborn.

Neshtar, as 'headwoman', organizes women's parties for these ceremonies – though not for her own family, as she explains.

Three days after a boy's born, we have the *nashra*. The boy's father buys sweets, raisins and fruit, then he goes to the mosque to ask the mullah and all the *tâlebs* to come tomorrow, and he announces that they're coming. Early in the morning the mullah collects all the *tâlebs* and turns up at the baby's father's home. He invites the villagers to come and eat the raisins and fruit.

Thirty or forty women and children gather, like at a wedding party. When they're assembled, the mullah recites the *nashra*. After he's finished, the boys say *Allahu-amin*. The mullah recites a lot of verses – they aren't like wedding songs, they're religious, from the Book. Ordinary people like us don't know them, only mullahs do. When he's finished, they spread a kilim and the mullah and his lads sit down. They give everybody some raisins, and they pay the mullah: 100 or 200 rupees if they're well off, 15 to 50 if they're not.

The boy's father bears all the trouble and expense, nobody else; but the mullahs and *tâlebs* do the actual *nashra*. We don't do it for girls, only for boys – and not all boys, only one who's taken his father's fancy, not if he dislikes him. A wealthy man's more likely to do it. A father does it to celebrate, for joy. But it's not essential.

I myself didn't do *nashra* for any of my sons or grandsons. Their grandfather – my late husband Akbar's father Mahd-Osmân – left instructions before he died: 'Don't do *nashra*, don't fire guns, I don't like it.' It was because so many of his children and grandchildren died at birth. At first, he did such ceremonies for his boys, but they all died. So he forbade guns and *nashra* – and now he has many descendants! If I have any more grandchildren, I won't do it for them either.

And I didn't do *tsalweshti* for any of my sons or grandsons, since their grandfather willed it that way. *Tsalweshti* is forty days after a baby boy is born. The parents don't do it; it's the older women, elders like me or my sister Hazâra here, or aunt Ghondak. These women sit together, laugh and bring out the baby. They make fatty bread, then they set the loaves up like this and pass the baby through. We say, 'God take this boy! God bring him up! God make him grow!' Then they divide the fatty bread and make it a sacrificial offering, distributing it among the women and children. We invite other women, saying, 'Today we're bringing the baby out for its *tsalweshti*, please come.' They'll cook fatty bread too, and bring it on the day with melons, grapes, sweets and other things. Some people do *tsalweshti* for a baby girl too, if she's light-skinned. As for boys, people do it only if they feel like it, when the baby particularly moves their hearts. It's up to the family.

My own father Golnur and his sons used to do these ceremonies, but they too decided against it. When his first son was born, they fired guns and did the *nashra*, but then, when the father died and the boy remained, it hit them hard; they said, 'Forget it, we won't do it again.' When my cousin Mahd-Rahim was alive, he'd do *nashra* and *tsalweshti* for his sons; some of them died, some lived; my cousin Mowzoddin's family doesn't do it any longer. This year, nobody's done *nashra* in this village, except Abdor-Rahmân Payu from Kandahar: he did a nice *nashra* when his son was born, a few days before you arrived. I didn't go, but we heard it going on. In twenty days' time, when Shahâboddin's boy is forty days old, they'll do *twalweshti* for him. Come and see for yourself.

Circumcision; childhood

Circumcision for boys is compulsory, and usually done early, with little or no celebration, unlike in many other Muslim societies. Baya-khân tells how it's done.

A baby boy may be circumcised after forty days. Some people wait for two or three years. A man with just one son may do the ceremony on his own; others collect five or ten neighbourhood boys to be done at the same time. They fetch a Jughi – we Afghans only get Jughi circumcisers, nobody else. We pay them in rice and cash. Rich men pay 200 to 500 rupees, and some rice – Jughi people are very hungry. If a Jughi barber comes by, a poor man will get him to do the circumcision right then, and pay 20 to 40 rupees.

The boy's parents will be present during the cutting; so will his brothers and sisters and other relatives. Some boys cry while they're being cut; but he's only a small baby, not a grown-up who might find it embarrassing. After the cutting, they take some *ârelang* – the plant I showed you the other day – and boil it in ghee; it releases its strength into the ghee, which they put on the boy's thing, and he'll soon recover. It's a very good medicine for fever; that's what we grow it for.

A rich man will hold a party for his son, for his reputation. He'll buy rice and ghee, slaughter an ox or a sheep, hire musicians, invite guests. The really wealthy invite lots of people; they'll dance *atan*; the women too will hold a party. Sometimes there's buzkashi; it's like a wedding party.

Baya-khân mentions an apparently one-off local practice. Interestingly, since 2001 many other instances in Afghanistan have received media attention.[4]

[*Pâkiza's brother*] Chârgol's wife Golmir wore boy's clothes when she was a girl. Her father Mahd-Omar had no sons, or his sons were tiny at the time, so he put Golmir in boy's clothes, with a turban and so on, and she behaved like a male; she grazed the lambs. Mahd-Omar had a hired hand who went with the camels; she was with the lambs, and she grazed them here, in the gardens near the house. When she was with the lambs, we called her Ghajak, and treated her like one of the boys; if you didn't know, you'd have thought she was a boy.

I'm not joking, ask around! Nobody else has done this. A year before Mullah Jabbâr engaged her to his son Chârgol, she put on women's clothes; she grew up and they kept her at home. Now she has a different name, Golmir, and she doesn't go outside the house. She no longer goes with the animals; people would talk, it wouldn't be proper.

Death and the Afterlife

Funerals

Death is only too closely associated with childbirth. Each village has its own separate graveyard. The Khârkash graveyard is beside the track linking the two main villages. Konjek's is on the edge of the steppe, beside the perimeter canal. In both, there are recent shrines, over the graves of murder victims. Piruzai who die away from home, usually on

---

[4] See Lindisfarne (1997: 65); *Wikipedia*, s.v. 'Bacha posh', and recent books and films listed there.

the migration trail, are brought back for burial; but if it is more than a day's journey away they are interred in one of the small Piruzai graveyards in the mountains.

Pâdshâh narrates the proper funeral process, and details what happens to the many infants who die.

If somebody's dying, we send a boy: 'Go and tell the mullah to come quickly.' A mullah should be summoned while the person's still alive and breathing; he should be there at the death. But if the mullah's far away, and hasn't arrived in time, then someone at home, like my father, will chant a few verses from the Holy Koran while the person's still breathing.

When this person's died, the women make a shroud from 12 to 15 yards (*gaz*) of white cotton cloth. They cut this into the right pieces and stitch them; then we take the body out into the yard, and if it's warm we put up a tent and work in the shade; not if it's winter. We heat several cauldrons of water for the mullahs, warm, not so hot it burns their hands; they wash the body completely.

(N) – Both men and women?

No, not women! Only men.

(R) – What if it's a woman who's died?

Let me finish telling about men first! Let's not get them mixed up or people in England won't be able to understand it properly. If I make a mistake, you'll blame me later!

So we wash the body; we do our best to make sure it's done properly and any dirt removed. Then – may God delay the day – we put on the shroud. We tie his big toes together and put his hands into a kind of bag, what we call a *katrun*; then we tie up the top of the shroud, like this, leaving no hole anywhere.

Then we make a bier, and place the body on it. The mullahs pick it up, walk with it for a few paces then set it down again. They do this three times, then the young men take over. If there aren't many people, they load it onto a camel or a horse; but if there are lots of people, four men can take it on their shoulders. We make the bier in such a way that four people can carry it, walking in step. Anyone can come along if they hear about it, they could be Hazâra or Uzbek, so long as people know them; but any Afghan, whether a friend or not, can come; anybody from these nearby villages.

Young men take turns carrying the bier on their shoulders for a few minutes until they arrive at the grave. They definitely won't argue about it; it's very serious business. You take a couple of steps and then if somebody wants to take over from you, you pass it to him; you don't say, 'I'll go on until I'm tired.' Absolutely not. You carry it, and if nobody takes it from you, fine, but if twenty people press you to pass it on quickly, no matter, everybody gets a turn. Most people take rapid turns and need a rest after a few steps. A dead body's very heavy – you must know how heavy it can be, no? But every step you take towards the graveyard, more of your sins fall to the ground, into your footprints. This has enormous merit, according to the Book. I don't know how many grams of your sins flow away, but God will forgive you any bad deeds, adultery and so on.

We take the body to where the gravediggers are digging and leave it beside the grave. They put up a tent for shade. As the gravediggers work, mullahs recite the Koran.

Anybody can be a gravedigger: Hazâra, Afghan, Uzbek. Whoever they are, anyone who digs earns great merit, there's nothing like it; in the other world his face lights up the whole place, like a huge torch in the dark. It's for merit that everybody brings spades and shovels and tries to help with the digging.

When they've finished the grave, the person in charge stretches out inside to test it for length; then they dig out a niche, and put the body in it, with the head facing Mecca. They put bricks, the size of your tape recorder, to cover the niche, like a plank, to prevent any earth or stuff getting in. When they've sealed the niche, they fill in the grave.

You've seen what graves are like. They put a couple of stones at the head and the foot, then they take the long white cloth strip tied to the body, and tie it to both stones – you've seen this, haven't you? The mullahs do a loud *do'â-o-takbir* prayer, then deliver a homily to the survivors, 'Try to keep to your religion, your prayers, your justice, don't tell lies, don't commit theft, adultery, and so on; whether we live a thousand or two thousand years, or one year, in the end, whatever country you go to, we all end up here.' When the mullahs say this, very pious people listen carefully. Others pay little attention; it takes all sorts.

When a woman dies . . . Wait, I've left some things out.

After the burial, the household head lets people know and perhaps he'll slaughter an animal, cook the meat and distribute it among the people at the graveyard; or he'll distribute money. Before the burial, I forgot, he collects cash: one or two thousand rupees, whatever people can afford; perhaps ten or twenty thousand from a respected person, even up to 50,000 or 100,000; it depends how wealthy people are. Now he'll hand the money to a mullah, who asks, 'How much is it?' and he answers, 'It's 10,000 rupees,' or whatever. The mullahs distribute the money to the poor and weak; nobody's left out, everybody, big and small, gets something. The mullah gets most, but others get 10, 20, 5 rupees, perhaps more. After that, they do *do'â-o-takbir* and the funeral's over.

Now he's dead and buried. On the third day, the bereaved household puts on a sacrificial feast. They slaughter a sheep, an ox or a camel, or cook rice, and they fetch mullahs for a Koran-reading. They feed the people, who give the mullahs 20, 50, or 100 rupees as they take their leave.

A few Fridays later, they do another sacrificial feast; and a year later, yet another one. If the survivors can afford it, they may well slaughter an animal and put on such feasts every year as long as they're alive; otherwise just once or twice.

Now when a woman dies, an older, grey-haired woman, they wash her thoroughly, make the shroud, then we take her to the graveyard and bury her, all in exactly the same way, except that, when we put her in the grave, at the last moment we uncover her face. Why? Because our Books say a woman's face is covered in this world, but in that world her face must be free. Her face has a small *ruyband*, they fix it so that her face is bare, and facing Mecca. A man's face is covered by the shroud; though of course it'll decay, the worms will eat it.

If you die a long way from home, your body's buried there. But your soul's free and it'll return to be with its family, its tribe. If the family has money they may fetch the body, by truck or plane, but it's a lot of trouble and costs a great deal. Rich people like Tâj-Mahmad Khân or Kheyr-Mahmad Khân, notable people like that can do it, others certainly can't.

When a household head himself dies, his family make the funeral arrangements together. If he has a son or brother, fine, but they'll get us all to help. If there are no men left in the house, only women, then a male cousin does it, gathers the people, fetches the mullah, slaughters the sheep, ox or camel, organizes the feast, does the distribution. Some people buy rice, but, if they can't afford it, relatives will help with bread or rice or an animal, or collect money. Whatever happens, there'll be a feast in the dead man's house. When a child dies, women don't normally go to the graveyard. If it was a nice young girl or a nice young man, and the mother's grief-stricken, she may go; one or two women may go, but no more. The mullahs and elders won't allow women there, but if they try really hard, then their hearts are moved and they're compelled to let them go and have a last look.

People aren't so sad when an old person dies. Women only grieve over their sons and daughters, and they cry to be allowed to go to the graveyard. For old people, there's only one death; it's the same person whether you see them here or there.

We say that a foetus isn't human until its hands, feet and eyes are distinguishable. If a mother miscarries a tiny foetus up to three months in the womb, it's just like a small piece of flesh, it's not human; we call it *achawunkey*. We wrap it up in a piece of cloth, take it away from the village and bury it – it doesn't matter where.

If its features, nails, hair, eyes, mouth and so on are formed, it's human, in which case for forty days the father shouldn't sleep with his wife; they can sleep together, but they mustn't touch each other; there should be a line between them, to prevent anything; she's forbidden to him. Why? Because for forty days she has this blood, this blemish. I don't know if it's the same for you people. Once this blemish is cured and the blood stops, then she's free. If a woman miscarries at six or seven months, the baby has recognizable features, and we must bury it in the graveyard like a live-born baby. We take a mullah, and people may come to the condolence ceremony (*fâteha*); it depends. If – God forbid – one of Haji's own daughters lost a child, then everyone would come. If my daughter died, some people would come to offer Haji condolences; others won't. For a five or six month baby, male or female, if the father's a big man, people will come; but not for people like you or me!

If I lost a premature daughter, my brother would come with me to bury her, or he'd go alone, or my uncle, or some other relative, or I'd send my brother-in-law Payz. But I might have to go alone with the mullah. The mother would never go, women never go to burials.

A premature baby will go to heaven. That's all in our Book. Once a newborn child just opens its eyes and sees something; then apart from the earth, which takes its due, Merciful God will forgive it everything else and it'll go to heaven and exist there in freedom. If a child doesn't understand, the earth takes its due, but it'll go straight to heaven. Until he's grown up like Manân [*his twelve-year-old half-brother*] here, or a little younger, a boy is responsible only to the earth; God forgives him the rest. When he's bigger and understands the ways of the world, starts wanting to do this and that with women or boys, then he'll have to take the consequences. Once he understands, for example, 'Someone's stolen my property, I'll retaliate by stealing something of his,' then we say he's grown up. A boy like Manân can't make babies if he sleeps with a woman – I guess it's like that with you too? – but when he's grown up, if he sleeps with his wife – so long as she's grown up too – they can have babies. Before that, no questions, they go straight to heaven, both boys and girls.

Among us, girls grow up quicker; I don't know how it is with your people. With us, males are like wheat, which is planted earlier and ripens later; females are like barley, which is sown later than wheat but ripens earlier.

While Maryam was a recognized midwife, Neshtar's speciality is as female body-washer at death.

Four years ago I learned from Mayoddin-jân Âghâ how to wash bodies. If – God forbid – some woman dies, I'll wash her. That is, the washing's my responsibility, but old women like Ghondak here, my sister Bibiwor, and two or three others help me. There are many women around as we work. We put up a tent or a curtain. We take the shroud and make two washcloths from it. Bibiwor sits by a big cauldron, washes the cloths very clean, fills the ewers with water – warm, not hot – and sends them to me. Mordamâl pours water from a ewer on my hands while I wash. We cover the left side while we wash the right. First we wash the right hand, then the left hand; then the mouth, the nose, the face, then the right arm, the left arm, then the right foot and the left foot; like the ablution for prayers.

Then we do the complete ablution, *ghosl*, for the right side, with plenty of soap. After we've washed the right side three times, we turn the body over and wash the left side three times with soap. When the body's completely washed, we put on the shroud.

The shroud has two sheets. We spread them out; two sheets make one long shirt. It's two spans wide, to cover the breasts and these places, down to the feet. We stretch it up to the neck, then tie a string around the neck, as with a baby. One side goes underneath, the other on top; one side of the head's up, the other down. So we tie the neck on the right side, then wind the sheet round, then the left side. Then there's the other sheet, two-and-a-half metres, which we wind round the top of the body like a man's headscarf. One of the two sheets makes the shirt, and the other's a chador, like a headscarf, which we use to hide her face up to here. That's how we do the burial shroud.

As we're washing the feet or the body itself, we all recite *la-ilaha-ila-Allah Mohammad-arrasul-Allah*; also as we're doing the shroud. When the shrouding's finished, the women say, 'God forgive her, she was a good woman, pious, dutiful in prayer.' Even if she wasn't so good, everyone still says she was, so that the angels who are sitting at her shoulder collect her quickly from the graveyard.

Next we get a good clean cloth, a prayer mat, or a clean blanket, to wrap round her. We make a bier – a framework of two poles with cross-pieces at both ends and rope wound between them – and put the body on it. Then four men carry it on their shoulders to the graveyard.

When someone dies during the day, we wash the body immediately. If it's Friday eve, we wash the body right away, and whoever's around stays up; someone reads from the Koran until dawn. If it's some other night, we also sit up and listen to the Koran, and we'll wash the body right away if it's not too cold – raining or snowing.

In every place, there's a woman who knows how to do it; in Khârkash, there's someone else for sure – though I don't know who, as I've never been present at a death there. I expect it's Nâder-shâh's sister Malek. In this village, they get me to do this sort of job. Elsewhere, like the Alizais, if there's no smart, sensible woman around, they may ask me to come. It makes no difference if they're a different tribe. This work has great religious merit.

The Book also says it's meritorious to give, so people give me something, according to their means; they also give aunt Ghondak something when she's with me. Perhaps a ten- or twenty-rupee note, or some tea. If they're poor, I don't take anything.

It's not important to learn from a mullah, as long as you do it properly, and think carefully what you're doing as you go along. If I hadn't learned from a mullah, I could learn from watching a woman who knows how. A young person can do it, so long as she's sensible. When I was young I didn't think about dead people, my heart wasn't there. Young people only think about who's there, about their feelings, that kind of thing. But now my hair's grey!

Sometimes I'm not at home; for example, with Khoday-râm's wife, I only arrived at the end, when they were ready to put the shroud on, and I did that. Pâr-khân's mother Shamayel did the washing; she knows how, but she's old and a bit scatter-brained. I'm younger, I can concentrate on what I'm doing, but when I get older . . .

Baya-khân and Seyyed-shâh/Golusar respond to my questions about strangers, graveyards for the nomads, and the continuing relationship with the dead, which brings merit (sawâb) in the afterlife.

(R) – If a stranger's body's brought to the village, who'll wash it?

(Baya-khân) – The mullah. It brings great merit.

(R) – Does it matter who carries the body?

(Baya-khân) – Not at all. It brings merit, and anyone in the village comes to help bury him. When a woman from another *qawm* dies here, her father, brothers and cousins decide where she's buried.

(R) – What if she has no close relatives?

(Baya-khân) – Wherever you bury her, distant cousins won't complain, but they have the right to decide. Her husband has no right; once she's dead, his rights cease.

(R) – What about her children, don't they have a say?

(Baya-khân) – No. It's not important. Her father may say, 'We'll take her to our graveyard.' Most people do that.

(R) – If a woman from Khârkash living here dies, they'll bury her in Khârkash graveyard?

(Baya-khân) – Yes, they'll take her there.

(Seyyed-shâh) – Haji Tumân's cousin Karâr was married to Kohandel in Khârkash; when she died we buried her in our graveyard. It was our privilege. They had nothing to do with it. Then there was Haji Ghâfur's wife, Tamâm, Khalifa-Patih's sister; she died up in Chenâr and they wanted to bury her there, but Khalifa-Patih sent a message, 'Bring her back, we'll bury her here.' They spent two days on the road, and it was evening before they got back. They'd already dug her grave, so they buried her the next morning.

(Baya-khân) – Some men and women make a will (*nesihat*): 'Take me and bury me in my own graveyard.' People will do just that, so long as it's not too far, like up in the mountains. If it's Chenâr or nearer, they'll bring them back.

(R) – If you pass the place where your sister's buried, or some other woman from your family, do you say a prayer for her?

(Baya-khân) – We say a prayer at any graveyard, even if there's no one from our family there.

(Seyyed-shâh) – On our way into town, we pray as we pass Khârkash graveyard, even though none of our sisters or relatives are there. They're Muslims, they need our prayers.

(Baya-khân) – Dead people get very unhappy; it's bad if you don't say a prayer for them.

(Seyyed-shâh) – If you say a prayer, they'll watch out for you in the next world.

(R) – The other day, when we went to the village graveyard, you went to your sister's grave but nobody else's.

(Baya-khân) – First I prayed for everyone, then I went to my sister's grave.

(R) – Ah. If there's a woman from a different village, you don't say a special prayer for her?

(Baya-khân) – First you pray for everybody; but then I went to my sister because if I didn't she'd be unhappy. You pray for someone from your own family three times. The mullahs know many verses for praying over them.

(R) – If you pass the graveyards of other people, like Arabs, do you say a prayer?

(Baya-khân) – Yes, we do. At night, if there's no house to go to, you can spend the night in the graveyard. It's good to sleep right there, because the dead watch over you even if you can't see them. Nobody can attack you. But if you pass a graveyard at night, they may set out to frighten you.

(R) – Who's buried in the middle graveyard, by the hill?

(Seyyed-shâh) – Mullah Jabbâr's crowd bury their dead there; so do the Âghâ-kheyl, and also a few people from Khârkash who can't get to the other graveyard; that's enough for them.

(R) – But nobody from this village?

(Seyyed-shâh) – No. All our village are buried in our graveyard; and a few up in Kachan.

(R) – Where in Kachan?

(Seyyed-shâh) – At the Tagawboy shrine. More are buried at Kuru – do you know it? Beyond Kachan, this side of Kajira village, there's a graveyard we call Kuru. Some of us are buried there.

(R) – Who, for example?

(Seyyed-shâh) – Akbar's wife, God forgive her, is there; so's a daughter of Kamaroddin; and many others.

(R) – Who's buried at Tagawboy?

(Seyyed-shâh) – Three of my father's brothers: Sangin, Dâdollah and Shâdi.

(R) – Who else?

(Seyyed-shâh) – There are others at Dangak and Cherâs.

(R) – Who's buried in Dangak?

(Seyyed-shâh) – Dur-khân's wife Shayesta. The graveyard doesn't mind where they come from. It's for the close relatives to say. But they're Muslims too, it doesn't matter where you're buried, there's only one other world.

(R) – Can you remember who died up in the mountains and was buried there, for example in the Adira graveyard?

(Baya-khân) – Any Piruzai who dies in the mountains, in Sar-jangal district, is buried in Adira; there's no other graveyard.

(R) – Once someone's buried, for example the martyr in your graveyard, can people petition to have his body taken home?

(Seyyed-shâh) – No. In his case, he was buried by their permission. His bones must now have crumbled away.

(R) – So it's not possible for a body to be reburied somewhere else?

(Seyyed-shâh) – That happens often. If you don't have the means, you first bury the body in this graveyard, which will look after it for you; then you fetch people to help dig him up and take him to be buried properly in your own place.

(R) – The second time, does the mullah come and pray again?

(Seyyed-shâh) – Yes, he does. After all, the first grave was only looking after the body; now it's being buried for good. They say further prayers, and on the third day they hold the sacrificial distribution; then, like when Hâshem went to town for his friend, if some respected person dies, all his descendants, his friends and relations will come to say the memorial prayers. They spread out kilims, serve tea or whatever they can afford, there's a mullah, and they pray.

Heaven and Hell

We did not hear any sermons in the village mosques, but from all accounts morality and the rewards and punishments in the afterlife were major topics. Pâdshâh and others articulate what the mullahs say, which is Koran-based but imaginatively elaborated according to tradition. Note the emphasis on the sins of theft, usury and adultery (zenâ). Legally, zenâ covers all heterosexual sex outside marriage; but speakers here mean adultery, where one or both partners are already married.

Pâdshâh explains.

If you do good in this world – if you help the poor, treat your family well, don't mess with other people's wives – then Merciful God will save you, you'll go to Heaven, with forty women-servants and I don't know how many men. There, you'll be carefree, free to wander as you please; among orchards, rose-gardens, and things that don't exist in this world. But if you've committed adultery, theft and so on, your place is Hell, where you'll be punished, and there you'll stay until the Day of Resurrection. Someone who goes to Hell will be there until the Day of Judgement; whatever he does, however much he cries out, he'll stay there and burn in the fire. Hellfire isn't like our fire, it's much worse. When your punishment's finished, they'll take you and put you in Heaven.

Only the soul is examined. Forget the body: the earth takes your dead body by the thread; three times it kicks you and brings you back to life, just as alive as you are now. It kicks your whole body three times, so that your bones break and catch fire, and the smoke's carried away, like cigarette smoke. After that, the body owes the earth nothing; it lies there in peace. Nobody's concerned with it, the worms eat it, it decays. It's the soul that has to deal with questions and punishments.

When a woman dies, it's exactly the same; if she's behaved justly, like a good Muslim, if she's taken things from her husband, openly or secretly, to help beggars and the poor, then Merciful God will award her merit. Whatever she's given to someone at the door, a piece of bread or 5 rupees, or scraps of wool or felt, so long as she didn't send them away empty-handed, it counts to her credit, she'll be rewarded.

When a tiny baby dies, say forty days or two months after birth, for some time its mother's breasts keep producing milk, which is very painful for her; so, our mullahs say, that tiny baby's parents will receive a lot of merit in the next world. If Pastuk or Torak or little Golabshâh here should die, it'll bring their mother and me merit.

Now, every dead person must cross the Sirât Bridge, which is thinner than a hair of one's head, sharper than a new razor blade, and invisible to the eye. A good Muslim who's said his prayers, etc. will cross that Bridge as quick as a flash, without worrying about the fire; but a sinner who's destined for Hell, at his first, second or third step on that Bridge, he'll fall off into the fire. It's the only route; you can't avoid Hell by sneaking around it on a detour by car.

When a baby dies, its soul stays on the Bridge; as every dead soul arrives, it sniffs them, until it recognizes its mother's or father's smell; then it'll starting crying, reach out and cling to them, and if they were about to be thrown into Hellfire, the baby will cry, 'I'll throw myself into the Fire too!' It's impossible to bribe them to let you go free; they'd say, 'Take your money back, child, what do we want with money? Let's throw your father into the Fire.' No, the baby will kill itself rather than let them throw one of its parents into the Fire. Until the Day of Resurrection, this child's soul will save them from the Fire, again and again.

These kids, too, only the earth takes its due from them. They don't go to the Fire, they go to Heaven, without being examined. There are scribes sitting there in an office, deciding whether each person's to go to Heaven or Hell, but there's no examination for children, only the earth has a claim on them. This is so until they're pretty near adult. Until then, they don't really understand the Book, and they don't know anything about the other world. They do pray, but their thoughts change every minute. They're still children; even if you tell them off a hundred times, they're liable to forget and go off and do mischief. A grown man remembers what he's told: he always remembers which path is the bad one that'll end up in Hellfire. A Muslim won't run the risk of Hell. A child doesn't think, so he won't be examined, but after he's grown up, even if he's struck down by madness a hundred times, he'll still be examined.

The trouble we see in this world, for instance when government puts us in jail or tortures us, what's that? It's nothing. It comes to an end. But in the other world, if you fall into Hell, it's for good. However much you groan and wail and leap, there's nobody there to help you out, to set you free. Here, your chief, whether Haji Kheyr-Mahmad Khân or the son of Yusef Boy Uzbek, will come and free you. There, wolves and dogs, bad and good, all drink in the same place. There's no trouble or torment in this world, Richard; it's all in the next world. This world is all talk.

If someone dies after being knocked down by a truck, our mullahs say he was sinless, as if he were returning from Mecca. He's suffered so much in the accident, if he dies his suffering's ended. But if he were run over while trading for profit and interest, people would say he was a usurer, so his place is Hell. If you're going along the road, with only your own money on you, whether 1 rupee or 10 or 100,000, and somebody kills you without cause – you hadn't even spoken with him – then you're a martyr and you won't be examined in the other world. You owe nothing to anyone – apart from the earth, which receives its due.

Among us, if someone's always squabbling with his parents, his wife or his parents-in-law, then if he dies without their forgiving him for any wrong he did them, people say that he'll suffer a lot in the other world, as though they'd cursed him. Then one evening they'll hear a little noise in the air, *chek-chek-chek.* You don't know what it is, and you can't see anything; it's like a cricket, chirruping away out among the melons, or in the corn, or in an orchard, you know? You realize it's one of the dead; you can't tell who it is, but it's certainly a relative. If your heart's at peace, you must forgive somebody who's recently died – like my poor sister-in-law, Bâdâm. 'If you're suffering because of me, I forgive you any wrong you did me. Please go back, don't do that *chek-chek* any more.'

That's all it is, we don't know anything else about the dead. Whatever other suffering God may have imposed, if it's a woman who's done wrong, slept with someone other than her husband, things we were talking about, well, God's punishment for her is another matter. But as far as you're concerned, if you get a wife for your son, and she quarrels with you, you must forgive her: God can't give anyone else permission to do so. It's your right. God demands a reckoning of what's due to him as Creator, but he can't give anyone else permission to forgive her on your behalf. God may put calm in your heart, give you patience so that you feel forgiveness, then you tell them, 'You're suffering now because you wronged me, you caused me suffering when you were alive, quarrelled with me; but now everything is forgiven on my part.'

Baya-khân and Kala-khân talk about sin.

(*Baya-khân*) – Afghans don't like usury (*sud*), taking interest. Our mullahs say that usury is very bad. According to the books they read, a usurer will suffer terribly in the other world; he'll get hung up by the tongue, thrown in the Fire; his soul will.

(*Kala-khân*) – It's as bad as sex with your mother or sister.

(*Baya-khân*) – The opposite of Hell is Heaven, where you can find everything God has made in this world waiting for you: food, or whatever you want. But people who've done wrong, like usury, get hung up by the tongue in Hell. It's all fire, and sinners are thrown into the Fire. Don't your mullahs tell you this?

(*R*) – Yes, but not for usurers, rather for murderers, thieves, and so on.

(*Baya-khân*) – For people who kill, yes, for thieves, yes . . .

(*R*) – Men who run away with other women, who don't respect father and mother . . .

(*Baya-khân*) – Ah!

(*R*) – Liars . . .

(*Baya-khân*) – Ah yes! We're the same after all. Nearly! Give us a couple of years together!

(*Kala-khân*) – All you have to do is recite the creed . . .

(*Baya-khân*) – Our mullahs say that, when they put you in the grave, the angels Nakir and Monker come and remove your soul from your body, and Almighty God takes it up. But if you've done bad deeds, God puts your soul back in your body, and sends scorpions and snakes; the scorpions bite you on this side, and the snakes on that side. If your deeds were very bad, you smell so awful that when the angels take your soul up to God they cover their noses. If you've committed adultery or usury, your soul gives out such a stench that, before you get close, God from afar orders the angels to drop you back to earth. So you fall and break up into small pieces like millet; they put the pieces together again and make them into a soul, and burn them in the Fire. Finally they forgive you, the mullahs say. If you've committed adultery, you suffer the due punishment, then they stop the torment, forgive you, and send you on to Heaven.

Good-doers smell very nice and go straight to Heaven; the angels are happy to take them right up to the presence of God Almighty. If you've done good and said your prayers, there's no examination. There in Heaven God has provided every amenity, it's a nice place, water and everything are abundant, you'll enjoy walking around all day, the mullahs say; that's where the good-doers go.

On his own, Pâdshâh gets intimate and confessional.

If you've got plenty of money, you might go after an attractive woman, who may or may not be married, and secretly spend the night with her, and make love to her. You'll spend money on her, buy her things from town, from Sheberghân, Mazâr or Kabul; things to eat or wear. In Afghanistan these secret affairs are very enjoyable, better than your own wife! It's good that I'm telling you this, no? You bring her nice jewellery, hair ornaments, scented soap, pretty clothes – you bring them for her, but not for your wife. And it's nobody else's business, only you and that woman will know; you don't tell a soul, family or friends.

But your wife might find out. Some man or woman might see you and tell your wife. She'll make a huge fuss, crying and screaming: 'What's the matter, am I blind, am I lame, skinny, lazy, why did you go and spend money on a slut? You've ruined yourself in this world, and you'll be punished in the other, they'll burn you in the fire!' and so on.

In fact, our Book says that such a woman will be hung up by her head-hair, like this; the man will be lying down, with his mouth open as in death; and the sperm that passed from his body into hers in life, in that secret affair, will pass back from the same place it went into her body, drop by drop, into his mouth. It's in our Book and it's true. On the Day of Resurrection all the dead, foreigners and Afghans, are brought back to life; but until then, this man must lie there, unable to move his head, and the woman must hang there by her hair, and the sperm will drip into his mouth. God the Creator says, 'We gave you a wife by Shar'i marriage; she was pure, nobody had been with her, why did you go with another woman? You should have been content with your wife, made love to her – she can do it too!'

It's very bad, according to the Book. But we're talking of the people of Afghanistan, who don't care. Some people are good, pious Muslims, who never look at anybody else's wife. Others pay no attention to their own wives, but like to look at other women and find ways to sleep with them, spending a lot of money. Does this happen in your place?

(R) – It happens everywhere!

Well it's like that among us. One year I spent a lot of money on a woman; Pâkhâl's mother heard about it, and both of them attacked me, went on and on about it. Now, though, she just asks why I did this to her daughter.

The skies

Human behaviour sometimes affects celestial bodies, signs of God's anger. There are several stories about this, and what humans can do about it.

Around a fire in his courtyard one evening, Haji Tumân and friends talk of the heavens.

The Prophet Star, *peyghambar storey*, is the Morning Star. In our Book, the Koran, when God first created the universe, the first star he made was our Prophet; he wasn't in the world. That's why we call our Prophet the first, because he was the first star to be created. There have been 124,000 prophets, and our Prophet is the last, the seal, there are no more. I don't know what your Book, your Gospel, tells you about this. Our Prophet was first because his star was the first created, and last because he was the last to be born.

Mowzoddin's son Mullah Kadir takes over.

The Prophet said to Gabriel, 'Who's first, you or me?' Gabriel said, 'I'm first.' The Prophet said, 'No, I am: of all the things created in the world, heaven and earth, mountains, what did you see in the sky?' Gabriel said, 'I saw one star.' The Prophet said, 'That was me.' Then Gabriel said, 'Without doubt, you're the first of all.' So Gabriel agreed that the Prophet's both first and last, Mohammad Rasulollah.

Tumân continues.

We call [*the Milky Way*] Deldel's Way, *dë deldel lâr*. Deldel was the horse of Ali, Lion of God. There was much evil and bad behaviour in the world, people didn't obey God's commands. Suddenly God sent a cataclysm on them. The heavens split in two, they say; the waters were released and came down, sent by the Prophet, through Deldel's Way. Prophet Noah built a ship, and the creatures entered it two-by-two, one male, one female. Everything else died in the flood. Mullah Kadir here says that all these hills and mountains were made from the foam of the floodwaters.

On another occasion Baya-khân tells of the Pleiades – a common season-marker for nomads.

When shepherds colour the sheep, it's for *peyrun*, the Pleiades: the group of stars, you know? It first rises in June, then every night it gets earlier; it disappears in spring. When it rises, shepherds dab some colour on the sheeps' tails, to prevent them from being '*peyrun*-struck'. On days when *peyrun* rises, to prevent the sheep from seeing it we herd them into the lee of a hill. After sunrise, it can't be seen, so it doesn't matter any more.

But it does strike the odd sheep. It doesn't kill them, they just won't get fat. If they graze all year without putting on weight, people say they've been struck by *peyrun*. If it strikes, it doesn't have an immediate effect, it doesn't strike all the animals, and it only occasionally happens, in some flocks, not all. Some people make charms for protection; they may or may not work. But shepherds do put a little colour on the sheep's tails, to guard against *peyrun*. When they shear a sheep and find it's good and fat, they colour it differently.

Pâdshâh, responding to the question 'What's at the end of the rainbow?' recounts what may be an attempt to account for transgender identities.

How should I know! Nobody does. We Afghans have a saying – whether it's an old one or newly made up, I don't know, but it's probably old – that at the beginning of the rainbow, a man who makes a fist in this direction will turn into a woman, while a woman who makes a fist in that direction will turn into a man. That's what happens with the rainbow!

Pâdshâh clearly links eclipses with human morality, then describes rain-making rituals.

When half the sun disappears in the middle of the day we call it *tranza*. Last year it happened to the moon. I was at home at that time. Part of its face suddenly disappears. The cause is an increase in sins, lies and bad deeds; particularly sins like murder. If we're going along the road, and someone kills us for money or something; or a married man has sex with somebody else's wife, or his daughter or his son, or his sister. It's sins like those that cause the moon to have an eclipse. The moon's without sin; but we who inhabit the earth under it, if there's a corrupt deed to do, we'll do it if we can. A good, respectable Muslim doesn't do such things, but villains are everywhere; if they can, they kill people, rob, steal, do things with women, even with their own daughters and sons. For all those sins, the moon suffers, like someone who's in prison.

Some people fire their guns, others beat a bread-making griddle, others beat an oil-drum. Some people recite the Koran. People do what they can. Then in the morning, some people sacrifice an animal: a sheep or a chicken. It's the same whether it's an eclipse of the moon or the sun.

In dry years, with no rain, like these last few years, there are various things we do according to the Book: special prayers in the mosque; a sacrifice; and one night we do what we call a *barambó*. We make a young lad into *barambó*; we stick a grey beard and a moustache on him, made out of goat hair or wool, and he goes round the camps and to neighbouring villages. At every house, people give him something, 10 or 20 rupees cash, a pound or two of wheat, barley, or flour; then they pour water over him. He isn't naked, he has clothes on, which get damp and cold; some people pour hot water on him, which burns him! We did this last year. It was Mahmad-gol Sufikheyl.

In the morning, he brings all the cash, flour, wheat, barley and corn that he's collected, and sells it to any buyer, or he may take it to town to sell; and he'll buy rice and ghee for the sacrificial feast. Elders and children go with him. This is an ancient custom for times of drought, from our ancestors.

Baya-khân on Plato

Though the Piruzai live remote, rural lives, they are lively participants in a far wider cultural world of traditions and stories. Here Baya-khân tells of how Aflâtun (the Greek philosopher Plato) cheated death.

Long ago, they say, when things were first created, there was a fellow called Aflâtun. He knew everything in the world, and he could make anything and do anything. He said to himself, 'One day they'll come to take my soul; I'll make something so that when they come I can pour it on myself, or drink it, and I'll be immune.' So he made three cupfuls of something we call *salasan*,[5] planning to make sure he'd come back to life by spreading it on himself before the two angels came to draw out his soul.

When Aflâtun's time came, God ordered the angels: 'His time's come, kill him and draw out his soul.' Now Aflâtun was so clever that he could foretell the future, so he knew a year in advance when he'd die; and he was determined not to let them take his soul. He rose into the air and made himself a room between earth and sky; he created thirty-nine people who looked just like him, and he sat there among them.

When the angels arrived on God's mission, they searched all over the earth and they couldn't find Aflâtun – although God knew where he was. They returned to God and complained: 'O God Almighty, forgive us, we looked everywhere but we couldn't find him.'

God ordered them to look 'in the air'. They did so, and they found forty people who looked like Aflâtun; they looked at them all, but couldn't tell which of them to take the soul from. They went back to God, complaining: 'There are forty people, they all look like Aflâtun. Which of them shall we take the soul from?'

God said, 'When you've greeted them and entered that nice cosy room, stare at the wall and say, "Oh dear, this panel's no good, it's broken!" The real Aflâtun will jump right up and ask, "What do you mean, broken?" Grab him, knock him down and remove his soul.' So back they went, entered the room, sat down, and said, 'Oh dear, this panel's broken.' Aflâtun jumped straight up and said, 'Which one?' and the two angels at once knocked him down and removed his soul.

Now, when they remove the soul, they take it through here, this fingernail. Well, they'd pulled at his soul, and got it out so far, when he shouted, '*A-salasan!*' – he called to his companions to pour on him the mixture he'd concocted, three cups of it. They brought the first cup of *salasan*, but the angels knocked it out of their hands and resumed pulling at his soul. As they got it a little further out, he shouted again, '*A-salasan wa-salasan!*' His companions brought the second cup, but again the angels struck it from their hands. He called for *salasan* once more, but this time, when the angels hit the cup, a few drops of the mixture fell on his body.

As a result, part of his body's still alive, while the rest is dead. People say that Aflâtun's up there in the air; he has a place, a small room, between earth and sky. He's half alive, half dead; he can't move but he still calls out, day and night, '*A-salasan wa-salasan!*'

---

[5] See *Farhang-e-'Omid*, p. 659: '*salâsa-ye ghosâla*: three cups of wine to be drunk in the morning, considered to be washing away the body impurities, and to wipe out sorrows; also called *seta*.' *Salâsa* is 3 in Arabic.

Aflâtun knew everything. Nobody in the air or on the earth was as clever as Aflâtun.

Disease and Curing

Piruzai have a detailed knowledge and experience of common diseases and ailments. They have – and seek – little access to 'cosmopolitan' medicine, which they see as expensive and ineffective: it is expected to consist of pills (which Nancy sometimes provides), injections (pich-kâri, which she doesn't offer), and dietary advice. Men and women most often consult mullahs and âghâs for advice and cures for a variety of afflictions. Diagnoses may involve jinns, as detailed later. Sufferers also seek relief at shrines.

Some diseases

This is a selection of diseases that Darwiza and Pâdshâh (and the rest of those present) are familiar with – others are mentioned and described at other times; some are classified by symptoms (diarrhoea, paralysis . . .), others by their appearance. I give likely nosological equivalents in square brackets.
    Darwiza on diphtheria/tetanus.

Khorzak [*diphtheria*] makes it hard to swallow. It attacks someone all of a sudden, taking him by the throat, as though someone were strangling him, and he can't breathe; his mouth is wide open, he's gagging and choking; he doesn't understand, hits out at everything. You must fetch a kid and kill it at his mouth, so that the blood goes in. If there's no kid, a chicken will do – a red one. If you kill it at his mouth, he'll get better.

If a human gets this illness, we call it *khorzak*. When an animal gets it, it's *amân* [*tetanus*], but really that's the same as *khorzak*. When a horse gets it, it's *amân*. Remember when your mare had it, and we had a kid killed at its mouth? There was no other cure for it, no charm. If there hadn't been a kid, a red hen – a white or black one wouldn't do. God sent everything that exists, so the mullahs say, according to the holy books that have come down to us.

Pâdshâh on the same, and others.

Khorzak and *amân* are much the same, though Fârsibân people say they're different. We call it *khorzak* when something rises in your throat and blocks the passage of food and water, and you choke; every minute it gets bigger and stops you breathing. With *amân*, your teeth stick together and your jaw just won't open; you can't talk or open your mouth, whereas with *khorzak* you can just talk a little, like this. You can tell *amân* from the smell: whether it's a horse, a camel, a donkey, or a person, their breath stinks, and you shouldn't hesitate to kill a calf or a chicken by their mouth.

Khorzak and *amân* strike suddenly, but neither are contagious; if one person has it, nobody else in the house need worry. It's fate.

An ordinary 'white cough' just means your nose is blocked and you cough a lot. With a 'black cough', *tura-ghara* [*whooping cough*], the coughing's very long and drawn out; it kills many small children.

Both *kawey* [*chickenpox*] – Fârsibâns call it *chichek* – and *sorkhakân* [*measles*] cover your face with spots. There's another disease, which we call *sharey*, and they call *gol* [*smallpox*]; it's much more dangerous, with huge boils, full of pus. It makes your face black, and if it hears a bad voice, it takes over the body. Seyyed-shâh[*/Soleymân*] had it. Once chickenpox or smallpox have found a place in the village, they spread.

We have another disease called *kowtsak* [*rubella*], which isn't such a killer. The spots it brings up cover the whole body; they're red at the base, but they're tiny, with narrow heads, like insect bites. It goes after two weeks, if you take good care of the patient.

Then there's *seyl* [*tuberculosis*]: the victim coughs, and brings up blood and black stuff. After a few years his blood slowly dries up, and he dries up himself and turns black. Old uncle Khoday-râm has a congested chest. Rawu had it for ten years.

The 'great disease', *loy-maraz* [*typhoid*], *mohreka* in Persian, is very bad, it kills people. All their hair falls off, they go bald. They're delirious at night; their eyes go red and they start talking nonsense. It takes less than a week to recognize this disease. God keep such a day from us! If it gets you, it also goes through the veins; it's very infectious; if you eat with Richard, he'll certainly catch it from you; and if Richard then eats with someone else, that person will catch it too.

My father and [*his sister*] Awâs, Dâdollah's wife, got *loy-maraz*; so did Shekar, Jân Mahmad's wife. That was when our houses were together, long ago, when I was tiny. They nearly died. It was a terrible time for them. But thank God, nobody in this house has died of it. We divided the household and put the healthy people in one room and the sick ones in another. One person took them food. If the person feeding you while you have this disease is frightened, it'll surely strike him too and knock him down. But if his heart's full, and he's not afraid of the disease, he'll feed you and take care of you without worrying about the consequences, and for sure it won't get him.

In *zharey-maraz* [*jaundice*] – *zardi* in Persian – the whites of the eyes go yellow; the body goes yellow. The mullah deals with it – he prays over it. It's rare, but you can find cases in this village.

With *wabâ* [*cholera*] – God prevent such a day – government doctors come and do injections. But among us, if the injections don't work, then the mullahs pray – not in the mosque, at home; they pray over each child. It comes every few years, but thank God nobody here has died of it, though it's killed some of our relatives and neighbours. For example, a Baluch who was living with uncle Dur-khân, he and his wife died of *wabâ* in Chenâr, at the rock near Awpânich. He was herding his sheep there, and suddenly it got him; in half an hour he was dead. *Wabâ*'s not infectious: it only gets those whose time has come. Some people who get it, they immerse them completely in water; or put them in a skin, and this'll cure them, if God allows; if not, they'll be dead within the hour. *Wabâ* is *wabâ*, it doesn't wait for anyone.

When the stomach runs very fast, with blood, it's *pich* [*dysentery*]. Many people in this village have it. Sometimes the bleeding lasts several weeks; it takes a long time to recover. There's a pill that cures it, which you can buy in the bazaar. Gol-Mahmad's still this way; his stomach's really bad. People don't die of it, but it's very painful when you take a shit. Our mullahs say it's a good disease, because it cleans your body; when you recover, your insides are as clean as glass. It stays away until you eat something bad. If you eat melon, watermelon, stew, and you get diarrhoea, it comes back.

There's another illness called *sorkh-bâd* [*erysipelas*]; your arms, face or some other place swell up red. It can kill you very quickly, it won't wait. Aunt Bibiwor knows something of this disease, but my mother Maryam knows all about it. My sister Zeytun had it one year, and so did Haji Ghâfur, and my mother cured them both; she was shown how by a Kachani, Mullah Hâtam, who's dead now. It nearly killed Zeytun; Haji our father got it too, but he recovered. You make a small incision with a knife, to release some blood; then take a piece of sandalwood, rub it with a stone and a little water until it's a paste, then apply it to the body, every morning, noon and evening. Do this for a week or two. Or take the victim to a mullah to chant over him. You should kill a goat, take its fat and wrap it round his stomach; or do a skin.

Baya-khân on scrofula ('the King's disease')

Seyyed-shâh's daughter Bakhtak has *khanâzel* [*scrofula*]: boils appear on her neck; they're very bad and never go away – and they quite spoil a woman's appearance. They swell up like a watermelon; if you remove them, next year more will appear. They may get her throat and kill her. That happened to Ghonchak, who died four years ago, two years after her wedding.

The skin cure

Pâdshâh gives detailed instructions on when and how to do the skin cure.

We do a skin if, for example, my back hurts, or my shoulder, or my knees. If I don't feel well for about a week, then for two weeks I'm okay, but in the third week I feel off-colour again, I'll put on a skin. It'll be sure to sort me out.

We do as follows. After slaughtering the animal, skin it from the arse upwards, making a bag. Don't rip it in half; peel off the whole skin, then turn it inside out, scrape it with a knife, removing all the blood and stuff, till it's as clean as a whistle. Then fetch some wormseed, what we call *mastyâra-tërkha* – you know, the women collect it the first day we come down from the mountains to the Kâshân river; it has a good scent – fetch some of this, make a small fire and warm the clean skin over it, so that it smells nice. Then turn the skin right-side out again, and put it straight onto the patient's body, putting his arms through the holes, with his head showing. Some people put it up to here, some up to there; it depends on the size of the skin.

Then lay him down. Put lots of clothes on top of him, blankets and felts. Ask him, 'Are you sweating? Is the skin sticking to your body?' The first time, it'll stick fast, like gum. As soon as he starts sweating, the skin opens up to receive him, like when you enter water; it sticks at first, but after he's sweated it'll get weaker and let him go; then he should pull the skin down to his knees, leave it there for an hour or so, then take it off and wash himself clean in hot water, with wormseed or some other herb. Then he should put his clothes back on; with trousers and leggings, an overcoat or cloak, and a scarf round his head if he's going out into the cold.

After removing the skin, for one week he must take special care: keep the leggings, put on warm trousers and a good coat, make sure all the edges are tucked in; he should stay in, sitting under a brazier or by the stove, not go out into the cold, relieve himself inside the compound, then it'll be all right. If he catches cold he'll get very ill and never recover. After a week, though, he can do anything.

In spring, when the sheep are grazing fresh green grass out in the steppe, their skins are no good; they'll just make you even sicker. You could buy a Wardak ram's skin from the bazaar, killed by the butchers; that'd do. Otherwise, use only the skin of a ewe that's been eating dry hay, or a goat, ram, or lamb that you've tied up and fed on dried hay or straw, alfalfa or barley. The skin of a ewe that's specially reared for six months on dry grass and barley will do for two people. For example, Nancy or you can use it, then I can use it too. If you've used it once, I'll turn it inside out and scrape it with a knife until it's as thin as paper, then I'll put it on the fire with wormseed again, and I'll wear it. A powerful skin may not do the first user nearly as much good as the second. Some will cure the first but not the second. Some skins will cure both. If the ewe was too old, or if you used a sheepskin and it should have been a goat skin, it may not work at all; it may make you twice as sick. Goatskins are best in June and July. From mid-August on, sheepskins are best.

When you've finished with a skin, the women can remove any remaining wool and spin it for thread. Then if the skin's any good, fold it down the middle to make it look bigger, and sell it in the market. You can sell it with its wool. If it's ruined, just throw it to the dogs. It doesn't matter.

Skins are good for all kinds of illnesses; perhaps not for typhoid, it's no good for that. Where you're well part of the time and sick and weak part of the time, your knees or arms or legs hurt a lot, night and day, or you have backache or your shoulders hurt from work – a skin is good for all these kinds of things. Some tuberculosis sufferers will put on an old black skin used for storing ghee. You turn it inside out, scrape off any fat and liquid thoroughly, then put it on, sew yourself into it and wear it for several days. It's also good for aches and pains that a normal skin won't cure.

Darwiza comments on how the skin behaves as though it were alive.

For some illnesses you must do a skin, quickly. The skin will suck out the illness. You kill an animal, skin the carcass, then leave the skin and it'll get hungry, because there's nothing left in it. Before, when the animal was wearing it, it was full and satisfied; just like us, if we're hungry and eat food, we're happy; but when we're hungry, our skin sticks close to our body; we're inside the skin and we can't help but say, 'let's have some food'. So the skin's just like that hunger: once you've removed it from the animal's body, leave it for a few hours, maybe a whole day, but not in a draught; it must be kept in a warm place, rolled up like bedding. When you put it on, if it fits, it'll stick to your body, so that you feel something gripping you tight. It has no mouth or teeth, but it sucks out the illness, whatever it is; it'll leave your body and enter the skin. Once it's full, the skin'll let go by itself. When you take it off, you'll see that the skin's relieved you of the weight of the illness. Then put on another skin – which you should prepare some hours before. This one'll cling to your body in the same way; you'll sweat profusely inside the skin, and it'll suck your illness out until it's full.

Fasting

Fasting and dieting sometimes help, as Pâdshâh explains.

Fasting's good for rheumatism, swollen joints, or any swelling on the body or the face – eyes or mouth – or arms; some weeks they're like this, some weeks they're okay. The sufferer shouldn't eat bread with salt; we cook him a special thin, salt-free bread called *pupak*; that'll do him good. Some people get mullahs or *khalifas* to do charms and amulets. If God wants him to be cured, then a mullah or *mowlawi* will cure him. Some people never get better, like Mahmad-wali's mother, the poor woman; you saw her, she died slowly. You could see the pain in her eyes. One week she was better, the next she was down again, and finally she died.

We don't abstain from anything else, like melons. But when a good mullah does an incantation, if he says, 'Eat this, don't eat that,' we do as he says. You do whatever the mullah or the doctor says. If you don't know, you want to eat melons, ghee, broth. Most people don't know about these things. Some who've observed what the mullahs and *mowlawis* do, learn from them, and if they're good people they pass it on. Among the women, the real experts have all died. Shâhpari was very knowledgeable, God forgive her. Haji Bakhtâwar has some knowledge; but there aren't any such women left, there's only Saduzi. It's the elderly women who know, because these are ancient matters. We young men don't think about such things; frankly we don't care much about them. Haji Wahâb knows, and our Haji knows; or Wazir here, he's seen things, or heard about them, and knows about them this way.

'Warm' and 'cool'

Cures (and diets) are influenced by the Islamic-Galenic humoral system, which usually includes the two dyads warm/hot vs cool/cold, and wet vs dry, producing four combinations. Local knowledge of the system is neither detailed nor consistent – as the following conversation shows.[6]

(*Pâdshâh/Parwiz*) – Now, to make a horse better, they give it barley straw, because it's cool. Wheat bread's warm, barley bread's cool. Mutton's warm, goat's cool, however it's cooked.

(*Baya-khân*) – In summer, goat's good. Camel's cool too; so's beef.

(*Pâdshâh/Parwiz*) – Cattle are cool too. Chickens are warm, like sheep.

(*Kala-khân*) – Chickens are warmest of all, warmer than sheep. Cattle are cool, horses are cool.

(*Pâdshâh/Parwiz*) – Nonsense, horses are warm; in the cold and the snow, you can take off their blankets and ride them; they're very useful! Many horses go loose in the steppe, in winter. Donkeys are cool.

(*Baya-khân*) – God rot the donkey!

---

[6]   Cf. Centlivres (1985), Tapper and Tapper (1986), Bromberger (2000) and references in them.

(*Pâdshâh/Parwiz*) – It's unclean. Goats are the coolest creatures in the world; they don't get fever, they just shiver. And chickens are the warmest. In this climate, there's nothing so good for you as chicken soup. It's very warm.

(*Baya-khân*) – Once upon a time, all the chickens would fly off in the morning, except one, which got left in the house. All the others would say, 'Tomorrow, God willing, we'll fly.' But this chicken didn't say 'God willing,' it just said, 'I'll fly too.' Up it went, but it fell down again and the rest went off without it. Our chickens are the descendants of the one that failed to say 'God willing.' Over in the forests of Qataghan, they say, there are many wild chickens; they're the ones that flew off.

(*Kala-khân*) – Mulberries are warm. Almonds are cool.

(*Pâdshâh/Parwiz*) – Tomatoes are cool. Onions are very windy, but they're cool too.

(*Baya-khân*) – Goat's milk is cool, sheep's is warm.

(*Kala-khân*) – Cow's milk is cool. If an animal's cool, so's everything that comes from it: milk, cheese, yoghourt and the rest. Green tea's cool, black's warm. Grapes are warm, so are raisins.

(*Pâdshâh/Parwiz*) – Watermelons are cool, melons warm.

(*R*) – Why?

(*Kala-khân*) – If you get stomach-ache then eat watermelon, it'll sort you out. It's cool, isn't it?

(*Pâdshâh/Parwiz*) – Melons have no medical uses, but watermelons have. But if you drink tea on top of watermelon, it'll spoil it completely.

(*Kala-khân*) – It becomes like this felt here; it can kill you very quickly.

(*Baya-khân*) – If you're on a diet, it's a bad idea to drink tea. It's also a bad idea to eat cheese on top of tea; if you eat meat with cheese, it'll kill you. There are two kinds of cheese: one's so hard that if you eat just a little, you'll be full the whole day.

(*Kala-khân*) – That's *pataka*; the soft one's *potsa*!

(*Pâdshâh/Parwiz*) – Apples are warm; they're good for everything.

(*Kala-khân*) – Apples are flawless; however many you eat, they won't harm you. Apricots are warm; but they'll make you sick if you eat too many.

(*Pâdshâh/Parwiz*) – Apricots are no good; they're windy.

(*Kala-khân*) – If you eat a few, it doesn't matter.

(*Baya-khân*) – Walnuts are warm too. If you eat walnuts, they don't cool your body.

(*Kala-khân*) – They're good.

(*Pâdshâh/Parwiz*) – Almonds are cool.

(*Pâdshâh/Parwiz*) – You can buy pills for diarrhoea; but better is dried whey, *krut*.

(*Kala-khân*) – If you knead it well, until it's sticky.

(*Pâdshâh/Parwiz*) – Sticky sheep's *krut* is very good. If your stomach's runny, eat some *krut* and you'll soon get better.

(*Baya-khân*) – We give it to the sheep too. When it gets inside the stomach it stops the flow.

(*Pâdshâh/Parwiz*) – It does a lot of good. Sour oranges are very cool; but oranges are better, they're warm. If you've made plain rice, take two oranges and put them on top, that's delicious. It doesn't matter how much you eat. Better than oranges, though, are lemons; they're good for any purpose.

(*Kala-khân*) – Of all the fruits in the world, lemons are tops.

(*Pâdshâh/Parwiz*) – They take the fire from your heart. When you don't feel like eating anything – meat, rice, or stew – take some lemon, and you'll soon recover your appetite.

(*Kala-khân*) – Dates are warm. Oleaster [*senjed*] is very good.

(*Pâdshâh/Parwiz*) – Rock sugar's warm, it's good for you; powder sugar isn't, it's cool, because … There are many kinds of person; some are cool by temperament, and cool foods don't suit them; but somebody who's warm by temperament will find that cool things like powder sugar suit them. Brown sugar's warm – have you seen it? It's made from sugar cane; there's a lot of it in Jalalabad, where I spent two years on military service. Rice is good, there's nothing wrong with it, it's very warm. Cooked in ghee or sesame oil, which is warm, it's very good for you. But it's no good cooked in vegetable oil, which is bad, it's cool. At this time of year rice isn't so good to eat, but in winter, it's very good.

(*Baya-khân*) – Wild antelope are cool too.

(*Pâdshâh/Parwiz*) – Corn is warm. So's corn bread, very warm. Salt's warm.

(*Baya-khân*) – Salt really heats up the stomach.

(*Pâdshâh/Parwiz*) – Black and red pepper are both warm. Turmeric's cool, cumin's warm. As for the grasses and plants of the steppe, we don't reckon those, since we don't eat them. But in the mountains there are some plants you can eat, like rhubarb (*chukri*) and peppergrass (*ghanduy*); rhubarb's warm.

(*Baya-khân*) – No, it's cool.

(*Pâdshâh/Parwiz*) – Yes, sorry; rhubarb's cool.

(*Baya-khân*) – Peppergrass kills the sheep in the mountains; it makes their bellies swell and kills a lot of them every year. But people eat it as a sweet; you cut it up, put it through a sieve, then take a little plain rice, mix them together in a saucer, and eat it. The rice absorbs it. If you put some salt on it, with some water, it settles down of itself.

The mullah

Someone with a persistent ailment will usually first consult a mullah, as Darwiza explains.

With you, when someone's ill, you expect the doctor to cure them. With us, most sick people don't go to a doctor, they go to a mullah. He'll consult his book and he'll soon see what's the matter, whether it's a disease. For someone with a bodily ailment, he'll recite a charm (*do'â*). There are different charms for different ailments: headache, stomach-ache, body-pain, the mouth, the eyes. Each ailment has its own charm, its own amulet (*timâr*), which the mullah will do for you. There's a kind of headache we call *nim-sarey* ['half-head'], when one side hurts and the other doesn't; there's a special amulet for that.

As for payment, it's like this: our mullahs say it's haram to ask for money. If you're a mullah and you demand 500 rupees to make me an amulet, I'll pay anything, because I'm in pain. If I say 'I haven't got that much, I'll give you 100 or 150,' and you say, '500 or no amulet,' then I've no alternative; you're the mullah, so I'll pay; but the money's haram for you. It's as though you'd stolen it. But if I really have only 100 rupees: 'Take it, it's all I have, don't ask for more,' and you accept, it's halal. Or if I just ask for an amulet and a charm to be recited, and the mullah asks nothing, then whatever I give is halal. In the old days, mullahs wouldn't demand anything. Now most of them do.

Have you seen the hole in [*Khâni-âghâ's son*] Tâjak's little finger? All the bone inside shows through. It wasn't like that before, he was as fit as the rest of us. Then he stopped eating or drinking, suckling his mother's breast, everything. His arms and legs shrivelled up. His father took him to a doctor in Sheberghân, who said, 'Buy a shroud; this child won't last your journey home, he'll die on the way. He's not a grown-up, it doesn't matter where you bury him.' So Khâni-âghâ bought a shroud and carried him home. Then we took him to Seyyed Meskin Âghâ, who recited a charm. We paid him 220 rupees, and Tâjak recovered, as you can see. After that we didn't take him to any more doctors. Thank God, he's growing up; he'll soon be a man.

These charms are from God. They came at the beginning, when this world was created. Only a mullah who learns them properly, prays five times a day, doesn't lie, steal or gossip, owes nobody anything, eats his own clean food, doesn't envy other people's property, doesn't cause shame for others, and day and night acknowledges that God knows best – only when such a man recites a charm, whoever it's for, will God ensure that it cures them. Such a man should also stop fights wherever he sees them. This has great merit. If you spread gossip and cause fights, then your charms have no effect.

Of course, not every good person can do it. For instance, look, when you write someone's name in your note-book, if you make a single mistake, nobody will understand it. It's the same with charms: if a single tiny thing gets left out – you forgot it, or wrote it down wrong – it won't work. The mullah must learn the charms correctly and get permission from two or three powerful mullahs to do them, then – if God allows – they'll work.

Haji Molk's son Gollu has been taken all round the country for his eyes: Mazâr, Pol-e-Khomri, Kabul. They spent so much money, and all the doctors promised to cure him, but none of them could do anything. Mullahs did amulets for him, but whatever they tried, it didn't work.

Now there's a very good mullah here, Khalifa-Nazar, who makes excellent amulets. He's unmarried, but he's made a woman his 'sworn sister', and she lives with him. She's a relative of ours, though he isn't. In spring, Shir's camel went crazy – was that after you arrived? You saw how crazy it was: when it was let loose it would rush off and wouldn't eat grass or look at a man. They didn't give it anything or take it to the doctor; Khalifa-Nazar just chanted a charm, and it was cured.

Aunt Haji Bakhtâwar asked Khalifa-Nazar to examine her son Gollu, to see what was wrong with his eyes. He said, 'Let me sleep for a night or two and see what I dream.' Then he said, 'In my dream I found that a *pari*'s fallen in love with him.' Then he looked at his book, and explained, 'Early one morning he must have trodden on a jinn and harmed it in some way: blinded it or broken its arm or its leg. It'll have seized some part of him and settled there; but it's fallen in love. If it's possessed his eye, you can't tell, even if you look at it all day long; Gollu himself can't see it.' Who can see his own illness? If some place hurts, for example my arm, you look at it, but the pain won't show. Khalifa-Nazar said, 'If God wills, I'll cure him.'

When I started going to Shir's house [*for bâzi with Shir's sister Sawur*], their dogs just wouldn't recognize me. Khalifa-Nazar gave me this amulet saying, 'Every night you go there, pin this on, so.' Now the dogs don't utter a sound! I've been going to Shir's for years now, and every time I pin it, or sew it, just here. But if I haven't got it on me, the dogs won't let me pass.

You can find such good people among us. Khalifa-Nazar's a very good man, a pure soul. He also speaks to God; day and night he does his five prayers; he doesn't lie or steal or envy other people's wealth, he doesn't look at their wives, daughters, sons, wishing they were his. If such thoughts ever came into his heart, his charms wouldn't work. If you make him happy, so that he favours you, then (with God's permission) he'll do you an effective amulet, and you'll get whatever you set your heart on. He isn't old; about the same age as my father. He's always done this work, but he didn't let people know at first. Now, if somebody's robbed, he comes to Khalifa-Nazar and begs him to show where the stolen property is; he can do that too.

Baya-khân mentions another good man.

Mullah Seyyed-Mahmad stayed here for a long time; people said it was because he was in love with Haji Bahâoddin's daughter, Bibi Zahrâ. He said himself, 'I don't want any other woman, I've fallen in love with her eyes.' Some people told Haji Bahâoddin to give her, it would put an end to his problems; but he married her to his nephew Komeydân instead. In the end the woman died. She was covered in boils, which opened up like springs and liquid poured out. It lasted for three years, then it killed her.

Mullah Seyyed-Mahmad would never leave us. He'd go away for a few years, but he always came back. He was very clean-living; he didn't steal or tell lies. All day long he'd chant the Koran and lament. He went around barefoot in the snow. He'd go without food for several days without noticing. He wasn't an *âghâ*, or a scholar, he hadn't studied much, but he was very ascetic man. After some years he made some *lang*; he didn't have any trousers, so he made long clothes down to here, we call that *lang*. Then one spring he came here for a few days, when Seyyed-shâh[/*Soleymân*]'s house was with us, then he left for good. Haji Bahâoddin's daughter had died – perhaps he'd cursed her. I don't know what happened to him, whether he's alive or dead; anyway, he didn't come back.

Charms, Curses and the 'Eye'

With life chances severely constrained by inequalities of birth, wealth, personality and luck, Piruzai believe in the potential of certain magical practices.

Love charms – and others

Darwiza tells how some mullahs can provide charms to influence other people's behaviour.

Suppose I fancy a girl, but I realize that her parents don't like me and won't give her, and perhaps the girl herself doesn't like me, but I'm so attracted to her that I simply must have her and marry her. I'll go to a strong mullah – Hazâra mullahs do this sort of thing well – and give him a lot of money, say 2,000 rupees; I'll show him her name and those of her mother, her father and her brother; he'll put them all in the charm and give it to me. I dissolve it in water, which I'll sprinkle on some sweets or raisins, and send these to her house. Or I'll sprinkle the water under their house, or pour some inside their butter-churn. I'll do whatever's needed. Either I'll go myself, or I'll ask someone else to go: 'I'm not known in that house, please do this secretly for me, take this charm-water, scatter it there, or get them to eat or drink some of it.'

Then the girl's heart will be mine – 'I want to marry him!' – and she'll elope with me like Rangin's daughter Kimyâ! Our mullahs know such excellent charms!

There's another kind of charm for her parents. For example, you go and ask for the girl, and they turn you down flat, demanding a huge brideprice, more money and sheep than you can afford. Or her father says, 'I like you, but my wife doesn't,' or 'My father or my brother doesn't like you,' or 'The girl herself doesn't want you.' Then you go and get this charm, to make her family like you. The household head will drink it too; it's just enough to make his heart warm to you. Then as soon as they're asked to give you their daughter, they can't refuse, they'll be pleased to give her without delay. All her relatives will tell them to give her: 'He's a nice young man, let's give him our sister, or our daughter; let's make him her husband.'

If the wrong girl drinks the charm, it won't work; even if there were a hundred others in that house, only the girl whose name was written on it will fall for you.

There's a charm for anything in the world. If I take a liking to your car – assuming I have the money – but you don't want to sell it, I'll bring along a charm that the mullah has recited on you. You're sitting by the hearth; I light the charm by you, throw it into the fire, and it'll get straight to work on you. Or I'll scatter it over some raisins, bread, broth or rice; or dissolve it into some tea or cold water for you to drink. When I come again and ask you for the car, you'll sell it to me without hesitation. You might want to buy someone's land; when you first ask, he doesn't need the money and won't sell. But if you do a charm on him, he can't refuse.

Only one in a hundred mullahs can do this kind of charm. And you must really please him. If I want to marry a certain girl and ask him for a charm on her, a major job like that calls for a lot of money. He'll take up to 10,000 rupees for such a charm. But if he likes you, he'll do it for free.

Some mullahs can also do charms to kill someone. He'll take a sheep's fat tail, pierce it with a needle, hang it on the wall, chant over it. As the fat gradually drips out, the victim gets sick; as the fat melts away, so does the person; he dries out, his breath falters. The needle in the tail was fine, but as soon as it blackens with rust, that person will die. This could be either a woman or a man.

A mullah can do a charm to scramble someone's brains, make him unconscious, unable to tell good from bad; he'll say anything, do anything. But he can't make a jinn possess someone.

Pâdshâh gives some examples.

Wazir's daughter Choghak was a good girl. She married Delbar Pakhizai's son Bâz-Mahmad. What happened was that Bâz's brother was a herdsman here, and he himself was often around, and eventually he fell for Choghak. He ingratiated himself with Wazir; he brought some rice, got a mullah to chant and sprinkle water over it secretly; he bought some meat, the mullah chanted over it too and made an amulet, which he hid in the house. He managed to get Wazir to eat the amulet; and he rubbed a *kharmora* on his body. Wazir then found that whenever his relatives asked him for Choghak, he refused and said he'd promised her to Bâz. Rawu asked for her; so did Haji, for Baya-khân; Haji Ghâfur for Joma-khân, and Pâdshâh for Dust-Mahmad. He turned them all down. That's why we now call him Crazy Wazir. He made a big mistake, and now he deeply regrets it. He wouldn't accept what any of us offered. After he's eaten a charm, or a *kharmora*'s been rubbed on his body, he can't open his mouth to speak with anybody but the person who did it.

A *kharmora* comes from a swelling on a donkey's face, just below the eye. When we see a donkey I'll show you. You cut it out and give it to a Hindu, who hangs it in a special place for sixteen days and chants over it. Then, say you fancy someone's wife, or a woman who doesn't like you, you take this *kharmora* and stroke her shoulder with it like this, three times, sh, sh, sh. If it's been properly processed, well matured – raw and untreated won't do – and you rub it three times on the woman's body, she'll come to you; whoever it is, woman, man, child, they'll come to you, they won't be able to resist and will do whatever you want. That's the power of *kharmora*. Another thing: once it's matured properly, it'll never age or wear out, it'll last for ever, as long as you live.

Afghans and Uzbeks don't generally make such magic charms (*ta'wiz, kudi*); but Hazâras do a lot, so do Hindus. Say you fancy a certain woman or boy. You ask around for a really powerful mullah, no matter the cost; the main thing's to get what you want. You tell the mullah – a Hazâra most likely – the woman's name and yours, as well as both your fathers. He writes them down: so-and-so's daughter and so-and-so's son, using special, nice-smelling, saffron-musk ink. Now this Hazâra, after he's eaten dinner and said his last prayers, goes and immerses himself in some water, like a pond or a tank. Then he takes the two names, calculates their horoscopes, finds where their signs are in harmony or not. Then he makes an amulet for you. He won't take money that day – perhaps 10 or 20 rupees, perhaps not – but he'll say, 'By God and the Koran, if this thing works, then give me 2,000' – or whatever amount is appropriate – 'and may the Koran strike you if it works and you don't pay my dues.' You shake hands over the Koran, and off you go with the amulet.

As he gives you the amulet, the mullah says, 'When this woman's away from home, bury this under a path you know she's likely to use when she goes visiting or to fetch water; or bury it at the edge of the hearth where she cooks; or if she fetches water from a tank, bury it at the water's edge; or get some close friend or go-between to hide it under where she sleeps.' Now, if the amulet's powerful enough, whatever her previous feelings for you, she'll find you irresistible; you'll be able to elope with her at night.

That's magic (*kudi*). But there are people who can make it void (*bâtel*). If the charm works, and you and the woman manage to get together, and then someone else notices and gets jealous, they can pay a good mullah a lot of money to write a counter-charm. He'll soak it in water and get you to drink the water, and your amulet will lose its power.

Or when he's sitting by the hearth, he'll throw the counter-charm on the fire, so that the smoke reaches your nose, and that'll ruin your charm.

A do'a is a charm with good intent; a bad-do'a *is the opposite, a curse, as Pâdshâh explains.*

If you curse someone, jinns have nothing to do with it. If God hears your curse and knows that you've been deeply hurt, that that person has caused you pain and trouble, then perhaps your curse will take effect and that person will die or suffer misfortune. But if you utter a curse that's insincere and you're really thinking of something else, nothing will come of it.

There's no cure for a curse; but it can be cancelled. A curse leaves the mouth like a wind; it'll go on and on, round and round, with nowhere to settle. It's nothing. Suppose I cursed you; or you cursed Richard, then he might say in Pashtu, 'The curse has left your mouth, may God put it back into your body again.' That's the response if the curse is uttered to your face. If it's said behind your back, in another room, then you don't know about it, but someone who's with the curser can say, 'May God put back in your body everything that's come out of your mouth.'

Darwiza tells how Majlun went mad.

Some people, the moment a wish leaves their mouth, God accepts it. Suppose they get left somewhere, tired, on foot; your car comes by and they say, 'Give me a lift; but I've no money.' If you don't stop, and he says, 'May your house be ruined, may your car break down, or may you die!' that's what'll happen. Someone cursed Payz-Mahmad like that, and his house was ruined: his wife died. The moment the curse, the *bad-do'a*, leaves such a person's mouth, his words reach God, and his hurt and anger take effect.

There are also charms that won't kill but can make someone crazy. You know Majlun in our village? Haji Jallât was jealous of Majlun's influence and wanted to bring him down, so he got a strong mullah to recite a charm on him, and it made him crazy, as he is today. He said, 'I don't want to kill him, just to cause him trouble, send him mad.'

Such a charm only works on the person named in it. If a mullah did one – God forbid – to kill Richard or make him crazy, then if you went to another mullah and said, 'My husband's sick, please look at him and see what's the matter,' this mullah will look at his book, and he will realize at once that Richard is under the charm of another mullah, who'll never admit it. But this mullah can 'blind' the charm and cure him.

Majlun was so crazy he was kept in a locked room day and night. He didn't recognize anybody, he didn't know who he was. He couldn't even eat. If he got out, he'd grab anyone he could, man or beast, and try to kill them. He'd try to throw himself into a well or a river, or off a cliff. Then a different mullah, Seyyed Mortazâ, came, and undid all the charms, except one. People promised him a camel, or a gun, but they didn't keep their word, so he left one out. Now Majlun's sometimes okay, sometimes still crazy. If the seyyed had undone all the amulets, he'd be completely cured. But it's too late now.

Baya-khân has another story about Jallât and Majlun.

Some fifteen years ago, when Haji Jallât was headman, he was scared of Khalifa-Patih's brother Majlun. Majlun too was a powerful man in his time; he was so strong he wasn't afraid of anyone. In those days the government wasn't as strict as today. People say that if you eat a donkey's brains, you'll go mad. They say Jallât surreptitiously gave Majlun a donkey's head to eat; he invited Majlun to a meal and gave him this donkey's head and he ate it. He went crazy: three people couldn't hold him down. He's been that way ever since.

The year before last they caught Majlun in Kabul. A soldier stopped him and asked, 'Where are you going?' He said, 'I'm going to Pakistan, across the border.' He was completely out of his mind. So the border guards arrested him, put him in a car and took him back to Kabul. They telephoned around, until someone identified him and told them, 'This fellow comes from Khârkash.' So they sent him in handcuffs under guard back to Sheberghân, then here. When we heard that he'd been brought back shackled, Majlun had been lost for two years.

Now he's living in his son's house; he's quite mad, poor chap. If you go to see him he'll speak nonsense with you; his words come from all over the place, all mixed up; he'll say, for example, that he has a car, but he really doesn't know who or where he is. There's no cure for him here.

The Evil Eye

There is wide literature on beliefs and practices relating to the Evil Eye in the Middle East and elsewhere. Certain men, commonly those with unusual blue or green eyes, are believed to have the power (often involuntary) to harm other humans and animals, sometimes fatally.

In Konjek, a notorious wielder of the Eye (stërga, nazar) is Sâleh (Neshtar's brother, who married his son Bâlu to his brother Rangin's widow, Golshâh Taymani, see p. 342), as Darwiza relates.

One man in a thousand has *nazar*, the Eye. Sâleh has it. If someone with *nazar* looks at a camel and thinks, 'I'd like that camel!' it'll immediately break a leg or die. If it's a person he takes a fancy to, they'll die, or go blind, or their nose will bend like Pordel's, or they'll break an arm or a leg – they'll suffer something bad. To get rid of his *nazar*, you must remove one of his teeth – any one – then he'll lose the power to harm people. It'd be the same if he did it himself, or a tooth just fell out.

Two years ago Mayoddin-jân Âghâ was very fat. One day after teaching, he was asleep in the shade of the mosque. Sâleh came up, I don't know why, and said: 'Hey, Âghâ-jân, you've really put on weight, today you look very well!' Mayoddin-jân denied it; but he was struck by Sâleh's *nazar*. From that time until today he's been unwell. He went to the doctor, but so far without success; some days he's well, some not. But he's such a good man, Sâleh's *nazar* didn't affect him so much.

It's God who gives someone *nazar*; not at birth, but when he's grown up. If you mention God's name – 'By God you're fat!' – *nazar* won't cause harm. But if you just say, 'You're fat!' when what you mean is, 'I wish I were that fat myself,' then his body will suffer. But there's a charm, an amulet: if *nazar* doesn't kill the victim on the spot, do this prayer for him and he'll recover. But a mullah's charm won't work on himself; his father, his brother or someone else must do it.

That's how it is with Sâleh's *nazar*. Once we had a wedding party, I don't remember whose; the drummer was Mahd-Akbar – he plays very well. Sâleh said to him, 'Uncle Mahd-Akbar, your drumming's fantastic, won't you play for us?' Mahd-Akbar got up to play, but when he struck the drum, one drumstick broke right through the skin. Such a thing had never happened to him before, however hard he played; but the moment Sâleh said those words, the drum broke.

Sâleh knows he has *nazar*. If he told you, 'How good-looking you are!' implying his heart had settled on you, and you replied, 'What a good eye you have!' then both his eyes would fall straight out, and he'd be blind! That's another thing about *nazar*, and that's why people never mention it to him. He doesn't do it to everybody; just occasionally when something really attractive takes his fancy. He thinks, 'That's really pretty, I'd like it,' and it'll be *nazar*-struck for sure; it could be a woman or a child. He did it to his own son, you know. 'Hey, Bâlu,' he said, 'Now you're grown up, you're a fine-looking young fellow!' Bâlu was immediately seized by a jinn. Bâlu hasn't recovered; there's no cure. If it were any other kind of jinn, this kind of ailment could be cured, but it's a *pari* that fell in love with him. God could remove it; but poor Bâlu's still afflicted today.

If Sâleh sees a nice fat ewe and thinks, 'I'd like that!' it'll die. One spring, when we put the lambs out with their mothers day and night, he said, 'What a lot of lambs so-and-so has!' Instantly they started to die, one by one. To stop the deaths, you must get a strong mullah to do a charm.

If you or I said such a thing, with or without *bismillah*, nothing would happen. If Sâleh says, 'By God, how many lambs there are!' then nothing happens, however bad his *nazar*. But if he says, 'What a lot of nice lambs!' without mentioning God, they'll start dying, or a wolf will eat them, or the cold will get them; they'll come to some harm for sure. That's what *nazar* can do.

Nobody else has *nazar*. If someone sells you an animal voluntarily for a good price, but then the same day regrets having sold it, you won't get any benefit from it; it'll either die or go lame or blind, and you'll be unable to sell it on. This isn't *nazar*, it's *delkashi*.

Baya-khân, Kala-khân, Manân and their cousin Jamâl-khân discuss the Eye.

(N) – Some people have blue eyes like ours, others black like yours; does this matter?

(*Baya-khân*) – Yes it does; some people say blue-eyed people have *nazar*.

(N) – Does everybody with blue eyes have *nazar*?

(*Kala-khân*) – Seyyed-shâh[/*Golusar*] here has green eyes, he's *nazari*. Sâleh has muddy eyes, he's *nazari* too; if he sees a nice animal, or a buzkashi horse, or a good man, he'll strike it at once.

(*Jamâl-khân*) – There are two kinds of blue eyes; those with yellow or red veins have a lot of *nazar*; but ordinary blue eyes are not so powerful.

(N) – So nobody with black eyes has the *nazar*?

(*Kala-khân*) – No, black eyes don't have *nazar*; people admire black eyes.

(N) – Tâjak's eyes are very black, while yours and Baya-khân's aren't so black?

(Manân) – They're speckled.

(Baya-khân) – They aren't blue.

(R) – Don't they say that Manakey's people [*Nasuzai, in Khârkash*] have *nazar*?

(Baya-khân) – Yes; Majid has blue eyes, haven't you seen? He has *nazar*.

(Kala-khân) – If you take out his tooth, his *nazar*'s finished.

(Manân) – Or if you cut his footstep.

(Kala-khân) – Follow him without his knowing; if he sees a horse or some other animal and says, 'How nice that is!' and goes on without thinking, then go and cut out his footstep with a knife and his *nazar* will be broken.

(N) – Doesn't a person with *nazar* know his power?

(Kala-khân) – He doesn't know until he sees the effect he's having, until something's suffered; then he'll realize. Sâleh has it, but his tooth came out and he doesn't have it any more.

(Manân) – Mâmuk [*close cousin of Rishmin and Rangin*] too has *nazar*.

(N) – Did he strike something?

(Manân) – Yes: once someone was riding by the pond beyond our house; the horse was Ahmad-shâh's [*a wealthy Khârkashi*], I think. Mâmuk saw it and said, 'What a nice horse!' It broke a leg and went lame.

(Jamâl-khân) – He says that whenever he looks at anything, at boys, they get struck by *nazar*, so he doesn't look any more.

(Kala-khân) – Nâder-shâh had a fantastic buzkashi horse. One year, a *châpandâz* called Maluk was riding it, and they were racing up to the Uzbek graveyard near Khârkash. It was much quicker than all the other horses, and people were clapping as it approached the canal. Then Sâleh cried, 'It's a racing pigeon!' Both horse and rider fell; he dropped the goat, and someone else got it. People shouted, 'Give it!' so Sâleh cut off a lock of hair and a piece of his coat; they took them to the horse, burned them, 'smoked' the horse, and it recovered. You take some hair or clothing or anything belonging to the person with *nazar*, and smoke them.

(N) – What happens if he won't give it?

(Kala-khân) – If he's struck someone, he will, or they'll take it by force.

(Manân) – He'd be afraid of being fined.

(N) – Are there any other cases where Sâleh used *nazar*?

(Kala-khân) – He says himself that he cast *nazar* on [*Haji Jallât's son*] Jânshâh's son and caused him to be shot. He was a very bright boy, studying here with the mullah.

(Manân) – No, his belly was cut open with a sickle.

(Kala-khân) – Really? A sickle? I didn't know! Sâleh said, 'How clever the boy is, how well he does his lessons.' There was a fight that very afternoon. He's better now; they took him to the doctor, who put dog's intestines into him.

(R) – What about Sâleh's teeth, haven't they been drawn?

(Kala-khân) – I don't know anything about his teeth.

(N) – People won't take a tooth by force?

(Kala-khân) – No. With luck, it'll come out by itself.

13

The World of Jinns

More numerous than raindrops

Piruzai commonly attribute illness and misfortune to a variety of jinns (pirëy, pl. peryân), God's creatures who live in a parallel, invisible world. They believe jinns to be vulnerable and vengeful if harmed. Precautions can be taken to prevent harming them, but jinns may possess an offender – usually a woman – causing illness and convulsions (epilepsy-like fits) and killing children in particular. Mullahs, shrines and Sufi pirs may intercede and force jinns to withdraw. Women unable to bear children, or in unhappy marriages, are most vulnerable to jinn attack.

Pâdshâh explains the danger.

Most of the time jinns live in ashes, the dung of sheep, cows and donkeys, old huts, ruined buildings, ditches and holes; not anywhere that's nice and new. There's only one way for a woman or man to go somewhere at night: until you get there, keep repeating *bismillah*, or say a *kulwallah* or *al-hamd*, *sobhân*, and such things, and even if there are millions of jinns, they'll get out of the way because these words burn their wings. They have wings like aeroplanes.

When you say *bismillah* that does them in. If you walk along without a *bismillah*, or if you're unclean, then you're liable to kick or squash a jinn, or kill one of its children, kick dust in its eyes or break its arm, or tread on its stomach. Whatever you do it'll do the same to you. If you trod on its stomach, it'll tread on yours. If you blinded it, it'll blind you, harm your eyes for sure. It'll continue to hurt until you find a strong mullah who can release you. If you don't find a strong mullah, eventually you'll die of it.

Jinns are more numerous than raindrops, they live in every country of the world, every single place, including England and Russia. The reason Afghanistan has so many is because we're believing Muslims, and they attack anyone who moves out of line. You people don't know about our Book, and you don't walk, you're always in a car or a plane; if you ever have to go somewhere at night, like from one apartment to another, you either go by car or walk along a main road. There aren't any jinns there. But we always have to go out to the steppe, or to look at the crops. You wouldn't walk from here to Rishmin's place at night if I gave you a lac of rupees, would you? Thank God, we're believers, we say our five prayers a day, and we walk. If one day we miss our prayers, or step out of line, steal or do something else bad, God will either see that we step on a jinn, or ... well, he'll do something to us for sure. God uses the jinns to frighten us.

Jinns take revenge if they're injured, that's their job. They can turn into anything they want, and nobody notices. Some mullahs have madrasas where the *tâlebs* study. Only the Hazâras don't have madrasas; they have mullahs in their mosques, but no *tâlebs*. Among Uzbeks and Afghans all mosques have *tâlebs*, throughout the year. Sometimes Muslim jinns study in the mosque or madrasa with other *tâlebs*, wherever they're from. They sit and eat and drink with the others. They help out, do their lessons, and live just like *tâlebs*; they study our Book in our language, and people talk with them without realizing they're jinns – absolutely not. Very few mullahs would ever stop anyone from entering a madrasa. Right now there are four *tâlebs* in our mosque with Mayoddin-jân. How can we tell they're not jinns? They won't ever say, 'I'm a jinn.' Other students won't recognize them; but a strong mullah or a powerful Sufi – a man who's honest and doesn't lie, who's pure and clean, says his prayers – he can tell if a *tâleb* is a jinn.

One year a powerful mullah caught a jinn-*tâleb*. There were twenty students in his madrasa. At night they'd sleep in the guestroom [*hojra*]. When a mullah's important, like Mayoddin-jân, the students serve him. Every evening this mullah asked for water; he was their elder, their master [*ostâz*], and they were his apprentices [*shâgerd*]; and each night he asked a different student. He asked this student to get up and bring him some water, which was in a different room. In an instant, without moving a muscle, the *tâleb*-jinn replied, 'Here's the water, mullah-seb.' The words had hardly left the mullah's mouth, when there he was. He hadn't moved, there wasn't even the noise of the door opening. The mullah and the other *tâlebs* immediately realized it was a jinn – a jinn can get through a hole as small as a needle's eye, and it's very nimble, quick as a flash – like when you turn on an electric light, it shines instantly. In Pashtu we say, '*pirëy-ta Ghaznëy tsë dëy*? What's Ghazni to a jinn?' This means, the jinn'll be in Sar-e-pol in the time it takes to say it.

Early in the morning the jinn collected its things and left. Once it knows it's been rumbled, it'll disappear off to another madrasa, to Seyyedâbâd, Sheberghân, Sar-e-pol, anywhere it isn't known.

That's the way with all *tâlebân*, such as the ones you photographed. None of us knows anything about them, whether they're jinns or not. But if they are, they're Muslims, not kafirs or evil ones; they find a place in the madrasa and learn their lessons, and they won't possess you or trouble you.

Darwiza tells more.

If you go out at night and walk over some blood or dung, a jinn may possess you. That's where jinns live; or they sleep under an old wall. If you go out at dusk to fetch some water, one may be sitting by the water, and you won't know if you knock it or tread on it, but if you do it'll enter your body, seize you and possess you.

Then go to a mullah, who'll chant a spell [*do'â*], and if he's strong enough he'll catch the jinn. You take him an animal – a sheep, a cow or a camel – or some cash, or a woven bag, whatever he wants. If he's satisfied, the mullah will hold the jinn and make it swear an oath.

Generally, if someone's possessed, the jinn makes them ill. Even if someone recites a spell, it won't show itself in the victim; it's inside their body, in their heart or head or eye or tooth; or they say their shoulder hurts. Sometimes – God forbid – it paralyses someone so that they can't feel a thing; they can't move their legs or go anywhere. Then you know it's a jinn. Occasionally a jinn makes someone blind, and it gets worse and worse until it kills them.

People can't see jinns. Suppose – God forbid – you're possessed and I'm a mullah. I'll talk with you, but you won't be conscious, since the jinn's seized you. You're unconscious, like a corpse, you're unaware of your breathing, of yourself, and you wouldn't know even if someone cut you with a knife. The jinn's sitting inside your body, talking through your mouth. Everything you say to the mullah is actually the jinn talking. He'll make it swear through your mouth; you take the oath, but it's the jinn speaking.

Jinns are such evil creatures. Some are very strong. We can't see them, but if you tread on one and kill it, it'll kill you too, if you don't quickly say a prayer. The moment it possesses someone, it'll make its presence known by knocking their mouth or their eye askew; or it'll make you so blind that you can't see your way. No doctor will be able to cure you. If you go to a shrine like Sakhi-Bâbâ, or a powerful mullah recites a good prayer over you, the jinn will let you go and you'll see again.

It's nothing to do with whether people behave well or badly, whether they're good-looking or ugly, whether someone bad-mouths them unfairly, or praises them in spite of their evil deeds, it's just that if a jinn takes a fancy to them, it'll possess them, whether man or woman – though women are much more vulnerable.

The world's full of mullahs. Not all can make amulets, only one who's a true believer, and he must get a permit from a stronger mullah. Nobody can do it by himself. Otherwise anyone who can write could do an amulet. With a permit from a very strong mullah, he'll be able to subdue all those jinns. If a mullah who hasn't got a good permit, or can't recite spells correctly, tries to exorcize a jinn, the minute it's exorcized it'll possess him or his wife, and if it can it'll attack his children and kill them. If it's strong enough, it'll go for the mullah himself. That's the kind of evil creatures these jinns are.

A strong mullah will do the job properly, he'll catch the jinn and it'll be helpless; it won't get either his children or his wife, and once he's done an amulet, he'll exorcize the jinn. Sometimes a mullah knows he isn't strong enough; he could exorcize the jinn, but it'd harm his wife or his children, so he won't exorcize it, he'll just chant some spells over it and pretend, saying 'It'll be all right.' Or he'll say, 'Go to some shrine, like Sayyâd-Bâbâ or Emâm-e-Khord.'

Haji Âghâ [*Mahd-Es'hâq-jân Âghâ*] made an amulet for [*Darwiza's brother-in-law*] Shir's wife Bâbak. Jinns don't harm her herself, but they kill her children. First she had a baby daughter. For three months she grew nice and fat, then she started crying at night; sometimes she took the breast, sometimes she wouldn't; day by day she grew thinner, until all her flesh had melted away. The poor baby was overcome by its illness. This was a jinn. Haji Âghâ made an amulet for Bâbak saying, 'I want an animal from her every year.' The child got better; but when the time came for Bâbak to give the animal, she tried to wriggle out of it; 'I'll give it to you today, tomorrow, I'll give you money . . .' In the end she never gave it. She never actually refused, but her heart was bad. So he stopped helping her, and the jinn killed the child.

[*Shir's half-brother*] Wazir's wife Sherang lost five or six children to jinns. She just couldn't give birth successfully; the jinn wouldn't let her babies live; if they were born, they soon died. Haji Âghâ made her one amulet when she'd nothing in her womb, and another when she was three months pregnant. He writes the amulet; they soak it in water and when the writing's dissolved she drinks it. He did another amulet when her nine months were nearly over, and again she drank the words. He told her to let him know once the baby was born, and whether it was a boy or a girl. Immediately the baby was born, Wazir went straight to Haji Âghâ, who wrote another amulet; he brought it back and hung it round the baby's neck. They dissolved one or two more, and Sherang drank them. Then he captured the jinn and it couldn't trouble her any more. Now every year, good or bad, without fail she gives him an animal for slaughter, such as a calf. Whenever they realize the child's sick, they know the jinn's trampling on it; but as soon as Haji Âghâ chants, it gets better.

If Haji Âghâ isn't strong enough – sometimes the jinn's too strong even for him – he goes to visit his father Nâju-jân Âghâ's grave, in the Korak graveyard – the other side of the river, beyond Behsud – and then the jinn will never possess her again.

They suspected Wazir's daughter Choghak had a jinn too. For a year or two they took her to doctors in Sheberghân, Mazâr, Pol-e-Khomri, but whatever they did the jinn wasn't identified. Anyone could see she was very sick. People gave her pills, potions, injections; they put her in a skin; they did many sacrifices in her name; they took her to a shrine; but she didn't get better. Then they took her to this Haji Âghâ; he chanted a spell, made an amulet, and got rid of her jinn.

They attack women and children . . .

Darwiza continues.

[*Another*] Sherang, wife of [*Neshtar's son*] Nasrak, is possessed too. The jinn seizes her when she's sitting down. When the mullah comes and chants over her, the jinn takes over and speaks through her mouth. He makes it swear an oath: 'By such-and-such a shrine, or by God, or by the Prophet, or by this Koran!' Once it's sworn, it'll never possess her again; it's finished with her, and she'll get better. The mullah will want something from her every year, in return for his spell; he'll expect a sheep, a kid, a cow, or some money – whatever they agreed. Keep the mullah satisfied and it doesn't matter if you don't go or take your daughter to him, he'll take care of her; if he's strong the jinn can't do anything while she's in his care.

Jinns don't declare themselves right away. If I tread on a jinn and break its leg or arm, or blind it, then – God forbid – it may rise into my body. Nobody knows it's happened, only God, not his servants; but my head will start to ache, or my stomach, my leg, or my eye. This goes on until, if it's a woman, she becomes pregnant; when she has the baby, the jinn won't let it live. When a baby's a month or forty days old and its mouth goes crooked like this; or its eyes go funny, in a squint, or go up and it stops feeling anything, this tells us – it's a tiny baby, it can't talk for itself – that it's possessed by a jinn.

When a woman has a baby, for forty days she mustn't be left alone. If she is, for sure she'll suffer some harm. For those forty days, our mullahs say, the mouth of her grave stands wide open, expecting her any day. Somebody must be with her, night and day.

We also leave a Koran with her; or a piece of bread. If she needs to go out, leaving her baby, you should leave the Koran with the baby; otherwise a jinn'll come and kick it to death. My sister Zeytun, the mother of these two kids, died the year before last. Her husband left her alone once, and she got frightened. When fright seizes someone, asleep or awake, she looks around fearfully, like this; even though there's nothing to see, once fear has settled in her heart, that's it, she'll be dead the next day. That's how it happened.

Generally, if a woman's left alone somewhere, she must keep a piece of bread with her, or a Koran. If she goes outside to fetch water, or to another house, or, pardon me, to take a piss, she must say *bismillah*, then bad things will get out of her way and let her pass. If she walks over ashes, blood, a discarded bone, or ground where an animal was killed – places where the jinn live – if she says *bismillah* they can't touch her. Whoever you are, man or woman, anywhere you go at night, you must keep saying *bismillah*, and you'll be fine.

Jinns aren't interested in older people; they sometimes possess them, but not often. They go much more for the young. Why do jinns kill small children? They like to possess things. It's like a hawk that sees a sparrow; you've seen how it dives straight down and eats it. It seems to be the same with jinns, though of course we don't know why; only God knows, not his servants.

You know Haji Bahâoddin's wife? She couldn't bear children, everybody knows. Mowlawi Golzâr and Mayoddin-jân Âghâ did amulets for her, and God gave her children; they're now grown up and jinns can't harm her, but she still gives a sheep every year, and she'll continue while they're alive. But now Mayoddin-jân Âghâ has his own son, and Mowlawi, who used to be so strong, has got rather weak. People say he doesn't make such good amulets for people, and he's no longer strong enough to exorcize jinns. Neither of them do. Mowlawi thinks, 'If I do the exorcism, the jinn will jump straight into my own children and kill them.' Jinns have killed several of Mowlawi-seb's children after he exorcized them.

If a jinn possesses a child of mine, once it's exorcized it won't go to one of yours, only to the mullah who did the exorcism: to his wife, sister, daughter, son or brother; but first, if it's strong enough, it'll try to kill the mullah himself.

Baya-khân adds.

Jinns go for women, they rarely attack men. When a jinn possesses a woman, it may settle in her heart, or occupy her whole body. She'll pull out her hair, or stick out her tongue – which goes black.

Sometimes jinns kill their victims. Once a jinn's killed a child, or caused the family some harm, it doesn't die, it flies off with other jinns. Jinns have wings, they're very light and can fly. I believe they eat food like us, because people say that if we don't say *bismillah* when we cook and as we remove food from the cloth, the jinns take it and eat it without our knowledge. Similarly, if you don't say *bismillah* when you take flour from the sack, they'll take it, though people don't see them doing so. Both Muslim and kafir jinns are frightened of *bismillah*. Whenever you say it, it'll get out of your way, even if it's in its own house. If you don't say it, and you walk over its house and hurt its children, it'll get you right away.

Maryam tells Nancy about her co-wife Pâkiza.

Men rarely have jinns, because they don't have babies. Women have babies, they care for them, and jinns attack the babies and kill them. It's good to say *Bismillâhirrahmânirrahim*, it keeps the jinns away. Men are good at saying this, but women aren't religious. If I go outside I'm scared, but men go outside at night, with the camels and the sheep; in the mountains, they're out with the sheep. Women are frightened; they never go outside the home.

Pâkiza had two or three miscarriages, very early on in pregnancy. For example, the one I told you about, without a head; people were scared when she had such a baby. A jinn killed it in the womb. She came and told me: 'Maryam, the baby inside me isn't moving; every day it's getting smaller.' 'What do you mean? How can it get smaller? You haven't done anything like lifting a heavy weight.' She said, 'I know it's dead, because it's stopped moving.'

We took Pâkiza to a holy man's mother, a really good doctor. She said, 'There's a baby in your womb, but it's dead. Let's hope it comes out.' Well, it was born dead. But God gave her a curtain, and stopped her stomach. The jinn didn't come back; it wasn't that kind of jinn. Sometimes, if you say something to her, when she's upset because someone scolds her, or tries to pick a fight, Pâkiza suddenly shrieks and falls down. Then she gets up again, as though nothing had happened. All she does is cry like a child, nothing else; it doesn't make her arm or her leg go funny, and it doesn't attack her sons or her daughters. Even her own husband Tumân says she's faking! 'That's no jinn, you're putting it on! You're not possessed!' She's not like Bâbak or Mumin.

... and animals

Animals too are vulnerable to jinns, as Maryam says.

If a *jinndi* [*possessed*] woman goes near a horse or a camel that's just given birth, the calf will die. My co-wife Sarwar was possessed; she had an amulet. My sons Khâni-âghâ and Pâdshâh were very fond of her, as they are of you; she was a really nice woman, very good company. When Sarwar was sitting there she'd lighten your heart; all the boys used to sit opposite her and watch her. She'd talk and joke and tease you. She'd amuse us all. My heart was happy, she was a good woman.

One night when she was with us, our red camel gave birth, some distance away. It was a nice big calf, jumping around like a lamb; Baya-khân and Kala-khân put a blanket on it and brought it home. Back home, Sarwar was joking: 'Tumân's sent me some clothes; what shall I do with them? I can't possibly wear them; give them to Pâkiza. He's brought her lots of clothes, but not for me. I won't wear them!' Khâni-âghâ was on horseback; she threw some clothes at him, and he spurred his mare and galloped off. They'd joke with each other. As he rode off, the camel was suckling its calf a couple of hundred metres away, and the calf heard Sarwar's words – she must have shouted, though she was just joking with Khâni-âghâ. The calf fell down, rolled over, frothing at the mouth.

Early next morning Jamâloddin came and told us it was dying. We cried, 'Why?' He said, 'A bad woman has attacked it.' 'Which woman?' we asked. He said, 'Pâkhâl.'

Pâkhâl said, 'It wasn't me, it was Sarwar; the calf heard Sarwar's words.' Then the calf just died.

Detective-jinns

Some jinns can find thieves and stolen property; Baya-khân, Pâdshâh, Jamâl-khân and Seyyed-shâh/Golusar give examples.

(*Baya-khân*) – [*Mowzoddin's wife*] Khiâl was sometimes possessed and Wazir her co-wife couldn't hold her down: she'd take her by the arm, which stood up stiff like this.

(*N*) – Did this jinn talk?

(*Baya-khân*) – If you beat her with a cane, it would talk a lot.

(*Pâdshâh*) – It said awful things. She didn't know what it was saying.

(*Baya-khân*) – Until someone had done some thieving or something; then it'd talk about the theft.

(*Jamâl-khân*) – Pâdshâh[/*Parwiz*]'s wife was the same. Ask a question and it'll answer; ask it whether so-and-so was the thief and it'll say yes or no.

(*Baya-khân*) – Mâmâzi, Jamâl-khân's mother-in-law, goes into a trance too and tells the names.

(*N*) – What does it say?

(*Jamâl-khân*) – Once, thieves stole two of her cows; when the jinn possessed her, we beat her with a cane and asked, 'Who took the cows?' It answered, 'Haji Jallât's son took them and gave them to Alijân's son; he sold them to the butchers and they were slaughtered. Go and get the cows back from Haji Jallât, or his son.' Whatever she says, it turns out to be true.

(*N*) – So she got the cows back?

(*Jamâl-khân*) – No, not the cows; she got five sheep and a thousand rupees.

(*Seyyed-shâh*) – Cows were cheap then.

(*N*) – Haji Jallât accepted what the jinn said?

(*Jamâl-khân*) – Yes.

(*N*) – Has she detected any other thieves?

(*Jamâl-khân*) – Once Mirzâ's son Seyyed-shâh lost three cows. The jinn said that Haji Jallât's son had given them to Qilich, who'd killed them.

(*N*) – Did he get the cows back?

(*Jamâl-khân*) – He got one cow and 4,000 rupees.

(*N*) – What relation is Seyyed-shâh to Mâmâzak?

(*Seyyed-shâh*) – Her husband's brother's son.

(*N*) – When the jinn took her, he asked it himself, and it spoke like this?

(*Jamâl-khân*) – Yes. It wouldn't name someone who hadn't done it; it named the real thief.

(*N*) – Who else has jinns like this?

(*Jamâl-khân*) – Gorey's daughter, Khâtima.

(*N*) – Ah, I know her.

(*Jamâl-khân*) – She had a powerful jinn. Last year, on our way to the mountains, it possessed her, from Shorshorak right up to Dangak; she nearly died. Finally they took her to the Seyyeds [*at Dangak*]. They killed some sheep and goats. At first nothing happened; then it spoke.

(*N*) – What did it say?

(*Jamâl-khân*) – It said, 'Haji Jallât's son Musâ has killed one of your ewes' – belonging to her father-in-law, Mahmud Pakhizai. They got a ewe back from Musâ, worth 200 rupees.

(*Baya-khân*) – They took a sheep for a sheep. Some people go by the sharia, which says that a sheep has twelve bones, and proper compensation for theft is one sheep for each of the twelve bones. That's the law, if you go to the government, the Qazi. But if it's a relative, they'll let him off.

Dreams

Dreams are a popular subject. Jinns are often blamed for bad dreams, as Pâdshâh says.

When you dream about something bad happening to a living person – for example, your son's burned to death in a fire, swept away by a flood, fell off a cliff, or shot by somebody – then as soon as you awake you should sacrifice whatever you can afford; if you're very wealthy, a large animal, an ox. If you can't afford anything, it doesn't matter so much.

It's a jinn putting such bad things into your dreams. It frightens you, but it passes. One kind of jinn throws itself over you when you're asleep and stifles you; it seems to want to kill you. You cry out, or sometimes it makes you laugh – there are all kinds. Then someone'll say, 'Wake up! Why are you crying – or laughing – like that?' You wake with a start, and say the *kelima*: *la-ilaha-ila-Allah Mohammad-arrasul-Allah*. This jinn won't kill you, it'll only cause you distress, in your soul.

It's not good to dream about a wedding. It's been that way since our ancestors' time. We say that if you dream about someone's wedding, that person will die; because the procession taking the body to the graveyard is like a wedding.

But there are some things it's good to dream about. Water's good; so's horse-riding; these are first class. Dreaming about water means your path ahead is clear. Horses are a blessing, so it's good to dream about riding. Dreaming about a donkey when one of your family's away means you'll get some news today. I dreamed about a donkey; let's see if Khâni-âghâ will come this evening. These things don't come from jinns, they're just thoughts, images that come into your dreams.

Jinn Tribes

It turns out there are several very different kinds of jinns, which attack different parts of the person. Pâdshâh and others try to identify them for us. The symptoms of each resemble some established ailments. (Likely nosological or other equivalents are given in square brackets.)

Many stories tell how leaders encounter and overcome some of the more dangerous jinns.

(*Pâdshâh*) – There are Muslim as well as kafir jinns, and many tribes [*tayfa*], just as in Afghanistan there are Hazâra, Turkmen, Uzbek, Jât. Every jinn tribe has its own king, its own authorities, government, capital city. Jinns too are God's creatures. They have wives; the Muslim ones take Muslim wives. After all, they have children. Both Muslim and kafir jinns possess people. Muslim jinns are careful, they don't cause much trouble, they'll keep out of your way; but some non-Muslim ones nearly kill people. This is a very sensitive subject.

Mirgey

Perhaps the most dangerous is mirgey [*epilepsy*], *for which there is no remedy. Darwiza.*

There are different kinds of jinns. For example, we're Piruzai, but Afghans are a hundred tribes: Es'hâqzai, Nurzai, Piruzai, Alizai. Jinns too are a hundred different tribes: there are *paris*, *divs*, *mirgeys*. Just like humans, there are believers and infidels among them, and both Shi'a and Sunni.

One jinn tribe is *mirgey*, which charms and amulets can't control. In the beginning, in the time of the ancestors of these shrines, all humans and spirits in this world came before God to do him homage, to put themselves under his seal-ring as his subjects. God told his soldiers and servants to make sure nobody was left out. Only *mirgey* failed to appear. God told his servants, 'Fetch *mirgey*, from the mountains or deserts or wherever he is, to come before us and become our subject.'

Now *mirgey* was a tiny orphan, with neither father nor mother – like this poor nephew of mine here, though he, thank God, has a father. *Mirgey* had taken the cows to graze on the hillside. The servants came back: 'Master, there's just one little *mirgey*, an orphan, more dead than alive, forget about him.' By God's grace, *mirgey* grew up, married, and his descendants multiplied, and none of them are under God's seal-ring. They've become a big tribe, stronger than all other jinns. Apart from God himself, nothing can cure this illness; no mullah, no Sufi *âghâ*, no shrine. That's what the mullahs say: it's all in the Book. And everything in the Book's true, there are no lies.

Mirgey can never be subdued by charms or shrines; but it's God's servant like you and me, and God can control it; if he doesn't, then it'll kill you. It's like a human, but nobody can see it, except perhaps a strong mullah. It may take on your shape, like a woman, or like Richard or me, then you might see it in the distance, and think it's somebody passing by; but it's a *mirgey*.

All kinds of jinns do this: we see them but we don't recognize them, we're blind. You can't grab its arm to ask who it is. But a good man, a straight Seyyed, or a shrine's living descendants, can recognize a jinn.

Of all jinns, these *mirgey* are accursed [*Qor'ânzada*], such an evil tribe. If their ancestor had been summoned when he was small, he'd have submitted, and all his descendants would have been God's subjects for a hundred generations. But since he didn't, they're out of control; just like rebels in a kingdom. Now the mullahs can't touch them; just as our king's arm can't reach a rebel if he's in the mountains, or has a big clan, and he'll never become a subject; for example, he won't supply recruits for the army. Everyone knows it; that's the way they are.

Baya-khân, Pâdshâh and Jamâl-khân give some examples.

(*Baya-khân*) – Khorjânak, Mahd-Akbar's wife, had a very bad jinn; nobody was ever as badly possessed as her. In the end it killed her.

(*Pâdshâh*) – It threw her in the fire.

(*N*) – Did it speak?

(*Baya-khân*) – No. It was a *mirgey*.

(*Pâdshâh*) – A jinn that doesn't speak must be a *mirgey*; nobody understands what it wants. Nobody knew when she was going to succumb. She lost consciousness. She was baking bread, and fell straight into the oven. If there'd been people around, they'd have dragged her out. That's what one kind of jinn always does; if you're near a fire or a well, it'll throw you in. Did you know about Abdollah-jân Alizai, Mahd-Rasul's brother, a relative of Jalâloddin? His family sent him to fill two water-bags, but he never came home. The poor chap was in the pond; he was on his own; we don't know if he was swimming or just trying to fill a water-bag; suddenly a jinn possessed him, the water pulled him in, and he drowned; but once he was dead, it sent him back up. His family knew he had a jinn. Some jinns just can't be exorcized. *Mirgey*'s like this: if you're near water, fire, a well, it'll attack suddenly, without warning.

(*Jamâl-khân*) – Haji Tabu's wife Malek has a bad jinn. Without anyone noticing, it takes her straight to a graveyard at night, and brings her meat; she eats the meat, and her hands get covered in blood. Once we camped near Mullah Shir's graveyard; it possessed her that same night and took her to the graveyard. When it was time to strike camp, Tabu said, 'Hey, where's Gëdëk?' [*laughter*]

(*N*) – What does that mean?

(*Baya-khân*) – He calls his wife Gëdëk, which means a little ram; she's very small!

(*Jamâl-khân*) – As we struck camp in the early hours, we looked around for her, and found she'd fallen in a ditch; her arms, her clothes, were covered in blood, her mouth reeked; it was terrible. We brought her back, lit a fire and washed her, and she got better. She put on new clothes. We tied her onto a camel, then we set off. At dawn, she vomited red blood.

(*N*) – Was this the first time it happened?

(*Jamâl-khân*) – No; the jinn came out whenever we got near a graveyard. If one of her sheep or camels dies, or a cow or a donkey, she devours the carcase; whatever she eats, her arms are covered in blood. I've seen it myself.

(*Pâdshâh*) – In fact the jinn sometimes gets her up at night, aunt Malek. She doesn't know what she's doing, she can't stop herself. She goes to Haji Âghâ's house, or anywhere in the village, or the graveyards, wherever the jinn takes her. Sometimes it throws her into a pit, or some water. In the morning her arms and mouth are all bloody. You can't tell what blood it is; dog, donkey or something else, you can't tell. Whatever she can reach, the jinn makes her eat it. It causes her such trouble and distress, taking her to this house and that, making her eat such meat.

(*N*) – Can't they get rid of it?

(*Pâdshâh*) – No. The problem is, Tabu doesn't want to pay to get her to a powerful mullah who can raise jinns and will demand something from him. He's too mean.

(N) – What kind of jinn is it?

(Pâdshâh) – That's a *mirgey* too.

Khâpëska

Nightmares are commonly attributed to khâpëska, *a jinn that resembles the Persian* bakhtak [*with the attributes of incubus and sleep-paralysis*].

(Baya-khân) – Another jinn is *khâpëska*. If you sleep on your back, *khâpëska* will jump onto you and press you down. It spreads itself over your body; you become aware of it and feel very sluggish. It's so heavy you can't move; it feels like the whole room's come down on top of you. But if you manage to say *bismillah*, it'll get off; or if you manage to touch your nose, it'll go; it hates noses.

I've had some bad ones. The first was the winter before last, when my father was on Hajj. I was out in the steppe alone, in the hut where you used to sleep; for some nights Pâkhâl and the rest hadn't come. The first time it got me, I was sleeping outside, with the sheep about as far from me as that door. Early that night it came and crushed me. It was very frightening, I couldn't move. It only released me when the shepherd called out that it was time to move the sheep on. But it attacked me again. When my sister died, everyone returned to the Valley, to Pâdshâh's house, but I had to stay a few nights in the hut to guard the things there. It attacked me then, when I was alone and terrified; it came like a cow, making a *pshasss* noise – some make this noise, others don't. As you lie there it spreads itself over your body. When you become aware of it, it's like a mountain on top of you, suffocating you; you can't say anything. You're conscious, you know what it is, but you can't move. You have to try and touch your nose.

Wobâ

Earlier (p. 373) Pâdshâh mentioned wabâ *as a terrible disease – and* wobâ/wabâ *is the Persian for cholera. But Kala-khân, Baya-khân and Abdol also identify it as a type of jinn.*

(Kala-khân) – *Wobâ* is also a jinn. Jinns make themselves into all kinds of things.

(Baya-khân) – Some years *wobâ* strikes people; blood and stuff come from their mouth, they soon die.

(Abdol) – One killed Nâder-shâh's wife, Sâtëk. Something cried out in the middle of the night; 'Sâtëk, Sâtëk, come here, I've got something for you.' She came out and asked, 'Who's calling?' But nobody could see anything. Then in the morning her lips were grey and her eyes were green, and shortly she died. That was a *wobâ*.

(R) – What's *wobâ* like?

(Abdol) – It's invisible.

(R) – It's not like a person?

(Abdol) – It has a voice; it calls out to people.

(Baya-khân) – It's terrifying. At this time of the year, in summer, there are lots of them.

(Abdol) – They're very bad in the Black Forty [*December to January*].

(*Baya-khân*) – One year, in the old compound near Dur-khân's, a *wobâ* came and called out loudly to my mother or someone, I don't remember who. They realized what it was and didn't make a noise but chained the door. In the morning, outside, where the butter-churn had been, everything had been flattened. It's a terrible thing.

Mordëzmâ

Another jinn is mordëzmâ *('my mother'), with some similarities to the Perso-Turkish* âl/mâdar-âl, *especially when it attacks pregnant women. But it also attacks men, aiming to frighten them to death, and only the strong and smart – village leaders – can resist, as Pâdshâh tells.*

There's a kind of jinn called *mordëzmâ*. It's found in the steppes and mountains, and in old campsites, in ashes and dung, or places like an old graveyard, or in holes in the ground, like those big ravines in the steppe. It turns into a rope, and lays itself out on the path; you pick it up innocently: 'Let's take this rope home.' You put it on your horse or donkey, or over your shoulder, and much further on, when you're close to home, it'll have turned into something else, a goat or a sheep, something impossible to carry – it's dragging its feet on the ground. At this point you think, 'What the hell is this?' Then you vow to sacrifice a sheep, a cow, a goat, a camel, whatever you can afford, and aloud you say *bismillah*, calling first on God, then on Sakhi-Bâbâ, the Saints, the Pirs, Emâm-e-Jafar, Emâm-e-Khord and so on, begging to be rescued from the creature. You hurl it off and spur your mount away; but it comes after you, mooing like a calf. It probably won't kill you, or even harm you, its only purpose is to frighten you. You fall ill, your nerves shattered, and later you may die of this very fright.

But there's one thing a smart person can do, someone like Mowlawi or my father. If you see a calf bleating like a goat, out in the steppe – not coming near houses and yards – cry, 'Get away from me, or I'll whip you with my pyjama-cord,' and start to loosen your cord; then it'll quickly make itself scarce. If you don't say that, it'll keep after you until you're nearly home. When you get home, the dogs will chase it away.

There's another kind of *mordëzmâ*. If you go alone into the steppe, it turns into a sheep, coloured nice and red. You say, 'Ah, I've found a sheep!' and it may let itself be caught, but it'll run off and you can't catch it. When you get close, it'll disappear, then suddenly reappear over there. It's a jinn. Sometimes it turns into a bird and produces little chicks, and you'll think that's all it is. Or it'll turn into a cow with calf, or a horse or a camel. It won't hit you or anything, it won't even touch you; it'll come near you, behind you or beside you, gambolling around like a calf. It just wants to give you a fright. The only way to get rid of it is to threaten it; it'll be frightened itself, and disappear.

Seyyed-shâh/Golusar.

A *mordëzmâ* turns into a calf, a dog or a horse, and jumps out at you; or it butts you like a goat, rubbing its head on you. A timid person could die. If you've just a little courage, and recognize it's a *mordëzmâ*, hit it with your pyjama-cord and it'll disappear; it's afraid of being caught. That happened to Shahâboddin's son Madat. One night, about four years ago, he said, he was with the sheep: 'I saw a horse making a *rassp* noise. I set the dogs on it, but they wouldn't go, they were scared. It jumped on me, going *maa* like a calf, and rubbed its head on me like this. For some nights,' he said, 'I wouldn't go out with the sheep. Then [*his cousin*] Kala-khân told me, "When the *mordëzmâ* attacks you, whack it with your pyjama-cord and it'll instantly disappear."'

Baya-khân.

Mordëzmâ is a terrifying kind of jinn. During the Black Forty there are many such things about, but particularly *mordëzmâ*. They're numerous out in the steppe, in the sheepfolds where the ground's compressed, there's blood from an animal slaughter, or lots of animal bones. It tries to frighten you. Sometimes when you're out with the shepherd, one will approach in the shape of a goat, a sheep, a camel or a calf, making a *boghassss* noise. Thinking it really is such an animal, you catch hold of it, tie it up and put it on your back. Then it'll scare you. It'll disappear, then suddenly reappear in a different place. When you're back in the sheepfold asleep, it'll turn into a sheep and bleat; then when you come near it'll disappear again. It frightens some people to death. If you realize what it is, it'll lose the power to frighten you. And if you untie your pyjama-cord and chase it, it hates that, and it'll disappear and leave you alone.

Somebody else – I can't remember who – said, 'As I was riding along a track in the steppe, I saw what looked like a thick rope, so I picked it up and made it into a crupper for my horse. On I went, without looking behind, but soon the horse was sweating and could hardly move, so I looked back. Riding behind me, holding me tight, was a creature shaped like a goat. I hit it, shouting *bismillah*; it fell off and I spurred my horse homewards. It cried out after me, "Hey, stop, I'm coming with you!" but I raced away and got home safely, leaving it behind.'

Manân tells some mordëzmâ *stories about his relatives.*

My maternal uncle Tella, God rest him, would tell how he was walking along the road at night and as he came to the hill he met a *mordëzmâ*. 'There, standing in front of me, was a small foal. Its face and forehead were white. I tried to pass it, then I realized it was a *mordëzmâ*. I was terrified, but I managed to get by. I didn't want to go all the way to Khârkash, it was too far and the thing might frighten me somewhere else, so I turned off the road at the graveyard by the hill and went round the back to Haji Malek-Mahmad's, hoping to find a farmhand or someone watering the wheat. As I was going along I saw a woman spinning. She asked several times where I was going. A bit further on, I cried out as I saw the foal again. Then there were people, dogs barking, and the thing took fright and disappeared.'

They say that one night two Kabulis were riding from Khârkash towards Haji Tabu's place. 'As we passed the graveyard at the hill,' they said, 'we were chatting together, when we noticed two nice young men, who called out, "Brothers, give us a ride, we're going to that village too." We said, "Why not?" So we each mounted one of the young men behind us. As we neared Pâdshâh/Parwiz's house at the head of the village, we slowed right down; the horses were so tired that they couldn't put one foot in front of another.

Each of us looked at the young man riding behind the other and saw that their feet were dragging on the ground. We found we couldn't move our own limbs, and we couldn't ask them to get off. But just then Pâdshâh's dogs started barking, and the two got off and disappeared into thin air, like when you burn a charm-paper.' These were *mordëzmâ*.

One winter night after dinner our father went out to water the animals in the steppe, riding a good, lively horse. On his way home, he said, 'As I passed the ditch at Haji Tabu's, a woman called out, "Hey, Tumân, stop! I've tethered one child, and there's one left. Stop, don't pass me by!" I pressed on to the Valley's edge, but I could still hear her calling, "Tumân, you're so powerful over your dead people that you managed to pass me." I left her behind.'

Mowlawi Golzâr was going to Kandahar. He said, 'I was walking along by myself through the desert when I came to a large canal. Suddenly I saw – begging your pardon – a donkey standing before me. It said, "Golzâr, won't you ride me?" So I said, "Of course," folded my coat, put it on the donkey's back and mounted. We came to a village and the donkey said, "Golzâr, dismount, we're near the village." I answered, "Over your dead body! If I weren't an *âghâ*, if I were someone else, you'd frighten me. Don't think I'm going to let you go! If I do, you'll go and frighten someone else." So the donkey swore by God and the Koran that it wouldn't harm anyone else, then it kissed his hands and feet and left. That too was a *mordëzmâ*.

My sister Zeytun's son Black-Manâp said, 'One winter evening we'd been out watering wheat or something. On my way back, as I passed the graveyard hill, suddenly I saw a black tent on the track ahead. I spurred my horse, but it took me half an hour to get past the tent. As I went on towards the village, four women were singing songs behind me; they called, "Won't you be our guest?" I said nothing, but they persisted, "We'll make you a fire." I said, "I don't need one, get lost!"' When he got home in the middle of the night, some of his teeth fell out. If you put blacking on your teeth they get better, so he did that. If he hadn't, he'd have been sick with terror for several days, but as it was he got better in one day.

Pari, div, ablij, rëwey, balâ

Very different are two types of jinn that commonly crop up in folk tales, where we've already met them: pari *[fairy, peri] and* div *[demon, giant]. Darwiza explains about* paris.

Suppose one day a good-looking young girl puts on nice clothes to go to a wedding or a party or festival, or just to visit another house, or another village; a really nice-looking girl, wearing a necklace, ornaments on her forehead, bangles on her wrists, nicely made up. If a *pari* sees such a girl and falls in love with her, it'll possess her.

But *paris* can possess boys too. Take Sâleh's son Bâlu: all the mullahs, all the shrines in the world, such as Sakhi-Bâbâ, have failed to cure him. Our mullahs say Bâlu's jinn is a *pari*. It can't be caught. If a mullah chants over him, the *pari* flies off and there's no way you can catch it; but when the mullah isn't around, it'll soon seize Bâlu. When the jinn gets Bâlu, he falls off a wall, or into a well or a fire. He's quite unconscious until it releases him. He won't notice even if he's burned. If you cut him with a knife when the jinn's possessed him, he wouldn't know he'd been injured. Several times Bâlu climbed onto a roof without people knowing, and when the jinn seized him he fell off. Once he broke his arm, other times he broke or hurt some other limb. This very summer early one evening he got onto the roof and fell off. All the shrines he's been to, the animals he's sacrificed, the mullahs who've prayed over him, all the money he's spent, he still isn't cured.

The *pari* fell in love with him and won't let him go. It's settled in him, and in the end it'll kill him. No doctor can cure him, even if you fetched one from Calcutta! The mullahs who've seen him say they're not strong enough; even the stronger mullahs said, 'Impossible!'

Many others have been possessed by *paris*. Kamaroddin's son Ali-khân has one; it gets him all the time, knocks his mouth askew, and his body too.

Once such a jinn fancies someone, whether woman or man, it turns into a human and makes friends with him, talks with him, without showing itself to anybody else. The jinn gets to know this person, and falls in love with him, if he's very good-looking. It makes him swear not to tell anyone about their friendship or what they say to each other. When he's alone, out in the steppe or in the house at night, it comes and talks with him, perfectly friendly. But once he (or she) tells somebody else about it, saying, 'I have this jinn friend,' then the jinn will seize him.

Ablij [*paralysis*] *is a type of* div; *Darwiza continues.*

You know Nâder-shâh's sister? She's been struck by an *ablij*, a *div*, a different kind of illness. May God preserve us, she can't move her arms or her legs. Not a bone in her body's left; you can see, they've all melted away, there's only flesh left. Only her mouth's alive, and even that doesn't work; her mother feeds her. When she needs to go to the toilet, begging your pardon, her mother takes her, putting some clothes over her head. She lifts her and pushes her; she can't move her arms or her legs. She looks at you with both eyes; but she's quite unaware of anything.

A *div* is like a human, but you can't see it. It flies like a bird, followed by its shadow on the ground. If its shadow fell on us, it'd harm us, we'd become like Nâder-shâh's sister.

Baya-khân, Manân, Hâshem, Pâdshâh and Kala-khân discuss divs, *then go on to talk about* rëwey *and* balâ, *two very dangerous types of jinn.*

(*Baya-khân*) – There are many tribes of *div*; there's Seven-headed Div—
    (*Manân*) – Four-Headed Div, White Div—
    (*Baya-khân*) – And also Black Div and Red Div; Yellow Div and White Div.
    (*R*) – Are they like people?
    (*Baya-khân*) – Yes, they're like men and women and they fall madly in love with *paris*. These creatures lack any self-control. When they see a *pari*'s face, they are lost, in love.
    (*N*) – How do you know if they're black or red, if you can't see them?

(*Baya-khân*) – We haven't seen them, but people tell tales, which we've heard.

(*N*) – Where do *divs* live?

(*Baya-khân*) – Long ago they lived in the steppes and mountains. They aren't there any more now, but people say they used to be.

(*R*) – Were they bigger than people?

(*Baya-khân*) – They were huge, and they could fly. Some men were stronger than them, and they'd tell these men: 'Don't kill me; get on my back and I'll carry you wherever you like.'

(*Hâshem*) – Prophet Solomon drove the *divs* out of these parts. He imprisoned them, people say, in Kuh-e-Kâf; and there they remain.

(*R*) – Is it just *divs*, or are other tribes of jinns there too?

(*Hâshem*) – There are *paris* too, and many other things.

(*R*) – Do you say jinn in Pashtu too?

(*Pâdshâh*) – Fârsi people say *jinn*, we say *pirey*.

(*R*) – *Pirey* and *pari* are different?

(*Pâdshâh*) – Yes; *pari* in Persian is *shâpirëy* in Pashtu. Everybody has their own words.

(*R*) – Is *ghul* a jinn?

(*Pâdshâh*) – What? There's no such thing as *ghul* in Afghanistan! [*Much laughter, people haven't heard this one*].[1]

(*N*) – We have them in our place.

(*Pâdshâh*) – What is it? Probably we call it something else.

[*R and N discuss what to say . . .*]

(*R*) – *Ghul* is like people's bones, without flesh, risen from a grave; it goes around at night frightening people; it's unclear who it might have been.

(*Kala-khân*) – Is it like a person?

(*R*) – Only the bones, no flesh [*finally getting some reactions*].

(*Kala-khân*) – Do you have it in your place?

(*R*) – I haven't seen it myself, but people say—

(*Pâdshâh*) – What they say is right. We do have them in Afghanistan, though I haven't seen one. I think it's what we call *rëwey*. They go around from camp to camp in the middle of the night; they aren't afraid of the dogs; they eat anything they see in the house, and make a mess. You can't see them; sometimes a woman or a man sees one and gets very scared; they may die of fright.

Khâni-âghâ's wife Bâdâm died in summer 1971; people identify the cause, probably correctly, as khorzak, *diphtheria. At the time, her brother-in-law Darwiza says, people thought it was a* balâ.

We can't see a *balâ* – may God never bring it here. If you're asleep and in your heart you feel that someone's hit you, whether by hand, with a stick or a clump of earth or a stone; suddenly you're overcome by fear, and cry out; then you'll die. If a *balâ* strikes someone like that, no doctor can't cure it. You must slaughter a goat or an ox at once, then wrap

---

[1] *Ghul* is listed in both Afghan Persian and Pashtu dictionaries as equivalent to *div*, or *div-e-sahrâ'i*.

the patient in the skin and put the heart in his hand. The skin will stink for a couple of hours; then take it off and kill another, and put him in the new skin with the heart in his hand; the heart will pass into his body, and calm his fright. Then do a *kheyrât* of the meat: distribute it among the people, the poor and needy and so on. When you've done two or three skins, he'll get better. If you didn't realize it was a *balâ*, but thought it was something else, and did the wrong charm, it'll finish him off.

Haji Tumân defeats the jinn

Haji Tumân had a terrifying encounter with a rëwey/balâ. He told us the story himself, but we didn't record it. His sons Pâdshâh and Baya-khân, however, give independent accounts.

Pâdshâh.

One year we camped at Sang-e-Solâkh in Qerghaytu, in front of Eskandar Aymâq's house. Not many people had gone that spring, there were only my stepmother Pâkiza, Dur-khân's wife Shayesta, Khâni-âghâ and Akhtar. They'd taken the camels up that gorge – you've seen it, it's very narrow, thickly wooded, with a fast creek coming down; a really bad place. Towards evening they collected the camels, but one female was missing. We'd sent its calf home from Kachan. The mother went looking for its calf and got lost in the woods at the top of the gorge. Khâni-âghâ couldn't find it and got scared; it gets very dark up there at night, you can't see anything.

When he heard this, Haji mounted a mare – it was a good mare, smooth as the wind – and rode far up the gorge; it was this time of evening, very dark. I don't know if he took his gun. When he got to the top, he found the camel and turned back. Suddenly, from up on the cliffs something went *pshasss*, like a passing car, or a cow pissing. He saw a great black thing, and he and the mare both took fright at the same moment, each trying faster than the other to get away; *hala–hala–hala–hala.*

He said, 'As I whipped the horse on, it was running with us, right beside me. It tried to get me to stop: "Take my child and I'll come with you." I vowed to sacrifice an ox; I called on every saint, all the Sufis and the Companions, crying, "O God and the Pirs, I beg you, come and rescue us from this evil!" Once I'd promised the sacrifice and said these things, it fell behind us and we escaped.' He whipped the mare on; it followed them down that tortuous track, but eventually they left it behind.

'When I got home,' he said, 'I called Akhtar and Khâni-âghâ to tether the camel, and take good care of the mare and cover it well, it was exhausted.' As soon as he'd dismounted, he crawled under the bedclothes and fell fast asleep – without eating anything. He was suffering from fright; that evil creature was quite something else. In the morning the mare's whole body was shaking. Both horse and camel were covered in lumps. Haji's own body was covered in swellings. He'd had a bad shock. For nearly a month he was really ill. He did one or two skins, took some medication, some pills. Finally he recovered.

That thing is called *rëwey*. Some people say they're *balâ* or jinn, but you can't tell what they are. God knows, but it's the sort of thing we can't recognize. With people you can tell an Afghan, an Arab, a Hazâra; with jinns, you can't tell by looking. The night's dark and so too are they.

Baya-khân.

Balâ is a very bad jinn. One year, long ago, when our households were joint but neither our family nor my uncles went to the mountains, and Haji Ghâfur's family stayed in Chenâr and Kachan, only my father Haji Tumân took the sheep up to Kuh-e-Kalân. The only people with him were Khâni-âghâ, uncle Akhtar and two or three women. I was small at the time. At Sarghân a camel's calf died. The following morning we moved on, down to Sang-e-Solâkh. In the evening we couldn't hold the camel back; it was thinking about its calf, and off it went, up the gorge.

My father followed it as best he could, riding a mare, but he couldn't catch it – camels move very fast once they get going. It was a very dark night. Around midnight he finally caught up with it, then, as he was turning it back, there was a *shrass* noise like a machine-gun from up on top of the rocks. The camel took fright at the noise; Haji was frightened too, while the mare was hot and sweating. The camel sped off for camp, and Haji hurried after it. The creature threw one of its breasts over this shoulder and the other over the other shoulder, and called out: 'Hey Tumân, stop! Hey Tumân, stop!' 'I spurred the horse,' he said, 'and when I looked behind I saw her hair hanging all the way down to her feet. I called on the Pirs to get me home, I begged them from the bottom of my heart, I called on Sakhi-Bâbâ and the other blessed shrines, but she kept after me, calling all the time for me to stop.' But it turned round and went off, and Haji got home safely. He was very sick, and for some days his mouth was swollen with boils. That was a *balâ*; it's very bad.

Sheytân

Sheytâns, devils, are rather different from other jinns. They inhabit everybody permanently, and cause bad thoughts and deeds, as Pâdshâh explains.

The *sheytâns* are a tribe of jinns, for example like Turkmens, Afghans or Hazâras. They divert you from the Muslim path, from saying your prayers or fasting. They turn you from the Right Path, the Way of the Book, onto the Wrong Path. That's what makes them *sheytâns*, that's all they do; otherwise they're a kind of jinn. If you're having sex with your wife, the *sheytân* makes you think of something forbidden, for example it makes you desire someone else's daughter or wife, or some boy. Or if you're about to do one of your daily prayers, the *sheytân* will press you to keep putting it off, until the time for prayer has passed and it's invalid.

That's the *sheytân*'s speciality; it turns you from Right to Wrong. If you're actually standing up and doing your prayers, it'll bring a hundred matters into your mind that wouldn't have been there at other times. When you're at your prayers, you should be concentrating on them; there shouldn't be anything else in your thoughts, like 'Where's that camel, or that donkey?' or 'I've forgotten something I was supposed to do.' No, once you've opened your prayers with the Allahu-Akbar, you must empty your mind of everything, and not allow anything in, because if you do, your prayers will be no good to you at all. It's at just such times that this bastard *sheytân* tries hardest to distract you so that you make a mistake in your prayers, or puts something else into your mind that would immediately nullify them, for example, 'Tomorrow I'll go to Pâdshâh's place,' or 'I'll go with Pâdshâh to the bazaar, where we have things to do.'

Sheytâns don't show themselves in your body like other jinns. No, they're inside your body, under the skin. Everybody in the world has them, including you. There's one of these buggers in every joint in your body. It cried out to the Creator, 'O God Almighty, you've made me a *sheytân*, a very unclean thing' – the most unclean thing in the world, according to the Book, though I haven't seen it myself – 'you've made me so bad that nobody likes me; just give me a place in that Muslim's body, so that I can be there under his skin and in his joints.'

When you go on Hajj, the morning you set off from Kandahar to Holy Mecca, then – if you say your five daily prayers, follow the Right Path and don't lie or do *sheytâni* – all your *sheytâns* will leave your body and stay in Kandahar, though you aren't aware of it. They can't go with you. You're clean, just like a glass bottle when you've washed it, as clean as when your mother bore you. You have no sin – until you return and get off the aeroplane in Kandahar. When you come home, if you have mean and bad feelings in your heart, or worry about the sheep, or plan to buy something cheap here and sell it there, or to steal something, or to take someone's land rights, then all those *sheytâns* come right back again into your body, without your knowing. They come back and once more divert you from the Right Path onto the Wrong Path. And they'll fit you up, and bring you lots of torment in the other world. In fact, the *sheytâns* will double in number.

It was God, not us, who created this heaven and this earth; perhaps you have the same idea? When God first created the world, all people were like angels or fairies. Then he made Hell, but it cried out to the Pure Creator, 'You created Heaven and the angels, why did you create me? Why don't you send me something to burn? Don't let everyone go to Heaven and leave me all alone with nothing for my fire to burn?' So that's why God created the *sheytâns*.

Sheytâns and unbelievers and all such tribes go to Hell, whereas a Muslim who says his five daily prayers, fasts, gives alms, and does pilgrimage to God's house, will go to Heaven, according to the Book – or so the mullahs tell us. Though it's not certain, it's up to God.

Neshtar articulates some conventional views of women and why they are inferior to men.

If a woman's sensible and doesn't quarrel, that's good. Happiness and laughter leave a good taste. So does kindness. If she acts like a man, organizes her life, works hard, that's excellent. It's not good to be weak, because people will call you stupid or slow-witted. A woman who's competent and pious will get things organized and go out to the steppe, to the bazaar, or to the mill to make flour. I myself went a hundred times to the mill, when my sons were small. Abdollah was with me, but he was a child. Both men and women approve of such a woman, and praise her and her work. She makes all her own arrangements, does her own work, and also looks after all the animals: horses, camels, sheep, cows.

A woman who's useless, who doesn't understand, we call *sheytân*. To hell with her! Dust on her head! Without a husband, a brother-in-law, work is too difficult for her, her animals go hungry; she should have looked after them, but she didn't bother, this good-for-nothing.

Men are free because they have few *sheytâns*, while women have many. Long ago, in the time of our Prophets, women too joined the congregation in the mosque. Then once, a woman sitting opposite the mullah gave him the finger [*guta*]! Get it? After that, they drove the women out, saying 'Women have too many *sheytâns*, it's wrong to let them into the mosque.' After all, men or mullahs among themselves wouldn't do such a thing. The mullah was talking about religious precepts, and she gave him the finger.

Women are bad, they have many more *sheytâns* than men. May God lessen them, so that a woman doesn't spoil things by doing *sheytâni*! Her grave'll be ruined, her face'll be blackened in the other world. If she doesn't do *sheytâni*, if she does good deeds, keeps her counsel, says good things, then she'll be all right. If not, she'll go black-faced into that world. But most women can't talk the way we two can, Nancy, I swear.

Women aren't so pure as men in religion, because, as you know, women have periods and become impure that way. After they've stopped their periods, it's all right for them to pray in the mosque along with the men, and many women do; or they go to Mecca like Haji Bakhtâwar. It's also correct to do your prayers outside the mosque along with the men, but it's difficult. My maternal aunt went on pilgrimage to Mecca. She wore white clothes and a white veil. She lives in Qataghan, I've been there to visit her. She does all her prayers standing right alongside the men. Since her pilgrimage, she's been one of them. Whenever men assemble in the mosque, she's there.

In this village they don't allow women go to the mosque with the men. It's difficult because when there are men and women, if there's a *sheytân* in the women's prayers, or in the men's, the prayers are invalid. For example, a man while praying might think, 'I really fancy that woman,' or if it was a woman, 'I really fancy that man.' That's why it's difficult.

It would be very good if women had their own separate mosque. We could do it, but we haven't. But women are *sheytân*; if that mosque were built, and there were twenty women inside, for sure there'd be twenty quarrels! If there are twenty men in one place, they don't squabble; but if there are only three women sitting together, there's sure to be some squabbling and the mosque will be spoiled, so will their prayers. Isn't it the same with you?

Of course men quarrel too, but it doesn't really matter; men have reasons for creating a fuss, such as something to do with the government. Men are otherwise very good, they don't do *sheytâni* – they don't gossip about what other people have said and done. But women gossip about everybody, they tell it all. Women! It's obvious that women have many *sheytâns*.

Birth of a Jinn

Pâdshâh recorded this tale on two different occasions; this is an amalgam of the two.

One spring night two or three years ago, they were camped in the Jamâli hollow below Wangar-e-Sorkh, or somewhere like that. Shirin's mother, Malek – Nâder-shâh's sister – was asleep. In the small hours, about 4:00 am, there was a cry, 'Hey auntie Malek, hey auntie Malek!' Thinking it must be one of her relatives, she quickly got up and answered, 'Yes?' just as you would if I called out to you. There was a woman outside, in Afghan clothes – chador, hat, shoes and so on. She said, 'Let's go, So-and-so's in labour, having a baby,' mentioning the name of some woman. Malek knows all about this; she's a midwife, helps a woman give birth – perhaps you people have them too.

Malek was still sleepy. She thought the woman was the wife of someone she knew, so she happily left her tent and joined her. Off they hurried, the woman ahead, Malek following behind. Malek soon realized they were going far from camp. About as far as Haji Âghâ's house from here, she noticed that, as they went along, the woman's clothes and her general appearance were shifting. It was a jinn, it had made itself human so as not to frighten her. Malek got very worried. She was too frightened to speak, to ask what was happening, or to turn back; she was afraid she'd be killed or something. She couldn't say anything aloud, but in her heart she asked God to save her.

They arrived at a big hollow at the head of the Shor valley. She was told, 'Come and join us!' There was a hurricane-lamp, and three women there, one having a baby and the other two sitting with her. On the other side were some men as well, all of them jinns. There was a lively conversation going on among the women and children; but Malek was terrified they'd kill her and eat her right there. She said, 'Hello,' and sat down and wanted to chat with them, but she was now trembling with fright and she couldn't utter another word.

Suddenly the woman gave birth, inside the circle – women gather round when one's having a baby. Some are experts and know about it, some just come casually, to see whether it's a boy or a girl. It was a boy. Malek took it up and found herself compelled to tell them, 'Bring the swaddling clothes' – what we bind babies up in, cloth and twine. They brought them, then she said, 'Fetch some ghee.' We mix a little ghee with sugar and give it to a newborn baby. But the jinns said to each other, 'We haven't any ghee, what shall we do?'

One of the jinn-women said, 'Wait a moment' and disappeared, saying, 'I'm off to get some ghee.' Now when a woman takes ghee out of her storage bag, if she says her five daily prayers, washes her hands and says *bismillah* before she puts them in, the jinn can't get close or it'll get burned. But if she doesn't wash her hands properly, or say *bismillah*, then the jinns can get some ghee as she does – she won't see them. So the jinn-woman went to a home where the housewife was known to be dirty and neglectful of her religious duties – some Muslim like you or me – and stole some ghee from her storage bag. If she'd been a good woman, clean and pious, the bag opening would have been closed; the jinn couldn't have got inside and would have been burned. This village is a swamp, you can find women who don't pray, or pray with their shoes on, or while talking to somebody.

Anyway, it was a mere instant before she brought back the ghee, lots of it. After all, she was a jinn, and 'What's Ghazni to a jinn?' Jinns are so fast, they can be in Kabul, or England, in the blink of an eye. 'So I gave the baby the ghee,' Malek said, 'and I wrapped it up.' Then she saw that the jinns were shape-shifting again. Terrified, she said, 'Now please let me go!' They said, 'Sit down a minute first.' Finally some of them said to her, 'O mother, be our sister, be our mother; we're jinns, we'll admit that now, but we have nothing against you, we'll neither kill you nor eat you; we're Muslims, not kafirs; don't be afraid of us; it was only because our midwife died, and we had nobody else, so when one of us was in labour we fetched you to help,' and so on. They gave her a scarf, which they'd stolen from someone's house – theft is easy for them, they can get in through the tiniest of holes – and said, 'Take this scarf as your reward!'

Malek was petrified – she tells this story herself – and desperate to get back home. Two or three jinn-women accompanied her for a long way, to make sure she didn't cry out about their being jinns. At first she was ahead, but when they got near her tent, about a hundred metres away, they tried to get in front and push her in the other direction. Malek ran as fast as she could, and as soon as she entered her tent she fell down, fainting from terror. In the morning she lay unconscious until very late. When she awoke she told her friends what had happened, how the women sat on one side and the men on the other, and so on. She was very ill for some weeks, then a mullah prayed over her and made amulets for her – for fright, not jinn possession. Now she's recovered.

The Tale of the Three Musicians

Many folk tales feature jinns of various kinds, notably pari *and* div. *This one, told by Baya-khân, has familiar elements, including a contest with a stupid* div.

There were three brothers: one played the pipe [*sornâ*], one the drum [*dawl*], the other looked after their three donkeys. They were all married, but they worked together. One day they quarrelled, so they split up. One of them got the three donkeys, one got the drum, and one the pipe.

The drummer said, 'We've nothing to eat here, I'll go round the villages and camps to earn some flour to bring home.' He went out, and travelled from village to village, but he had only his drum, no pipe; although a few people gave him some flour, most didn't. If you have both pipe and drum, everybody will give lots of flour, but if there's just a drum or just a pipe on its own, people won't give you anything!

Afternoon came and he said, 'I'm having no luck here, let me go out into the steppe,' somewhere like our spring campsite. The sun was setting as he headed into the steppe; on he went, until he found himself in a dry valley, and there beside the track was a cave. In the cave's mouth there stood a fox, a wolf and a leopard, and in the cave behind them were all kinds of creatures. Scared for his life, he took up his drum, and started beating a lively march rhythm. The wolf and the other creatures were petrified: 'What's this creature standing there in front of our cave?' He was scared of them, they were scared of him! He was so frightened, he went on drumming until dawn; 'If I stop drumming,' he thought, 'they'll come out and eat me!' But they were so frightened, they didn't dare come out.

In the morning, as the sun came up, he saw a caravan in the distance, coming from a neighbouring country. The caravan was long, the camels had great bells hanging from their necks, and they were loaded with precious cloth, which they were bringing to trade in another country. As the caravan came up, the leader didn't notice the cave and said, 'What on earth are you doing, drumming out here in the steppe, exhausting yourself for nothing? Why don't you go to some populated place, where they might give you something for your pains!' He grabbed the drummer's arm; as he did so, the drummer stopped drumming and the fox leapt out of the cave, followed by the wolf, the leopard and all the other creatures. The drummer seized the caravan-leader's reins: 'Curse you, I put the padishah's zoo in this cave, and I was standing at the entrance drumming to stop them escaping. Either you go and round up all the animals and put them back in the cave, or I'll have to take you to His Majesty.'

The caravan-leader was frightened that he'd be taken to the padishah, who'd send him to the cannon's mouth or the gallows. He begged the drummer, 'Take a camel with its load of precious cloth, and for God's sake let me go!' 'No way; I'm taking you to the padishah.' By now this fellow knew he was onto a good thing, putting on these airs, and was determined to get what he could from it; he repeated, 'If you get all those wild animals back inside, I'll let you go; otherwise I'm taking you to the padishah!' The caravan-leader kept pleading with him to take one of the camels, but he refused; he offered two camels; finally, after he'd offered three loaded camels, the drummer accepted and let him go.

Once the caravan had gone, the drummer smashed his drum to pieces in front of the cave. He mounted one of the camels, twirled his moustache, and set off home. When he arrived, they were delighted that he'd brought back three camel-loads of precious cloth, which he added to his household goods.

Next day, the piper's wife came to the drummer's house and saw how wealthy they'd become. She wondered, 'Did they hide something from us? How did they get hold of all this precious cloth, these camels?' She didn't ask, but rushed off home to her husband and upbraided him: 'You split up with your brother, and now he seems to have got hold of camels and cloth, and you sit here in front of our house, doing nothing, earning nothing. Off you go, play your pipe around the tents and houses, earn some flour, find some wealth for us too.'

So off went the piper round the houses, but he too had no luck. A few people gave him some flour, most didn't. Nobody wants a pipe without a drum! When evening came, he thought, 'Nobody in this valley's going to give me anything, I'd better go out into the steppe, there are lots of Afghan nomads there with their flocks, they're well-to-do, they're good people, they'll give me some flour.' So he headed into the steppe, to a place like our spring campsite; but the nomads had migrated and there was nobody there. He found a long thin rope, and wound it round his waist.

In another campsite he found a sparrow. He thought, 'What are you doing out here in the steppe, little sparrow, I'll take you to some water' – sparrows really like water, they splash around in it, don't they? He picked it up and put it in one of his pockets.

In a third campsite, he spotted a partridge in a cage – the nomads had forgotten it when they moved off. He broke open the cage and put the partridge into another pocket.

By now it was night-time. Far away over the steppe he saw firelight. He headed towards it, and as he got closer he saw it was a *div*, who'd killed a large ox, skewered it on a spit, and was turning it over the fire.

The piper approached and said '*Salâm aleykum*'. The *div* said, 'If you hadn't said *salâm*, I'd have ripped you apart.' The piper answered, 'If you had, you'd have regretted it!' Terrified that he'd be killed and eaten, he was bragging and laying it on.

Well, when the *div* had cooked the ox, he gave some to the piper, saying, 'Have some of this meat.' The piper answered, 'No thanks, I ate a couple of oxen over there before I came, and now I'm full, I can't eat any more.'

So the *div* ate the whole ox himself. When he'd finished, he twirled his moustache and sat back; he was full too. When a *div*'s hungry, he doesn't see much. Now that he was full, he looked at the piper and said, 'Let's compare the length of the hair on our backsides.' The piper said, 'Okay.' The *div* measured his own, and it came to a metre and a half. The piper took the long thin rope that he'd picked up from the campsite, unwound it from his waist, and it turned out to be much longer than the *div*'s hair.

At this, the *div* said, 'Let's compare our fleas'. The *div* picked off one of his fleas, which was as big as a sheep's dropping. The piper took out his partridge and released it. They were sitting in the *div*'s house, and the partridge flew up, calling *kawkakawk*. The piper told the *div*, 'My people's fleas all sing like this!'

The *div* admitted that he was bested in this one too. So he said, 'Let's compare our lice', and took out one that was as big as a camel's dropping. The piper took out the sparrow he'd found on the campsite, and released it; it did *mush-mush* and *korkor*; and he said, 'Our lice all sing like that!'

Well, in all these comparisons he'd bested this huge *div*, who could have eaten him in one gulp. The *div* was afraid, 'He's stronger than me!' But the piper too was really scared the *div* would kill and eat him.

Then the *div* suggested they compare farts. The *div* farted, and the piper was blown as far as from here to the edge of the well – he had a really powerful fart! Then the piper took up his pipe and played a loud blast on it for five minutes. The huge *div* realized, 'He's stronger than me in every way, he's bested me in everything,' and he leaped up and fled. As he did so, the piper leaped after him, his pipe in his hand.

Well, the *div* soon got far ahead of him, as far as from here to Chârbâgh, with several mountains in between, so the piper returned to the fire, where the *div* had eaten the ox, and he searched the *div*'s house, which was nearby and was full of wheat, gold and silver. The piper found some camels, loaded them with all this and took them home.

When he got home, after a night or two, the wife of the third brother, who'd received the three donkeys, came to visit her two brothers-in-law, and saw how much precious cloth the first had brought, how much gold and silver the second had brought, and how rich they'd both become, and she immediately reproached her own husband, 'Why are you sitting here at home, while your brothers have become rich, bringing home precious cloth and gold? Why haven't you been out in the steppe, looking for some food for us?'

So the third brother went out, driving the three donkeys before him; he went round village after village, and people gave him a little flour, a little barley, a few coins. Evening came, and he headed out into the steppe. He came upon a rat, standing at the entrance of the burrow it was digging. He said, 'Hey ratty, don't tire yourself!' and he tied one of the donkeys at the mouth of the burrow, instructing it to help the rat move the earth. The rat, frightened by the sight of the donkey tied up at the mouth of his burrow, scurried down inside.

He went on, and saw Sleep; he felt sorry for it, so he tethered a donkey there, thinking perhaps Sleep might have need of it.

He went on and found a dung-beetle, which makes dung-balls and pushes them along; he said, 'O dung-beetle, how tired you must be!' so he gave it the last donkey, to help carry the dung-balls.

He was left with nothing. It was night when he got home. Now that same day, his wife, who was very beautiful, had gone to the river to wash their clothes, and the padishah passed by with his retinue. The padishah saw her and exclaimed: 'What a nice-looking woman, I wish she were mine!' He asked, 'Whose wife is this?' and somebody mentioned that she was married to a musician, the one with three donkeys. He said, 'What does he want with such a nice woman?' and he called a servant, 'Go and put her on your horse and we'll carry her off.' So when the man got home, he had nothing, and there was no trace of his wife either. There was nothing he could do about it, so he just sat there with his children.

That evening the padishah planned to hold the wedding ceremony. When the rat heard about it, he went to the dung-beetle and said, 'That man was so nice to me, he left me a donkey to help carry the earth for me,' and the dung-beetle said, 'He left me a donkey to help move all my dung, he was really nice to me.' Sleep joined them and said, 'He was good to me, and gave me a donkey too.' So the three of them got together to decide what to do about the padishah's plan to marry the poor man's wife that very evening.

Nobody can see Sleep, so he jumped onto the padishah and made him fall asleep. The rat came, chewed a hole in the padishah's pyjama trousers, and told the dung-beetle, 'In you go!' As the padishah slept, oblivious to everything, the dung-beetle entered his backside, crawled all the way in and thoroughly emptied the padishah's innards of shit. When the padishah awoke – nobody had dared wake him to prepare for his wedding – he saw that his trousers were filthy, full of shit. So he told everyone, 'This night's no good, we'll do the wedding tomorrow night.' They dispersed, and the padishah went to a watercourse, washed himself and his trousers, and put on fresh clothes.

The next morning, he told the people, 'Tonight is a good night for the wedding, come early.' So, early in the evening everyone gathered, the ministers and all the court. They ate their dinner, but as soon as the conversation turned to the marriage contract, Sleep spread itself over the padishah again. Once he was asleep, the rat came and made a hole in his trousers, and the dung-beetle went in. When he got inside, he saw a carrot sticking out of the padishah's arsehole, so he came out again and said, 'Uncle Ratty, he's blocked up his arse with a carrot.' The rat said, 'But that's what all my family eat, my parents, all my ancestors; give it to me, I'll eat it!' And the rat polished his teeth and finished off the carrot. Meanwhile the dung-beetle went inside again, and cleared out the padishah's insides, clean as a whistle. When the padishah awoke, he found his trousers dirtied once again; and again he told the people, 'Tonight's no good, tomorrow night we'll do the ceremony.'

But the next day, the padishah said, 'This musician with the three donkeys must have many trousers; two nights I've tried to have a wedding, and he's played this trick on me.' So he sent someone to fetch the musician, and gave him back his wife and put him on the throne for forty days.

And I came this way and they went that way.

14

Shrines, Sufis, Exorcism

Pilgrimage to Shrines

There are shrines (ziârat) – graves or buildings associated with martyrs and saints – in the graveyards and in the surrounding country, as well as at well-known spots along the trek to the mountains. Sar-e-pol town contains several, most prominently Emâm-e-Khord ('Little Saint') and Emâm-e-Kalân ('Big Saint'), the former being more important. Another much-visited shrine is Sayyâd-Bâbâ, twelve kilometres south-west of Sar-e-pol. Far the most potent in the area is a day's journey away in Mazâr-e-Sharif, the main city of northern Afghanistan; here is the shrine of the Prophet Mohammad's cousin and son-in-law Ali, known locally as Sakhi-Bâbâ, the object of international and local pilgrimage. At the New Year in March, there is a spring festival at the shrine, the climax of which is the famous ceremony of Jenda-Bâlâ, *raising the standard. There is a smaller standard-raising ceremony at the Emâm-e-Khord shrine in Sar-e-pol. (See Map E)*

Baya-khân enumerates the shrines known to the Piruzai, including those on the annual migration route.

(R) – In Konjek and Khârkash there are some shrines, martyrs' graves; some are well known, some not; people go and give prayers . . .

(Baya-khân) – Yes, there are some martyrs' graves in our graveyards – and also among the Baluch. The ones we have were Afghans; we know their names, but we don't know anything about them. One shrine we call Ziârat-e-Mullah-kâkâ.

(R) – Where's that?

(Baya-khân) – In the Khârkash graveyard. Women go there.

(R) – Not men?

(Baya-khân) – Mostly women.

(R) – When do they go?

(Baya-khân) – Whenever they have aches or pains, they visit such a shrine. In the Qoshtepa graveyard there's the shrine of Pakir-jân Âghâ.

(R) – The one behind the Wardaks?

(Baya-khân) – Yes, on that hill beyond the Wardak lands. If someone's killed for no reason by a stranger, we call him a martyr. Women visit such a martyr's grave.

(R) – Where, for example?

(Baya-khân) – Two years ago, three people were martyred in one night.

(R) – You mean those Baluches?

(*Baya-khân*) – Yes. The women go there. It's on the same hill. After the burial, the Seyyedâbâd Arabs say, for three nights they saw lights shining on the hill, like hurricane-lamps – they can see the graveyard from their houses. After all, they were innocents, real martyrs.

(*R*) – Who were they?

(*Baya-khân*) – Abdol-Hakim, his son – I don't know his name – and a servant called Majlun.

(*R*) – Are there other martyrs buried around here?

(*Baya-khân*) – One is buried in our graveyard: Samad's father Mullah Ebrâhim. He died long ago.

(*R*) – In the feud?

(*Baya-khân*) – Yes. People go there too. Women visit Mullah Ebrâhim's grave for backache; they take a little dust from by his head, and eat it. We call this dust *khorda*. But someone with smallpox pustules on his face – smallpox killed one of my brothers [*Sadr-e-Azam*], and many other people – or a child with chicken-pox, or a sheep with pustules under its tail or on its face, fetches dust from the grave of Shâhpari's son. If you scatter some of his dust among the sheep, or in the sheep's mouth, the sheep soon recover.

(*R*) – Shâhpari's son? Mir-Hamza's brother?

(*Baya-khân*) – Yes; her elder son Darwiza. He wasn't a martyr; he died of smallpox, eight or nine years ago. The reason I mentioned him is that ever since he was buried, people have found that the dust from his grave cures and prevents sheep-pox, like *khorda* dust from a shrine.

(*R*) – Are there other shrines in this graveyard?

(*Baya-khân*) – Another martyr, Lala Âghâ, who died last winter, is buried in our graveyard. When such an *âghâ* dies – someone who's read a lot of books and has many murids – his grave will become a shrine. People with ailments like backache go there to be cured. Then there's Khoja Shkâra-Bâbâ, on top of that hill opposite Nawakey. I've never seen it, but people say there's a shrine there; our women go.

(*R*) – Are there other martyr's shrines near the village?

(*Baya-khân*) – No. Except the Kamuzai who was killed in Neymadân last year, he's a martyr too.

(*R*) – Sâtu?

(*Baya-khân*) – Yes. Many people go there; didn't you see it?

(*R*) – I haven't seen his grave.

(*Baya-khân*) – Women also go on pilgrimage to Emâm-e-Khord and Emâm-e-Kalân in Sar-e-pol; to Sayyâd-Bâbâ; and to Sakhi-Bâbâ in Mazâr-e-Sharif. They also go to Seyyed Farrokh-shâh Âghâ's shrine, by the road. Then there's another *âghâ*, I can't remember his name, over in the Behsud graveyards; the women often go there. Wherever there's a shrine, women go; men too. Women also go to Cheshma-ye-shafâ ['*Healing-spring*']: you must have seen it.

(*R*) – Near Angut? I haven't seen the spring, but I know where it is.

(*Baya-khân*) – Just below Angut. It's a beautiful place; many people go there. There are lots of trees, and water emerges at the foot of the hill. People say that long ago this country belonged to kafir people, and when our Sâhebs and Pirs and Prophets were fighting with them, they realized that their numbers never decreased; however many they killed and wounded, every morning there they were, back again. It seems that whenever one of them was wounded, so long as he got to the spring and into the water in time, he'd be cured at once.

There are more martyrs' graves up at Mayda-Qâsem – you saw them last year on the trek.

(R) – Oh yes, the Shinwâris. What was their story? `

(Baya-khân) – They were traders, and a while ago they were going some place on trade. They climbed up to Mayda-Qâsem, where they were killed – was it Aymâqs or Hazâras who killed them? Being quite blameless, they were martyrs; their graves became a shrine. When their Kabuli kinsmen go there on pilgrimage, they spend two or three nights and have a big sacrificial feast. Other people go too.

When you get to the Kâshân and Balkhâb rivers, there's a mountain range in between; *mâldâr*s from Kandahar, from Band-e-Teymur, come that way. In there's the Peghola valley, and the shrine of Mir Seyyed-Ali Âghâ; many people go there on pilgrimage.

(R) – Was he a Hazâra?

(Baya-khân) – People say he was a Seyyed, a Sunni, but we don't know; he died long ago. It's supposed to be an excellent shrine, which cures many people. People go there for various ailments; some sacrifice a sheep or a chicken. There are some amazing walnut trees, so big that three of them would fill our yard. It's a lovely, fertile valley, with lots of orchards.

People who drown aren't martyrs; it's God's will, it's the water that killed them, after all, not other people. Some people drown, others die of fever; it's fate.

Nancy asks Baya-khân and Pâdshâh/Parwiz if women could be martyrs.

(Baya-khân) – It's certainly possible, but I've never heard of one.

(Pâdshâh/Parwiz) – If she's killed for no reason, for instance if she's shot or clubbed on the head, she'll be a martyr. But not if she dies by her own hand, or by drowning or falling off a horse.

(N) – Would people make pilgrimage to her grave?

(Baya-khân) – No, this never happens for a woman.

A pilgrimage to Mazâr-e-Sharif

Maryam tells how she and others took her Uzbek co-wife Sarwar on pilgrimage to Sakhi-Bâbâ in Mazâr-e-Sharif, to ask the shrine to help her get pregnant.

In spring, as the ewes were lambing, at the time when they raise the *jenda* standard at Sakhi-Bâbâ's shrine, we took my co-wife Sarwar there to ask God to give her a child. With us were my sons Kala-khân, Manân and Kayum, my son-in-law Lâljân, and my brother-in-law Dur-khân; no other men, but several other women: Bibiwor, Bibikuh, Saduzi, and Gol-Ahmad's wife Negâr. [*See Fig. 23*]

We went by truck. Sarwar was carsick; she really vomited. We stopped in a place called something like Biâbân – a nice big open space, where there were some tents and sheep. We laid her down in the open; she was prostrate, half-conscious; her stomach was all upset. There were many people passing by, trying to see, but we stood there and held our chadors over her like this, to hide her. She kept crying, 'What's wrong with me? I'm dying! I shouldn't have come.' But she recovered, so we went on to Âqcha, where we

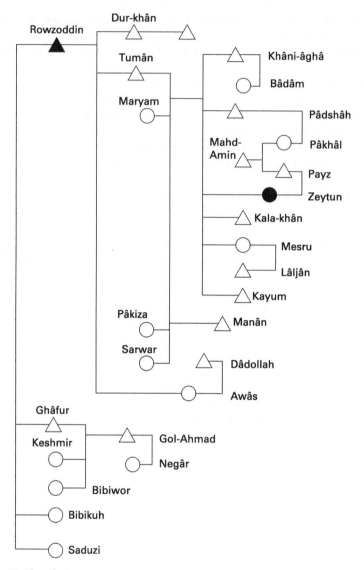

Figure 23 The pilgrims.

spent the night. In the morning she was better, so we got back in the truck, and eventually we arrived at Mazâr-e-Sharif, and did the pilgrimage at Sakhi-Bâbâ's shrine.[1]

We spent two days there. There was such an atmosphere, so many people, horses, cars, trucks; many women were singing. People were rushing about this way and that, all round the shrine. The lame were sitting there, the blind, people without arms, people with nothing, tiny but with long beards. One man had a huge head but a small bottom, and no arms or legs! Have you seen them, Baya-khân? In Sakhi-Bâbâ's garden?

---

[1] For another personal account of pilgrimage to the shrine, see R. Tapper (1986).

When I was there, other women came too; one was blind and lame, with a tiny baby. In one place a car had fallen off a bridge into the river. Another woman got down from a truck crying, 'What's that green stuff? Is it water?' She'd been blind, but even before she reached Sakhi-Bâbâ her eyes suddenly opened; she was so happy to see the water and the car that had crashed into it! People gathered around and explained things to her. She went on to Sakhi-Bâbâ and when she got inside, to the place of the blind and lame – you must have seen it, Nancy, when you went there – her eyes opened again and she could see. I saw it myself, Kayum here saw it, so did Bibiwor, Saduzi and Bibikuh.

When they cried out that the woman's eyes had opened, a huge crowd gathered; people snatched at her clothes and tore them to shreds, until she was sitting there naked! They found her some clothes and took her to a government office, where one of the khans, Ahmad-shâh Khân, gave her some nice clothes, a chador, a tunic, some old trousers, which she put on, and round her head they bound a pretty white scarf. They also gave her some nice spectacles and told her, 'Cover your face for several days, don't expose your eyes.' She came out again, people gathered round, they beat the drum, people shouted. God had restored the light to her eyes.

We got back in the truck and started the drive home. We stopped off in Balkh for a couple of days and visited Shamayel's castle[2] and Muslim Pâdshâh's palace. Have you seen them? They're still standing, in good condition. Shamayel's castle's painted red. Then we went on to another place with shops, then to Âqcha. The truck had a puncture, so we got down and paid someone to watch over our stuff; it was late and nobody was talking much. Finally we got back to Sheberghân, and it was there that Dur-khân's little son disappeared. Everyone rushed around calling his name, but they couldn't find him. He was lost! Dur-khân was nearly in tears.

All the women got down, but Negâr and another woman climbed into the cab, without saying a thing. Bibiwor and I laughed, saying 'Why are you sitting in the driver's place? What's the matter with you? Get down!' They didn't answer but hid themselves. It was night. Dur-khân was still rushing around crying, 'Oh God, my son's gone!' The boys were looking everywhere. In the end, after people had retired for the night, Lâljân and Dur-khân found the boy, way over at our shepherd Dastagir's place, and they brought him back. We cried and kissed him. The women's hearts were full, and we slept.

When morning came, we got the women together again and looked for the truck, but it had disappeared. There we all were, far from home, how could we get another truck? When the sun was high, we found our truck. We got back in and *hala–hala–hala* we came home. It was dark when we reached Shamshiri, Âghâ-Mahmad Khân's place – do you know it? People were asleep by the time we got to Hoseyn's house, Mahd-Amin's Hoseyn.

While we were there, all the women came to see Sarwar, Tumân's new bride. But she sat there crying and saying, 'It hurts, I'm dying, I'm going to lose the baby!' 'My God,' I said, 'Don't let her lose the baby! Hold on, help her!' So women came to help her and gave her medicine, made her some whey-and-ghee, and finally Sarwar went to sleep.

---

[2] See the tale of Jallât Khân and Shamayel in Chapter 10.

In the morning she was absolutely fine, so we put her on a donkey and came back to the village. We stopped off at my daughter Zeytun's – she was still alive then. I sat and had a long chat with Zeytun, while Sarwar went to Dâdollah's house, where they treated her well, fed her and served her tea, and she put on nice clothes. Eventually the boys brought donkeys and horses and we rode home.

All the women were so happy: 'You've been to Sakhi-Bâbâ, what have you brought us?' I'd brought nothing, just a couple of handfuls of sweets. Bâdâm, Pâkhâl, Pâkiza and all the children came, asking, 'Mum, what did you bring?' 'Nothing, just a little candy!'

Sarwar did not get pregnant, and shortly after this returned to her village in Chârkent.

Exorcism

Unlike some other Muslim societies where cults are devoted to the taming and celebration of possessing spirits (see Lewis 1989), Piruzai try to get jinns exorcized for good, as Pâdshâh explains.

A woman with a jinn should be taken to a good Sufi or a mullah like Haji Âghâ or Mayoddin-jân Âghâ. He should be strong; not all mullahs have power over jinns. When he's chanted over her, the jinn will possess her and start talking with the mullah. With everybody sitting there, the jinn can't stay silent, it'll talk through the woman's mouth; in Pashtu, or Persian if she's Persian-speaking.

The mullah tells the jinn to let the woman go; 'Why are you making her suffer? What has she done that you cause her such distress? Let her go or I'll beat you!' If the mullah's weak he won't have much success; the jinn will reply, 'No, you bastard, you're not man enough to exorcize me!' Then the mullah beats the woman with a whip or a switch; it doesn't hurt or harm her; she'll have a few bruises and marks, but the important thing is that it doesn't hurt. All that happens is that she's a little out of sorts, like someone who hasn't slept; she suffers no other harm.

Shrines and jinns

If a mullah can't cure a possessed woman, Darwiza says.

They'll take her to another mullah; if this one isn't strong enough either, they'll say, 'By God, we'll make a pilgrimage to Sayyâd-Bâbâ, and we'll offer a sacrifice there!' Then the jinn thinks, 'That's too much for me!' So they kill a calf, a chicken, whatever they can afford, and ask the shrine, 'Please get rid of this affliction.'

When you go to a shrine, you must do proper ablutions and your clothes must be clean, so that you can declare that you're pure enough for prayers. Without clean clothes, we don't pray. Five prayers a day are obligatory for us; if we miss them, our punishment in the next world will be heavy. You must go with a pure heart, with no bad thoughts. The shrine knows what's really in your heart, whether your heart is pure or impure.

Suppose I'm the *jinndi*: I go to the shrine and make a petition; what I say is known to God and the shrine; the shrine will talk to God: 'Dear God, this person came to me, trusting first in you and second in me, and now I'm petitioning you to take his affliction away. He's come so far and he's tired, come, let's release him.' Then God will cure me and I'll no longer be possessed. If you go to a shrine it's up to God to cure you. After you've been there and got cured, the shrine imprisons this jinn right there; it won't trouble you again. It's like, if someone commits a crime, robbery or murder, our king has him arrested and put in jail. He's a prisoner, he can't go anywhere, and he won't be freed while he's alive. But, like you or me, he has relatives; when they hear he's in jail, they'll bring him food.

Some people imprison the jinn by putting a knot in a piece of thread; when they pull it tight, the jinn's captured and can't move. My sister-in-law Bâdâm – God rest her – was possessed. Wherever we took her, it didn't work. Then she went to Seyyed Meskin Âghâ's place. He's still alive, they say he's 220 years old; he lives beyond Emâm-e-Kalân. There's a small garden there where the trucks pass, do you remember when we went there? He doesn't make amulets; he ties some camelhair thread and puts it inside a thing like an amulet – there's one on Lâl-Mahmad's neck, you must have seen it? When he chants a charm over it, the jinn disappears at once. Every year we give him money for this. He also said, 'Take her to Sayyâd-Bâbâ shrine, she'll get better.' After she went to Sayyâd-Bâbâ, the jinn couldn't do anything; sometimes it would seize her, but it didn't make her so tired, and it didn't hurt her children. [*But Bâdâm died two months ago, some say from jinn attack*]

Sufi pirs and *âghâs*

Many Piruzai say they are murids of Sufi pirs or âghâs, especially the Hazrats of Shur-Bâzâr ('Hazrat-seb') from the Mujaddidi family, Naqshbandi pirs based in Kabul. Others (including women) are followers of Qâderi pirs, notably the family of Shir-Âghâ Naqib Gailâni. Each pir or âghâ has a langar *– strictly speaking a lodge or base where he welcomes and feeds all-comers – but many, including the ones known to the Piruzai, travel widely round the country among their murids, teaching, conducting* halqa *(local term for zikr) ceremonies and other rites, and collecting dues; they are usually accompanied by one or more dervishes* (malang), *who often behave like professional mendicants.*

In late April 1971, a Sufi pir comes round the mâldâr *camps. Kala-khân later explains.*

He's a descendant of Hazrat-seb. We're all his murids. Without his permission, nobody can do anything, such as making amulets. He had a dervish with him, from Konâr, a murid of Shir Âghâ. When he went to Dur-khân's house, the dervish saw a nice coat that someone had just put down, and said, 'Give it to me!' Akhtar said, 'I can't, it's borrowed.' 'If you don't, you'll regret it!' Akhtar took fright and handed it over.

When he came to Khâni-âghâ's house, the dervish said to Bâdâm, 'Give me something.' She replied, 'I haven't got anything.' 'Look under your pillow, there's money there.' She lifted it up and there was a ten-rupee note, so she gave it to him. When I arrived, he clapped me on the shoulder and asked Akhtar, 'How's he related to you?' Akhtar replied, 'He's my brother's son.' He gave me an amulet and a little thread, then he came here to our house. My father gave him a ten-rupee note.

Then he went to Abdol's; Abdol wouldn't come out, so he said, 'Come on out, or you'll regret it!' Abdol refused, but he gave [*his son*] Sepâhi a two-rupee coin for the dervish. Then he put on the coat and announced, 'We're going to Haji Tabu's.' He took things by force, he was that sort of dervish. He went house-by-house, asking who was sick. If someone was jinn-possessed, he gave an amulet; for the sick he gave a charm or an amulet, asking God Almighty to cure them.

Mowlawi Golzâr does not have Piruzai murids in Konjek, but travels himself. Baya-khân explains.

Mowlawi used to associate with famous pirs, especially with Hazrat-seb, who was a very great *âghâ*, without equal in all of Afghanistan; he died some twenty years ago. The whole valley here were his murids; he was our pir. Some of our elders kissed his hand. Mahd-Amin and Mowlawi went to his place once. He came here on tour, but he went back again. His family never came, they're in Kandahar, where he had a great durbar. He fed the people; he had a huge *starkhân* (food-cloth) like a blanket; it took two people at each end to raise it; they'd cover it with food and put it before the people. He had many guests; his lodge was always busy and full of his murids. People brought camels and cows; someone gave him a car. There was no one like him in all Afghanistan.

One year, Hazrat-seb's grandson came to Mowlawi's place; there were many *halqas*. Alijân was here too – that place we went the other night, remember? The big old room on the west side; he hadn't yet built this other one. The room's very tall but Alijân could reach the roof-beams if he stretched up. He went into trance several times.

Shortly before we leave in September 1972, Nur-Alijân Âghâ, a Sufi pir of the Qâderi order, spends a few days in Konjek accompanied by his acolytes: a dervish and four murids. He conducts halqas *and exorcizes jinns in several private houses. Nancy witnesses several exorcisms, and I attend a number of* halqa.

One afternoon, before we know of the âghâ's arrival in the area, we drive a party of women, including Bâbak (Haji Ghâfur's daughter, wife of Shir, who is on military service) and Mahbuba (Haji Amir's daughter, wife of Shir's half-brother Kamaroddin), chaperoned by their cousin Pâdshâh, to the shrine of Sayyâd-Bâbâ. There, Mahbuba and Bâbak separately have possession fits.

Bâbak's exorcism

Back in the village, in Shir's house, Bâbak has another fit. Present are Bâbak's mother Bibiwor; Shir's mother Piruzat; Shir's brother Kolakhtiâr's wife Mabi; Shir's brother Nik (unmarried); Shir's sister Sawur (engaged to Darwiza); and Pâkhâl and Maryam, who describe the scene. (See Fig. 24)

(*Pâkhâl*) – Bibiwor spread out a blanket saying, 'I'll make this flour into dough.' Sawur wasn't there, she'd gone to Gol's house. Piruzat told Bibiwor, 'Don't make dough, we'll get Sawur to do it,' but she said, 'No, Bâbak's my daughter, I'll make the dough.' Bâbak came and said, 'Am I a new bride that you should make dough for me? Has my mother come to your house to do her daughter's work? Thank God I'm all right; but I won't do

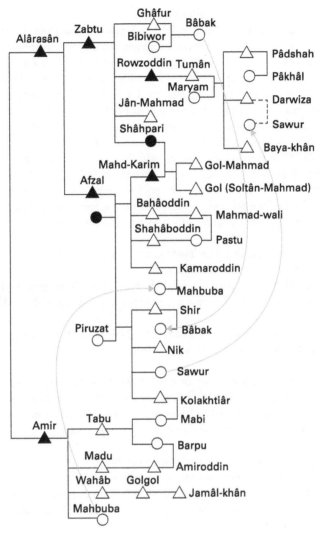

Figure 24 At Bâbak's exorcism.

it today, I'll do it tomorrow.' But Bibiwor got up, swept the place, spread the blanket and the flour cloth, got the water-skin and said, 'I'll go and get some water.'

(*Maryam*) – They were quarrelling.

(*Pâkhâl*) – Then Bâbak said, 'Don't you go, my brother-in-law Nik can get water.' Nik arrived and said, 'Sister-in-law, straighten the place up, the *âghâ's* coming.' She said, 'My mother's going to fill a water-skin, nobody else will do it.' He said, 'Why let your mother do it? I'll do it myself; I'll take a donkey right away.' Bâbak laughed and said, 'My mother's also making dough.' He said, 'Aunt Bibiwor, don't, I'll be upset if you do, and I swear I won't eat any of the bread.' So Bibiwor got up and sat aside. I told her, 'I'll do it for you.' Bâbak and the rest were sitting there as I said this.

(*Maryam*) – There was a competition.

(*Pâkhâl*) – Bâbak said, 'Don't you make dough, your daughter will cry; my brother-in-law will fill the water-skin, we'll make the dough.' Nik laughed, 'Aunt Bibiwor, are you going to make bread for me? Why? This is intolerable!' Suddenly Mabi said, 'Well, I'm not going to do it, why should I? I'm not your brother's wife, Bâbak is. If I got an amulet from the *âghâ*, you wouldn't pay him for me. We share the housework, but we don't share money and things; if you earn 200 rupees, I don't get a share of that. I'll do my own turn, but if Bâbak doesn't do her turn, I'll be damned if I'll do it for her. Anyone else who wants can do it, I don't care, I'm still not going to.'

At this, all the women laughed. Bâbak said, 'Now you're clearly shameless!' Mabi retorted, 'Am I shameless or are you? You laughed at me, saying I wasn't jinn-possessed; I was flat out here on the veranda, and you pricked me with a needle and jeered at me; and now you've become possessed yourself. Now you too may die. God's made you shameless, you've become a laughing-stock. Men and women gather around you: "Look how shameless she's become!"'

Bâbak said, 'It isn't like that, I can't help it, it's something God sent.'

Mabi replied, 'Mine too was sent by God.'

(*Maryam*) – Then Bâbak cried out, fell to the ground and thrashed around groaning; and Piruzat said, 'For God's sake come and hold her down!' I was frightened and didn't go near.

(*Pâkhâl*) – I looked at her today, and her hands were like this; she was completely blue. She couldn't talk, all her mouth was hurting.

The following afternoon, Bâbak has another fit and is judged 'very ill'. As Nur-Alijân Âghâ is around, Pâdshâh asks him to help. He conducts an exorcism, which seems to work. Neither of us is present, but Pâdshâh describes the event for us shortly afterwards, with Baya-khân, Seyyed-shâh/Golusar and Jamal-khân present.

(*N*) – Tell us what happened, from beginning to end!

(*Pâdshâh*) – I was watering the sheep, when Nik came for me: 'Please come, my sister-in-law Bâbak's in distress, there's nobody else from your family. God forbid, she may die. Times are bad; anyway you're her cousin.' So I went. She was indeed in a bad way, completely out of it.

(*R*) – She was unconscious?

(*Pâdshâh*) – She was so unconscious, Richard, she wasn't there! She wasn't breathing. You could just tell, something was just moving. Then suddenly she sat up, and she bit anything she could reach, like a dog. If you let go of her arm, she'd pull out her hair.

(*R*) – Who was with her?

(*Pâdshâh*) – Apart from me there were Mabi [*Kolakhtiâr's wife*], Barpu [*Amiroddin's wife*], Pastu [*Mahmad-Wali's wife*]. Her mother-in-law wasn't there, but then her mother Bibiwor arrived. At first I held her head myself firmly, like this. She was attacking us like a dog, biting and scratching, and she would try to hurt herself, wherever she could reach. After Bibiwor arrived, I held one side and Bibiwor the other, and sometimes Pastu helped.

(*N*) – Pastu's big, she can!

(*Pâdshâh*) – We were very upset; Bibiwor kept shrieking, 'My dear Bâbu, my dear Bâbu!' as though someone was dying. These jinns dislike such nonsense! I told her, 'Don't shout like that! She's not really sick; it's a jinn, it won't kill her; God willing, she'll recover. Once it lets go, she'll be a normal healthy human being again.' Then I rushed off, looking for a mullah, but none of them would do anything.

(*N*) – Which ones did you try?

(*Pâdshâh*) – For example, Haji Âghâ and his son. Mayoddin-jân wasn't around, and Mowlawi-seb wouldn't come out – he doesn't do these things. So I sent Jân-Mahmad to fetch you, thinking that – with Richard's permission – we'd drive her back to Sayyâd-Bâbâ.

After Jân-Mahmad left, Bâbak got worse, not better. Suddenly I thought, what about that Nur-Alijân Âghâ; he comes from a Sufi *tariqa* that's famous for dealing with jinns, amulets and such things; so I sent a boy to fetch him. He had no success, so I sent Shitty-pants Gol-Mahmad, but he's absolutely hopeless! He went and just sat and chatted, while Bâbak here was close to death. I went up onto Shir's big roof to watch for him, but there was no sign.

I jumped down behind the house, and rushed off to Rangin and Rishmin's place. As I arrived at Rangin's house I banged on the door, and Nur-Alijân came out. I got him to come. He asked, 'What sort of jinn is it? If it's heard my voice, throughout Sar-e-pol and Khârkash, how dare it turn up here? Hasn't it heard of me?' I said, 'Âghâ-seb, I don't know; the dead are in the hands of the living, we're blind, we're dead and can do nothing unless you cure her; you have the power [*shim*].' Then he said, 'By the power of God, the Saints and Sufi Pirs, if I don't manage to raise up cripples, don't call me my father's son!'

As he arrived many people gathered to greet him. The women grasped his hands and kissed them, and so did the men. We took him in, and we held Bâbak like this [*demonstrates*]; I held her here, her mother held her there, and Pastu there. As we held her, the *âghâ* sat here, with Bibiwor in the middle holding her, thus; she tried to pull her hair out, and her legs thrashed around, sometimes kicking people. It was quite a business!

The *âghâ* wrote three long amulets, on fresh paper, with Koranic verses on all three, each of them so long. He told me, 'I'll chant them over her; you stay, but don't let anyone else come in.' Then he gave me the three papers, saying, 'Light each of them, and waft the smoke over her like this,' and he indicated: near her nose. I took the papers and held them in one hand, and with the other – a boy struck a match behind me – I set light to them and held them by her nose until they went out. The mullah began to chant, and after some verses his other murids, who were sitting behind us, started up a zikr, so enthusiastically that all the women gathered in the room.

(*N*) – Did the women join in the zikr?

(*Pâdshâh*) – Some were crying, weeping, all were emotional.

(*R*) – They didn't lose consciousness?

(*Pâdshâh*) – Mabi did; his power sent her straight into a fit. The other women all cried a lot, but nobody else fainted that way. Several men did; Kheyru, for example, Âghâ-Mahmad Nurzai's son, fainted; and this other boy, Seyyed-Gholâm's son, he knows a lot of zikr *ahâl-o-hâl*, he does it very well; and the three or four murids, they too went over. As he chanted, they loosened their hair and shook it this way and that

– the *âghâ* too has very long hair. Two of the murids he brought with him were Omarzai; another was our Gol Âghâ; and another of his own murids – there were four altogether.

(R) – Was it a jinn, or God's spirit, that possessed them?

(*Pâdshâh*) – No; you see, the *âghâ* comes from a great Sufi *tariqa*, which is why people are easily drawn into ecstasy. He can do that because he's powerful, a pure man. With just an ordinary pir, mullah or dervish chanting, we'd feel nothing, we'd just sit there. But a powerful man like that can cause some people to fall unconscious into a fit.

He continued chanting, then he started beating Bâbak, on the side—

(N) – With his hand?

(*Pâdshâh*) – No, with a crop. He beat her repeatedly, like this, very hard. For some time the jinn didn't speak; then he blew on her like this [*demonstrates, knocking his son over*] – sorry, Pastuk! – then he chanted again several times, then again.

Finally he demanded, 'Why don't you speak? Are you happy now I'm burning you? I'll burn you so much, I'll set fire to seven generations of you! Why don't you come up? What's this poor woman done to you? Why've you possessed her, so that she nearly died?'

But the jinn still wouldn't speak. Once more he chanted, once more he beat her, and again he asked, 'Why don't you speak?' At last it spoke: 'What should I say? She's killed four of my children, what do you expect me to do? I won't let her live, I'll kill her!'

The *âghâ* said, 'You want to kill her? Don't you know who I am? Now you'll see what I'm going to do to you, how I'll burn you! I'll burn you so that nobody will even find your ashes. Why won't you let her alone? What's the matter with you, what's she done to you?'

The jinn repeated, 'She's killed four of my children, what do you expect?'

The third time he blew on her body, he said, 'Release her, now!' The jinn cried, 'By God, I'm sorry, I'm sorry, you've burned my wings, you've set me alight, release me and by God I'll release her! Enough, by God, I'm sorry, let me go and I'll let her go!'

The *âghâ* said, 'No, by God, I shan't release you until you swear me an oath. If I release you now, once I've left this house, when I'm not there, you'll seize her again. You must swear me an oath, by King Solomon's sandals and staff.' He forced it to swear by the Koran to leave Bâbak alone.

When he'd done this, it started talking to him just like I'm talking to you now. It said, 'I'll leave her alone, but not her children; even if she has babies for a hundred years, I won't leave them alone; whenever she has a son, I'll kill him; a month old, a week, twenty days, three months, a year, I'll kill him, because she's killed mine. She trod on our blanket and killed the children underneath; what did I do to her to deserve this? I came, Âghâ-seb, I was here and I saw this crazy woman' – it said – 'I gathered up my children and took them to another place; then I saw this woman coming there too, so I picked them up and came here; I moved them three times, trying to get out of her way. Finally, this woman was blundering about all over the place; and right here, she trod on them! How can I let her go? I won't let her go until I kill her.'

The *âghâ* said, 'Now won't you let her go?'

The jinn said, 'No-o-o-o-o,' stuttering just like that; it was afraid, it couldn't talk properly.

He said, 'I won't release you until you release the children too; what sin has a little child committed that you should kill it?' It replied, 'No, she's killed my children, I'll kill hers.'

The *âghâ* went on beating her hard with the crop, chanted over her, blew on her, and his murids, with bare heads, made a grand zikr, *hey-hâl-o-hu-o-hâ*, and crowds of women, children and men gathered to watch the show.

Finally he made the jinn swear; the jinn said, 'By God, I'm really sorry, I'm on fire, my wings are burned, by God I won't do this again, I'm sorry, I won't possess her!'

The *âghâ* said, 'No, you must swear four times.'

(N) – What was the oath like?

(Pâdshâh) – It was like, 'Do you swear by the sandals *(chawât)* of King Solomon the Prophet that you won't possess her?' It answered, 'Yes!' 'Swear again, by the staff [*lakare*] of King Solomon the Prophet, that you won't possess her!' And it answered, 'I swear by that too!' Then he said two more: 'By the Holy Koran,' and once again it swore by the Koran that it wouldn't seize her again. The end!

King Solomon lived a long time ago; he had great spiritual power, and so did his sandals and his staff – you know, what old folks use for getting about.

When it had sworn the oaths, he asked, 'What animal do you want, to compensate for your children that she killed?' It said, 'A lamb or a sheep, but it must be pitch black, like this chador, with not even a pin-head's-worth of white, yellow, or any other colour. Let her kill such an animal; all I want is the blood; she can distribute the meat.'

When he'd finished, the *âghâ* told Bâbak, 'Sit up, woman!' She came round at once, and sat up just like you are. He asked, 'What do you want to eat?' She said, 'Nothing.' Âghâ-seb said, 'You're very tired.' 'Now,' she said, 'I know what's happening; before, I didn't; now I feel as though I've been chopped up with an axe. My whole body hurts. I'll eat something later.' 'No,' said the *âghâ*, 'You must eat something, my daughter, or you'll go to sleep hungry.' Then he took a small piece of melon, put it in his mouth like this, then gave it to Bâbak.

When she'd eaten that, he told her to recite the profession of faith. She did so three times, and he spat three times on her left shoulder, then let her go. She sat there; the *âghâ* sat here, I sat here, and other people were sitting behind us. They brought some bread, cut open a fresh melon for the *âghâ*, and he and the murids ate the lot; and they had some tea. Then the *âghâ* rested there, while the party broke up and everybody left.

He talked with Bâbak; he prepared some wild rue – you know, what we throw on the fire – gave her half-a-dozen amulets, told her where on her body to put each one, and what colour to wear them with, red, white or green, with full instructions. After he wrote each amulet, he spat in her mouth three times, then chanted over the rue and gave it to her, saying, 'That jinn's a kafir, not a Muslim; one day, you can't tell when, it may come back; it won't possess you, but if you're feeling out of sorts, put some of this on the fire and take a whiff of it. Don't go into this room any more; store small things like grain here, but don't come in yourself, and use another room for your clothes.' The jinn had said, 'Unless you keep her out of this room, I'll really do her in. There was an old bread-oven underneath; my children were there when she trampled and killed them. If you keep her out, I've sworn to leave her and her children alone. But if she comes back here to sleep, sit or work, I won't let her go.' In the morning she took all her stuff into the room next door.

The *âghâ* agreed to keep her out, when he got the jinn to swear the oaths. He didn't ask it, 'If I get her out, can other people come into the room?' And the jinn didn't mention anybody else, it only said, 'Take her out, she's killed my children.' It wouldn't possess anyone else without cause; only someone who'd hit or injured it. Jinns have a rule that they can't possess anyone without cause.

The jinn said, 'I didn't come out before, only after she'd trodden on my children. I had no other problem with her. I was in her but I only attacked her children. Whenever she gave birth, after some time I'd kill the child. But now she's been to Sayyâd-Bâbâ: Sayyâd-Bâbâ's powerful, and I was like a thief.' The shrine exposed the jinn. Previously, Bâbak wasn't known to have a jinn, but all her babies died. Everybody discussed it, women and men, and we realized it was a jinn.

(N) – Yesterday at the shrine, did you know the jinn would rise like this afterwards? Did it speak when you were there?

(Pâdshâh) – No. After you'd left the shrine, I tried hard to get it to speak. I asked: 'What do you want? Why are you causing this pain? What offering do you want, so that we can give it to you!' But it didn't say a word, only made odd noises. Whatever I said, it didn't say anything that I could understand. But even if I couldn't understand what it wanted, when we came back in the car I realized that she was distracted [*bi-churt*] – didn't you notice too? Unlike the other women, she was distracted.

(N) – What do you mean by 'distracted'?

(Pâdshâh) – I mean she was very upset; she was clearly in pain, moving around all over the car. These jinns cause such trouble. May God keep it from us, but sometimes I get like that in the middle of the night. Your body aches, you tremble; your eyes go funny, like the eyes of these murids as they do the zikr; and their mouths are crooked.

(N) – Was she like that today?

(Pâdshâh) – Yes. Her mouth was like this, her tongue was blue and hung right out; we had to stop her biting it off. There's no illness in the world as bad as what jinns cause!

(N) – Didn't Bâbak go to Sayyâd-Bâbâ and Mazâr-e-Sharif last year? I took her myself.

(Pâdshâh) – So you did. But when you took her, she wasn't possessed, was she? Did you notice?

(N) – No, and I didn't hear anything about it.

(Pâdshâh) – Well, she wasn't. Bibiwor said so today; so did Bâbak's mother-in-law Piruzat and all the women. Now, one woman will go to a shrine sincerely, that means with faith, without bad thoughts or feelings in her heart. But another woman will declare, 'Nancy, I'm ill, I'm in pain; take me to the shrine at Mazâr-e-Sharif!' but she's not really in pain, she's going just for fun, an outing. People said that, until now, whenever Bâbak went to shrines such as Emâm-e-Khord or Sayyâd or Mazâr, it was for fun, not because of a jinn. But this time, when she left home, she knew it was serious. This time her faith was pure, and the shrine exposed her jinn. If she'd told you she was going on pilgrimage, while she was really just going for the ride, without pure intentions, then nothing would have happened. But if someone does that, neither shrine nor *âghâ* like it.

(N) – Will Bâbak's jinn return? Has it been killed, or what?

(Pâdshâh) – No. It can't be killed, but it can be badly hurt: its wings got burned, it said so. You can't tell what's going to happen. If there's a powerful mullah or Sufi around, it'll be scared to come out. After being released, she may – by God's will – tread on it or its children again, or on some other jinn – there are so many of them on this earth – or the same jinn in a different place. But if it's God's will, the jinn may never return.

(N) – If the jinn realizes later that the *âghâ's* gone, won't it come out again?

(Pâdshâh) – No. It's scared of the amulet the *âghâ* gave her, of the oath and Koranic verses he wrote on it. That's why he leaves the amulet, to frighten the jinn so that it won't come again; if it does come near, it'll burn, like someone who falls into the fire.

I told Nik, Bibiwor and Piruzat, 'This was a serious matter, your Bâbak might have died. You must keep this *âghâ* here tonight. Here's 100 rupees: go and buy a chicken, a half-kilo of ghee, a half-seer of flour; cook a meal, feed him and his murids, so that his work takes effect properly, and the jinn disappears. You must keep the *âghâ* happy.' They already had some ghee, so I bought them a small chicken for 35 rupees and killed it, skinned and cleaned it.

Then along came Haji Âghâ's son, with the message, 'This must be our party. This very *âghâ* was my mate for two years on military service; so we'll be very upset if you don't let us entertain him.' Haji Âghâ's a very good man. We fixed it with him, saying, 'If you've come to fetch him, that's fine with us, our two houses are one.' We told the *âghâ*, 'Come back tomorrow, and we'll cook the food here then.' So he accepted Haji Âghâ's invitation for that evening.

The rue's for whenever she feels a little down, as sometimes happens; then she should burn some and waft the smoke by her nose, like this; it smells good. Rue's an excellent thing. Every family keeps some, just in case. But nobody anticipated nor imagined that such an *âghâ* would come for Bâbak that day; and nobody knew what he intended to do or ask for; how could they?

They'll sacrifice the animal tomorrow, I think; it's Friday. We gave them a nice lamb. They'll gather round and pray over it. The *âghâ* permits you or me to slaughter it, or he gets one of his murids to do it. It's not his business; once he's given permission, it doesn't matter who kills it.

A woman with jinns knows which [*langar*] lodge she's in. Bâbak's in Nur-Alijân Âghâ's *langar*. She'll never go to a different *âghâ*. Wherever she is, if (God forbid) a jinn possesses her – not this one, it's sworn not to, but another one – if she treads on its children, she'll have to return to this *âghâ*, or get him to come.

Other women are already followers of Haji Âghâ or Mayoddin-jân or some other *âghâ* – there are many such dervishes and Sufis, and they all say they're better than each other. Such a woman won't come to Nur-Alijân Âghâ; she's afraid, 'The jinn will kill my children or cause me harm; I belong to Haji Âghâ's *langar*. If they have a power struggle, I'll be caught in the middle and killed, or my child will.' Jinns really hate it if someone jumps into another *âghâ's langar*.

All the shrines – and they are many; God bless them all – have *langars* too. When the jinn possesses her in the shrine, you ask, 'Speak, what do you want for an offering?' If the shrine's powerful, like this *âghâ*, it'll raise the jinn into her mouth, and it'll ask for a grey sheep, or a black or brown one, or a cow, a calf or a camel: 'Kill it, and I'll release her.' That's what the shrines can do: expose the jinns. Of course the shrine's just a building, it doesn't speak itself. But if you ask the jinn inside the shrine, it'll speak and say what it wants.

Yesterday in the shrine, Sherang's jinn talked too; it also said, 'You've killed my child, you've trampled our quilt!' She cried a lot, you remember? The jinn didn't ask for anything. But she's in Mayoddin-jân's *langar*; she won't come to this *âghâ*. Neshtar wanted to bring her, but she wouldn't come: 'The jinn'll kill me if I go.' If she went to another *âghâ*, her jinn would seize her that very day, knock her over, hurt her a lot. If the power of two *âghâs* comes together in one place, the jinn's power is mightily increased, and it could well kill the victim. If she hadn't been in Mayoddin-jân's *langar*, this *âghâ* could have released her today.

Mayoddin-jân Âghâ is strong, and he could free her; but he wouldn't, for the sake of his children and his brothers; Sherang didn't know this, nor did Neshtar. If someone says, 'I'm an *âghâ*, a pir, I can do such things,' who knows if he can or not? First God knows, secondly he knows himself in his heart, but nobody else does, even someone in his *langar*.

In this village, and in Sar-e-pol district, a hundred women have put themselves in Nur-Alijân Âghâ's *langar*. He's their pir, they're his murids. It doesn't matter if they compete for his attention. He's like a shrine; he's only one, but even if there are ten thousand women, or ten thousand men, there's enough of him for all. Once his prayer's left his mouth, it'll reach them all. 'If you're all in my *langar*, and I've prayed over your bodies, released you all from jinns, the same goes for all.' Whatever prayers or verses came from the Koran, sent by God, it's all one. Nancy can't say, 'I'm best of all, I came first.' Nor can Hâshem say, 'I got left until last, there's nothing left for me.' No, it's the same for everyone.

Each woman in his *langar* does her own offerings, in her own time. They don't all get together at once. Whatever the jinn's asked you to kill, you must do that every year on the same day, as long as you live. Even if you've got nothing for dinner, or you have to pawn something, sell your clothes or other things, you must kill whatever animal the jinn demanded, to fulfil your obligation to it. It's up to you to kill it every year, whether chicken, cow, camel, sheep or goat.

A jinn's children are tiny, according to the Book; if you tread on one, it's so thin, it'll die. The close relatives will take revenge. Anybody would do the same, for a son, sister, husband, father. Bâbak's jinn stopped her entering that room because she'd killed its children there. It won't matter if she just comes in to fetch something, but she won't sleep there. Of course, the jinn would be happy if she did, because it'd be able to possess her again. It's scared of this *âghâ*, but it won't ever forget its children. If you kill someone's child, they'll always try to kill you, if they get a chance.

Bâbak's jinn has no grudge against any other woman, unless she came into that room and trod on its children; then it'd possess her too. Otherwise, it'll leave her alone. If you go somewhere, and say *bismillah* three times, any jinn will get out of the way; it burns the jinn.

Almost all possessions are of women; when women have fits, the criterion men (and some women) use to judge whether they are genuine or faked is not the skill of the 'performance' (which we used) but the social circumstances of the victim: are they likely to be possessed?

This emerges in conversation with Pâdshâh, Seyyed-shâh/Golusar and Jamâl-khân

(N) – Nanawor [*Habib's wife*] too has a jinn, which *langar* is she in?

(*Seyyed-shâh*) – Her jinn isn't serious.

(*Pâdshâh*) – Some women, Nancy—

(N) – Not serious?!

(*Jamâl-khân*) – But it really abuses her, throttles her, makes her unconscious.

(N) – Does it talk?

(*Jamâl-khân*) – No, it doesn't. If it talked it'd just be swearing.

(*Pâdshâh*) – Let me tell you straight. Most women don't have jinns. She's just trying to attract her husband's attention. She's pretending, putting on a show: 'I'm possessed! Take me to the shrine! Take me by car, or in a *godi* [*taxi-cart*]! Take me to Emâm-e-Kalân, Emâm-e-Khord, Sayyâd-Bâbâ, Mazâr-e-Sharif!' She wants to endear herself to her husband. But it isn't a jinn, she's just faking it. A real jinn was this one today.

(N) – Of course women know that some are faking; don't men know? I imagine, if I told Richard I was possessed, he'd tell me to get lost!

(*Pâdshâh*) – If you were to tell Richard, 'I have a jinn, take me to the shrine,' and you acted like a jinn, making all the right noises in front of him ... of course you don't have a jinn and you're already dear to Richard! But if the rest of us told him to take you, Richard would be disturbed. 'If everyone says it,' he'd say, 'perhaps these women are right.'

(N) – What about Negâr? Her husband Gol-Ahmad doesn't love her: her jinn must be a real one?

(*Pâdshâh*) – Yes, it is; it possesses her children, not herself. She's in Haji Âghâ's *langar*. Her jinn doesn't throttle her like Bâbak's, but it won't leave her children alone.

Mahbuba/Khurey's exorcism

The morning after Bâbak's exorcism, Nur-Alijân Âghâ conducts several more, followed by a halqa *zikr in Pâr-khân's house. In the afternoon he does another exorcism, of Khurey (aka Mahbuba), Haji Amir's daughter, wife of Shir's half-brother Kamaroddin. Nancy records most of the dialogue between the* âghâ *and the possessing jinn. Later the same day Kala-khân listens to the tape, translates the dialogue into Persian for us and explains what's happening – which is very close to Pâdshâh's earlier narrative of Bâbak's exorcism.*

It takes place in a room in Shir's house. Apart from the protagonists and the âghâ's *dervish companion, four accompanying murids, and the local dervish Gol Âghâ, five female and two male close relatives of Khurey are present. The session begins with a complex ensemble: while the* âghâ's *dervish leads a* halqa *of the murids, chanting the shahâda profession of faith, the* âghâ *himself chants Koranic verses loudly and rapidly over Khurey, in order to 'burn' and 'raise' the jinn. She has meanwhile quickly fallen into trance; she is lying down, tossing around, but with stiff, taut arms. The* âghâ *repeatedly pauses to blow on her, commanding the jinn to utter the shahada, known locally as* kelima, *the 'word'. Occasionally Gol Âghâ chimes in with some Pashtu religious verses. After about a minute, the spirit 'rises', singing out in Pashtu, 'God you are One (Allah yaw-ye)!' In this case (it later emerges) there are ten possessing jinn, nine Muslim but one kafir; it seems it is the latter that speaks, in a quavering voice. The* halqa *quickens pace and the chant becomes just 'Allah, Allah!' The jinn echoes this, alternating with hesitant repetitions of the shahada. After another few minutes, while the* halqa *and Gol Âghâ continue in the background, the* âghâ *initiates the dialogue. At first the jinn doesn't respond, chanting nonsense. Then . . .*

We'll do a sacrifice for you; what do you want? Show me what sacrifice you want, and stop troubling Khurey.

(*Jinn*) – Kill a black ram.

(*Âghâ*) – Good. Every year I'll give you a black ram. You won't oppress her?

(*Jinn*) – I won't, I won't!

(*Âghâ*) – I'll give it to you myself, if Khurey doesn't.

(*Jinn*) – Allah, let me go!

(*Âghâ*) – I'll slaughter it myself; leave Khurey alone! She's my sister, don't bother her.

(*Jinn*) – If you do it, I'll be your servant. [*sings: Allah yaw-ye, Allah yaw-ye!*]

(*Âghâ*) – This is my word, I'll give you my hand. I promise I'll give it to you every year, whether or not she does. Now say the oath with me. I'll give you a black sheep. Say the *kelima*: *La ilaha ila-ellah, Mohammad arrasul-allah.*

(*Jinn*) – I can't do it . . . [*tries singing it out*]

(*Âghâ*) – Say it properly for me! Say it, say it! She's my sister, I'll give you a sheep, say it!

(*Jinn*) – *La ilaha ila-ellah, Mohammad arrasul-allah.*

(*Âghâ*) – Say, 'By Shâh Soleymân . . .'

(*Jinn*) – *La ilaha ila-ellah, Mohammad arrasul-allah.*

(*Âghâ*) – Say, 'By Shâh Soleymân, I swear I've no grudge against her children.' [*Repeats this several times, insisting that the jinn recite the oath after him, phrase by phrase; which it eventually does, though the first time it doesn't come out right*]

(*Jinn*) – By Shâh Soleymân the prophet, by his sandals, the jinns' oath, I won't oppress Khurey or her children any more. I'm your slave, leave me alone! Once you've gone, I'll seize her again.

(*Âghâ*) – No, no, that won't do, I won't let you get away with it. Don't you recognize me? All the jinn know me, seven generations of jinn, all of them oath-bound to me and my ancestors; I won't let you go, you're oath-bound to me; why should I let you go?

(*Jinn*) [*voice constricted and quavering, but loud*] – For sure, your family is powerful! There's no doubt you're a strong Muslim, a friend of religion. Don't forget my animal. You'll forget to give it to me.

(*Âghâ*) – I won't forget it, don't worry. A man with a sister never forgets her, so don't worry. I won't forget you, don't worry. If God asks me, I've done it. Don't move, don't talk, don't throw yourself about. I've released many other jinn-possessed women. You help me too. Now recite the words once more: by Shâh Soleymân—

(*Jinn*) – Go and release those other women.

(*Âghâ*) – Okay. Now repeat it after me: 'By Shâh Soleymân the prophet, and by his sandals, the jinns' oath, I won't possess Khurey, her children, or her arms, again.'

(*Jinn*) – He's a pure prophet, and you've freed me.

(*Âghâ*) – Repeat it, all of it. 'By Shâh Soleymân, the prophet's seal, the jinns' oath, I swear I'll no longer trouble Khurey, or her arms.' By the four Books. When you've sworn the oath, I've said I'll give you a black sheep, after I let you go. I'll kill it for you. Do you doubt my word? Why don't you say it? Look at me; I'm stronger than you!

(*Jinn*) – You're stronger than anyone in the world.

(*Âghâ*) – Say the words.

(*Jinn*) – You're a religious man.

(*Âghâ*) – You know the world of jinn.

(*Jinn*) – For sure, for sure, for sure, for sure!

(*Âghâ*) – Well, don't you know my father and grandfather?

(*Jinn*) – If you trample my eyes, I shan't complain!

(*Âghâ*) – By Shâh Soleymân; the prophet; by his throne; the jinns' oath; all ten of us swear; no more to hurt Khurey; or her children. By Haji Bâbâ's shrine, it's the same for all of us.'

[*The jinn repeats the oath quietly after him, phrase by phrase*]

(*Âghâ*) – Good! *Bismillahirrahmanirrahim! La ilaha ila-ellah, Mohammad arrasul-allah.*

(*Jinn*) – [*repeats three times after him*] *La ilaha ila-ellah Mohammad arrasul-allah.*

(*Âghâ*) – So, don't trouble her any more. I'm a Muslim, I don't break my word.

(*Âghâ*) – [*starts talking to Khurey*] – Khurey, get up and shake your skirt three times. Then sit down and I'll give you an amulet. Go, out this way.

[*The âghâ then chants a brief, rapid Arabic do'a. The halqa comes to a close, and normal conversation resumes.*]

Before he left, Nur-Alijân Âghâ agreed to be interviewed on tape; unlike most of our other recordings, there was a large audience, all devotees, so R confined his questions to formal and obvious topics.

My name is Nur-Alijân Âghâ, son of Abdollah-jân Âghâ, son of Haji Lâljân Âghâ; from the province of Maymana, the district of Dawlatâbâd.

(*R*) – And your *qawm* is Mahmudkheyl?

(*Âghâ*) – Mahmudkheyl.

(*R*) – Good; so when and how did you enter the Qâderi *tariqa*?

(*Âghâ*) – Long ago.

(*R*) – From your father? When you were a child?

(*Âghâ*) – Yes, from my father. The father of Haji Lâljân Âghâ was Khalifa Moshk Sâhib, then Khalifa Khân-Mahmad Sâhib, then Lâl-Pakir Atâ-Mahmad Sâhib from Band-e-Teymur; originally from Kandahar.

(*R*) – Are there others in Maymana from the Qâderiyya *tariqa*?

(*Âghâ*) – Our lineage [*awlâd*] is four houses; and one family of murids. Mahmudkheyl is a large *qawm*.

(*R*) – Are they all your murids?

(*Âghâ*) – Yes.

(R) – Are there other *tariqas* in those parts, like Sohrawardiyya?

(Âghâ) – No, there are no Sohrawardiyya or Chustiyya, only the other side of Kabul, over towards Pakistan. But there are Naqshbandi.

(R) – Are there more Qâderiyya, or Naqshbandi? Who is more powerful?

(Âghâ) – Qâderiyya. Shir Âghâ and Naqib-seb are Qâderi; Shir Âghâ in Kabul, son of Pir Seyyed Hasan Âghâ; they are the lineage of Pirânapir-seb of Baghdad.

(R) – Now the zikr that you do, are there different kinds, or only one?

(Âghâ) – There are different kinds; the names of God, e.g. *La ilaha ila-allah*; also *Allah*; *Allahu*; *ilellah*; there are many *sabaqa*.

(R) – Did you learn the *sabaqa* from your father, or from someone else?

(Âghâ) – From my father, and he from his father, and so on, from Lâl-Pakir Atâ-Mahmad Seb, who got them from Pirânapir-seb; Shir Âghâ and the rest, they're all together.

(R) – And do you yourself take some people as *khalifa*?

(Âghâ) – Yes, I take murids and among them I choose *khalifas*, give them certificates [*reshâd*], then I send them to other places and they too get murids.

(R) – Have you taken many *khalifas*? Or only a few?

(Âghâ) – I have numerous *khalifas*, all over. I've given them all certificates: in Farah province, near Bakwa and Gereshk; in Qala-ye-Naw, Herat, Maymana, Qataghan, Sar-e-pol, and over towards Ganda and Aqsay, Khoja-Yegâna.

(R) – And do you sometimes go to Kandahar?

(Âghâ) – Yes.

(R) – Is your pir there, or in your own house?

(Âghâ) – My pir is my own ancestors. They are dead and buried in the lodge. My grandfather's buried in Shur-Daryâ; my father in Farah, but great-grandfather's buried in Sharbati in Bakwa, others in Nawzâd in Gereshk, in Qala-ye-Sarang where there's a shrine. The rest, like Lâl-Pakir Atâ-Mahmad, are in Band-e-Teymur. Band-e-Teymur is beyond Gereshk, when you stop at Khâk-e-Chopân.

(R) – When you meet somebody, for example staying in the same place, and you find you're both from Qâderiyya, do you greet each other?

(Âghâ) – Yes; we respect each other.

(R) – What is the meaning of the word *tariqa*?

(Âghâ) – It means a road, a smooth road. It's Arabic, it comes from Sheykh Abdol-Qâder Jilâni [*Gailâni*], the *tariqa* of Pirânapir-seb. Qâderiyya comes from his name, Sheykh Abdol-Qâder. He's the original great *khalifa*, Pir-e-Baghdâdi, from Baghdad. Have you been to Baghdad?

(R) – Yes, but I didn't see much; it was very hot!

Later, Baya-khân, Jamâl-khân talk about those who joined the langars *of different* âghâs.

(Jamâl-khân) – Some time ago Wazir went to Maymana. God didn't give him any children, so he became murid to Nur-Alijân Âghâ, and his wife entered the *langar* too. They both entered the *langar*; he tied both ends of her chador; then God gave her two children. So Wazir gave him 2,000 rupees and bought him a nice teapot worth 200 rupees; last year he gave a set of women's clothes.

(*Baya-khân*) – People give all sorts of things: guns, camels, horses worth 10,000 to 20,000 rupees.

(*Jamâl-khân*) – Uncle Zarghun's wife too didn't produce any children, so he put her in Haji Âghâ's *langar*, and each year they give him a sheep. Now God's given her a daughter.

(*R*) – If a woman's in an *âghâ*'s *langar*, what does she do? Do women do zikr?

(*Jamâl-khân*) – No, she won't do zikr; he'll make amulets for her.

(*Baya-khân*) – She'll tell him, 'I throw myself at your feet!' and he'll make her an amulet and tie it at her collar with black thread.

(*Jamâl-khân*) – He ties the two chador-ends, reads from the Book. For Zarghun's wife he made two amulets, one for morning, one for noon; one she ate, one she burned for the smoke, one was at her collar, one on her back; as a result, God gave her a child.

(*R*) – How long ago did she become a murid?

(*Jamâl-khân*) – Two years ago.

(*Baya-khân*) – If you're a murid, you're supposed not to steal and so on, because the sin is much greater. If you're going to steal, it's much better not to be a murid!

(*R*) – What about people who work with government, can they be murids?

(*Baya-khân*) – They too can be murids, if they want; some don't. Most people can't keep it up.

(*Jamâl-khân*) – Most murids still rob and steal, take other people's money. That's not being a proper murid; God will punish them.

The Tale of Seyf-ol-moluk and Badri-jamâl

Baya-khân tells this well-known Arabian Nights tale.[3]

Once upon a time, long ago, there was a padishah, and he had a vizier. Neither vizier nor padishah had a son. They would ask visiting dervishes for help and advice, but to no avail.

Then one day a dervish came and stood at the padishah's gate, begging for food. A maidservant came out and gave him some flour, but when she'd done so, she knocked it out of his hand and slapped him on the head crying, 'A curse on all you dervishes!'

'Sister, what's the matter?' the dervish asked. The maidservant said, 'Bibi' – she meant the queen – 'Bibi told me to slap any dervish who called. "So many dervishes come round every day and get flour from us, yet they never give me an amulet nor chant a charm to ask God to give me a son."'

The dervish told her, 'If that's so, ask Bibi to come here.' When the queen arrived, he told her, 'Take this stick of mine, throw it into that tree, and see how many apples fall; give one to the vizier's wife, eat another yourself, and give the third to the padishah. If only one falls, cut it into three; if three fall, that's one each; if more than three fall, share the extras among you.'

When the dervish had gone, the maidservant threw the stick into the tree, and three apples fell to the ground. The vizier's wife ate one, the padishah ate the second, and the queen ate the third.

---

[3] See Shackle (2007), 'Manal' (2016).

Nine months later, while the padishah and the vizier were out hunting, God bestowed sons on both of them. The people were so happy that the padishah and his vizier now had sons, after such a long time. They fired their guns in the air, and on the padishah's return home they rushed to meet him, to get the reward – when you go to the padishah and give him the good news, 'Your son's been born! Give me my reward!' the padishah will be so happy – it's a son after all – that he'll give you something as a *zirey*, some money for example.

It so happened that a poor old man was the first to tell the padishah the news, so he claimed his reward from both him and the vizier. They were both delighted and gave the old man lots of money, clothes and other things, which made him very happy too.

When the padishah got home, he named his son Seyf-ol-moluk, while the vizier named his son Saad-moluk. The boys grew, and when they were old enough the padishah said to the vizier, 'Let's put them into school; let them learn their lessons.'

The padishah gave orders for a large cellar to be dug underground, with a beamed roof and a covered entrance. They put the boys inside, and gave them water, food and clothes. They stayed there night and day, seeing nobody except a mullah who came to give them their lessons, with the help of a hurricane-lamp. When the mullah came and went, the door was locked behind him. He'd come and teach them from morning to noon; then he went to fetch the boys their food and water, and then, after some more lessons, he left them again for the night.

Time passed, and Seyf-ol-moluk grew up into a nice-looking young man. Now there was a *pari* called Badri-jamâl. One night she saw Seyf-ol-moluk in a dream, and fell in love with him. When she awoke, she turned into a dove – in those days, all the *paris* would turn themselves into doves in order to get about – and flew around until, spotting the cellar down below, she alighted on top of it and started picking at the earth with her feet until she'd made a hole through into the cellar. She looked through and saw Seyf-ol-moluk and Saad-moluk.

She looked, but she did nothing. The sun came overhead and shone in through the hole she had made, casting a beam onto the floor inside, like a torch. The boys were amazed at this light; they wondered what it was; it must be a flower – and each claimed the flower as his own. They started fighting; they fought bitterly until the sun had moved on and the beam disappeared, at which point each accused the other of hiding his flower. They went on hitting each other until both were covered in blood, though Seyf-ol-moluk proved stronger and beat Saad-moluk really rather badly.

When the mullah got back, he saw what had happened: 'Boys, what silliness is this? What are you fighting about? What could have come between you? Was it a plot of land or something? You've had your lunch, you should've been relaxing and talking happily together.' Saad-moluk said, 'Seyf-ol-moluk hid my flower and wouldn't give it back', and Seyf-ol-moluk said, 'Saad-moluk took my flower and kept it from me.' They were talking about the sunbeam, but of course the sun had gone and it was no longer there.

The mullah said, 'Why did the padishah lock you in here? You should get out and see the country, the sunlight, people, farms, summer and winter crops, all the blessings of God; they all belong to you, yet you know nothing of them, or of what's happening out there in the world. There's buzkashi, fun and games; and you're shut in here, complaining about a hidden flower! You should get out into the light, there's so much going on out there!'

So they told the mullah, 'Go and ask the padishah to let us out, otherwise we'll break the door down ourselves. Why did he shut us in like this, in the dark? We too are Muslims, why did he do this to us? We assumed that everybody lived like us; how could we know otherwise if he shut us in? You can go around outside in the sun just as you like, while we're stuck in this room all day long. By God, if he doesn't let us out we'll cut ourselves in two with a sword! We'll stay here tonight, but if he doesn't let us out in the morning we'll either break the door down or cut our heads open. We don't want this life any more.'

The mullah went and greeted the padishah: 'Sir, you must do something about the boys; today a sunbeam fell on them, and they thought it was a flower and each claimed it as his own, and they beat each other up over it. Now that they've heard about the world outside, you can't hold them back.'

The padishah said, 'Mullah, tomorrow morning I'll go and let them out.' And with musicians playing and guns firing, he came and released the boys, and they had a great party.

The boys were soon grown up, and they'd spend their days out hunting, not coming home until evening. That was their sole occupation. Each day they might shoot an antelope or a pigeon or a duck, and they'd bring it home in the evening.

One day, Seyf-ol-moluk had a dream in which he saw a beautiful woman – it was Badri-jamâl – and he fell passionately in love with her. From then on, he fell daily deeper into melancholy, and nobody could lift him out of it because he was in love.

Then one day when they were out hunting he saw a domed roof, and on it a pretty dove. It was Badri-jamâl; he really liked the look of the dove, though of course he didn't recognize her. The dove threw down a little box of kohl, which you put in your eyes; remember, she was in love with him too. He saw what it was and applied the kohl to one of his eyes, and when he opened it he could see half of Badri-jamâl's body. He put kohl in the other eye, and he could see all of her – he was astonished. But Badri-jamâl flew off, all the back way to Bâgh-e-Arâm Garden, to Kuh-e-Kâf Mountain, which is where all the *paris* and *divs* live. She went to join her sisters Zârâ and Bibi-Zârâ; they all belonged to the tribe of *paris*.

When she'd gone, Seyf-ol-moluk was devastated. He told Saad-moluk, 'It's no good, I can't stay here, I'm in love with Badri-jamâl and I have to go after her.' Saad-moluk said, 'Brother, if you're going, I'm coming too. We grew up together; if you leave me, my life will have no meaning; I have to go with you; if we're to die, let's die together; if we survive, we'll come back together.'

They saddled their horses, collected plenty of money, and went to say goodbye to the padishah. Seyf-ol-moluk said, 'I can't stay here, I'm going after Badri-jamâl.' The padishah begged him, 'My son, I'll bring all the people; you can take your pick of the girls, and I'll organize a fantastic wedding!' But Seyf-ol-moluk answered, 'No, I can't stay,' and he took leave of his father.

For many months Seyf-ol-moluk and Saad-moluk searched for clues as to where Badri-jamâl might be. One day, they met an old man and asked him, 'Old man, if you've seen any trace of Badri-jamâl, tell us and we'll give you all the money you want.' He answered, 'Don't worry, no problem, I've seen her!' Seyf-ol-moluk was overjoyed to hear this. He put his hand in his pocket and gave the old man a fistful of silver.

The old man was pleased, and told Seyf-ol-moluk, 'There's a lake nearby; every Wednesday all the *paris* come and swim there. There's only one way you can catch her. Great flocks of *paris* come down in succession, all of them in the form of doves. When they land, they take off their special *pari*-clothes to swim, and afterwards they fly off again. Last of all come three *paris*. Two of them land at the edge of the lake, take off their clothes and jump straight into the water, but Badri-jamâl circles the lake three times, and only then does she join them. Keep concealed until they've all entered the water; then come out and sit on their clothes. When they see you from the water, they'll change into leopards, wolves or lions and threaten to eat you, but don't be afraid; whatever they look like, they can't do anything to you.'

So early next Wednesday morning they went to the lake and built themselves a hide – a *khaza*, which we make when we go hunting, to sit in, hidden from the outside – and they settled in there, watching for the *paris* to come.

The sun was up by the time the *paris* arrived. They went swimming in the lake and then flew off, one after the other. At the very end came the three *paris*; Badri-jamâl sniffed the air, and could smell Seyf-ol-moluk – she was in love with him, after all – then called to her sisters, 'I can smell a human, I'm not going in the water.' She looked around; now Seyf-ol-moluk was wearing boots, and she spotted his tracks, so she sang out to Zârâ:

'I won't go into the water, sister Zârâ, because Seyf-ol-moluk's boots left their tracks on this path.'

Zârâ answered, 'Sister, why're you being so silly? It's a major road, caravans are passing day and night, hundreds of people go by, what makes you think Seyf-ol-moluk is here? Think how far away his home is! There's no way he could be here.'

Now Seyf-ol-moluk had a dagger in his pocket; as he was turning it back and forth, suddenly it made a noise – *shrrannng*! Hearing this, Badri-jamâl sang out:

'I won't go into the water, sister Zârâ, because the *shrang* of Seyf-ol-moluk's dagger reached my ears.'

Her sisters, Zârâ and Bibi-Zârâ, both begged her, 'Come on in, he's not there!' In the end they forced Badri-jamâl to come in; she didn't believe them, but she went into the water. As soon as she did, Seyf-ol-moluk and Saad-moluk jumped out and sat on the *paris'* clothes.

As Zârâ and Bibi-Zârâ came out, Seyf-ol-moluk and Saad-moluk easily caught them both. They knew that Seyf-ol-moluk and Badri-jamâl were in love, and he'd catch her that day or the next. They sang:

'Brother-in-law, give us our clothes, we know you and Badri-jamâl are in love. Let us go, we'll fly off and leave you two to yourselves.'

So he gave them back their clothes and off they flew, leaving Badri-jamâl in the water.

She turned herself into a leopard and told Seyf-ol-moluk, 'I'm going to eat you!'

Then she turned into a wolf, then a lion, but she couldn't do anything, and whatever shape she took, he refused to give her her clothes.

Finally she begged, 'Please, for God's sake, give me my clothes, or a whale will eat me!' – have you seen a whale? People say it's a huge fish like a camel, which swims around in the Ocean of Kuh-e-Kâf.

Seyf-ol-moluk said, 'Swear, by King Solomon the Prophet's sandals, that you won't fly away.'

So she swore by Solomon's sandals, and she came out and he gave her back her clothes, and she put them on. Having sworn the oath, she couldn't fly off.

They set off for the old man's house, which was a little distance away, Seyf-ol-moluk and Saad-moluk in the lead, Badri-jamâl following behind. But she'd never had to walk before; and she didn't manage more than twelve steps ... her feet were so soft that by the twelfth step they were already bleeding; after all, she was a *pari* and had never walked before. So she sang this verse at him:

'They're both in love with each other, Seyf-ol-moluk sat on the clothes, with both his eyes open.'

After she'd taken twelve steps, she cried: 'Seyf-ol-moluk, you've forced me to walk twelve steps; if I ever get free from you, by God I'll give you twelve years of trouble! My place is Bâgh-e-Arâm, in Kuh-e-Kâf, and you'll never find me there.'

Hearing this, Seyf-ol-moluk took her *pari*-clothes from her and hid them, in case she flew away, even though she'd sworn not to. He dressed her in Afghan clothes, sat her behind him on his horse, and they headed home. They spent about a week on the road; during the day they went hunting and brought back some meat, then they'd stay overnight in some inn. Eventually they came to a town, and he sent word ahead to his father, 'Tell the padishah I've brought Badri-jamâl, so that he can come out to greet us with musicians and courtiers, and prepare a party and some games.'

The padishah received the news with joy, and sent out a whole army of people to greet Badri-jamâl; the women went out singing, the men fired their guns. Then they had a really huge wedding party, for three whole days, with meat and rice, buzkashi, and lots of fun and games.

After it was over, Seyf-ol-moluk took Saad-moluk off hunting again; he was a real hunting fanatic. They shot pigeons, pheasants, partridges and rabbits and then came home at dusk.

Now Seyf-ol-moluk had locked those *pari*-clothes in a trunk, and given his mother the key, telling her, 'Here's the key to that trunk, with the *pari*-clothes inside. We're going out to the wild where it might get lost. I warn you that Badri-jamâl or someone else may come and ask you to give her back her clothes; but if she puts them on, she'll fly off again, all the way to Kuh-e-Kâf, and I'll spend the next twelve years searching for her, and I may not live that long. So, mother, don't give anyone the key.' So saying, he left to go hunting.

After he'd gone, all the women of the village came to the padishah's wife, 'Show us your new bride; let's see this "moon" that Seyf-ol-moluk fell in love with: what does she look like? Is she so beautiful that he fell in love with her instead of one of our girls?'

When they saw the *pari*, who was dressed in Afghan clothes, well, someone who's not in her own things isn't that attractive, is she? These women said to each other, 'For God's sake, this *pari*, this Badri-jamâl, she's no better than any of us!'

The *pari* told them, 'My sisters, my mothers, you can't see me properly; let me wear my own clothes, then you'll see what I'm really like! Seyf-ol-moluk's mother has the key.'

So the women begged the padishah's wife, Seyf-ol-moluk's mother, to give the *pari* her clothes. 'You must let her wear her own clothes; let's all wear our own things so that we can be seen at our best.' She couldn't resist this argument, but she warned them that the *pari* was liable to fly off if she put on her *pari*-clothes, so they promised to stop her doing so. There was a hole in the roof, and one said, 'I'll go and block that hole.' Others said, 'We'll take the doorways; she won't be able to get through.' So five or six women took one entrance, five or six took the other, and more were lying on the roof and watching through the hole.

Now the *pari* knew a lot of special dances; and once she got her clothes she went round the room two or three times, dancing, and the women outside the door fell down entranced, so did the women inside; and the women on the roof fell off, they were entranced too. The *pari* flew out of the room and sat on the roof. Seeing that all the women were unconscious, she took a little water, recited a spell over it, and sprinkled it over them; as they regained their senses, she flew away.

Seyf-ol-moluk had gone hunting, but he'd failed to hit anything but a partridge, and he was very down. As they were collecting sticks to build a fire and cook the partridge, he said to Saad-moluk, 'I feel bad; we've had no success at hunting, and I think something awful's happened.'

Just then Badri-jamâl arrived and flew over the fire; she kept settling on a branch, then flying off and settling on another. Seyf-ol-moluk immediately realized it was her, that his mother had given her clothes back and that she'd escaped. He took up his bow and arrows and said to Saad-moluk, 'Come, let's shoot her, I'd rather she died than we had to spend another twelve years chasing her, that would be too much!' So he shot at her and missed, as she flew off; when she settled again, he shot and missed again. Finally Badri-jamâl sang to him: 'Seyf-ol-moluk, you forced me to walk twelve steps; but my place is Kuh-e-Kâf, and by God you'll spend twelve more years chasing me before you see me again!' Saying goodbye, off she flew, all the way to Kuh-e-Kâf, to join her sisters and the other *paris*.

It was late afternoon when Seyf-ol-moluk got home, so furious with his mother that he wanted to cut off her head. He'd been clear: 'Don't give anyone the key, don't let her have her clothes,' but she'd let him down. He was so angry, people had to restrain him, and they told his mother, 'Go and hide, or he'll kill you; he'll never forgive you for letting the *pari* escape. He'll look everywhere, so you'd better hide well.' So she went into hiding, and Seyf-ol-moluk was unable to find her. He was very depressed, and in the morning he told his father, the padishah, 'I'm going after Badri-jamâl.' His father said, 'Don't go, you won't return alive.' But he insisted, he wouldn't be held back. So his father gave him some men, and sent Saad-moluk with him, and a mullah, and off they went.

They travelled night and day, heading for Kuh-e-Kâf, eating a little food and asking directions on the way. Eventually they came to a vast river, impassable by man or beast – it was a long time ago, when there were no ships or aeroplanes. They stayed several nights beside this river. Seyf-ol-moluk had a dream about a great black crow: 'It's coming near me, let me take it by the foot, then Saad-moluk can take my foot, the mullah can take his, and so on ...'

When he awoke, a huge bird really did come. Seyf-ol-moluk grabbed its foot, Saad-moluk grabbed his foot, the mullah his, and the servant the mullah's, and the bird took wing. When they got to the banks of the great river, the servant's hands slipped, and he called to Seyf-ol-moluk, 'Goodbye!' and fell into the water. Further out, the mullah called out, 'Goodbye, Seyf-ol-moluk!' and he too fell in. Further on still, Saad-moluk called, 'Goodbye, brother Seyf-ol-moluk, I'm going!' and he too fell; he wasn't that far from the other bank, but as soon as he fell, a whale swallowed him up in a single gulp, and the water carried them away. Only Seyf-ol-moluk was left; he hung on until they reached the far bank before he fell.

For a couple of days Seyf-ol-moluk lay unconscious where he had fallen. When he awoke, he sat up, pulled himself together and looked around. He saw four or five apes – *bizu* as we call them – jumping around. Apes are sometimes very bad, but it turned out to be the country of the apes. They greeted each other. Now apes don't choose a padishah from among themselves – an ape never submits to another ape – instead, they find a human, a Muslim, put him on the throne and call him their padishah. When these apes met Seyf-ol-moluk, they consulted each other. A long time ago they'd taken a padishah, but he was now an ancient greybeard, so they decided he was too old and useless, it was time to eat him and replace him with Seyf-ol-moluk. So they took him off to their country, telling him, 'We're going to put you on the throne.' Seyf-ol-moluk couldn't plead a previous engagement, because there were too many of them and he was afraid they'd eat him.

Having dragged the old man off the throne, they were about to eat him when Seyf-ol-moluk asked, 'What are you doing?' They said, 'We've put you on the throne, now we're going to eat him.' He ordered them not to kill the old padishah; after all, if he was now padishah, he could give any orders he liked and they had to obey: 'Don't kill him, he can keep me company and serve me in some way.' So they released the old man, who was very pleased not to be eaten!

Meanwhile Saad-moluk, if you remember, had been swallowed by a whale. One day some fishermen caught the whale; when they'd landed it and cut open its stomach, a man emerged – it was Saad-moluk. They asked him, 'What sort of man are you, living inside this whale? Where did you come from?' Saad-moluk told them the whole story, about falling into the river and so on; 'I had some companions, including a mullah, but I've lost them all.' Saad-moluk set off to look for Seyf-ol-moluk.

For three or four years, Seyf-ol-moluk ruled the apes. Every day, he gave them orders like, 'Go and kill that ape and eat him; and that one.' The apes had a rough time; he got them all fighting each other and caused them no end of trouble. Of course, he was doing all this on purpose, and eventually he told them, 'I've had enough of being your padishah, and you've had enough of me; let me go!' They thought, 'This Seyf-ol-moluk has finished us off; that old man never gave orders like these, perhaps he wasn't such a bad padishah,' and they told Seyf-ol-moluk, 'We're going to restore the old man to the throne, you're free to go wherever you want.' Once they'd got him off the throne, they decided to eat him. However the old man remembered what Seyf-ol-moluk had done for him, and once he was back on the throne he gave orders that they weren't to touch Seyf-ol-moluk, so they let him go.

Seyf-ol-moluk resumed his search, and came to a place where there was a White Div, who took him on as a servant for six months. At night, Seyf-ol-moluk got very depressed, and when the six months were up, the *div* asked him, 'What's the matter, why are you so down?' Seyf-ol-moluk answered, 'In the six months I've been working for you, you've never asked me anything about myself: "where are you from, where are you going?" and so on.'

The *div* said, 'Forgive me; let me ask now: what's up, why did you come, what's going on?' So Seyf-ol-moluk told him his story: 'I'm after Badri-jamâl, I'm in love with her.' The *div* said, 'I'll take you to my brother, Blind Div Shâdnâm's place; I'll give you a letter for him, and he'll get you to Kuh-e-Kâf, he knows it very well.'

So the *div* hoisted Seyf-ol-moluk up, and they flew a long way – like between here and Khârkash – then he set Seyf-ol-moluk down, handing him a letter and sending him to Shâdnâm. Seyf-ol-moluk approached him, holding the letter over his face; if he hadn't held the letter like that, once the *div* spotted him he'd have eaten him whole. Shâdnâm saw him – he was blind in one eye only – and his anger was aroused; he said, 'I'm going to eat him whole!' But when he saw the letter, he went silent, wondering, 'What's this letter, let me read it.' He read the letter. His brother the White Div had written: 'This is Seyf-ol-moluk, he's served me for 6 months, treat him well and be sure to get him to Kuh-e-Kâf.'

So the Blind Div greeted Seyf-ol-moluk politely and took him home. He had 500 goats, and a huge underground cave, and at night he'd put all the goats in there. A large billy led the flock like a goatherd. The *div* was very fond of his billy-goat. It had little ears, what we call *buchey*; and it had bells knotted into the hair all around its neck, so that it jingled like a *godi* taxi-cart as it moved. All the other goats followed it, grazing all over the hills, until towards evening it led the goats back down the mountain and into the cave, where Shâdnâm slept at the entrance.

Seyf-ol-moluk was very unhappy. He saw that Shâdnâm was still full of anger and wondered what to do. 'I've got to do something, or I might have to stay for another couple of years working for him; he's not going to take me to Kuh-e-Kâf any time soon.' So one evening, when the goats came home, he managed to enter the cave by clinging onto the billy's side. Shâdnâm felt for him among the goats, but he managed to slip by.

The Blind Div went to sleep at the mouth of the cave as usual. Now *divs* sleep very heavily – we have a saying, if we can't wake someone up, that they're 'sleeping like a *div*'. In the middle of the night, Seyf-ol-moluk collected some goat-droppings for fuel and made a fire; he found an iron spit and heated it until it was red-hot, then he thrust it into the *div*'s good eye. The *div* bellowed with fury and felt all round him, but Seyf-ol-moluk had disappeared into the depths of the cave. Shâdnâm shouted, 'I'll stay at the mouth of this cave, there's no other way out, and by God, I'll kill you and eat you!'

Seyf-ol-moluk stayed in the cave for several days, too frightened to come out. 'Even if the *div*'s blind, if he catches me, he'll eat me.' He wondered what to do. Finally, he realized that the only thing to do was to kill the billy-goat. Every evening when it came in, the *div* would feel it as it entered the cave at the head of the goats, and the billy, which was very fond of the *div*, would caress him with its horns as it passed. In the middle of the night Seyf-ol-moluk took a knife and killed the billy, skinned it and put the skin on himself, tying the head to his shoulder like this. In the morning he approached the Blind Div, and caressed him with the horns, and the *div* felt the head, thinking, 'It's my billy-goat, leading the goats out to the hills.'

When Seyf-ol-moluk got out, he shouted, 'I'm out, I've killed your billy-goat and escaped, and you can't do anything about it! You're blind, you can't see me!' The Blind Div felt all round him on the ground, and struck out into the air, but it was no good; he said, 'You win: I can't see you, I can't touch you, I can't eat you.' Seyf-ol-moluk quickly made good his escape.

Now the Blind Div had a sister called Golnâz, Beauty. Whenever she pissed, her pee would drive a mill for twenty-four hours; she'd fashioned 180 onions into a necklace and hung it round her throat – you can see that this Golnâz was a real beauty! She heard what Seyf-ol-moluk had done to her brother, how he'd blinded him and caused such mayhem. She soon found his tracks and caught him, swearing, 'I've got you, and after all you've done to my brother I'm going to eat you!'

Seyf-ol-moluk realized she was serious, and that she was too strong for him, so he started sweet-talking her, complimenting her on her looks, 'Perhaps she won't kill me.' As she had 180 onions round her neck, he sang to her:

'Golnâz's tresses are the colour of flowers, she has 180 onions as her necklace.'

Golnâz was a little mollified; he spent some time with her, continuing to flatter her and so on, hoping she wouldn't kill him. Then one day he said, 'I'm going to your brother's house, to the White Div.' She said, 'You have three days' leave, then come back.'

But Seyf-ol-moluk simply took off. Kuh-e-Kâf was not far away, so he made his way there, asking around. When he got nearer, he came to a huge palace. He went inside and saw a lake surrounded by tall trees; it was a really nice place. As he wandered around, he came across a *pari*; when she saw Seyf-ol-moluk, she cried and laughed at the same time. 'Why did you laugh and cry?' She said, 'I cried because when the Black Div who lives here comes back from the wild, he'll see you, and by God there won't be a drop of your blood left on the earth. But I laughed, because I've never before seen a human being; where did you spring from?' He told her, 'I'm starving, parched and exhausted.' So she fed him a lot of rice and stuff, and he ate until he was full – he'd been very hungry.

When the *div* arrived, the *pari* hid Seyf-ol-moluk. The *div* sniffed around, threatening her: 'I can smell a man here. Show me where he is!' The *pari* cried, 'What do you mean, you fool, how could there be a man? This is Kuh-e-Kâf, and thanks to you *divs* no human being can ever come here. There's only the sun and the sky and my servants and I.'

The next morning, the *div* went off hunting, and the *pari* got Seyf-ol-moluk out of his hiding place and they sat and enjoyed each other's company. He spent two or three months like this with her; when the *div* went off in the morning, he came out and spent the day with her; when the *div* came back at night, she put him back into hiding.

One day he said, 'I'm in love with Badri-jamâl, and it's her I've come for.' He told her the whole story, how Badri-jamâl had said, 'I'll give you twelve years of trouble.' The *pari* said that the twelve years were nearly up, there were only a few months left. She added, 'Badri-jamâl's place is nearby; up on Kuh-e-Kâf there's a lake, they come to bathe there.' He asked, 'If I catch her, will she come with me or not?' She said, 'She's a *pari*, she's given you her word, so when your twelve years are up, if you catch her she'll go with you.'

He said, 'When the Black Div comes back this evening, pretend to be very sad, and when the Black Div asks you, "Pari, why are you so sad?" you should answer, "How will you die? One day somebody may come to kill you, how would they do it?" See what the *div* says.'

So that evening when the *div* came home, she seemed very dejected. Now the *div* was in love with the *pari*; he asked her, 'Pari, why are you so down?' She said, 'Of course I'm sad; one day you'll go to the mountain and somebody will kill you, and I'll know nothing; how will you die?' He was suspicious, and he told her a lie; he said, 'If my fireplace breaks, I'll die, but so long as it's intact, I'll be all right.' In the morning the *div* went hunting. After he'd gone, the *pari* took some mud, and made a very nice fireplace of mud reinforced with iron. When the *div* came back, he saw the fireplace from a distance and smiled, 'What a nice fireplace she's made, reinforced with iron! So she loves me, she doesn't really want me dead! I shouldn't have told her a fib.' He came up and kicked the fireplace to pieces. The *pari* grabbed him and said, 'For God's sake, don't do that!' But he laughed at her, 'That's not how I'll die! I told you a fib, my death will come some other way.'

The *pari* had tricked him herself. Now she asked him, 'So tell me, in case some day somebody tries to kill you, how will you die?' This time he told her the truth: 'There's a river, in such-and-such a place, and in the middle there's a tree; the tree-trunk is hollow and inside there's a small box; in the small box there's a jar and in the jar there's a parrot. If you cut off the parrot's leg, my leg will be cut off; if you cut off its head, my head will be cut off. My life depends on the parrot's life; so long as it's intact, I'll stay alive.'

The *pari* asked, 'How do you get to this tree?' He said, 'Nobody can get there, nobody can cross the river.' She was delighted; 'If that's so, if nobody can ever get there, you've shown me that your death's impossible!' The *div* went on, 'Nobody can get there, unless they have this ring of mine' (it was on his finger). 'If I take this ring to the river, the waters will part and I'll be able to get to the tree. Nobody else can get through that great river.'

The *pari* begged him, 'Let me look after the ring, in case some day when you're out hunting it falls off and gets lost,' and she tricked it off him.

The next day, while the *div* went to the top of Kuh-e-Kâf, she and Seyf-ol-moluk made their way to the river with the ring. When they got there, the river parted and let them through. At that moment, up on the mountain, the *div* felt a fever coming, and realized what was happening. He leapt up and headed for the river himself.

The *pari* broke the tree-trunk open with an axe, took out the little box and opened it, handing the jar to Seyf-ol-moluk, who held it in his hand and said, 'Let the parrot alone for now, let's wait until we've got back to the palace before we cut it up.' But the *pari* got really angry with him; 'He's on his way now, he'll eat us both! Cut its head off right away, so his head will be cut off too.' Seyf-ol-moluk saw the *div* in the distance, approaching rapidly, so he cut off one of the parrot's legs, and the *div* immediately lost one of his legs; but he came on with just one leg. Then Seyf-ol-moluk cut off one arm, then the other, until the *div* had lost all his limbs; but he kept on, squirming along on his stomach, begging them, 'For God's sake, don't kill me!' Finally the *pari* cut off the parrot's head, and the *div* lost his head too.

So Seyf-ol-moluk and the *pari* were very happy, and they stayed there together for a few months, until he said, 'My twelve years are nearly up, I should return to my own country; I miss my parents a lot and they'll be wondering whether their son's disappeared.' He asked the *pari* to show him where Badri-jamâl could be found. She said, 'Why do you want to go home? Let's go and fetch Badri-jamâl and bring her here, this is a nice place with a nice house, plenty of water, plenty of everything.' He answered, 'I must go; there's no place like home [*khpël watan bëlbël watan*]!'

Now the *div* had a magic carpet, which King Solomon had given him; if he said his prayers on the carpet, the carpet would fly him to whatever place he had in his mind. The *pari* knew about it, so they both did their prayers on the carpet, and it took them to the lake of Kuh-e-Kâf, a big lake where all the *paris* come. Seyf-ol-moluk hid himself with his *pari* and after a while the same three *paris* came; all three *paris* landed and took off their clothes, and Seyf-ol-moluk sat on the clothes of Badri-jamâl. He caught her; and again he made her swear by King Solomon's sandals that she wouldn't leave him again, and he gave her back her clothes.

He took her and the other *pari*, and they spent another two or three months in that nice palace. In the end he said, 'I really must go home.' They accepted it. A mullah was called, and he performed the marriage contract for both Badri-jamâl and the other *pari*. Badri-jamâl fetched her other clothes, and they got onto the carpet and said their prayers. They ordered it first to set them down on top of Kuh-e-Kâf; so it took them and set them down on the very top of the mountain. Then Seyf-ol-moluk told the *paris*, 'I'm bored, dance for me.' They danced a lot for him, and he was very happy with them, and told them, 'I really liked that!' They were all very tired, so they spent a few nights on top of Kuh-e-Kâf.

In the morning he said, 'Let's go home now.' They sat on the carpet and did their prayers, and it flew them all the way to his home country. There was such a reception: people came out with guns, drums, fun and games, because he'd brought back Badri-jamâl and the other *pari*.

But his father was old and blind, so was his mother. Moreover, Seyf-ol-moluk was very unhappy to learn that another padishah had conquered his kingdom. This other padishah had a daughter, who was a great fighter, better with the sword than any man. Two or three years after Seyf-ol-moluk had left, his father went blind, and this warlike princess came with her army and fought and killed a lot of his soldiers. In those days, long ago, each village had a padishah; it was a time of warlords, and whoever proved stronger would take the other one's land and possessions.

Seyf-ol-moluk was upset to hear about all this, how she'd taken the kingdom when his father was blind, and so on. He swore, 'By God, I'll get my country back.' The *pari* said, 'Let me fight the other padishah's daughter,' but he replied, 'No, I won't let you, I'll fight her myself.'

In the morning, the armies came out to do battle. Seyf-ol-moluk wanted to take back his kingdom in single combat, or to die in trying. In those days, single combat was fought by turns; they took turns to raise their sword and strike each other. Seyf-ol-moluk told that woman, 'It's your turn first, I'll take mine afterwards.' So she raised her sword to strike him; Seyf-ol-moluk was very cunning, he slid down his horse's flank, and the sword missed. Then with his own sword he cut her horse's girth, and that was the end of her.

Thus Seyf-ol-moluk got his kingdom back. His father was very old and sick, so Seyf-ol-moluk took over the kingdom and sat on the throne, and the people became his subjects. That's what happened; his name remains.

15

Epilogue: The Piruzai Since 1972

Haji Tumân on 'The End of Times'

One August evening in 1972, as we sit in his yard with some of his friends, Tumân reflects on how times have changed.

The year of the flash-flood, we had 180 milking ewes and we made 200 kg of ghee. In those days there was plenty. We'd get 1 kg per ewe, now you're lucky to get 500 g; with 200 ewes you'll get only 20 kg of ghee. Then, if you sowed 45 kg of wheat on the dry lands, you'd reap over a thousand; in recent years – not this one – one kg sown scarcely bears 5 kg. Times of plenty have gone, out of the window. Money comes and goes like water. If you fill the sacks full of flour, it's gone in a month or two.

In those years there was so much snow and rain on the trek. Now – except for this year – by God's will, we don't see any rain or snow after we leave the village until we reach Dangak, nor any of the troubles we used to see. Last year, when you and I went together, there was no rain or snow at all. But formerly we could camp wherever we wanted and there'd be grazing and browse for the camels. The sheep would be off with the shepherd; we'd arrange a rendezvous for him to come and collect flour, then he wouldn't come back for ten days. He had plenty of milk and meat and everything. In spring, food was plentiful in Afghanistan; wherever you went and said you were hungry, people would give you a sack of flour.

I don't know, perhaps it's the end of times. Our chronicles say we shan't reach the end of the century; we shan't reach 1400, they say. One of our calendars is solar, one lunar. In the solar calendar this year is 1351, in the lunar it's 1391 or 1392. Some mullahs say that we won't reach the next century, but how do they reckon it? Some mullahs say it's this lunar calendar; others say no, it's the other one. When time finishes and the world comes to an end, will it be one day before the year 1400, or two days, or one year or half a year before? Others say no, if we finish this century, we'll make it to the next. Such rotten mullahs! There are no proper mullahs who can say for sure which calendar it is! They just don't know, and there are no prophets or saints or sheykhs any more.

The sheykh of today, curse him, is no sheykh. If he can find lies, he'll never tell the truth; if he can find sin, he'll never do what's right; if he can find haram, he won't eat halal. That's where we've got to. Now when you and I talk with each other, it tastes very good on the tongue, but God knows what's in our hearts. That's how it is, I swear!

With you people, your words are at one with your conscience. As for the people of Afghanistan, as I said, even a sheykh's word isn't at one with his heart. What he has in his heart, only God knows; when talking to you he'll say something else. That's how it is; it's the end of times!

Our original chronicles say that one in a thousand will go to Hell; but our latest chronicles declare that one in a thousand will go to Heaven, the rest to Hell. I'm not joking. The chronicles say that at the end of time truth will be lies, people will trample truth underfoot; that's the way things will be. Who will then go to Heaven?

And prayer, where is it now? Not ten in a hundred pray. If you pray just once a week, I don't call that prayer. If you're obliged to do your ablutions because you see someone else doing it, that's not prayer. That's just fear of what people will say. Such a person doesn't say, 'God created us, sent us a Prophet who commanded us, "Pray five times a day, repent your sins, tell the truth, don't tell lies, don't steal other people's property, give alms and tithes, stay on the Right Path." There's none of this left. It's all gone to ruin.

That's what's happened. What can we do? To tell the truth ... [*laughs*] I can't go on!

The Islamic lunar year 1400 began in November 1979 CE, *shortly before the Soviet invasion of Afghanistan. Truly, the world as Haji Tumân and his Piruzai knew it ended then, as decades of war, upheaval and suffering began.*

What happened to the Piruzai?

After we left Haji Tumân's family in 1972, Nancy and I had intermittent correspondence with them, and we planned to return for further research in Sar-e-pol in 1978–79. Political events prevented this, and indeed ended our communication with our Piruzai hosts, apart from a short, uninformative letter in 1991 from Mastu-khân (Kuk), eldest son of Bakhtâwar (Tumân's aunt and Hajj-companion), apparently sent from a refugee camp in Quetta, Pakistan. I responded with my own family news and asked for his, but I heard nothing more.

Mastu-khân's letter suggests that the Piruzai became refugees and spent at least some time in Pakistan. The only other evidence of their story since we left is a GoogleEarth image of May 2004, which shows most houses in Konjek and Khârkash clearly as long-abandoned – roof-beams gone, house and compound walls ruined, farmlands uncultivated.[1]

Without further specific evidence, I cannot complete the Piruzai story. I shall simply summarize my best guess, drawn from scattered references to Es'hâqzai Pashtuns in the multifarious literature on the country's tragic history since 1972.[2] Most of it is speculative; perhaps publication of this book will result in more information becoming available.

---

[1] Map H; compare Google Maps, 'Abrishamin'. In Google Maps, the historical images, for 31 December every year since 1984, are much lower resolution, but suggest that Konjek and Khârkash lands (and not their neighbours') were abandoned in 1987. Some nearby villages are still occupied and the lands farmed.

[2] See Appendix 2 and bibliographic suggestions there.

The Piruzai almost certainly left Sar-e-pol in the 1980s, during the Soviet occupation of Afghanistan. Newly empowered Arabs, Uzbeks and Hazâras drove them from their rich valley lands and their mountain pastures, and they fled to Quetta, to join the millions of Afghan refugees in Pakistan. Their villages were long deserted by 2004.

Some Pashtun refugees from Sar-e-pol and Jawzjân returned in the early 1990s during the mujahidin government, then again under the Taliban (1996–2001), but most, driven out once more by local hostility, or by the catastrophic drought in 1998–2001, gave up and went back south, either to Pakistan or to camps near Kandahar. In the early 2000s, after the Taliban defeat, the return of refugees, and of Internally Displaced Persons (IDPs), was sponsored nationally and internationally, but was no more successful among the refugees from Sar-e-pol. Some Piruzai may have joined those who tried, without managing to recover their lands; *mâldâr* who returned to Jawzjân and Sar-e-pol were driven out again as recently as 2005–6.[3]

Studies of the large Zhare-Dasht and Spin-Boldak IDP camps near Kandahar show a high proportion of both 'kuchi' and other refugees who fled persecution in the north since 1992, the largest group coming from Sar-e-pol.[4] Piruzai may be among them. At the time of writing, Sar-e-pol in the north and Helmand (notably Nawzâd and Musâ-qala districts, once held with difficulty by British and American troops) in the south are among the provinces where the resurgent Taliban are most active. If any Piruzai stayed in Sar-e-pol, or resettled there successfully, they probably joined the Taliban, at least to the extent of accepting their protection against local warlords and the government. But they may also have returned to their ancestral homes in Nawzâd and Musâ-qala, which have for some years been among the main centres of opium poppy cultivation. If they resumed semi-nomadic pastoralism or started farming, they are unlikely to have found water and grazing conditions any better than in the north.[5] Prominent among those controlling the Helmand opium trade have been local Es'hâqzais such as Mullah Akhtar Mansur, Mullah Omar's successor as Taliban leader.[6] In December 2015, 'The Taliban can also count on the sympathy of the Ishaqzai tribe, who constitute a sizeable part of the province's population. The current Taliban leader, Akhtar Mansour, and many in his close circle, are Ishaqzais and the tribe was alienated by the US forces and their Afghan allies in the early years after the fall of the Taliban regime.'[7]

In Appendix 2, where I sketch the recent history of Afghanistan in more detail, it becomes clear that an issue of increasingly vital importance in the country has been control and ownership of productive land. Both legitimate claims to original ownership, and illegitimate land-grabbing by warlords and others, and the endemic corruption at

---

[3] Numerous press columns between 2001 and 2006; see especially IRIN reports.

[4] Marsden and Turton (2004); Schmeidl et al. (2010), who give an excellent summary of the fates, both of the Sar-e-pol Pashtuns become IDPs in the south and of those who attempted to return and resettle in the north.

[5] In 2002, the Nawzâd council (*shura*) informed UNHCR that the district hosted IDPs from Sheberghan, Maimana, Sar-e-pol, and elsewhere. 'They have built houses on governmental land, as the local community are reluctant to accommodate them on their land/houses' (UNHCR 2002:4).

[6] On Es'hâqzai in Nawzâd (Helmand), see Coghlan (2009: 120f., 136), Gordon (2011), Martin (2014), Ali (2014), Amiri (2016), Linke (2016); and for 'Isakzai' in Helmand in the 1970s, see Scott (1980).

[7] Osman (2015).

all levels of government and society, have meant that large numbers of returning refugees and displaced farmers and pastoralists have been unable to return home. The Piruzai almost certainly lost their 'golden tent-peg' in Sar-e-pol many years ago.

Readers of this book may be struck by pre-echoes of what has since been reported of the actions and policies of the Taliban. Narrators describe actions and express opinions that may shock Western sensibilities today, though just a few generations ago this would not have been so. In a recent article, I explored the disconnect between the moderate, humanistic Islam that Nancy and I found among the Durrani of 1971–72 and the puritan revivalism that the media portray as the beliefs, policies and behaviour of the Taliban. I see elements of Taliban Islam among the Piruzai – they are there in Haji Tumân's musings quoted above, and he might well have welcomed the emergence of Taliban leader Mullah Omar as a 'proper mullah' or 'sheykh'. Taliban ideology surely echoed Piruzai ideas of the righteousness and power of the *woles* community. But Taliban fanaticism was, first, only an extreme version of one strand in Piruzai culture and society, and second, a temporary response to an extreme crisis.[8]

As for Pashtun society generally, the oppression of women, and customs such as *bacha-bâzi* and *baad/bad*, have been widely publicized since the 1990s, largely thanks initially to the postures of American personalities commenting on Taliban rule and justifying the 2001 invasion, followed up mercilessly, and with little understanding, by legions of journalists since. The stories narrated here will provide some of the social, cultural and political context needed for a fuller understanding of such customs – and indeed, I hope, of some Taliban practices.

[8] R. Tapper (2012).

Appendices

1 Ancestors

Gholâm-Rasul Khân Bâbakzai (see Chapter 2) relates the origins of the Es'hâqzai. His account differs little from some shorter accounts we heard later from tribesmen in Sar-e-pol.

There are two divisions of the Es'hâqzai: Hawâzai and Mandinzai. Es'hâq had two wives, Mandin and Hawâ. The Hawâzai are Mesrikheyl, Omarzai, Idizai, Pakhizai, Kutizai, Dawlatzai. [*See Fig. 25*]

The Mandinzai descend from two brothers Omar and Musâ. The elder, Omar, had four sons, Abu-bakr, Sheykh-Hasan, Bahrâm and Nahâm. Their descendants are the Bâbakzai, Sheykhânzai, Bârânzai, and Nâmanzai. Musâ, the younger brother, had five sons, Kamu, Khâni, Chokhâ, Mahmud, Nazar, ancestors of the Kamuzai, Khânikheyl, Chokhâzai, Mahmudkheyl and Nazarzai.

Omar and Musâ's father was Seyyed Joghadâr, son of Seyyed Cherâgh, son of Seyyed Abu-Moslim-e-Bokhâri. We don't know the ancestors of Seyyed Abu-Moslim, but they join up with the Koreysh people, Arab Seyyeds. In those days they lived in Bokhara, under Tyrant Hojâj. Hojâj was angry with the Seyyeds, and he ordered them to be killed wherever they were found. 'We'll turn the mills with Seyyed blood!' Abu-Moslim laid himself down across the mill, to prevent other Seyyeds dying; they killed him and the mill ran with his blood.

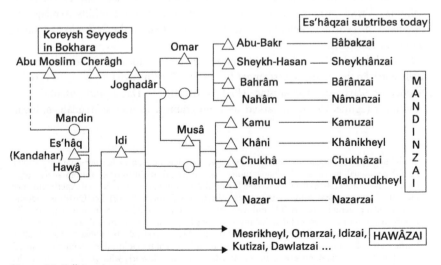

Figure 25 Es'hâqzai ancestors.

The rest of the Seyyeds fled from Bokhara to Kandahar, young and old, including Seyyed Joghadâr and his sons Seyyed Omar and Seyyed Musâ; and also a Seyyed woman called Mandin. They took refuge with Es'hâq. One morning Es'hâq quarrelled with his wife Hawâ, and swore, 'If I don't find another wife before nightfall, I'll divorce you!' Mandin went to look for a wife for him, but couldn't find one. Evening came, and she said, 'I'll agree to marry you myself, to release you from your oath, but don't expect to sleep with me.' Es'hâq went to Mandin, thinking to sleep with her; but she was a Seyyed, descendant of the Prophet, and he found himself impotent.

Es'hâq and Hawâ had a son called Idi, and Mandin arranged for Idi's two daughters to marry Seyyed Omar and Seyyed Musâ. So the Mandinzai are Es'hâqzai on their mother's side, and Seyyeds on their father's side – and on their mother's side too.

The Kamuzai divided after generations into Akhtarkheyl, Sufikheyl and Amânkheyl. So also, Abubakr left four sons: Jân-Mahmad, Dawlat, Ahmad-khân, Adu, and the four lineages Jânikheyl, Dawlatkheyl, Ahmadkhânkheyl, Aduzai, are now separate.

2 Afghanistan and Sar-e-pol, 1972–2016[1]

The PDPA

Following his government's failure to respond effectively to the terrible famine of summer 1972, Zâher Shah was deposed in June 1973 by his cousin Dâ'ud, who founded a republic. The Sar-e-pol region continued to be dominated by Es'hâqzai Pashtun khans, both politically and through their possession of farmlands and pastures acquired by their ancestors after their arrival from the south. Economic conditions for ordinary Pashtun villagers and semi-nomadic *mâldâr* improved: they resumed seasonal treks to the mountains in the years immediately after we left, and karakul prices rose. But the khans further alienated the local population by increased oppression. Non-Pashtuns – Uzbeks, Arabs, Hazâras and others in the northern foothills, Aymâqs and Hazâras in the central mountains – had every reason to eject the Pashtuns as soon as conditions allowed.

Meanwhile Islamist and socialist opposition parties, formed among the urban intelligentsia in the 1960s, grew stronger. In April 1978, with Soviet support, the People's Democratic Party of Afghanistan (PDPA) overthrew Dâ'ud and established a communist regime, which embarked on a programme to abolish 'feudalism', break

---

[1] The bibliography of Afghanistan since 1972 is large; I can offer here only a few personal suggestions. Useful annotated or classified bibliographies can be found at: https://afghanistan-analyst.org/. Centlivres-Demont (2015) is a very accessible collection of articles by international experts from her journal *Afghanistan Info*. Another important collection is Shahrani (2018). Lee (2018) is a recent, monumental general history. AREU and AAN stand out among local NGOs for producing regular reports based on intensive and detailed investigations by researchers thoroughly familiar with the country: one is Antonio Giustozzi, who has also published several valuable books, notably (2009). Ruttig (2013) is an excellent brief summary of twentieth-century political, economic and social developments, especially on events in the decade after our fieldwork, with good sources on the drought of 1969–71 (2013: 11–12).

down ethnic, tribal and sectarian barriers, promote the working masses and improve the position of women. The PDPA's violent repression of opposition, infighting among its leaders, and mujahidin risings outside Kabul, led in December 1979 to the Soviet invasion.

From 1979 to 1989 the Soviet occupying forces supported the PDPA governments of, first, Babrak Karmal, then Najibollah. They controlled the main towns and roads; in the rural areas they conducted a ferocious, prolonged but ultimately unsuccessful military onslaught on the mujahidin resistance. The most prominent mujahidin were the seven mainly Pashtun parties based in Peshawar, variously encouraged and financed by the USA, Saudi Arabia and Pakistan, but much of the active resistance inside Afghanistan was conducted by the Tâjiks Ahmad-shah Massoud in the north-east and Ismail Khan in the west, and the Iran-backed Hazâras in the centre. The chief dimensions of the conflict were indigenous resistance to foreign occupation, Islamism versus atheist/secularist communism, rural versus urban, and 'traditionalism' versus 'modernity'; other dimensions – ethnic, tribal, sectarian, class – were merely dormant. In a decade of appalling suffering for the Afghan people, perhaps a million died; many more were disabled or displaced and about six million took refuge abroad, mainly in Pakistan and Iran.

In the years following the 1978 PDPA revolution, Sar-e-pol was best known for the oil wells at Angut, and as the home-town of Abdol-Hakim Shar'i, Minister of Justice until the Soviet invasion.[2] Politically and socially, the main change was the end of Pashtun dominance. The PDPA government, though largely Pashtun, was hostile to tribalism and 'feudalism' and encouraged resistance to the Es'hâqzai khans and Pashtuns generally. Some or all of the khans lost their vast estates, possibly in the radical Land Reform of PDPA Decree No.8, implemented in Jawzjân between 1979 and 1982.[3] Meanwhile, Hazâra villagers of Kâshân and Lâl-o-Sar-jangal denied the Pashtun *mâldâr* access to their mountains. Some of them found pasturelands in Aymâq country further west in Ghor province (where their ancestors had once summered), others joined those using the Band-e-Turkistan mountains closer to Sar-e-pol town.

In 1988 Sar-e-pol sub-province was made a province (*welâyat*), carved from the southern parts of Jawzjân together with the district of Balkhâb, transferred from Balkh province. But with only a dirt road providing access to Sar-e-pol town (from Sheberghân) the new province remained among the most remote and neglected in the country. In Sar-e-pol, Jawzjân and Fâryâb, warlords emerged. Many were militia commanders with links to government, but their chief interest was to defeat rivals and extend their local control. General Dostum, based in Sheberghân, led the most powerful militia, predominantly Uzbek. Some Pashtuns allied with Dostum's local ally Ghaffâr Pahlawân, and supported the government against the mujahidin; others joined the latter.[4]

Overall, Arab, Uzbek and Hazâra villagers, armed and empowered, re-appropriated lands taken from their ancestors many decades earlier, driving ordinary Pashtuns from their homes and farms and the steppe pastures nearby. Some joined the *mâldâr* still

---

[2] Our cook Hâshem's first cousin, see pp. 35f; though we never met him.
[3] Grötzbach (2015: 16), Shahrani (1984: 15–25).
[4] Giustozzi (2004: 9–10; 2009: 61, 103f., 141–2).

practising migratory pastoralism, but this was a more precarious existence than before, for political and climatic reasons. Denied access to their traditional pasturelands, and deprived of their powerful patrons, the northern Pashtuns faced a series of tribulations that made their lives difficult or impossible: discrimination from the regime and violence from non-Pashtuns, land-grabbing, livestock theft, mechanized farming, as well as increasingly catastrophic flock losses from drought. From the 1980s, waves of Sar-e-pol Pashtuns joined the millions of Afghan refugees in Pakistan. Most refugees were landowners; mainly Es'hâqzai, both khans expelled from their vast estates and small farmers such as Piruzai, as well as *mâldâr* who had lost pastures and flocks and were destitute.

The Soviet military withdrawal in early 1989 left Najibollah exposed, though some advisers and considerable materiel remained, and powerful local forces, such as General Rashid Dostum's northern militia, continued to support Najibollah's government. After the collapse of the Soviet Union in 1991, Dostum converted his militia into a new party, Jombesh-e-Melli. Though Dostum and the Jombesh were secularist in orientation, they now allied with Ahmad-shah Massoud's mujahidin of the Jamiat-e-Islami.

The mujahidin

In 1992 Kabul and the PDPA government fell to Dostum and Massoud, and the mujahidin established a new Islamic State of Afghanistan, dominated by Jamiat with their leader Borhânoddin Rabbâni as president. Massoud's deadly enemy, the Pakistan-backed fundamentalist Golboddin Hekmatyâr, wanted to be sole ruler, and refused to join; his Hezb-e-Islami forces bombarded Kabul, causing massive damage and loss of life. In the provinces powerful warlords – notably Dostum in the north, Massoud in the north-east, Gol-Agha Shirzai in the south and Ismail Khan in the west – established relative peace, but Afghanistan was in a state of civil war, and the behaviour of the mujahidin in Kabul threw their Islamic and political claims to legitimacy into serious question. In 1993–94, alienated by Massoud in Kabul, Dostum took his Jombesh to join Hekmatyar. Their forces, allied with Abdol-Ali Mazâri's Hazâra Hezb-e-Wahdat in west Kabul, invaded the city, but Massoud's forces prevailed, and eventually drove them out. The northern cities of Mazâr-e-Sharif and Konduz meanwhile saw major clashes between Jamiat and Jombesh.

After the Soviet withdrawal, some Pashtun exiles from the north returned but met renewed antipathy and violence from Uzbeks, Arabs and Hazâras, who had repossessed their farmlands, refused to allow *mâldâr* onto their pastures and looted their flocks. Many were forced again to flee to Pakistan or to camps in Kandahar.[5] Dostum and his allies successfully resisted Pashtun attempts to regain control, and rejected Najibollah's Pashtun administrative appointees. Returnees from Pakistan increased once the mujahidin captured Kabul, and some got central government help in litigation over their land. In Sar-e-pol and nearby areas ethnicity was important in determining political allegiances, but so were local loyalties and conflicts.[6] For some years, Jombesh in the

---

[5] See esp. Schmeidl et al. (2010).
[6] Giustozzi and Reuter (2011: 11).

north ran 'the only functioning administration in the country', with revenue from taxing trade and local industry as well as resources such as the Angut oil well near Sar-e-pol, natural gas in Sheberghân and the Andkhoy salt mine.[7] The bulk of Dostum's Jombesh party were Uzbeks, but they attracted many Tâjiks and Arabs, and even some Pashtuns. Most Tâjiks, Aymâqs and Pashtuns followed the Jamiat-e-Islami leaders, notably Dostum's main northern rival, the Tâjik Atâ-Mohammad Noor. The Hazâras, especially those in Balkhâb and Sangchârak/Toghzâr districts, were mostly with Wahdat.

The Taliban

In late 1994 the Taliban emerged in Kandahar, supported by Pakistan, which had given up on Hekmatyâr. The Taliban routed Hekmatyâr and attacked Kabul, now in a state of devastation, but were beaten off. Over the next two years they defeated the warlords and mujahidin parties in the east, south and west, and in September 1996 they took Kabul and established their Islamic Emirate, bringing law and order but imposing their strict version of Islamic law – as well as restoring Pashtun ethnic dominance.

As the Taliban consolidated their control of Kabul and other parts, in the north local conflicts continued between Dostum's Jombesh and Noor's Jamiat. In Sar-e-pol, Jombesh were led by Ghaffâr Pahlawân, and Jamiat by Haji Rahim of the Sangchârak Aymâqs. Haji Rahim had resisted the PDPA regime (and Dostum) since the 1970s; Jombesh defeated him in 1994, but he recovered Sangchârak in 1997. That year, the Taliban drove through Fâryâb and Sar-e-pol to attack Mazâr-e-Sharif, though Jombesh and Wahdat forces beat them off.

Dostum and Massoud were reconciled and, together with the Wahdat, formed the Northern Alliance (United Front), but in 1998 the Taliban finally took most of the north and the Hazârajât. Their conquest was accompanied by massacres of Hazâras and others, in which some local Pashtuns participated.

After the Taliban formed a government, they attracted foreign attention by a number of extreme measures and acts, notably severe restrictions on women, public executions, prohibition of music and images, massacres of civilians as well as prisoners, violence and discrimination against Shi'is and non-Muslims, and the destruction of the Bamyan Buddhas. The Taliban war economy was based on opium trade, smuggling and decreasing foreign aid – and their guests Osama bin Laden and his Al-Qaeda were making their mark with attacks on the USA in East Africa and elsewhere.

It is unclear how many Sar-e-pol Pashtuns supported the Taliban, or how far. Probably the majority were not actively involved, but at least welcomed the security brought by co-ethnic Taliban. More refugees returned to Sar-e-pol, including some active Taliban supporters, and tried again to recover their lands and pastures – and to seize more;[8] the *mâldâr* may have briefly recovered access to their Hazârajât pastures, though it appears the Taliban tried to restrict this. But 1998 was the first year of a severe drought that lasted until 2001. Catastrophic flock losses and crop failures, and further

[7] Gossman (2005: 107).
[8] Alden Wily (2003: 49).

deterioration of living conditions for most of the population, led to a renewed outflow of refugees, especially of destitute farmers and *mâldâr*.[9]

The Taliban now controlled nine-tenths of the country, aided by thousands of Pakistani troops and arms sent by General (later President) Musharraf, Arabs led by Osama bin Laden, and other foreign elements – not least American support for plans to run oil and gas pipelines from Turkmenistan through western Afghanistan. Only a guerrilla resistance was maintained, with some Russian and Iranian support, by Massoud in Panjshir and the north-east, and small groups of Jombesh, Jamiat, Wahdat and others in remote northern and central districts. Various groups in the mountainous southern districts of Sar-e-pol, notably Balkhâb, continued to defy the Taliban; Haji Rahim led the Jamiat until he was again expelled and took refuge in Panjshir, returning in 2000. Around Sar-e-pol town the Arab brothers Abdol Chirik, Haji Amroddin, Kamâl Khân and Haji Payenda led the Jombesh forces, until the first two were killed in action in 2000–2001.

Post-2001

The main US response to the Al-Qaeda attacks of September 2001 was to bomb the Taliban in Afghanistan and to help the Northern Alliance in driving both the Taliban and Al-Qaeda from power. By the end of 2001 the Taliban were defeated, but both their leader Mullah Omar and Osama bin Laden escaped capture, and Afghanistan was left in an exhausted and lawless condition. In the ensuing years, US-led NATO/ISAF forces supported the formation of a new government and constitution, and a general programme of disarmament, reconstruction and development.

In the north, Dostum and his allies returned to Fâryâb, Jawzjân, Sar-e-pol and Balkh. While the general population were suffering from drought and famine, the ethnically based Jombesh, Jamiat and Wahdat militias (whose leaders were made ministers in Kabul, though Dostum remained in the north) took violent revenge for years of oppression and killing by the Taliban. Their chief targets were Pashtuns, all of whom were suspected of Taliban sympathies.[10] There were widespread reports of land seizure, looting, rape and massacre. For the first few years Sar-e-pol and neighbouring provinces also experienced violent conflict between Dostum and Atâ-Mohammad Noor and their respective parties and local representatives.[11]

Lands and flocks slowly recovered from the long drought, and 2002 and 2003 saw exceptional harvests, though these were unable to stem a steady labour migration from villages to cities, especially Sheberghân and Mazâr-e-Sharif. Many refugees returned from

[9] See numerous IRIN reports from 2001 onwards, e.g. IRIN (2002).
[10] HRW (2002: 44). Pashtun nomads, it seems, had been particularly associated with the Taliban, and supplied many recruits; in return they were helped in recovering access to pastures.
[11] On Sar-e-pol, there have been regular reports since 2001 by AAN, AREU and IRIN, and news items in English from PAN and Tolo. From 2012, Obaid Ali wrote several reports for AAN on Fâryâb, Sar-e-pol and Ghor (including Lal-o-Sarjangal). Larsson (2008) includes a very useful survey of Sar-e-pol. From 2002 to 2004, GAA (2004) did studies of villages in some Sar-e-pol districts, including Sayyâd; which was also the focus of further studies by AREU: Grace (2004), Pain (2004), Pain and Grace (2004), Shaw (2010), Kantor and Pain (2010). See also Giustozzi (2005, 2009, 2012) and Giustozzi and Reuter (2011).

Pakistan at this time, but vengeful Uzbeks and others beat them off, and several hundred thousand northern Pashtuns fled south again, to Pakistan or the Kandahar refugee camps.[12]

The violence cooled after 2004. Dostum, who had regained his base in Sheberghân, yielded control of Mazâr-e-Sharif to Noor, who was appointed Governor of Balkh province and conceded areas to the west to Jombesh. Subsequently Dostum's focus gradually shifted to Kabul – where, despite the Tâjik-Uzbek Northern Alliance having driven out the Taliban, Pashtun hegemony was being reintroduced.

Climate change has had drastic effects; reportedly there has been less snow and rain in the mountains, consequently much less water in the main rivers (Balkh, Sar-e-pol, Maymana); the distribution system is even more corrupt than before, so no water at all reaches the lower end of the irrigation networks. Further severe droughts in 2006–8 and 2011, alternating with devastating spring floods in 2005, 2009 and 2012, have led to further waves of emigration.[13]

The Taliban reformed and reorganized as an armed opposition, attacking both government and foreign forces and agencies. From 2004 they gradually recovered control of many areas of the country. A variety of factors led to the Taliban resurgence: a double game played by Pakistan, the return to power of the warlords, both locally and in government, and popular Afghan perceptions of the Karzai and then the Ghani-Abdollah governments as corrupt and ineffective. Not least, the cultural and historical insensitivities of the foreign 'invaders', their savage treatment of suspected insurgents, and the toll of civilian casualties they inflicted, steadily increased the determination of many Afghans to expel them.

In the north, by 2007 the renewed anti-government insurgents were usually termed 'Taliban', though their relation to the Taliban elsewhere is unclear. Non-Pashtuns were increasingly prominent among them, and arms apparently poured into the area. Some reports suggest the drug barons were behind them, others that the southern Taliban, to help their main efforts, were creating diversions in the north.

In Sar-e-pol, Arab, Hazâra and Uzbek warlords competed for position. Jombesh dominated the centre under the Arab brothers Kamâl Khan and Haji Payenda – though after 2004 Kamâl Khan disarmed and started business activities, while Payenda remained politically active and became a delegate to Parliament. Haji Rahim had retaken Sangchârak, and restarted Jamiat. In 2008 Sar-e-pol was reckoned 'the forgotten province', one of the poorest in the country. The estimated 2011 population was around 514,000; Sar-e-pol town was 145,500.[14] Violence and conflict continued. Failure to bring any warlords to justice for war crimes meant that they could not be excluded from candidacy in the 2010 parliamentary elections, and several stood again, including Haji Rahim.

As we have seen, Pashtun exiles returned north to try to recover their lands at various points: under the mujahidin, then the Taliban, and then the US-supported government of Karzai – whenever fellow-Pashtuns were in power and political conditions seemed

---

[12] Many press reports in spring 2002, esp. IRIN (2002), Giustozzi (2005), Schmeidl et al. (2010).
[13] 'This pattern of long droughts, poor harvests and flash floods has been a growing trend for the people of northern Afghanistan, with experts largely in agreement that the climate is becoming more extreme. A new report identified Afghanistan as one of 11 countries globally at extreme risk of both climate change and food insecurity' (Dyke 2014).
[14] Saltmarshe and Medhi (2011: 80).

favourable, or they thought they could use the courts. Returnees included some Es'hâqzai khans, who hoped to recover their estates, and some *mâldâr*. Continued local hostilities, or climatic problems, usually frustrated these hopes, and life was hard for both farmers and *mâldâr*: local warlords and commanders were 'reluctant to allow the sustainable reintegration of Pashtun returnees and provide for their protection'.[15] Government attempts to send Internally Displaced Persons (IDPs) back to Sar-e-pol (and other areas) were rarely successful. In 2009, refugees returning from Iran and Kandahar were finding difficulty surviving in Sar-e-pol, where security was sharply declining.[16]

Some Pashtuns, however, both semi-nomadic *mâldâr* and settled landowners, had remained and found niches where they could survive, even if confined to the vicinity of Sar-e-pol town. These were mainly non-Es'hâqzai; but some landless and stockless Es'hâqzai and others probably stayed too, owning little or nothing to attract rapacious and vengeful non-Pashtuns, with whom they may well have become better assimilated over time.

The *National Multi-Sectoral Assessment on Kuchi*, based on field studies by teams of investigators in the spring of 2004, presents detailed information on the state of pastoralism in most parts of the country. In Sar-e-pol they found 5,381 households (59,843 individuals) of 'kuchis', including both migratory and settled people. They had lost access to summer pastures in Kohestânât and other mountain areas further south, in Ghor and Bâmyân. Some 2,171 households (40 per cent) that previously migrated to Kohestânât were now settled. The migrants, numbering 3,090 households (57 per cent), wintered near Sar-e-pol, moving in summer to nearby pastures in Suzma-qala, Sangchârak and Seyyedâbâd districts; a few summered in neighbouring Balkh province. For most migrants, around half the community did not migrate. At the time of the survey, over half the 'kuchi' owned rainfed farmland in Sar-e-pol, an average of 49.3 jeribs each, but virtually none had irrigated land.[17]

Subsequently, *mâldâr* from Sar-e-pol and Fâryâb regained some access, at a price, and not without conflict, to mountain pastures in the southern districts of their provinces, and some even to the mountains of Lâl-o-SarJangal, Chaghcharân and elsewhere in Ghor – where they met *mâldâr* from Helmand and the south.[18]

These reports do not specify 'kuchi' tribal affiliations; they likely include Maleki, Baluch and Breti, who may well have stayed in their villages in Boghâwi, Suzma-qala and Sangchârak. There are no mentions of Es'hâqzai or other Durrani Pashtun tribes, except as landowning khans, especially those near Seyyedâbâd, which was the former khans' main home. Haji Kheyr-Mahmad Khân, whom we knew in the early 1970s as the young head of the Es'hâqzai khan family, left in the 1980s, then reappeared briefly in Sar-e-pol under the Taliban. Following his election in 2003 by Quetta refugees to the Kabul

---

[15] Schmeidl et al. (2010: 48).

[16] Saltmarshe and Medhi (2011: 80).

[17] de Weijer (2005: Annex IV). There are some excellent studies of nomads since 2001, both general (e.g. de Weijer 2002, 2007; Alden Wily 2004b, 2013; Barfield 2004; Foschini 2013) and regional; but only passing references to those in Sar-e-pol and neighbouring provinces. There are many reports on the conflict between Hazâras and Pashtun nomads over access to pastures in the Behsud region (e.g. Alden Wily 2009, 2013).

[18] de Weijer (2005: 16–17); Alden Wily (2004a).

Constitutional Assembly, he returned to Sar-e-pol permanently. He was then little respected locally, running unsuccessfully in the 2005 Parliament elections (aged seventy); but President Karzai favoured him, and in 2013 appointed him to a fourteen-man forum charged with reducing the numbers of candidates in the next presidential election.[19]

As for the other khans, his cousins, in 2007–8 there are reports of land seizures and murders of several Es'hâqzai 'khans' of Seyyedâbâd by the Arab Jombeshi warlords Kamâl Khân and Haji Payenda. Recently returned refugees from Quetta are said to have been forced to go straight back as a result of Kamâl Khân's oppression.[20] Again, in 2010 it was reported that 'There is a community of Ishaqzai Pashtuns in Sar-i-Pul, some of whom have been victims of land-grabbing attacks from powerful warlords and commanders', including Kamal Khan and his brother Payenda Khan.[21] Payenda, the MP, claimed that 'The land issue involving the Is'haqzai tribes is not a secret. President Karzai even knows about this. The Is'haqzai's claim to the land is baseless'.[22]

Dostum had since 2001 controlled the oil wells at Angut, close to Sar-e-pol town, and used the oil on a small scale. In 2011–12 China signed an agreement with Afghanistan to exploit the wells, but withdrew after interference by both Dostum and local 'Taliban'. Insurgents were confronting with increasing strength both government and Jombesh and Jamiat forces, despite expeditions by Dostum to clear them out. They were concentrating in Sayyâd, Kohestânât and Suzma-qala districts. Those in Sayyâd were clearly linked with 'Taliban' in the neighbouring districts of Darzâb in Jawzjân province and Belcherâgh in Fâryâb; those in Suzma-qala provided bases for attacks on Balkh province. Among them now there were certainly both local Arabs and Uzbeks and activists from Central Asian republics, as well as many of the remaining Pashtuns, who found Jombesh control intolerable.[23]

Appointed Ashraf Ghani's vice-president in 2014, Dostum maintained his local links, leading further campaigns to deal with the growing insurgencies in both Fâryâb and Sar-e-pol provinces. From early 2015, Da'esh (Islamic State Khorasan Province) were reported to be recruiting in the area. But there were also uprisings in Sar-e-pol against the militants, though they lacked weapons. At the time of writing, Kohestânât and Sayyâd districts and much of Fâryâb province were reckoned to be under 'Taliban' control.[24]

3 Recording and Editing the Stories

'Fieldwork' involves 'collecting' materials[25] for research and analysis. But these materials are not just the product of observation, recording and note-taking; they are given meaning during the interaction between fieldworker and informants, who share

---

[19] *Dawn* 20 Nov. 2003; *PAN/Sada-ye-Azadi* 12 Oct. 2013.
[20] Roshangar (2008).
[21] Naval Postgraduate School (n.d.: note 1).
[22] Sherin (2009).
[23] Giustozzi and Reuter (2011), Giustozzi (2012), Ruttig and Ali (2012).
[24] Ali (2015, 2017).
[25] For these and many other metaphors, see Salmond (1982).

ownership and authorship of the results. As articulated in the Ethical Guidelines of our professional organizations, our prime obligations and responsibilities are to our informants, who make both our discipline and our personal careers possible. What we do in the field, and whatever we publish as a result, should not cause them harm.[26]

Journalists, while protecting their sources, are responsible to their employers and the 'public interest' before their subjects, who do not 'own' what is written about them. Like novelists, they are also strongly motivated by ambition: career advancement, money, prizes, fame. Academic anthropologists may have similar ambitions: when we write for colleagues, competitors and evaluators, we seek to display originality and theoretical sophistication, but if we are concerned about our readers, we too are tempted to sensationalize, to elaborate, even to fictionalize.

While not completely disavowing such ambitions, I regard the people whose voices are heard here as at least co-'owners' of this book. If I am credited as 'author', it is not as originator of the stories but as the main translator, compiler and editor. Here I present my edition to an English-reading public, with the hope that it may start a process of returning the stories to the narrators, their descendants, and those who have direct dealings with them. If they wish and are able, I hope they will re-edit and re-publish these stories themselves, or even publish alternative stories.[27]

When deciding how to construct and present this book, I had three priorities: it should be both intelligible and interesting to readers without previous knowledge of the subject (Afghan rural life); it should keep close to the words of our narrators – a term I prefer, in the context, to 'informants', 'respondents', or 'research participants' – with a minimum of accompanying explanation and comment; and it should present a variety of voices and of situations. The book is not intended as a comprehensive ethnography of a particular community, let alone an account of 'Afghan culture'. The stories do not necessarily depict 'what actually happened' or what the narrator believes or thinks; they are best understood as giving meaning to what is narrated, for instance expressing ideals or explaining realities and deviations from ideals.

I hope readers will be able to recognize how the events and actions described relate to the narrators' conditions of existence; to respect them as complex people with knowledge, humanity and humour as well as ignorance and prejudice; and to discern both difference and sameness, both oppression and agency, both helplessness and ingenuity. I hope the book will prove a worthy companion to Nancy's *Bartered Brides*.

Recording

We were both involved in most recordings, though often one of us was the more active interlocutor, depending on the subject. In some cases only one of us did the recording. Sometimes narrators made efforts to check that we were following them; often – as

[26] See statements by the Association of Social Anthropologists (https://www.theasa.org/ethics.shtml) and the American Anthropological Association (http://ethics.americananthro.org/category/statement/).

[27] Some of my Shahsevan hosts in the 1960s and their relatives and friends have read some of my publications about them (in English or Persian) and have commented in print, online or directly to me. Similarly, I have had responses from Turkish colleagues to my (still few) writings on Turkey.

narrators commented on several tapes – we were all exhausted at the time, and we did not always understand what was being said as well as we might have wished. But we usually took notes during the recordings, and were able to check questions, terms and so on afterwards.[28]

Our narrators were happy to talk on almost any subject. Who were they, what were their interests and motives? Did they claim to represent their community and its values? Did they want to be heard as individuals, asserting a distinct version of the truth for their own purposes, knowing that there were other versions? Many narrators told us that they saw it as a duty to make tapes for us. It was certainly a novelty for them to be able to speak so openly and in such detail to strangers, whom they had come to trust neither to judge them nor to use the recordings against them. For some, perhaps, speaking for the tape recorder was therapeutic. In many cases entertainment was the prime motive, for example with folk tales, for which there were appreciative audiences of up to a dozen people.

In making this compilation, I have included stories from a range of narrators, male and female, old and young, rich and poor, powerful and weak. There was much agreement among our hosts, a convergence of views and perceptions on values and priorities. But women's and men's narratives tended to differ, in style as well as in content, for various reasons: not least, most men spoke better Persian, and their daily practices allowed them to maintain greater concentration and to produce more sustained narratives than most women. Older and wealthier men would articulate more formal 'representations' and ideals, younger and poorer men would focus more on practicalities. But if women talked about gender roles and differences, it was usually to echo dominant male opinion, even if their actions sometimes deviated radically from accepted values.[29]

Our time among the Piruzai was brief and busy. The months we spent with them did not include a full annual cycle of pastoral and agricultural activities. Most of the tapes date from our shorter second visit in 1972. We asked our hosts to tell us about their lives in autumn and winter, the seasons we had missed. The winter between our two visits turned out to be the harshest for a generation, with pastoralists in particular devastated by livestock losses, and in 1972, for the first time, no Piruzai trekked to the mountains. Of course, even if we had passed a complete year with them, we would not have seen the full spectrum of bounteous and disastrous years and their very different effects on the local economy, society and politics. Moreover, like all ethnographers, we witnessed only episodes in ongoing social and political affairs, and we relied on our hosts to explain them by narrating their contexts and origins; by making them into 'stories'.

Rather than spending valuable time in the field analysing tapes and notes, we decided to give priority to accumulating what materials we could, and to postpone

---

[28] We took with us, on loan from our university, one 4-speed mono Uher 5″ reel-to-reel recorder, with separate mic, and one cassette recorder, the latter being replaced in 1972 by a second 5″ reel-to-reel machine. Apart from the stories, our recordings and note-books include systematic materials on land and livestock holdings, agriculture and pastoral activities, hundreds of household and marriage histories, accounts of social events in which we participated, maps, plans and genealogical diagrams, as well as thousands of black-and-white and coloured photographs and a short 8mm silent film.

[29] See N. Tapper (1991: 12, Chapter 10, and passim).

translation and analysis until we returned to England. When we left, we expected to return before long to discuss the materials and our analyses with our Afghan hosts; but this was not to happen. An important factor in our decision, though, was our hosts' time. They – men and women – actively encouraged us to make recordings whenever we could. They wanted to help us 'write a book', and they wanted their words to be heard. But without exception they were busy making a living and pursuing social activities. We – and they – wanted to spend what time they had for us on making new tapes, rather than laboriously examining previous ones. They controlled the timing: sometimes two or more individuals wanted to make a tape at the same time; many preferred to talk late at night after a hard day's work, and then nearly fell asleep while talking. None of our narrators were reluctant to speak for the recorders. As they frequently told us, 'filling tapes' was their duty to us as guests who had come so far to live with them; but they also talked of it as entertainment. If we had spent the relatively slow winter months with them, tape recording – and conversation generally – might have been both more leisurely and more entertaining for us all.[30]

Representation

We translated most of the recordings during 1972–73, right after leaving the field, and they were an important part of the materials that we later drew on in our writings. We soon realized the richness of the stories. Inspired by Blythe's recent *Akenfield* (1969) we determined that, while Nancy worked on her doctoral thesis (which became *Bartered Brides*) I should edit some of the stories into a book that would be a community 'self-portrait'. Other commitments delayed my work on the recordings, while revolution, invasion, occupation and other disasters launched Afghanistan and its people into decades of violence and misery on a scale unimaginable during our stay. Meanwhile, we had all the reel-to-reel tapes copied onto cassettes. In 2007 I digitized all the tapes, and started work on constructing this book.

Over the years my thinking and rethinking about how to present these stories has been much influenced by watching, discussing and teaching about documentary film, and by my developing understanding of differences between verbal and visual modes of representation and their respective advantages and limitations, a subject of long-standing debate. It is commonly recognized that visual representations of 'other cultures' rarely communicate effectively without words in some form: titles, subtitles, narratives or writings; while written texts, despite a long history of academic privileging of the verbal over the visual, can be more effective with illustrations and are sometimes incomprehensible without.

Written text and film differ in significant ways, both as media of representation and in the techniques and problems faced by respective editors. Generations of students and television viewers have experienced how well-shot and -edited documentaries can persuade viewers, more effectively than any printed description,

---

[30] We never paid narrators or informants, nor did they ask to be paid; but we did at various points give our hosts substantial loans and presents, and we also did our best to help with supplies and transport (except on the trek to the mountains) and in other ways to ensure that we were not expensive guests.

that they are 'there'. This is achieved by a combination of visual (even if two-dimensional), aural and verbal (voice-over or subtitled) messages that communicate not just acts and words but intonation, facial expression and bodily movement, extraneous sounds and images, as well as pace, space and colour. Little, as they say, is left to the imagination; as they also say, though with less justification, the images speak for themselves.

As regards the ethnographic practices and materials from which representations are constructed, it is perhaps more useful to make a different distinction: between the visual and the oral/aural. Ethnographers observe action, and record what they see in visual form (note-books, maps, tables and diagrams as well as film and still photography). But they also converse with their subjects and record oral texts (narrative descriptions and explanations of actions, events, customs, usages; statements of values, beliefs, meanings, intentions; stories, myths and poetry). Here again, it is important to recognize that the visual and the oral, observation and conversation, are mutually indispensable: observed actions cannot be understood without taking account of actors' explanations, and oral texts are situated in contexts of social action. Socio-cultural anthropology has always attempted a balance in what is crudely summarized as a dialectic between what people do and what they say.

One dimension of the fluctuation in fashions in anthropological theory and practice, at least in the United Kingdom and the United States, has been the degree to which one form of ethnography is privileged over the other. Thus, a key element in Malinowski's 'revolution' of the 1920s was his stated aim 'to grasp the native's point of view'. He and his 'functionalist' and 'structuralist' successors spectacularly failed to take this aim seriously, however, in their concern to theorize anthropology as a science, whether in terms of functions and needs or of notions of structure, comparisons of social structures, and explanations of behaviour. They continued laboriously to collect oral texts, and sometimes presented them at length in the course of monographs, but treated them as documents for 'scientific' linguistic/semantic analysis rather than as valid depictions or analyses of social or cultural practices.

Until the 1970s, academic anthropology set somewhat narrow boundaries for what were acceptable methods of fieldwork and styles for presenting the results. As with film-making, limits were partly set by available technology. From the 1960s, changes set in: prompted by post-colonial pressures, and aided by technological developments, fieldworkers began to take 'the native point of view' more seriously. Audio-cassettes made recorders more user-friendly, and new light-weight, synch-sound cine-cameras allowed more naturalistic, participatory filming; in particular, the MacDougalls' films of the Jie and Turkana pastoralists of East Africa revolutionized ethnographic film-making, representing 'the native point of view' through long, subtitled interviews and conversations, with little or no commentary.[31]

Many different ways of representing 'other cultures' became ethically and academically respectable. There was a general (post-structuralist) withdrawal from

---

[31] The documentary film *To Live With Herds* (1972) and the trilogy *Turkana Conversations*, by David and Judith MacDougall. Cf. Nichols (1991), Loizos (1993).

'theory', scientific pretensions and generalization, and the recognition of a 'crisis of representation' in ethnographic writing and film-making. A questioning of the authority of the ethnographer (and film-maker) led to more 'honest', 'reflexive' accounts of the fieldwork process and the power relations involved, and to increasing publication of 'indigenous ethnographies'. Where anthropologists once sought collective representations of 'culture', the focus – in both writing and film-making – shifted towards individual subjects, their experiences, values and priorities, and how these can be variable, changing, multiple and contradictory. Data 'collection' was recognized as a matter of inter-subjective negotiation between ethnographer and informants, with 'culture' as the product. Ethnographers also began to recognize the importance of multi-vocality (*which* native's point of view?), and to question the authority of informants who were male, wealthy, old or powerful.[32]

Blythe wrote *Akenfield* mostly in the words of his fellow-villagers; it was not 'ethnography' strictly speaking, but 'oral history', informed by the writer's deep local knowledge. In the 1970s, anthropologists who had worked in more exotic locations were beginning to publish similar 'experimental' accounts, using the voices of the people among whom they had lived. Since then, this mode of 'representing' other people has become conventional, while anthropologists have discussed at length the methodological, ethical and other issues involved. Among early 'experimental ethnographies', which focused on 'ethnographic conversations', multi-vocal representations, and a greater use of recorded texts, were some from the Arab world, notably Morocco.[33] As for Afghanistan and Afghans or Pashtuns, while there are notable studies by 'indigenous anthropologists', there have been few experimental or text-based ethnographies.[34]

Cultural styles

Ethnographers intending to represent their subjects through oral texts must consider several methodological questions. Answers to two general questions will determine many of the answers to more specific issues of transcription and editing: First, how can outsiders represent 'points of view' other than their own? Second, who are the intended readers?

In representing specific peoples and cultures, there is considerable variation in the degree to which the medium – whether film or written text – is appropriate. David MacDougall suggests 'that the dominant conventions of ethnographic film make some societies appear accessible, rational, and attractive to the view, but applied to a society with a very different cultural style they may prove quite inadequate and inarticulate.' He contrasts his film-making experiences in two very different contexts: among East

---

[32] For texts that exemplify the literary turn in Anglo-Saxon anthropology and ethnographic writing, see Clifford and Marcus (1986) and Marcus and Fischer (1986).

[33] See Eickelman (2001: 356–60).

[34] 'Indigenous' anthropologists include Shahrani (1979), Ahmed (1980). Early 'new' ethnographies include Doubleday (1988), Mills (1991) and Grima (1992); and recently Klaits and Gulmamadova-Klaits (2005).

African pastoralists and Australian aborigines. With the former, he and other film-makers found an 'openness and eloquence in the cultural style ... a positive value placed upon explicitness of speech, expression of personal emotion and opinion, and the public resolution of conflict'. But his experience of Aboriginal society led him 'to think that it systematically resists approaches based on conflict structure and most of the other expository conventions of ethnographic cinema. This is partly due to a style of discourse which ... is highly allusive and, when not formal, is often laconic and multi-pronged. Speech here does not provide an open channel to personal feeling and opinion'.[35]

Such differences of 'cultural style' clearly affect audio recording too. I found a similar contrast in my experiences of fieldwork with the Shahsevan in north-western Iran and the Piruzai in northern Afghanistan. With the Shahsevan, initially (in the summers of 1963 and 1964) I made considerable use of a tape recorder, partly to compensate for my linguistic shortcomings, but influenced by a positivist assumption that oral texts would be a concrete source of data about history and culture. I recorded several formal texts about custom, and accounts of historical events by old men and women. Later, during my main fieldwork (1965–66), when my Turkish was relatively fluent, I recorded little other than some rather formulaic stories. My hosts would discuss most things informally, but they rarely allowed me to record talk of personal matters. They had strong notions of privacy and secrecy: statements of ideals, narratives of recent events, especially those involving conflict, should be kept from outsiders; they were not to be discussed openly or recorded.[36] Spoken words – oaths, promises, public statements – were powerful, possibly dangerous, and expected to be true, while written words – books, letters, official documents – were probably misleading if not lies. This, I decided, was to be expected from a disadvantaged minority: they were both non-literate Turks in a highly literate, Persian-dominated state, and tribally organized nomads under a regime determined to settle and detribalize them.

We found the Piruzai, by contrast, open and eloquent. Their attitude to spoken and written words too was different: speech could be powerful, but spoken words were 'air', they could be lies, and they could always be denied. People often spoke of something written ('black') as fixed, and therefore more powerful, and expected it to contain at least some form of truth.[37] As members of the dominant linguistic-tribal group in the country, Piruzai had a pronounced sense of their own moral worth and nobility, and little to fear from the authorities, whom they saw as remote and ignorant of their affairs. Knowledge for them was less a matter of private information to be guarded, than a public reality to be claimed and negotiated.

The book celebrates the people and events of that time – importantly, in their own voices, even if mediated by my role as translator, compiler and editor. In many respects this book is, like *Akenfield*, an 'oral history',[38] even a memorial to a way of life that no

---

[35] MacDougall (1992: 92, 93, 96). Cf. Abu-Lughod's (1993) reservations about life-stories.

[36] See Eickelman (1989: 382) for similar reasons for a refusal to allow tape recording.

[37] The words in a charm written by a mullah must be accurate to be effective.

[38] As I completed this book, I read another account of British rural society, Rebanks' excellent *The Shepherd's Life* (2015), which resonates more closely with parts of this one.

longer exists. Yet my reading of recent sources on the lives of rural Afghans suggests that many features of their life have not changed as much as might have been expected after the catastrophes they have experienced in the intervening decades. Afghan nomads and farmers at the time of writing (2019), and researchers who have worked among them in the years since the 1970s, will, I feel sure, find much familiar in these pages.

Translating, selecting and editing

Nancy and I went to northern Afghanistan with a working knowledge of Persian and some training in Pashtu, our hosts' mother tongue. Pashtu and Persian, though mutually unintelligible, are Indo-Iranian languages. In both Pashtu and Afghan Persian, Pashtu is commonly termed 'Afghani/Awghani'. Afghan Persian is the mother tongue, in various dialects, of the Tâjiks, Arabs, Aymaqs and Hazâras of the north. In 1964 Afghan Persian was officially renamed 'Dari', and has since been known as such in official circles, but in the 1970s, in both Persian and Pashtu, it was still 'Farsi/Parsi', i.e. Persian. Uzbeks and Turkmens speak Turkic languages.

The Piruzai spoke the Kandahari ('Western') dialect of Pashtu, with some Persian and occasional Uzbeki vocabulary, drawn from their local environment. We found that all men and boys and most women and girls spoke fluent Persian, the local lingua franca. Despite our initially poor understanding and fluency in Pashtu, we asked our hosts to make tapes in that language, expecting that our Pashtu would progress and we would come to understand the texts fully later. We all continued to converse in Persian, however, and we and they soon decided that it was easier and more intimate to record the tapes in this shared language. So the vast majority of the stories are in Persian, some of them duplicating narratives earlier recorded in Pashtu. The Persian of the stories is Hazâra-influenced in many ways, but also keeps a few Pashtu words.

Every text and opinion expressed is the original narrator's, though I have sometimes shifted sentences and paragraphs, or combined texts from different recordings, confident that the narrator concerned would approve. In editing the translations, I have been fairly free with colloquialisms in an effort to convey both the sense and the flavour of the originals. Literal translation of the idioms and figures of speech that make up most people's ordinary speech is practically impossible.[39] Given that most narrators spoke with heavy use of cliché, I have often used English clichés that, while not usually identical, preserve the original sense.

Particularly in the tales, narrators often used 'obscenities', which I have avoided in the English except where it seemed necessary to keep them. Sometimes these are gendered in ways that readers may find offensive: but I felt it was better to have 'son-of-a-bitch' in place of the literal 'father-dog', which has the same strength. For the literal but improbable 'go fuck your mother', addressed to a woman, I have preferred 'shameless bitch'. The frequent fruity curses and epithets don't translate easily, so I've attempted more or less conventional colloquial renderings. For example, in Pâdshâh/Parwiz's

---

[39] Not forgetting Asad's discussion of 'unequal languages' (Asad 1986).

story of his father's wooing of Shamayel, Shamayel calls to her ex-husband (Persian) *Boro bar pedar-e tu sag nâlat shawa*, literally 'Go, curses on your dog of a father!' This combines two conventional insults: *pedar-nâlat (la'nat)*, 'cursed-father', and *pedar-sag*, 'father-a-dog'. I've chosen to render it as 'Piss off, you bastard', which is no translation but conveys the flavour of Shamayel's cry. 'Bastard' is also the best and simplest rendering of the common Persian epithet/insult *khâna-kharâb* (Pashtu *kur-spera*), literally 'house-ruined'.

Introductions and comments (including those in square brackets) on the stories are italicized. Matter in round brackets is either a vernacular term (italicized) or its translation.

Transliteration and usage

When translating, I found numerous words I didn't know, but identified most of them with the help of the dictionaries listed in the Bibliography. With personal and place names, and transliterations of Persian or Pashtu terms, I have sought simplicity and reasonable consistency.

The vowels 'a', 'e' and 'o' are short, 'i' and 'u' ('oo') are long. This differs from common Afghan Persian transliteration, where 'u' is short, as in 'Kabul', and 'o' is long, as in 'Dost'. I use only two diacritics: a macron to distinguish the long 'â' from the short 'a'; and a dieresis for the Pashtu shwa 'ë'. *'Ain* and *hamza*, which are barely sounded in Pashtu or Afghan Persian, are omitted.

Diphthongs: 'ey' is pronounced as in 'hey', 'ay' as in 'pie', 'aw' as in 'how', 'ow' as in 'owe'. Ai, as in the *–zai* end of tribal names, is properly *za'i*, not a diphthong. Note that I've kept the conventional singular *–zai* ending for all tribal groups and persons, though the Pashtu plural-collective for tribal names is properly *–zi*: 'Piruzi', Es'hâqzi.

I have also ignored the Pashtu retroflex versions of the consonants 'r', 'n', 'd', 't' as well as several important distinctions in Pashtu, such as the different final sounds represented here by 'ey', as in *khoshey*. Pashtu has no *qâf* ('q'); turning it into 'k' in all Arabic and Persian words: the Arabo-Persian *qawm* is Pashto *kâm*. The 'q' in non-Pashtu names such as Aymâq, Qoshtepa is retained, but Karakul for *qaraqol*. Inconsistently, I have Kandahar rather than the Persianized Qandahar, but Es'hâqzai not Es'hâkzai – and here the apostrophe indicates that the second sound is not 'sh'.

I keep the standard forms of proper names: Afghanistan, Pakistan, Turkistan, Kabul, Durrani (but Dorrâni when a personal name).

Local terms not in English dictionaries are italicized throughout, and translated or explained on their first occurrence, in a note or bracket. Those that occur more than once are listed in the Glossary. I have retained in their anglicized (and roman) form local terms that can be found in standard English dictionaries with recognizable definitions: (local version in brackets): bismillah (*besmellah*), buzkashi (*bozkashi*), crore (*karur*), dervish (*darvish*), Haji, halal (*halâl*), haram (*harâm*), jinn, jirga (*jerga*), kafir (*kâfer*), lac (*lak*), madrasa, maund (*man*), mujahidin (*mojahedin*), mullah (*mollâ*), murid (*morid*), nikah (*nekâh*), pir, rupee (*rupya* = Afghani), seer (*sir*), shahada (*shahâda*), Taliban (*Tâlebân*), tariqa, zakat (*zakât*), zikr (*zekr*). But I have used *seyyed* for sayyid and *sheykh* for sheikh.

Glossary

ablij – kind of *div*, that causes paralysis
âghâ – holy man, Sufi master; Seyyed, descendant of Prophet Mohammad
alâqadâr – district governor
alâqadâri – district of sub-province
anj – asafoetida (Persian: *hin, row*)
arbâb – local water-master (see *mirâb*)
ârdâwa – dough-balls
arri – two-humped Bactrian camel
ârwânâ – female *râsta* camel
âsh – dish, usually of noodles and yoghourt, presented by women *âshnay* on the trek
âshnay – 'acquaintance', *mâldâr* trading partner along trek route
atan – Pashtun-Afghan national dances
awi – of sheep, watered every day
awlâd – lineage, descendants
bâbirey – extra brideprice demanded by bride's father if she is pregnant before wedding
bacha-bâz – pederast
bacha-bâzi – pederasty, hiring 'dancing boys'
bad-do'â – curse
badi – feud, vendetta
balâ – disaster; jinn that causes fright, kills
barak – thick cloth, woven by Hazâras
barakat – blessing, abundance
barapay – putting new lambs out to graze with mothers
bâzi – 'marital' visits to bride before wedding, sometimes leading to pregnancy
bëni – cloth bag filled with sweets, sent by bride's family to groom's at *khoshey*
beswa – one-twentieth of a *jerib*; 100 sq. metres
bismillah – in the name of God
boy, bay, bey – rich man, boss
bugarey – small separate plot given to a hired *dehqân* to farm for himself
byetsa – mountain fodder plant
chakman – cloth, inferior to *barak*
chapân – embroidered coloured cloak, often of silk
châpandâz – leading buzkashi rider
chelaw – plain rice
chella – 'Forty'; 40-day period during the winter
chol, also *dasht* – the steppe-desert of the north
churi – jewelled ornament
dehqân – a farmhand, contracted for the year
digil – Karakuli sheep, bred for astrakhan lambskins
div – jinn demon, giant; strong but stupid; invisible but has shadow; falls in love with *pari*
do'â – charm, spell, prayer, with good intent

do'â-o-takbir – prayer, invocation of blessing

du-shkamba – two-rumen, an uncommon variant among sheep

dur-andish – 'far-looking', popular etymology of Durrani

entepâk – family solidarity

fâteha – first chapter of Koran; betrothal, see *târ*

gang – tick

gangi – person who can remove ticks

gelim – kilim

gerow – pawning or mortgaging, usually land

gharib = *khwâr*

gharibkâr – labourer, usually casual

ghërey – fatty layered bread

gheyghân = *byetsa*

ghosl – complete ablution

godâm – godown, warehouse

godi – horse-drawn taxi-cart

gurwân – cowherd

haft-posht – seven generations, limit of *qawm* ancestry

hâkem – governor, sub-governor; see also *woleswâl*

halâl – religiously permitted, clean; of an animal that has been properly slaughtered

halqa – circle; zikr ritual conducted by Sufi master

hamsaya – 'neighbours', clients

harâm – religiously forbidden; of an animal that dies without being properly slaughtered

harâmi – implied illegitimate, disowned by father

inâr – of sheep, watered every other day

jenda – standard, flag-pole, associated with shrine

jerib – areal measure, approx. 0.2 hectares

jinndi – possessed by jinn

joft – yoke of oxen, ploughland; 44 *jerib*s in Khârkash and Konjek

kâriz – underground water-channels

këley – hamlet, small village

kelima = *shahâda*

kepanak – felt cloak, part of shepherd's due

keshtagar(i) – sharecropper(ing)

khâklewa – late winter period when rain brings up new grass

khalifa – deputy of a pir, religious figure

khâna, kur – house

khanâzel – scrofula

khâpëska – jinn that causes nightmares; incubus

kharmora – charm, from swelling on a donkey's face

kheyl – camp, hamlet, small community

kheyrât – sacrificial distribution of meat

khish(ân) – in-laws

khishi – in-law relationship

khoja-khedri – daily bread, due to cowherd

khorzak – diphtheria

khoshey – ceremony after which groom may come to *bâzi*

khwâr – poor

komâla – sweet-smelling mountain plant

kotorey – bowl with a needle-hole, for measuring time (e.g. for irrigation)
krâst – large black felt made by *mâldâr* on the trek
krut – dried whey
kuchi – nomad; common term for *mâldâr*
kumâch – thick loaf of bread, cooked in the embers
kur – house, trousseau
langar – Sufi master's base, lodge
leyti – sweet broth distributed after a birth
luk – male *râsta*
mahr – bride's dower, paid only on divorce
maji – she-camel before first birth
malang – dervish, disciple of pir
mâldâr – pastoralist, nomadic or semi-nomadic
mâldâri – pastoralism
maraka – delegation, e.g. to propose marriage
mâya – hybrid camel
mëkhi – direct exchange marriage
mirâb – canal and province-level water-master
mirgey – jinn that causes severe harm; probably epilepsy
mish-band – 'ewe-string', to waken shepherd when the flock moves
mordagaw – pimp, cuckold
mordëzmâ – jinn that terrifies esp. pregnant women
mowlawi – mullah who has done advanced study
mozdur/mazdur – waged worker: herding assistant, farming assistant, houseman/
    domestic servant
nârawâ – forbidden sexual relations, see *zenâ*
nashra – ceremony held three days after birth of a first son
nazar (stërga) – Evil Eye
netsey – small grey felt made on the trek
neyza-bâzi – tent-pegging
nimawri – contribution to wedding expenses
pâdawân – cowherd
pari – fairy, peri; jinn that falls in love with attractive humans
paruney, porëney – 'veil'; gifts to new bride
pataka – hard cheese
paykâl – 1,800 hectares
peyrun – Pleiades
pirëy (pl *peryân*) – jinn
pishkhur – pre-selling/fore-buying, see *salam*
pituki (155) – extra payment given to shepherd
plâr – fathers, descendants of an ancestor
push – 'bridal shower'
qariyadâr – headman
qawm – meanings range from family to tribe to ethnic group, according to context
qawmi – tribal solidarity
qerân – an old coin worth half an Afghan rupee; the rupee was replaced by the Afghani,
    colloquially still called the rupee (*rupya*)
qorukhmâl – field-warden
rag – strain (in heredity)

râsta – one-humped dromedary
rëwey – jinn, causes fright
rowgha – peace
ruybâr – go-between
salam – pre-selling something, for delivery later (at originally agreed price)
sar – 'head'; premium over agreed price
sar-kheyl – headman of camp
sar-neyza – turban tied to rifle-barrel as a standard
sar-saya – 'head-shade'; zakat
sarwandarey – 'for the milking-rope'; a return of one sheep from brideprice
sawâb – religious merit
senjed – oleaster
seyyes – kind of monster
shahâda – profession of faith
shâpirey = *pari*
shapp – neighbouring plot-holder, who has first option in case of a land sale
sheytân – devil, jinn present inside each human, causing naughty or malicious behaviour (*sheytâni*)
shir-khowla – medicinal mountain plant
shpun, chopân – shepherd
shurwa – broth
simorgh – '30-birds'; phoenix
sir – full, well off
starkhân – food-cloth for meals
storey – star
sud – usury, lending money on interest
tahsildâr – tax collector
takbir – reciting of Allahu-Akbar'
takila – communal collection of contributions to a payment, e.g. of a fine or bribe
takir – highly valued skin of Karakul lamb killed just before or after birth
tâleb(ân) – religious student(s)
tanga – old coin, half a *qerân*
taqawi – advance delivery (of grain) to be paid for later
târ – betrothal ceremony; strip of turban given by bride's father on this occasion; nowadays a tray of scarves
târat – ablutions before prayer
tarawi – night prayers during Ramazan
tariqa – Sufi order, brotherhood
tazkira – ID card
tol – gathering of people
toy, or *wâdë* – wedding feast, when bride is brought to groom's house
tsalweshti – ceremony forty days after birth of a son
ushr – tenth of grain harvest, given as zakat
wabâ – cholera
wakil – representative, member of *wolesi jerga*
wâli – governor of province
watan – home, homeland
wëkrey = *târ*, betrothal ceremony
welayat – province

wëlwar – brideprice; see N. Tapper (1979: 66)
wesh – division of property among heirs
wobâ – jinn that causes severe internal illness; cf. *wabâ*
woles – community, larger village or wider
wolesi jerga – lower house of parliament
woleswâl, hâkem – governor of sub-province
woleswâli – sub-province
zâbet – recorder, bailiff, assistant to *arbâb*
zenâ – illicit heterosexual relations, esp. adultery
ziârat – shrine, pilgrimage to shrine

Bibliography

Abbreviations

AAN Afghanistan Analysts Network
AREU Afghanistan Research and Evaluation Unit, Kabul
FAO Food and Agriculture Organization
GAA German Agro Action, Kabul
HRW Human Rights Watch
IRIN Integrated Regional Information Networks, Kabul
PAN Pazhwok Afghan News, Kabul
PRT Provincial Reconstruction Team
UNCHR United Nations High Commission for Refugees

Abu-Lughod, Lila, 1993. *Writing Women's Worlds*. Berkeley, University of California Press.
Ahmed, Akbar S., 1980. *Pukhtun Economy and Society: Traditional Structure and Economic Development in a Tribal Society*. London, Routledge and Kegan Paul.
Alden Wily, Liz, 2003. *Land Rights in Crisis. Restoring Tenure Security in Afghanistan*. AREU Issues Paper Series.
Alden Wily, Liz, 2004a. *Rural Land Relations in Conflict: A Way Forward*. AREU Briefing Paper.
Alden Wily, Liz, 2004b. *Looking for Peace on the Pastures: Rural Land Relations in Afghanistan*. AREU Synthesis Paper Series.
Alden Wily, Liz, 2009. *Recommended Strategy for Conflict Resolution of Competing High Pasture Claims of Settled and Nomadic Communities in Afghanistan*. Kabul, United Nations Environment Programme.
Alden Wily, Liz, 2013. 'The battle over pastures: the hidden war in Afghanistan'. *Revue des mondes musulmans et de la Méditerranée* 133:95–113.
Ali, Obaid, 2014. *Armed, Disarmed, Rearmed: How Nahr-e Seraj in Helmand Became one of the Deadliest Districts in Afghanistan*. AAN.
Ali, Obaid, 2015. *The 2015 Insurgency in the North: Case Studies from Kunduz and Sar-e Pul provinces*. AAN.
Ali, Obaid, 2017. *Non-Pashtun Taleban of the North (2): Case Studies of Uzbek Taleban in Faryab and Sar-e Pul*. AAN.
Amiri, Rahmatullah, 2016. *Helmand (1): A Crisis a Long Time Coming*. AAN.
Anwari, Hangama, et al. 2004. *BAD, Painful Sedative, Final Report*. Kabul, Women and Children; Legal Research Foundation.
Asad, Talal, 1986. 'The concept of cultural translation in British social anthropology'. In Clifford and Marcus, *Writing Culture*, 141–64.
Azoy, G. Whitney, 2012 [2003]. *Buzkashi. Game and Power in Afghanistan*. Long Grove, Illinois, Waveland Press.
Balland, Daniel, 1988a. 'Baṛēc(ī)', *Encyclopædia Iranica*, accessible at http://www.iranicaonline.org/articles/bareci-a-pashtun-tribe-in-southern-afghanistan
Balland, Daniel, 1998b. 'Esḥāqzī'. *Encyclopædia Iranica*, accessible at http://www.iranicaonline.org/articles/eshaqzi

Barfield, Thomas, 2004. *Nomadic Pastoralists in Afghanistan; Reconstruction of the Pastoral Economy*. Washington, Bank Information Center.

Barry, Michael, 2002 [1984]. *Le royaume de l'insolence. L'Afghanistan (1504–2001)*. Paris, Flammarion.

Blythe, Ronald, 1969. *Akenfield. Portrait of an English Village*. London, Allen Lane/Penguin.

Breckle, S. W., and M. D. Rafiqpoor, 2010. *Field Guide Afghanistan: Flora and Vegetation*. Bonn, etc., Scientia Bonnensis.

Bromberger, Christian, 2000. 'Eating habits and cultural boundaries in Northern Iran.' In Sami Zubaida and Richard Tapper (eds), *A Taste of Thyme. Culinary Cultures of the Middle East*. London, I.B. Tauris, 185–201.

Centlivres, Pierre, 1972. *Un bazar d'Asie Centrale. Forme et organization du bazar de Tâshqurghân (Afghanistan)* (Beiträge zur Iranistik). Wiesbaden, Harrassowitz.

Centlivres, Pierre, 1985. 'Hippocrate dans la cuisine: le chaud et le froid en Afghanistan du nord.' In Pierre Centlivres (ed.) *Identité Alimentaire et Altérité Culturelle*. Recherches et Travaux de l'Institut d'Ethnologie 6, University of Neuchâtel, Faculty of Letters, 35–58.

Centlivres, Pierre, 1992. 'Le jeu des garcons.' In Jacques Hainard and Roland Kaehr (eds), *Les Femmes*. Neuchâtel, Musée d'ethnographie, 55–80.

Centlivres-Demont, Micheline (ed.), 2015. *Afghanistan: Identity, Society and Politics Since 1980*. London, I.B. Tauris.

Clark, Kate, 2012. *Plants of Afghanistan 1: Centre of Global Biodiversity*, and *2: the Koh-e-Baba Foraging Top Ten*. AAN.

Clifford, James, and George E. Marcus (eds), 1986. *Writing Culture: The Poetics and Politics of Ethnography*. Berkeley, University of California Press.

Coghlan, Tom, 2009. 'The Taliban in Helmand: an Oral history.' In Antonio Giustozzi (ed.), *Decoding the New Taliban. Insights from the Afghan Field*. London, Hurst, 119–53.

Cooper, Merian C., and Ernest B. Schoedsack, 1925. *Grass: A Nation's Battle for Life*. 16mm film (available on DVD at Milestone Films).

Doubleday, Veronica, 1988. *Three Women of Herat*. London, Cape.

Dupree, Louis, 1980 [1973]. *Afghanistan*. Princeton, New Jersey, Princeton University Press.

Dyke, Joe, 2014. 'Climate change: Afghans on the front line,' *IRIN News*, 4 November.

Eickelman, Dale F. 1989 [1979]. *The Middle East. An Anthropological Approach*, 2nd edn. Englewood Cliffs, New Jersey, Prentice Hall.

Eickelman, Dale F. 2001 [1979]. *The Middle East and Central Asia. An Anthropological Approach*, 4th edn. Englewood Cliffs, New Jersey, Prentice Hall.

Favre, Raphy, 2003. *Grazing Land Encroachment; Joint Helicopter Mission to Dasht-e Laili 25-27 March 2003*. Kabul, FAO/Afghanistan.

Ferdinand, Klaus, 2006. *Afghan Nomads: Caravans, Conflicts, and Trade in Afghanistan and British India, 1800–1980*. The Carlsberg Foundation Nomad Research Project. Copenhagen, Rhodos International Art and Science Publishers.

Foschini, Fabrizio, 2013. *The Social Wandering of the Afghan Kuchis. Changing Patterns, Perceptions and Politics of an Afghan Community*. Thematic Report, AAN.

Frederiksen, Birthe, 1995. *Caravans and Trade in Afghanistan. The Changing Life of the Nomadic Hazarbuz*. The Carlsberg Foundation Nomad Research Project. Copenhagen, Rhodos International Art and Science Publishers.

GAA, 2004. *Livelihood System Analysis II of Selected Villages in the Provinces Sar-e Pul and Jawzjan in North Afghanistan. Final Report*. Bonn, Deutsche Welthungerhilfe/Kabul, German Agro Action.

Ghobar, Mir Gholam Mohammad, 2001 [1999]. *Afghanestan in the Course of History*, transl. by Sherief A. Fayez. Alexandria. Virginia, Hashmat K Gobar.

Giustozzi, Antonio, 2004. 'The demodernisation of an army: Northern Afghanistan, 1992–2001'. *Small Wars and Insurgencies* 15, 1:1–18.

Giustozzi, Antonio, 2005. *The Ethnicisation of an Afghan Faction: Junbesh-i-Milli from its Origins to the Presidential Elections.* Working Paper no.67. LSE Crisis States Research Centre.

Giustozzi, Antonio, 2009. *Empires of Mud: Wars and Warlords in Afghanistan*, London, Hurst.

Giustozzi, Antonio, 2012. *The Resilient Oligopoly: A Political-Economy of Northern Afghanistan 2001 and Onwards*, AREU.

Giustozzi, Antonio, and Christoph Reuter, 2011. *The Insurgents of the Afghan North.* Thematic Report, AAN.

Gopal, Anand, 2014. *No Good Men Among the Living. America, the Taliban and the War Through Afghan Eyes.* New York, Metropolitan/Henry Holt.

Gordon, Stuart, 2011. *Winning Hearts and Minds? Examining the Relationship between Aid and Security in Afghanistan's Helmand Province.* Tufts University, Feinstein International Center.

Gossman, Patricia, 2005, *Casting Shadows: War Crimes and Crimes against Humanity: 1978–2001.* Kabul, Afghanistan Justice Project. Accessible at https://www.opensocietyfoundations.org/reports/casting-shadows-war-crimes-and-crimes-against-humanity-1978-2001

Grace, Jo, 2004. *Gender Roles in Agriculture: Case Studies of Five Villages in Northern Afghanistan.* AREU.

Grima, Benedicte, 1992. *The Performance of Emotion among Paxtun Women.* Austin, University of Texas Press.

Grötzbach, Erwin, 2015. 'The land reform of 1979 and its aftermath'. In Centlivres-Demont, *Afghanistan: Identity, Society and Politics Since 1980*, 15–18.

HRW, 2002. *Paying for the Taliban's Crimes: Abuses Against Ethnic Pashtuns in Northern Afghanistan.* Human Rights Watch Afghanistan Reports, Vol.14, No.1(C).

Hudson, W. H. (William Henry), 1910. *A Shepherd's Life.* London, Methuen.

Ibrahimi, Niamatullah, 2017. *The Hazaras and the Afghan State. Rebellion, Exclusion and the Struggle for Recognition.* London, Hurst.

IRIN, 2002, 'Focus on nomads and the drought', Kandahar, 20 March; accessible at https://www.irinnews.org/feature/2002/03/20/focus-nomads-and-drought

Javadi, Hasan, 2009, 'Köroğlu i. Literary Tradition'. *Encyclopædia Iranica*, accessible at http://www.iranicaonline.org/articles/kroglu-i-literary-tradition

Jebens, Albrecht, 1983. *Wirtschafts- und sozialgeographische Untersuchung über das Heimgewerbe in Nordafghanistan unter besonderer Berücksichtigung der Mittelstadt Sar-e-Pul.* Universitat Tübingen, Tübinger geographische Studien, 87.

Kakar, Hasan Kawun, 1979. *Government and Society in Afghanistan. The Reign of Amir 'Abd al-Rahman Khan.* Austin, University of Texas Press.

Kantor, Paula, and Adam Pain, 2010. *Securing Life and Livelihoods in Rural Afghanistan. The Role of Social Relationships.* AREU.

Klaits, Alex, and Gulchin Gulmamadova-Klaits, 2005. *Love and War in Afghanistan*, New York, Seven Stories Press.

Krasnowolska, Anna, 2009. 'Ḵeżr.' *Encyclopædia Iranica*, accessible at http://www.iranicaonline.org/articles/kezr-prophet

Larsson, Katarina, 2008. *A Provincial Survey of Balkh, Jowzjan, Samangan and Saripul.* Kabul, World Bank and Swedish PRT.

Lee, Jonathan L., 1996. *The Ancient Supremacy, Bokhara, Afghanistan and the Battle for Balkh, 1732–1901.* Leiden, Brill.

Lee, Jonathan L., 2018. *Afghanistan. A History from 1260 to the Present*. London, Reaktion.

Lewis, I. M., 1989. *Ecstatic Religion*, London, Routledge [Penguin 1971].

Lindisfarne, Nancy, 1997. 'Questions of gender and the ethnography of Afghanistan'. In Jacques Hainard and Roland Kaehr (eds), *Dire les autres. Reflections et pratiques ethnologiques. Textes offerts à Pierre Centlivres*. Lausanne, Editions Payot Lausanne, 61–73.

Linke, Lenny, 2016. *Helmand (2): The Chain of Chiefdoms Unravels*. AAN.

Loizos, Peter, 1993. *Innovation in Ethnographic Film*. Manchester, Manchester University Press.

MacDougall, David, 1992. 'Complicities of style'. In Peter Ian Crawford and David Turton (eds), *Film as Ethnography*. Manchester, Manchester University Press, 90–98.

'Manal', 2016. 'Saif-ul-Malook – The Complete Tale'. Accessible at https://windsweptwords. com/2016/04/25/saif-ul-malook-complete/

Marcus, George C., and Michael M. J. Fischer, 1986. *Anthropology as Cultural Critique*. Chicago, Chicago University Press.

Marsden, Peter, and David Turton, 2004. *Preliminary Study of Assistance to Internally Displaced Persons in Afghanistan*. Report submitted to the Danish Ministry of International Development (DANIDA), September.

Martin, Mike, 2014. *An Intimate War. An Oral History of the Helmand Conflict 1978–2012*. London, Hurst.

McChesney, Robert D., 2002. 'Architecture and narrative: the Khwaja Abu Nasr Parsa shrine. Part 2: Representing the complex in word and image, 1696–1998'. *Muqarnas* 19:78–108.

Mills, Margaret A., 1991. *Rhetorics and Politics in Afghan Traditional Story-telling*. Philadelphia, University of Pennsylvania Press.

Monsutti, Alessandro, 2005. *War and Migration. Social Networks and Economic Strategies of the Hazaras of Afghanistan*. London, Routledge.

Monsutti, Alessandro, 2018. *Homo Itinerans. La planète des Afghans*. Paris, PUF.

Mousavi, Sayed Askar, 1998. *The Hazaras of Afghanistan. An Historical, Cultural, Economic and Political Study*. Richmond, Curzon.

Nasar, M. Ibrahim, 2005. 'Muhammad Gul Khan Mohmand'. Accessible at http://www. khyber.org/people/a/Muhammad_Gul_Khan_Mohmand.shtml

Naval Postgraduate School, n.d. [2016]. *Sar-i-Pol Provincial Review*. Program for Culture & Conflict Studies. Accessible at https://my.nps.edu/web/ccs/sar-i-pol

Nichols, Bill., 1991. *Representing Reality: Issues and Concepts in Documentary*. Bloomington, Indiana University Press.

Nuri, Mohammad-Gol (comp.), n.d. *Melli Hendâra* (National Mirror). 2 vols in 1. Peshawar, Habib Bros.

OCHA, 2014. *Hilmand Province District Atlas*. UN Office for the Coordination of Humanitarian Affairs, accessible at https://www.humanitarianresponse.info/en/ operations/afghanistan/infographic/hilmand-province-district-atlas

Osman, Borhan, 2015. 'Why capturing Helmand is top of the Taliban's strategic goals'. *The Observer*, 27 December.

Pain, Adam, 2004. *Understanding Village Institutions: Case Studies on Water Management from Faryab and Saripul*. AREU.

Pain, Adam, and Jo Grace, 2004. *Rethinking Rural Livelihoods in Afghanistan*. AREU.

Parenti, Christian, 2011. *Tropic of Chaos. Climate Change and the New Geography of Violence*. New York, Nation Books.

Rebanks, James, 2015. *The Shepherd's Life. A Tale of the Lake District*. London, Allen Lane/ Penguin.

Roshangar, Bahram, 2008. 'Forced taking and seizure of the properties of the people of Sar-e-Pul', *RAWA News*, 3 April. Accessible at http://www.rawa.org/temp/runews/2008/04/03/forced-taking-and-seizure-of-the-properties-of-the-people-of-sar-e-pul.html

Ruttig, Thomas, 2013. *How it All Began. A Short Look at the Pre-1979 Origins of Afghanistan's Conflicts*, AAN Occasional Paper.

Ruttig, Thomas, and Obaid Ali, 2012. 'Protests and factional conflict in Saripul'. AAN.

Sakaoğlu, Saim (collected and translated), 1969. 'The fox and the miller', narrated by Mehmet Köksal. Accessible at http://aton.ttu.edu/narratives/wmVol_42-1270_The_Fox_and_the_Miller.pdf

Salmond, Ann, 1982. 'Theoretical landscapes'. In David Parkin (ed.), *Semantic Anthropology*, London, Academic, 65–87.

Saltmarshe, Douglas, and Abhilash Medhi, 2011. *Local Governance in Afghanistan. A View from the Ground*. AREU.

Schmeidl, Susanne, Alexander D. Mundt, and Nick Miszak, 2010. *Beyond the Blanket: Towards More Effective Protection for Internally Displaced Persons in Southern Afghanistan*. A Report of the Brookings-Bern Project on Internal Displacement, The Liaison Office (TLO). Washington DC, The Brookings Institution.

Scott, Richard B., 1980. *Tribal & Ethnic Groups In The Helmand Valley*, Occasional Paper #21. Afghanistan Council, The Asia Society, New York. Accessible at https://easterncampaign.files.wordpress.com/2009/08/scott1980.pdf

Shackle, Christopher, 2007. 'The story of Sayf al-Muluk in South Asia', *Journal of the Royal Asiatic Society* (Series 3), 17, 2:115–29.

Shahrani, M. Nazif, 1979. *The Kirghiz and Wakhi of Afghanistan*. Seattle, University of Washington Press.

Shahrani, M. Nazif, 1984. 'Introduction: Marxist "revolution" and Islamic resistance in Afghanistan'. In Nazif Shahrani and Robert Canfield (eds), *Revolutions and Rebellions in Afghanistan: Anthropological Perspectives*. Berkeley, Inst. for International Studies, 5–57.

Shahrani, M. Nazif (ed.), 2018. *Modern Afghanistan. The Impact of 40 Years of War*. Bloomington, Indiana University Press.

Shaw, Tom, 2010. *Afghanistan Livelihood Trajectories. Evidence from Sar-i-Pul*. AREU.

Sherin, Lal Aqa, 2009. 'Afghanistan: stolen land and political power', *Inter Press Service/Killid Weekly*, 20 August.

Tapper, Nancy, 1979. Marriage and social organization among Durrani Pashtuns in northern Afghanistan. Unpublished dissertation, University of London.

Tapper, Nancy, 1981. 'Direct exchange and brideprice: alternative forms in a complex marriage system'. *Man (N.S.)* 16:387–407.

Tapper, Nancy, 1983 [1973]. 'Abd al-Rahman's north-west frontier: the Pashtun colonisation of Afghan Turkistan'. In Richard Tapper (ed.), *Tribe and State in Iran and Afghanistan*. London, Croom Helm, 233–61.

Tapper, Nancy, 1991. *Bartered Brides. Politics, Gender and Marriage in an Afghan Tribal Society*. Cambridge, Cambridge University Press.

Tapper, Nancy, and Richard Tapper, 1989. 'A marriage with fieldwork'. In Ilva Ariëns and Ruud Strijp (eds), *Anthropological Couples*, special issue of *Focaal, Tijdschrift voor Antropologie* (Nijmegen) 10:54–60.

Tapper, Richard, 1984. 'Ethnicity and class: dimensions of inter-group conflict in north-central Afghanistan'. In Nazif Shahrani and Robert Canfield (eds), *Revolutions and Rebellions in Afghanistan: Anthropological Perspectives*. Berkeley, Inst. for International Studies, 230–46.

Tapper, Richard, 1986. 'Peasant's pilgrimage: a religious ballad from Afghan Turkistan'. *Asian Music* 18, 1:20–34.

Tapper, Richard, 2008. 'Who are the Kuchis? Nomad self-identities in Afghanistan'. *Journal of the Royal Anthropological Institute (N.S.)* 14:97–116.

Tapper, Richard, 2012. 'Studying Pashtuns in Barth's Shadow'. In Benjamin D. Hopkins and Magnus Marsden (eds), *Beyond Swat: History, Society and Economy along the Afghanistan-Pakistan Frontier*. London, Hurst, 221–37.

Tapper, Richard, 2013. 'One hump or two? Hybrid camels and pastoral cultures, an update'. In Ed Emery (ed.), *Camel Cultures: Historical Traditions, Present Threats, and Future Prospects. Selected Papers from the Camel Conference @ SOAS*, London, SOAS, RN Books, 149–62. Accessible at https://www.soas.ac.uk/camelconference2011/file74604.pdf

Tapper, Richard, and Nancy Tapper, 1986. '"Eat this, it'll do you a power of good": food and commensality among Durrani Pashtuns'. *American Ethnologist* 13, 1:62–79.

Thomas, Vincent, with Mujib Ahmad Azizi and Ihsanullah Ghafoori, 2013. 'Water rights and conflict resolution processes in Afghanistan: the case of the Sar-i-Pul sub-basin'. AREU.

UNHCR 2002. *District Profile Naw Zad*. UNHCR Field Office Kandahar, 31/12/2002.

Weijer, Frauke de, 2002. *Pastoralist Vulnerability Study*. Afghanistan Food Security Unit, World Food Programme.

Weijer, Frauke de, 2005. *National Multisectoral Assessment on Kuchis*. Kabul, Ministry of Rural Rehabilitation and Development.

Weijer, Frauke de, 2007. 'Afghanistan's kuchi pastoralists: change and adaptation'. *Nomadic Peoples* 11, 1:9–37.

Youssefzadeh, Ameneh, 2009. 'Köroğlu ii. Performance Aspects'. *Encyclopædia Iranica*, available at http://www.iranicaonline.org/articles/kroglu-ii-performance-aspects

Dictionaries

Afghani-nevis, Abdollah, 1956. *Afghân Qâmus* (Persian to Pashtu dictionary), 3 vols. Pashtu-Tolana, 1335.

Afghani-nevis, Abdollah, 1958. *Loghât-e-Âmiyâna-ye Fârsi-ye Afghânestân* (Dictionary of the Colloquial Persian of Afghanistan). N.p. [Kabul?], 1337.

Amid, Hasan, 1978. *Farhang-e-Fârsi-ye-'Amid*, 2 vols. Tehran, Amir-Kabir, 1357.

Aryanpur-Kashani, Abbas, and Manoochehr Aryanpur-Kashani, 1976. *The Concise Persian-English Dictionary*. Tehran, Amir Kabir.

Nuri, Mohammad-Gol, 1951. *Pashtu Qâmus* (Pashtu to Persian dictionary), 2 vols. Pashtu-Tolana, 1330.

Acknowledgements

Nancy and I have both written about the Piruzai (Maduzai), independently and in joint papers (see Bibliography). Our research in 1970–72 was supported financially by the Social Science Research Council (Grant HR 1141/1) and SOAS, University of London.

The late Neil MacKenzie patiently introduced us to Pashtu; we remember him fondly as a teacher and friend. Also in London, we acquired some fluency in Pashtu with the help of Habib Pashtoonzoy.

We remember many friends with whom we have shared our Afghan experiences; sadly, several of them are no longer with us. We are grateful particularly to Jon Anderson, Gholam-Rasul Khan Babakzai, Asen Balikci, Daniel Balland, Fredrik Barth, Hugh Beattie, Bob Canfield, Pierre Centlivres and Micheline Centlivres-Demont, Veronica Doubleday and John Baily, Bernard Dupaigne, Louis and Nancy Dupree, Klaus Ferdinand, Bernt Glatzer, Tony Hyman, Albrecht Jebens, Schuyler Jones, Hasan Kakar, Hashim Kamali, Martin Kuhn, Laurence LeBrun and Pierre Lacombe, Margaret Mills, Haji Kheyr-Mahmad Khan Nazarzai, Jan Ovesen, Pribislav Pitoeff, Robin and Michelle Poulton, Aparna Rao, Olivier Roy, Philip Salzman, Qari Azim Sarepoli and his family, Nazif Shahrani, Badruddin Sharifi, André Singer, Greta and Mark Slobin, Peter Snoy, Brian Spooner, Bahram Tavakolian, Malcolm Yapp, as well as members (in 1970–72) of the British legation and of the French, German and British Institutes of Afghan Studies in Kabul. We are also indebted for support from members of the Afghan Foreign Ministry and colleagues in Kabul University. Other Afghan friends and numerous people in Kabul, Sar-e-pol, Jawzjân and Fâryâb gave us hospitality and assistance, but it is inappropriate to give their names at this time; we remember them all with thanks.

In more recent decades, for comments in seminars, classrooms and elsewhere that I have discussed our work in Afghanistan, I thank numerous colleagues, students and friends, especially Fariba Adelkhah, Akbar Ahmed, Liz Alden Wily, Len Bartlotti, David Edwards, Enrico Fasana, Jonathan Goodhand, Rob Hager, Shah Mahmoud Hanifi, Benjamin D. Hopkins, Deniz Kandiyoti, Charles Lindholm, Magnus Marsden, Robert D. McChesney, Sayed Askar Mousavi, Adam Pain, Gabriele Rasuly-Paleczek, Nasir Saberi, Torunn Wimplemann.

Micheline and Pierre Centlivres, Sarah Hobson, Trevor Marchand, Thalia Marriott, Ziba Mir-Hosseini, Alessandro Monsutti, Jonathan Neale, Nazif Shahrani, Nicholas Wade, have read all or parts of the text and I have benefited greatly from their comments. To all of them, and all those other friends, colleagues and relatives who have asked repeatedly over decades about the book of Afghan stories I was 'finishing', thanks for your interest and patience; I hope you are not disappointed with the result. Iradj Bagherzade at I.B. Tauris has been particularly patient and encouraging, up to and beyond his retirement.

We owe so much to the Piruzai, not least for providing models for child-rearing that we sought to follow with our two sons, Ruard and Edward, born in the mid-1970s. During their early years we fully expected to return to Afghanistan *en famille* in 1978–79. Unable to do so, we turned to fieldwork in Turkey, where Ruard and Edward accompanied us between 1979 and 1983. The experience proved hugely formative for them and for us. They grew up talking Turkey, while they have been living Afghanistan vicariously through us ever since (see Tapper and Tapper 1989).

As Nancy wrote in *Bartered Brides* in 1991: the Piruzai 'often said that they liked our being with them because we afforded them an amusing way of passing the time. If this is what we gave them, it is so little compared with their warm friendship and the great trouble they took for us throughout our stay. We care very deeply for them. When we left them in 1972 we wished for them, as they did for us, that their land would always be green. Now, after the changes, losses and suffering they must surely have experienced, we can only hope that they have preserved something of their cultural integrity and some degree of self-determination.'

I have suggested in Appendix 2 how much more suffering ordinary Afghans such as the Piruzai have endured in the decades since. More than likely, there are few survivors of the repeated violence from multiple hostile forces. At the very least, they have been displaced, lost their homes and lands in the north, been forced to take refuge hundreds of miles away to the south, and had to deal with unprecedented climatic and political insecurities.

This book, like Nancy's *Bartered Brides*, is offered as a humble tribute to them and as a record and memorial of their way of life as it was in those distant times of peace.

Index of People and Places

People are referenced only when they are mentioned on more than one page, and when they act or speak. Characters in tales are not indexed. Cities, regions, countries are not indexed, nor are Konjek and Khârkash villages. References in bold are to Plates.

Index of Subjects

The Table of Contents indicates where many subjects are discussed; the following brief index is supplementary.